CONNECTICUT

BRASS VALLEY

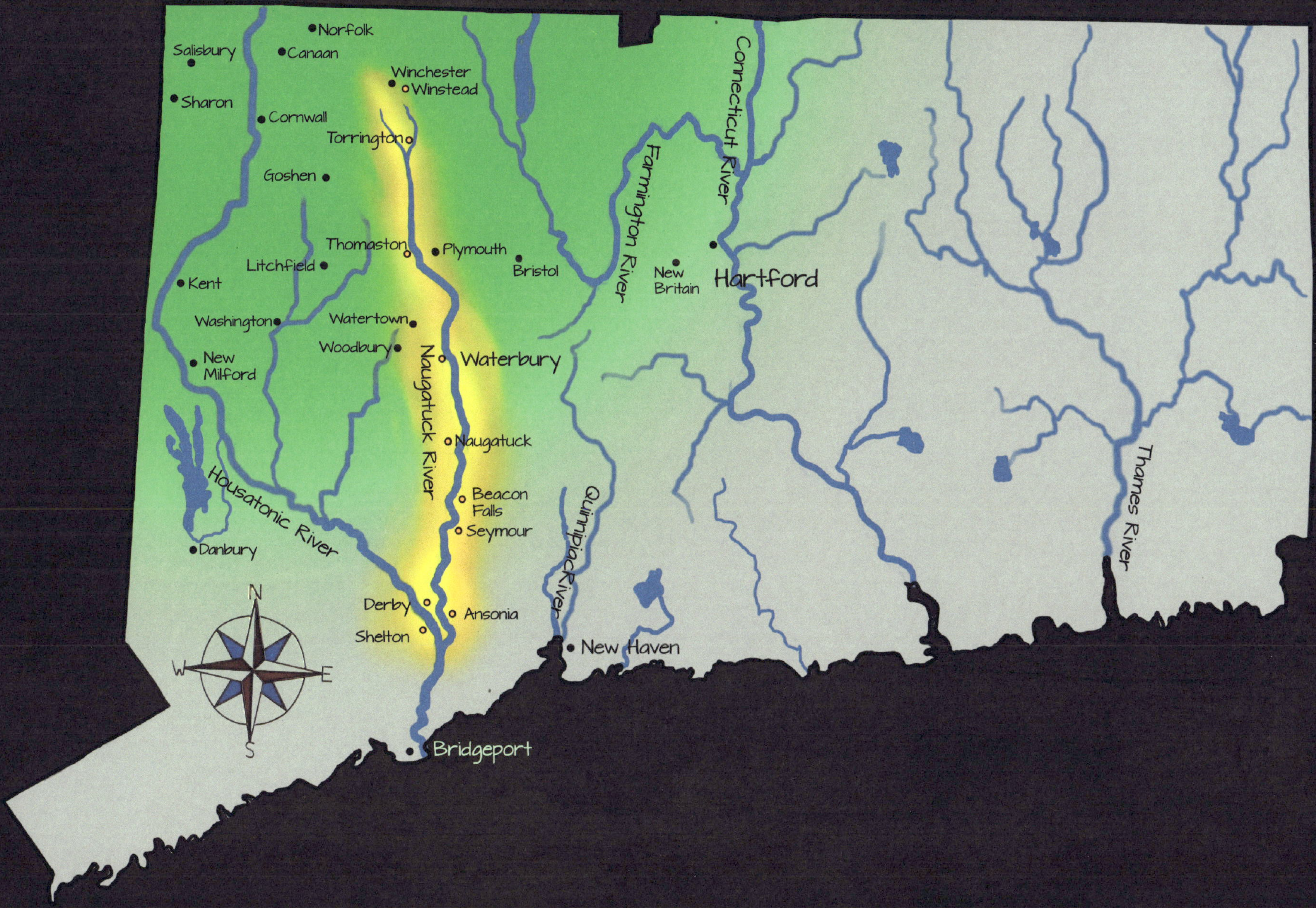

Emery Roth II

BRASS VALLEY

MADE IN AMERICA

Schiffer® Publishing Ltd

4880 Lower Valley Road • Atglen, PA 19310

Library of Congress Control Number: 2015940353

Cover design by Justin Watkinson
Type set in Augus/ Times New Roman

ISBN: 978-0-7643-4930-0
Printed in China

Published by Schiffer Publishing, Ltd.
4880 Lower Valley Road | Atglen, PA 19310
Phone: (610) 593-1777; Fax: (610) 593-2002
E-mail: Info@schifferbooks.com

Other Schiffer Books on Related Subjects:

Mine to Mill: History of the Great Lakes Iron Trade: From Sault Ste. Marie to the Lower Lake Ports, Phillip Stager, 978-0-7643-4901-0

Mine to Mill: History of the Great Lakes Iron Trade: From the Iron Ranges to Sault Ste. Marie, Phillip J. Stager, 978-0-7643-4767-2

This Was Sawmilling, Ralph W. Andrews. 978-0-8874-0594-5

This Was Wheat Farming, Kirby Brumfield 978-0-7643-0188-9

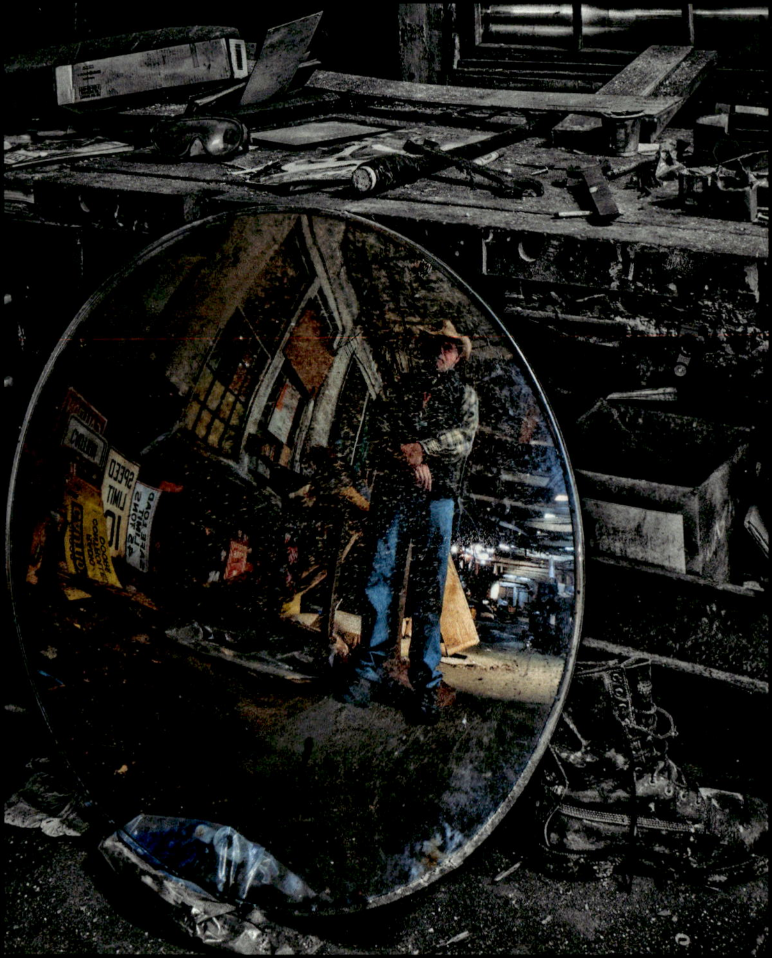

DEDICATION

For John Barto and everyone at Ansonia Copper & Brass, for inviting me into their world and for patiently explaining and helping me understand much that I didn't know.

....and for Jane who, as always, puts up with me.

CONTENTS

When Ted Roth first approached me about photographing our industrial era mill, I was very unsure of his motivations. I agreed to meet Ted and discuss his reasons for wanting to photograph our workplace. It had long been the policy of the business to forbid outsiders from taking pictures of the mill since we were the last mill of our kind in the United States producing specialty tubing for the US Navy. The company had a strong desire to protect our process from duplication, especially in a foreign country. Furthermore, I asked myself, why would anyone want to photograph a rundown mill struggling to survive in difficult economic times?

When I met Ted, though, he appeared to me a seasoned hobbyist who seemed quite thoughtful, and he did not seem to be the type with a hidden agenda. Ted was very clear on why he wanted to photograph Ansonia Copper & Brass, Inc., as he had recently shifted his focus to "industrial decay." This phrase wasn't the easiest thing to hear as the person in charge of the site, nor was it the easiest thing for an artist to state such a purpose to the leadership of his intended subject. Thus, our relationship began.

Ted eased me into the concept by sharing the works of others within the stated genre. One in particular struck a chord: *Detroit Disassembled*, by Andrew Moore, a very thought-provoking and at times stomach-churning photographic tour through a city that was once a proud example of the American dream.

Through Ted's daily photo blog I soon learned that he was also an avid historian with a thirst for knowledge, and he possessed an incredible insight. Seeing Ted's work and reading his words on a daily basis has become something I always look forward to. I believe that it is through this photo blog medium that the realization of the book was born.

Ted has spent the last several years artistically documenting the final days of a company that was erected in the nineteenth century on the banks of the Naugatuck River and thrived through both world wars. Although the historic Naugatuck Valley is the subject of Ted's journey, there is an unquestionable focus on the history and slow decay of the once-mighty brass works that served as the economic engine of Connecticut. Ted is tireless in his craft and extremely dedicated, often working ten-hour days in hopes of getting just the right lighting conditions to capture just the right moment as he envisioned it. Along the way Ted has shared his work with all of our employees, being very careful to make sure no one was left out.

Through my association with Ted I came to realize that he is anything but the "hobbyist" I had originally thought. Rather, he is a professional with an incredible eye for capturing images that tell a story, beg questions, or proliferate mystery.

JOHN W. BARTO
Former President of
Ansonia Copper & Brass, Inc.
Cheshire, Connecticut

INTRODUCTION

As art became displaced—abandoning representation and the place-consciousness of the American impressionists and muralists of the Great Depression—its role in service to place, past, and community fell by the wayside. But we aren't so global and homogenized that it no long matters—not yet. Art has a role to play in helping us see the grace and wonder of our surroundings.

In *On the Beaten Track: Tourism, Art and Place*, art critic Lucy Lippard challenges artists to explore, know deeply, and help shape the cultural identity of their locales by making art that invests in and is inspired by the physical and cultural environment. She challenges working artists to explore the interplay between art and environment in ways that help us see and engage. It's about being creatively observant, and it is not a new idea. Among the many things artists do—or used to do—is to help us SEE our world imaginatively.

Writer and National Humanities Medal recipient Wendell Berry observes that "the vitality of a local economy is strikingly related to the vitality of local community. A strong local economy depends on a love of place which depends on the stories we repeat to another....When a community loses its memory, its members no longer know one another, no longer trust one another, and can hardly avoid harming one another."

This is the central challenge of citizenship. As Wendell Berry further advises, "If we are to protect the world's multitude of places . . . then we must know them . . . by heart."

Knowing them by heart is what Emery "Ted" Roth's work is about.

The son of a renowned New York architect and grandson of another, whose name he carries, Ted spent most of his adult life teaching in the public schools of Connecticut. To dive into his *Brass Valley: The Fall of an American Industry* is to be immediately overwhelmed with evidence of his great eye and heartfelt affection for the dying embers of Connecticut's illustrious industrial age.

Sadly, in the world of historic preservation we have a concept known as "doc and destroy"—where preservationists assure that historic resources in the crosshairs of "progress," indifference, or economic failure, are at least well documented before they are destroyed.

As early as 1906, George Dudley Seymour (1859–1945), one of Connecticut's legendary pioneers in historic preservation and urban planning, commissioned photographers to document New Haven's historic buildings before they were demolished as Yale's prolific expansion rebuilt much of the city's northern Nine Squares. In countless instances we are almost helpless to imagine the lost chapters of our lives—as villages became cities and urban renewal, creative destruction, and the out-migration of Connecticut industries decimated cherished, built environments.

Ted Roth is observant, curious, has an extraordinary sense of composition, and is a wiz in the "darkroom" that is picture-editing software. The photography —for this is mostly a book of pictures—is extraordinary.

This is a journey of discovery and affection for a place he's made it his business to know deeply. It's the story of the Naugatuck Valley—the riparian spine of western Connecticut.

Connecticut is a story of rocks, moving water, valley farmlands, and the sea. Connecticut is polycentric. We have no single dominant city. We have 169 towns and as many more boroughs and villages. Connecticut was the only state in the union that spent almost a century trying to decide where to locate its state capitol. Until 1879, we had two —one each in New Haven and Hartford.

Water defines us—and made us rich. The book opens, on the inside cover, with a map of Connecticut, the spindly fingers of a half a dozen major river regions reaching northward from the sea into the interior of New England. Along these riverways, and especially the small brooks and tributaries, hundreds of small and large water-powered mills and factories were built, beginning as early as the seventeenth-century with small grist and saw mills, then blossoming into light manufacturing—a chair factory here, woolen mill there— until the 1850s when, with the arrival of railroads, coal, and the steam engines that enabled year-round production, Connecticut became an industrial superpower.

It has been said that if you walked into any hardware store in the country in 1880, half the items on the shelves were made in Connecticut. Even before the Civil War, our clocks, firearms, machine tools, and electroplated silver were known and sold the world over. Eastern Connecticut was known for its textile mills, New Haven and the Connecticut Valley for machine tools, firearms, and precision manufacturing. The Naugatuck Valley became famous for its copper and brass mills—mills that eventually produced most of the world's supply of brass and copper products.

This book is an elegy to the century and a half when brass—its products, processes, and environmental effects—shaped the economy and identity of a region. Ted weaves poetry, prose, and eerily gorgeous photographs into a journey of reverence and reflection, showing us places such as the Hendey Tool Company in Torrington, the Seth Thomas clock factory in Thomaston, and Holmes, Booth & Haydens, a company that cornered the market on the silvered-copper plates used by the first generation of American photographers —"Dageurrean artists" they were called.

It is a tale of ruins and fading glory holding on for another breath. Ruins reek of yearning and remembrance, and so we revisit these places—Torrington, Waterbury, Ansonia, Derby—to see towering cathedrals of industry, their windows now shattered and empty shop floors strewn with evidence of evacuations. The evacuations were rarely abrupt. The region's industrial core was reduced by a thousand cuts—and one epochal flood in 1955.

Like nothing else that exists in our art or literature, without being pedantic or precisely analytical, this book documents a world we have lost—the machines and inner workings of an iconic industry cluster. Most residents of twenty-first-century Connecticut will find it hard to believe how much is still standing or was recently, as some of these environments have already been or will soon be demolished. Today, Connecticut has perhaps a million square feet of empty factory space.

Ted's prose is poetic and suggestive. He writes of "the foundry [as] a place of Stygian magnificence," the "air viscous and sooty," and clocks "sold to a growing clientele of the newly parlored."

While a sense of loss and decline permeates, it is not all soot, grime, and extrusion. Among the most haunting images are the three opera houses built in Derby, Ansonia, and Waterbury—Victorian-era emporiums of culture for places suddenly rich enough to afford some. The patrons and patriarchs—the factory lords—with their sense of civic pride and accomplishment left a trail of architecturally magnificent libraries, churches, opera houses, genteel mansions, and the classical exuberance of the Birmingham National Bank in Derby. These are landmarks, as are the factory floors now mostly in ruins. What haunts most are the opera houses neglected or in ruins, notably Ansonia's with every imaginable thing to recommend it—except a contemporary patronage base affluent enough to support it. It is hard to look at Ted's starkly direct portraits and interior details of this building without pangs of emotion. If these all are, in the end, lost, then Ted has done a tremendous service by capturing the dying embers of a passing age of grandeur.

All is not lost—not yet. The centerpiece of the book is Ted's extraordinary access to and capturing of the inner workings of the casting furnaces and extrusion mills of the American Brass Company plants—still operating, barely, in Ansonia and Waterbury. Sparks and steel and liquid copper, pickling tanks, and massive extruders: archeologists one thousand years from now may not quite resurrect the workings of an industry from these pictures, but almost—the pictures are so evocative you can almost hear, smell, taste and feel what you see.

The rest is love. Ted was not born in the Valley. He's lived near there for forty years and has packed generations of affection into this remarkable artistic journey.

Wendell Berry observes that "my own experience has shown me that it is possible to live in and attentively study the same small place decade after decade, and find that it ceaselessly evades and exceeds comprehension."

Ted Roth would surely concur with Berry that "if one spends much time here and feels much liking for the place, it is hard to escape the sense of one's predecessors...I am surrounded by associations; everywhere I look I am reminded of my history and my hope."

My hope is that current and rising generations will not forget nor lose sight of from whence we came. Our lives are built on the toil and often the suffering of those who came before. *Brass Valley* is a gorgeous and poetic homage to that toil and accomplishment—a place in time, in Connecticut, the Naugatuck Valley. The photographs are, individually and collectively, works of art—as compelling as anything we will see in our art museums and galleries, this year or next.

WILLIAM HOSLEY
Enfield, CT
Hosley is the author of numerous books and articles including Colt: *The Making of An American Legend*

ONCE

In our parents' day people who didn't pay cash often paid with a check, or they told the clerk, "charge it," and at the end of the month each merchant sent a bill and expected to be paid. It is a long way from that world to automated self-checkout lines, PayPal, and online banking, shopping, dating, poker, anything! Many shops on Main Street have closed as a consequence, and shopping malls are looking ragged. Our parents' Main Street that we took for granted feels not merely old, but creaky and antique even as the earlier world of our grandparents is soundlessly sliding from antique to ancient, and companies are bought and sold faster than a human mind can formulate a thought—faster than the snap of a picture.

This is the story of Brass Valley. It is a meditation on the past as present and the present as past. It is about dreams and the places they take us, how they turn and shift like smoke over rooftops, twisting soundlessly or whispering, mingling or dissipating, but sometimes eddying into an ennobling mythology that unites people and gives form and purpose to the whirl of time. How that happens is as mysterious as transmuting base metal into gold.

Brass Valley, through which the Naugatuck River flows, is the long valley east of the Shepaug, where I live in Connecticut's Northwest Hills. I've lived in these hills half my life and listened to talk of "hill people," and "valley people," their differences and their politics. Because I'm not a native, I never really understood.

While the Shepaug River was tapped for drinking water and stayed mostly wild, the Naugatuck Valley became the brass- and copper-making capital of the world, through two world wars, and then the community of purpose seemed to wash away like winter snows down storm sewers. The Naugatuck River was to brass and copper what the Monongahela was to steel.

I've lived in the hills by the Shepaug River for forty years. To learn the story of Brass Valley, I decided to follow the tracks along the Naugatuck's banks, and put my thoughts into pictures and words. Those thoughts reflected here in the "Photographer's Journal" evoked a parallel narrative, "Our Stories," like voices of time remembering our beginnings. Let the journey begin.

"The best journeys are those in which you ask questions you didn't know you had when you started."

—Doug Tompkins, adventurer and founder of NorthFace in a TED Talk

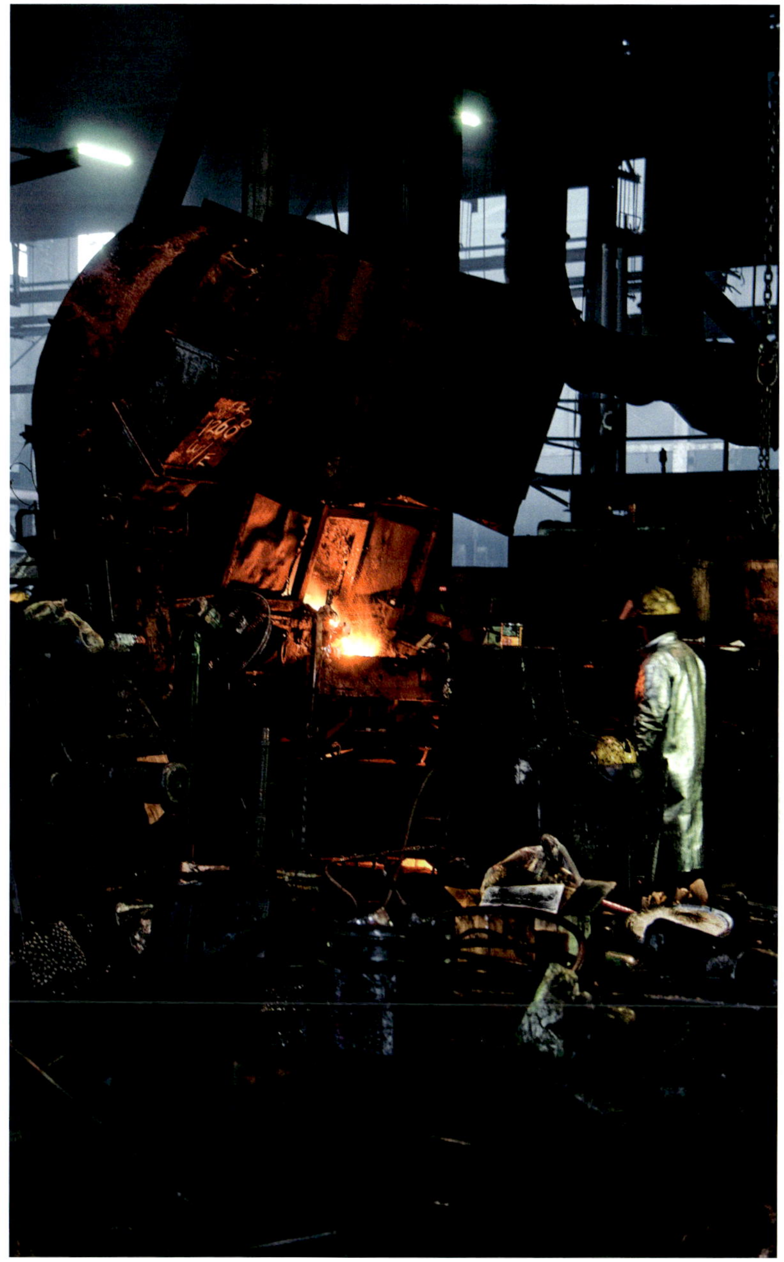

PART ONE:

FOLLOWING TRACKS

On tracks of discovery from Torrington to Waterbury

NAWKATUNK

The first settlers
followed the tracks
the native people used
that followed the river
they called "Nawkatunk."

It was the easy way
through wilderness boscage
where native people hunted
and fished
and where settlers soon built mills,
developed a local expertise in
brass and copper
and later rubber,
and where imaginative people
built what they imagined.

When railroads shot up the valley
like bindweed up a sycamore,
opportunity drew laborers
sprouting families, churches, schools,
saloons and selectmen,
societies and brotherhoods,
sisterhoods and neighborhoods,
unions and country clubs,
parties and alliances,
relationships that helped
communities
endure and thrive.

Huntington, Paugasuck,
Birmingham, Humphreysville,
Nyumph, Naugatuck,
Mattatuck, Plymouth Hollow,
Wolcottville, and Winsted became
the towns that made the world's
copper and brass.

Somewhere
along the river by Rimmon Falls
in the time before the settlers,
near where the brass mills used to be,
it's told,
there was "this old tree,"
"Naw-ka-tunk,"
in the native tongue,
a sweet place in the shade
prized for good fishing.

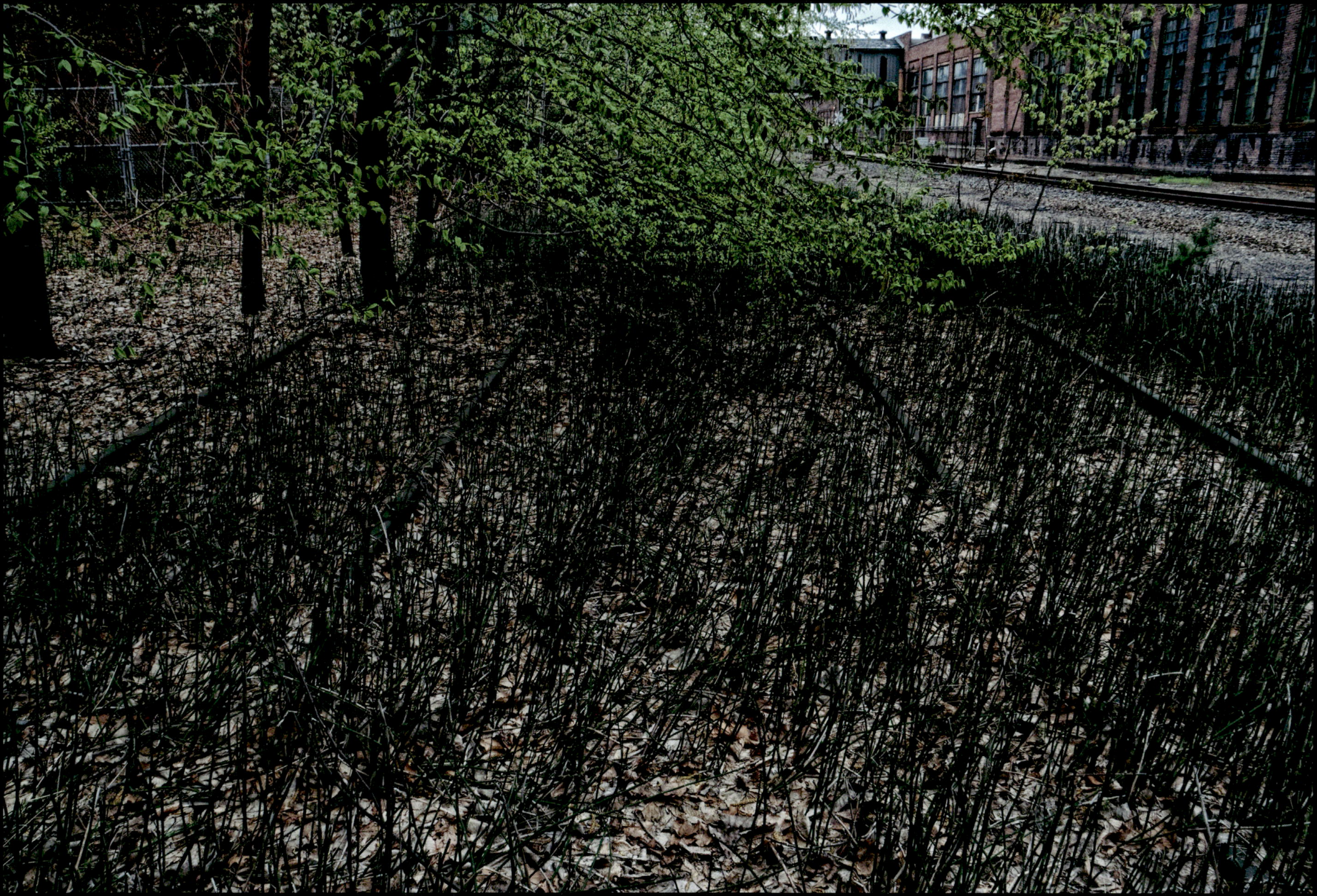

"A report by the Connecticut Sewage Commission dated 1899 stated that the Naugatuck River had reached the limit of permissible pollution due to the discharge of industrial wastes and municipal sewage. A subsequent report by the state Board of Health in 1915 described the river as badly polluted throughout its length and listed six municipal and 29 industrial waste sources on the river. This grossly polluted condition was essentially unchanged into the late 1960s and early 1970s."

—BOB GREGORSKI,
A Brief History of the Restoration of The Naugatuck River and Its Tributaries, 2007

NAUGATUCK SPRING

Rail corridor through Farrel Corporation and American Brass, Ansonia, CT

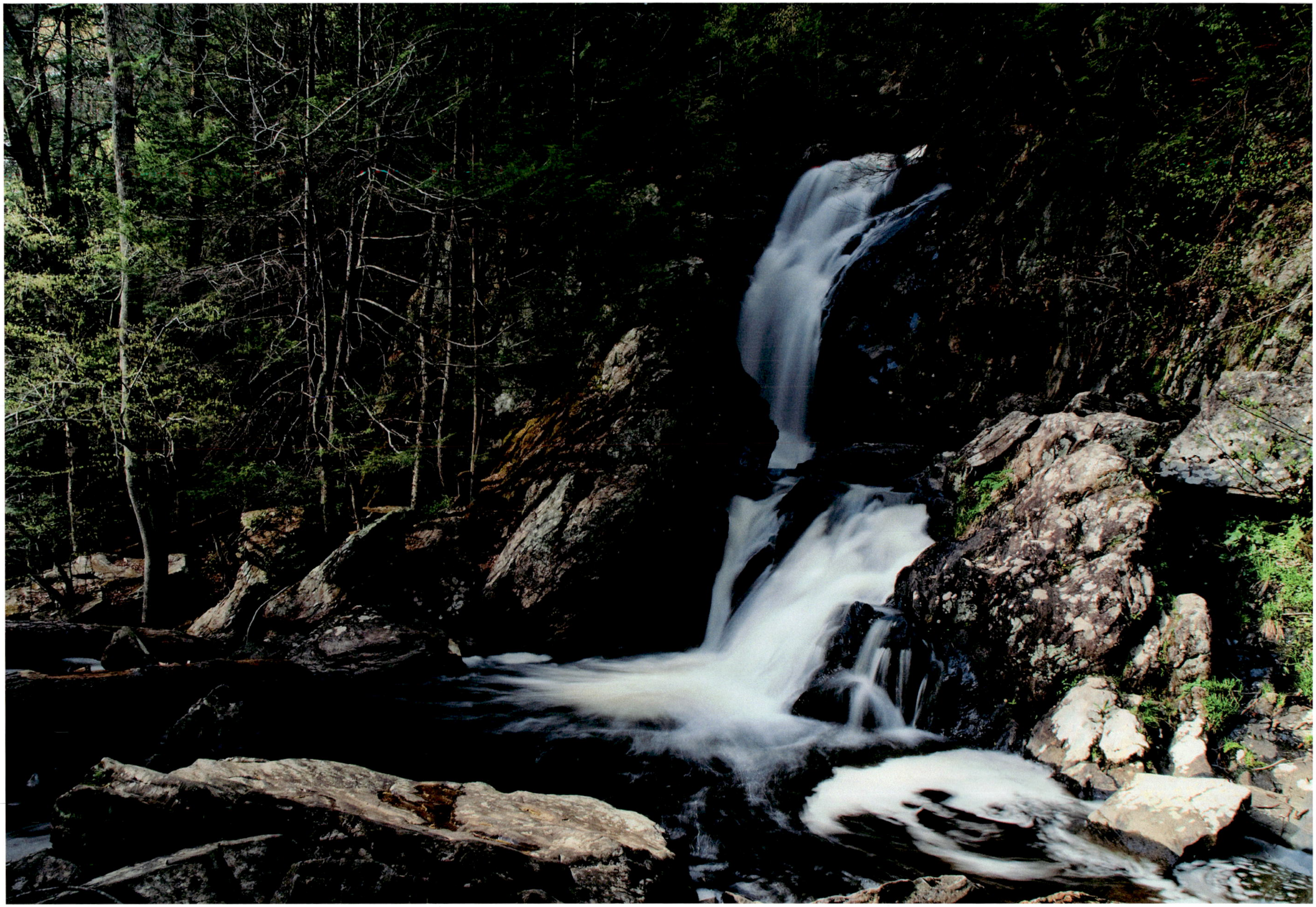

OUR STORIES:

Fertile Soil

We came as trappers, traders, and woodsmen to a land of English puritans who told us of a shining city on a hill. We brought music that held our wisdom, and we sang it to our children in a land of English hymns. Once there was a sawmill here at Campbell's Falls, high up in Connecticut's hills and just west of the Naugatuck Valley. Later we dug rock and made it metal, and we turned the wood to charcoal. But industry played out early, and we moved on. Tranquility has had the upper hand ever since, and farming, and the rivers run clean. Water that passes here takes the long route to Shelton and Derby via the Housatonic. Rain that falls just a bit west follows an express route via the Naugatuck to the same destination. It's all chance and wind, which way it flows.

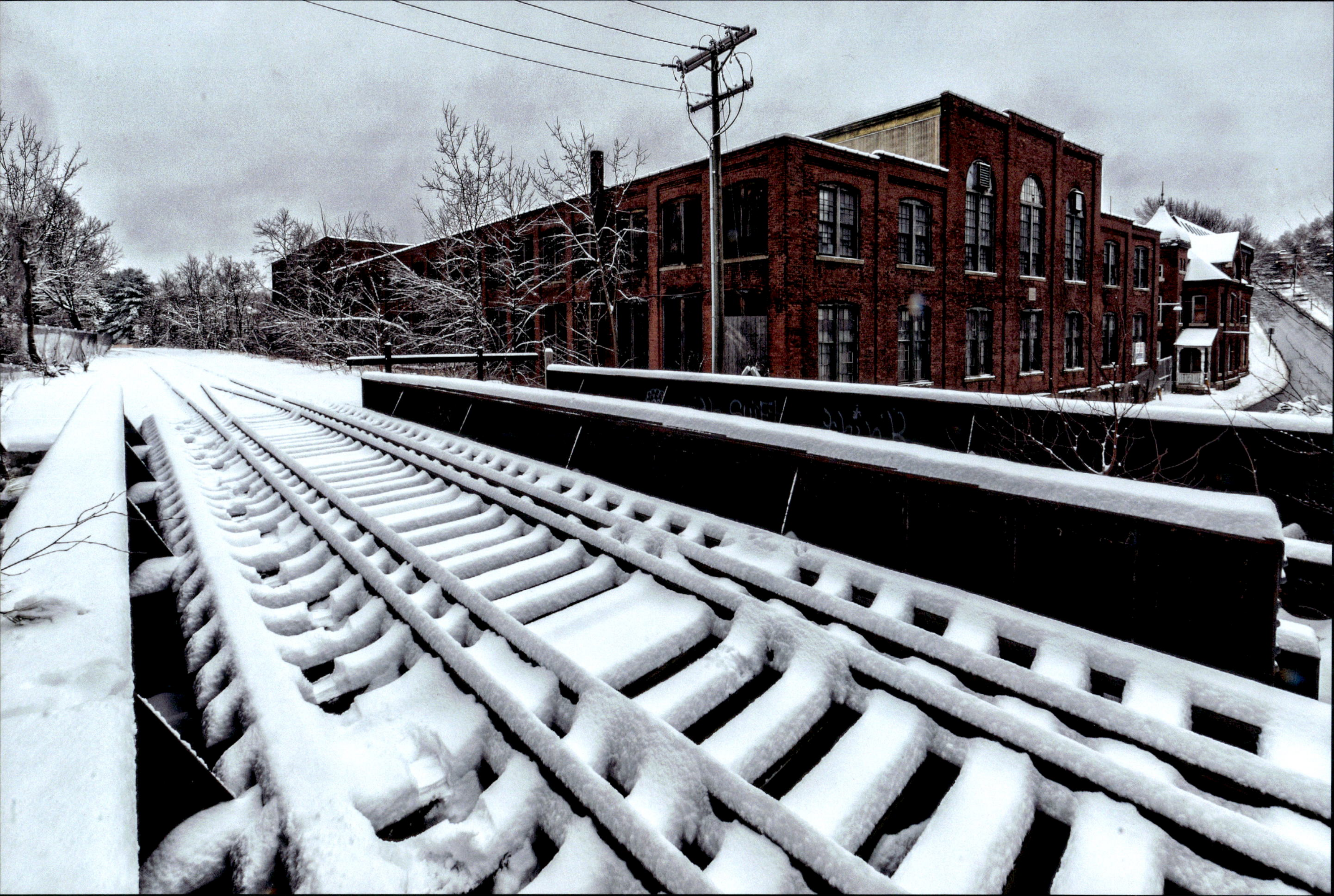

PHOTOGRAPHER'S JOURNAL:
Time, I'm told, moves along a line like a train along a railroad track vanishing into a dark, damp tunnel, but when I looked, I saw it falling in layers, settling like snow on scaly leaves and popped acorn caps, and when I brushed layers aside, I saw our barefoot prints lithified into stone.

I like to follow the tracks even in winter. I live in the north, so I began here by the hollowed out, old Hendey Tool Company sheds in Torrington, once Wolcottville, near the top of the valley. Workers here once turned out the finest quality, precision industrial lathes that one could buy, and the business was run from the original 1880s Victorian offices just beyond the 1908 factory shed.

HENDEY MACHINE COMPANY

Factory building and company offices, Summer St., Torrington, CT

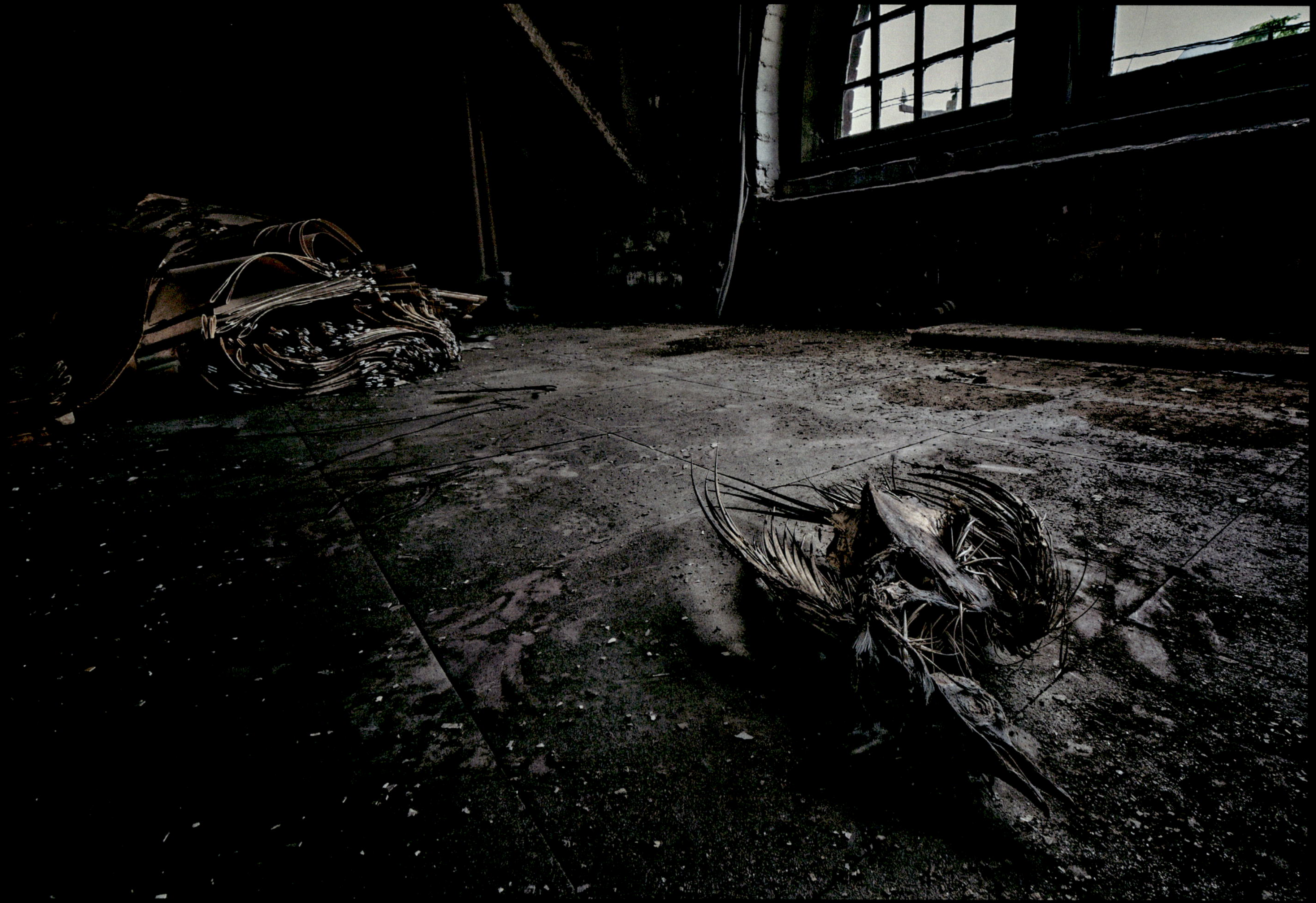

PHOENIX-LIKE

Hendey Machine Co.,
executive tower, Torrington, CT

PHOTOGRAPHER'S JOURNAL:
According to the laws of physics, energy can be neither created nor destroyed, only transformed, and the whole is never greater than the sum of its parts. Is it bird that still burns in the desiccating bird? Do the old habits of organization linger in the dissipating heat or drift among dust motes? What does spirit weigh? What is the coefficient of conversion for wisdom passed from old to young, and what happens to those energies when the wisdom is garbled or lost?

PHOENIX-LIKE

Fluttering
in the updraft
attic of the
Hendey tower

where attic vandals'
rocks chipped
the mansard
smashed the window,

hanging green folders,
analog bequest
of Hendey Corporation,
creep across the floor.

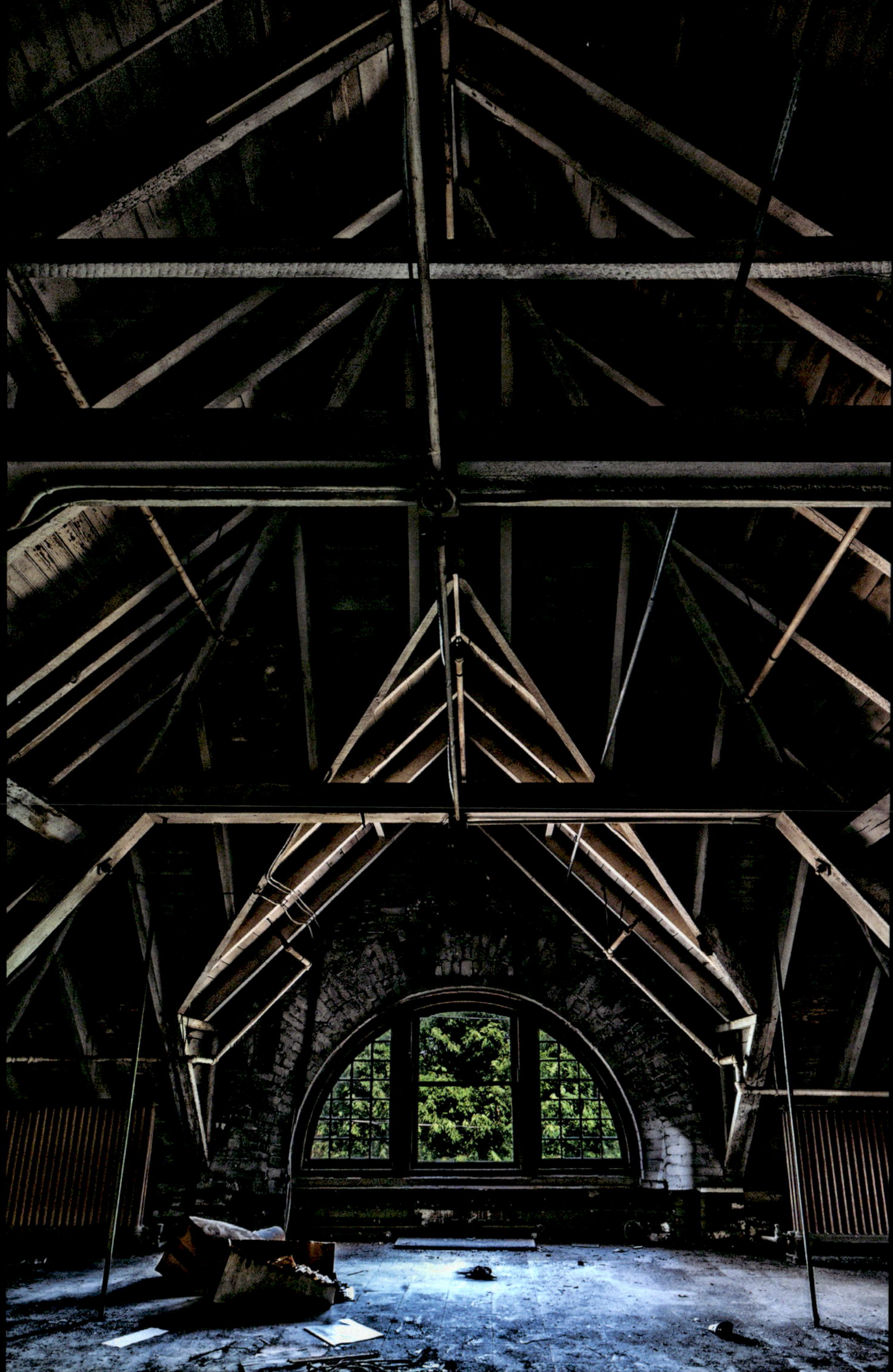

ATTIC REST
Hendey Machine Co., executive
tower, Torrington, CT

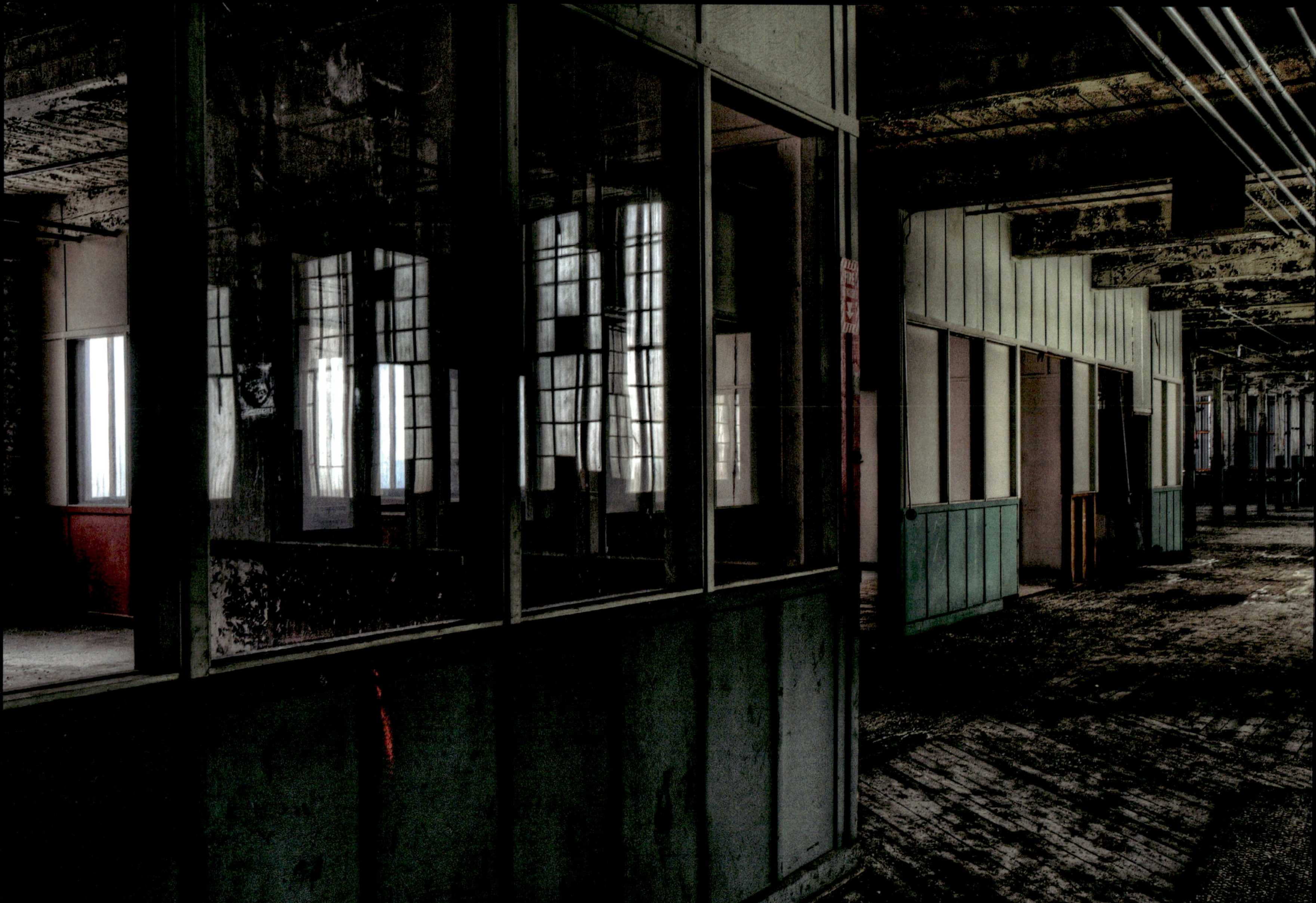

THROUGH WINDOWS

Hendey Machine Co., Torrington, CT

PHOTOGRAPHER'S JOURNAL:

The track that passes the Hendey Company is no longer maintained. It doesn't go far, the buildings are hollow, and the yards are used to store empty freight trucks. I've followed the broken rails north to the old station, but after that even the right-of-way disappears until the new bike path north of town where the track once went on to Winsted.

At the Torrington Historical Society, there is a room devoted to the Hendey Company. Gleaming industrial lathes sit silent inside glass cabinets. The lathes were made here, and old-timers remember the traditions of tool-making that go back to when people referred to the town as Wolcottville.

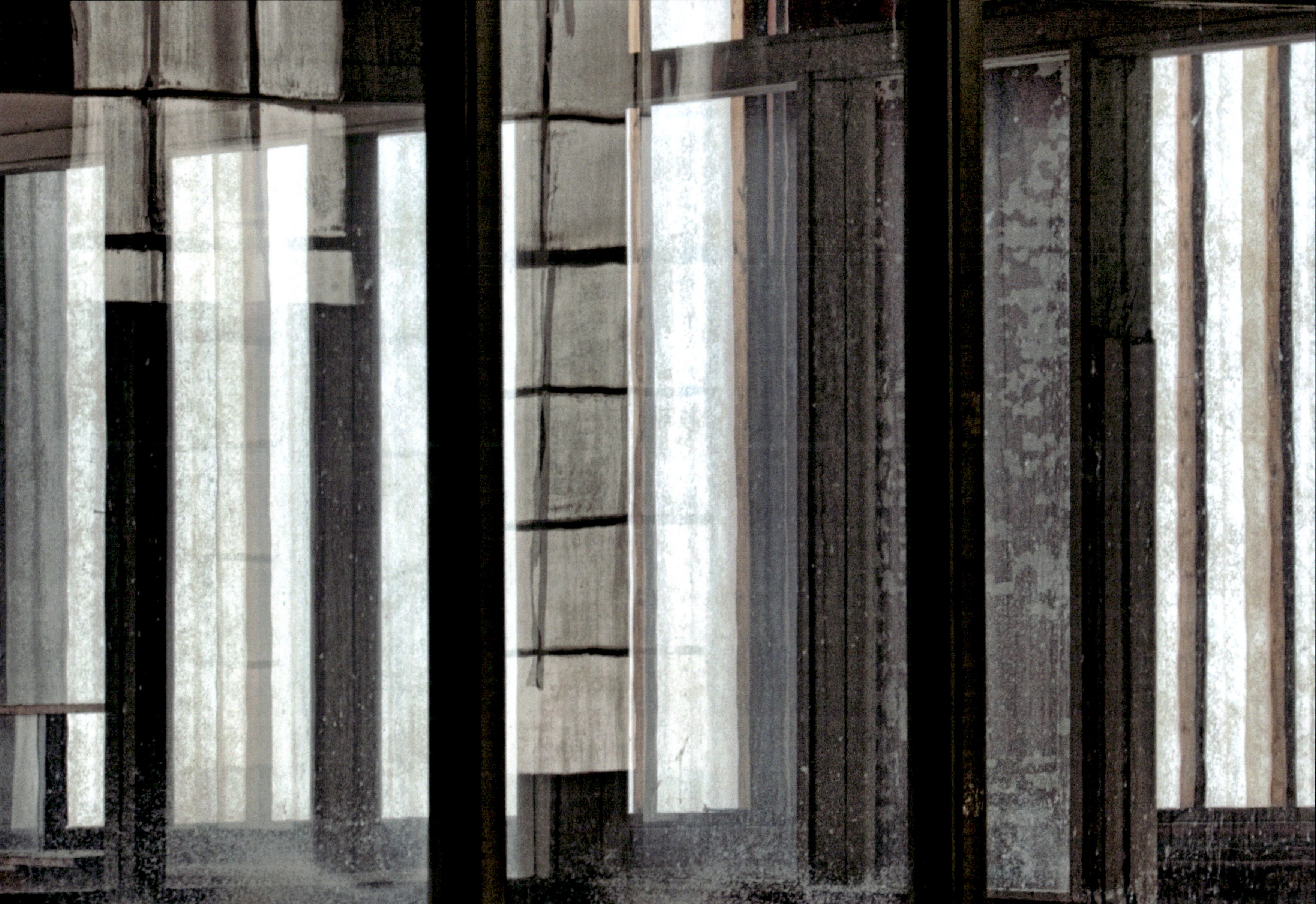

WINDOW GLASS
Hendey Machine Co., Torrington, CT

OUR STORIES:

Wolcottville Brass and Battery

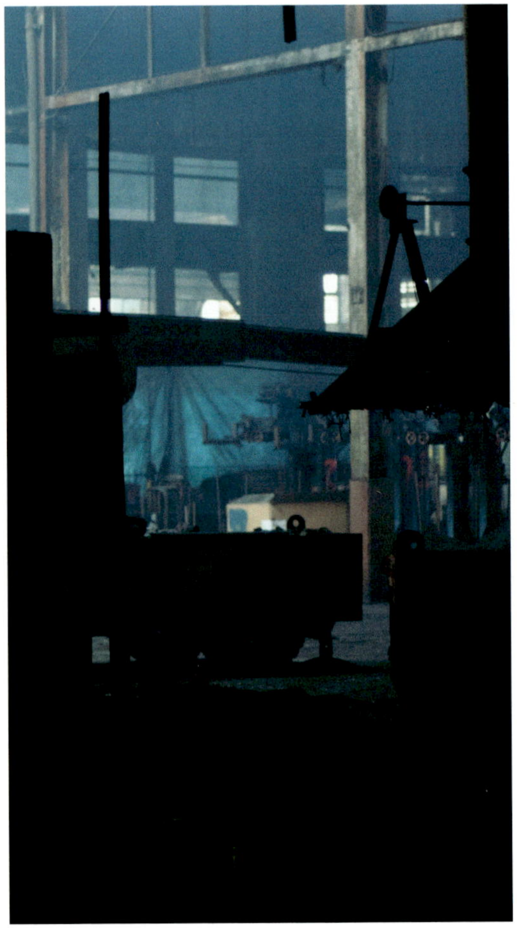

FOUNDRY EXCERPT

Casting shop, American Brass, Ansonia, CT

Under British rule we were not permitted to manufacture things in the colonies. For most of us, clothing was homespun and manufactured buttons came from England. Even so, when the crops were poor, button-making and tin-smithing brought us a bit of cash. For many it became a cottage industry, a sideline for some farm blacksmiths especially around Waterbury. That was a day's ride south along the river and no place for a farm. If we didn't peddle our buttons and tin goods door to door, we paid a Connecticut "Yankee peddler," who traveled the rough roads widely, and went south in the winter with a wagon full of goods.

Before the railroads, it's said, "good land governed Connecticut." The land the rest of us could afford was stony, but if it had a good creek we might build a small mill to grind grain or make cider. Clever, ambitious working folk could make a good living on a rocky creek, but wealthy people with power wanted fertile land, and they clustered around hill towns like Woodbury, Middlebury, Litchfield, and Goshen, places of bounteous harvest where we lived by the sun and the seasons.

That's the way it was even after the revolution up until the 1830s. It was that way in 1813 when Frederick Wolcott, Oliver's son, having learned the truths of common law from Tapping Reeve, came down the Litchfield hill from the law school there and opened a mill for making woolen broadcloth here in the valley by the Naugatuck River, where a bit of a settlement had begun to cluster; soon we would call it Wolcottville. Until then we lived off the land. If we needed a kettle, it came from Birmingham, England, and we treasured our hand-me-downs and had to make do.

Israel Coe was a local farmer and silversmith and a descendent of one of the town's first inhabitants. John Hungerford was a local businessman. There was lots of talk when we learned they partnered with Anson G. Phelps, a New York entrepreneur, to make brass kettles in Wolcottville along the river north of the woolen mill. There was nothing like it anywhere in the country. In 1834, some of us even left the farm and found work battering out kettles and casting buttons for Wolcottville Brass on the Naugatuck's west branch where channeled water made mill wheels turn. Newcomers came looking for work; soon there was a rolling mill as well.

Alas, the brass we made lacked the beguiling golden patina and the rock bottom price of English brass. We lacked their alchemy. The story has been told many ways. Sometimes the telling includes mysterious trips to England made under false pretenses. Sometimes there's talk of kidnapping and the name "Holmes" is whispered. At midnight, we're told, English platers, founders, dyers, and die-sinkers were sealed into casks, to avoid English authorities, and rolled aboard waiting ships—sails raised hastily, stories repeated endlessly later.

Israel Holmes was a junior partner at Wolcottville Brass in charge of manufacturing. He needed expertise and equipment to roll brass. In Birmingham, England, they had been manufacturing brass since the Renaissance and had by the 1780s mastered the secret arts of blending zinc and copper. Here's how an ancient history book tells the story of Israel Holmes:

> Mr. Holmes went to England for the purpose of procuring machinery and workmen. His efforts in this respect were hindered by every possible ingenuity and power of those interested in the same kind of manufacturing in that country, but after a time he sent two battery men to Philadelphia, one of whom died the next day after his arrival. Subsequently he procured others and thirty-eight men, women and children in one vessel arrived in New York. Considerable trouble was experienced in transporting them without a railroad to Wolcottville. When they were landed here, the mill was not ready for operatives, and thereby the troubles were multiplied. The men received their pay and, having nothing to do, most of them gave themselves to dissipation and the disquietudes of disposition. In the meantime Mr. Pope [one of the skilled workers] bargained with other parties for a rival concern and took three of the men with him. This was at first thought to be an injury but eventuated an advantage as these men proved to be worthless in the business. However, some of the workmen remained, and the quick eye and ready hand of Wolcottville Yankees soon secured experts in the making of brass.
>
> —Samuel Orcutt,
> *The History of Torrington, Connecticut*, 1878

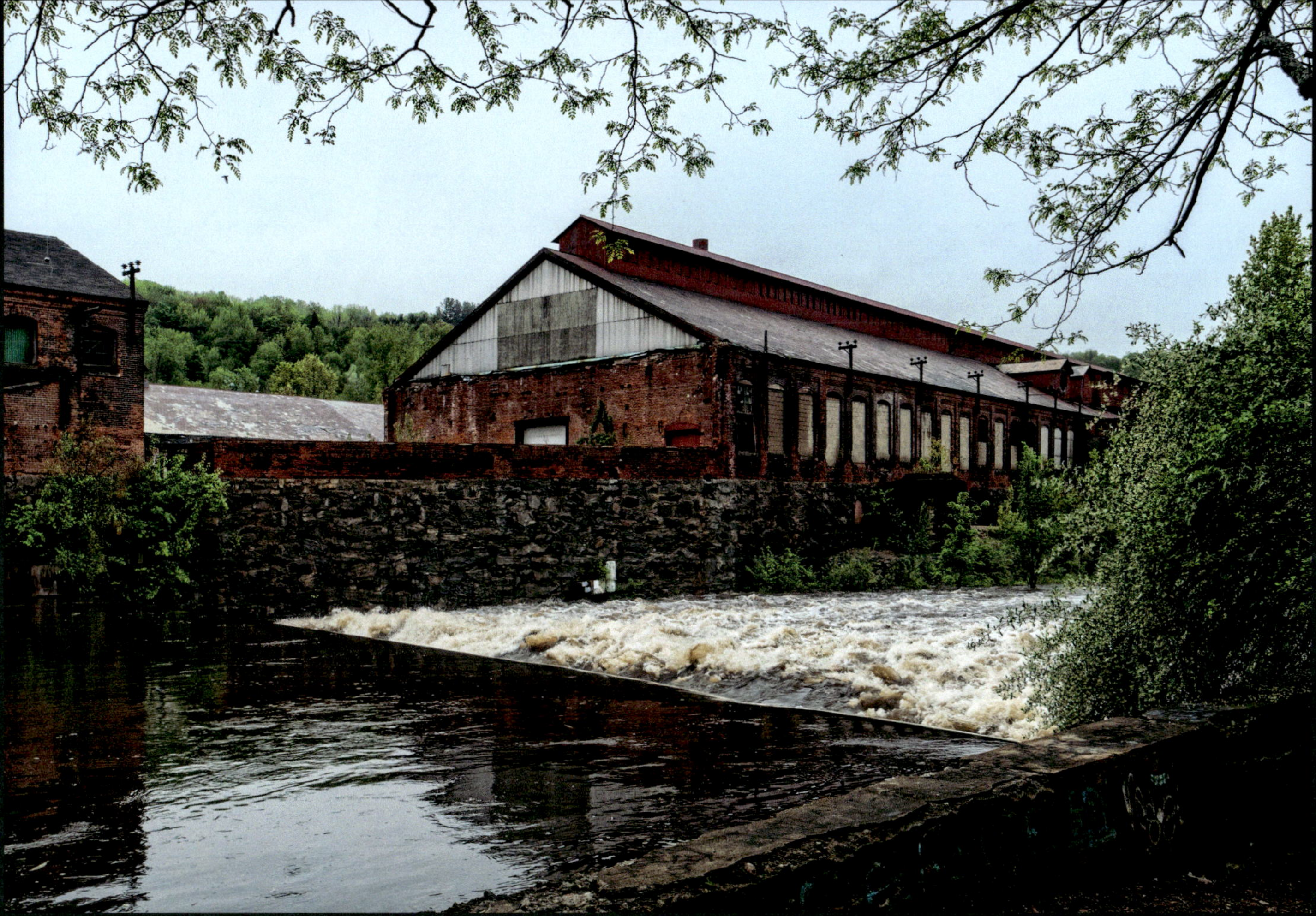

PHOTOGRAPHER'S JOURNAL:

Below Torrington the east and west branches of the Naugatuck unite. The rail finds the river as the valley narrows and deepens on its way to Thomaston, where a flood control dam protects the lower valley, and the track passes along the side of the dam.

Thomaston was called Plymouth Hollow until Seth Thomas built a factory on the river in order to manufacture clocks. Thomas was a joiner who, like a number of other joiners, learned clockmaking from Eli Terry, a clockmaking wizard. The first clocks were wooden. Terry invented what has come to be called the "American System" of manufacturing. His shop was up the hill in Plymouth. Seth Thomas Company clocks followed Terry's manufacturing methods, but he put them in fine cases that looked hand-crafted and he sold them to a slowly growing clientele of the newly parlored who sought the dignity of a fine timepiece ticking softly, solemnly chiming the hours as the Naugatuck flowed and Thomaston grew. And Seth Thomas kept on selling grandfather clocks long after grandfather clocks had passed on.

Three dams remain below the headwaters of the Naugatuck River today: this small one is beside the hollowed out Plume and Atwood plant that was originally built by Seth Thomas to roll brass for clock movements. The large dams are downstream at Rimmon Falls and Kinneytown, where they are building fish ladders.

THE NAUGATUCK AT PLUME & ATWOOD

Formerly Seth Thomas factories, Thomaston, CT (demolished, 2013)

OUR STORIES:

The Man Who Warped Time

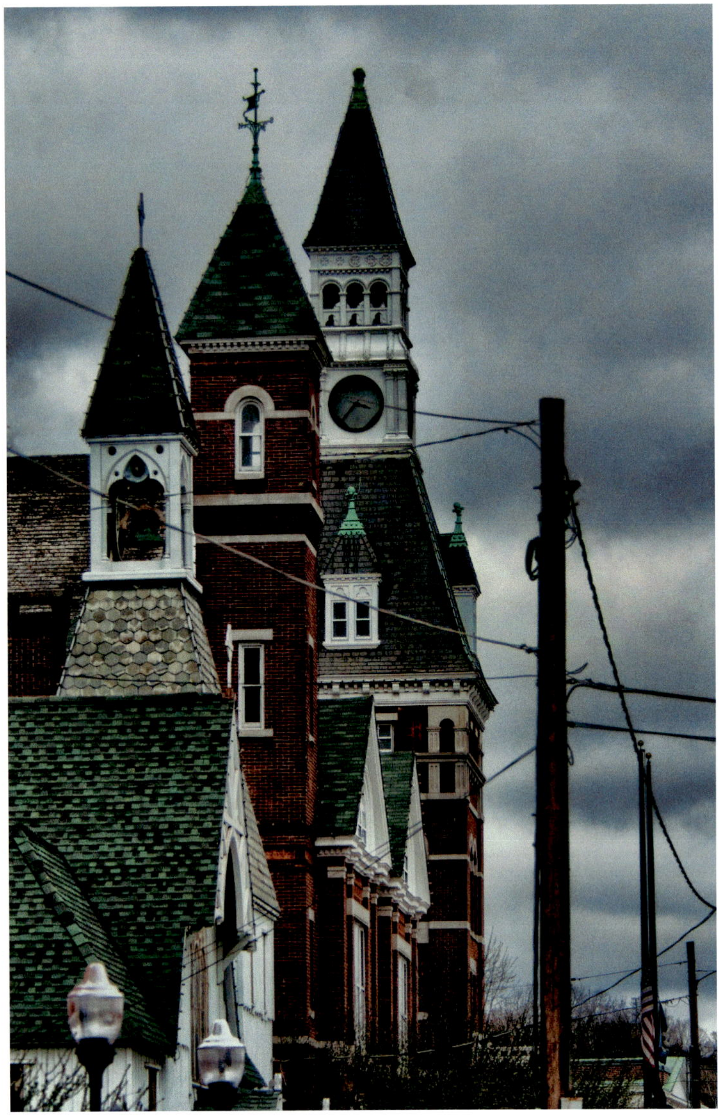

THE THREE TOWERS

Trinity Episcopal Church and Town Hall/Opera House, Main Street, Thomaston, CT

Once our lives orbited with the seasons. We thought time was our natural inheritance, God-given, a sacred trust to be used wisely, not subject to earthly tampering; but time was the first to change. The clockmaker's wizardry looks intricate, consisting of astronomical calculations and tedious tinkering with gears and escapements, teasing out tiny efficiencies and tuning verges to mimic the heavens and meter out our moments precisely. We scarcely understand or remember how the clockmakers came to possess and warp time, nor can we recall those tattered circadian harmonies bequeathed us by ancestors even to those with gills, who knew time from beneath the surface of a pond.

Clockmakers were in the Naugatuck Valley early, working in wood even before the first brass mill rolled metal, and it's hard to overestimate their influence. In 1801, Eli Terry registered the first United States patent for a clock mechanism. It was a clear sign of genius. The mechanism, called "an equation clock," modulated the flow of clock-minutes to mimic sun time, perceptual time, time as it was given by the orbits of the heavens.

It was no simple thing to get a clunky machine to figure the tilt of the earth and the living flux of days as they varied in length; to get escapement and verge to lay down 86,400 even moments in the ever-changing span between every sunrise and sunrise. Today such a clock would be an antique, always hopelessly wrong. It measured old time, nature's time, the time most people knew, but it would never have made Eli Terry famous or wealthy in the times ahead.

Most of Eli Terry's clocks were not equation clocks. They were ordinary clocks that beat in even moments. His clocks became famous because they made time cheap. In 1806 he accepted a contract to make 4,000 wooden, 30-hour shelf clocks in three years at $4 each. Creating a 30-hour shelf clock in wood presented technical challenges, and skeptics laughed at the thought of producing any clock for $4. Nobody could make 4,000 of them in three years when the most a single clockmaker could turn out in a year was under a dozen. Before Eli Terry, clocks were enlightenment "tech toys" for aristocrats, or they were purchased as a common community resource.

Terry formed a partnership with Silas Hoadley and Seth Thomas, two young joiners, and spent the first year designing the clock and the systems and jigs to mass-produce it. If parts could be uniformly made, much time could be saved in precision finishing. The partners spent the remaining two years refining methods and producing the required number. Terry was mass-producing time and selling it at prices we could afford; it was a milestone in mass production comparable to Henry Ford's a century later. Terry knew what he had, and he knew how to perfect it.

He sold his share of the business to his joiner partners and took all he had learned about clocks and mass production, and he applied it to the design of a wholly new, made-for-mass production, 30-hour shelf clock; in 1816 we began manufacturing the first machine of any kind made from wholly interchangeable parts. By 1825 Terry was making 10,000 clocks a year, and his clocks delivered time to the rest of us, and they dominated clockmaking for twenty-five years until clocks of wood were replaced by clocks of brass. In 1833 Terry retired, wealthy from the manufacturing of clocks. He spent the next twenty-two years quietly, patiently making unique, fine, precision timepieces the old-fashioned way, fitting each wheel to its place in a singular clockwork, while around him in the hills men discussed matters of gravity and imagined a clockmaker God.

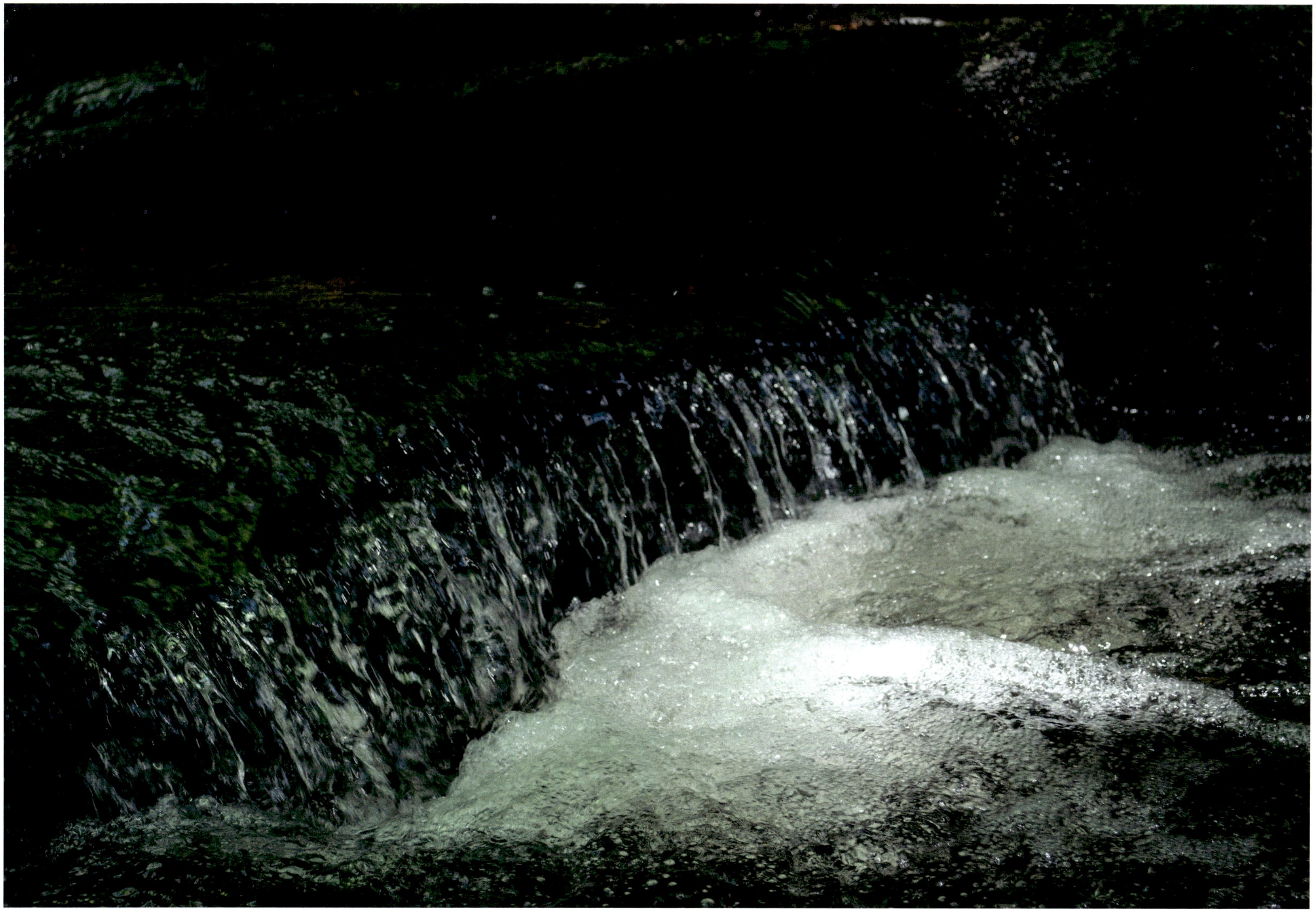

EYELASH FALLS
Shepaug River headwaters, Upper Reservoir, Warren, CT

OUR STORIES:

Farm and Mill

Litchfield was Connecticut's cultural center, intellectual capital. Tapping Reeve opened the first law school on a hill in Litchfield and his students spread those principles of law across generations. It was the home of Oliver Wolcott and the Beechers, a place where men and sometimes women discussed the things that followed from self-evident truths, and their ideas rumbled across horizons toward a more perfect union.

The steep, rocky land around the Naugatuck River Valley remained mostly wild, while Litchfield became the fourth largest town in Connecticut, but after the revolution the valley towns began to spin. In the flat, stony land of Waterbury, many rivers joined the Naugatuck. So it was there that we built the most dams, and the gravity of water soon turned the most mill wheels. Build a few mills and you start thinking about wheels and dams and millraces and things of gravity. Up and down the valley, what we spun from our mill wheels was not just power for manufacturing but also a community of know-how, competing and forming bonds, mixing metals and spinning wheels differently. We were trying things that had never been tried before; successes were contagious.

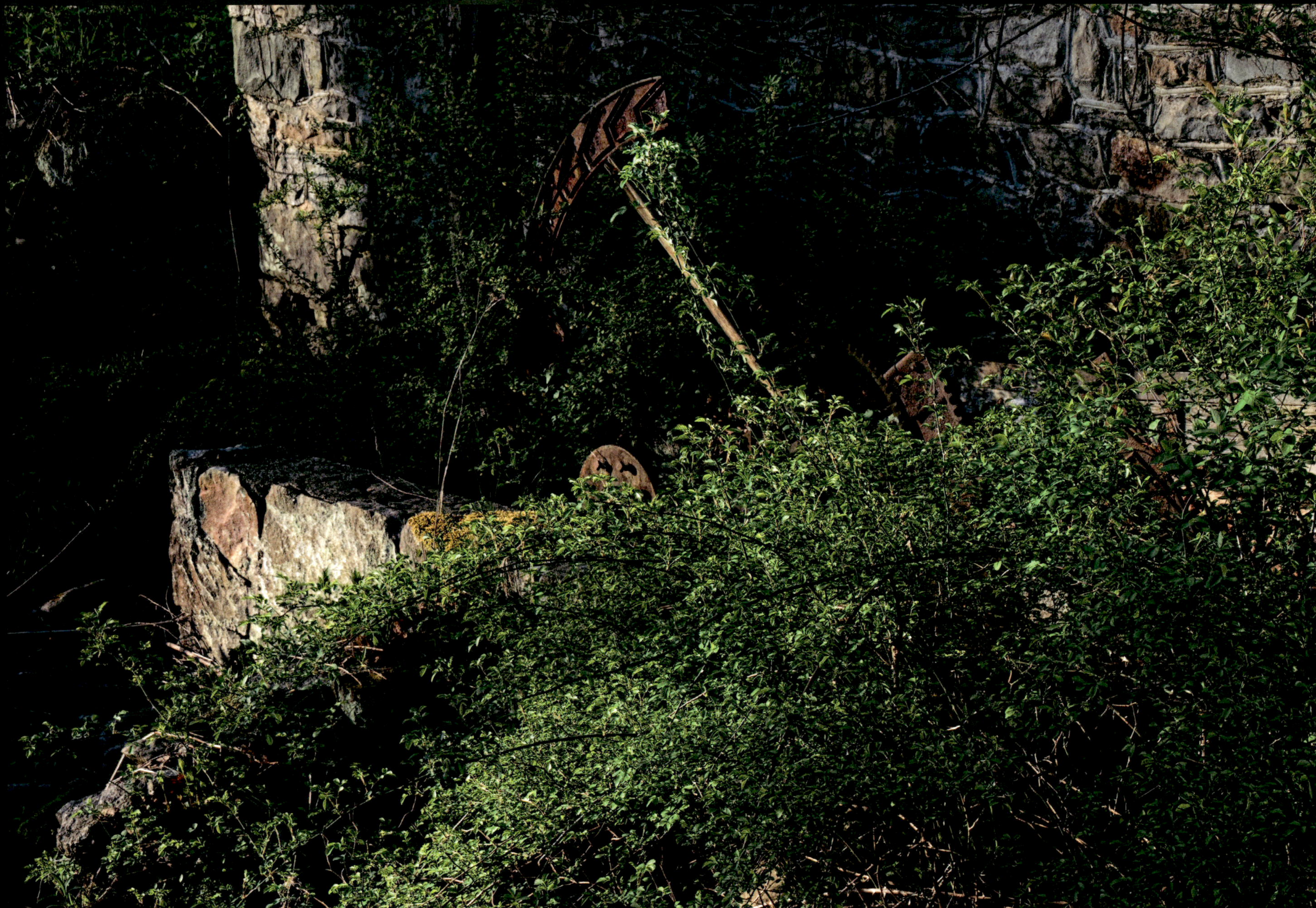

MILL WHEEL

Old farm mill wheel and mill race.

TRUNDLING SONG

The wheel turns with the river.
It never turns back,
until one day it stops,
but the river keeps flowing,
always
always
always

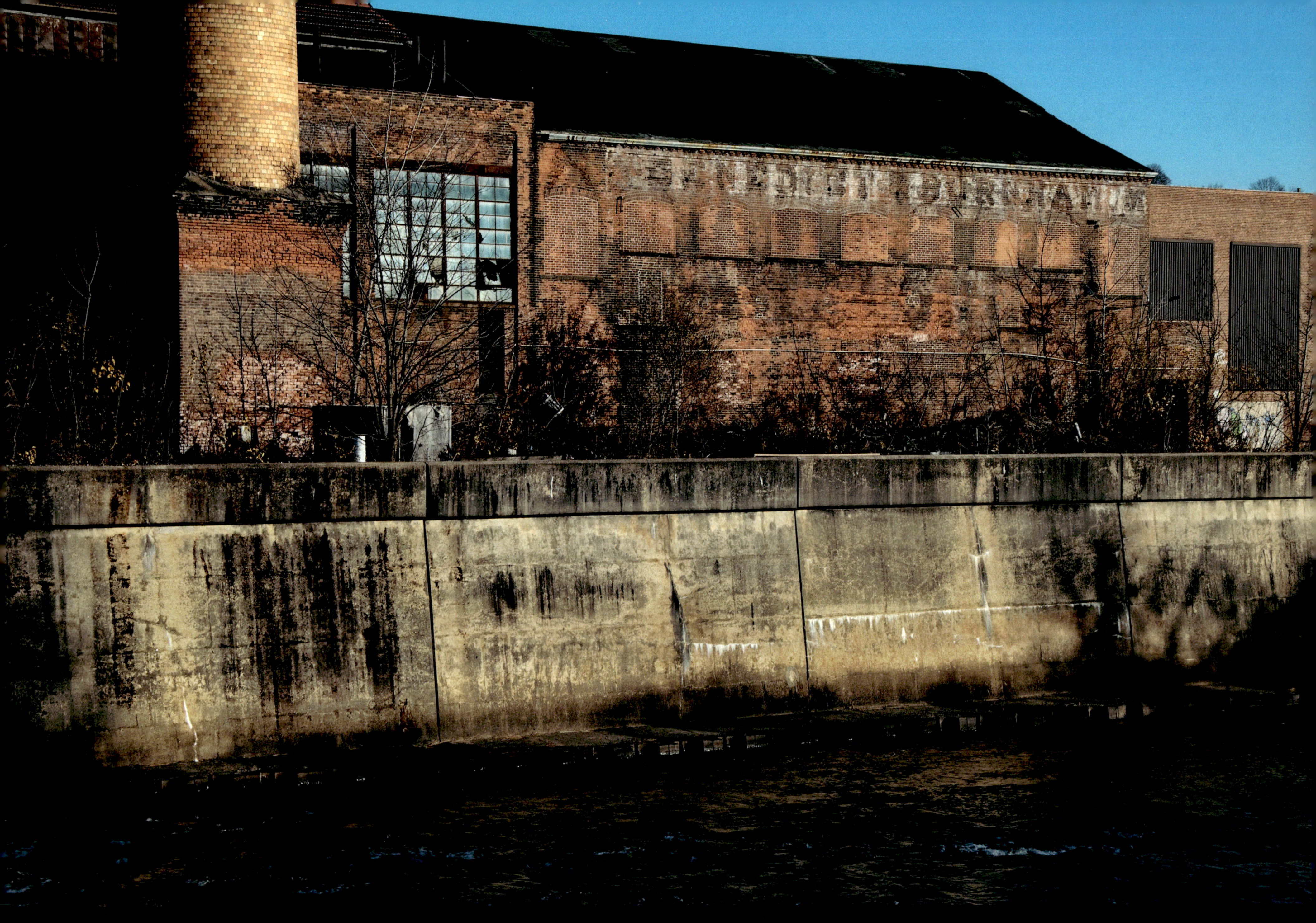

SHADOWS CAST BY BENEDICT & BURNHAM

Powerhouse, American Brass, Benedict Street, Waterbury, CT

OUR STORIES:

Benedict & Buttons

They told us it all began with buttons, mostly brass ones. We imagined retired Yankee colonels from the recently won revolution wanting something a bit spiffier than those they wore at Valley Forge and chagrined to realize the best brass buttons still came from Birmingham, England. Perhaps it's hard to take buttons seriously, but think of what you're wearing, and imagine removing every button, clip, hook, eye or fastener, every bit of elastic, every buckle, zipper or inch of Velcro tape. Take off your suspenders, and appreciate the power of buttons.

By one account it began in 1790. Under the flag of the new nation, three brothers—Silas, Henry, and Samuel Grilley—began making pewter buttons in a small shop on Main Street in Waterbury. Before the revolution it would have been seditious. Their buttons were cast whole and finished by hand, but a pewter button was a poor substitute for shiny British brass.

The Grilley brothers joined forces with Abel and Levi Porter and set up shop in the grist mill John Hopkins had built on the Mad River on what came to be known as Mill Street. The Porters had been trained as tinsmiths. The newly formed Abel Porter & Co. began melting scrap copper and infusing it with zinc to make ingots of brass. It was a technique stolen from English masters.

Porter & Co. paid us to load the ingots on wagons and haul them up into the hills of Litchfield, where the flourishing iron industry had a mill that could roll the ingots into rough sheets. We then loaded the sheets back onto wagons, and we coaxed the horses down the winding road to Waterbury, where horse-powered rollers finished the rough sheets, and craftsmen with dies stamped and finished buttons of brass. The road to a gentleman's trousers or to a lady's starched bonnet wound over many hills. In spite of the labor, we all thought our American buttons still looked paltry, like they were "gilded with dandelion water." The company the Grilleys and Porters started would become Scovill Manufacturing. It would one day be one of the brass industry's "Big Three."

In 1812 we were again fighting the British, and war cut off the supply of British buttons and new metal. More than the nation's regimentals were in jeopardy. Button supplies had become a matter of national, if not personal, security. Some claim it was the Scovill Brothers and some say it was Aaron Benedict. Whoever it was, we began salvaging every pot and kettle we could find, and in 1812 Waterbury manufactured enough buttons to keep the nation's colors flying; it has been said that Francis Scott Key was probably wearing Scovill buttons as he sat in Baltimore's harbor, detained by the British, and watched the banner yet "gallantly streaming."

Whatever Aaron Benedict's role, he has been called the father of Waterbury's wealth; in 1824, he and James Croft, an Englishman, revolutionized the way brass was rolled so it would outshine British brass; in times to come nobody would roll the way Connecticut rolled. Benedict and Burnham became the largest maker of appliances in the United States. Aaron Benedict began and ran landmark companies where we made everything from pins to door knobs, buckles, clocks, badges, burners, and jobs. They pioneered the manufacturing of seamless tube. Some say Aaron Benedict is the one who made brass golden.

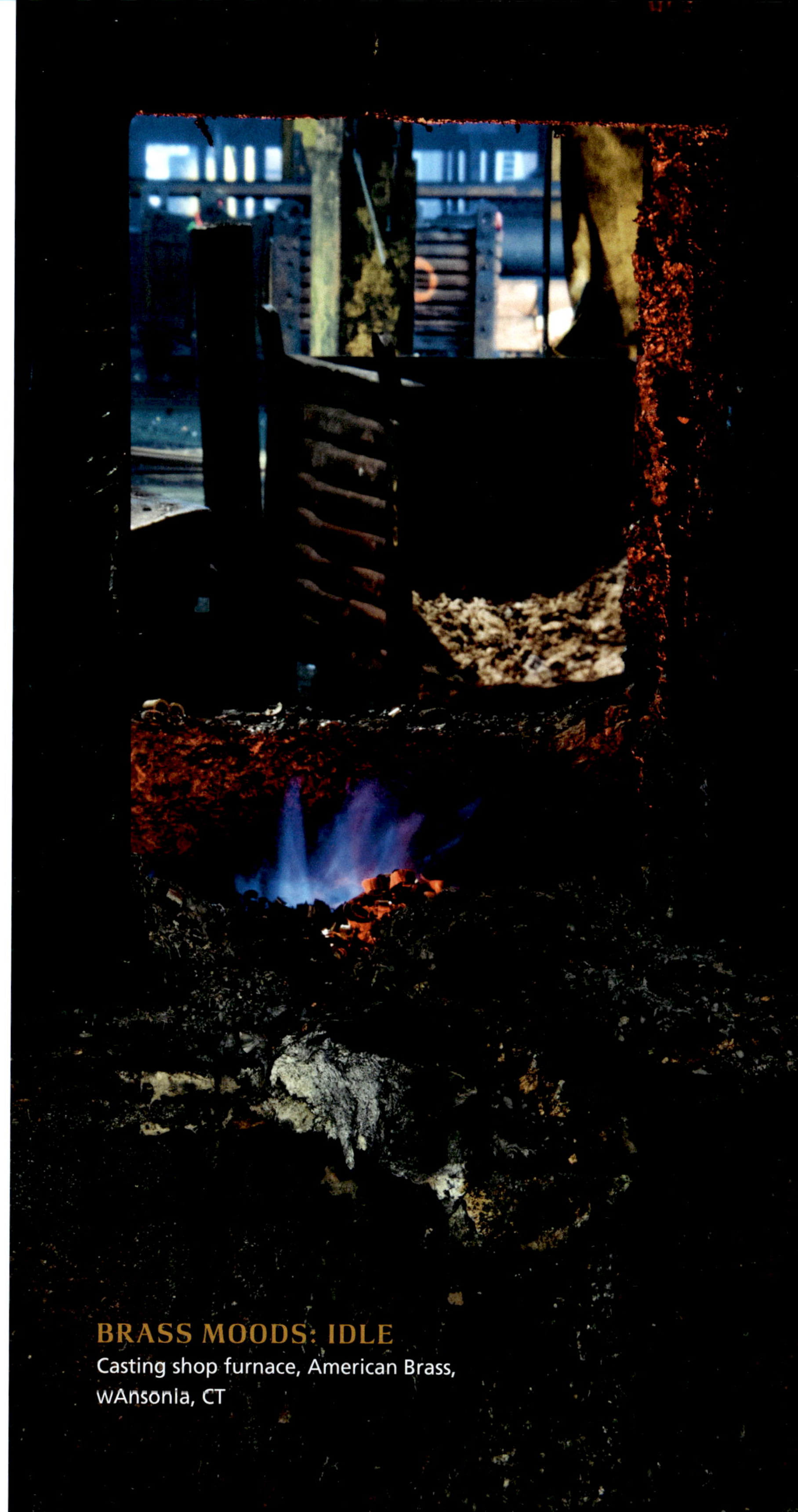

BRASS MOODS: IDLE
Casting shop furnace, American Brass, wAnsonia, CT

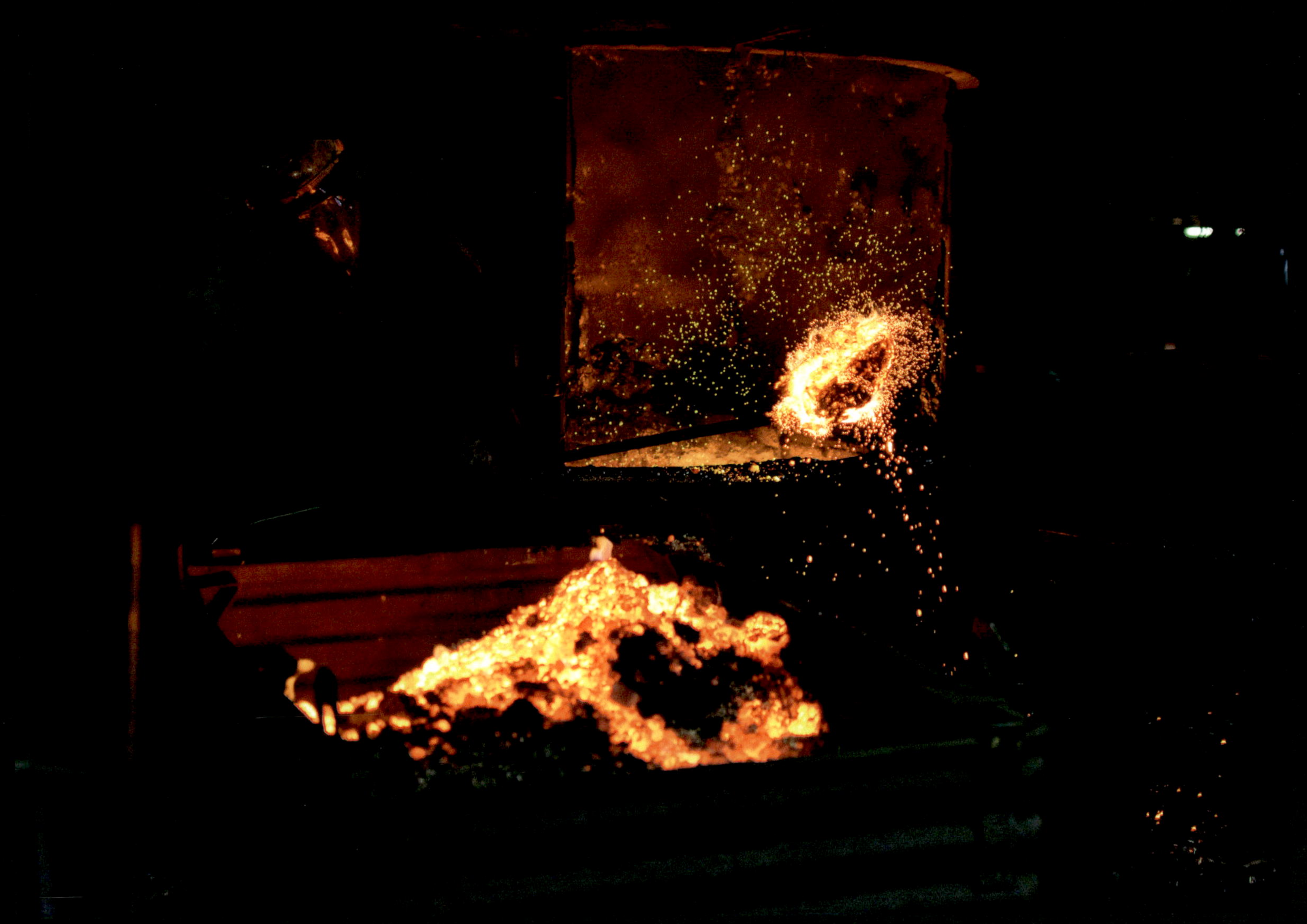

SHOVELING SLAG

Casting shop furnace,
American Brass,
Ansonia, CT

PHOTOGRAPHER'S JOURNAL:
When I began following the old tracks through Brass Valley, I wanted to photograph what was left of its industrial past. I was looking for rust and a glimpse of another age. It's funny where tracks can lead. I never expected to find myself in a time warp, photographing where giant hydraulics are still whining, steel clanking, hot glowing metal flying through the air, where the steam still rises from old pickling vats, and men are still charging furnaces in buildings where the soot has had a hundred years to cake, and the air at casting time is tasty. I never dreamed such a place still existed. I heard about the casting shop from a man in Thomaston who managed a small copper mill there. He, too, was one of the last of brass; he told me about the brass mill in Waterbury where they were still making tube seamlessly. He said I had to see it, photograph it.

The tracks are still maintained between the flood control dam north of Thomaston and Waterbury, but there's no regular train service over them except in summer when hobbyists run weekend rides for children and tourists. I followed the tracks past the old Chase brass factories before they were knocked down, and eventually reached Waterbury. I had little idea what I would find, and no trains passed.

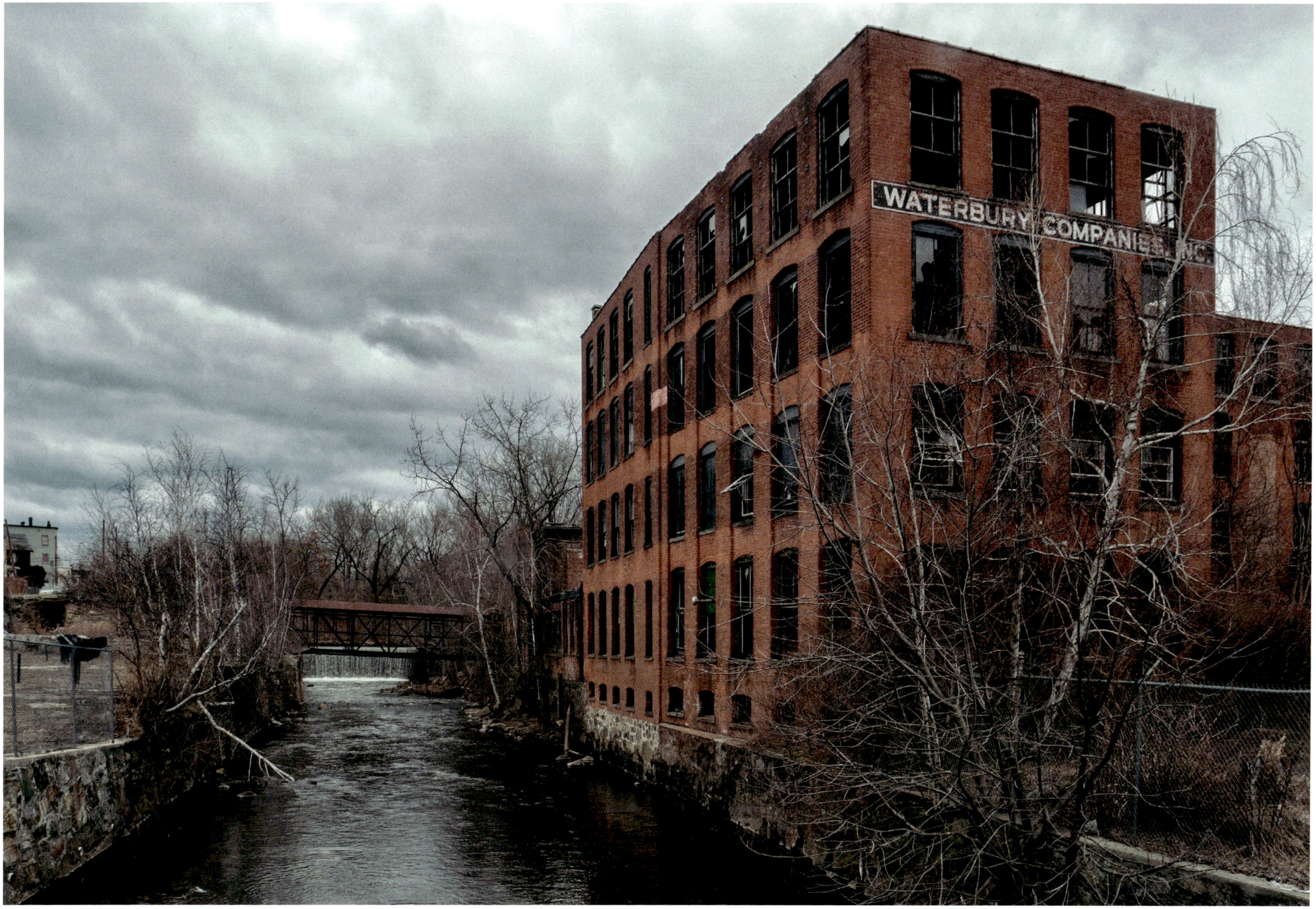

BETWEEN RIVER & MILL STREET, SPRING, 2013

Waterbury Companies, Inc., River Street, Waterbury, CT

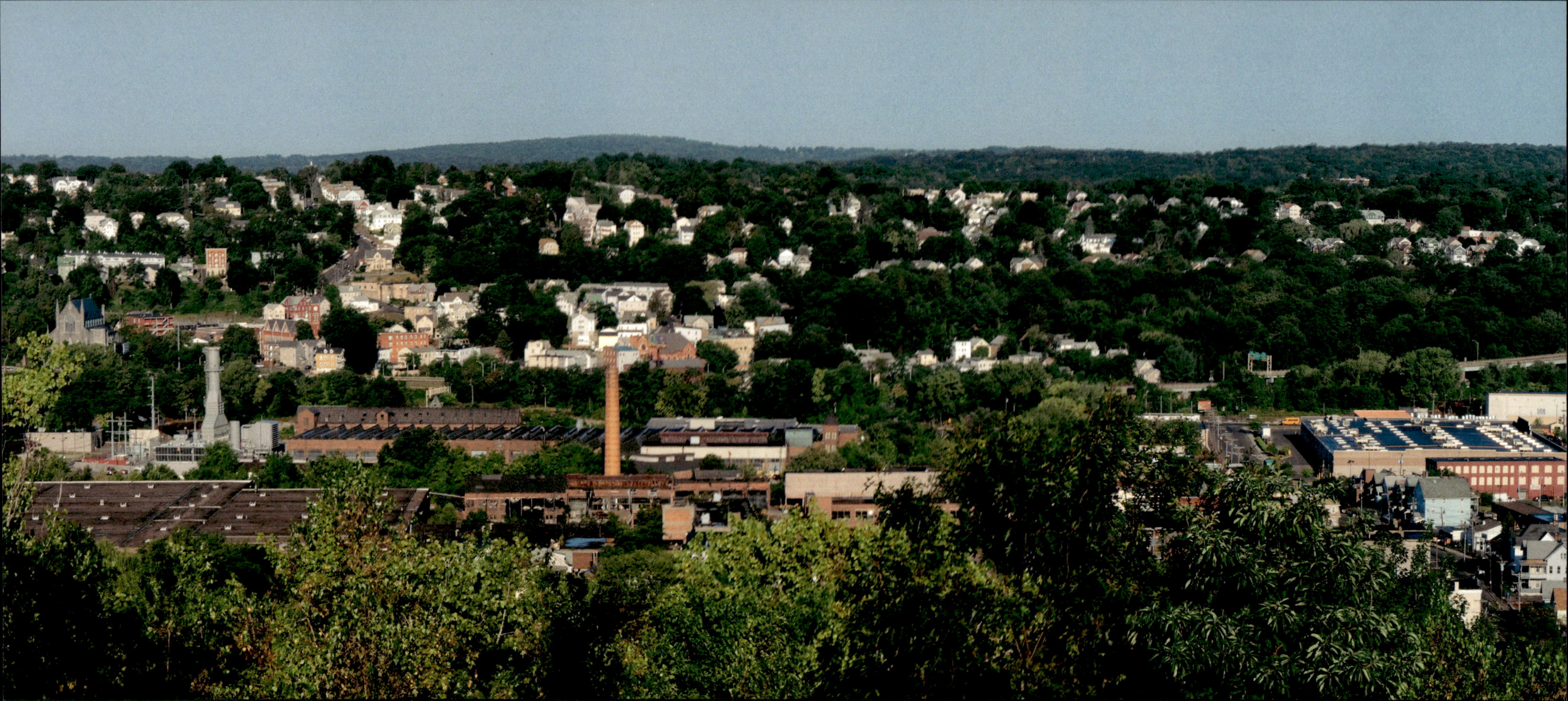

PHOTOGRAPHER'S JOURNAL:
I'm standing in Holyland. Holyland looks down on the Naugatuck Valley and over Waterbury's South End to keep them holy. Near here, the first wheels rolled brass.

The large factory complex with the two chimneys was once the primary manufacturing facility of the old American Brass Company. It is the direct descendent of many of the companies founded by Aaron Benedict, arguably the father of Brass Valley. This campus is a small part of what once was American Brass. They turned a river of new brass into stuff. Once they made two-thirds of the world's brass stuff.

Inside the long shed with the sawtooth roof, three-ton billets of brass are still processed into brass tubes. The brass is cast into billets down river in Ansonia. The tube mill was built in a hurry in 1917 to meet the needs of World War I. Today, it is the last factory in the United States where specification-critical, large-diameter, seamless brass tubing is made. Some of the mill equipment is original. Much of it dates to 1930 when the mill was updated. Some, I'm told, was in use here in 1903, the year the Wright brothers became airborne. I've seen plans for one of the metal-working benches dated 1897.

The sawtooth roof wraps around the 1880's lampworks built by Holmes, Booth & Haydens when their 1850s factory on this site burned. The strip of trees between the two rows of factory sheds follows the Naugatuck River. Once both sides of the river belonged to American Brass. Men still work on the west side of the river, who once worked on the east side, before the east side was sold and abandoned and the connecting bridge across the river was fenced and padlocked. Holyland sits on top of Pine Hill, along the east ridge of the valley.

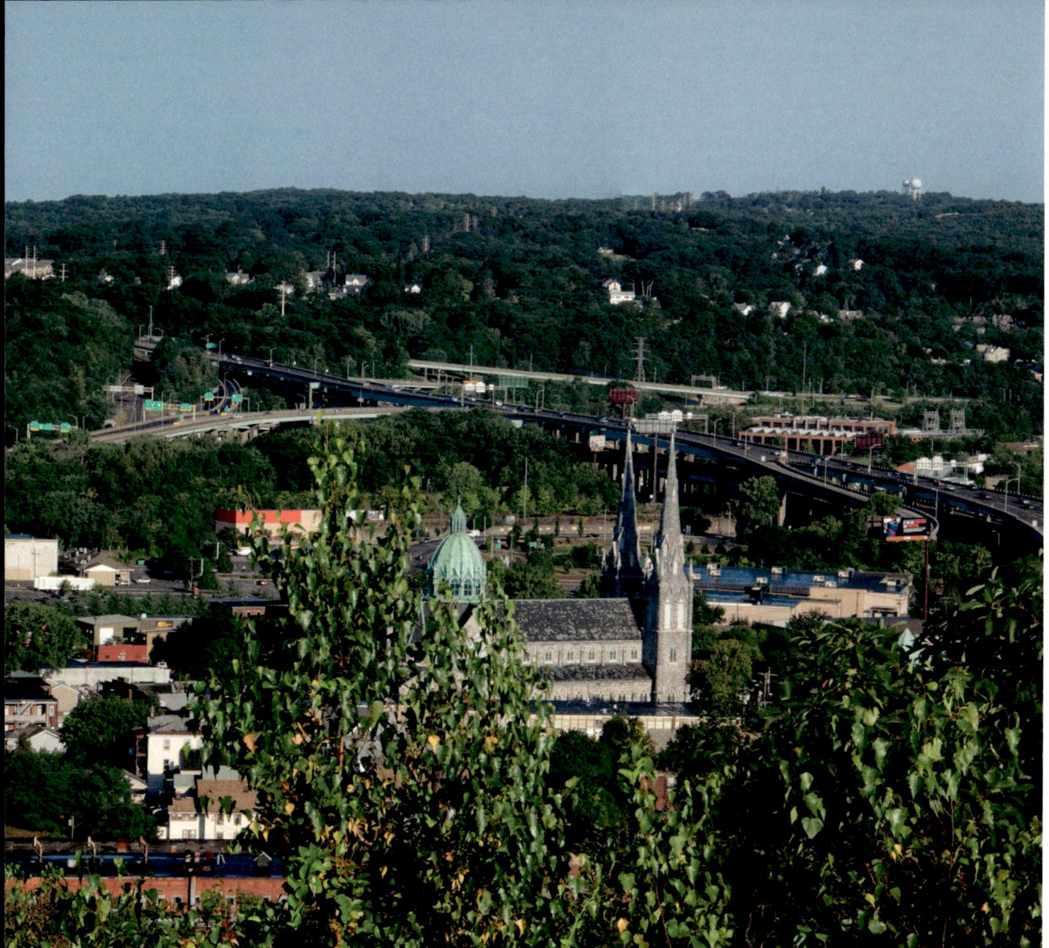

Holyland was the private park where, in 1956, John Greco set his cross and eventually welcomed 40,000 visitors a year from all over the country. They came to stroll through a miniature Bethlehem and Jerusalem that he and neighbors sculpted by hand using chicken wire and plaster. They were mostly South Enders, Italians from the mills who built Holyland, and before his work on Holyland ceased, Greco had added a sad tribute to the martyrdom of Martin Luther King. John Greco's cross became a landmark for travelers, regardless of color or faith, from everywhere heading up Brass Valley on Route 8 or across it on Interstate 84 and for those as well who lived beneath its glow in a place variously known as "Waterbury," "Dirty Water," and "Sin City." Holyland, today, is another one of Brass Valley's ruins.

OUR STORIES:

Pine Hill

We've climbed to the top of Pine Hill to look across Waterbury's South End where many of us lived and died.

Waterbury sits approximately halfway up the Naugatuck Valley. It is the land of many rivers where the valley spreads out. It has always been too wet and rocky to farm, but mosquitos thrive. The local tribes called it "Mattatuck," the land without trees, and wondered why white men, who came over the hills from Farmington, would want to live here instead of at Rimmon Falls where one could hear the song of water, and could fish in the shade of a tree. The settlers called Mattatuck "Waterbury" and built mills on the Naugatuck and on abundant tributaries to manufacture buttons and kettles and stuff folks needed.

Hidden in the foliage are the rivers we lived by. The Mad River flows behind vanished factory sheds of Scovill Brass Company. The river is masked beneath the foreground trees. The Naugatuck River flows through the strip of trees between the two stacks of the mostly abandoned factory sheds of American Brass Company. Waterbury Button and Waterbury Buckle were down there, too. Most of us found our way from distant places and cast our lots with the industries here, and a short lifetime later we were neighborhoods and our children took our places. The names say it all: proud to be from Washington Hill or from Abrigador (in Portuguese, "refuge," or "shelter") or from Hopeville. We lived where Scovill and American Brass emptied their coolants, wastes, and pickling tonics and where dyes from the Princeton Knitting Mill colored the river gaily. In the center of the South End, the Mad River joins the Naugatuck, and the brews of American Brass and Scovill mixed to a more potent potion, but the streets were safe for stickball, and across back alleys our chatter stitched us together with people on the next street until someone called the hillside a "crazy quilt," and it stuck.

Stickball is gone, and so is Scovill, and what's left of American Brass churns slowly, has retreated to the west side of the river, and Waterbury's proud motto, "Quid Aere Perennius," or "What is more lasting than brass?" is no longer uttered rhetorically. From Pine Hill the view is like that over any of the mill towns that blossomed into neighborhoods along the Naugatuck Valley. Derelict factories lie decomposing like amnesia, and we get by as best we can.

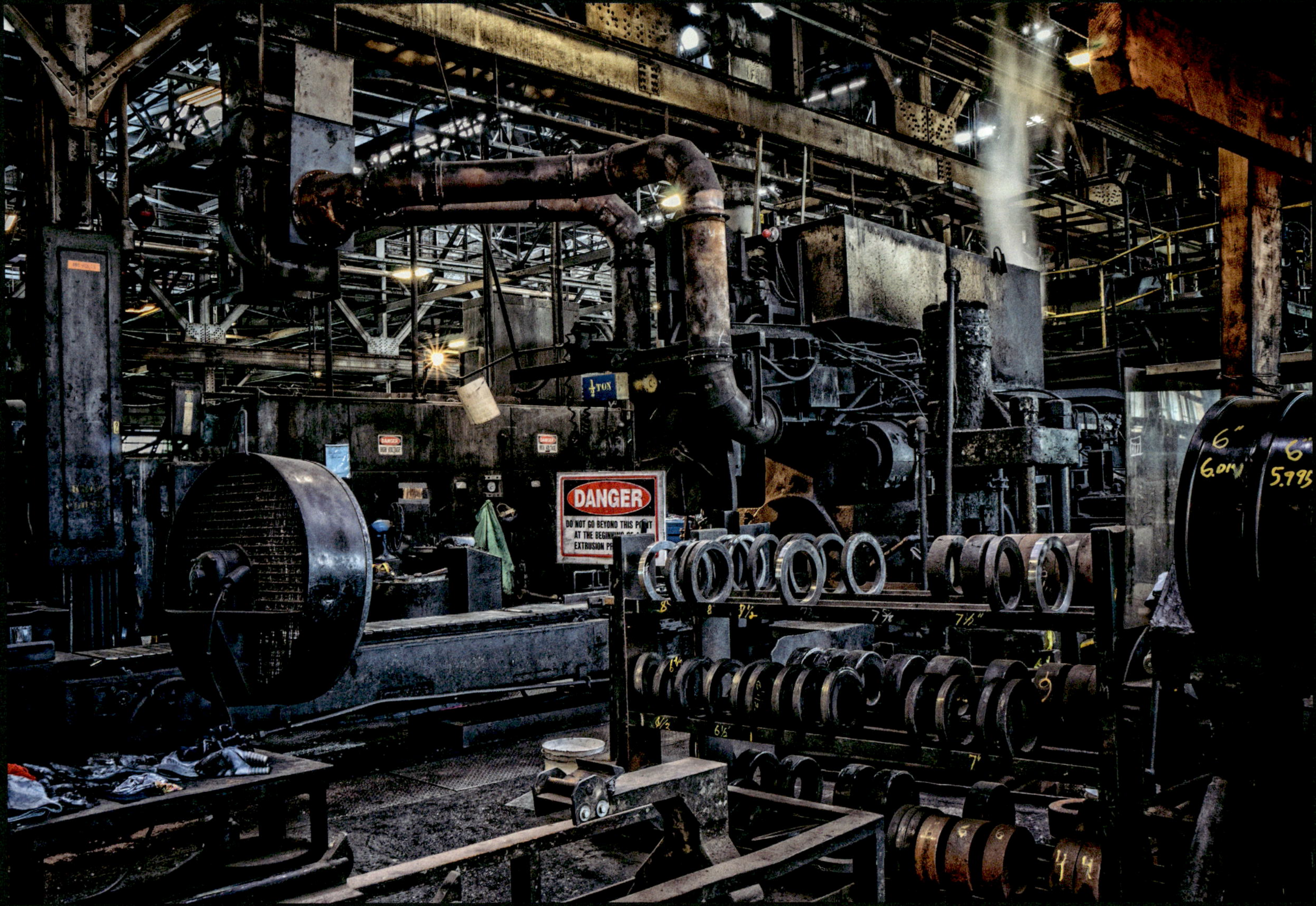

PART TWO:

FOUNDER'S ALCHEMY

Down river to the last industrial brass foundry in the Valley

I LOOKED IN THE DIRECTION OF THE STEAM AND CLICKED

Extruder, American Brass, Bank Street, Waterbury, CT

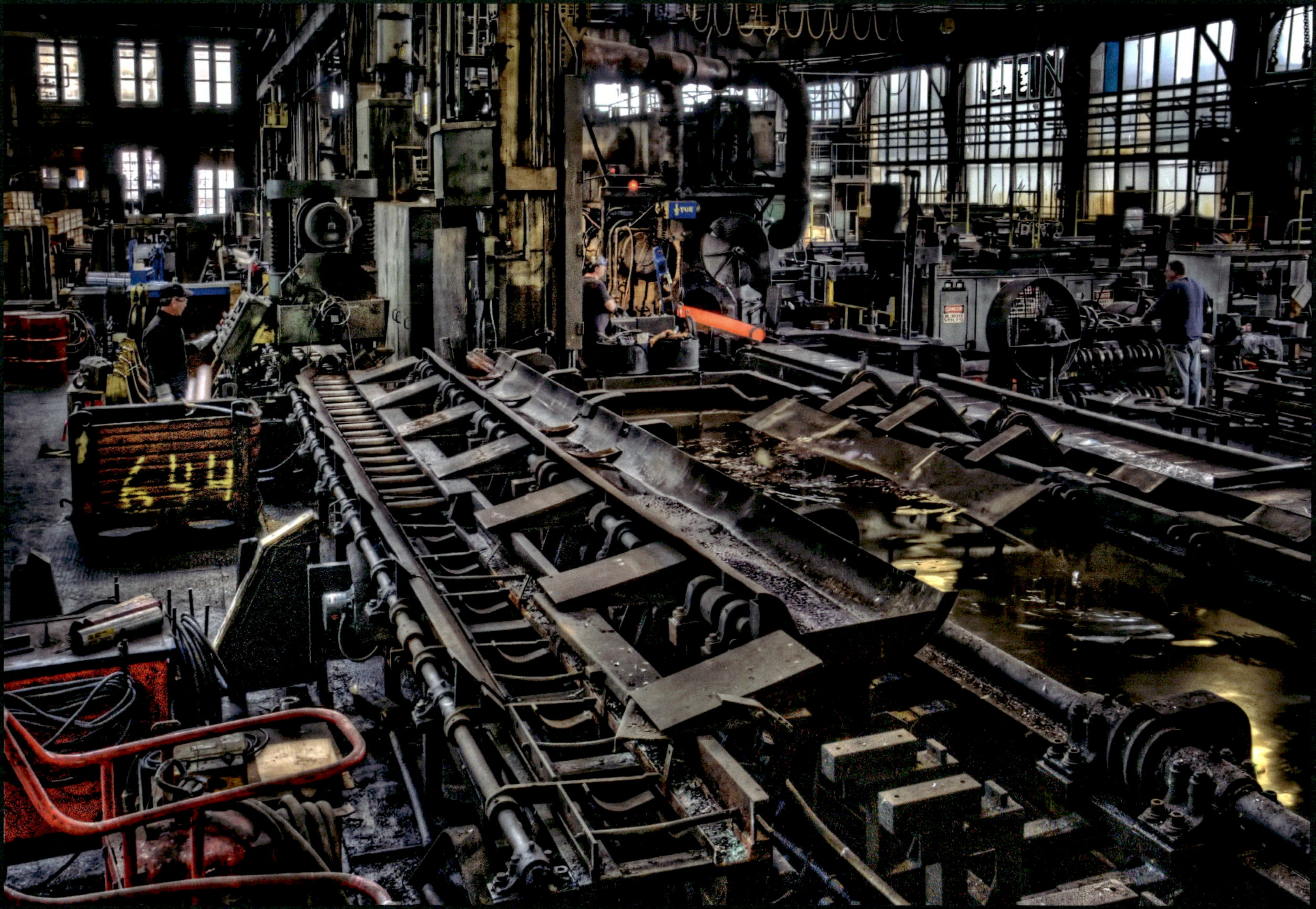

PHOTOGRAPHER'S JOURNAL:

The first time I entered and photographed in the shed with the sawtooth roof, all was chaos. I looked around—saw a plume of smoke or steam puffing steadily into the joists of the factory shed in the northeast corner, and I turned my camera that way. I later recognized that was where the howl of straining engines came from, and the heavy clank of steel striking steel so you felt it in the souls of your feet. Without realizing it, I had composed a photo of the extruder. It was the most important piece of equipment the company owned, I learned, the last of its kind, nothing else like it in the country. It is as large as a dragon.

Because of the extruder, the company maintains and runs a complete production line. It begins at the foundry downstream in Ansonia where metal is mixed and cast into billets, and it ends at the benches, here, in Waterbury, where finished, large-diameter tube is tested and crated and loaded for delivery.

Master mechanics, machinists, and machine operators still work here. Once even the unskilled grunts, living by the load they carried, inhaled the culture of the toolmakers and got promoted. Thousands once worked here; now there are fewer than a hundred.

EXTRUDER FROM COOLING TANK

American Brass, Bank Street, Waterbury, CT

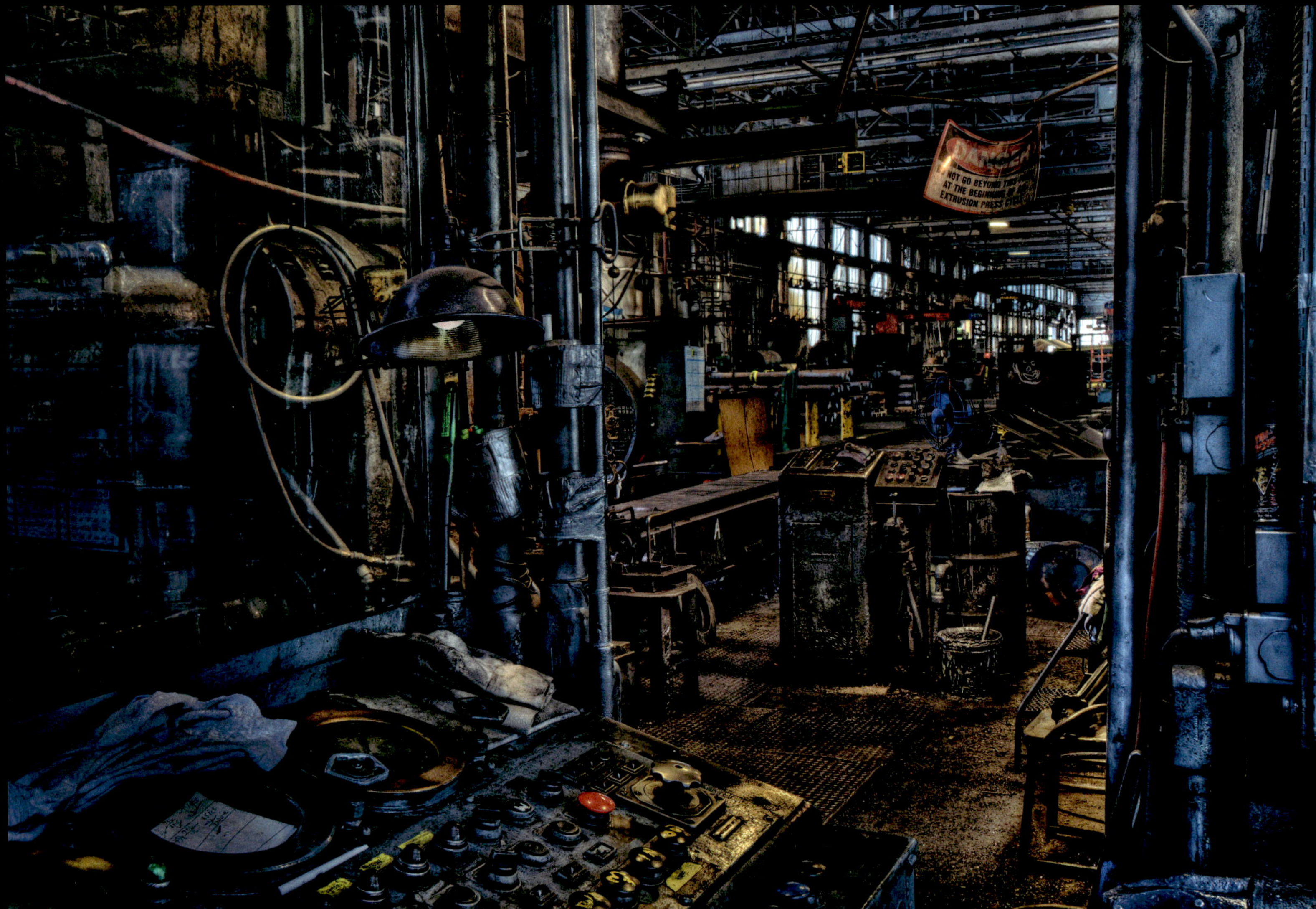

EXTRUDER FROM THE MASTER CONTROLS

American Brass, Bank Street, Waterbury, CT

PHOTOGRAPHER'S JOURNAL:
Mythologist Joseph Campbell advises, "Follow your bliss and doors will open where you didn't know there were doors." I had followed the tracks to photograph rust and passed through an unexpected portal into a mill with a nineteenth-century tempo and machines that had worked metal for more than a century, but the production line began further down the track where new metal and scrap are cast into billets of brass.

The story of the brass mill should begin there, so I followed the tracks south. I was headed to the spot where a few commuter trains a day still pass through the center of the foundry property. It's near the bottom of the valley, just before the Naugatuck joins the Housatonic.

Below Waterbury, the track passes the ruins of the old Bristol Company then on to Naugatuck, famous once as the home of Naugahyde. Soon the valley narrows and the rail hugs cliffs beside the river as they wind together through a wild, narrow ravine, where an amusement park once flourished beneath High Rock. I climbed to the top and looked down—High Rock, which is remembered still for the freed Indian slave Toby, who stayed among the settlers, and whose history is muddled with a jug of rum and an Indian princess leaping from the summit.

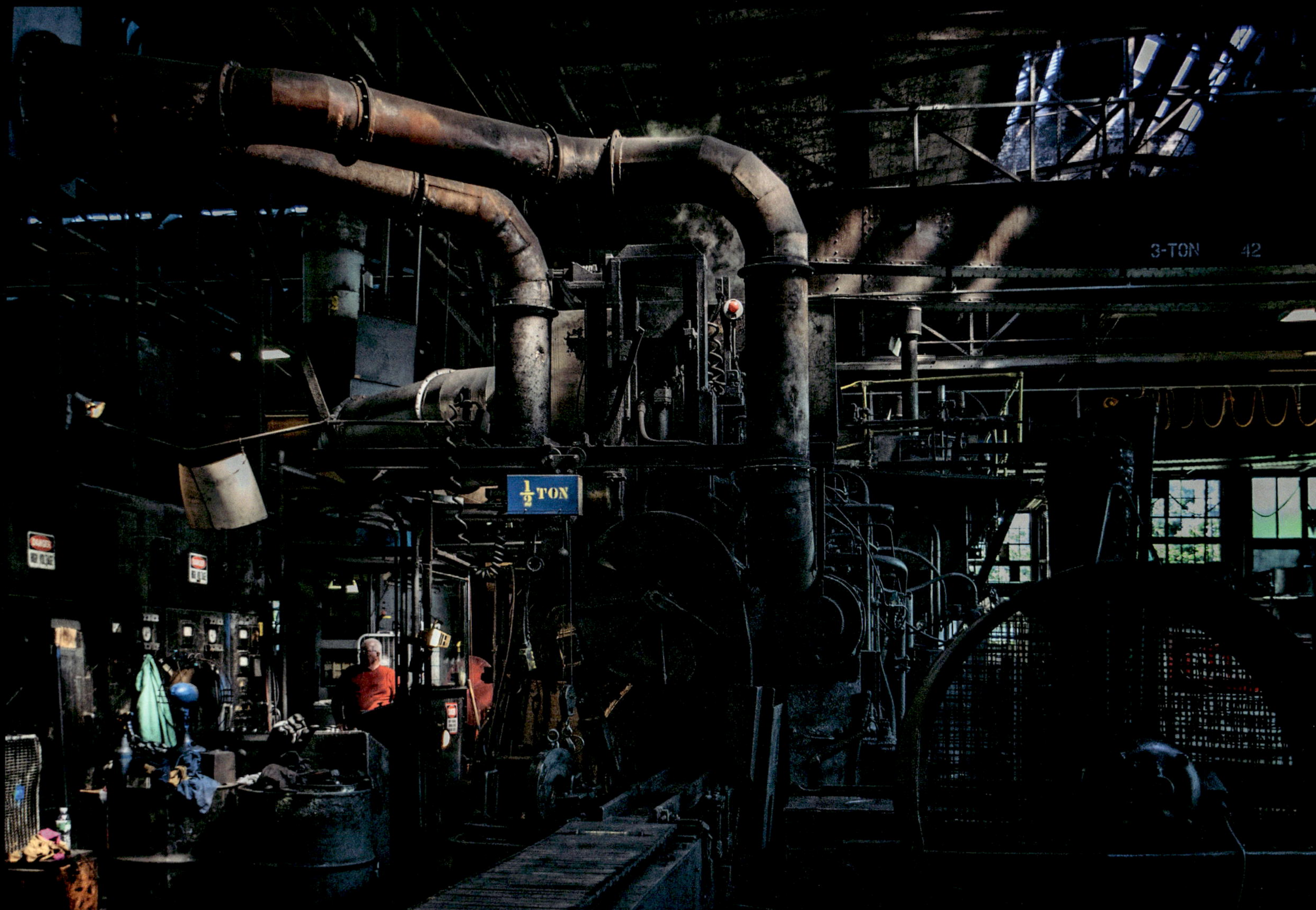

There's barely room for track to pass until Beacon Falls, where wooden matches were first made. Further on the rails pass Rock Rimmon, so named, they say, because it looked like frontier into which savages fled; this is the lower valley. Beside Rimmon is Seymour, the town built around the Naugatuck River's "great" falls, once cherished as fishing grounds before the river was channeled for power. The track follows the east shore, as the river swells wide and still as a mirror on many mornings, restrained by the Kinneytown Dam. Below the dam, the train rides on a sliver of land between the rocky river and the sullen canal, long forgotten, that Almon Farrel built in 1845 to power the first mills of Ansonia. That was the mill site I was headed to, to the ancient foundry of the American Brass Company and to stage one of the last brass production lines of old Brass Valley.

It's a peaceful walk along the track beside the flowing canal for more than a mile, hidden under a jungle canopy. It's terrain known mostly by birds, squirrels, possums, and turtles before the track and canal reach the edge of the brass company where the canal goes quietly underground, and the track passes between the brick factories of old American Brass, Ansonia. I had never been in a working foundry, didn't know what to expect.

EXTRUDER AT REST

American Brass, Bank Street, Waterbury, CT

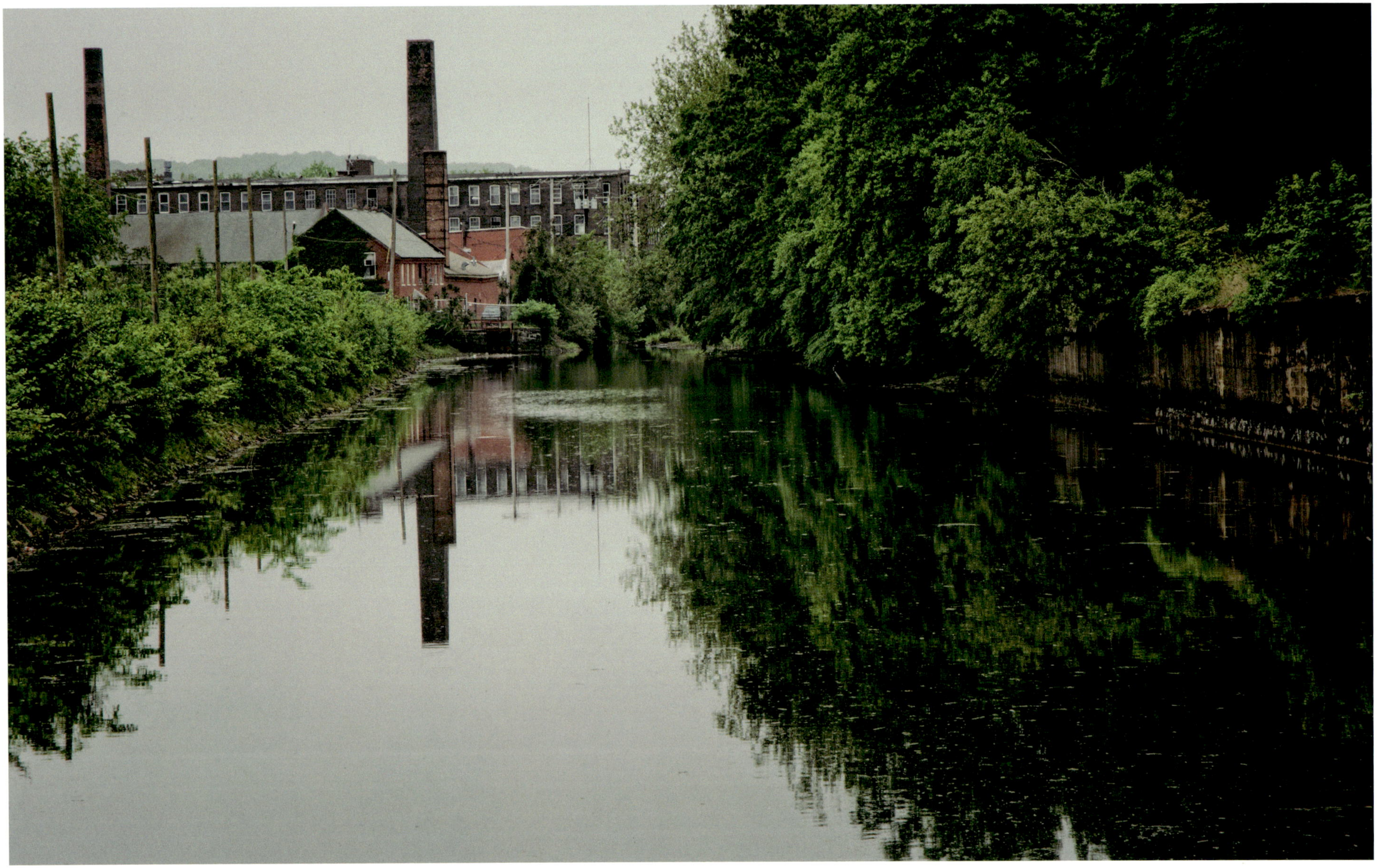

OUR STORIES:

Derby Landing

THE SHELTON CANAL

Factories between the old canal and . the Housatonic River, Shelton, CT

Water from the Naugatuck River flows into the river we called Ousatonic at Paugassett, the township now known as Derby. That was the top of the Housatonic River's tidewater, a place of beauty where the great artists of the day painted, and where once we sometimes smelled the salt air. It was as far upstream as the old sailing ships could navigate. We cherished the quiet beauty of the rivers' confluence and the richness of the fishing grounds there. We built a landing where the rivers joined and built a double-width road up from the shore, and it became known as "Derby Landing." Derby Landing provided sheltered harbor, well upstream, and became an early center for shipbuilding and trade. Ships from Derby Landing served the East Coast and traveled as far as the West Indies with local fish and produce. By 1730 we had built mills not only in Derby Landing, but on the eastern shore in the area that became Ansonia, and on the west in the area that became Shelton. A century later the area at the tidewater was a hotbed of industrial innovation and a bustling manufacturing center where we produced cotton and woolen goods, paper, sheet metal, wire, and anything small in shaped

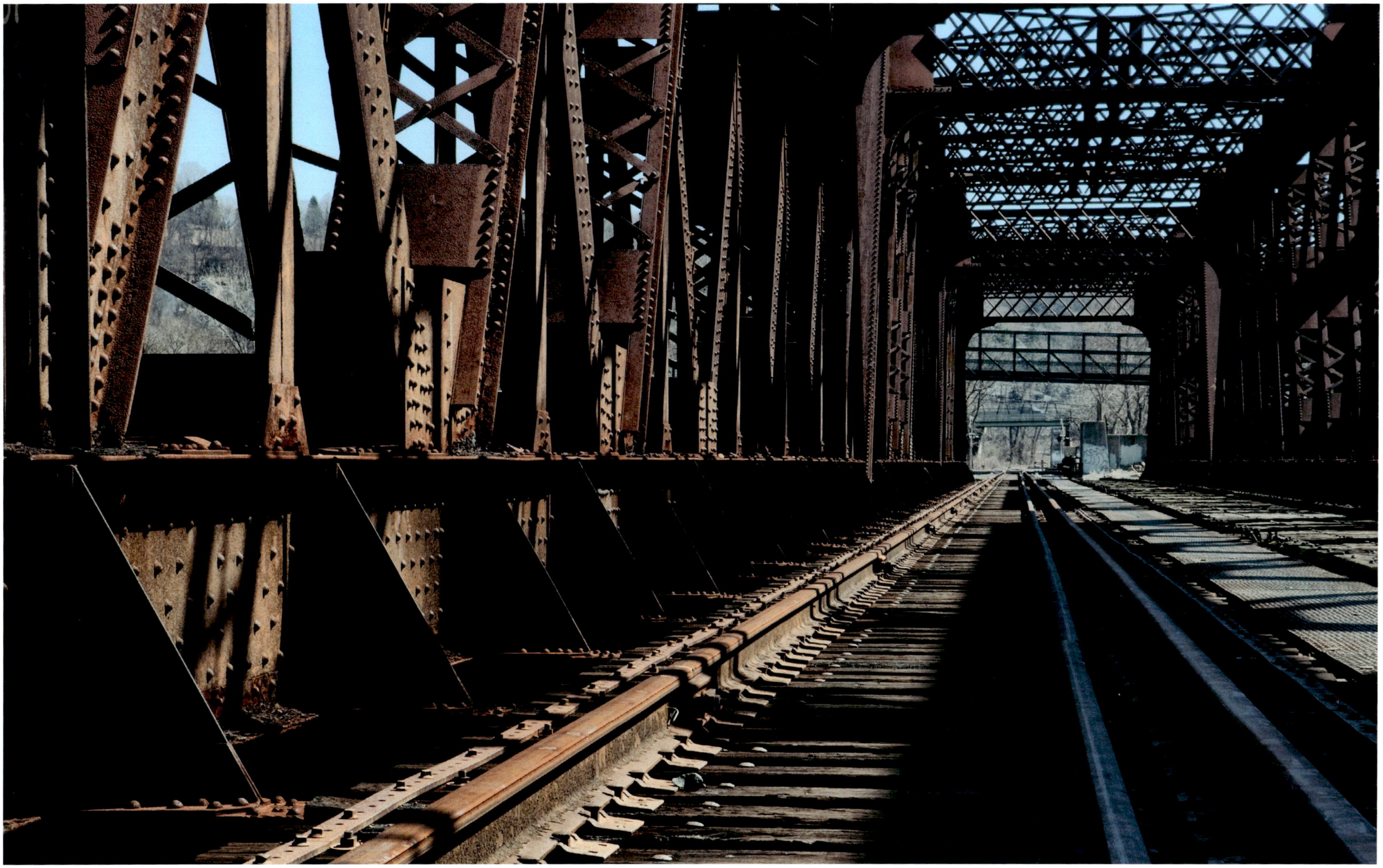

metal from augers to pins. Between three young settlements lay the valuable resources of our rivers' confluence and above them the energy of the Housatonic and Naugatuck headwaters. Here, on two rivers, was energy for industry in close proximity to the ports of New Haven and Bridgeport and the sea.

While the Housatonic River wanders, the Naugatuck tumbles with unusual swiftness, thirteen feet per mile. It is the largest Connecticut river with waters that lie entirely inside the state. In 1849 the Naugatuck Railroad would conquer its inclines and narrow passes as far north as Winsted, permitting water-powered manufacturing to thrive and providing new access to markets for farm goods produced inland, and we heard it was a land of opportunity and started coming even before the building of the railroads, before the slow shift of wealth and power began to move from fertile fields toward barren, rocky soils.

HIGH IRON 1 – SHELTON TO DERBY LANDING

Abandoned railroad spur from Danbury to Derby

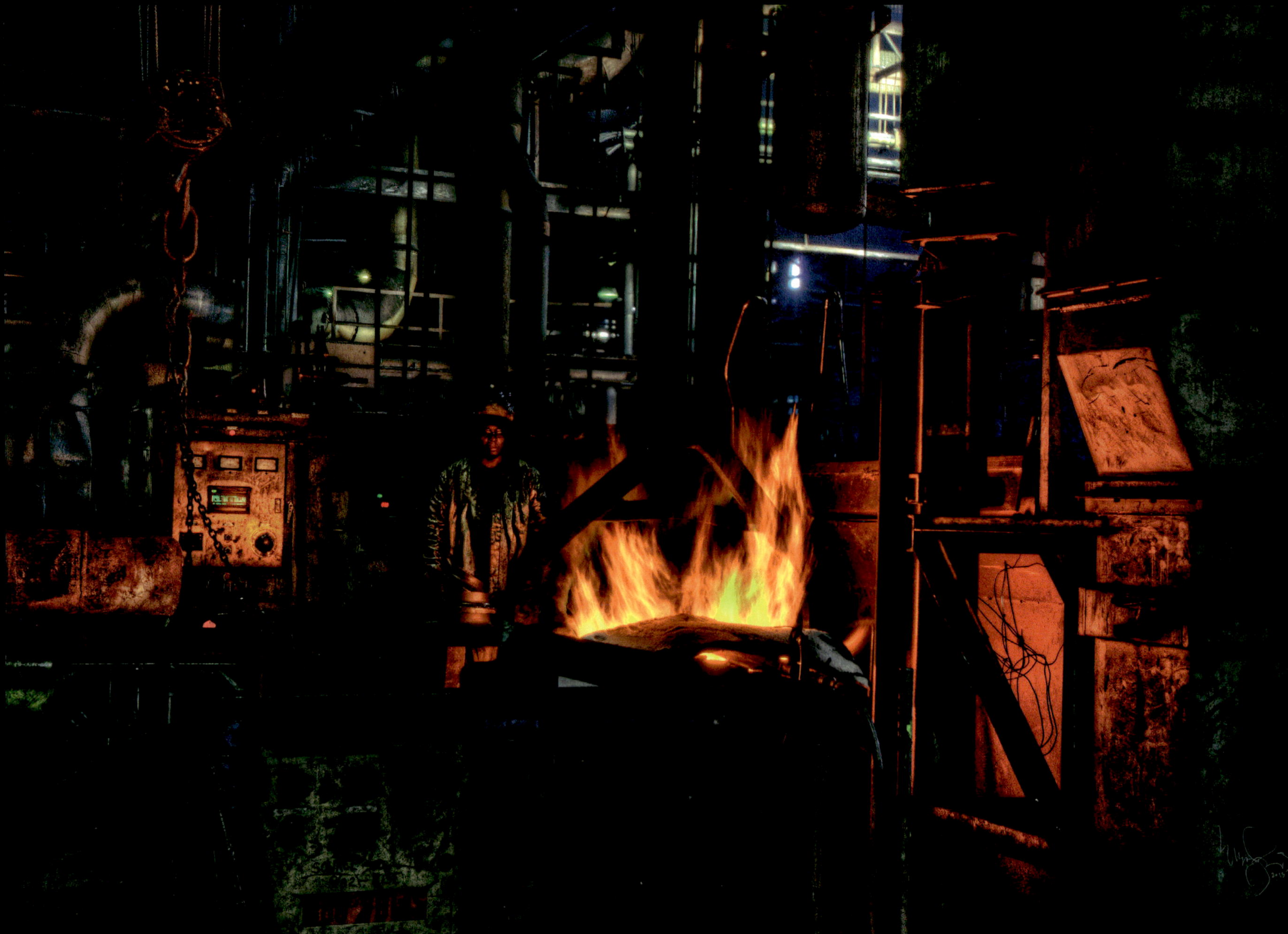

HEATING THE CHARGE
Willy preparing the charge to prime the furnace, American Brass, Ansonia, CT

PHOTOGRAPHER'S JOURNAL:
The truth of the foundry is its darkness except where there is light, and then truth comes in flashes, flares, and flourishes. Whether beautiful or ugly, they snag on my lenses and make pixels bleed. In the sooted darkness, even bare, fluorescent tubes among the trusses of the shed glare explosively on my images and must be avoided or removed by photographers' magic.

On Monday, repairs were completed on the casting furnace. Willy has just lit the fires for priming it. Damir, Lucio, Mike, and Willy all said priming was a photo op, but I only had a vague idea of what to expect. Willy explained the process to me and suggested a good place to catch it, but much preparation and waiting followed.

First a small amount of metal, "the charge," was heated in a small furnace at the far end of the shed. Beside it was a crucible to transport the metal. It was also heated. Everything had to be at the right temperatures in both these vessels and at the main furnace. It was more than an hour later when Willy, Lucio, and the crane were suddenly in motion, Soon Damir reappeared. The dials were all in sync, and it was time to prime.

They poured the glowing, liquid brass from the small furnace into the waiting crucible. The crucible was then lifted and taxied gently by crane down the shed to the casting furnace, which had also been prepared. The electrical metal "element" that would carry the charge that would heat the furnace would be made of liquid brass, insubstantial like the ash that glows inside a propane camping lantern. Willy slowly tipped the crucible, and for a moment a ribbon of white light connected to the open casting furnace; it closed the circuit as the air ignited. A blinding squall of sparks roared from the mouth of the furnace, singed and spun like a whirlwind into the trussed roof. I was stunned! Blinded! The utter darkness of the cavernous shed sucked up the plume of yellow and orange that kept rising from the furnace while at its base the short, still, white stripe glowed motionlessly where molten brass flowed furiously. It was a mash-up of blinding light and blinding dark, a hollow rush of energized air.

Of course, when I looked at my exposures later, the plume of sparks rising into the dark vaults of the shed was bigger and taller than my wide lens could grasp, the light brighter and darker than my camera could record, and exploding sparks challenged available shutter speeds. To put it plainly, I missed the shot.

When the plume died away, Willy, Mike, and Lucio put the hood back on the furnace and loaded scrap metal for casting the first pair of billets. The furnace is kept running 24/7 so priming is infrequent and it was many months before I got another chance at the shot.

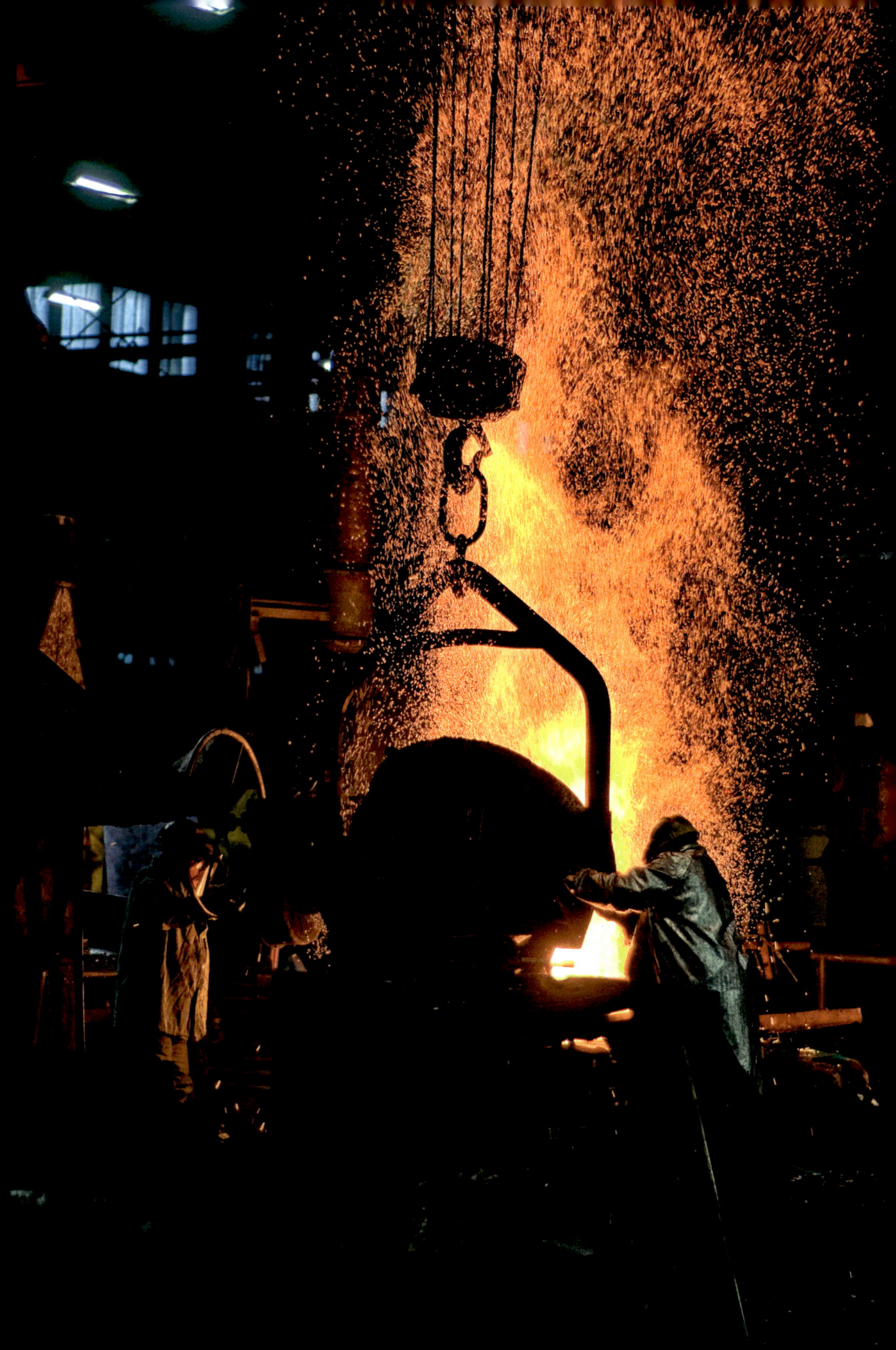

PRIMING THE FURNACE
Casting shop, American Brass, Ansonia, CT

HOLLOW TOGETHER

Hillside barn
hollow with age,
no longer fit for the stacked hay,
even,
stares into the valley
where the works have closed.

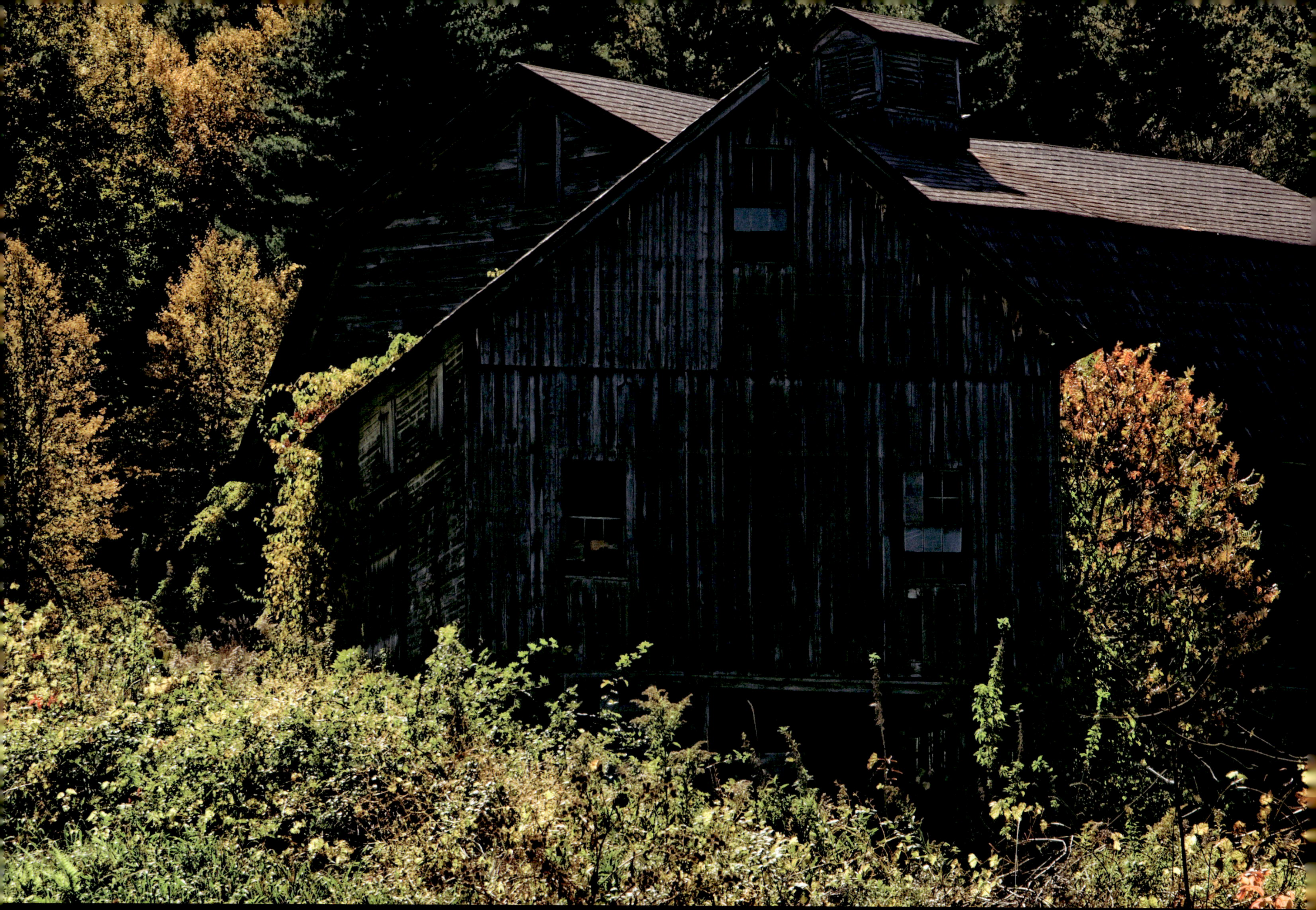

HILL BARN

Former dairy farm, Cornwall, CT

OUR STORIES:

Smithville

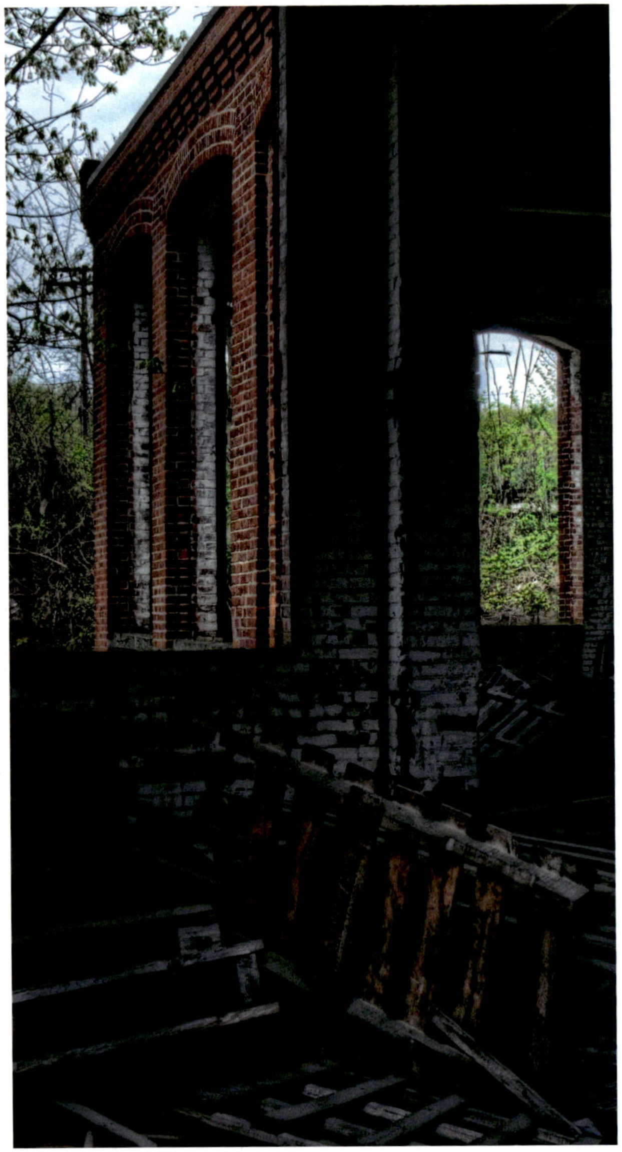

CLOISTERED AT PLATT'S MILL
The Bristol Company, Waterbury, CT

Sheldon Smith was born in 1791 and, like most of us, received only the most basic education in the little schoolhouse near where the brook enters the Narrows on the Ousatonic River in Derby Landing. At age fourteen he was taken in as an apprentice to learn saddle and harness making from Edward Peet, and seven years later he was taken in as a partner and manager. That was the way things were supposed to work.

The year was 1812; like many among us, he served in the war, and when he returned he had a vision for Derby. He was thinking beyond bridles and leather. Was he inspired by Humphreysville, a visionary, Utopian, factory community that was developing upstream at Rimmon Falls? Colonel Humphreys had built homes and schools for his factory workers! It's unclear what part Utopia played in Smith's vision, but it was definitely about factories and water.

When we rejected Smith's ideas for Derby, he went to New York. In New York, he met Anson G. Phelps, a trader and, like Smith, a former saddle maker. Phelps had been investing in copper and other minerals. Smith continued to Newark, New Jersey. When Smith arrived, Newark had an extensive water system of springs and reservoirs, and a stringy patchwork of bored, wooden pipe that delivered drinking water to each family in the city for twenty dollars a year. In 1822, under Smith's leadership, the old system was replaced with a new one to provide water to everyone in Newark through a revolutionary system of iron pipes. It's unclear what prepared Smith for the task, but here's the way our history book passed the story on:

> Mr. Smith showed himself a public benefactor to the city. He introduced, and supplied at his own expense the inhabitants of the place with good water, a sanitary want much needed. This enterprise at first was looked upon as visionary, and Mr. Smith was laughed at for the undertaking by capitalists, but when the blessings of pure water, by the citizens, were realized, he was importuned to sell out to an envious corporation, giving it control of so valuable a public improvement, which he did without profit or loss to himself, satisfied to confer a lasting benefit on a place in which he had been so much prospered. The citizens of Newark to-day owe the introduction of water into their city to the enterprise of Sheldon Smith.
>
> —Samuel Orcutt,
> ***The History of the Old Town of Derby, Connecticut*, 1880**

In the 1830s, Sheldon Smith returned to Derby, to the point of land between the Naugatuck and Housatonic rivers and the sheltered tidal basin. He came back to his birthplace and brought us a new plan and a backer. Derby was in decline following the revolution and in need of revitalization. Smith had bought the old, run-down grist mill. He called his vision "Smithville," and he went to work. He and his New York City friend, Anson Phelps, laid out our streets and built our housing and created our shining town green high on the hill, with our business district slightly below. They also built the Derby reservoir and a dam on the Naugatuck River and a mile-and-a-half canal system drawing Naugatuck water though town to the Housatonic River. Smith was thinking big. The canal would power a considerable industrial village and serve many manufacturers.

In the end, the name that was chosen was not Smithville but Birmingham after the center of England's prized copper and brass industry. It was a shrewd choice.

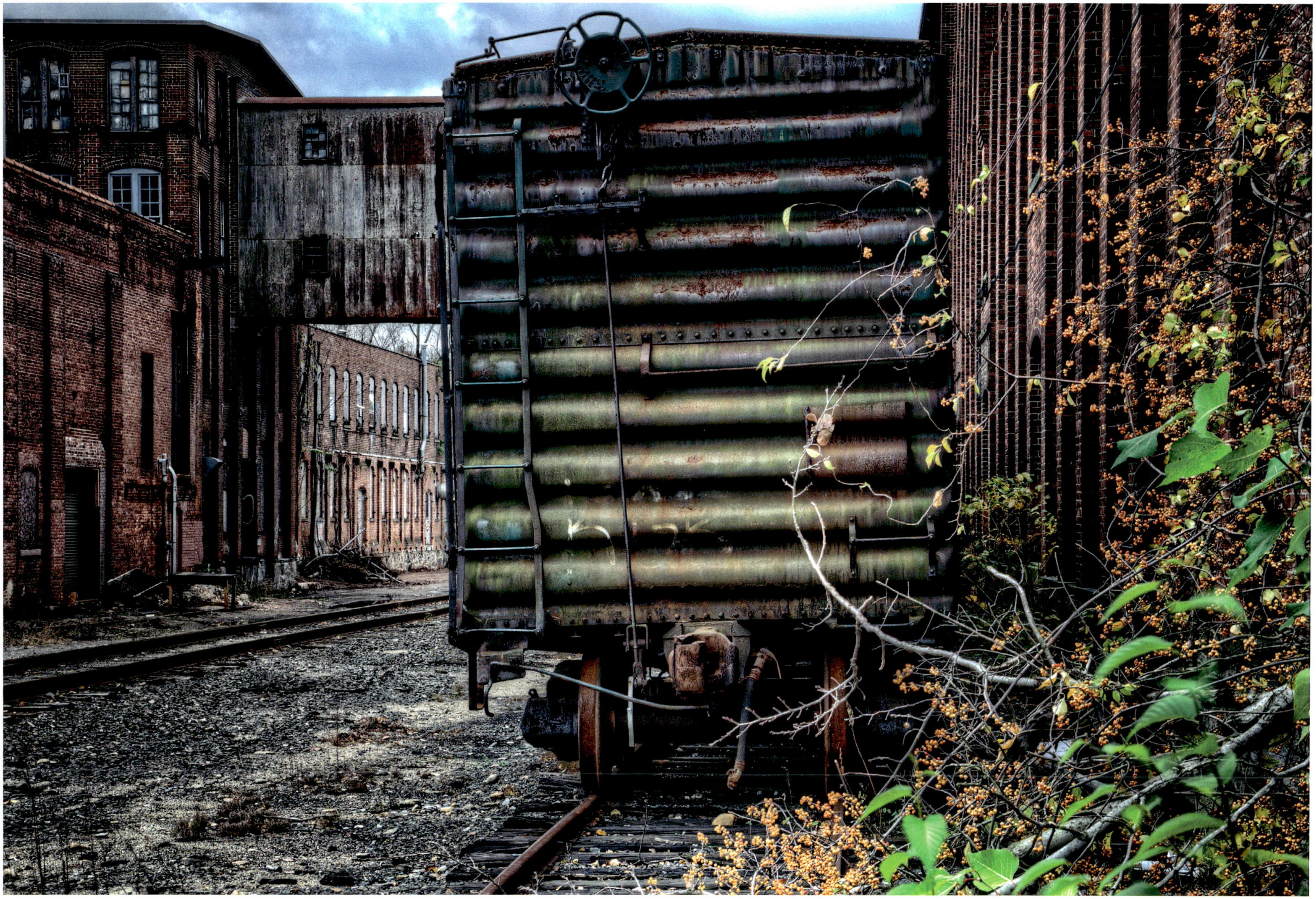

SIDETRACKED BESIDE SCOVILL

Scovill shops and foundry, Thomaston Avenue, Waterbury,

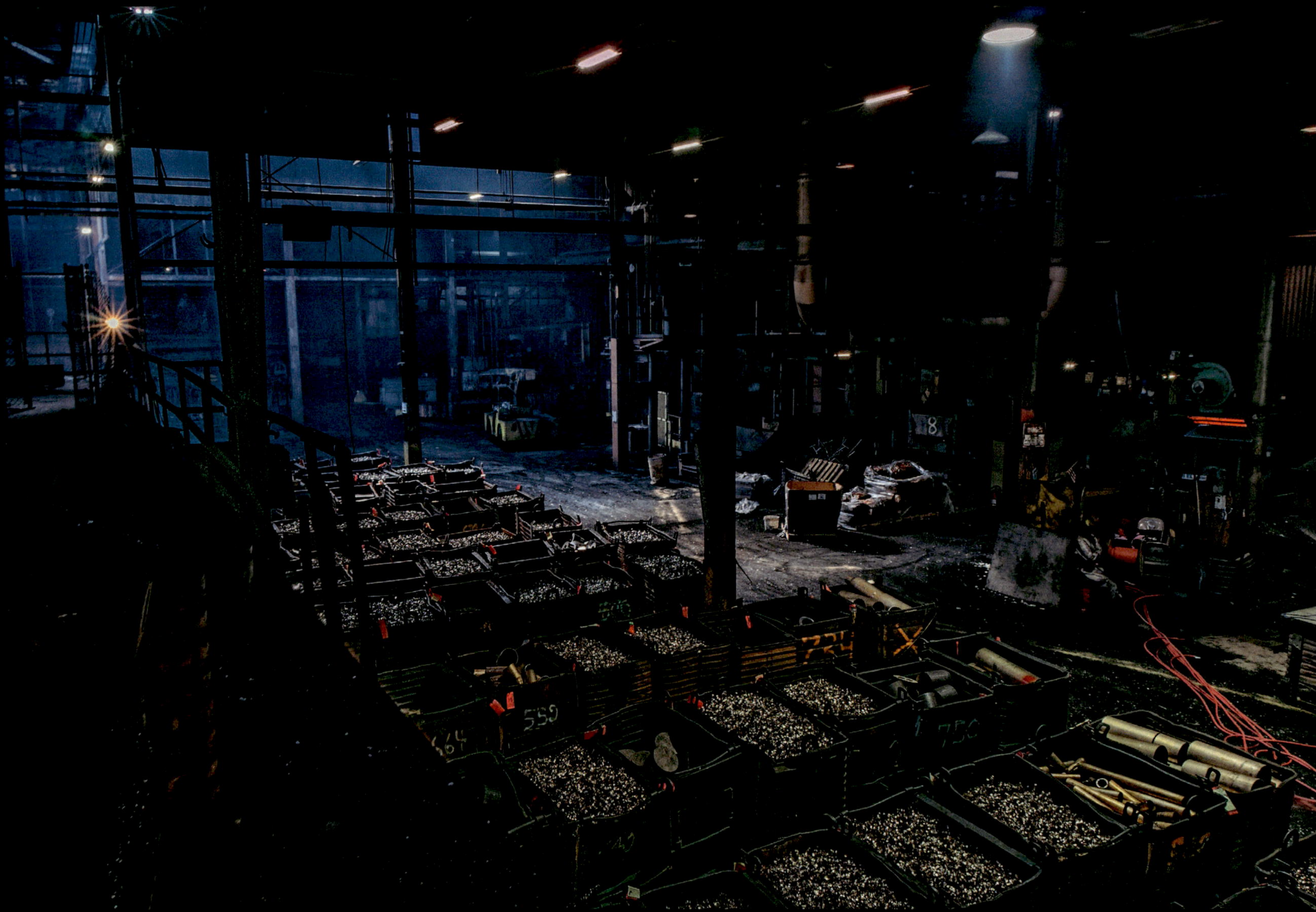

SOOTED & STILL

Casting shop, American Brass, Ansonia, CT

PHOTOGRAPHER'S JOURNAL:

The foundry is a place of Stygian magnificence. Although the end of the shed is open to fresh air and daylight, inside the air is viscous and sooty, and one sees as if through cataracts into a tarred and dusted world that sucks up light and then suddenly sparkles and flares. A truckload of scrap has recently been delivered. Along the edges of darkness are bins of recycled, scrap brass from the factory upstream and gleaming bricks of "new" scrap copper wire pressed tight the way unwanted cars are pressed tight at the auto junkyard. Wherever light catches the edges of the bricks or the bins of shavings, they gleam like chests of treasure.

The shed is extensive and lofty, and daylight glares from the indistinct perimeter. It is strewn with ruins of the brass industry's past, paleolithic conveyors and compressors, tanks, pipes, ducts, strange engines the size of cabins, rusted relics. Most appear to be crumbling in place, but along the back wall, as if from the depths of a cave, a giant furnace

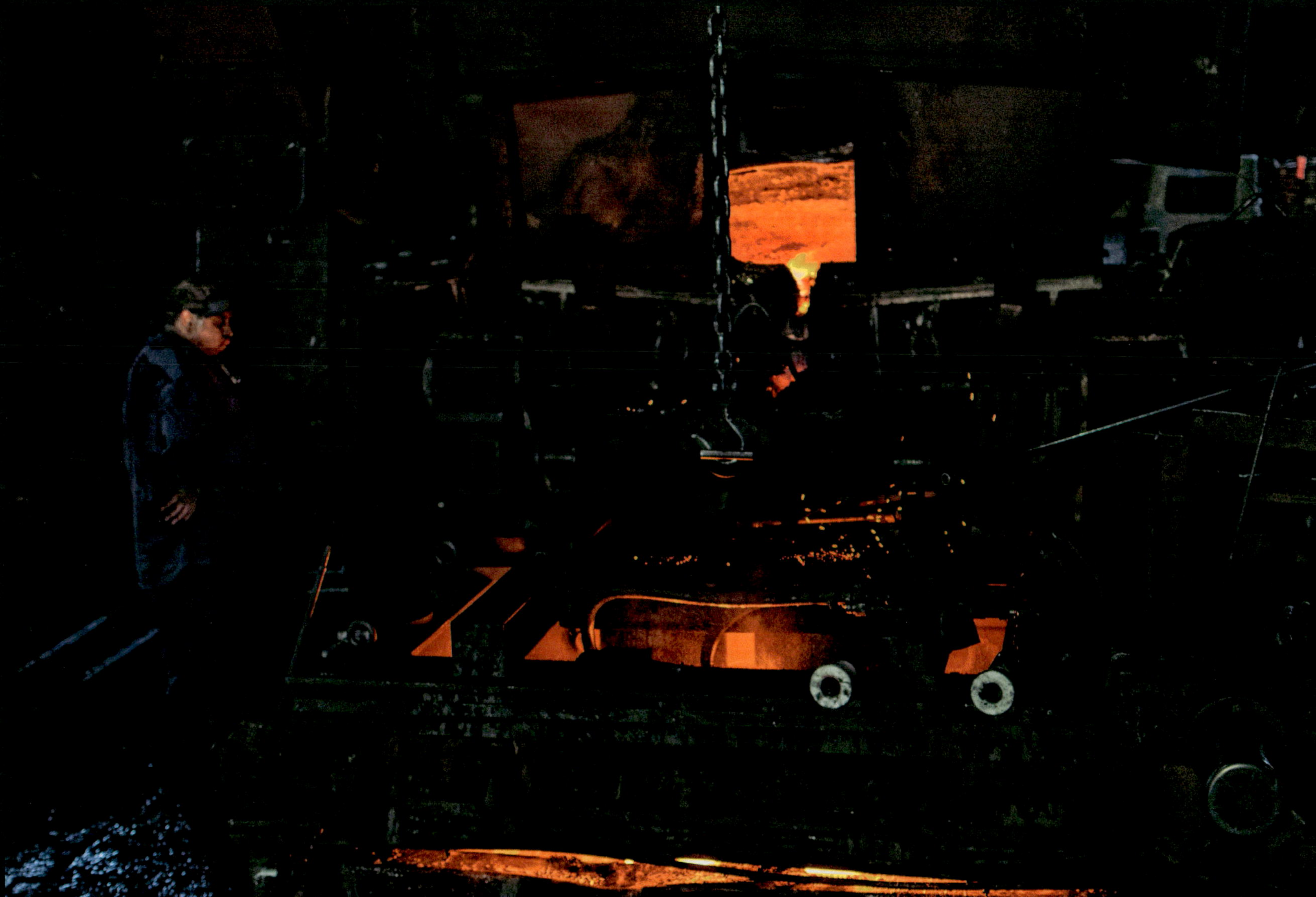

still purrs, simmers, seethes, and softly roars. It is a fiery thing, spewing like a dragon and surrounded by the sound of rushing water.

As Mike pushes a button, the crucible tips, and white-hot brass flows into two molds below the floor. Cooling water flows through the molds, gushing from their sides, and luminous water glows from the pit below. Searing brass and cooling water are explosive and must never touch.

It takes a long time for the molds to fill, but once they are loaded and gently cooled, Mike will hoist out two pillar-like billets, glowing red. I put on my fastest lens, stop it all the way open, turn the ISO up to 1600, and try to squeeze out acceptable exposures at an eightieth of a second while dodging lens flare. I can't see to focus, and at f/1.8 focus must be precise. Sometimes I have trouble seeing the compositions through the viewfinder, and as I work, my hands and gear turn black and buttery. It is a nasty place for taking pictures, and I know I'll be back for more.

FOUNDER & FURNACE

Casting shop, American Brass, Ansonia, CT

42

CLEAN HANDS TO GO, WYPALL

Spirits in the old foundry shed,
sweeping time aside,
do you hold the missing keys?
"Begin the Beguine" plays
from the silent boom box,
new numbers chalked
on old lockers,
and vintage grime,
allure of the corded desk phone
in biscuit tan,
the scent of lime,
and who will it be
at the end of the line
on the other side
where time has stopped
at quarter to four
in May of two-thousand and nine?

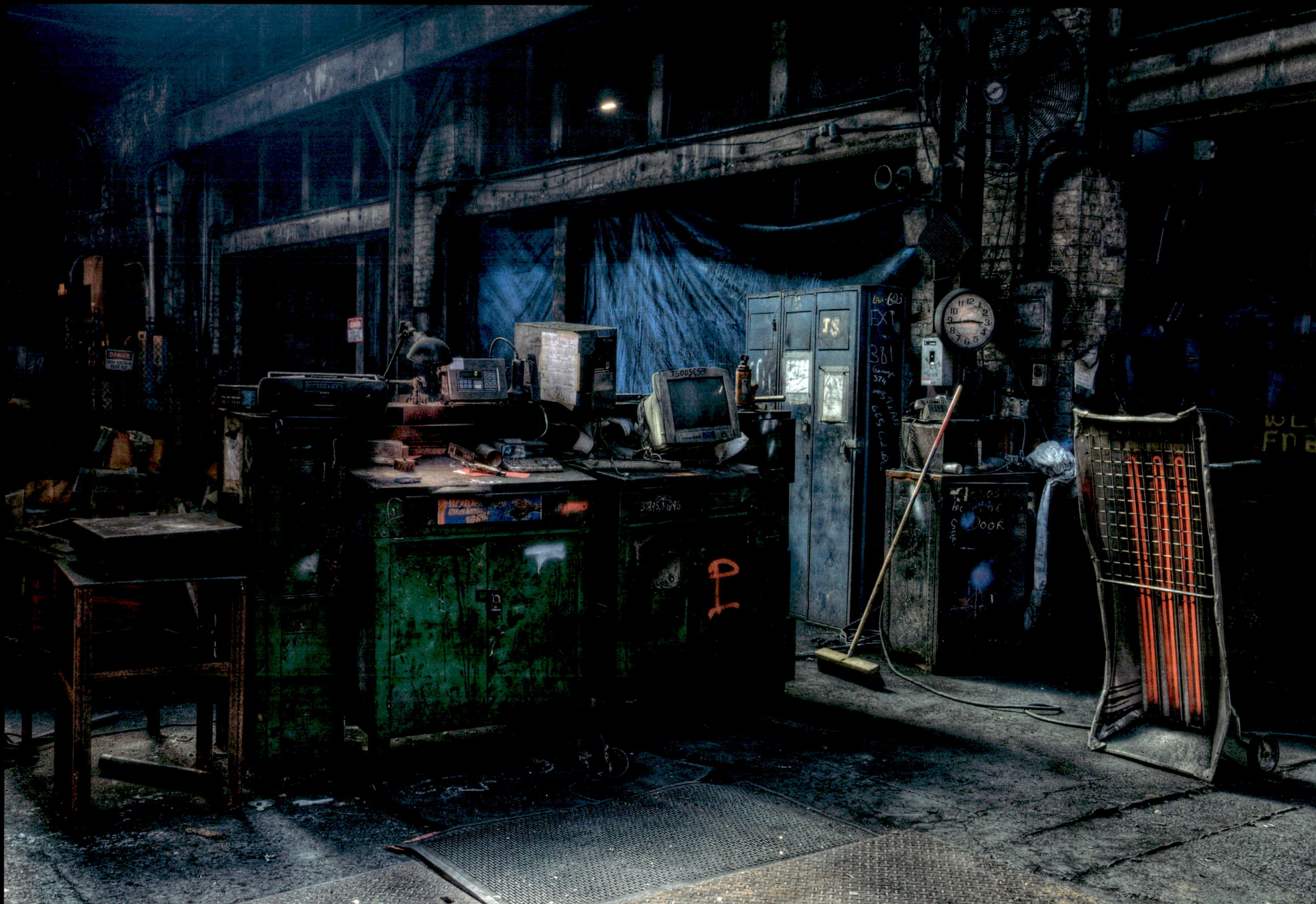

PHANTOM STATION, 11 AM, 2012
Casting shop, American Brass, Ansonia, CT

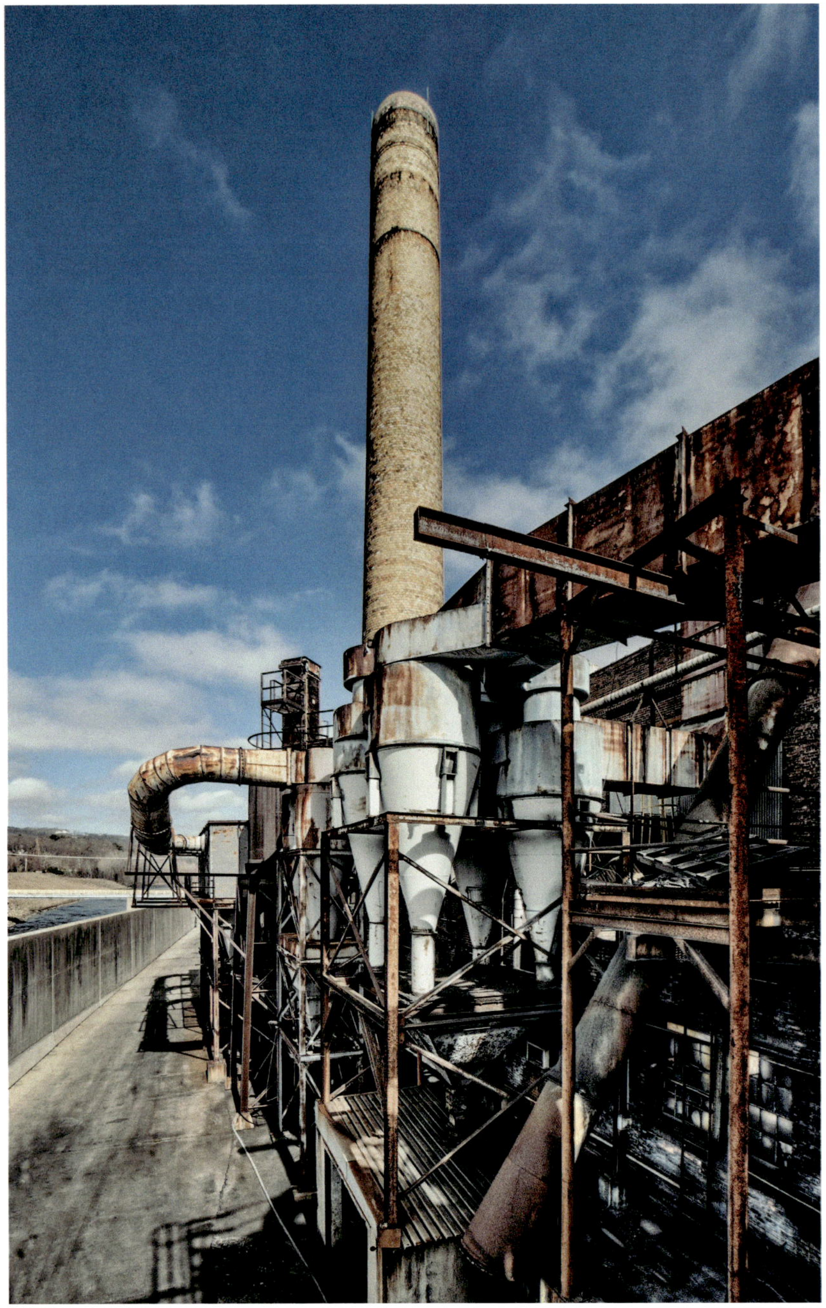

AIR OVER ANSONIA

Furnace filtration, casting shop, American Brass, Ansonia, CT

OUR STORIES:

Phelpsville

Sheldon Smith's Birmingham project was a success. By 1836 he and his New York partner Anson Phelps had attracted a range of independently owned, small industries to the site, and they began hiring us to make sheet copper and copper wire. At his industrial village, Phelps invested in entrepreneurs such as John Howe and his revolutionary machine for manufacturing pins. When Howe patented the technology for sticking pins in paper folders, pins became plentiful. Suddenly everyone could afford a paper of pins, and, though it took fewer people to make a pin, they needed more of us to run more pin-makers and pin-stickers.

In other mills we made augers, carriage springs and axles, and some of us made nails and tacks. There was even a factory where we made flannels and satinets, but the biggest of all was the Birmingham Foundry, which manufactured machinery and equipment for using river water to power mills and which later pioneered giant machinery for processing rubber and paper and much more.

Ansonia Copper & Brass was owned by Smith and Phelps. Upstream Phelps co-owned Wolcottville Brass and Battery. It was said he made money in importing, and he knew how to invest it. The future looked bright for Birmingham, so we could only speculate why Sheldon Smith sold his interests and left town.

Phelps went on building, up and down the valley. When expansion on the west side of the Naugatuck became the subject of haggling, he bought land on the east side, and started a new factory village to be called Phelpsville. His millwright was Almon Farrel. In 1844, Phelps bought the four-year-old Kinneytown Dam and put Farrel in charge of building a canal, power system, and the new brass mill. The dam was at the edge of Humphreysville, below Rimmon Falls in Kinneytown, and we heard that a mile and a half of canal had to be dug along the east side of the river to sluiceways that powered the massive wheels to spin more copper into gold. The dam is still there and the canal still leads water to the old American Brass factories, though most of us have forgotten there was a canal.

Anson Phelps spoke of Phelpsville, but when we were finally a town he called us Ansonia. Ansonia Brass and Battery eventually spun off Ansonia Clock Company. Clockmakers were switching from wood to brass and recalibrating time, and Phelps recognized opportunities.

History, however, knows Anson G. Phelps mostly as the co-founder of Phelps Dodge. Phelps Dodge, famously "Christian merchants," was closely associated with the Presbyterian church. Phelps Dodge began by trading cotton for metals, but its wealth and power came from copper mines and tin mines.

Anson Phelps lived in New York City and contributed heavily to The American Bible Association, overseas missionary organizations, and efforts to establish Liberia, as well as to societies for the poor and the blind. In his will he left $5,000 to each of his grandchildren with the injunction:

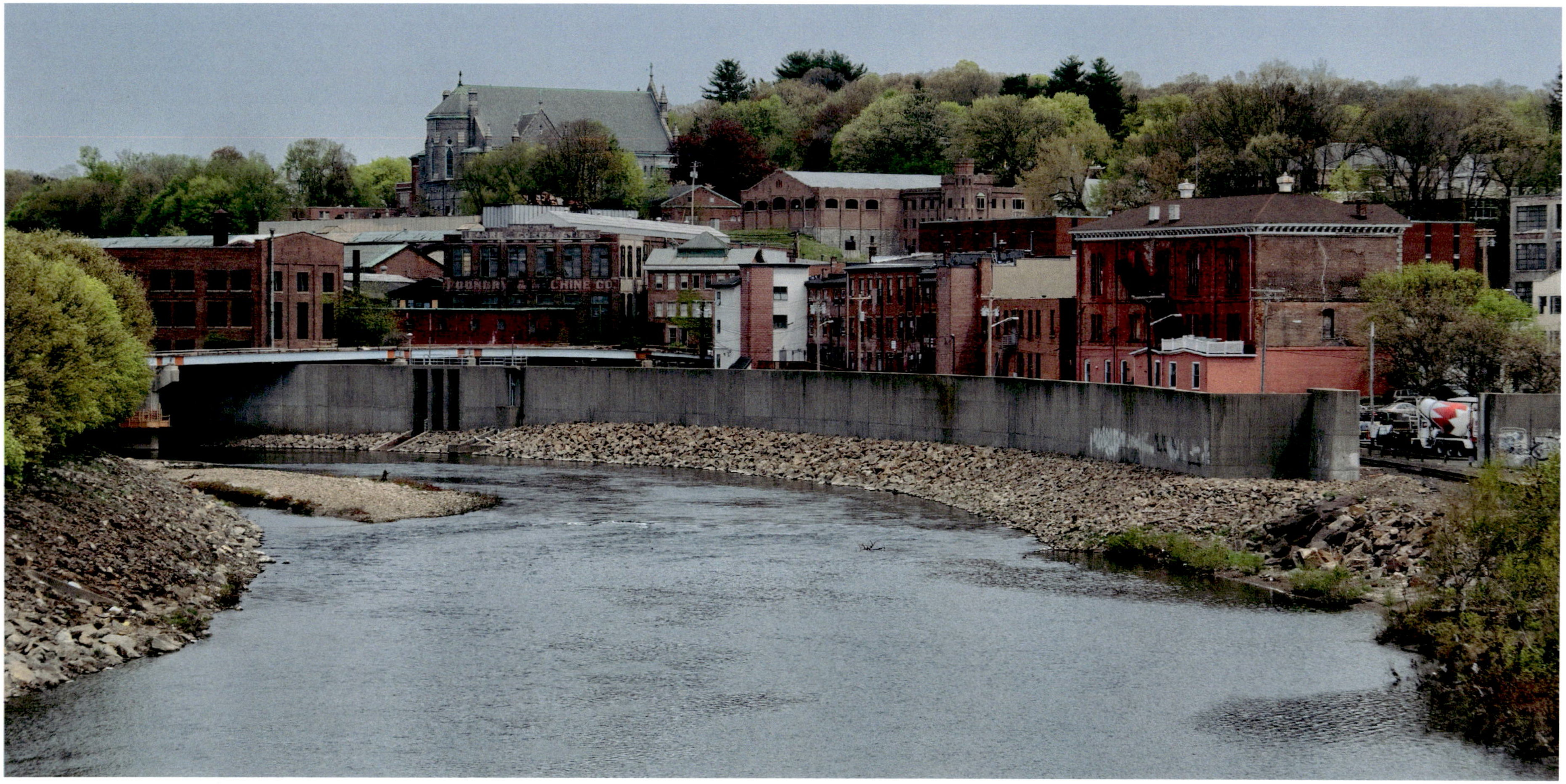

"I give and bequeath to each of my grand-children, living at my decease, the sum of $5,000, to be paid them as they severally attain the age of 21 years. This latter bequest I direct to be accompanied by my executors with this injunction: –That each of my said grand-children shall consider the said bequest as a sacred deposit, committed to their trust, to be invested by each grand-child, and the income derived therefrom to be devoted to spread the gospel, and to promote the Redeemer's kingdom on earth, hoping and trusting that the God of Heaven will give to each of that wisdom which is from above, and incline them to be faithful stewards, and transmit the same to their descendants, to be sacredly devoted to the same object.

"I know this bequest is absolute and places the amount so given beyond my control; but my earnest hope is that my wish may be regarded as I leave it, an obligation binding simply on their integrity and honor."

Anson G. Phelps died in 1853. In the later nineteenth and the twentieth century, Phelps Dodge earned notoriety for its union-busting tactics and the infamous 1917 Bisbee Deportation—1,300 striking, Arizona mine workers who refused their chance to denounce the union were seized and loaded into cattle cars under the watch of machine-gun-bearing deputies, and taken through the desert without food or water for 200 miles to New Mexico, where they were left and warned never to return. Meanwhile company executives seized telegraph and telephone lines to keep newspapers from reporting what they had done. When word got out we were told they were Red agitators, and Bisbee was far away. The war made steady work, and we were getting by, but it was a bad start for deportation policy in the United States.

ANSONIA SKYLINE

Irish Catholic Church of the Assumption Above Farrel Works, Downtown Ansonia, and the Opera House Naugatuck River at downtown Ansonia, CT

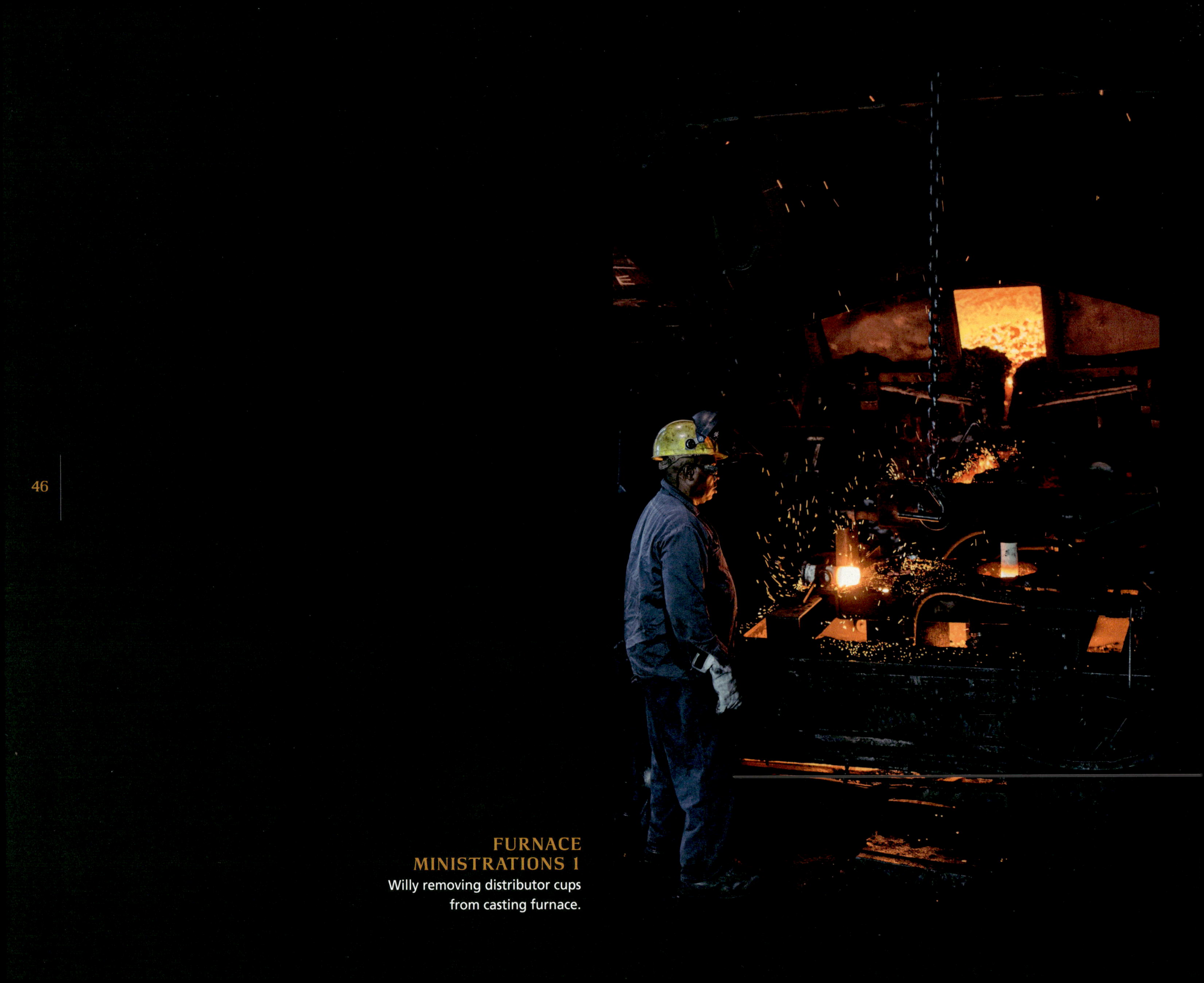

FURNACE MINISTRATIONS 1

Willy removing distributor cups from casting furnace.

PHOTOGRAPHER'S JOURNAL:
Except when the billets are pulled from the form, the founder generally works alone. The console lets him monitor the all-important temperature of the brew and control the melt. He sprinkles it with manganese that explodes like firecrackers of white light, or with lampblack that makes thick, black smoke and sparks.

When the time is right, he tips the crucible and corrects the flow. The brass must be poured slowly so no gas pockets form, and the molds are large, so much of his time is spent waiting beside the furnace, monitoring temperature and flow while seasoning the stew. Periodically he rakes out the channel through which the molten brass is flowing, and the rake showers him in sparks.

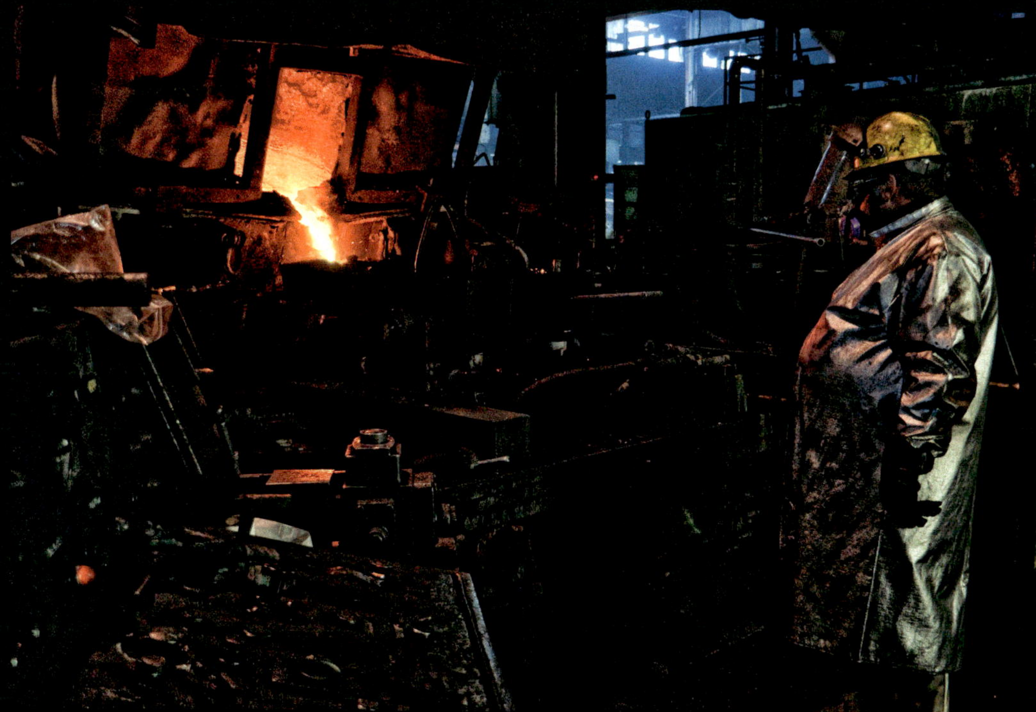

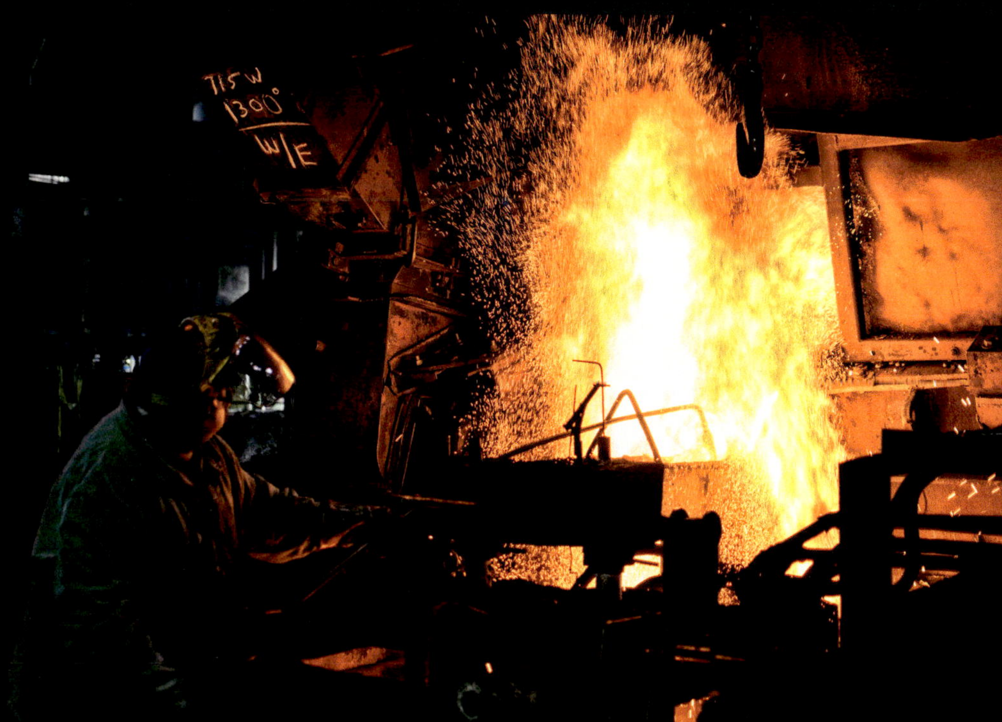

FURNACE MINISTRATIONS 2
Mike monitoring the flow of metal...

FURNACE MINISTRATIONS 3
and raking the runner box when flow is sluggish.

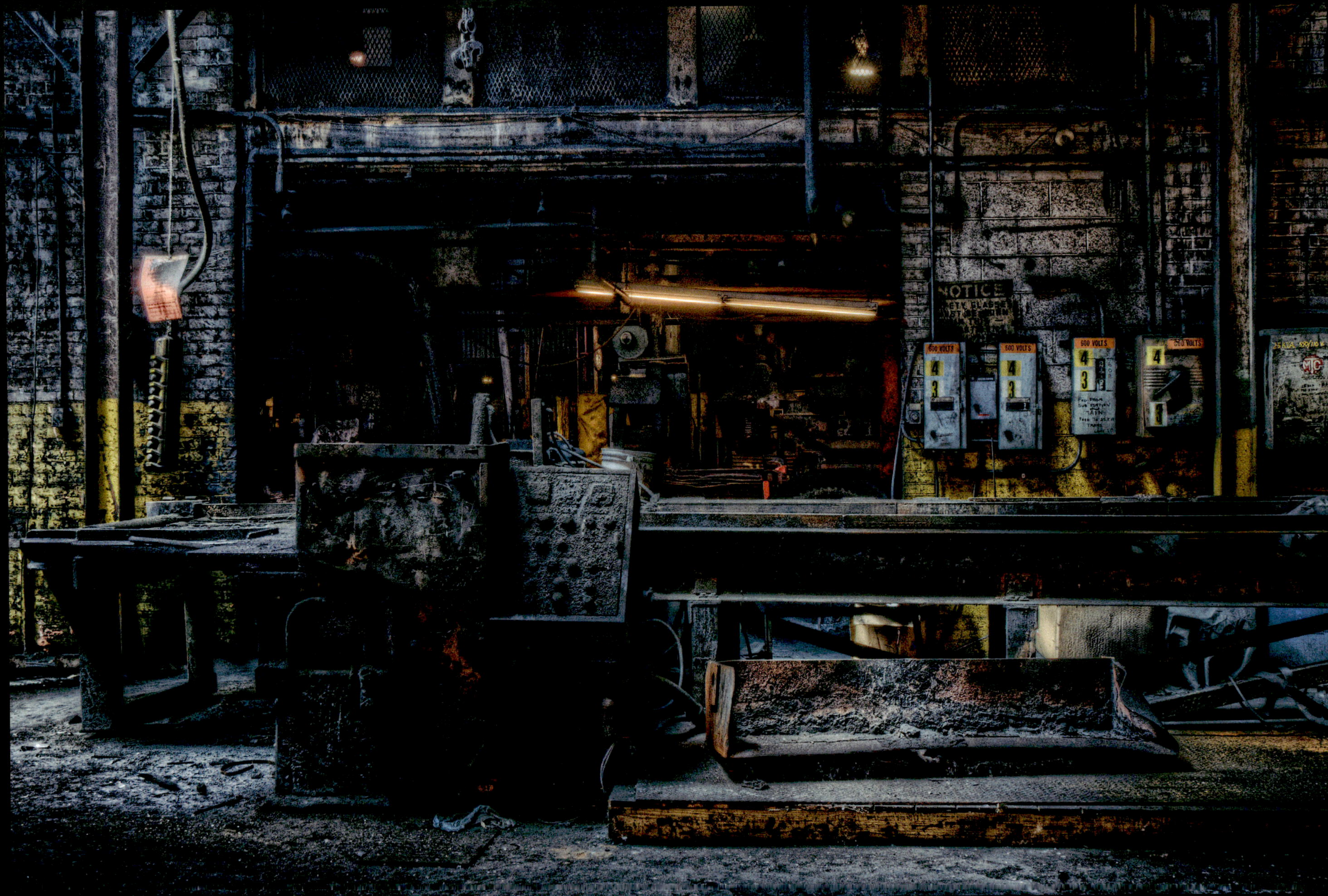

AT THE CUTTING EDGE, NO.2

Saw bench, casting shop, American Brass, Ansonia, CT

SHIFT

Amid the foundry's ruminations:
shapes of idle benches trace
forgotten paths of spectral pipe
that circumnavigated the globe,
and a sign from OSHA rots and warns
where grease of absent fingers plays
on buttons that hang from the overhead crane,
and here where power no longer surges;
oh, where are the hard hats and safety glasses
for the queued shadows of the next shift?

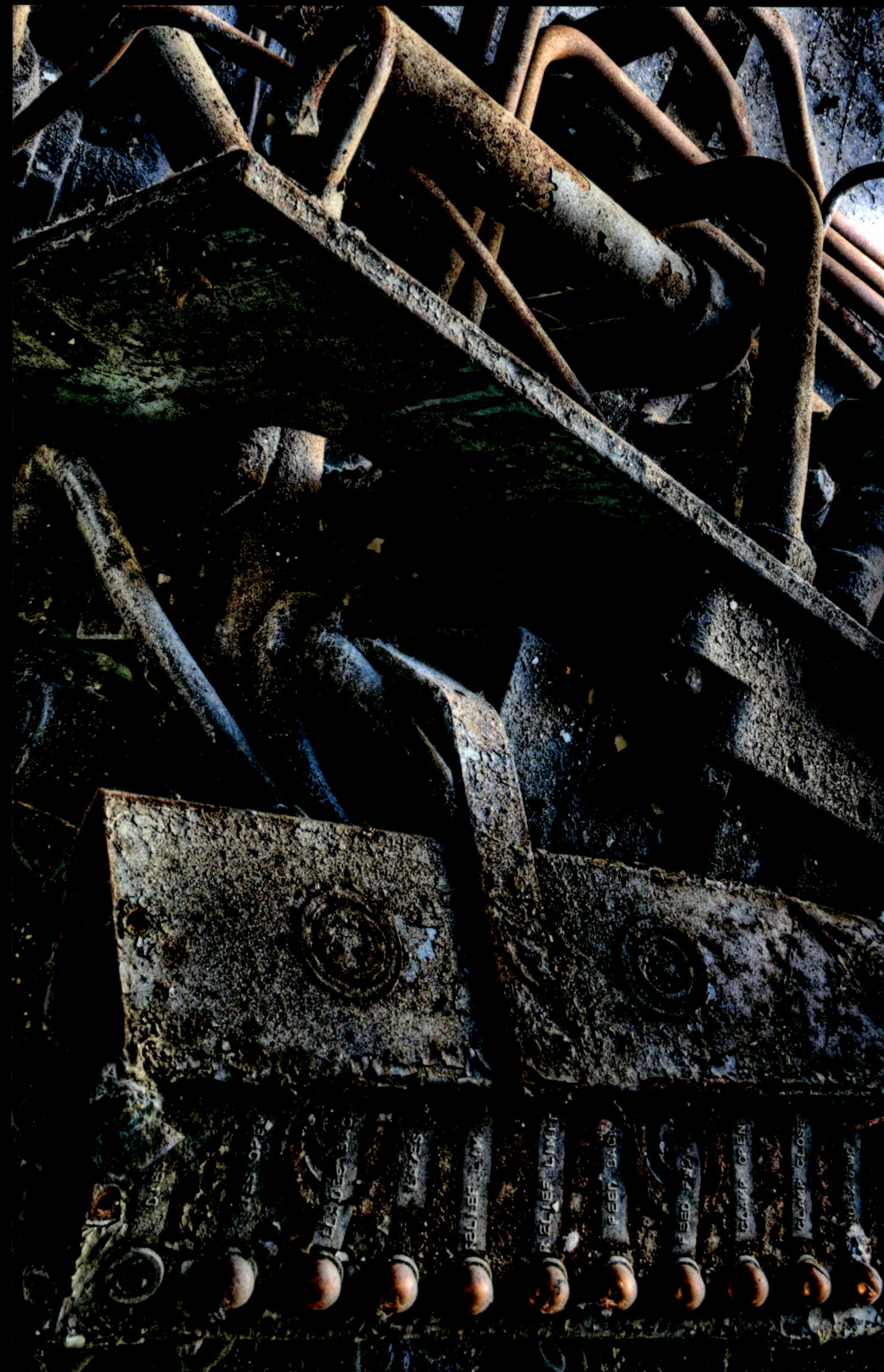

MR. BUNDLES
Abandoned machine, American Brass (Benedict & Burnham), Benedict Street, Waterbury, CT

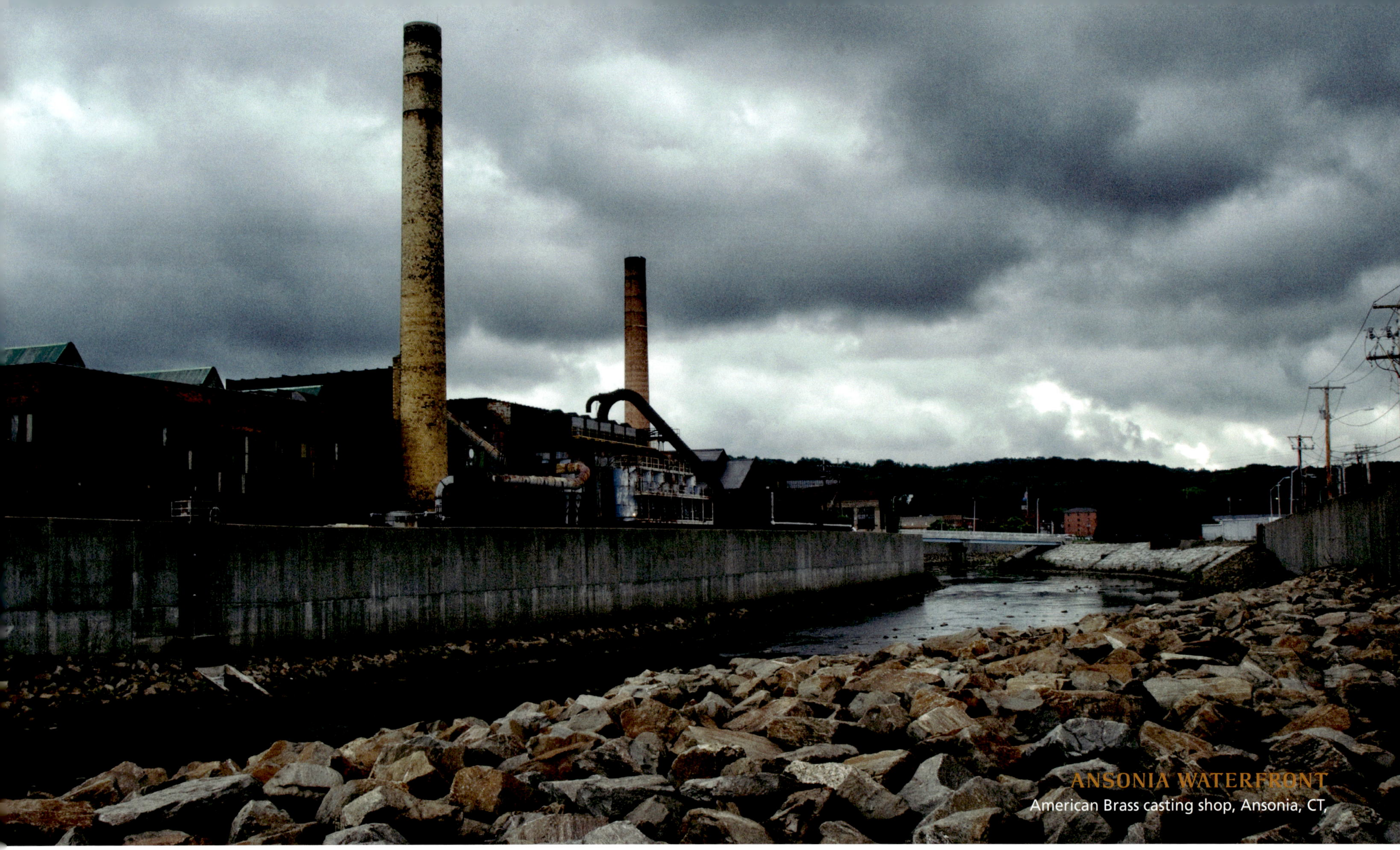

ANSONIA WATERFRONT
American Brass casting shop, Ansonia, CT,

OUR STORIES:

Postdiluvian Calculations

The floods of 1955 reorganized the valley, and we accepted the cost to human spirit to see the river so channeled. The river smelled back then, and it was dead, and perhaps the channel was a fitting sarcophagus, and next to it were the furnaces and milling machines that kept the living world spinning.

This is the property around which Anson Phelps built Ansonia. It is a descendent through numerous mergers, buyouts, and divestitures of Anson Phelps's original Ansonia Copper & Brass Company, which once stood here. After the floods, Brass Valley was never the same. More and more manufacturing went elsewhere. Once, 400 of us worked in the rod and wire mills here, and inside this building we kept forty furnaces casting billets around the clock. Today just one furnace makes the billets for the extruder upstream. After it was American Brass, it was called Anaconda, but now the names keep changing. Lately it's been Ansonia Specialty Metals.

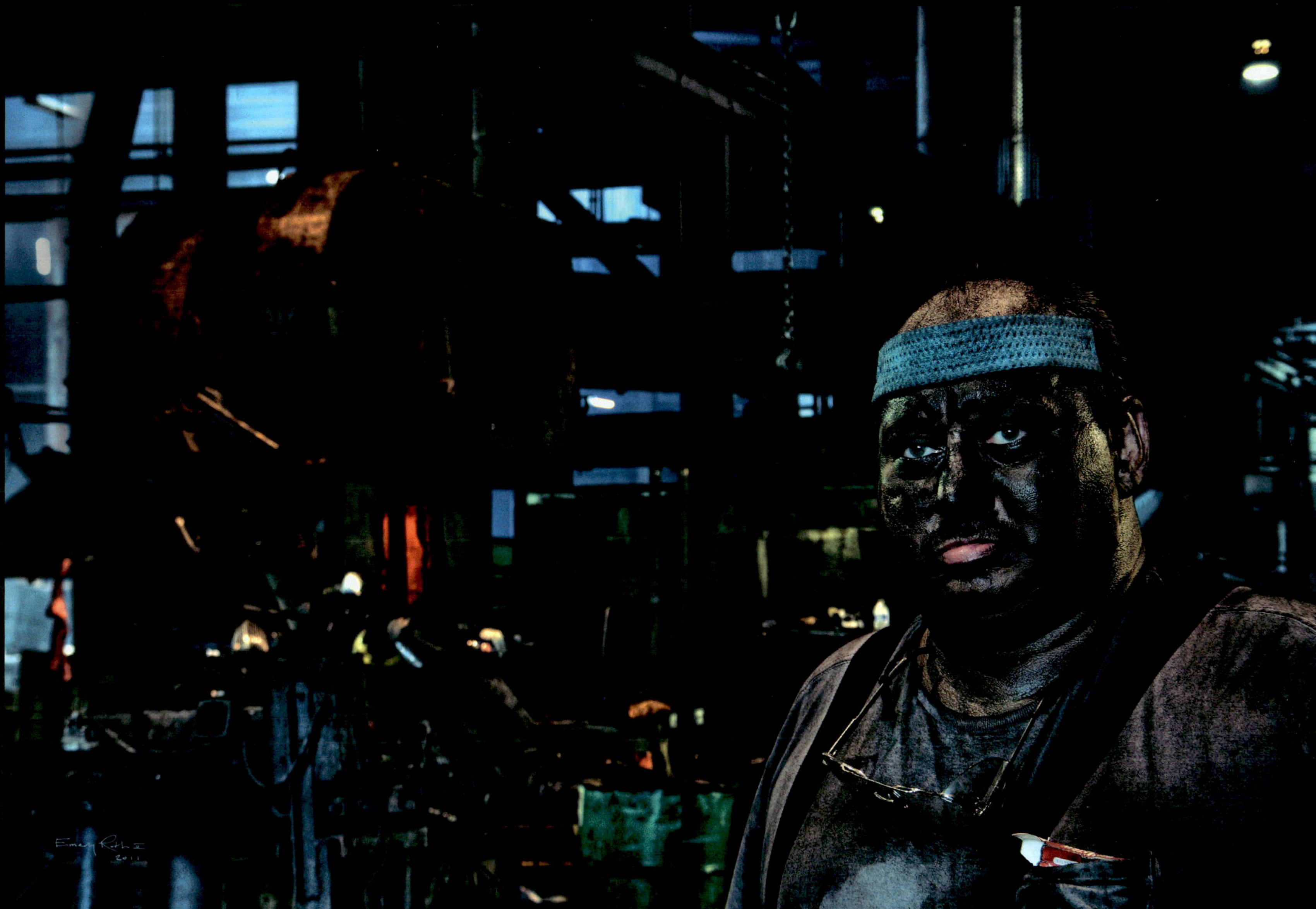

PHOTOGRAPHER'S JOURNAL:
On the day I took this picture of Mike, the temperature outside was pushing past 100 degrees, and it was considerably hotter beside the furnace. The normally waxy air was pudding. After Mike finished pulling the billets and charging the furnace for the next pour, I positioned myself to catch a candid of him with the dragon in the background as he headed off for his break and a smoke, but as he turned my way and saw the camera pointed at his face, he stopped, tried to wipe away the grease and pasty perspiration, looked into my lens, and posed proudly.

MIKE, THE FOUNDER
Before the casting furnace, American Brass, Ansonia, CT

STILL LIFE

The
still life
tells
the story
of life
not quite still,
still
life.

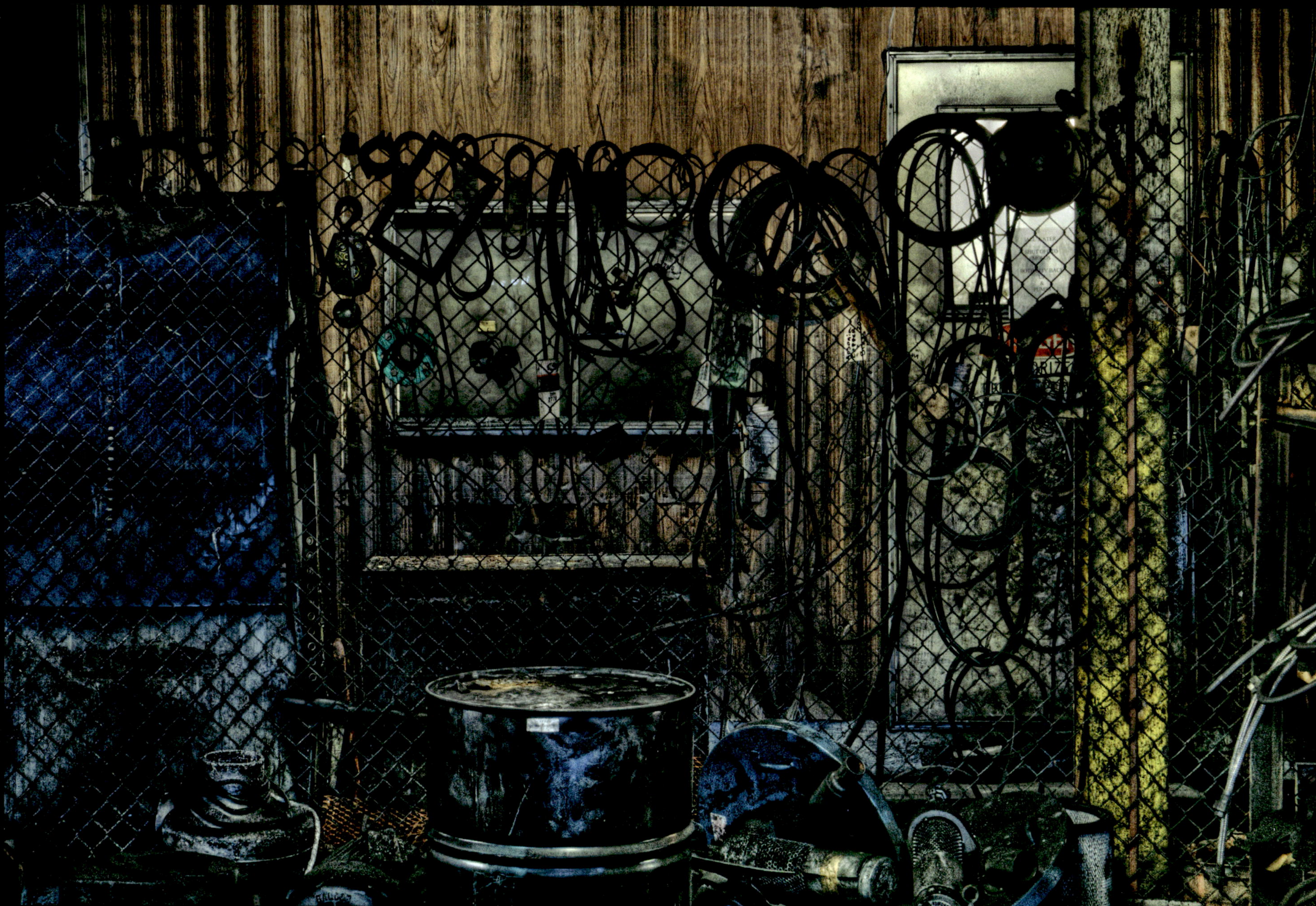

STILL LIFE
Casting shop, American Brass, Ansonia, CT

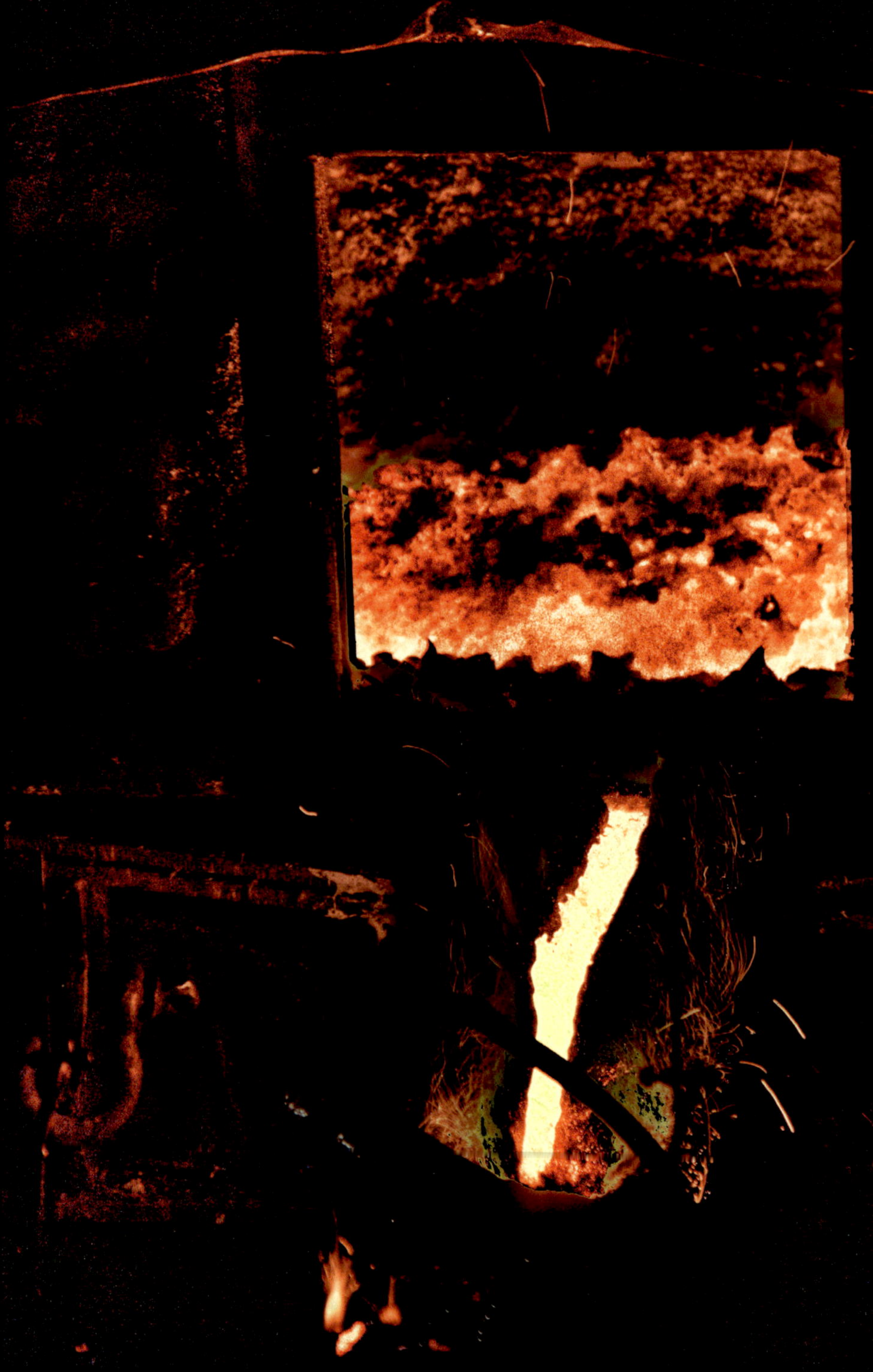

PHOTOGRAPHER'S JOURNAL:
"Foundry"! I'd forgotten the origin of the word, from fundus, bottom, or base. The founder was the one who gave rock life by revealing base metal's form and properties; he managed the fires, measured out the precious earths and elixirs, and invoked hidden powers to transform its crystal core and align electrons. The great ages of humankind are named by metal's secrets: We call them, "Stone Age," "Copper Age," "Bronze Age," "Iron Age," and "Nuclear Age," while we long for a lost "Golden Age."

BRASS MOODS: WHITE

Casting shop, American Brass, Ansonia, CT

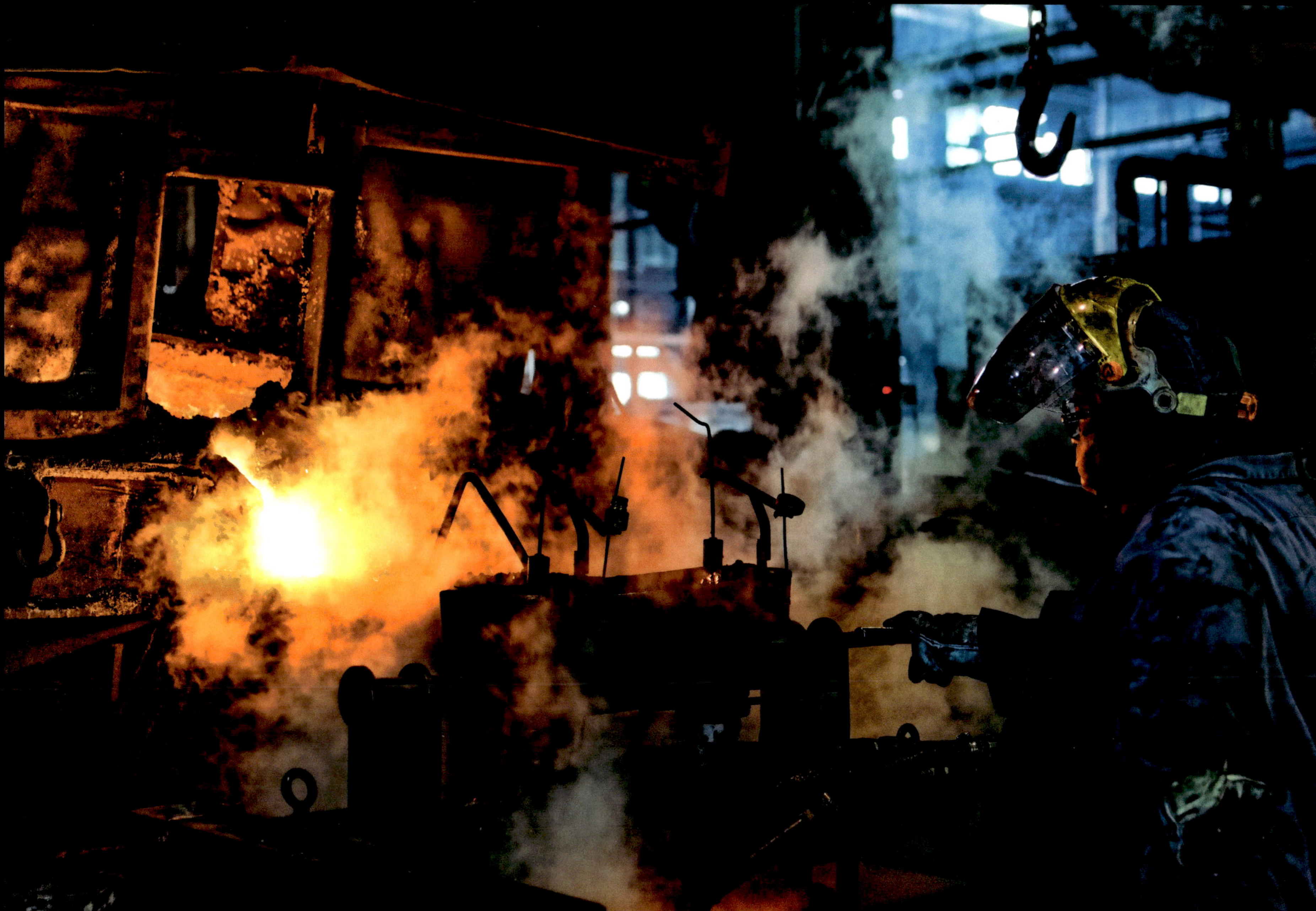

BRASS MOODS: SMOKING

Casting shop, American Brass, Ansonia, CT

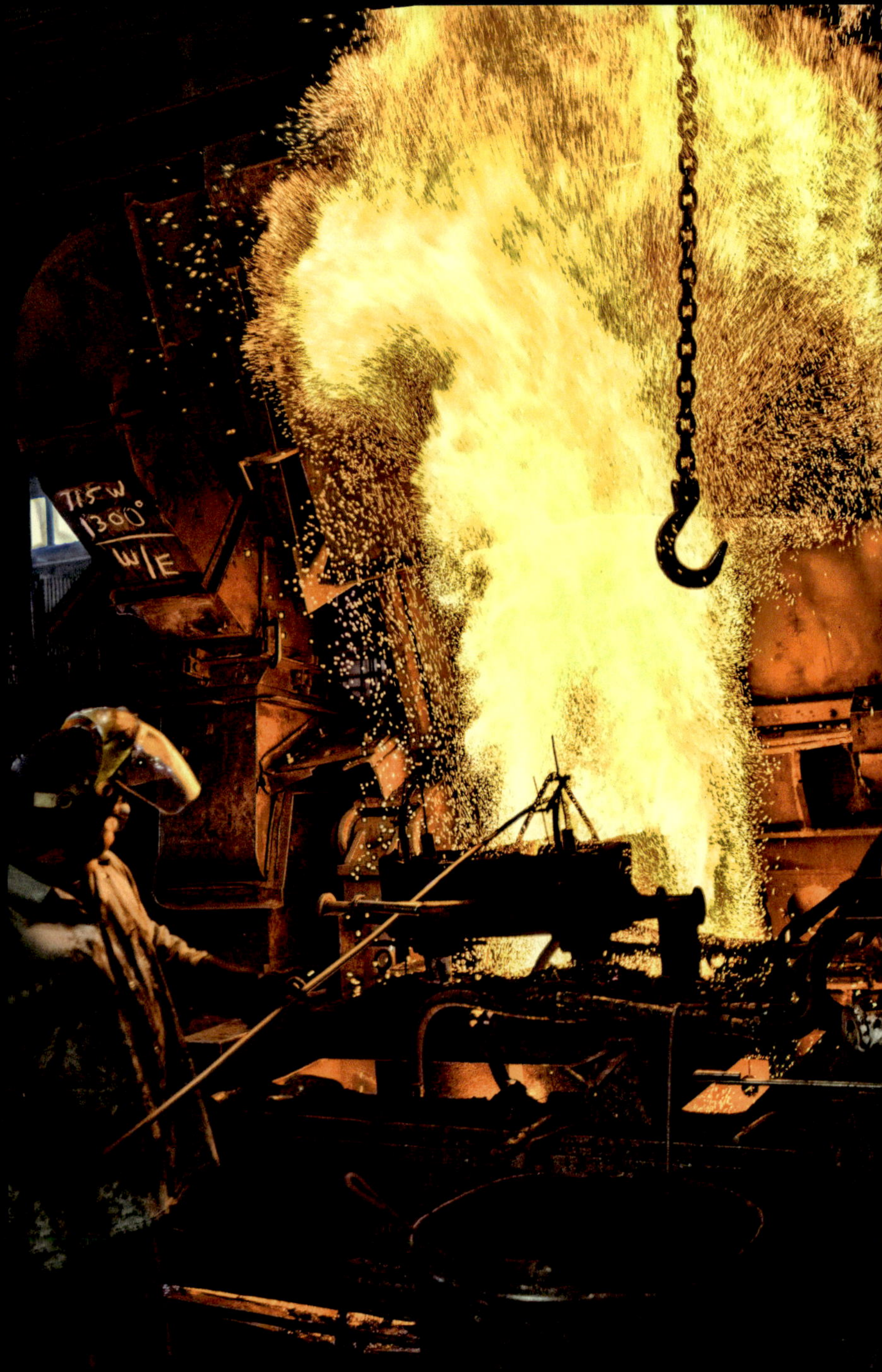

PREPARING TO REMOVE THE RUNNER BOX

All images: American Brass casting shed, Ansonia, CT

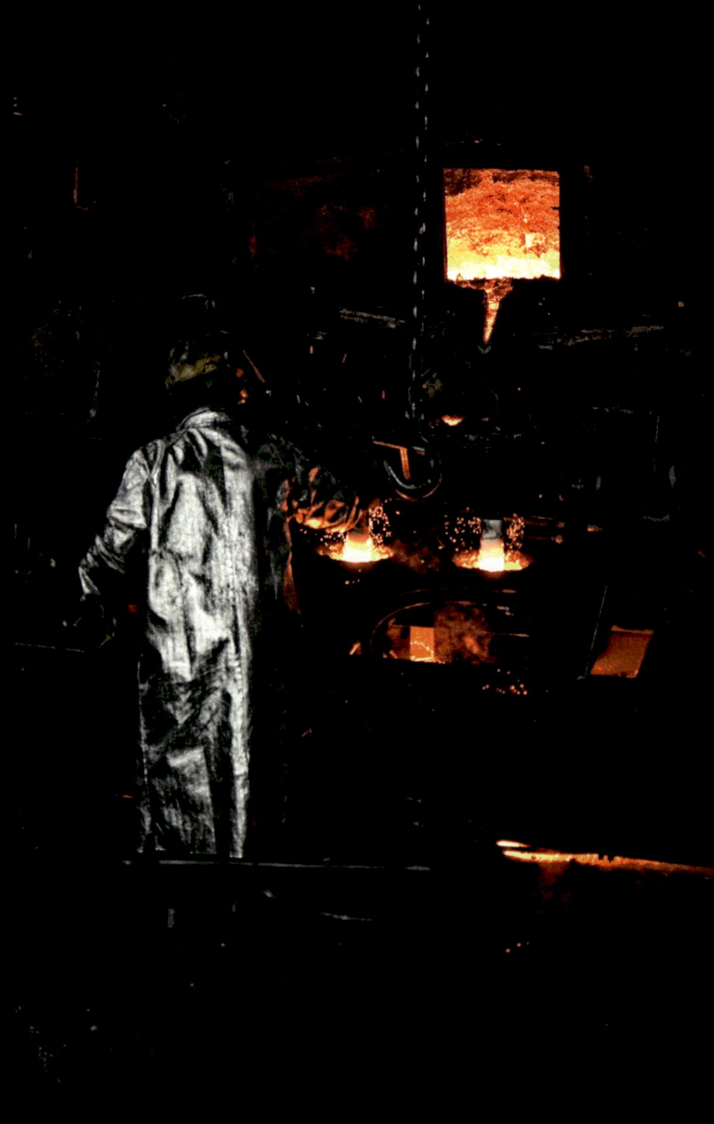

DISTRIBUTOR CUP RITES

PHOTOGRAPHER'S JOURNAL:

I've been reading about brass. Before 1781, its production was almost accidental. Some traced its secrets to knowledge given to Adam at creation. Others traced them through Egypt and the writings of Hermes Trismegistus and Thoth. Wherever they originated, they were lost arts, the subjects of alchemical investigation. The secret that turned copper to brass lay hidden in calamine until William Champion and James

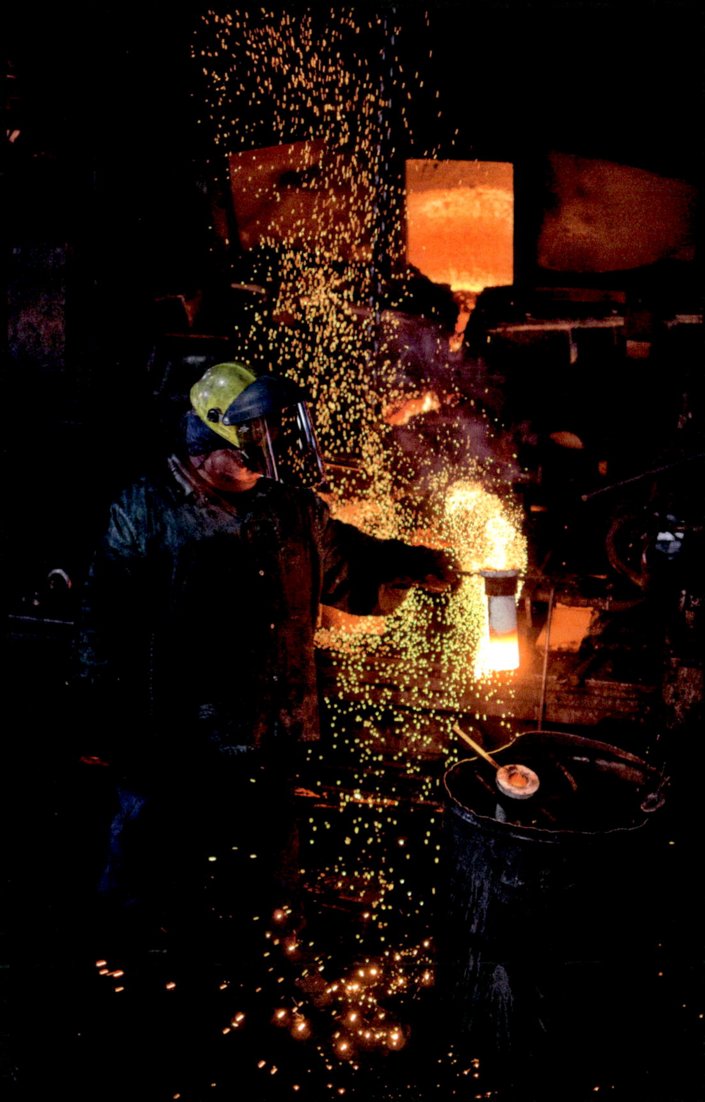

FOUNDER'S THURIBLE

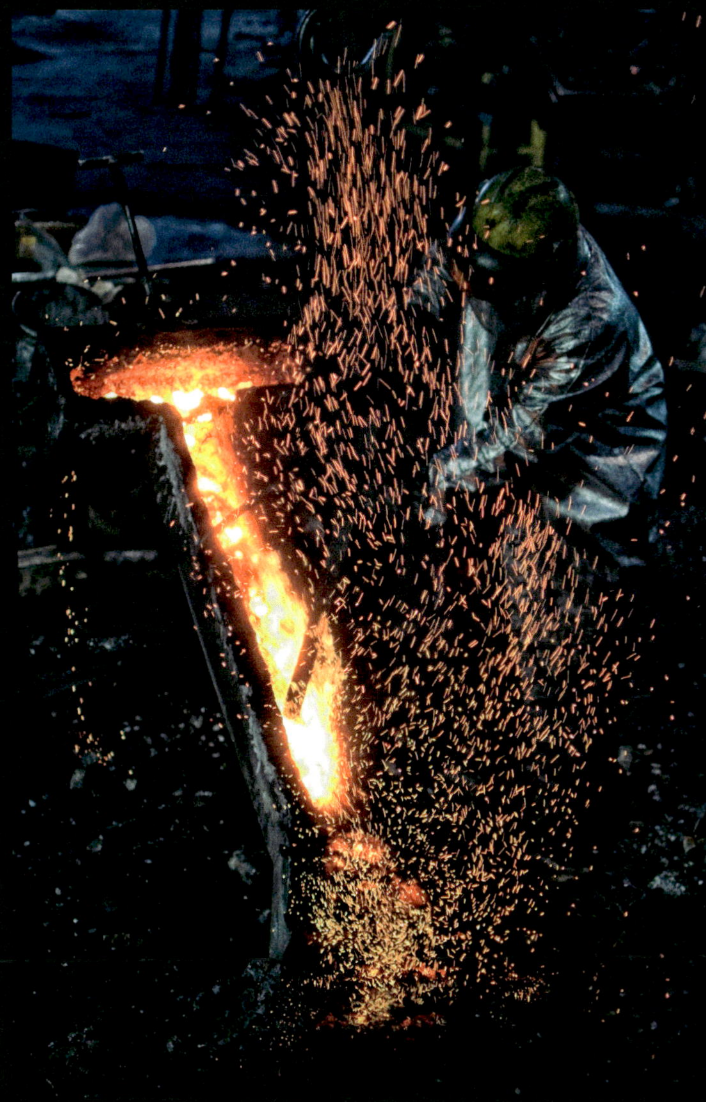

RAKING OUT THE RUNNER BOX

Emerson devised smelting methods to obtain pure zinc to accurately control the properties of the brass.

They were stolen secrets brought to Brass Valley by men Israel Holmes smuggled from Birmingham, England, and by the Englishman James Croft. These new Americans were men the Yankee brass men had to respect and compensate. From that start, Brass Valley developed its own alchemists; they summoned furious fires and tempered their burn, charged the crucible, melted the charge and balanced the melt with alloys, and refined it to purge unwanted gases, and they determined, at last, when the time was right for tapping. They were magic men, crystal gazers, who toned and tuned molecules and engineered machines and factories that turned base metal into wealth and power, law and community: Truly an alchemical transmutation!

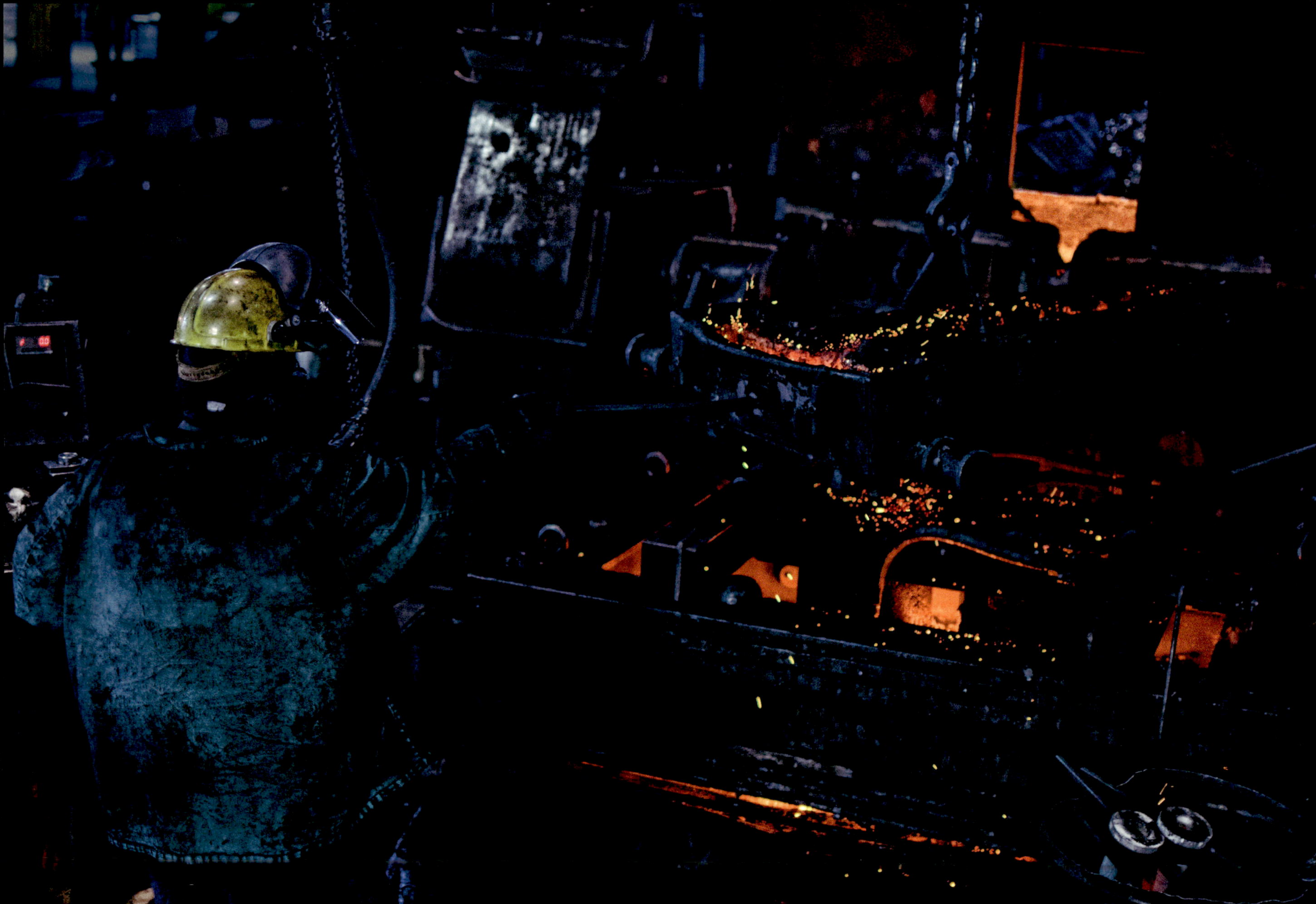

RUNNER BOX BOOGIE-WOOGIE

Mike removing the runner box, American Brass, Ansonia, CT

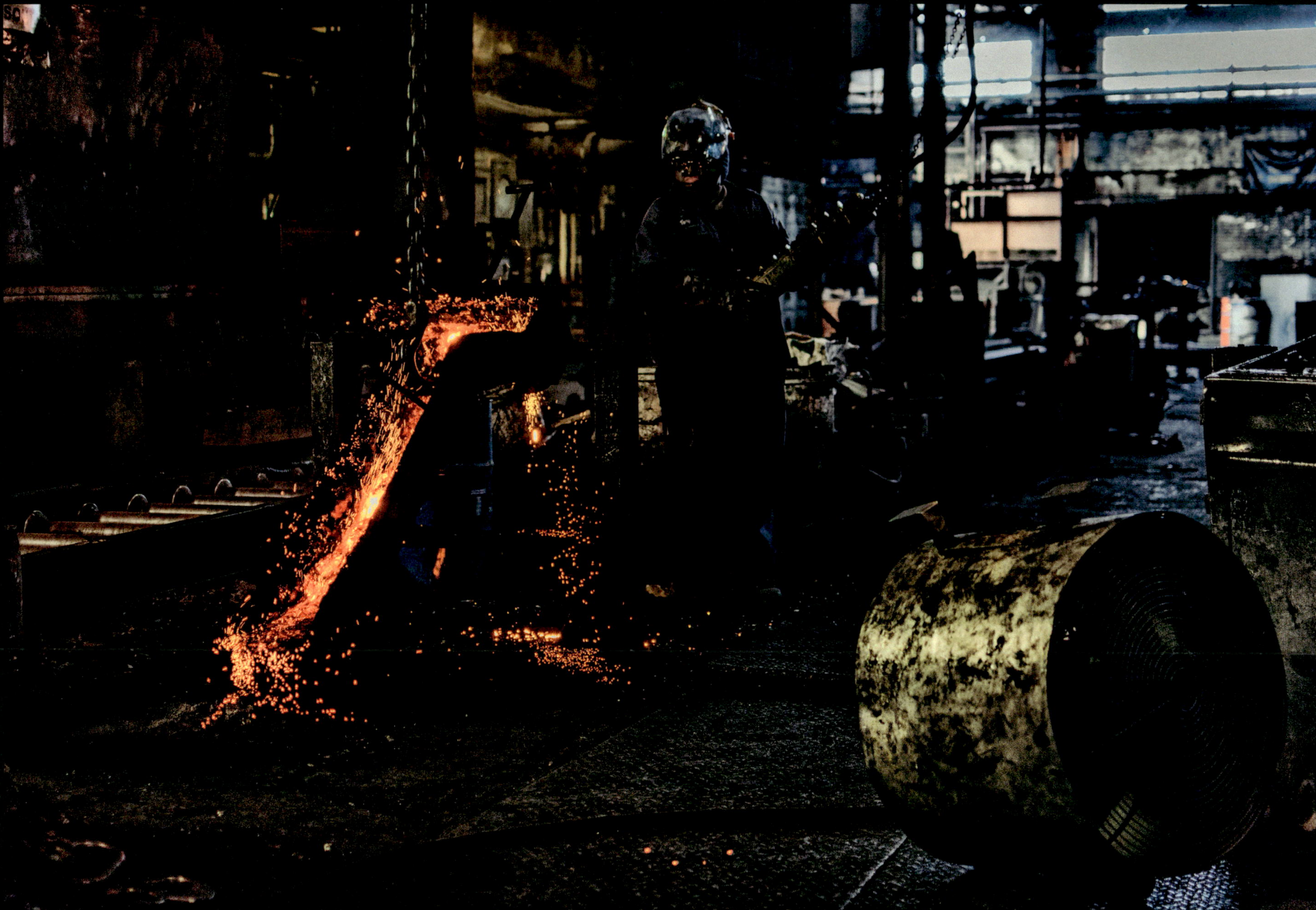

PREPARING TO OPEN THE SANCTUARY
Mike sets the runner box aside in order to swing the cover and remove the billets

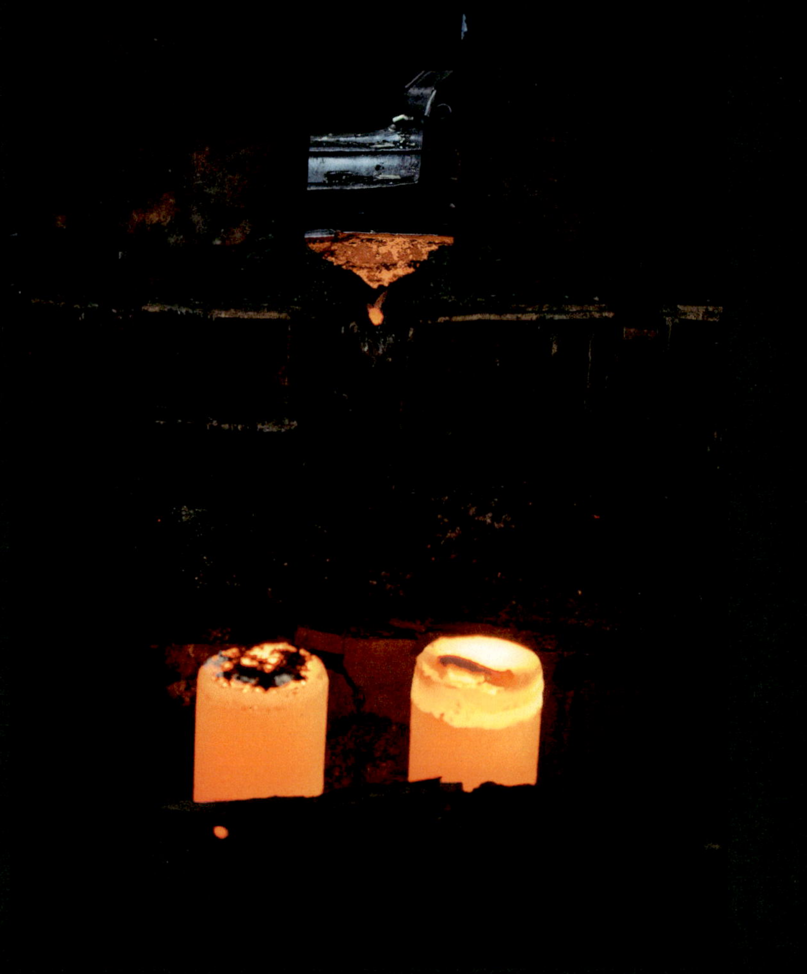

BILLETS REVEALED

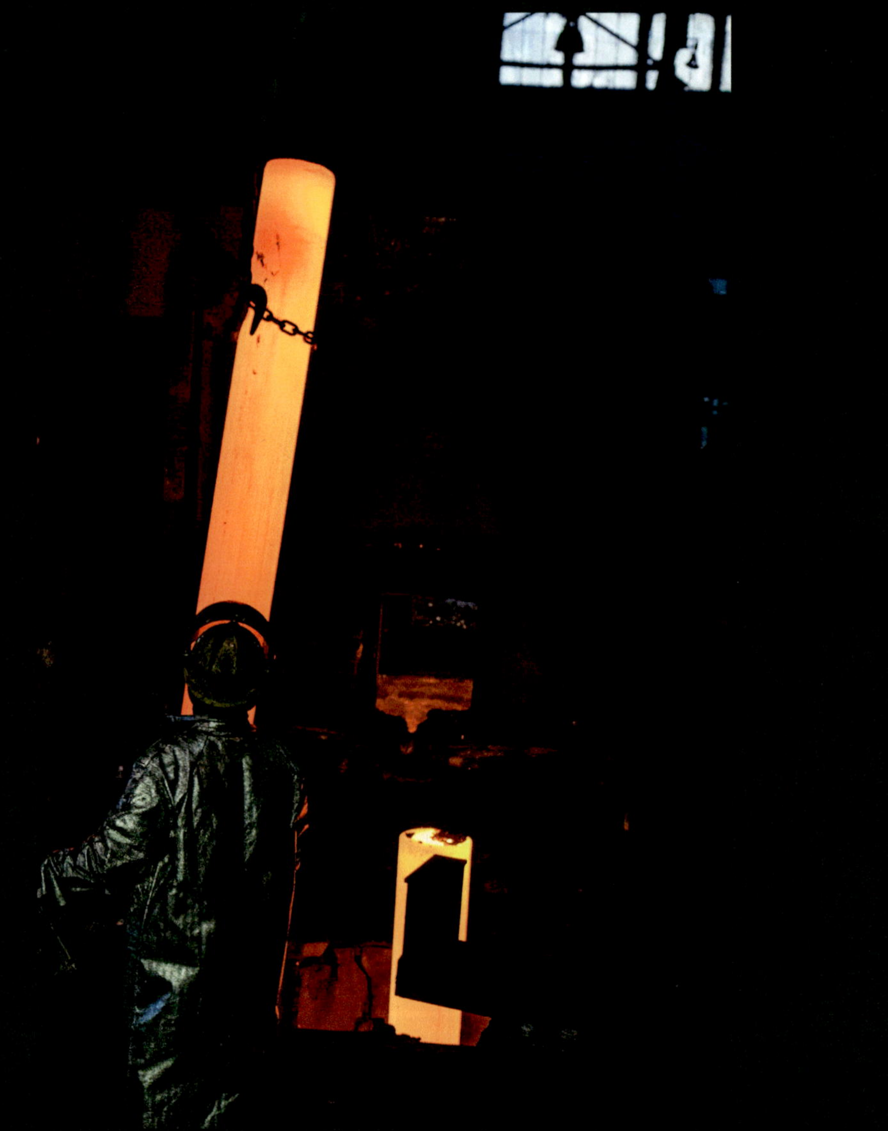

LIFT

PHOTOGRAPHER'S JOURNAL:
The Faustian beast still rumbles and roars, the fire in its belly kept hot by a few machinists, engineers, and conjurers with a supply of parts, grease, and belts. They repeatedly rebuild the furnace and make parts, keep water flowing, power surging, motors turning, hydraulics pumping, gas jets burning, and generally fix and patch anything that needs fixing or patching. They are the keepers of the philosopher's stone that makes copper sweat with golden dew, though as I look at them, they look like machinists and tool makers.

Here at the foundry in Ansonia, the fire is reduced, and the output of brass is a trickle, but they still know how to mix the zinc and the copper, when to

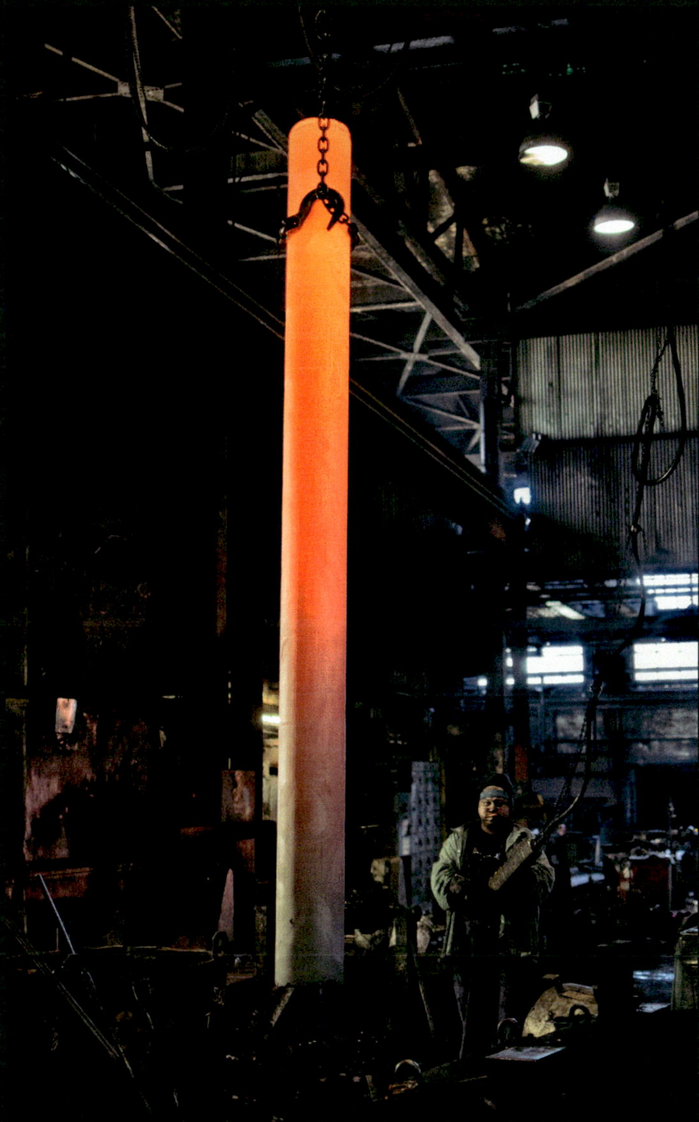

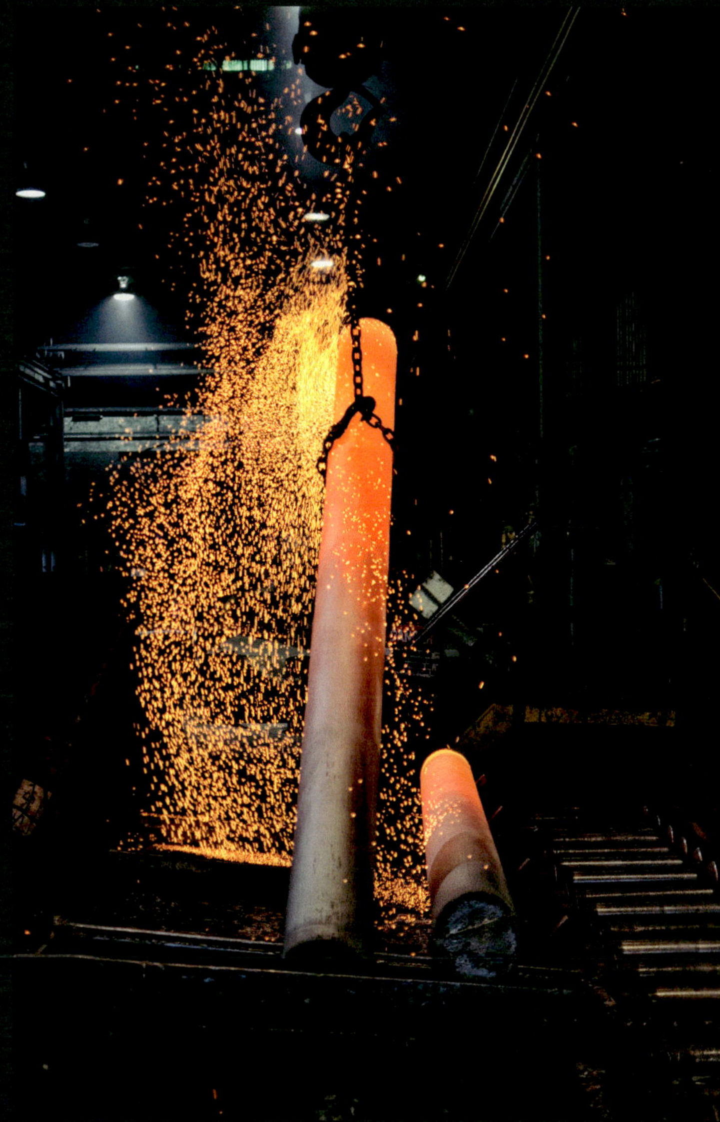

TRANSPORT

REST

All photos: Damir & Mike, casting shop, Ansonia, CT

sprinkle manganese or magnesium, which brews need nickel, lead or other metals. Looking closely around the rusting stacks and pipes, bins and tanks, someone with knowledge could read a machine-age history in the alterations, adaptations, and innovations, encrustations wrought by earlier generations to make founding foolproof. The dragon is no longer fed by someone shoveling coal. Electric heat is almost hands-free. Even so, the jobs have gone where labor's cheap and regulations are lax. Abandoned machines sit idle and corroding, becoming fossils, even as core operations churn slowly. This foundry is the last of its kind, the end of a line. In it are alchemists' secrets. Where have the alchemists gone?

A GORDIAN KNOT

Worm-like,
wriggled free of earth,
conjured in mind's alchemy
to charge and channel the forms of mind,
but where did mind wriggle from, and
where is it heading?
Truly a can of worms!

COMPOSITION IN SCRAP
"New" scrap to be added to recirculating tube scrap, American Brass

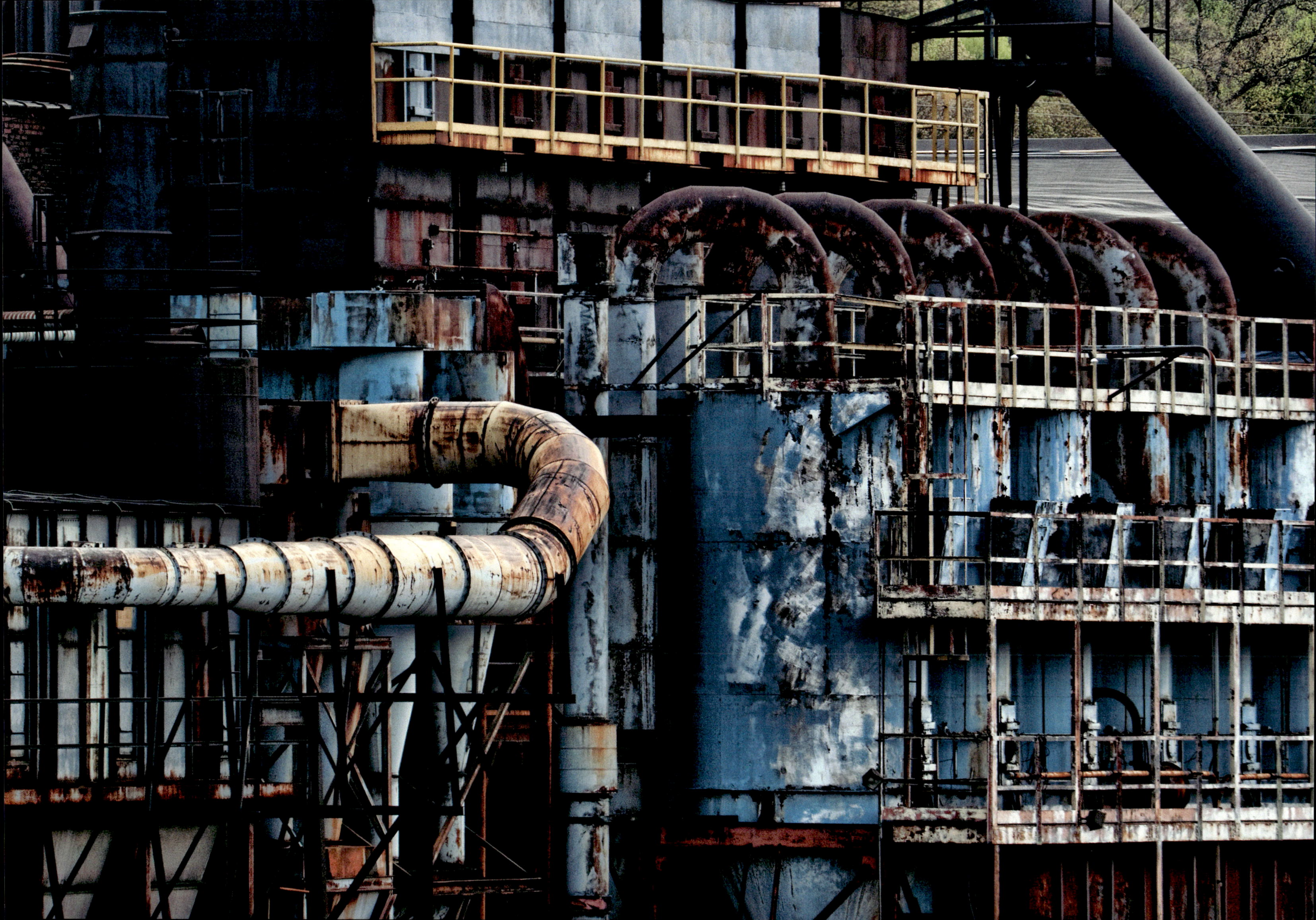

COMPOSITION IN FILTRATION

Casting shop, American Brass, Ansonia, CT

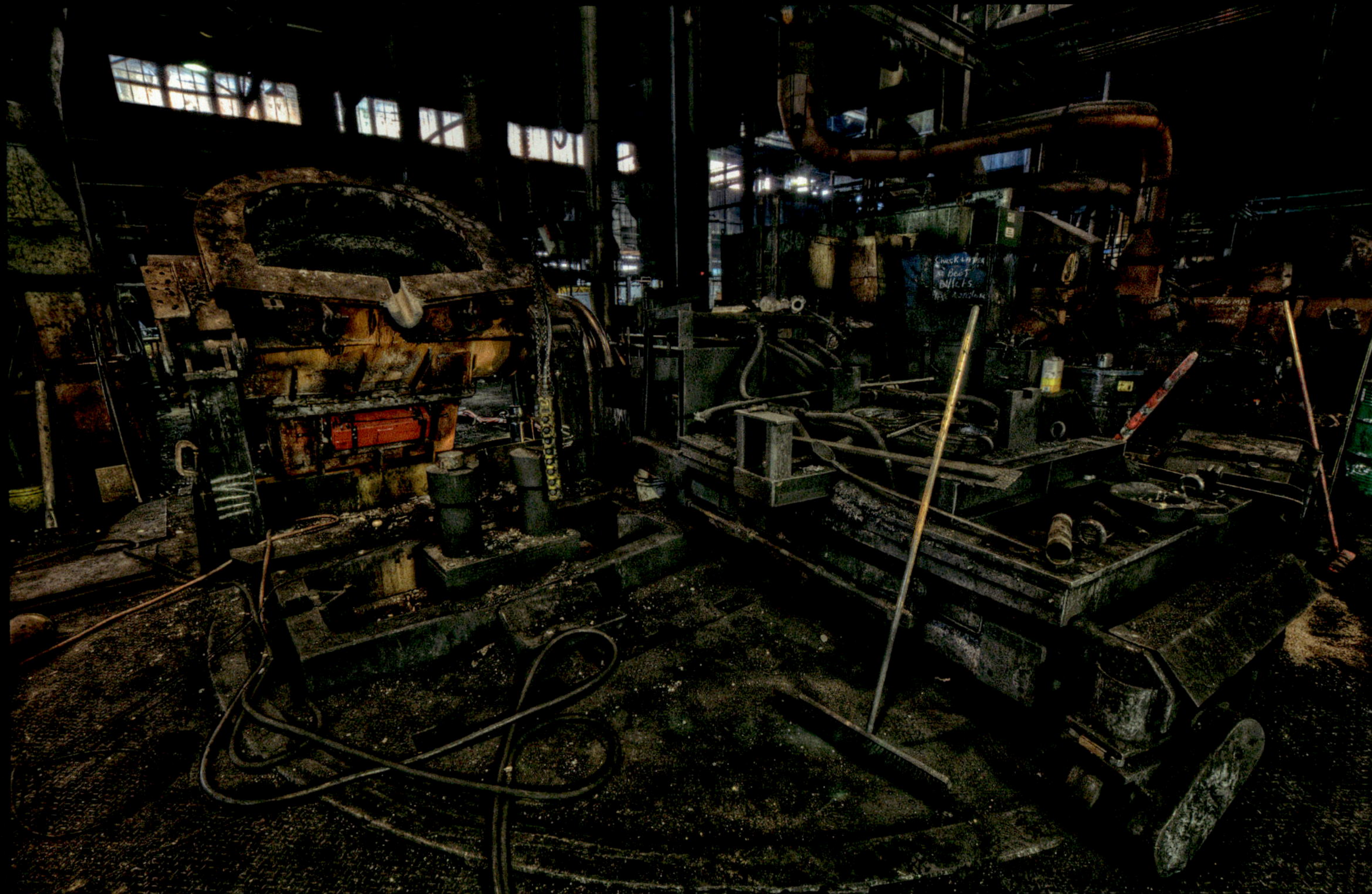

THE FURNACE

Open and with hood removed, American Brass, Ansonia, CT

PHOTOGRAPHER'S JOURNAL:
Today when I returned to the foundry it had been taken apart, and I could see behind the magic to things previously concealed. Willy pointed to the furnace, but I couldn't recognize it; the fiery dragon was gone. Where were the molds from which I'd seen him draw billets? Mike took me to a pile of metal parts and tried to explain, but I was still clueless. I saw two short cylinders sandwiched between rusty metal plates; they were two feet deep and open at both ends. How could they make twelve-foot-long billets? Then he took me to one of the unused furnaces and showed me forms that looked like what I had imagined: slick, black tubular holes into the floor, too deep and too dark to see bottom, like giant candle molds. "We don't use forms like that any more."

We went back to the short, rusty sandwich that had been pulled from the furnace, and Mike pointed back at the two stubs, like fire-hydrants, where the furnace had been—he called them "plugs," and they seemed to fit. I asked again: How could the long, glowing billet I had seen, come from a short, bottomless form? Mike was patient with my failure of imagination, and he again explained how, as the billet cooled, it became solid, and Mike used hydraulic elevators to lower it into the pit even as new molten brass was pouring from above. The billets grew downward. I had watched him lower the elevators without realizing what was happening.

When the furnace is shut down, the men who regularly run the foundry work on refitting and repairing it. Lucio, Damir, Mike, and Willy were all busy. Other men were there, too, engineering staff with the tools to install and test new hydraulic and gas lines and electrical circuits. There is no repair man to call to fix equipment like this, no books from which to order the custom part; what breaks, you fix, what fails, you remake. When conditions change, you innovate.

Unfortunately, the repairs happened in tight spaces and in watery pits beneath the floor, so I went off to shoot in the abandoned wire, rod, and tube mills that once processed the foundry's brass. In my explorations I passed through what must have been the main engineering shop, row after long row of immense tools and benches, bits and chucks and widgets all hung, stacked, or pegged in neat, graduated sequences, enough to keep at least one hundred engineers busy repairing, sharpening, building new. Several hours later I returned to the foundry where a half-dozen men labored repairing the only piece of equipment in operation on the campus.

While I was gone the crew had remounted the crucible on the new hydraulics they had been installing, and the hydraulics were extended, tipping the crucible steeply. It seemed the perfect shot to explain the anatomy of the furnace. In front of the crucible are the plugs that close the bottom of the short billet molds. The plugs have been raised high, more hydraulics refitted there; the molds were not yet in place.

When the furnace was put back together, the metal tipped from the crucible flowed through the runner box to two distributor cups above the molds. As the brass cooled, the founder lowered the plugs and the solid end of the billet dropped down and became the new plug. Gradually the founder tipped the crucible to keep metal flowing toward the molds. Damir was relining the runner box with some sort of material like clay, and others were testing fittings. They expected to prime on Tuesday. I planned to be there.

At the center of the foundry the last furnace rumbled. Its ducts and stacks disappeared among the dark trusses of the foundry's roof. It was hard to find its edges, to find a place to stand back and take it all in, to use photography to clarify the twisting, sculptural pile of ducts, pipes, wires, and stacks, but now that I'd seen them take it apart and put it together I realized, it was only a tin dragon with a pot of gold in its belly.

The truths of Brass Valley all depend on people. I thought about the small cohort repairing and maintaining this lone furnace, the bonds they developed, the genius they shared, something more than mere camaraderie; then I multiplied that many times as it was when the valley was filled with factories and families whose children rose through the mills. Then I thought about the dark sheds around me, not the empty benches and idle tools, but the culture that had filled those spaces as dampness fills them now. What an engine of intuition, initiative, innovation, liberty! What a generator also of soot, smoke, sickness, and early death. I've been told to beware, that's the way it is; there is a devil's cost in our alchemy.

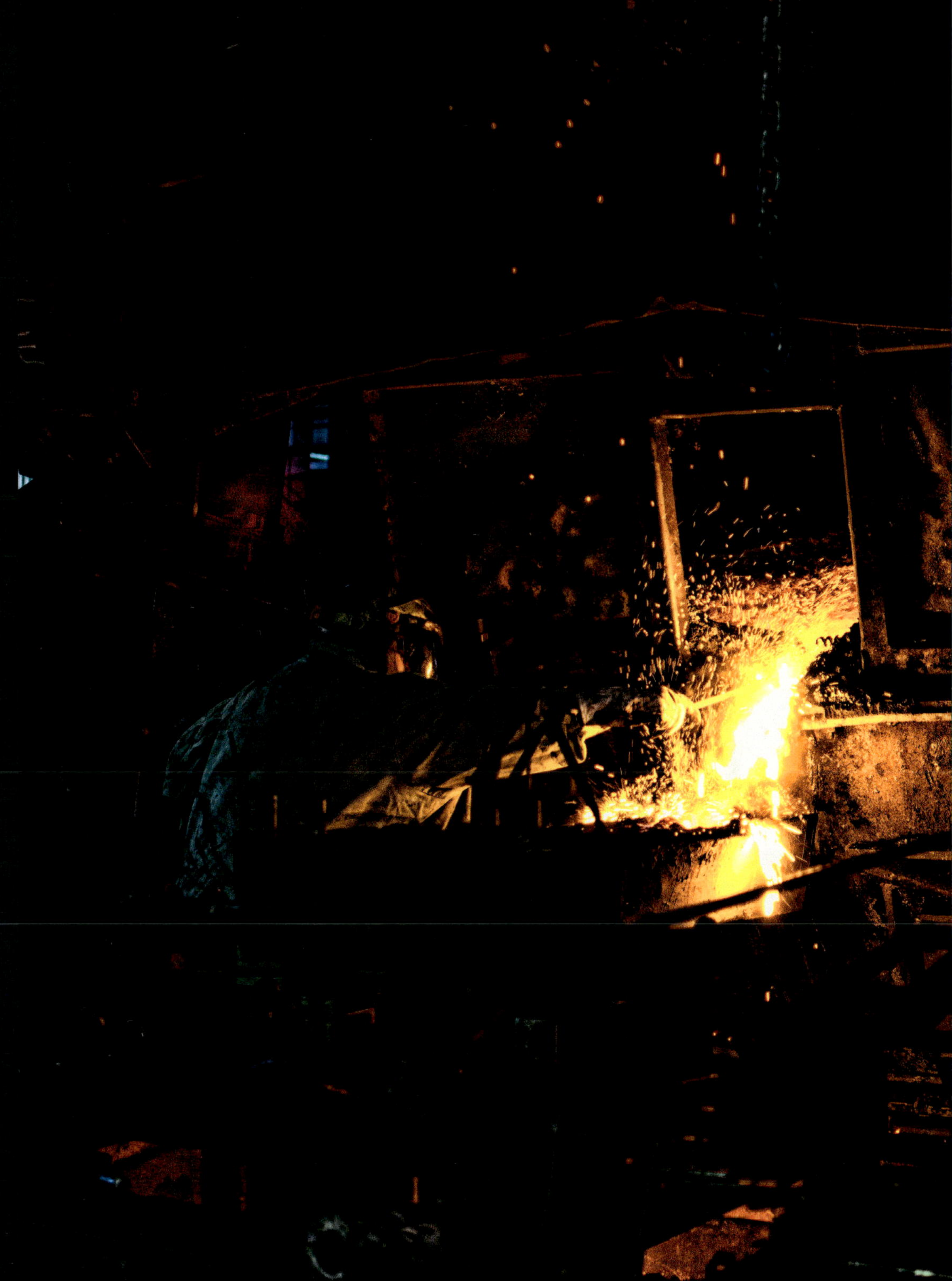

OCCULT KNOWLEDGE
Testing the charge, Ansonia, CT

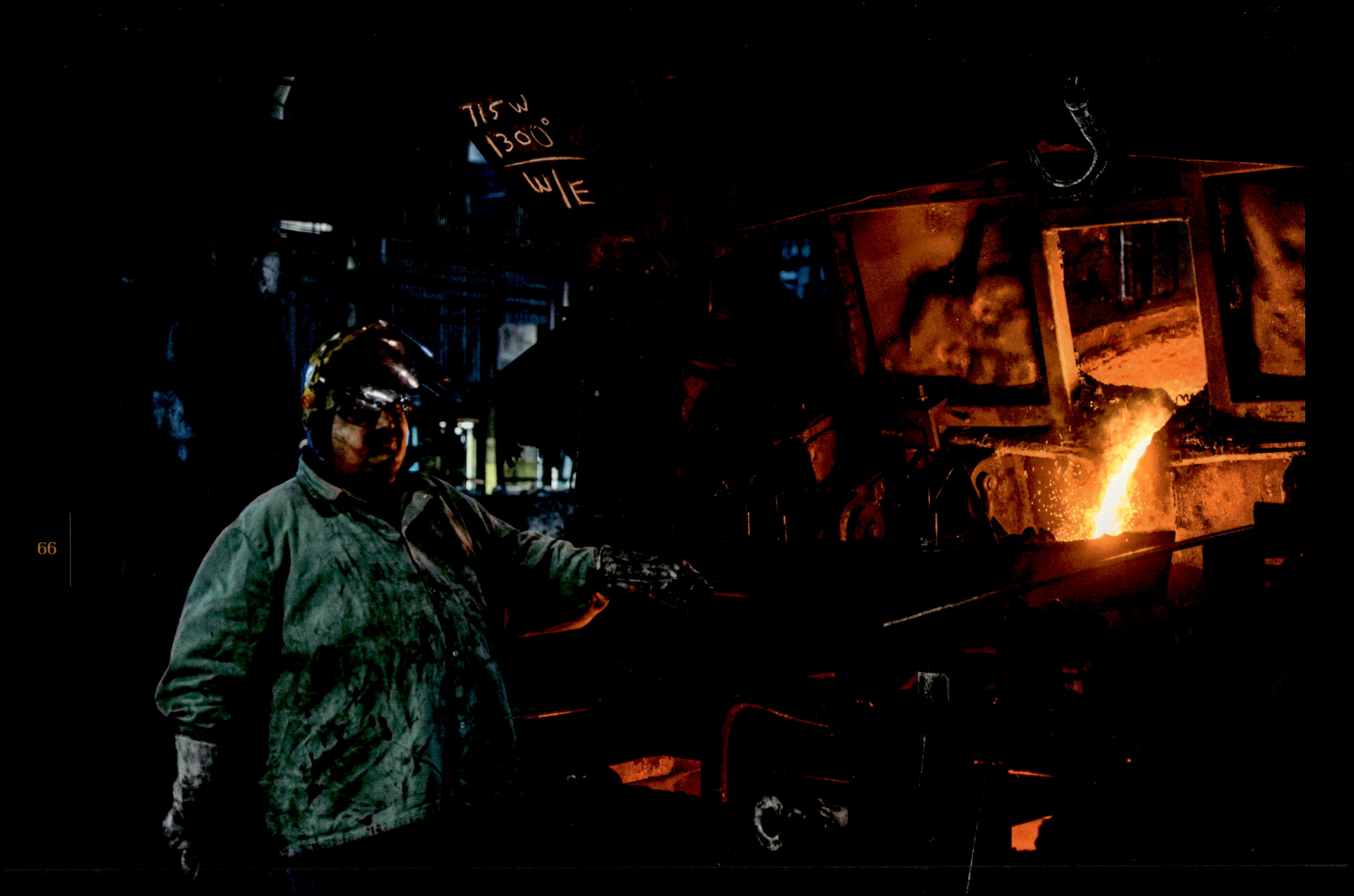

MIKE
American Brass, Ansonia, CT

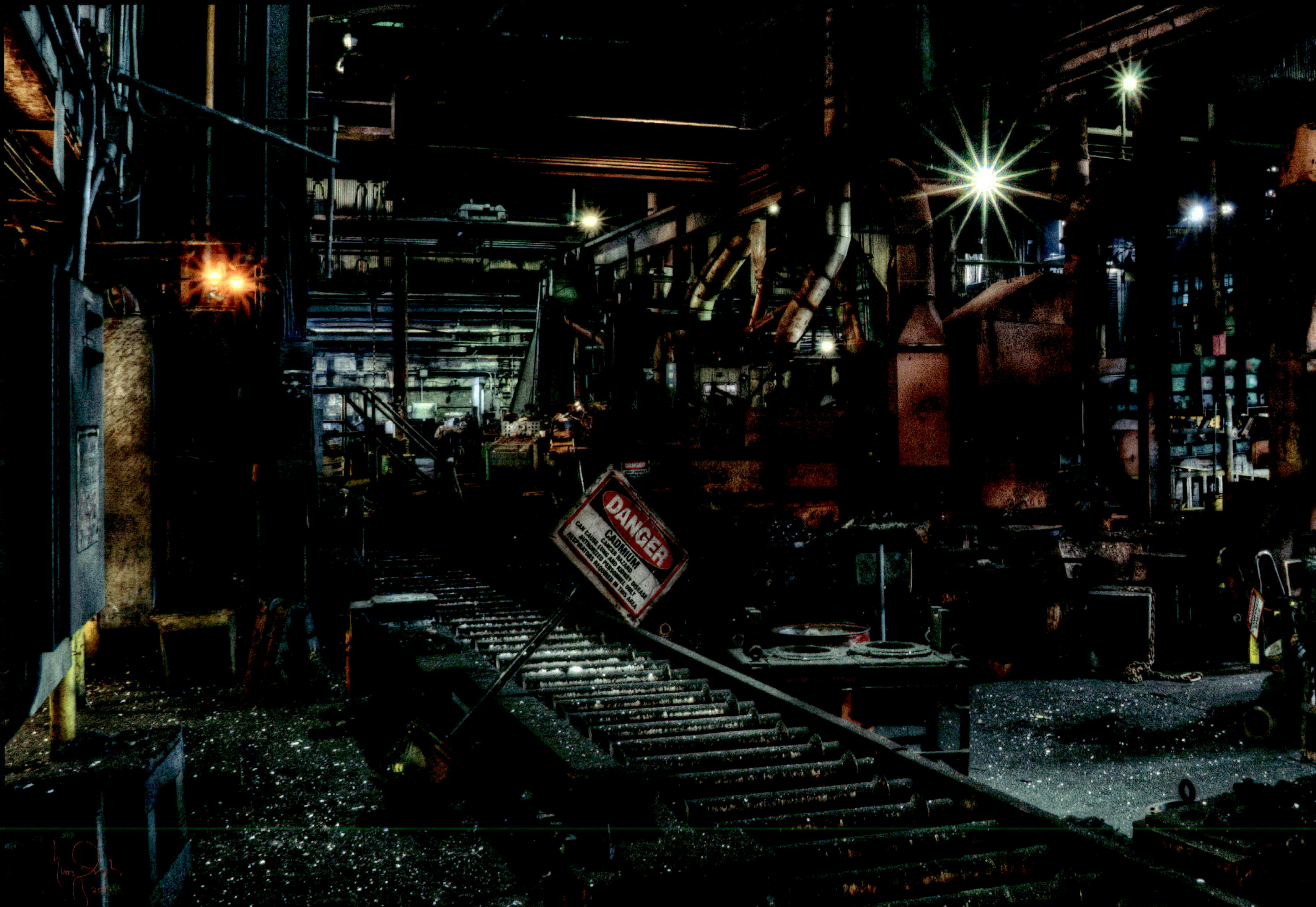

THE DRAGONS

Conveyor & row of large casting furnaces, casting shed, American Brass, Ansonia, CT

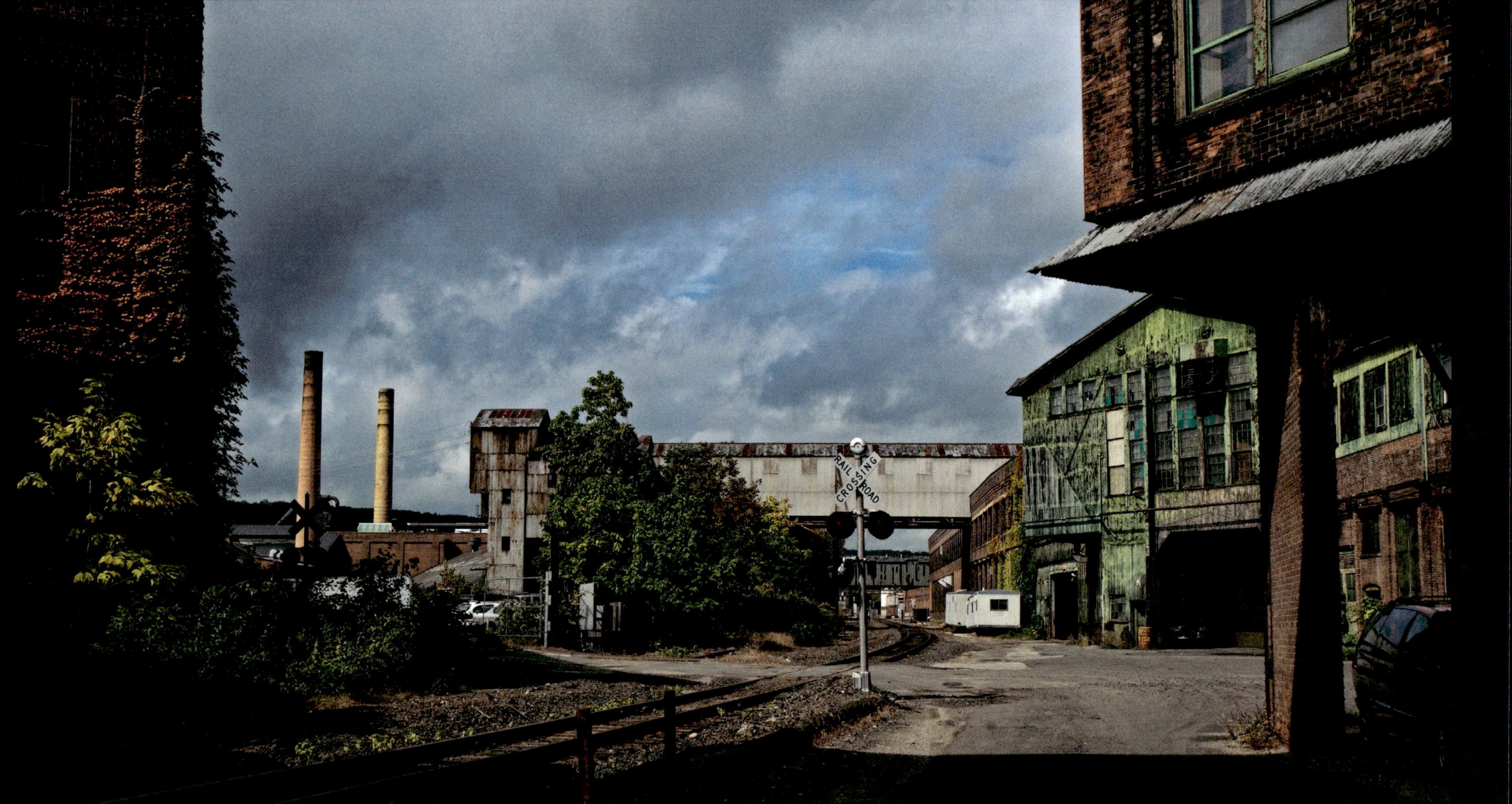

FARREL WORKS, ANSONIA, CT

Naugatuck Railroad corridor between Farrel work sheds and American Brass, Ansonia, CT

PHOTOGRAPHER'S JOURNAL:

The track that passes by the foundry continues to the old Farrel Machine Company campus before it reaches Ansonia Station. I've continued across the Naugatuck River, along the tracks, and into the old Birmingham section of Derby at the point where the Naugatuck River ends, and I've crossed the track to Shelton on the western bank, where the waters of the Naugatuck mix into those of the Housatonic. These three cities—Ansonia, Derby, Shelton—once formed a vital industrial core at the bottom of Brass Valley where the track goes on to New Haven and Bridgeport.

The corridor where the track cuts through American Brass and Farrel Corporation was once one of the busiest places in the valley. Machines as big as buildings were made here and shipped around the globe. Now, even on the busiest days, one rarely sees more than a few cars passing in and out, and buildings that once made giant machinery and where thousands worked are now just storage. Time plays tricks with multiple incarnations of Farrel & Company signs that haunt the terraced parapet, and a bend in parallel Main Street makes for interesting geometries that hint to me of lost land contours and a forgotten canal. Today this is one of the rustiest places in Brass Valley. People ask me, "What do you find there to photograph?"

I photograph what's gone.

OUR STORIES:

Farrel Works

We were Irishmen fresh from building the railroads and looking for jobs when Almon Farrel brought us in to work at his new mill.

Almon Farrel was a millwright and the son of a millwright. He had grown up in Waterbury where the confluence of many streams and small rivers watered many mills. He was Anson Phelps's millwright when Phelps bought the Kinneytown dam, and it was Almon Farrel with his seventeen-year-old son Franklin who dug the Ansonia Canal and set the foundations of the waterworks. We worked beside them when they installed the first wheel and set it turning beneath the channeled waters, turning the force of gravity into power for new mills. Like Smith before him, Almon Farrel was pioneering a new scale of industrial power generation in a pristine valley, learning as he built.

The railroad was the future. He saw opportunity and, on the canal near the factory he had built for Phelps, he opened a small foundry and machine shop of his own. Almon Farrel & Company manufactured things for manufacturing and eventually supplied heavy machinery to manufacturers throughout the Naugatuck Valley and around the world. By the 1850s, Farrel had a second factory in Waterbury. He was the millwright's millwright and in direct competition with the Birmingham Foundry on his canal in Birmingham. It is said that Farrel spent $15,000 to establish his mill, and from that point on his company produced all its own capital.

At about the same time Charles Goodyear patented his process for using sulphur to harden rubber. He called it "vulcanization." His brother Henry Goodyear had built the Goodyear Metallic Rubber Shoe Co. upstream in Naugatuck. Charles Goodyear famously died penniless, but vulcanization made rubber useful for shoes, tires, gaskets and seals, elastic bands, bumpers, and balloons. Long before plastics, everything rubber turned to gold except for the man who invented the essential vulcanization process. Rubber fired imaginations, changed how simple things were done. It brought much new work to the valley, and added a robust, sulfurous mix to the valley's flatulence.

Both Birmingham Foundry and Farrel Foundry began manufacturing the equipment to manufacture rubber and soon paper, and the entire Naugatuck Valley was becoming a powerhouse of industry just in time for the Civil War and riches to be made from cannons and machines for rolling bayonets that let soldiers get up close and personal. Brass Valley was the vital point for manufacturing them.

In the nineteenth century, cane sugar was a rare and costly luxury item, and we treasured our bit of sweet honey and maple sugar. In the 1870s, under Almon's son Franklin Farrel, Farrel Corporation began manufacturing machines for grinding sugar cane. A single machine filled eighty freight cars on its way down to Bridgeport, where it filled an entire ship bound for Cuba, and Franklin Farrel and others bought sugar estates in Santo Domingo and Cuba as inexpensive sugar became affordable for all of us here in the United States, and other businessmen saw opportunities for investing abroad, as uprisings were "manageable" in the Caribbean but they became "tense" with labor sometimes at home. During World War I, Farrel Works was running round-the-clock shifts. Labor troubles came to a head in 1919 and 1920.

That was then. Long ago the Farrel Corporation merged with the old Birmingham Foundry. Franklin Farrel IV resigned as assistant secretary of the Farrel Machinery Group on May 6, 1981, ending family participation in the business. Today Farrel has offices in more than thirty countries, but the worldwide headquarters are still here in Ansonia, and there are still some machinists doing finishing work in a few of the old buildings.

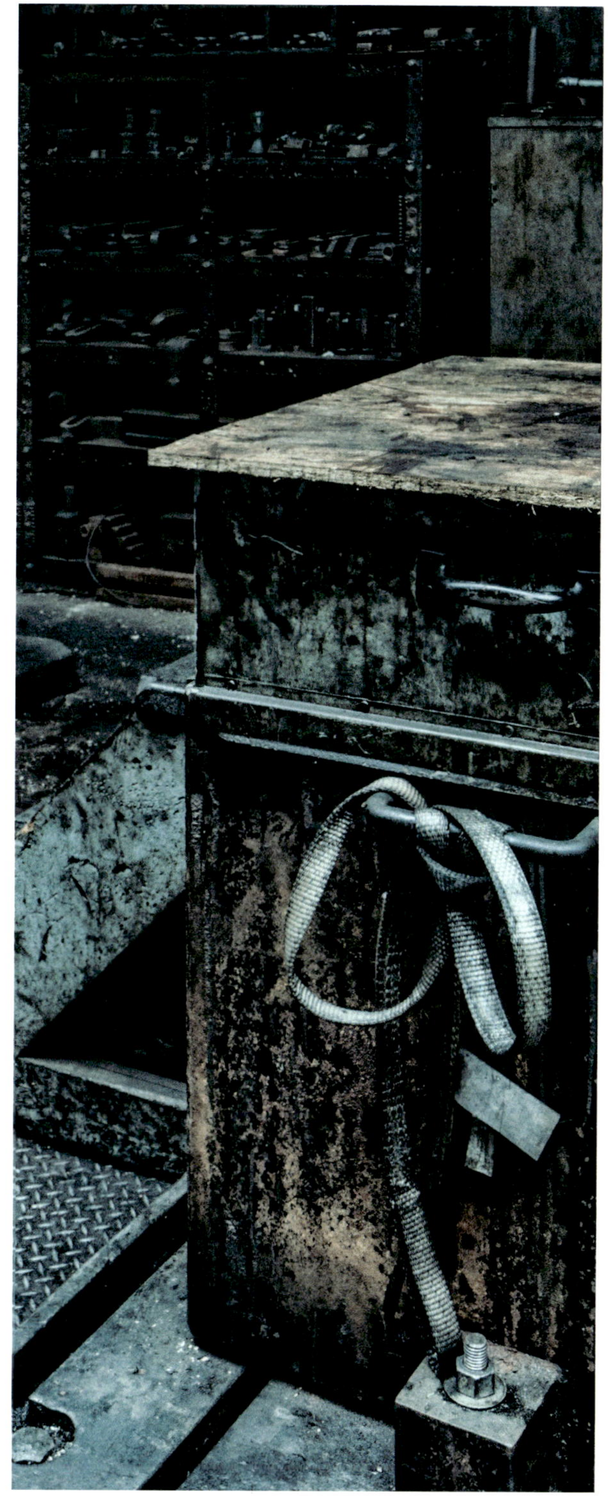

MACHINE SHOP

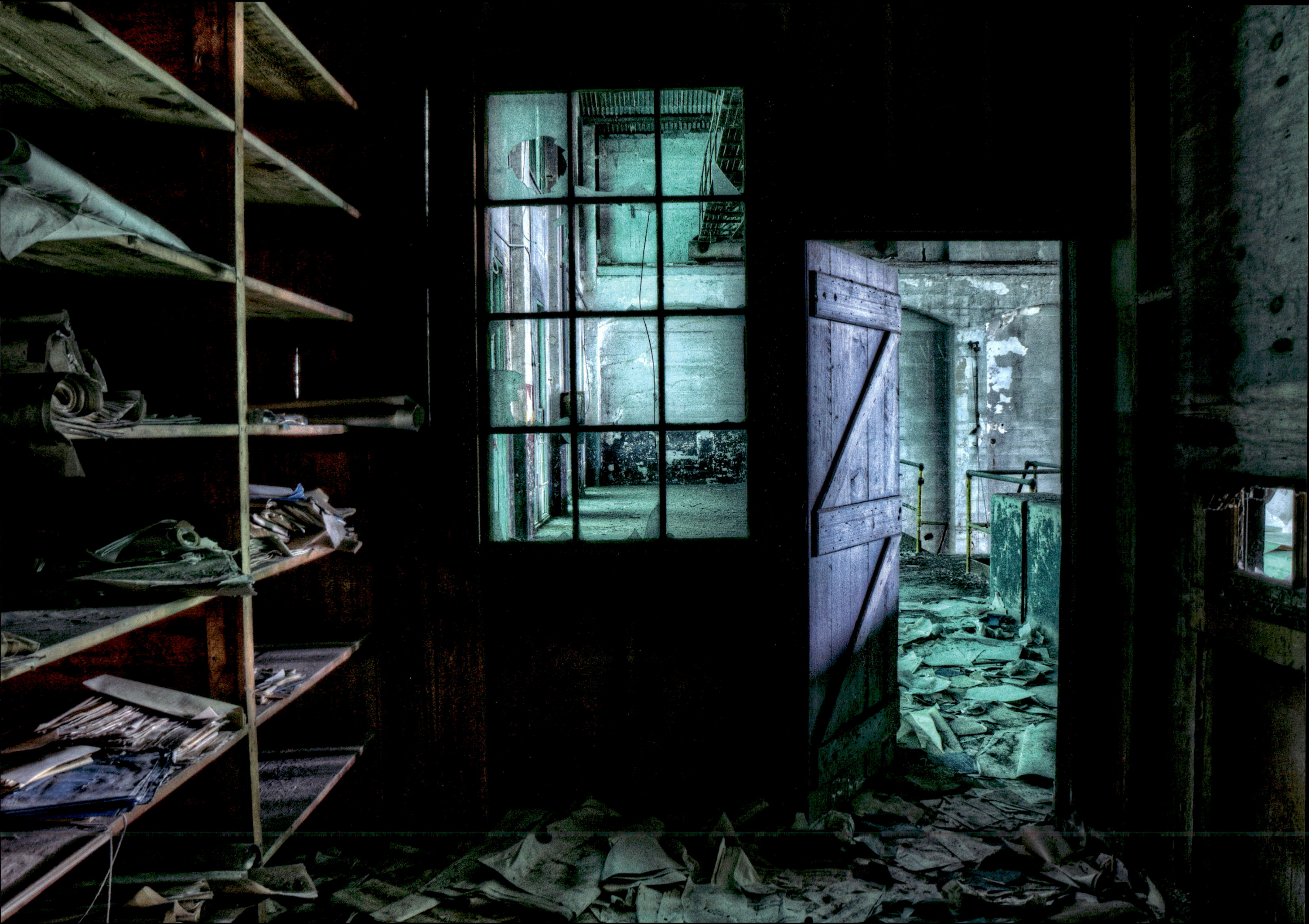

PAPER TRAIL

Abandoned concrete factory

PAPER TRAIL

Factories closed,
vagabond files loosed on the wind,
wretched refuse of the pre-digital world,
teeming on our shores.

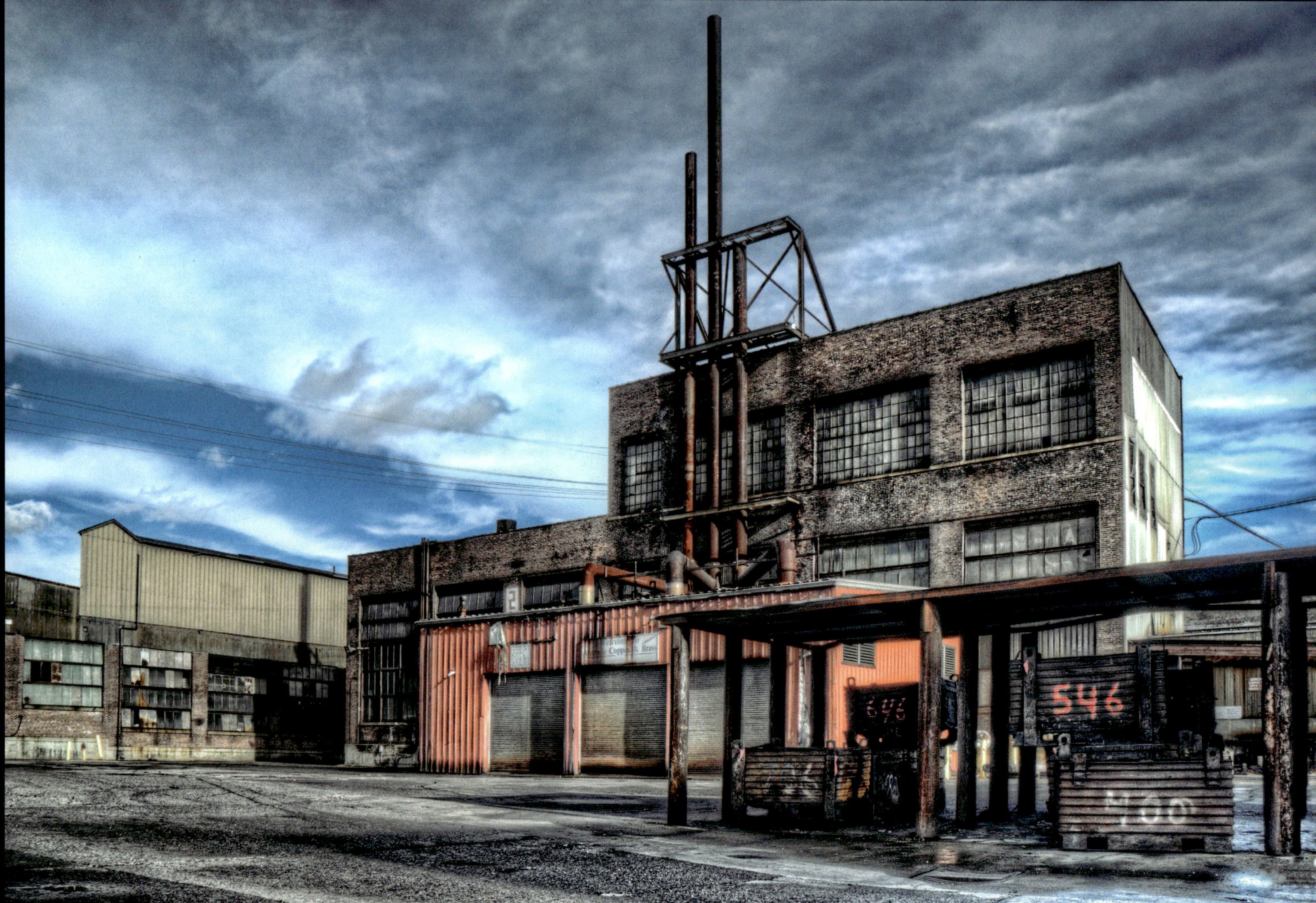

WAITING SCRAP HAMPERS BESIDE THE CASTING SHOP

Rod mill and powerhouse, American Brass, Ansonia, CT

PHOTOGRAPHER'S JOURNAL:

I've seen buildings like this before, photographed in them. Every large industrial campus had a powerhouse. This one powers the casting shop so it still drips and buzzes, and, unlike others I've visited, it has not yet been closed and looted. Its muscle once powered and heated a large wire mill, two rod mills, executive suites, labs, accounts offices and the foundry.

The powerhouse contains two brick furnaces as big as houses. The crew says they date to the Civil War and that the current building was built

large fire boxes that originally burned coal and were later converted for oil. They are surmounted by large boilers that generated enough steam to keep all of the buildings of the campus warm; the powerhouse provided heat by the acre and met the power needs of the whole complex.

Stairs and catwalks climb between and over the two furnaces and further up to the top of a large atrium whose purpose has been lost; there are also the remains of something that was in the floor that nobody is able to identify.

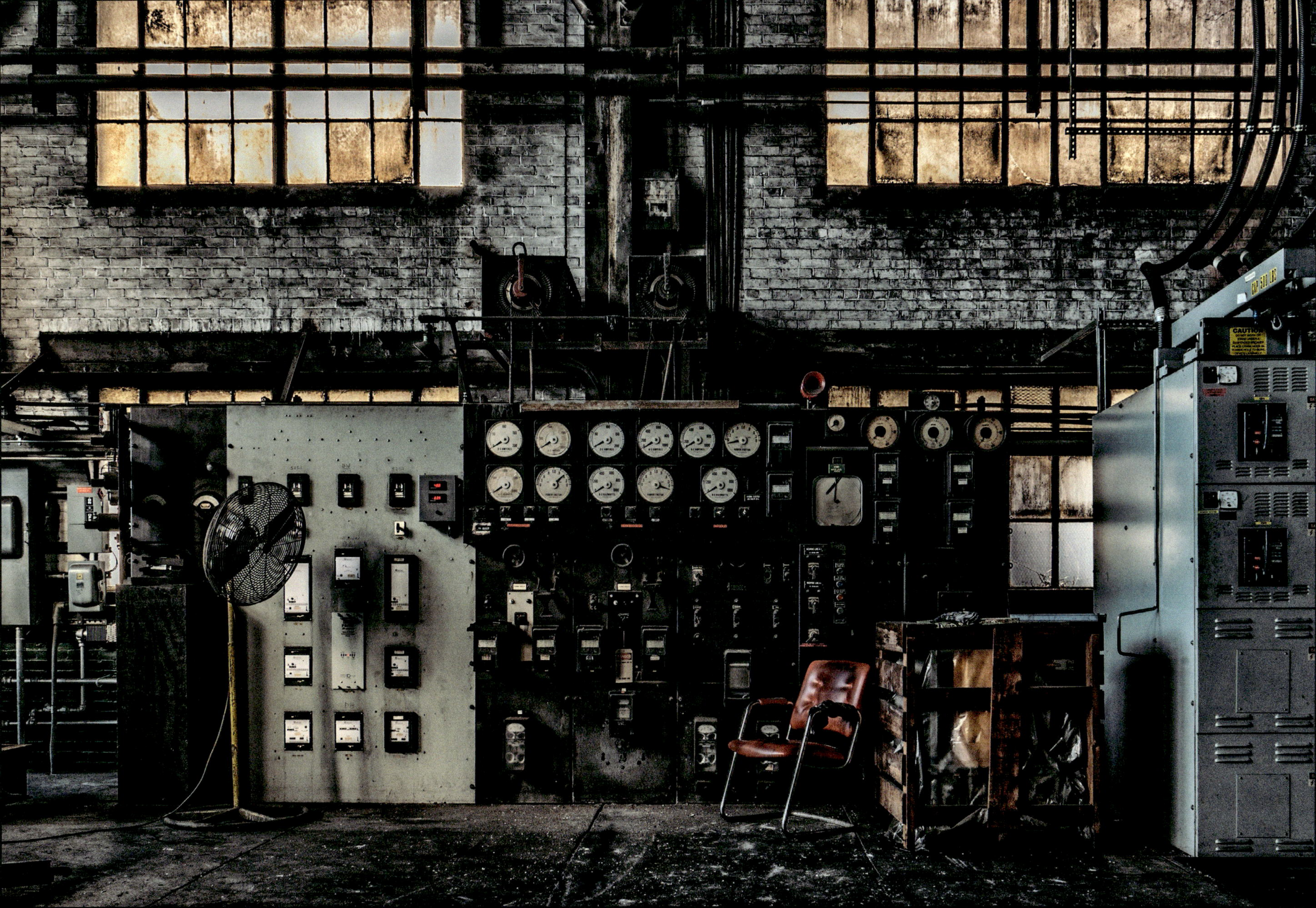

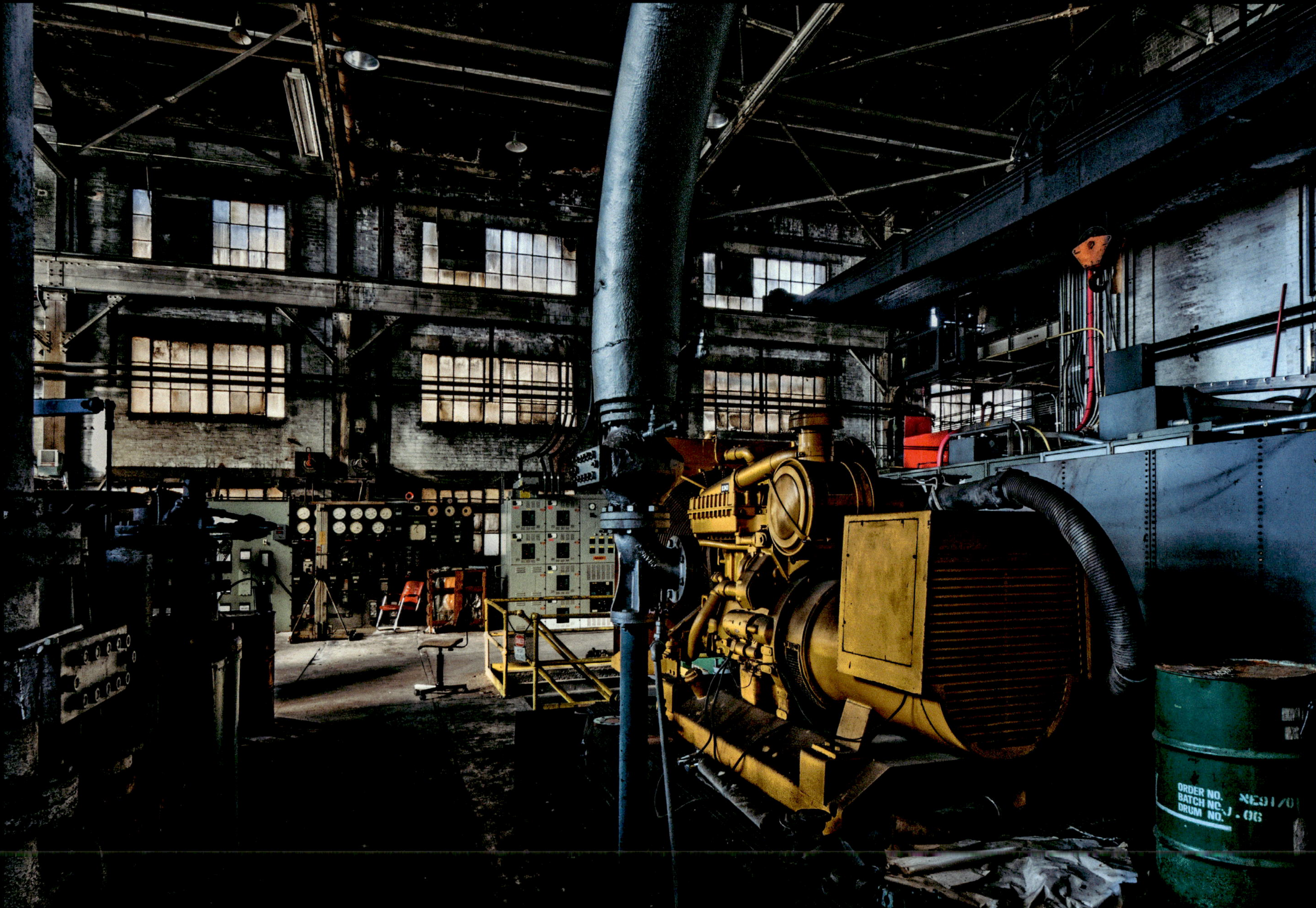

THE YELLOW BACK-UP COMPRESSOR
Powerhouse, American Brass, Ansonia, CT

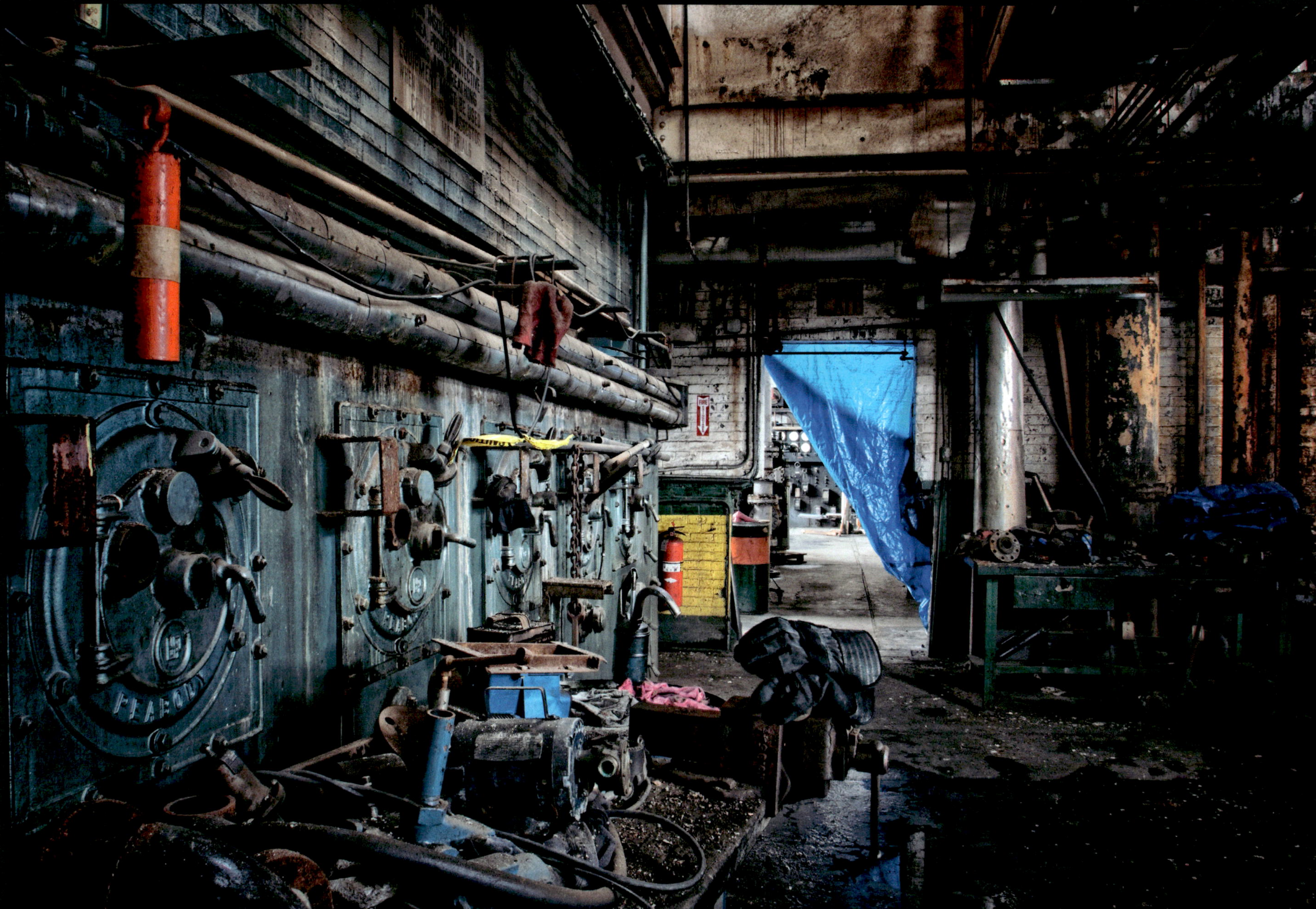

HANDLERS

North furnace bank, American Brass, Ansonia, CT

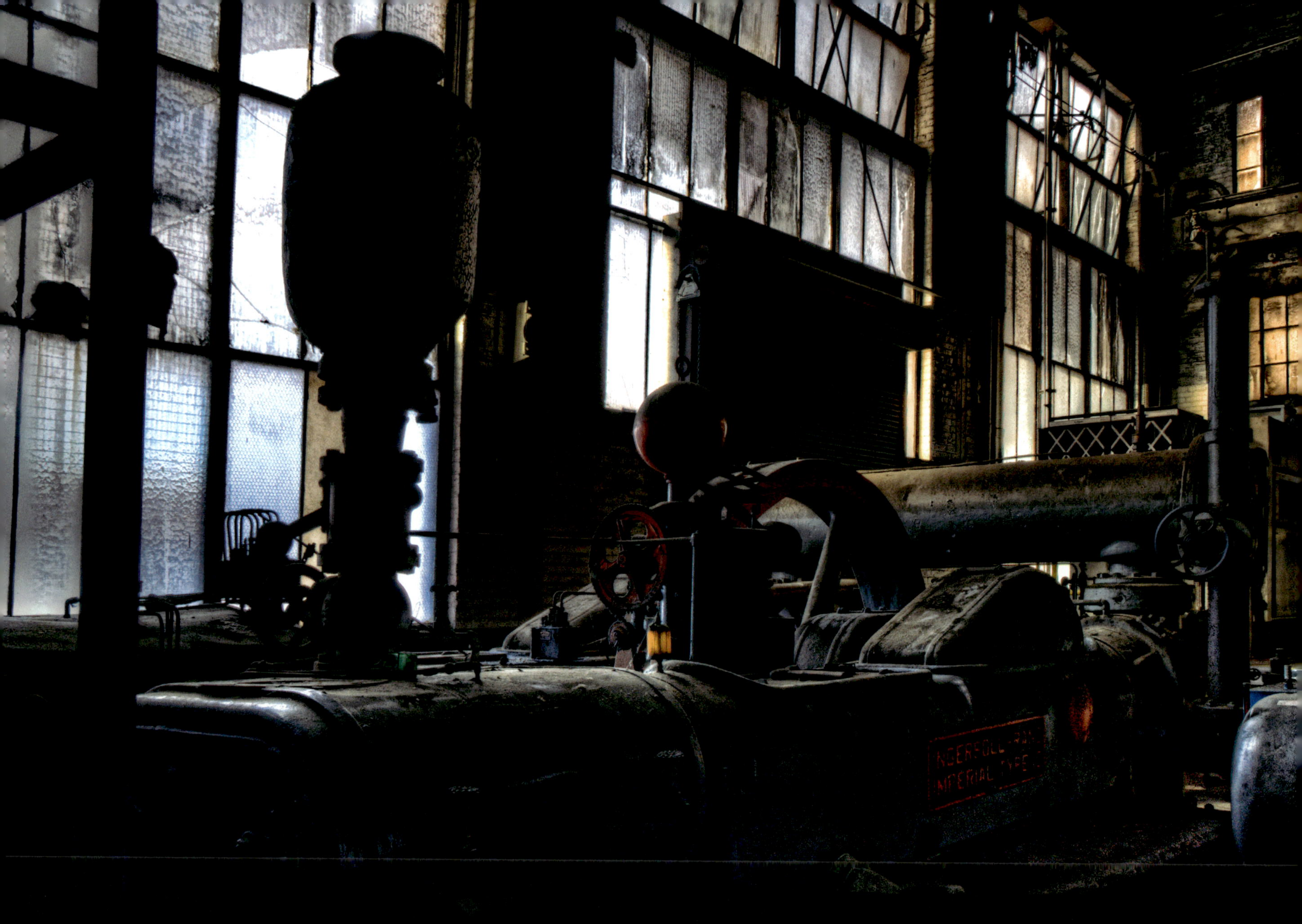

NGERSOLL COMPRESSOR, GREAT HALL OF DINOSAURS

PHOTOGRAPHER'S JOURNAL:
I'm a stranger here in need of a tour guide. The powerhouse is a bit like the old Natural History Museum that I remember from my childhood, giant rooms quiet and hollow enough for footsteps to echo, but here it is water dripping that resonates and a ceaseless buzz. A guide would help me sort the triassic from the jurassic and explain all the wheels and globes, pulleys, and valves and what they do, and a real expert would know that each limb and appendage on the torso of the dinosaur had a bit of a story. I can only gawk at the glint of alchemists' dreams in the silent machines.

The powerhouse consists of two great halls. The smaller Hall of Dinosaurs contains free-standing pumps, motors, compressors, turbines, and panels of electronics and meters and graphs.

The larger hall holds the furnaces and a high atrium that begins a floor below grade and rises four-and-a-half, column-free stories. It's almost heroic in its height and broad enough to hold another pair of furnaces and mostly empty. The furnaces are topped with ducts, pipes, valves, and barnacles.

Behind the boilers are dark masonry chasms where the floors are always damp and dripping. Metal catwalks climb from the dank hollow between the boilers, up through and around ducts to the top of the hall where the air is hot, dusty, and dry.

The powerhouse is in the center of the factory property between the other sheds. The sheds contain rusting, silent machines, left as when work stopped, not yet salvaged or sold. Pedestals and gaping pits mark where machines once stood. When the wind blows, tin rattles and echoes inside and out.

The vast works are variously maintained or abandoned, and haunted by disappearing cats, but in the powerhouse there is real activity, even if there are few people—a steady buzz and a glow of light that lets me know the casting shop is at least smoldering and turning out brass billets to be trucked up the valley to Waterbury. Mike says they've been at it here since the time of Anson Phelps.

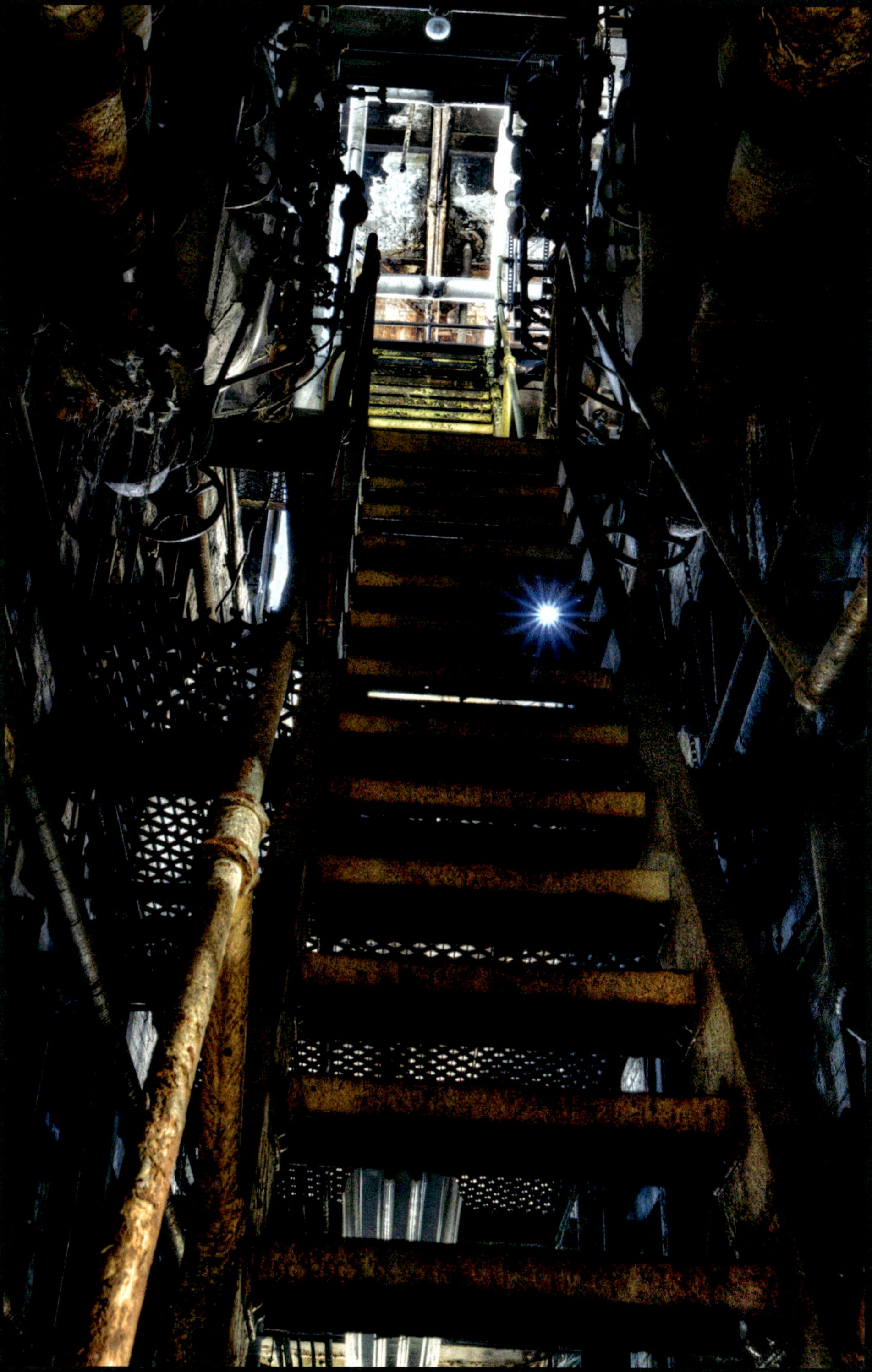

TO THE CATWALK
Between the furnaces, powerhouse,
American Brass, Ansonia, CT

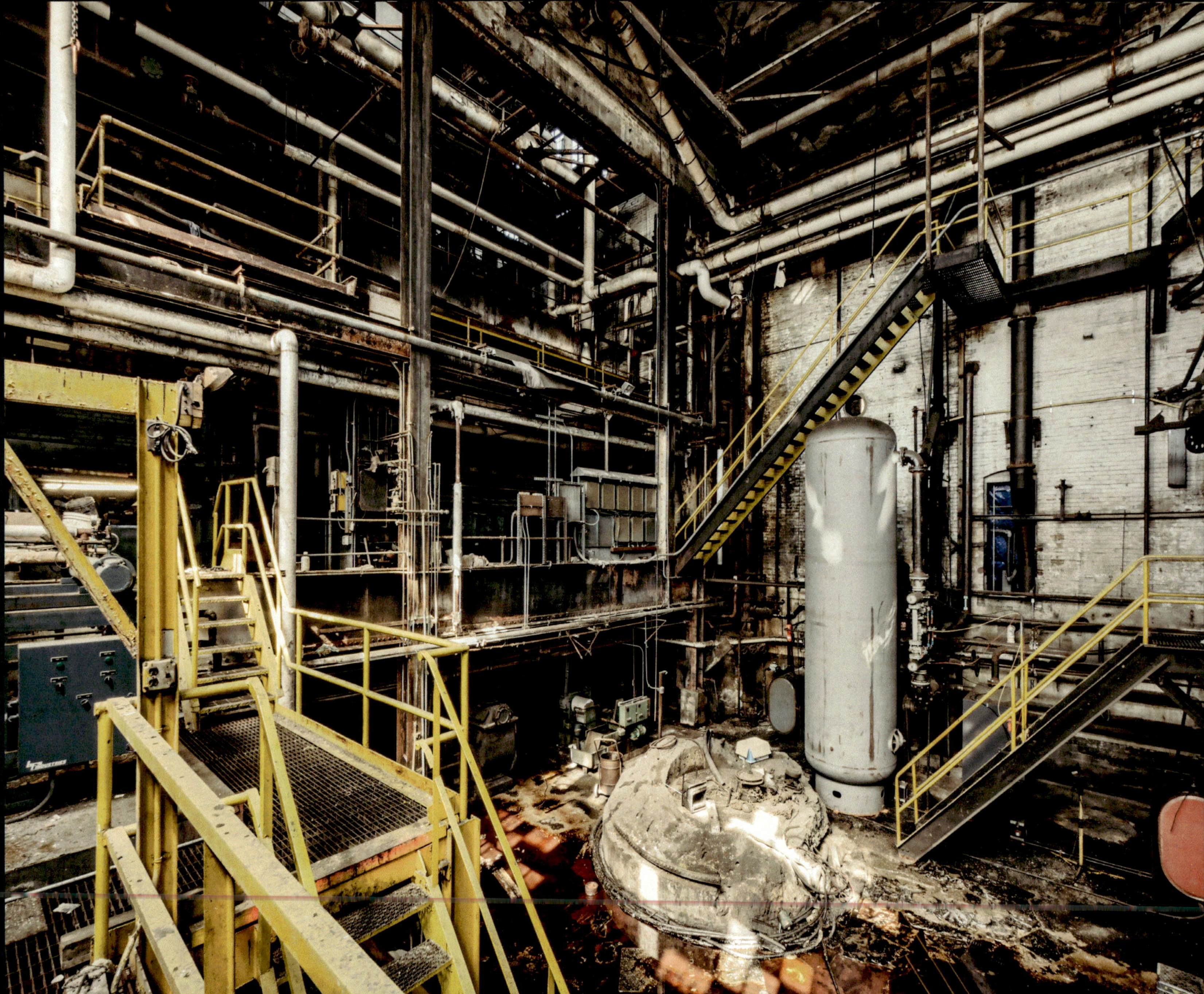

MOONWALK

High atrium, powerhouse, American Brass, Ansonia, CT

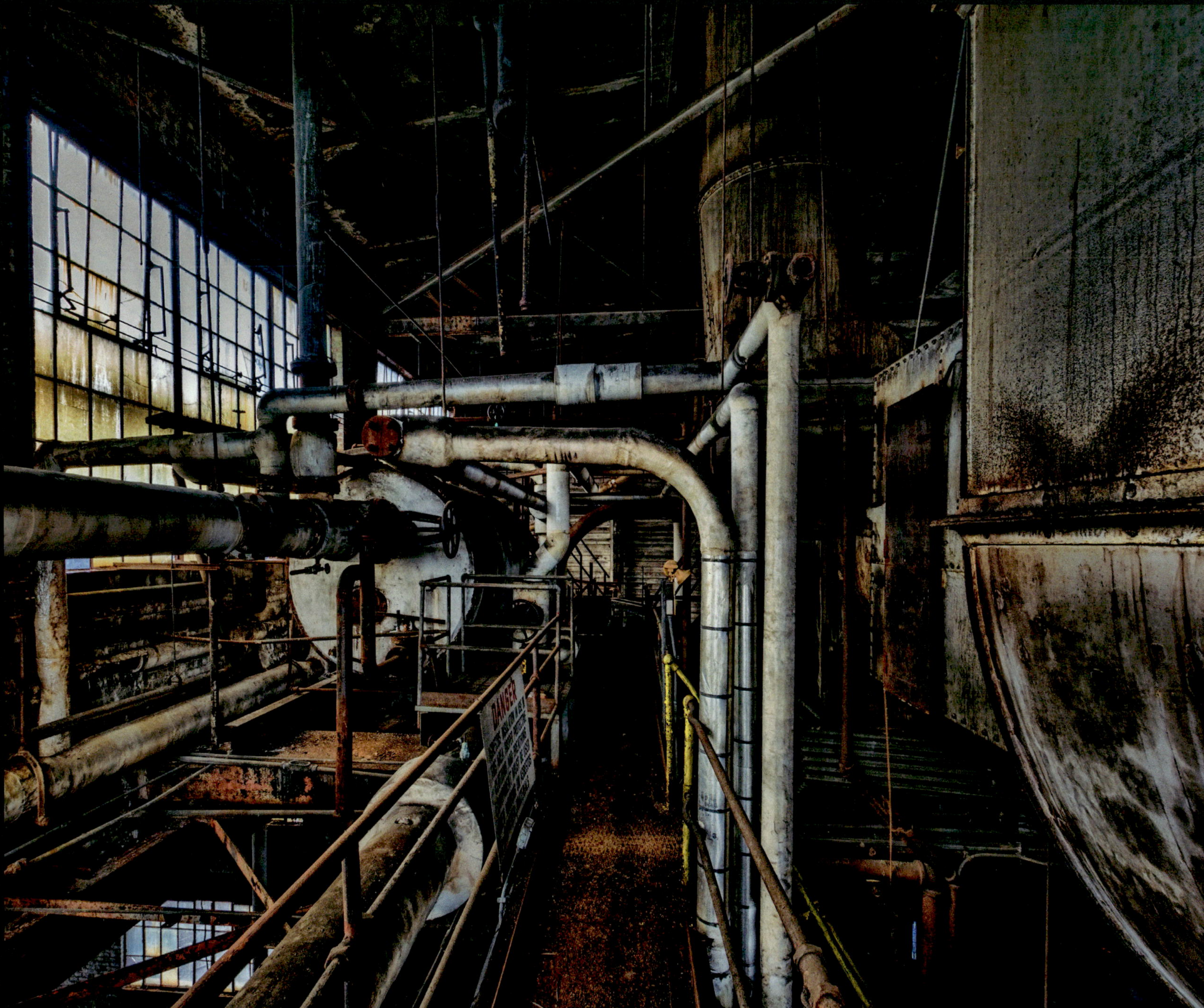

CATWALK

Above the atrium, powerhouse, American Brass, Ansonia, CT

BREAK TIME

In the whoosh
of the closer
opening,
bathroom secrets
hushed.

To be told later.

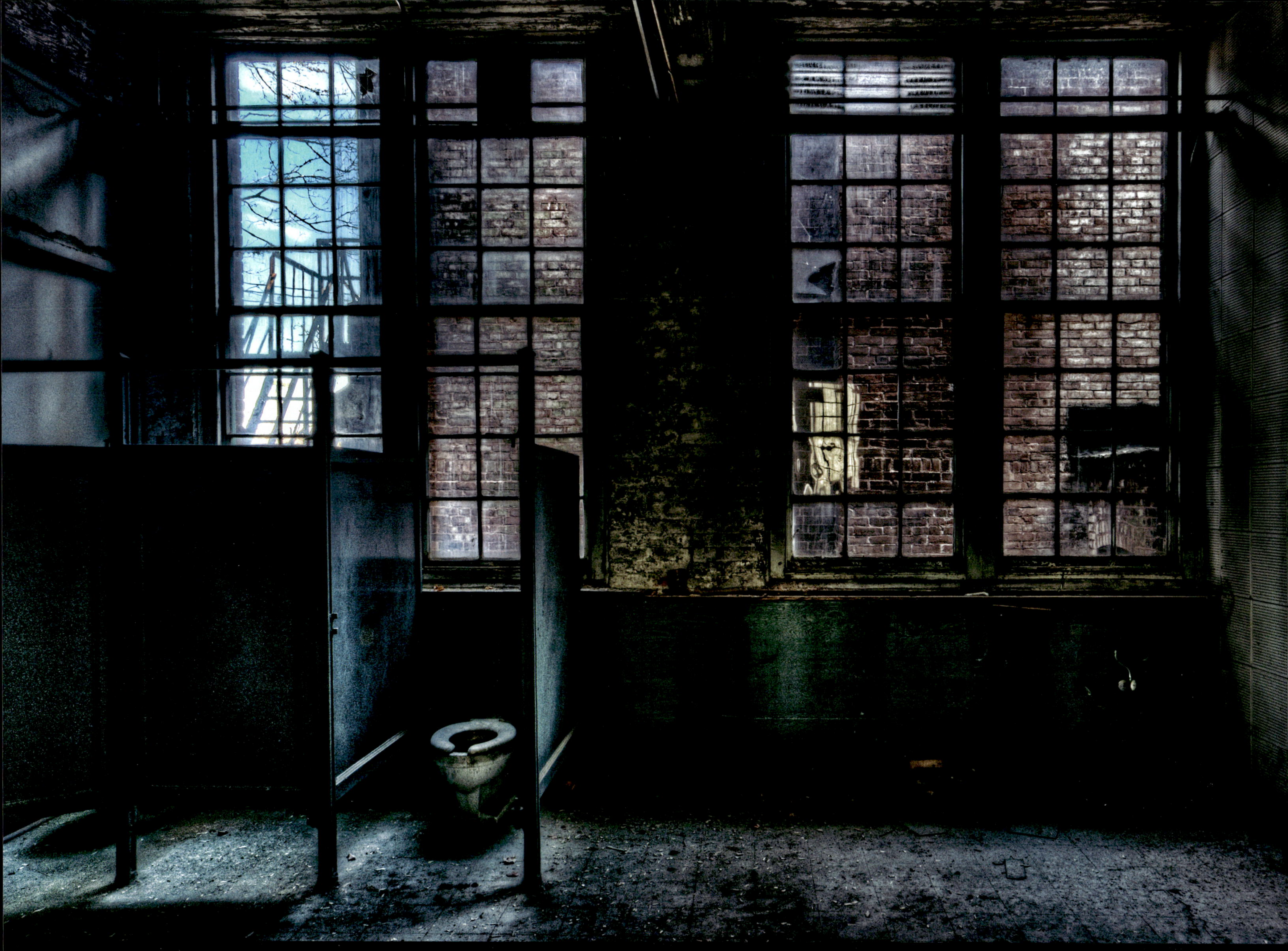

HENDEY COMPANY BATHROOM

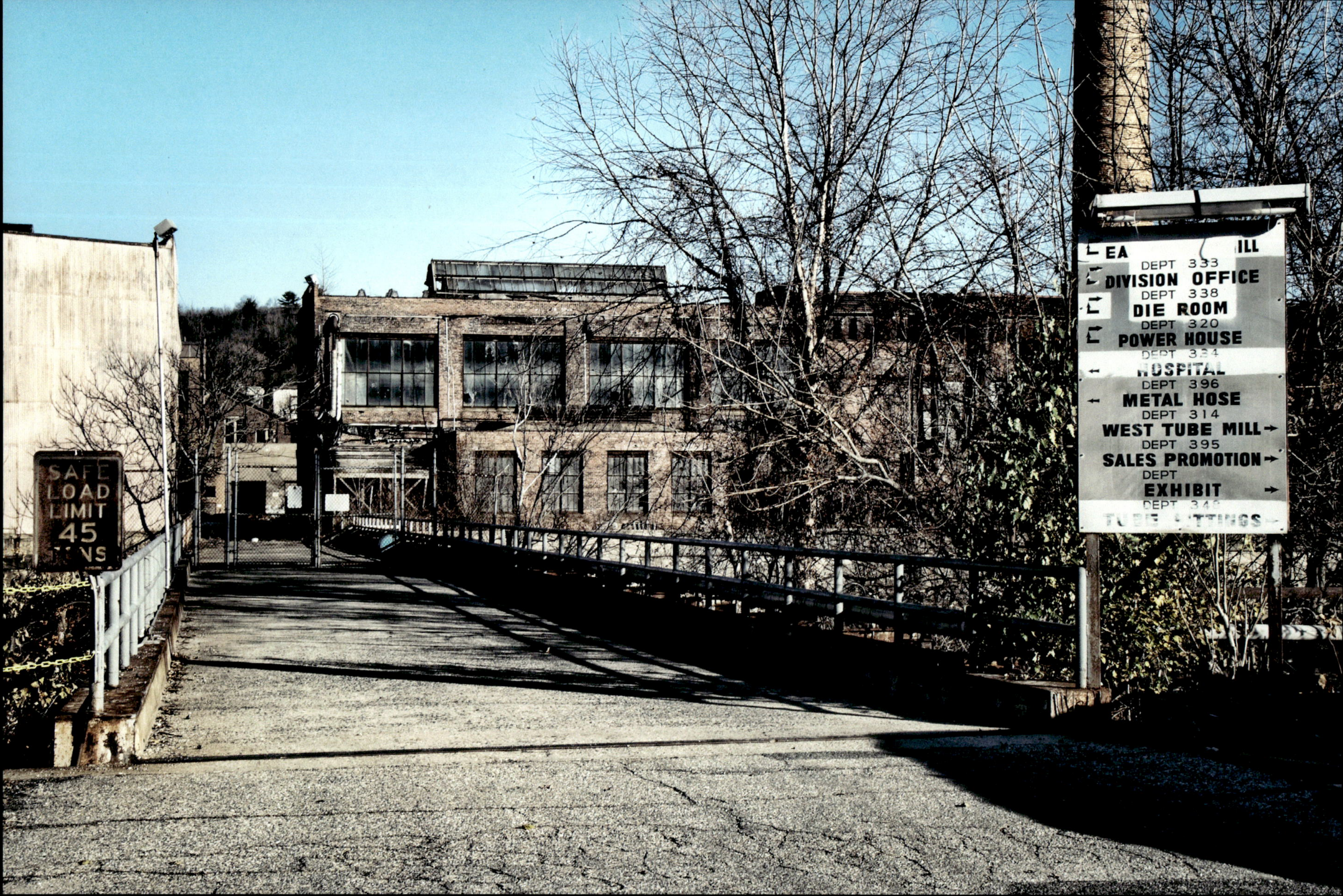

BRIDGE TO THE EAST CAMPUS
From American Brass (Holmes, Booth & Haydens), Bank St., Waterbury. CT

PART THREE:

BRASS ABANDONED

Of ruins that speak

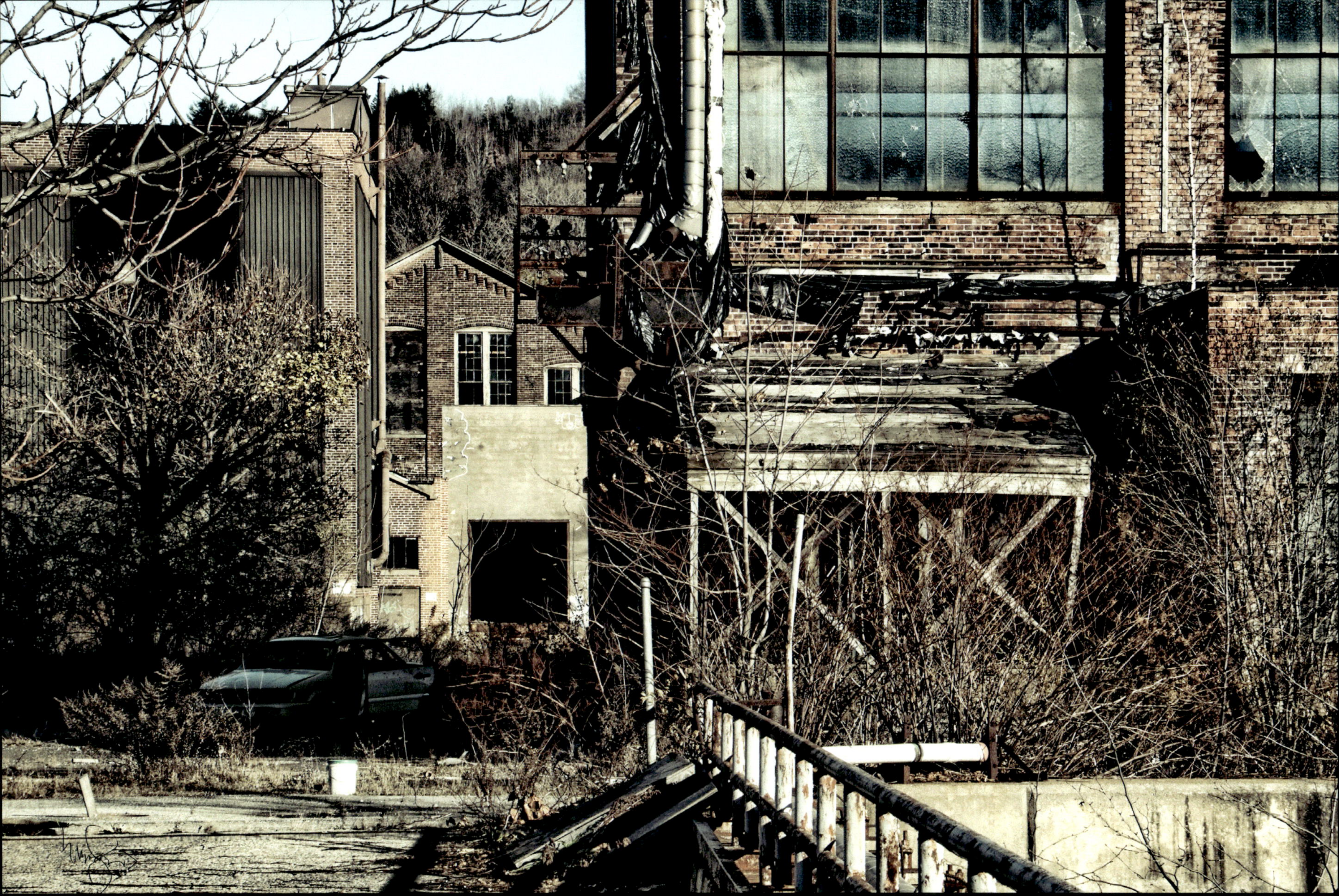

PHOTOGRAPHER'S JOURNAL:

Behind me is the last working vestige of American Brass, where the old extruder still pumps out tube from billets cast in Ansonia. In front of me lies the abandoned eastern campus of the company and its abandoned powerhouse. A sign still directs us over the bridge through weedy spaces, hollow and still.

Break time is over inside the brass mill, but across the river it is always break time, and no motors purr. I'm told the Pope now tweets in five tongues, and we live in a different world today than when these bricks were set in wet mortar. Yet we still partly live inside these old walls even as new walls rise, invisible and ubiquitous, and twittering ominously across newly formatted frontier terabytes.

ABANDONED!

Powerhouse and worksheds, American Brass (Benedict & Burnham), Benedict St., Waterbury, CT

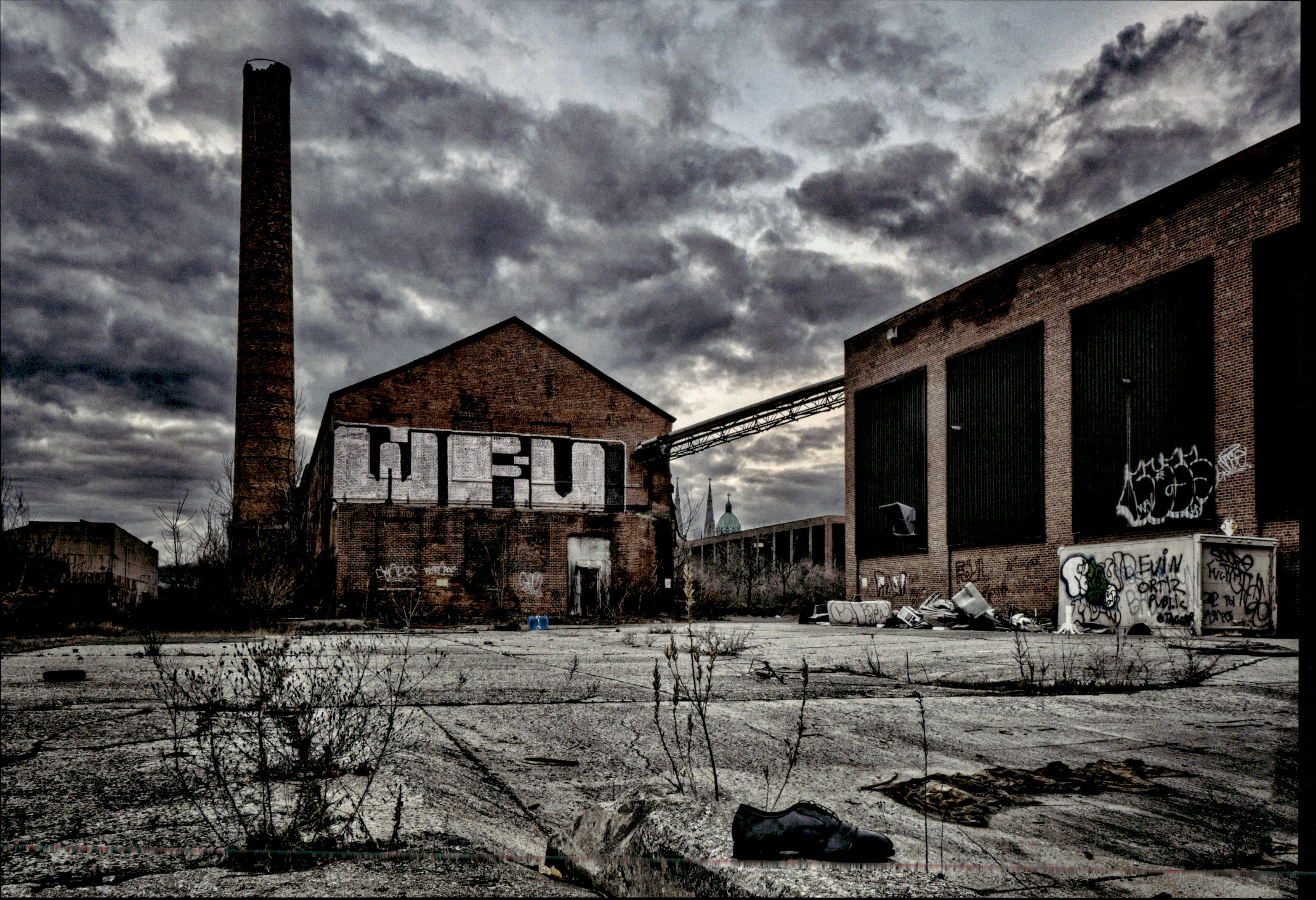

WAITING, NO. 2

Looking north toward powerhouse and work sheds, American Brass (Benedict & Burnham), Benedict St., Waterbury, CT

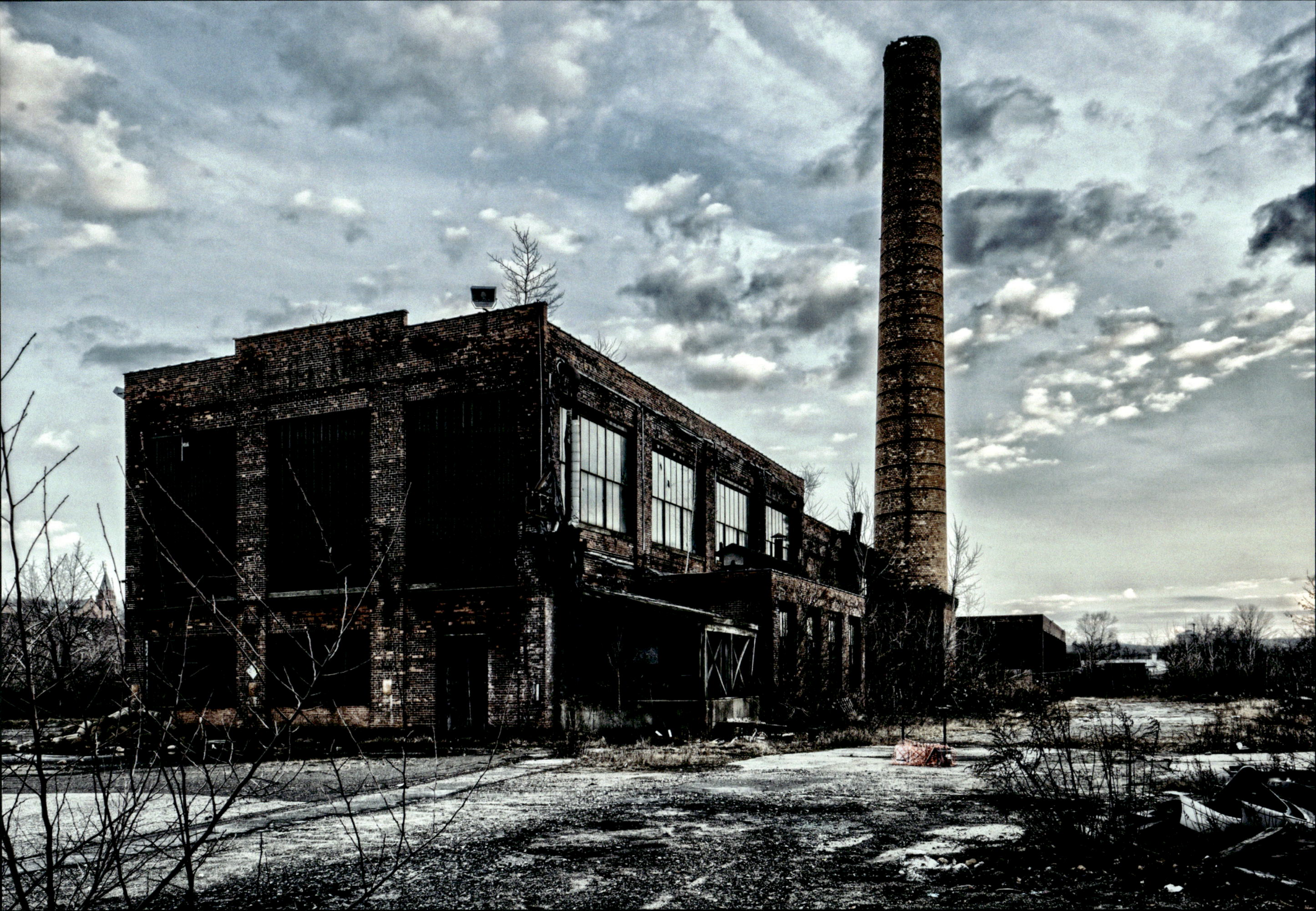

FROSTED POWERHOUSE
Looking south toward powerhouse, American Brass (Benedict & Burnham), Benedict St., Waterbury, CT

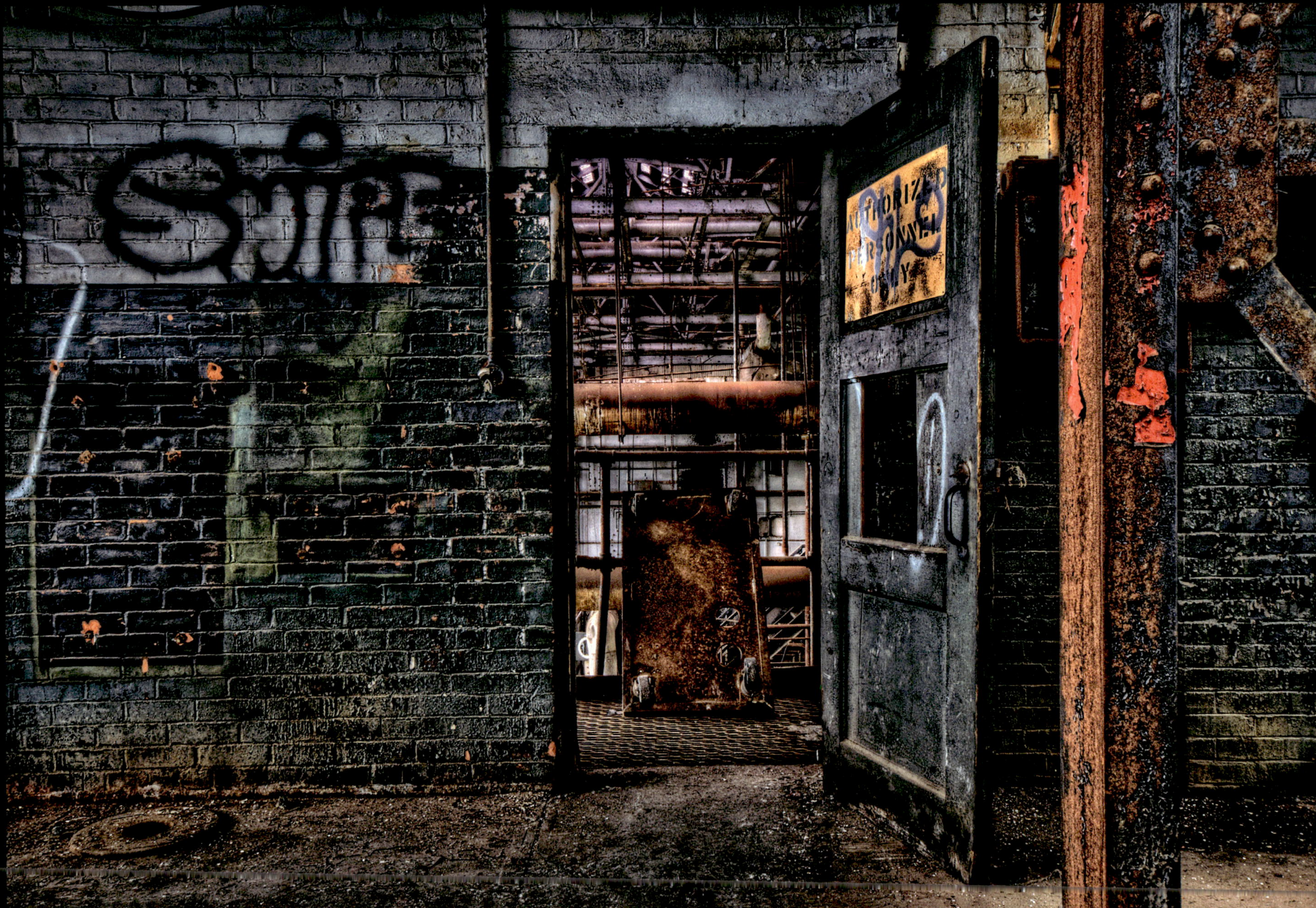

SNIPE

Powerhouse, second floor, American Brass
(Benedict & Burnham), Benedict St., Waterbury, CT

PHOTOGRAPHER'S JOURNAL:

My friend and I have learned how to slip through the gate soundlessly, inconspicuous in the shadows, and we always close the gate behind us, but inside the fence we must follow the remains of the train tracks across the large loading plazas where we are easy to spot. Inside the gate is no-man's land. A busy city hums all around us, but nobody knows what goes on here. The manhole covers were among the first things to disappear. The plazas are now booby-trapped with shafts that end in darkness. Drop a rock, and wait to hear it splash.

Metal salvage is only one of the things that brings people here. In one of the plazas a couple of lawn chairs and a table have been set up next to a small, covered storage trailer, well plundered. The back gate of the trailer was miserably disfigured by the break-in. A TV with a cracked picture tube rests on the edge, ready for the Superbowl; faded scarves and wet pillows, a Sony Walkman and a few dozen vinyl LPs from the trailer lie strewn across the plaza with a three-legged sofa that must have limped down the loading ramp as the party grew. Over several months I've observed no changes to this oasis of domestic tranquility. I have no further explanation.

One day we arrived and found the gate wide open, and when we reached the entrance to the largest shed, we saw a car, clean and shiny, parked inside. We called out several times but got no reply. We continued our shoot, though staying close.

Old factories are wind instruments, and parts of this one are tin. On almost any day there's enough breeze to raise a variety of flaps and flappers, chattering out tunes, and tapping and clacking to uncountable syncopations. Narrow stairs lead up to a warren of offices, and at the top floor there are views over the city and down on the roofs of some of the factory sheds. On this particular day the band featured a couple of soloists, and we watched as they sawed and banged to remove the large, rusty ventilation covers from the lower rooftops. It was one more insult to the old buildings that would speed their decay. I was pretty sure the metal thieves didn't want to be seen, and I was certain we felt the same. We all dance the Ruins Boogie-Woogie.

On the way out we met the owner of the car. By his looks, he was in his late twenties. He told us he spent the night here because his girlfriend threw him out. He assured us that he had closed the gate when he drove in the evening before. He was like a kid making excuses to the teacher for the bit of drifter etiquette that he had ignored, and it made me feel my age. The people we meet are only sometimes the people we expect.

Most interesting of all the buildings is the powerhouse; it is the pillaged, defaced cousin to the one in Ansonia. It also has a high atrium, housing great brick furnaces and boilers and pipes and ducts and motors and parts we didn't understand. Once again there were catwalks to reach valves and gauges high on the sides of equipment and up near the roof, but everywhere limbs had been looted and the buzz had died. Behind the main atrium, a second building of equal height was divided into two floors. It took us several visits before we discovered the cave-like lower story. The entrance had been hidden behind slouching, plastic tarps fallen from the façade. They had once been hung to cover the gaping, three-story-high window-wall of glass. It had been too much temptation for local thugs with pellet guns and rocks instinctively marking their territory, their tiny piece of time. The tarps were a doomed effort from the start; they fell as yard garbage as the site decayed and now we crawled beneath them to get in.

The upper floor of the powerhouse was another museum hall with rows of machines on pedestals, like species of jungle cats set side-by-side for easy comparison and defying identification. In the corner was a large metal tank with interesting rust and rivets, catching shadows in a way photographers find irresistible. I had photographed the tank once, but I wanted to improve my shot.

When I finally got my chance to return, it was clear the metal thieves had been through again. They had begun removing catwalks. Here and there steps were missing from some of the ladders and stairs. I might have mistaken it for an effort at security had it not been so random. As I climbed the metal stair to the upper floor of the back building where the boiler stood, I had to step over the space where the third stair had been removed. I was glad the thieves had left sufficient treads to reach the top. Once there, I saw the landing had been removed, and I had to go back down and find a plank to bridge the gap.

I climbed back up, put the plank in place and crossed into the room, and when I got inside, the metal tank that I had come to photograph, that had once stood two stories high and as big around as a silo, was gone. I gazed in amazement as I realized the only way they could have gotten it out was to cut it into door-sized pieces. The museum had been looted; save for a few metal stumps that could not be moved without a crane, the balcony had become a hall of empty, concrete pedestals and monster torsos.

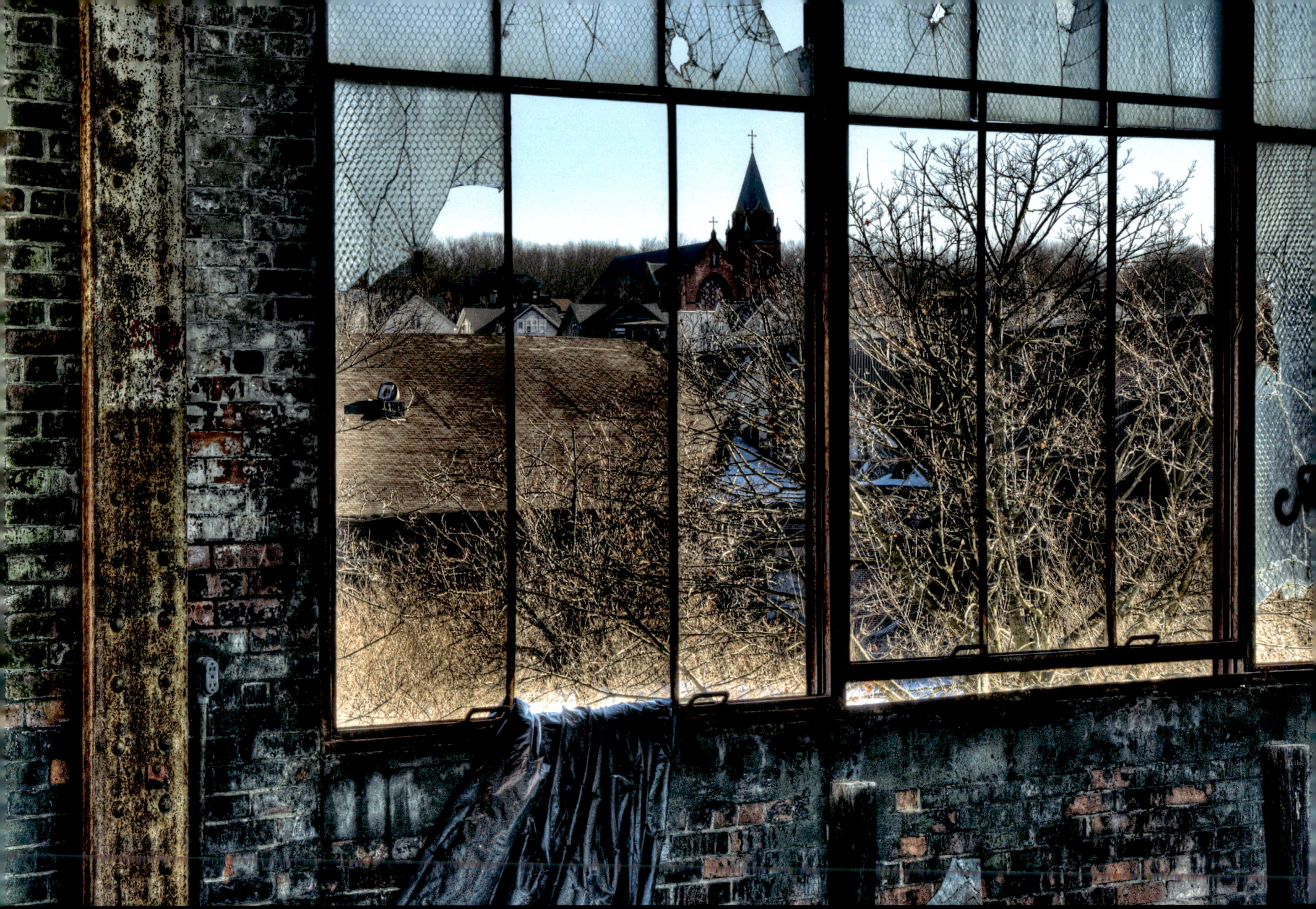

ST. FRANCIS OF THE MILL

The Church of St. Francis Xavier, Washington Hill from powerhouse, American Brass (Benedict & Burnham), Benedict St., Waterbury, CT

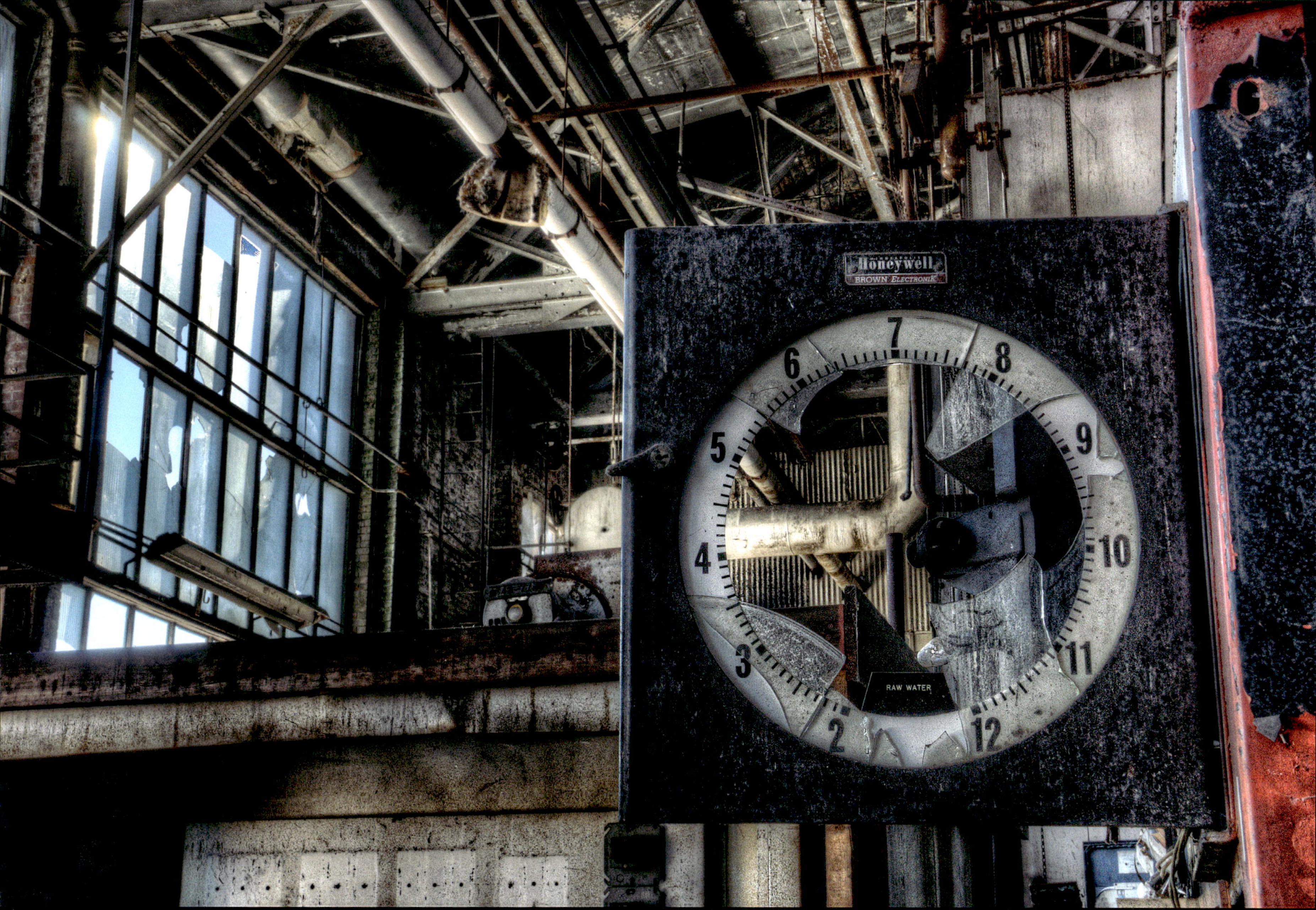

RAW WATER

Powerhouse, American Brass (Benedict & Burnham),
Benedict Street, Waterbury, CT

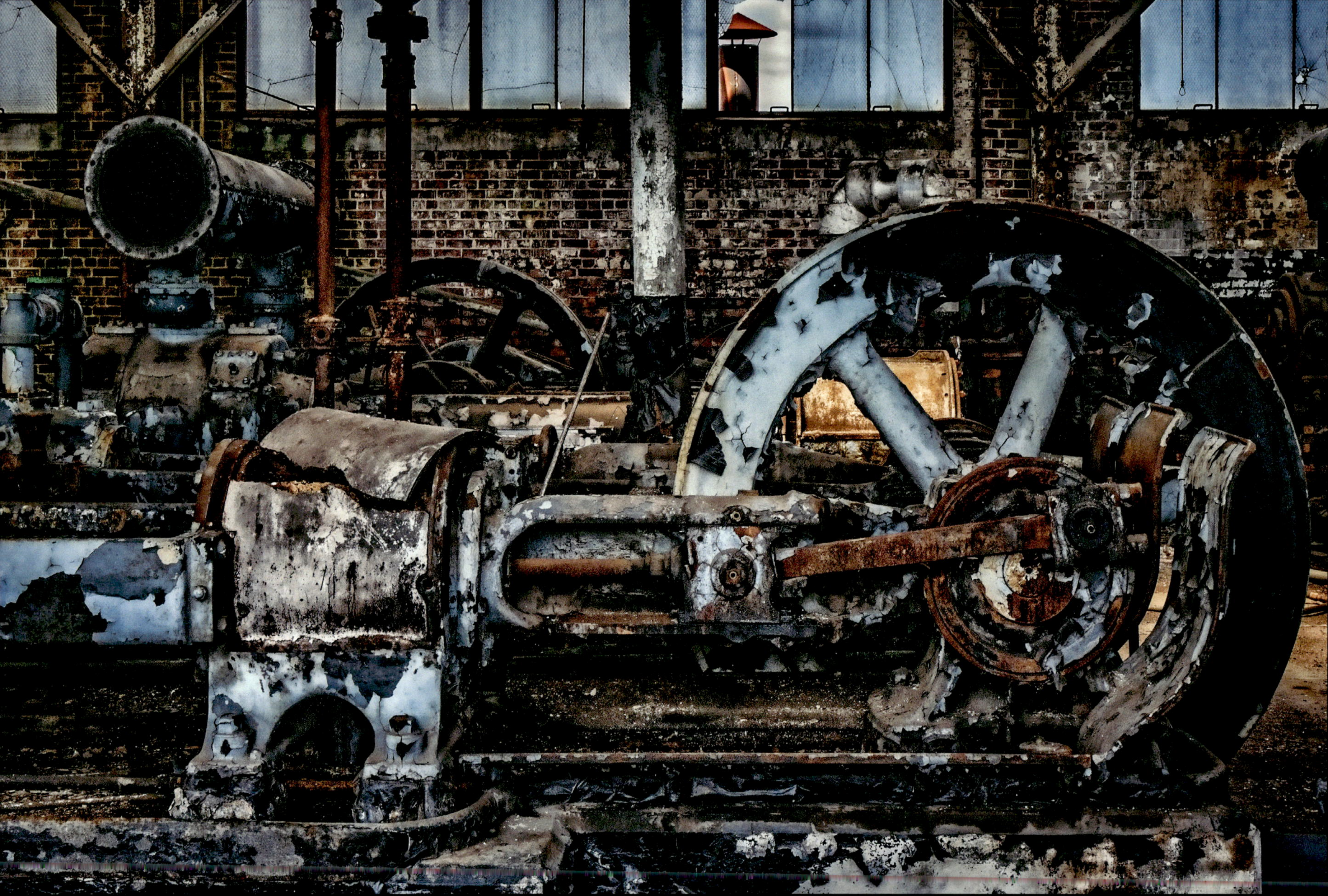

COMPRESSOR 1

Powerhouse, American Brass (Benedict & Burnham),
Benedict Street, Waterbury, CT

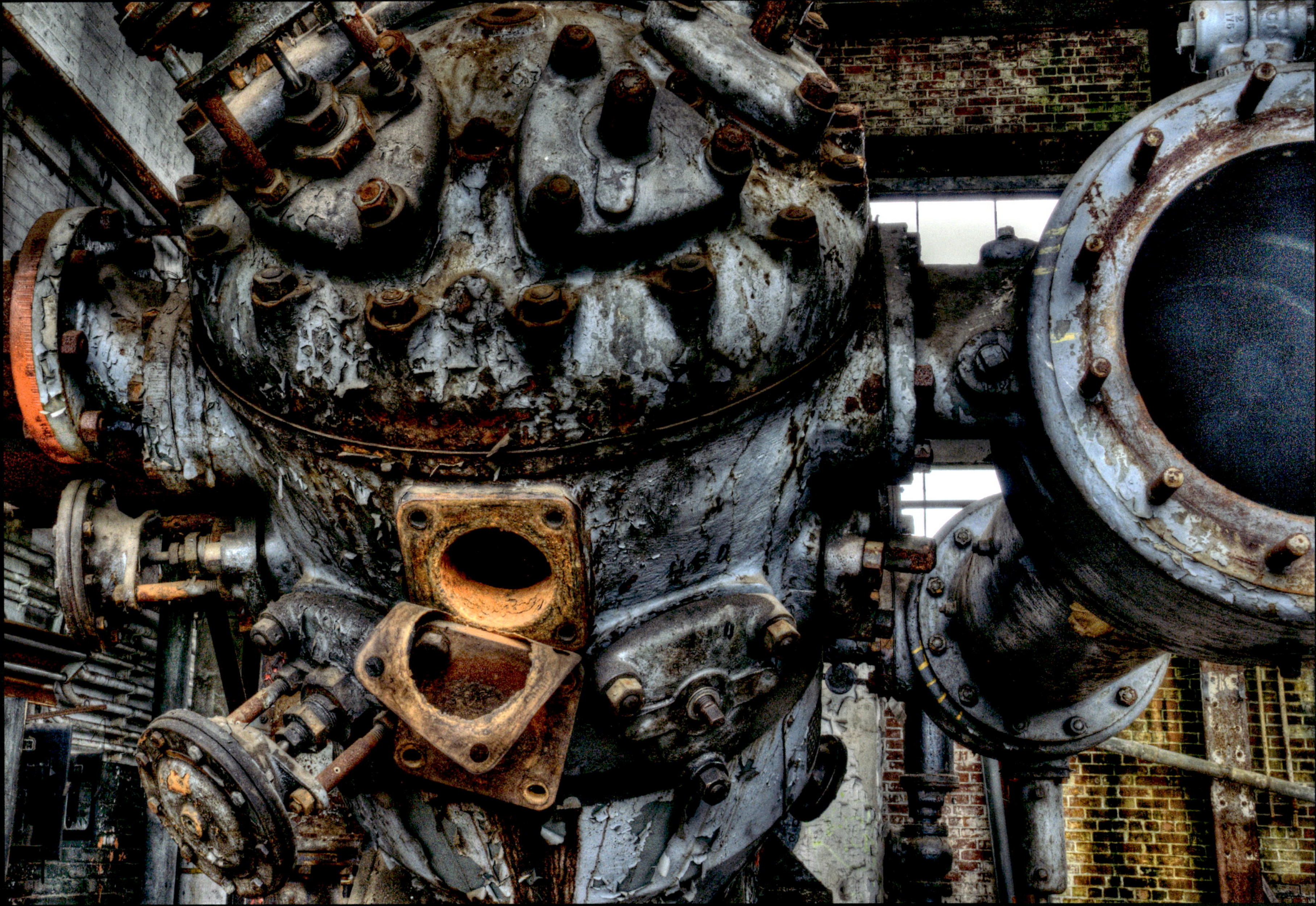

COMPRESSOR 2

Powerhouse, American Brass (Benedict & Burnham),
Benedict Street, Waterbury, CT

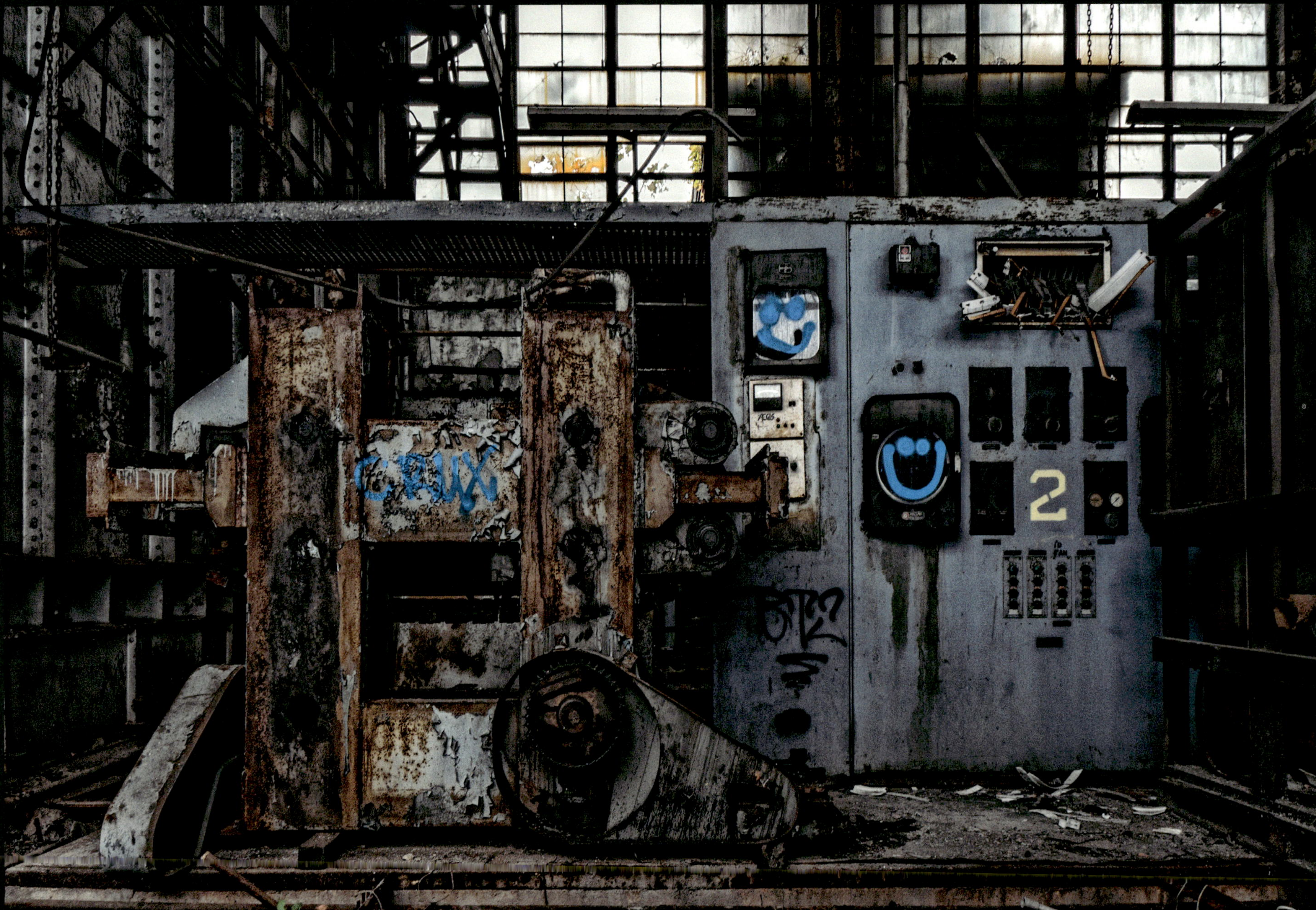

NUMBER TWO

Powerhouse, American Brass (Benedict & Burnham), Benedict Street, Waterbury, CT

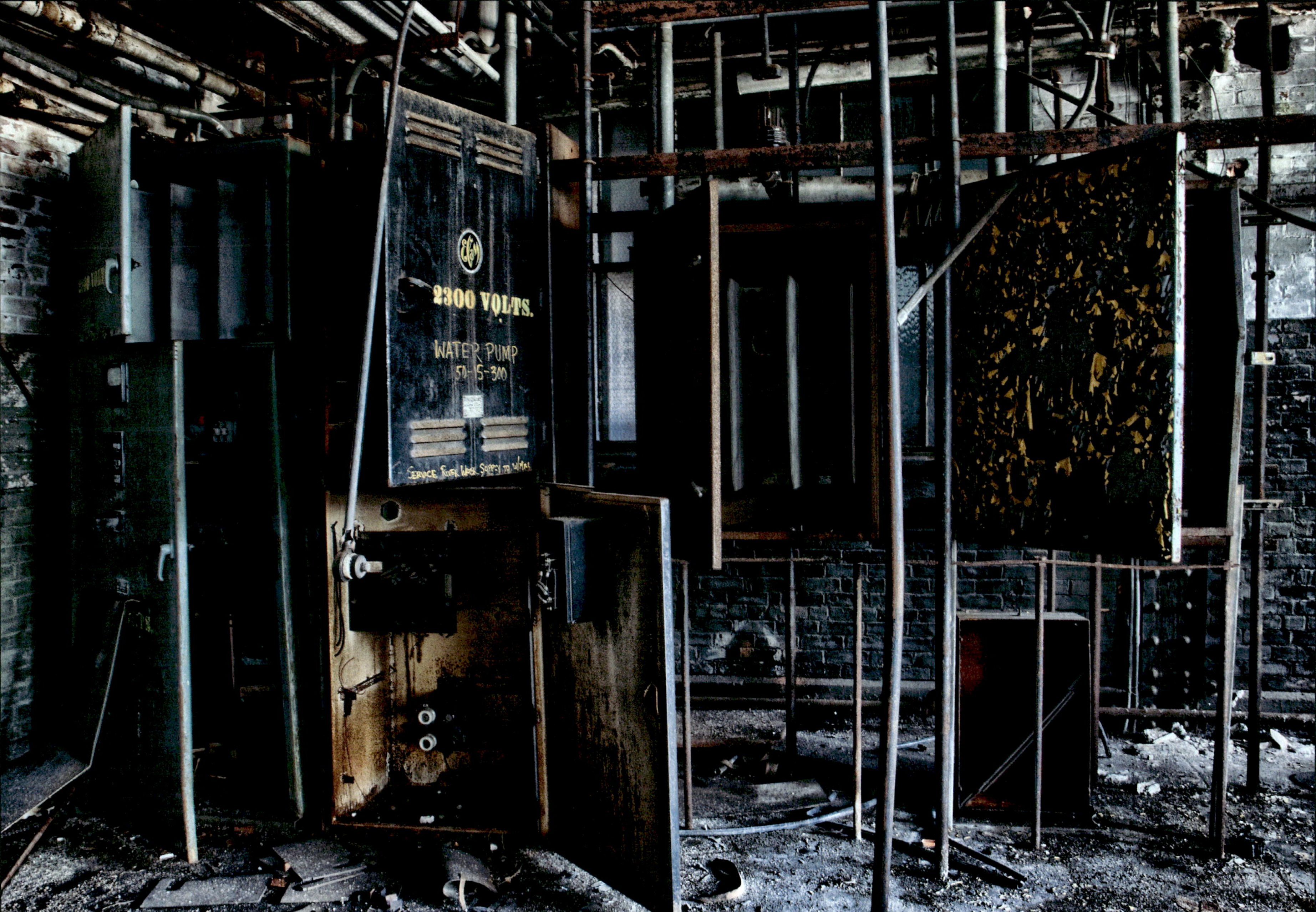

WATER PUMP 50-15-300

Powerhouse, American Brass (Benedict & Burnham),
Benedict Street, Waterbury, CT

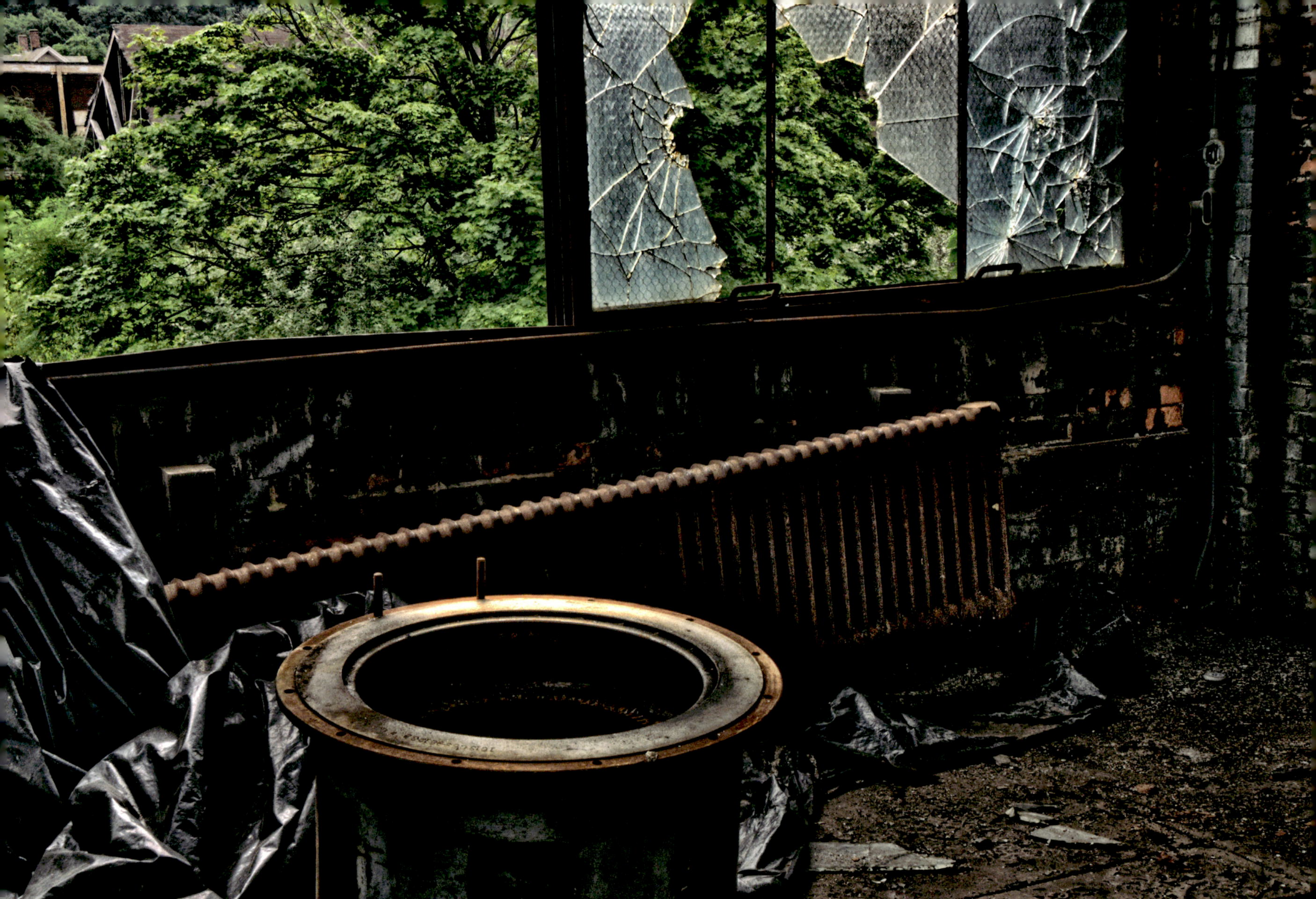

CIRCLE, SQUARE & TRIANGLE
(COMPOSITION IN DECOMPOSITION)
Powerhouse, American Brass (Benedict & Burnham),
Washington Avenue, Waterbury, CT

Opposite: COMPRESSOR 3
Powerhouse, American Brass (Benedict & Burnham),
Washington Avenue, Waterbury, CT

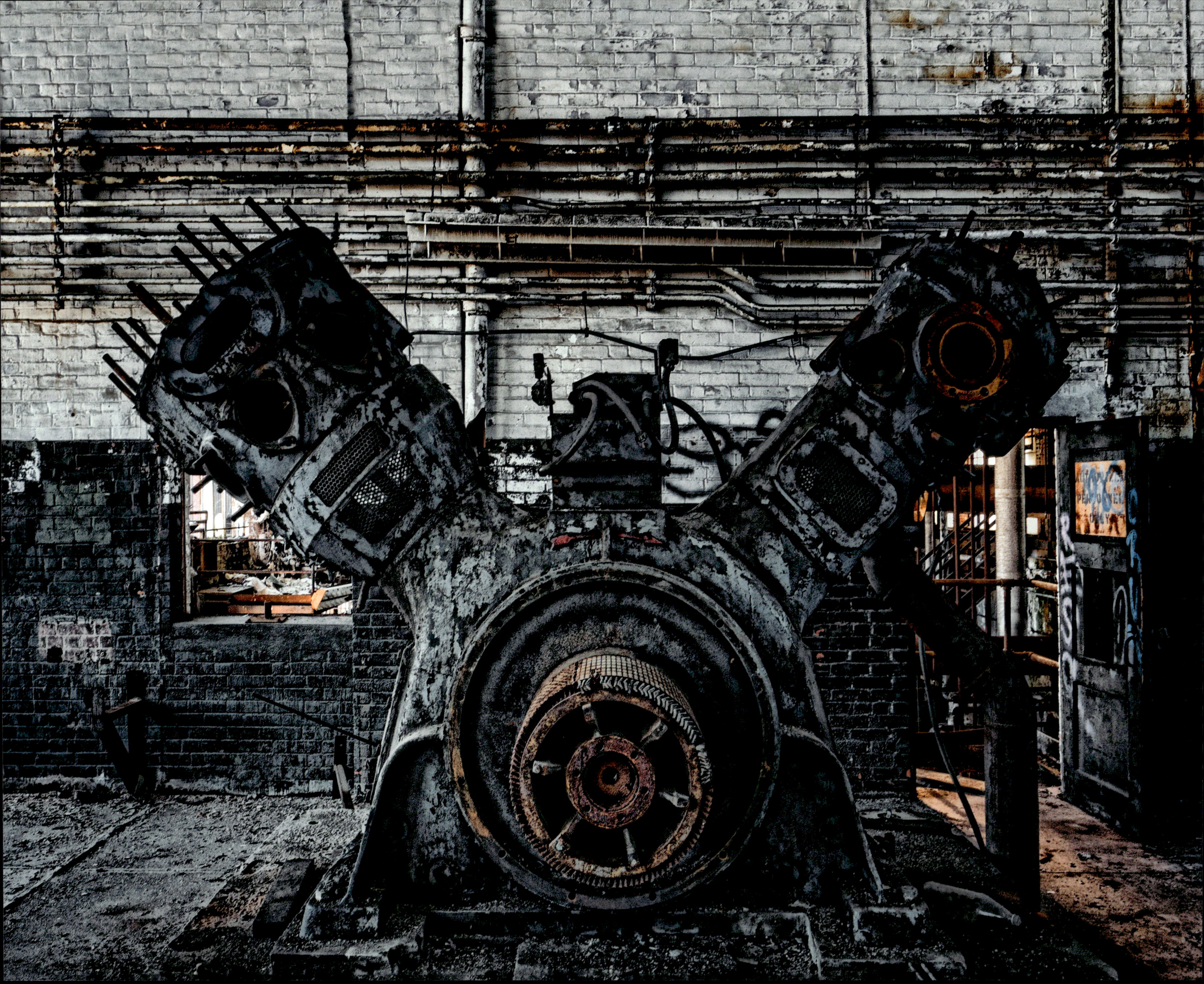

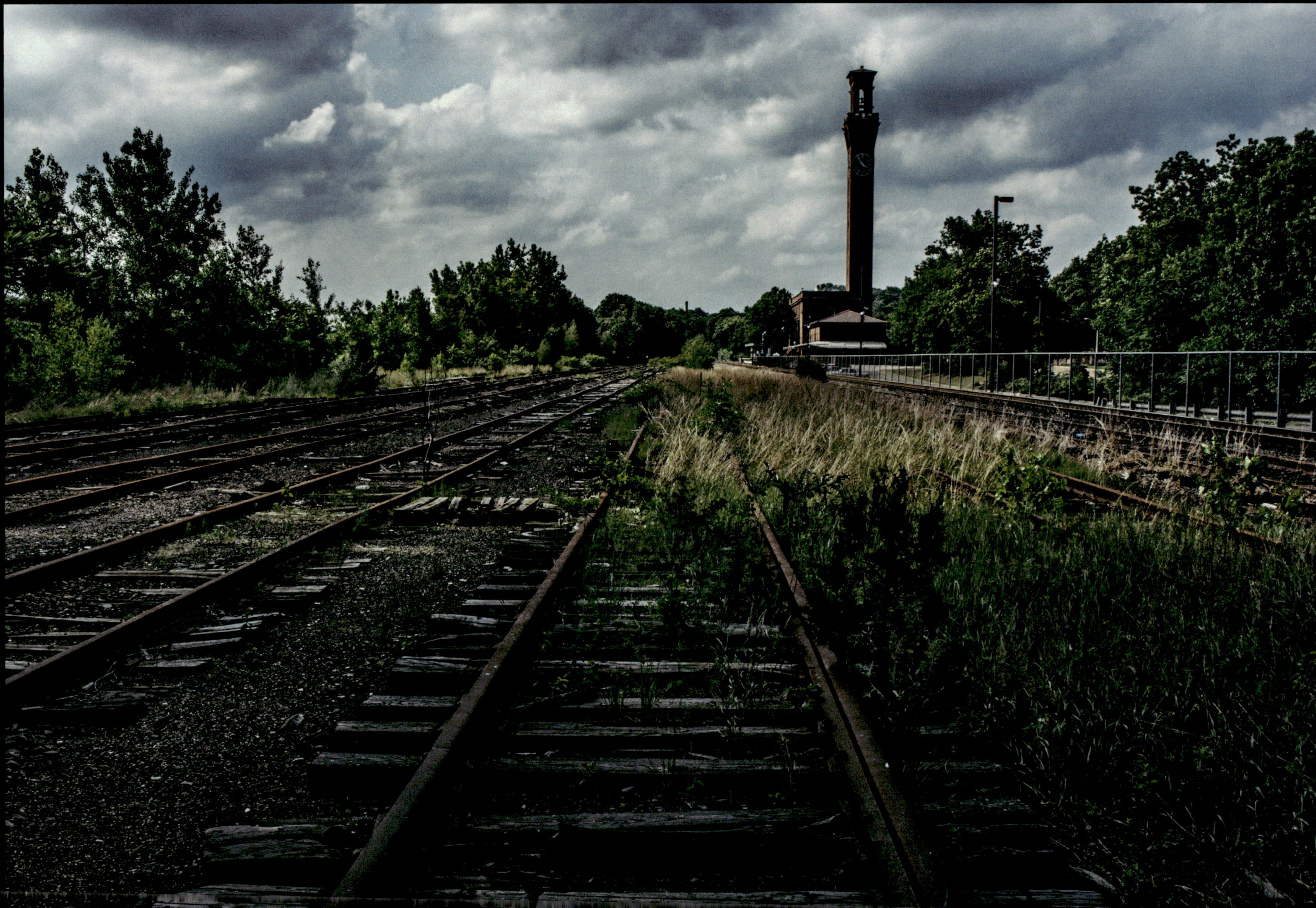

RAILYARD SUMMER
Union Station, Waterbury, CT, from the south

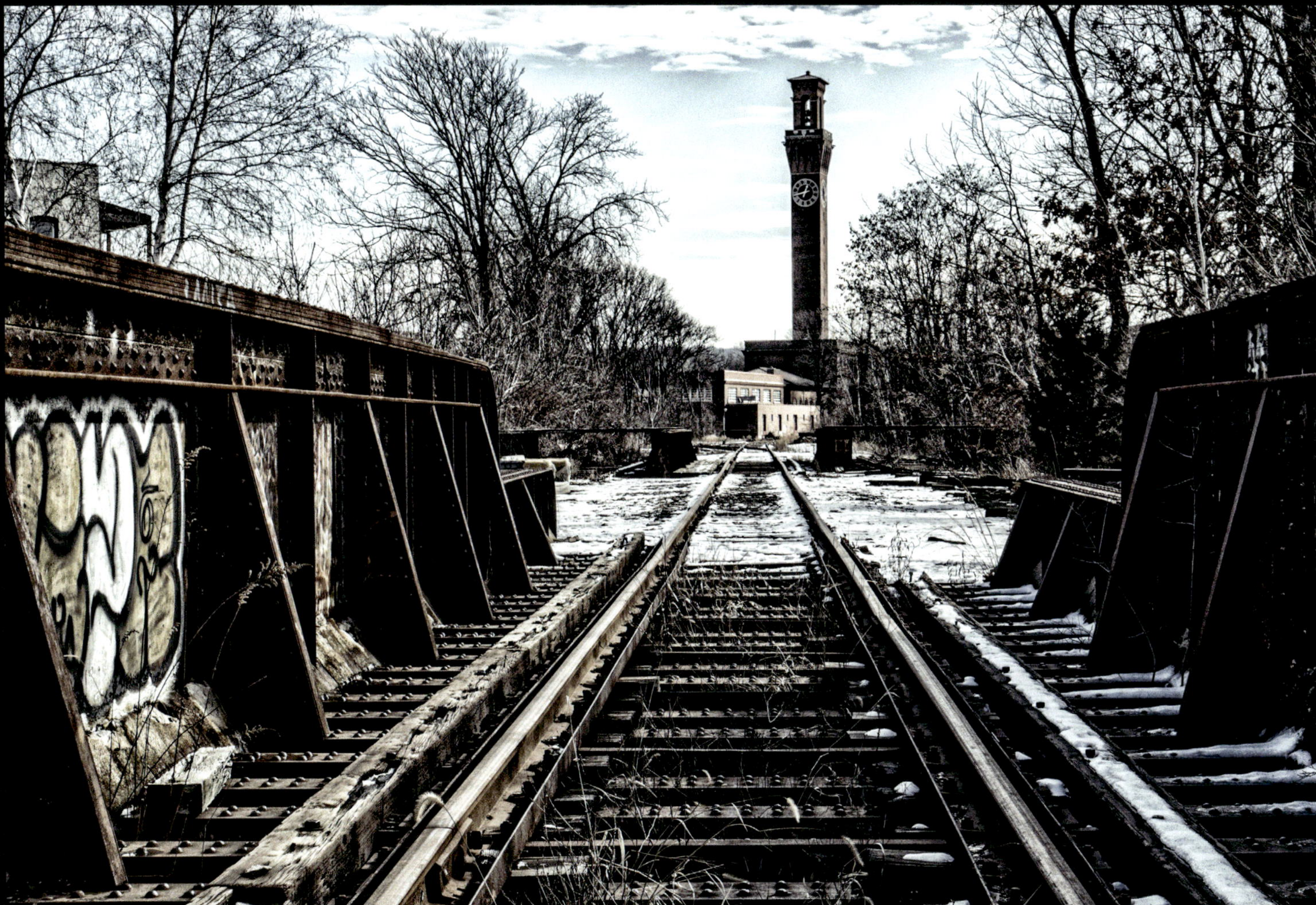

A DREAM OF BLACK TRACK

Union Station, Waterbury, CT, from the north

PHOTOGRAPHER'S JOURNAL:

Over the winter I had a dream of black track crusted in snow, and the angle of my dream opened a window into the past that I had not suspected. For a year I had been walking a spiral around Union Station, viewing it from all angles, wondering about its meaning, trying to clarify its place in the story of Waterbury and the valley. The once-powerful New Haven Railroad had long ago moved out. As soon as the snow was crisp, I climbed an embankment north of the station, looking for the place in my dream, but I found only thin snow and one, sometimes two tracks, including the active line.

I don't know what made me resume my quest this spring. I was trying to get closer and soon found myself in a wilderness beneath highway ramps near the center of the spiral I had been walking, and in front of me were the remains of the pulsing rail yard that was once the heart of Brass Valley. I counted sixteen branch lines between station and river, hidden under brush and sometimes with large trees growing between the rails.

I found satellite images, and I can see how it once may have spread to be twice as large, and half of what's left is hidden in brush. These yards served Union Station before the era of the Interstates, when sixty or seventy trains per day came and left, and a significant yard was needed here to handle the traffic. From here, one could take the pulse of the valley, and I can still follow the tracks to most of Brass Valley's ruins, though nothing pulses beyond the main line, and the world has spiraled on

PICNIC BY THE MILLPOND, 1968,
THE GIRL, THE CAR, THE MOON!

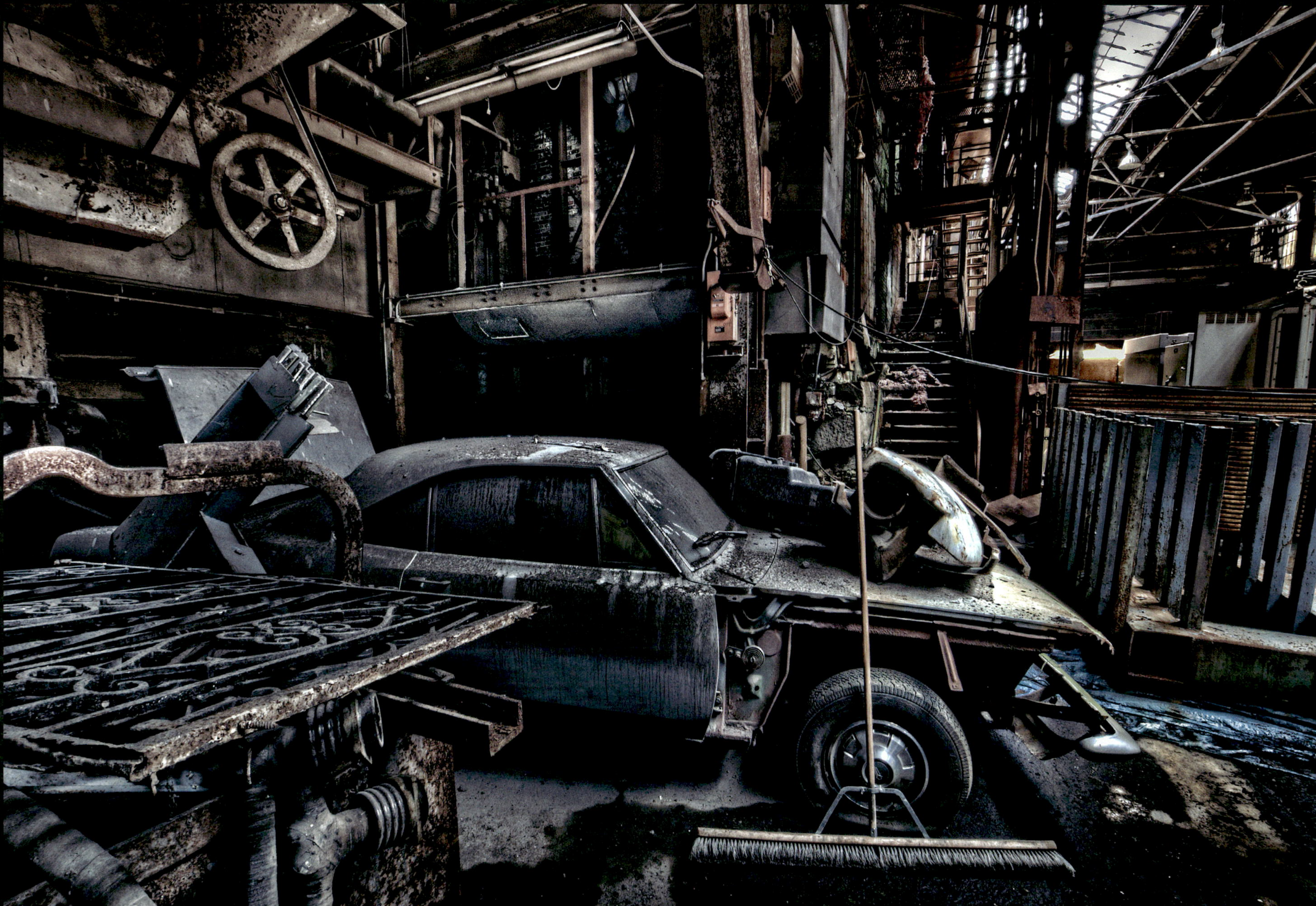

STAIRWAY TO HEAVEN
Farrel foundry, Ansonia, CT

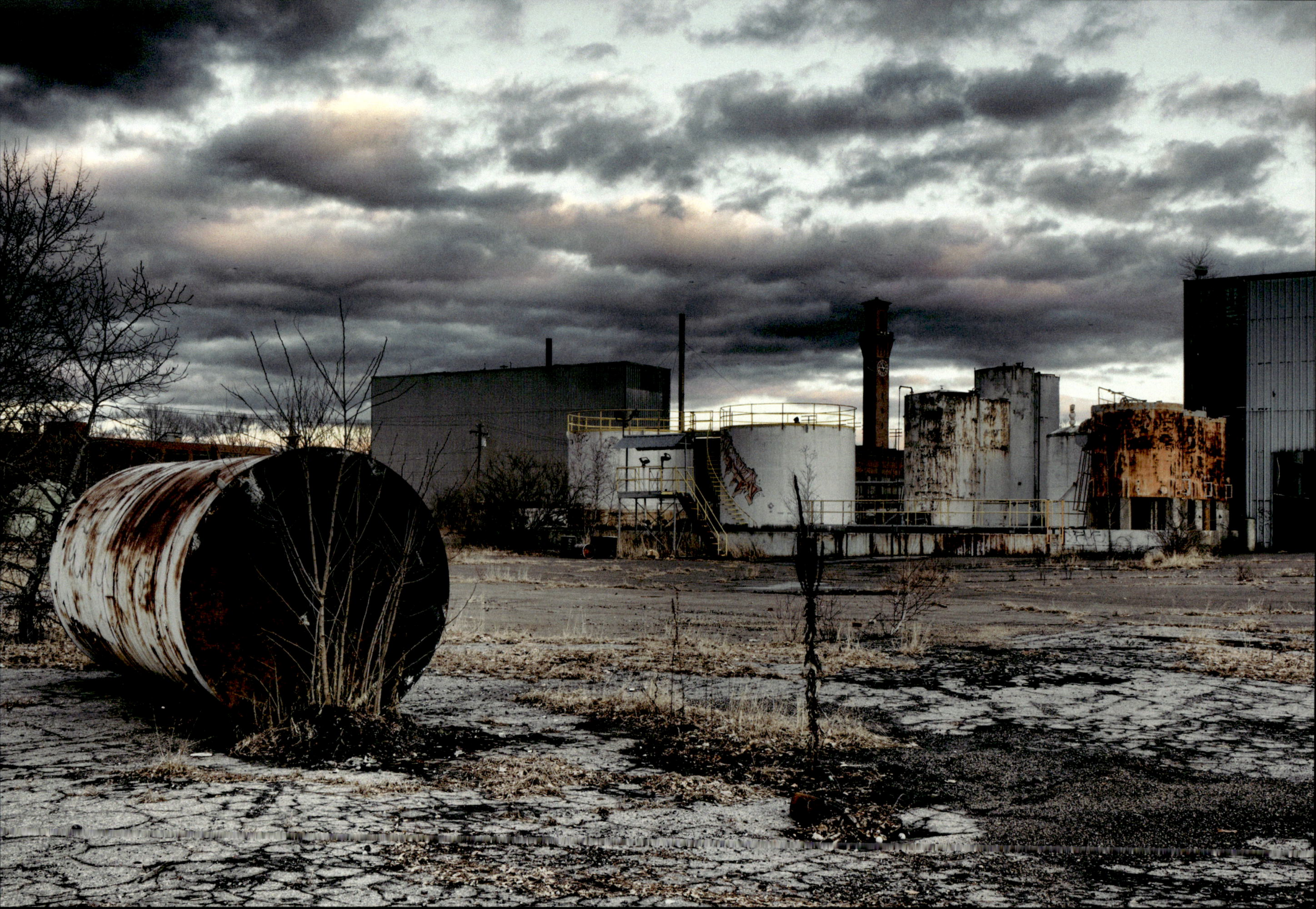

TANKS NESTING BY UNION STATION

American Brass, Freight Street, Waterbury, CT

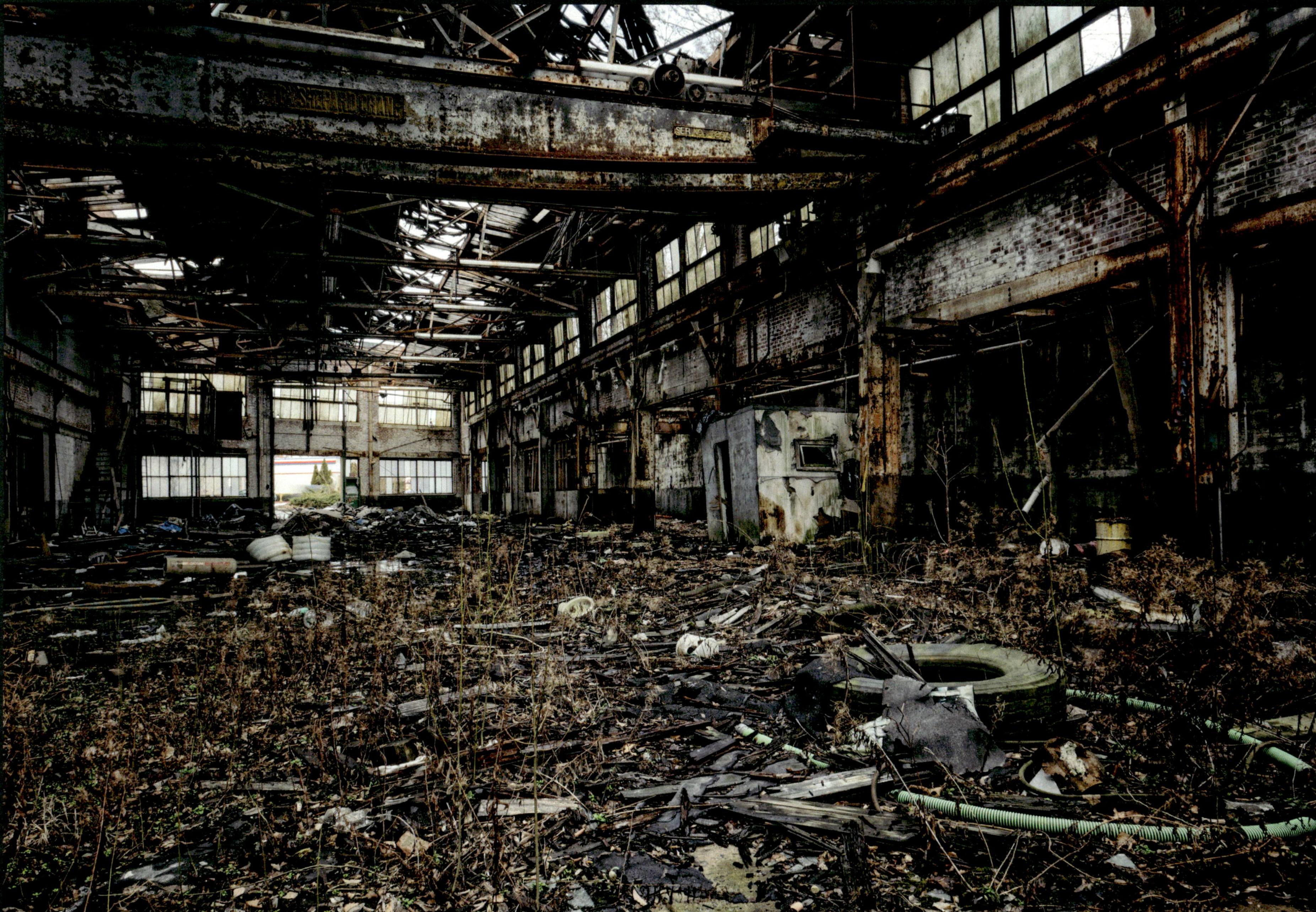

FINAL SKID

American Brass, Freight Street, Waterbury, CT

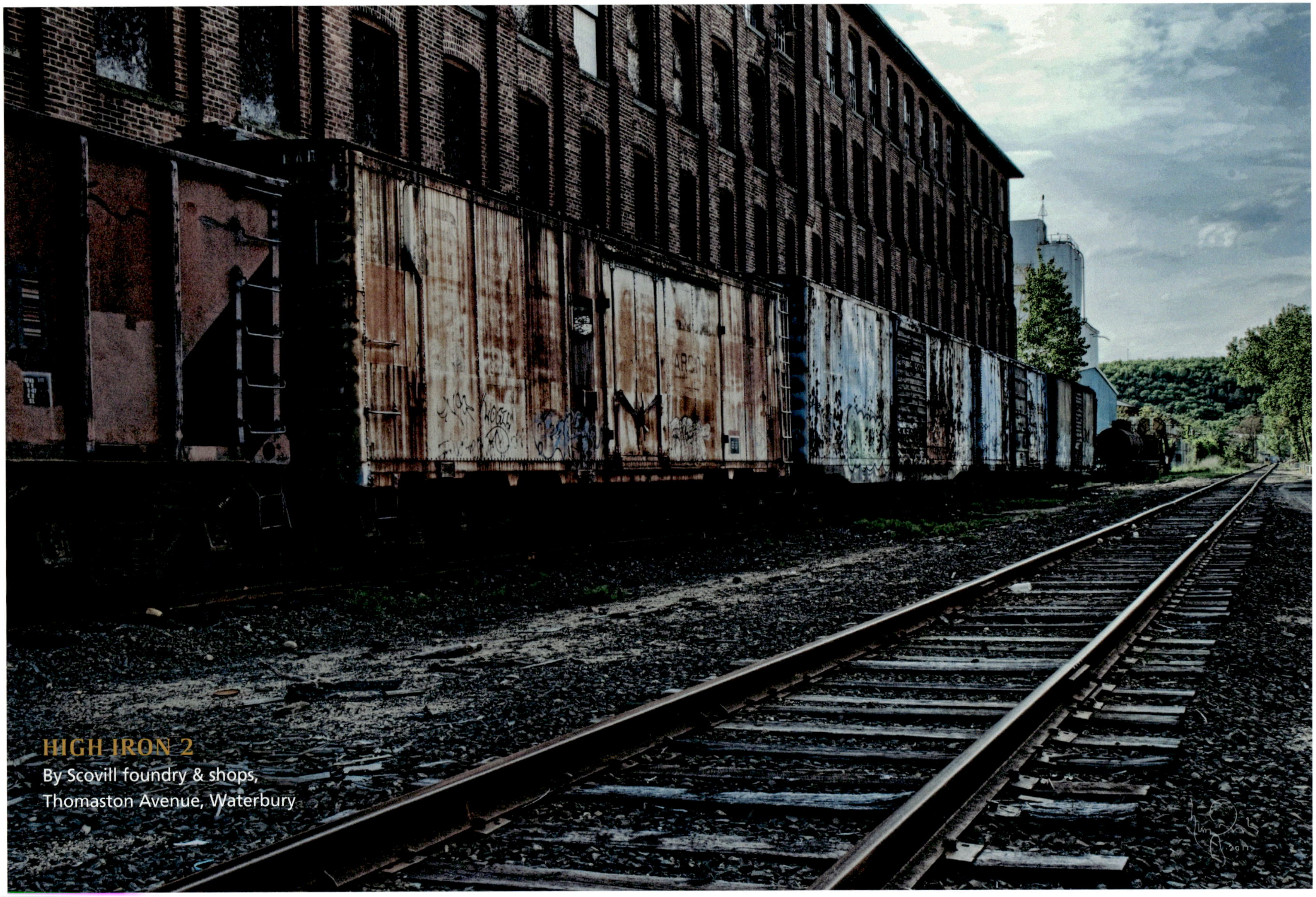

HIGH IRON 2
By Scovill foundry & shops,
Thomaston Avenue, Waterbury

OUR STORIES:

Railroads and Civics

The 1845 potato famine in Ireland coincided with the building of the railroad up the Naugatuck Valley, and so we were hungry and mostly illiterate, unskilled men with brogues who leveled the roadbed and laid the track along the river all the way to Winsted. The Yankees who hired us were mostly descendants of Puritan settlers and didn't much like us, but they needed men with strong backs, and they tolerated the work songs we sang that kept us steady, and a few of them even liked our fiddlin'.

Before the railroad, a turnpike had replaced the dirt trails between Derby and Waterbury, and we were already lugging more than a ton a week of metal in cartloads from the docks on the Housatonic in Derby Landing up the road to Waterbury. Time for us was money, and whether we spent it to survive, sent it home to Ireland, or drank it, there was never enough of it. In 1848 the new railroad opened the valley to industry, carrying its products to Bridgeport and the world. Trains brought coal, copper, zinc, tin, jobs, and more Irishmen and took away buttons and kettles, pins and pipes, clips and clocks. Brass was the plastic of its time; uses were burgeoning, and the Naugatuck Valley was trying to compete with Birmingham, England, a region rich in all the things needed to make brass. They tell us Israel Holmes was the driving force behind the great puffing railroad up the Naugatuck Valley, but a good deal of the muscle in his driving force lay in our arms and backs, and we took many of the aches with us to our graves.

During the Civil War, output fluctuated, but industry boomed at the mills, and after the war the rest of us came, and the valley began to fill up. The trains brought Italians and Lithuanians, Portuguese and Russians, along with raw materials. Like the Irish, many of us were illiterate and unskilled. Unlike them, we spoke no English. Even so, after the war, as the nation nursed its wounded, we learned that at Appomattox both Lee and Grant wore buttons by Scovill, and we heard our first negro spirituals and sang the songs of marching and grief.

Mill owners built villages to house us and systems to provide water and food, to keep the peace, and to manage town affairs. It was a massive undertaking to create civic institutions and infrastructure that would support the growing population. We built the cities first in wood, and we rebuilt them in stone as town fathers hired prestigious designers like Cass Gilbert, McKim, Meade and White, and Olmstead Bros. to design civic buildings and public spaces and eventually public schools that would reflect the confidence of the region and provide a foundation of hallowed permanence. But before any of that, in churches, taprooms, social clubs, and street corners we figured out how to make life livable and then, how to make a living while we struggled to make a life.

At the mills, there was a marked difference between skilled and unskilled labor. The skilled "Birmingham" workers from England, who had assured the mills' success, guarded their secret knowledge and passed their jobs to other Englishmen or occasionally to Irishmen who were in positions of seniority and had apprenticed in the shops, and when there were chances for promotion, we often knew the fix was in.

The policemen and firemen were mostly Irish, and the rest of us spoke little English and resented their superiority, as they resented the superiority of the old Yankee families who ran the mills and the towns, but we all formed clubs, gangs, factions, and unions with others of our kind and lived in settlements around churches and saloons where there was good talk in a tongue we understood and drinks to make us bold or lead us astray. Those who became citizens were encouraged to back political candidates and vote. Banding in groups of our own kind, we struggled over identity, flexed muscle, and sometimes, at work or school or wherever our communities collided, we rumbled, but we all cherished our overseas mail and helped our brothers and sisters and fellows to follow us. When they got here we shared our rooms, and if one of us worked the night shift, even our beds. Very few of us went back.

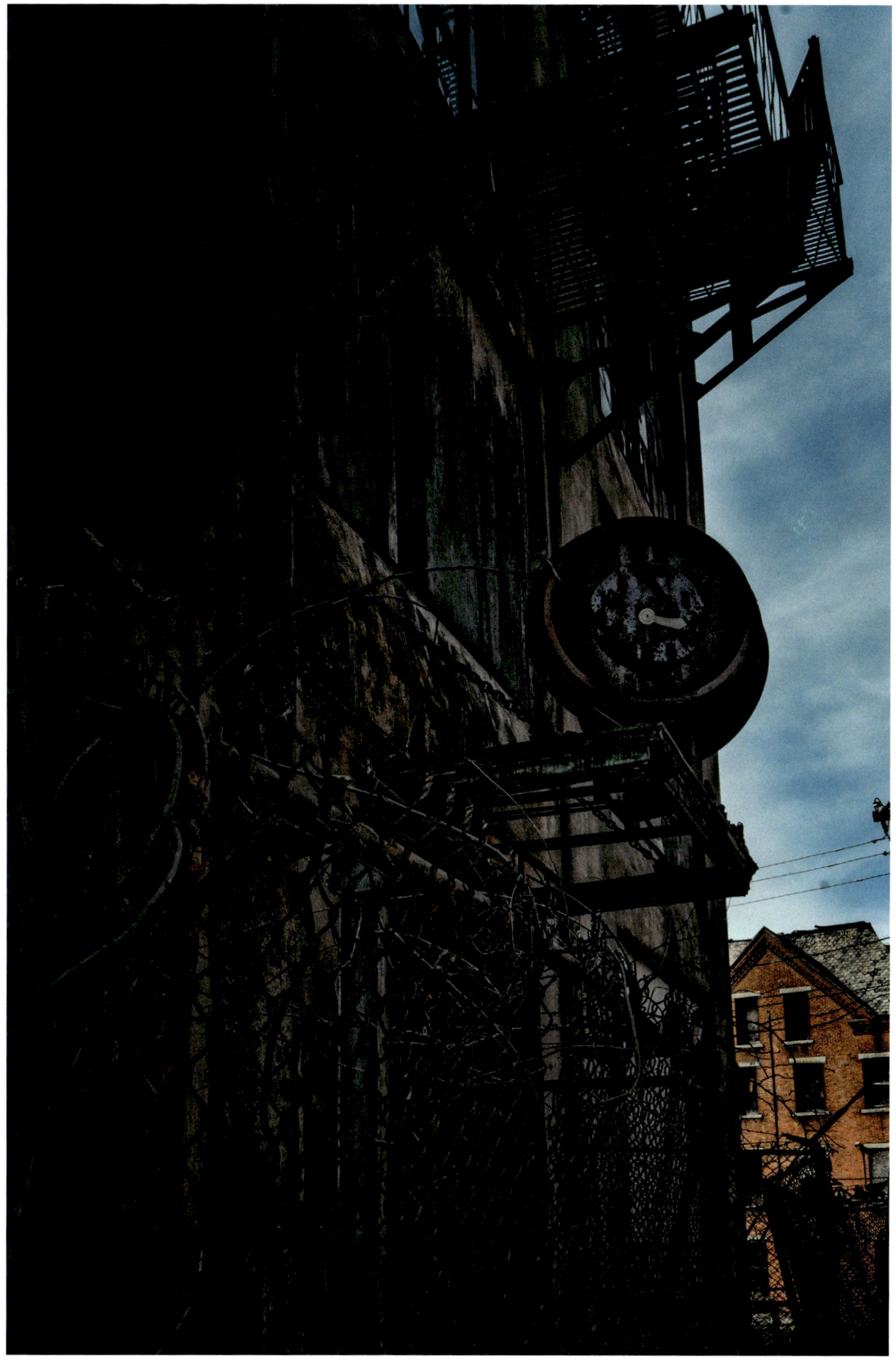

BULOVA BUILDING
Waterbury Clock Company, Cherry Street, Waterbury, CT

ROOSTING

Earl C. Banner was first,
penciled faintly, May 10, 1937.
Ed Trewline worked here in '58,
Rich Brodman or Brosman 9-23-82 wanted us to know,
and in 1940 CK & BH marked the date;
so did G. D. Cool and sucks unintelligible in 1972;
and Totes was here in '78,
neither first nor last,
perhaps he was meanest,
He carved his name deepest
in the attic of Anaconda
where pigeons roost and coo.

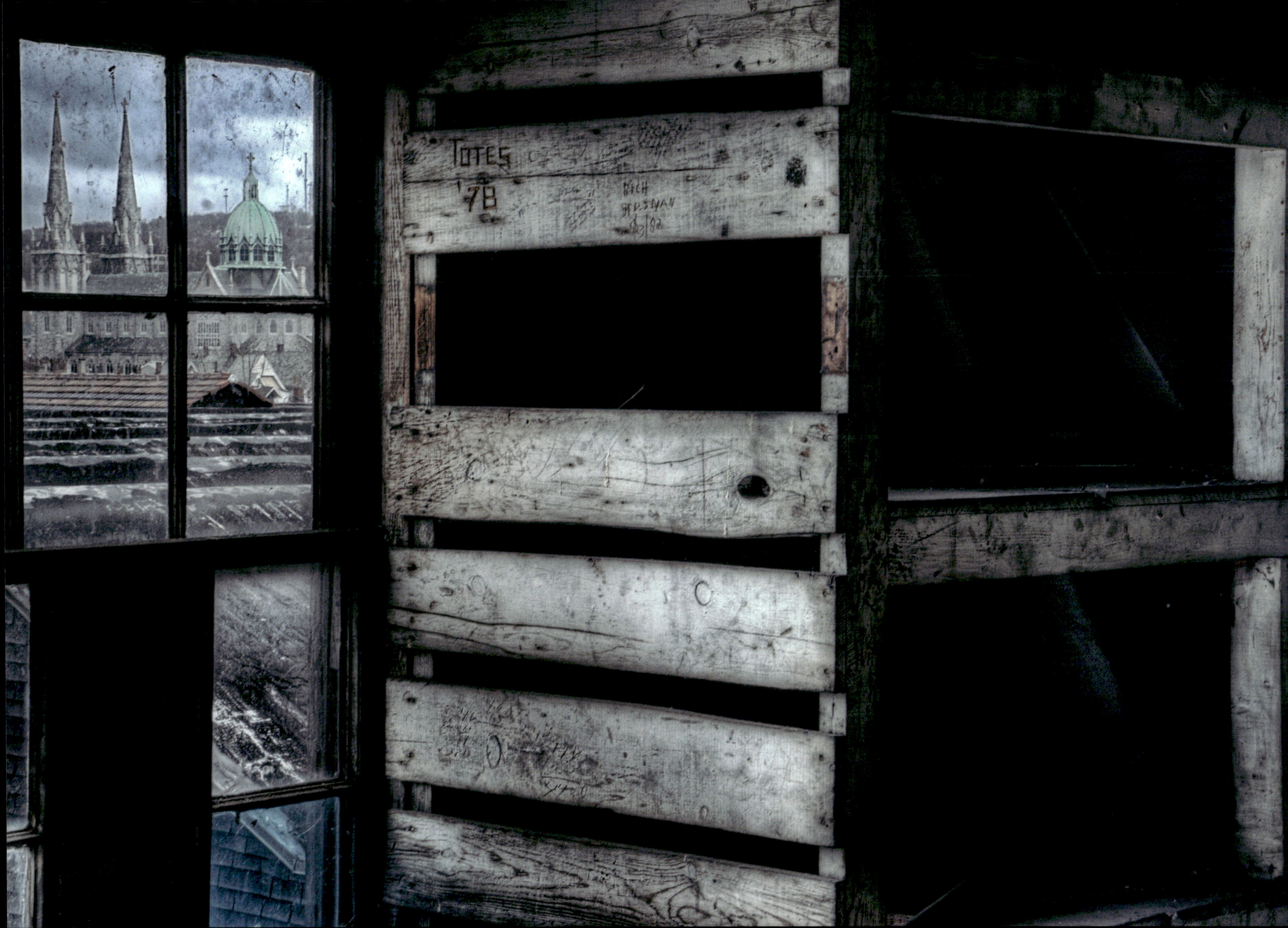

TOTES '78

Attic window, Holmes, Booth & Haydens burner factory,
American Brass, Bank Street, Waterbury, CT

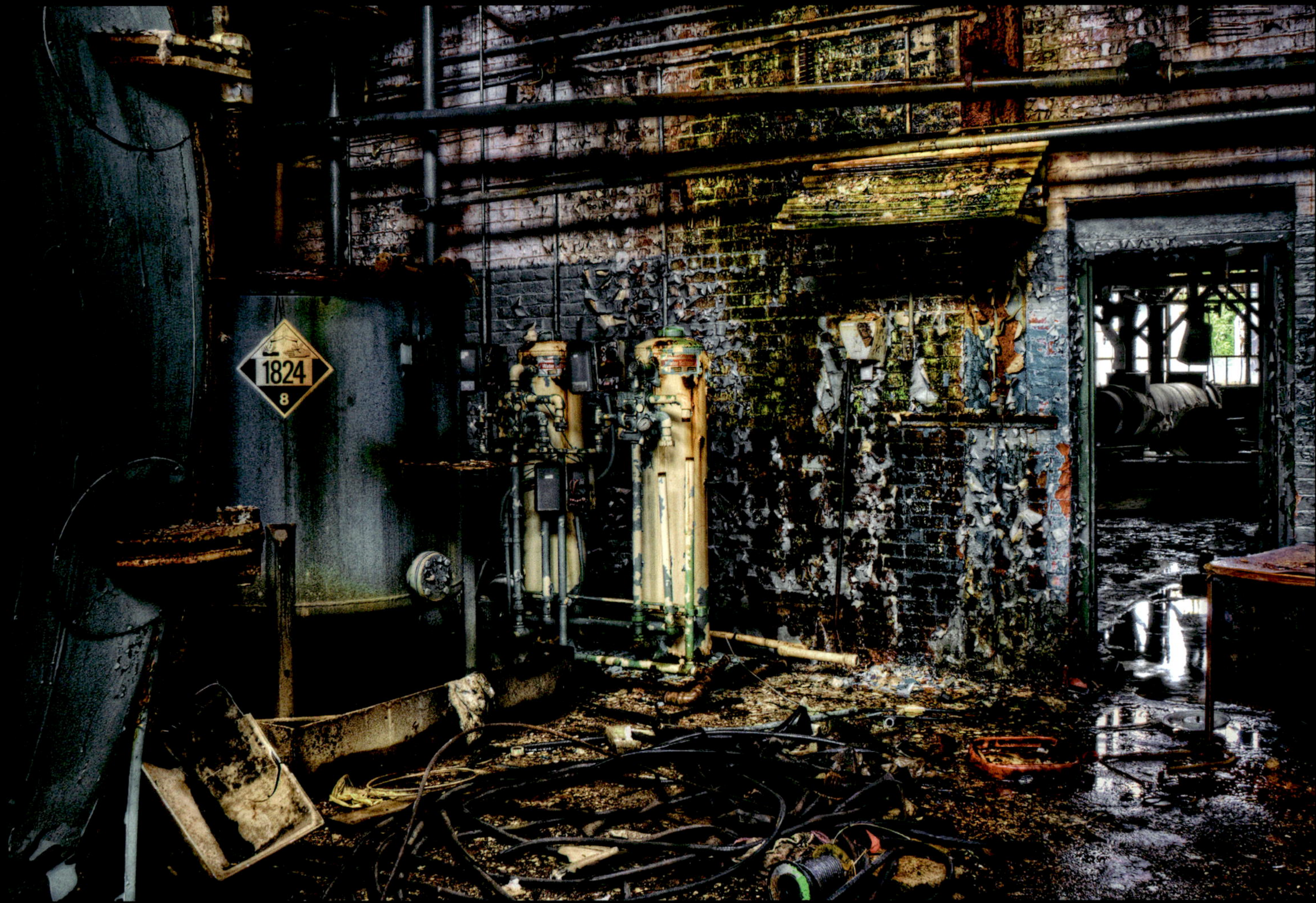

1824
American Brass, Freight Street, Waterbury, CT

PHOTOGRAPHER'S JOURNAL:

I used all my powers to persuade the man to let me photograph. I followed him into the building as I made my case, until we stood halfway down a long basilica-like space where a trailer served as his office. The sheds came together at odd angles and were encrusted with rusted barnacles, survivals of past operations. They promised a funhouse of adventure. He explained, the new owner had hired him to clean up.

He was alone, one man in a basilica five stories high and long enough for a small battleship and loaded with equipment, some rusting and dead, and some that looked like it must be the salvaged booty of failed enterprises; it was warehoused and awaiting new life. The ceiling was leaking, and the floors were greasy. He said "Ya gotta watch for falling glass." In all directions the room disappeared into shadowy bays and grease-black crevices. I saw stairs disappearing down into an impenetrable underworld. Was that part of his job—to clean down there? I saw other dark doorways at grade level and off of catwalks high in the rafters. I hoped he had a big crew coming. He considered my request slowly while he told me about electroplating shops where he had worked in Shelton, and other things he had done. He showed me a brass Scovill button on his keychain that his grandfather wore in the Pacific during World War II and a small copper cartridge shell that hung by a ring and that he said his mother had made as a kid in one of the shops. He didn't seem busy, nothing but time.

. . . several stories later, "Sure!" he said, "You can shoot."

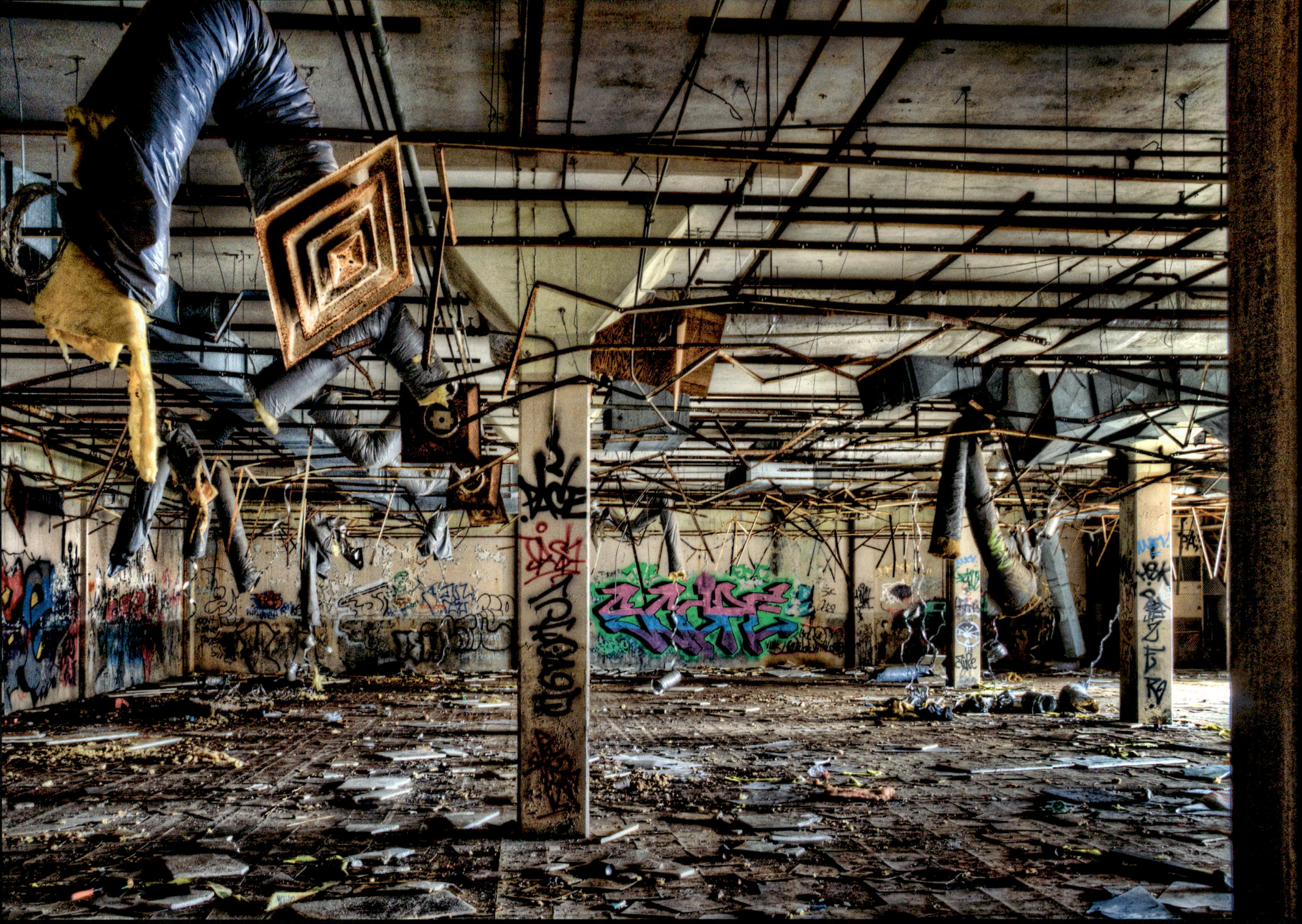

AFTER THE PARTY

The Bristol Company, Waterbury, CT

108

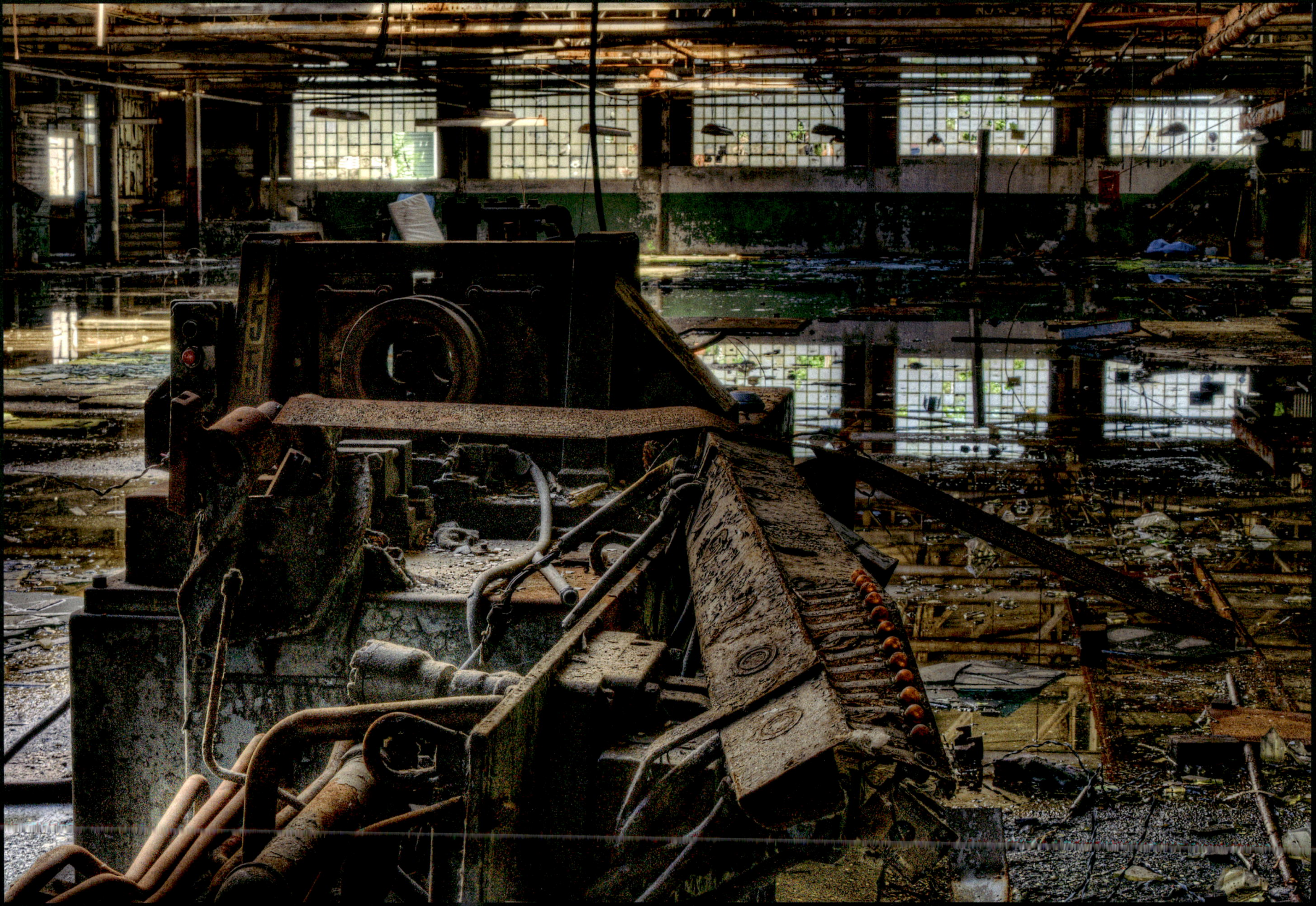

THE LAST MACHINE
American Brass (Benedict & Burnham),
Benedict Street, Waterbury,

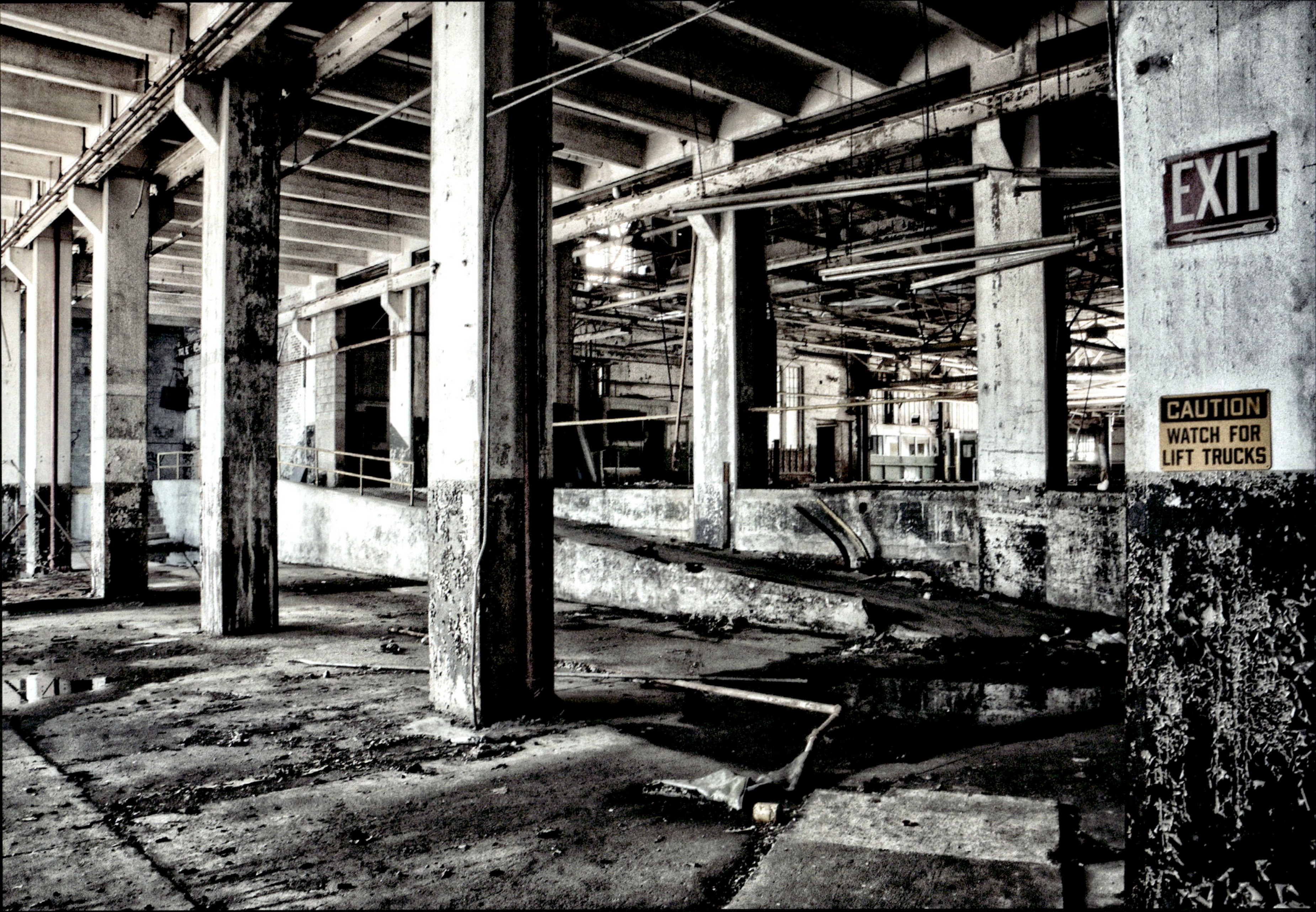

CAUTION, INTERSECTION
American Brass (Benedict & Burnham),
Benedict Street, Waterbury, CT

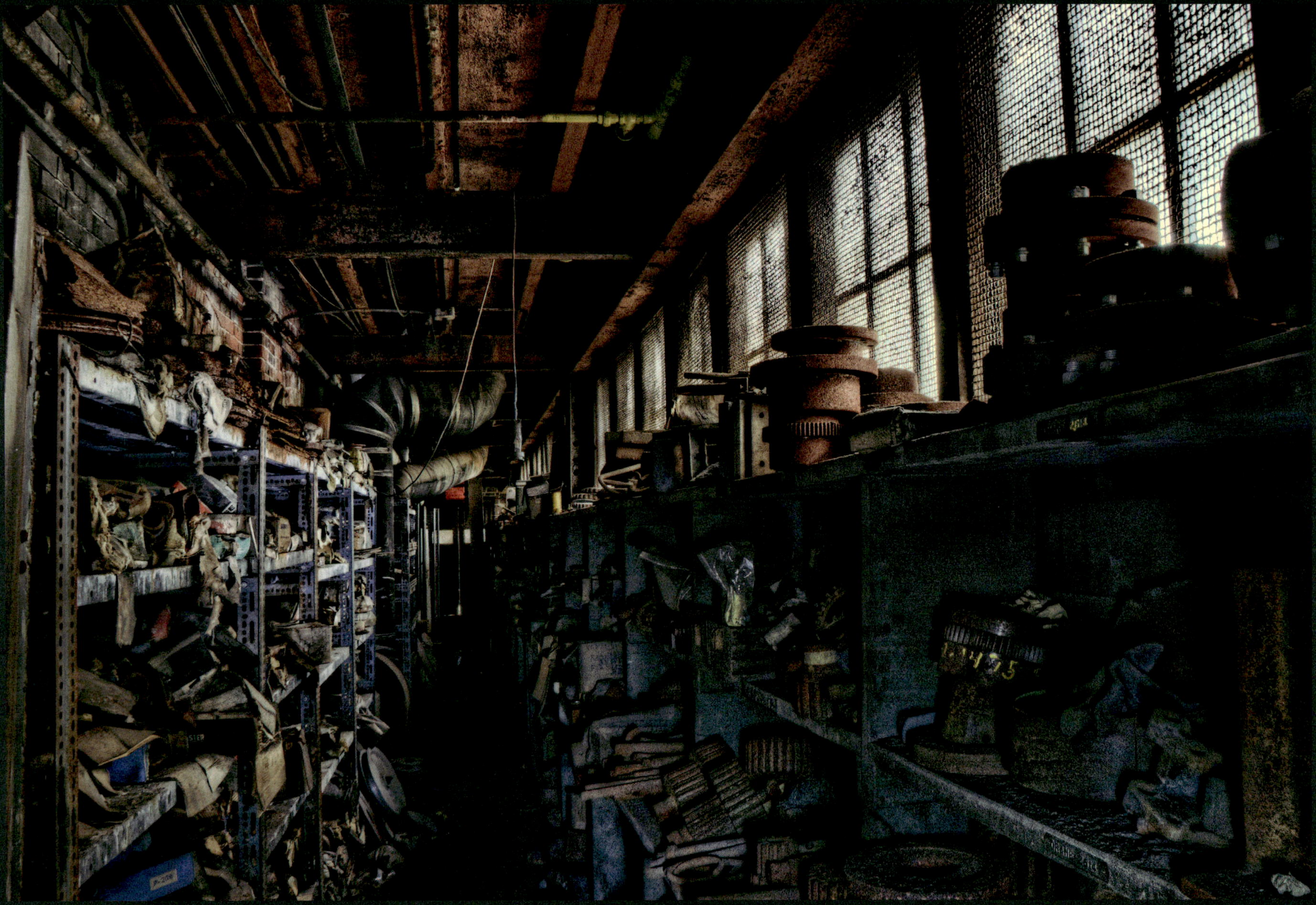

PARTS
Farrel foundry, Ansonia, CT

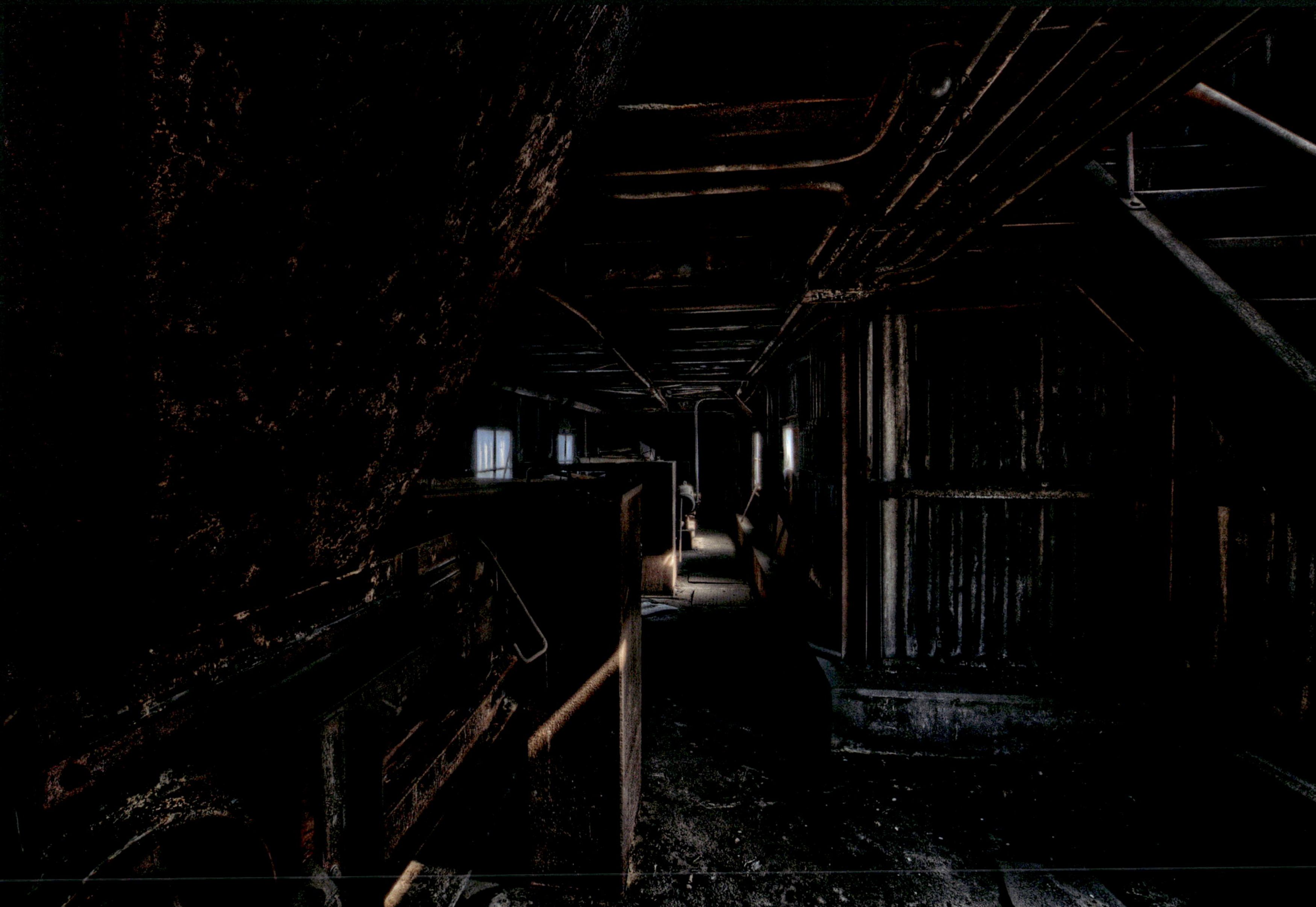

PHOTOGRAPHER'S JOURNAL:
I noticed a narrow doorway, and I followed down a few steps into a passage that went on like a long tunnel. Dust grew like fur on screen-covered windows on my right. Below the windows and along the wall on my left were bins filled with spare parts, gears, wheels, bearings, cams, axles, things for which I had no names, all woven together over time by cobwebs and rust. They were pieces to a puzzle that no longer needed solving. The hall went on like Alice's tumble down the rabbit hole, and I pointed my flashlight to try to paint a picture from the darkness, even if I couldn't quite see to the end of the rabbit hole. I advanced cautiously. I was three stories up. It was dark, and I knew nothing of the floor. I listened and watched intently for the glow of eyes or anything that moved.

FACTORY OVERPASS

Scovill foundry, Thomaston Avenue, Waterbury, CT

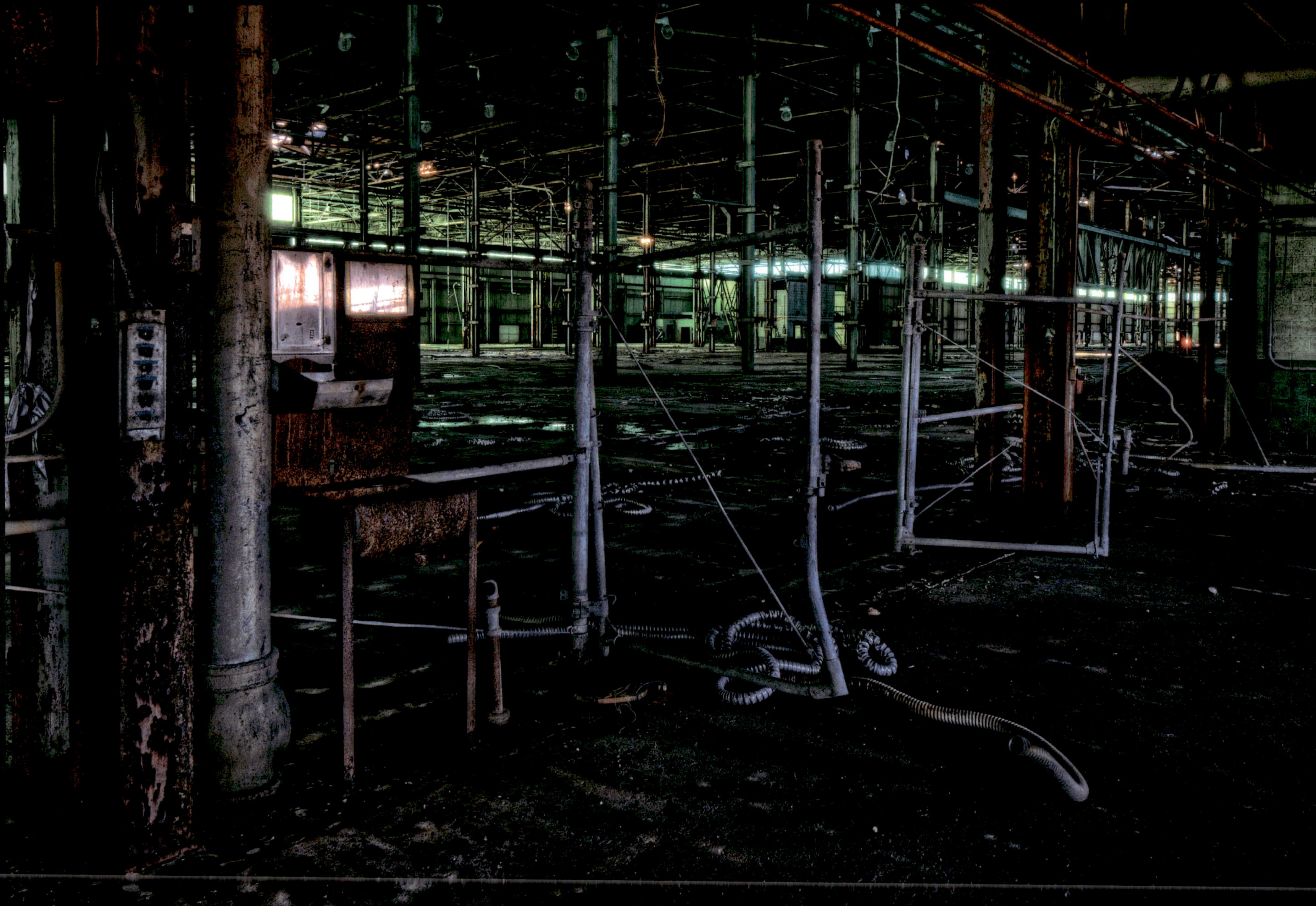

WASHUP
Century Brass, New Milford, CT

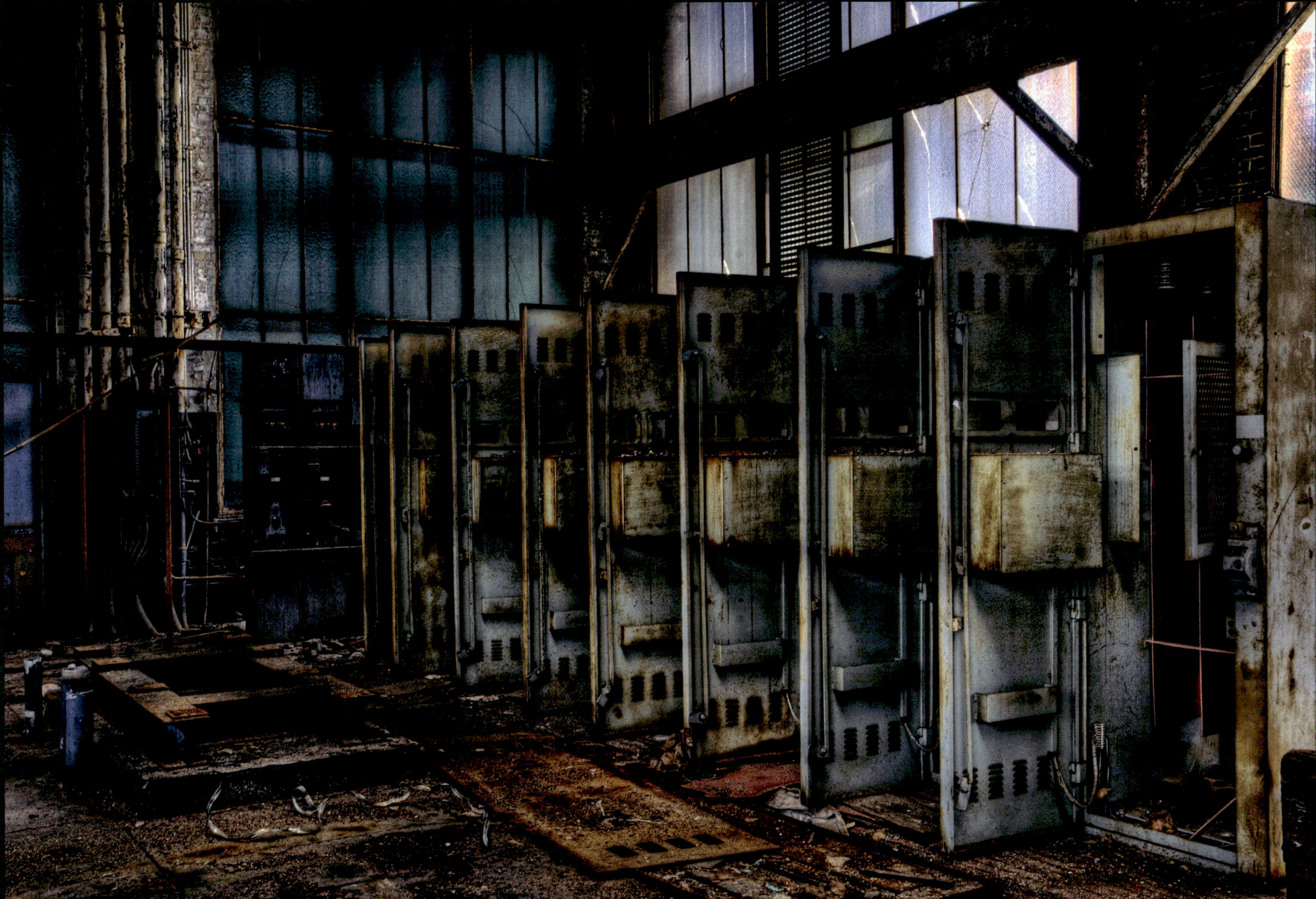

POWER CLOSETS
Powerhouse, American Brass (Benedict & Burnham),
Benedict Street, Waterbury, CT

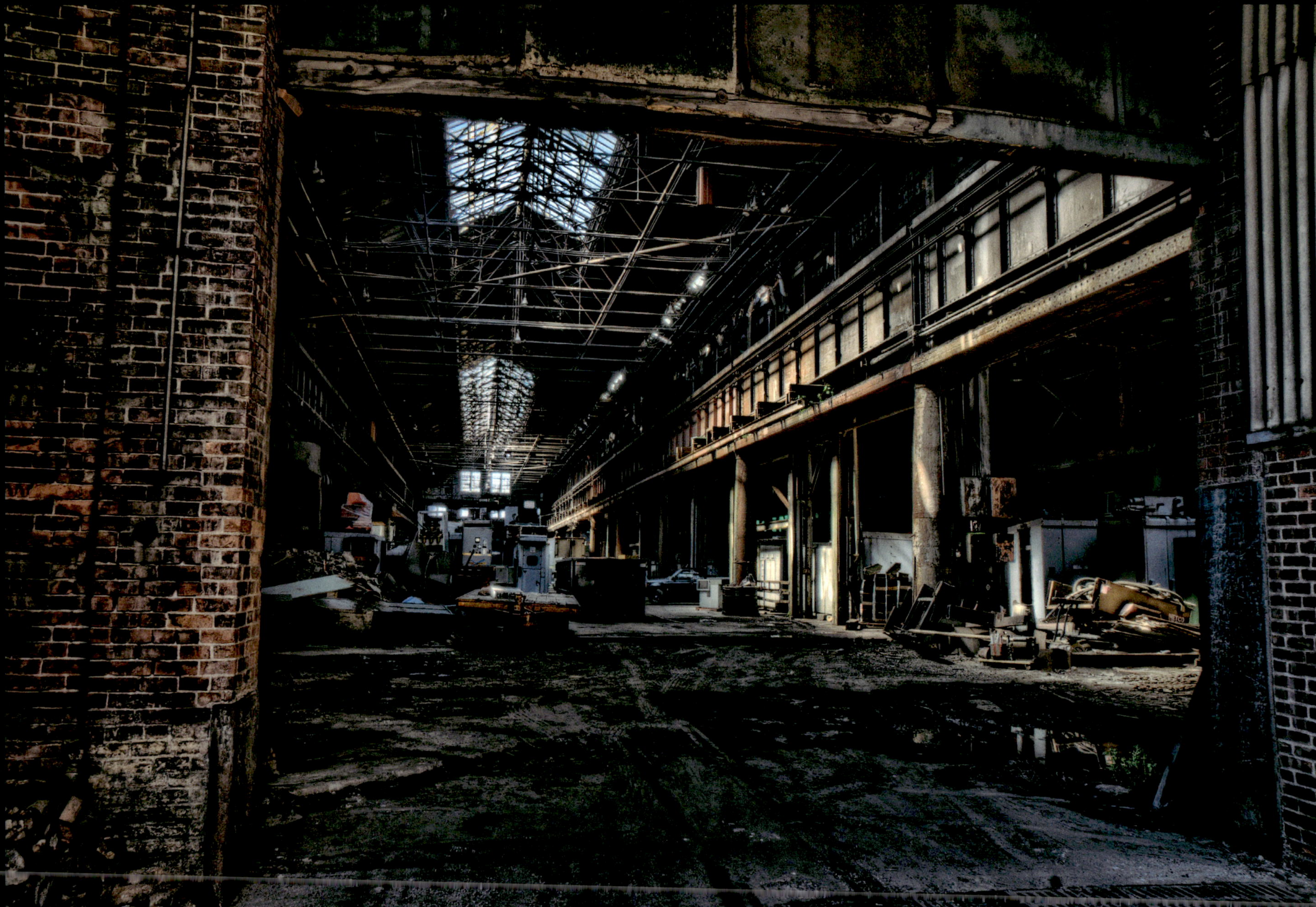

INDUSTRIAL CATHEDRAL

Farrel Foundry, Ansonia, CT

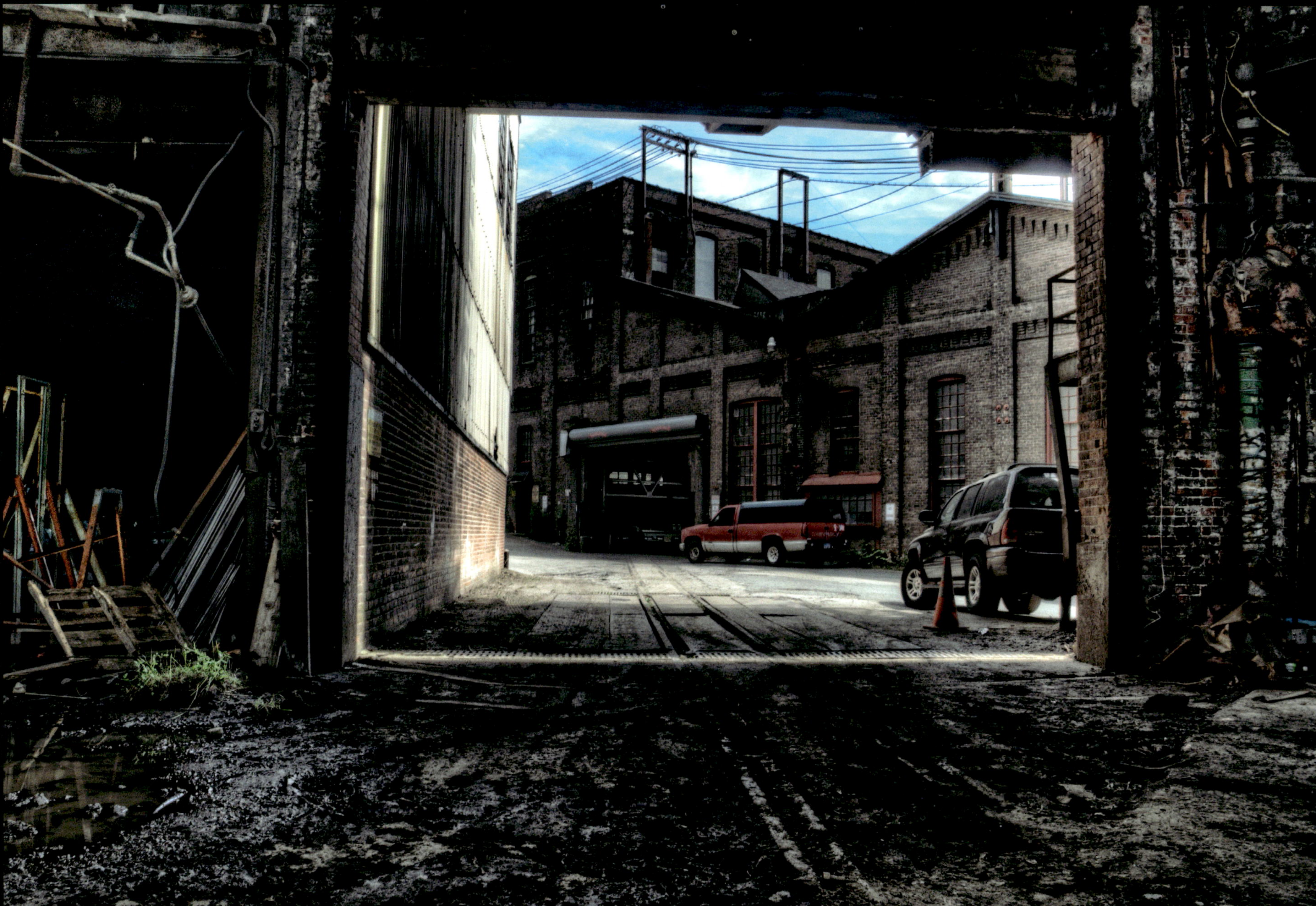

TRACKS
Farrel Company, Ansonia, CT

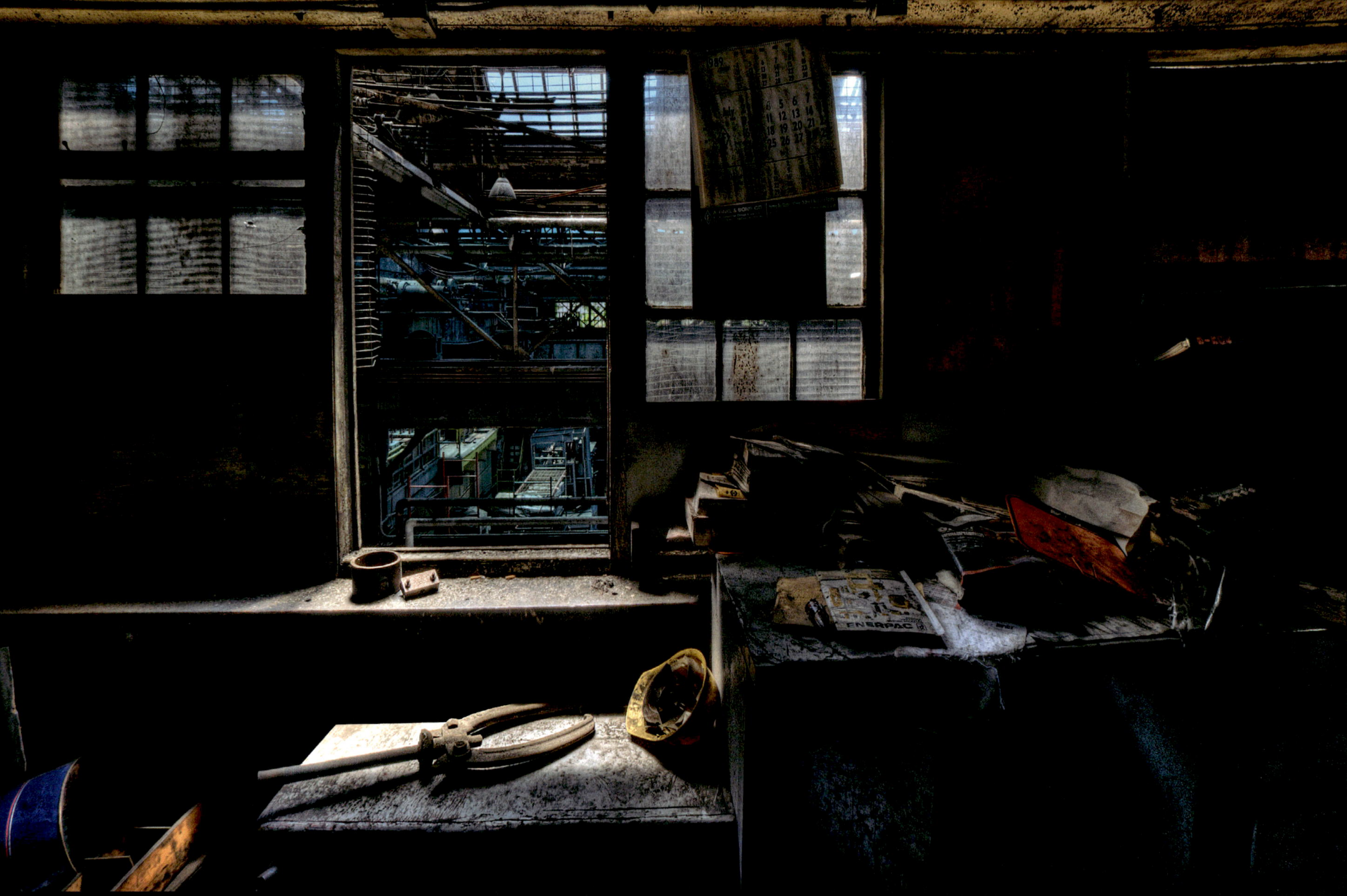

OFFICE OF THE CHIEF ENGINEER

Farrel foundry, Ansonia, CT

PHOTOGRAPHER'S JOURNAL:

A chill of hesitation made me turn back. I never reached the end of the rabbit hole and followed brighter mysteries. There were places of mostly wires, and places filled with sweating pipes, and other dark places, shiny with grease, but many turns and stairs later I entered a room that looked as if there had been a brawl. It was clearly the engineers' office. A large table on the back wall was covered with dusty plans and schematics, and a calendar indicated I'd slipped back a few decades to July of 1989. A window by a desk was open and overlooked a work floor where men used to assemble large machinery. I could almost reach out and touch a crane rated at sixty tons. This was a position of power.

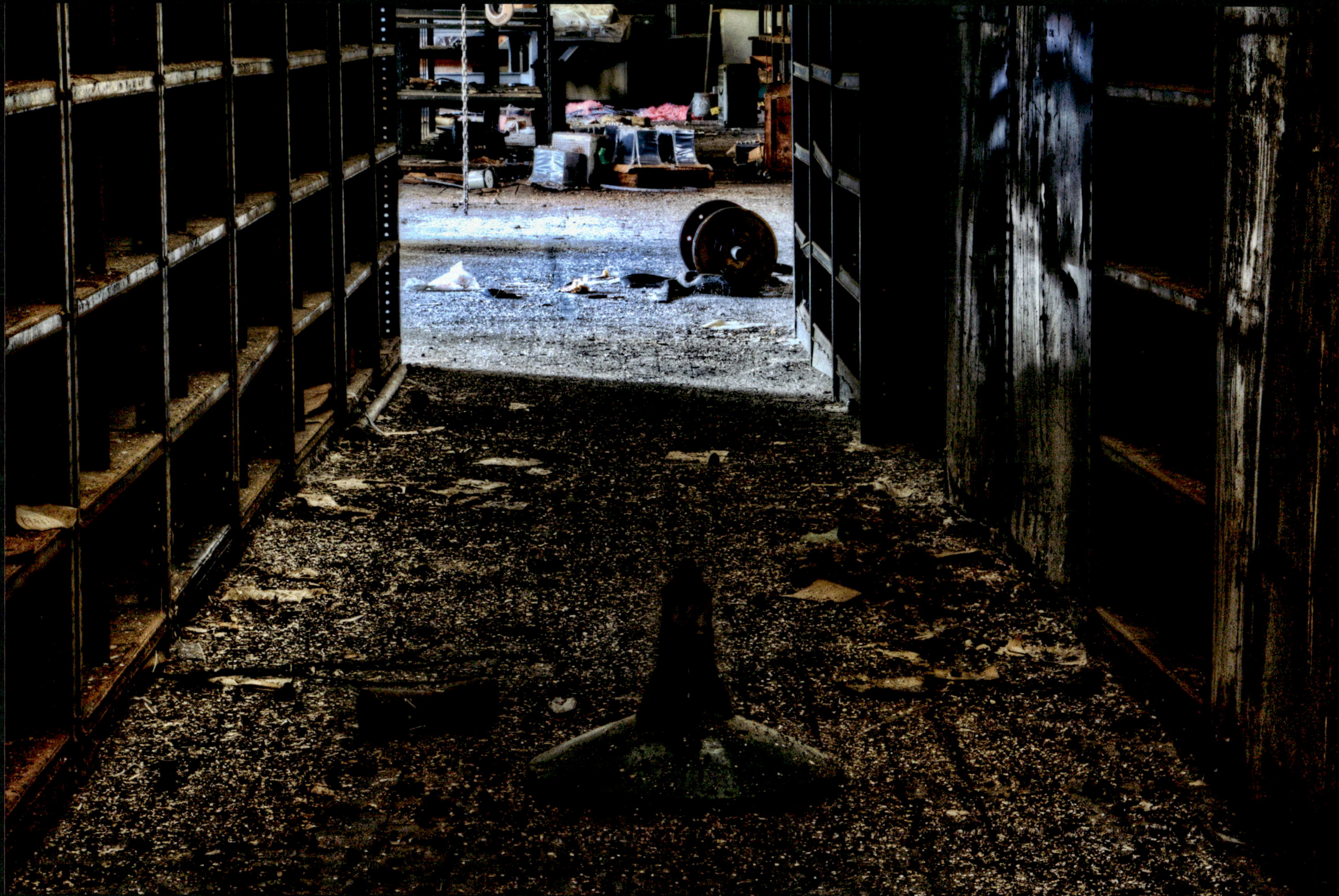

DE LUX

Storage building, American Brass,
Ansonia, CT

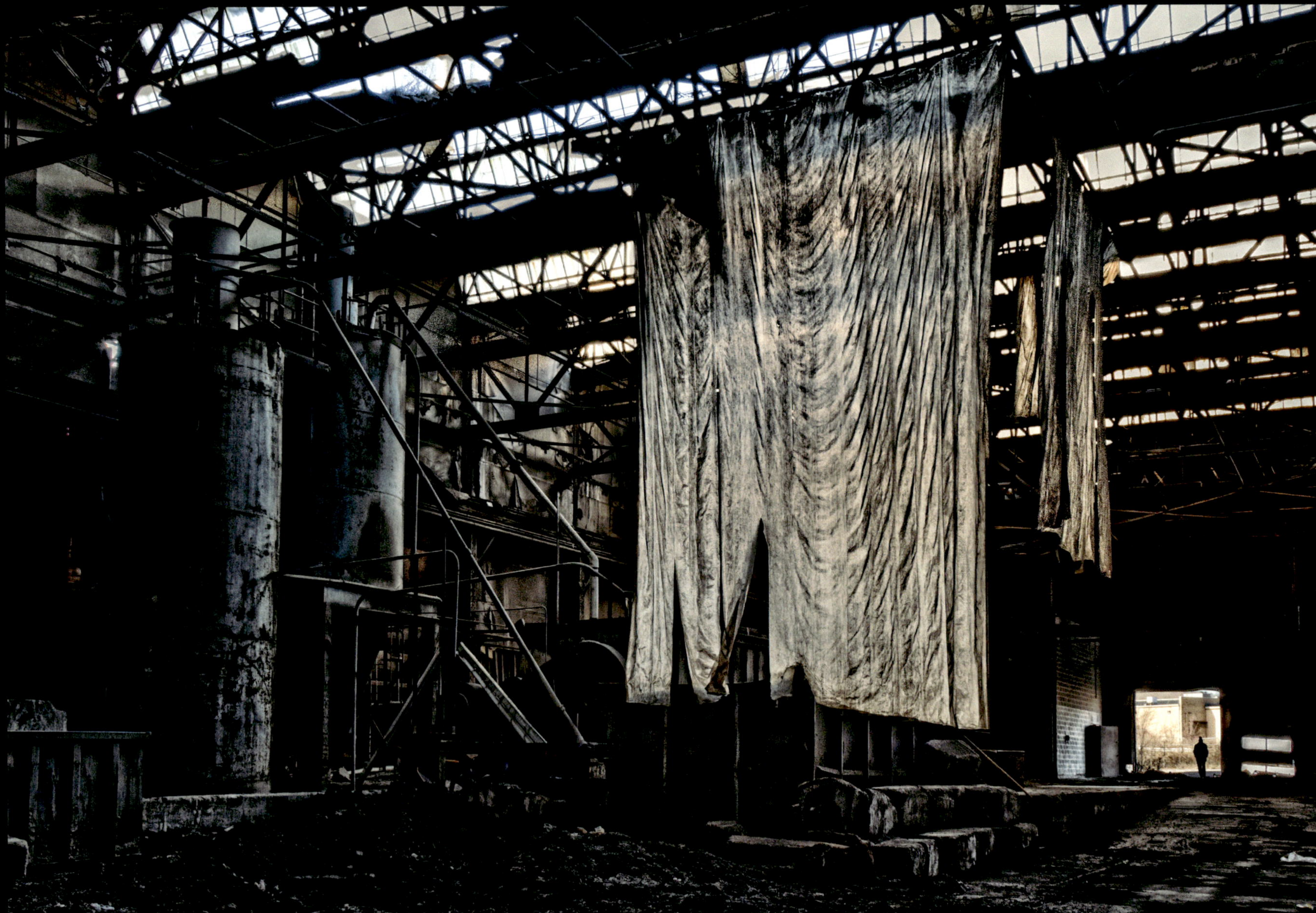

VALLEY SHROUDS
American Brass, Freight Street,
Waterbury, CT

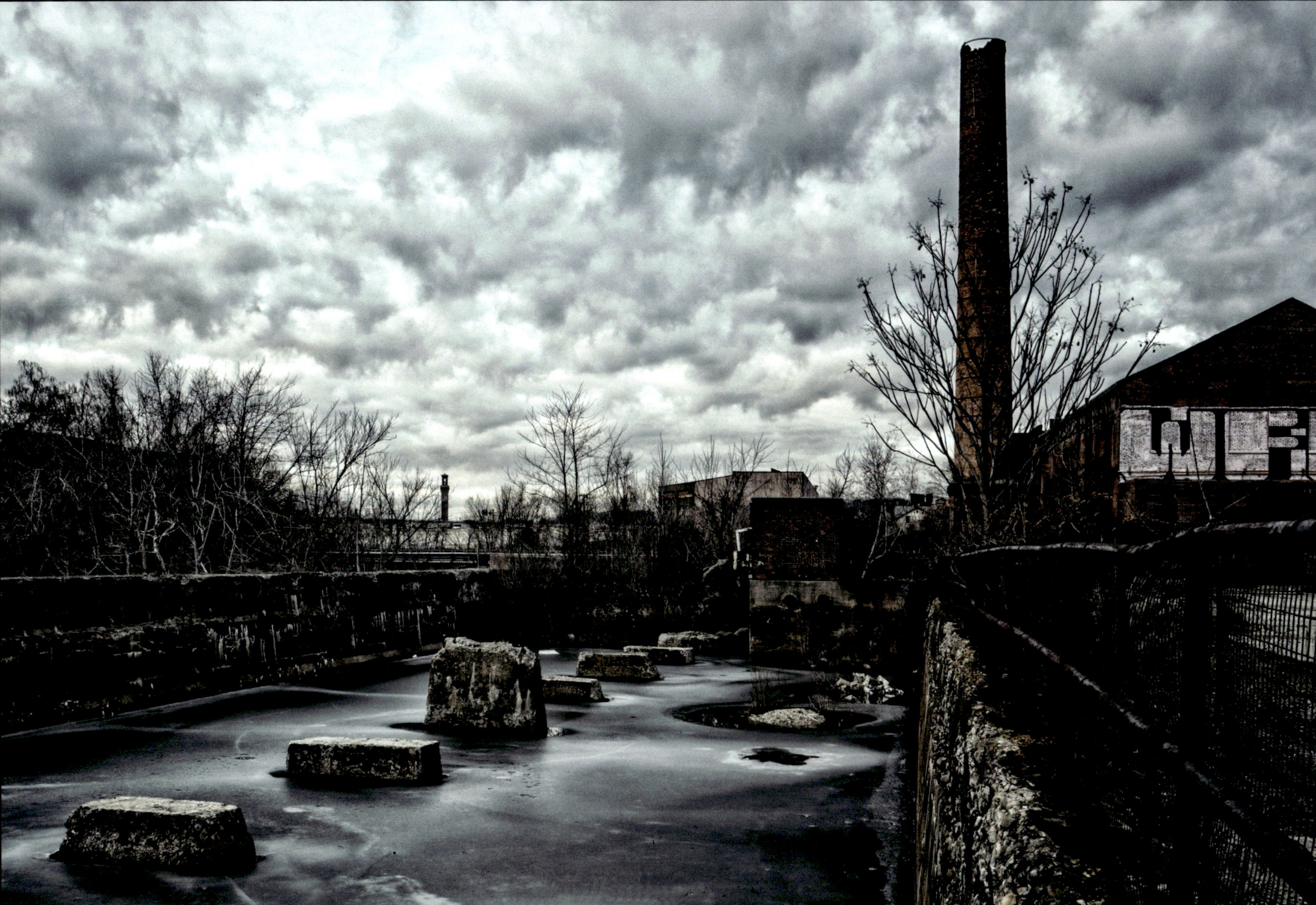

PHOTOGRAPHER'S JOURNAL:
A spur of track runs beside the abandoned powerhouse. Once it brought coal through the factory yard to feed the furnaces that puffed through the hollow stack of hand-piled brick. In the distance is the tower of Union Station. I study to compose their rapt dialogue over Waterbury. Behind Union Station the rails spread out into yards, and the ties rot in a garden of bramble beneath reckless highway interchanges. It is a view that encompasses much wreckage. Between the powerhouse and the river is a settling basin with broken piers that once held a large duct or pipe. What was it that was regularly spilled here to settle or cool before the fluid was drained to the river below? In spring and fall I've imagined there among the transient geese a place for naiads in Gotham.

VALLEY TOWERS & POOLS

Settling basin by the Naugatuck, American Brass (Benedict & Burnham), Benedict Street, Waterbury, C

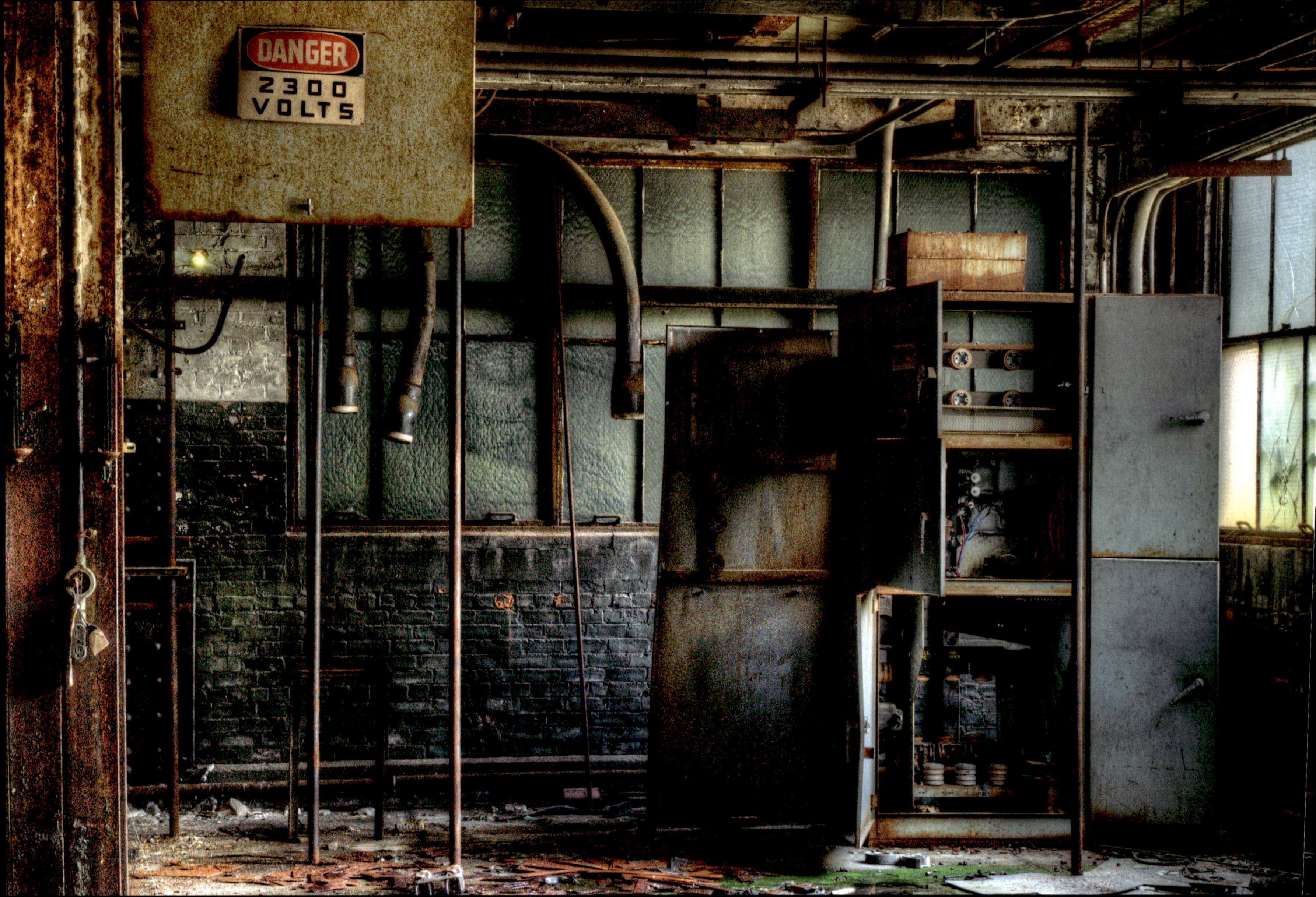

DANGER

Powerhouse, American Brass (Benedict & Burnham)

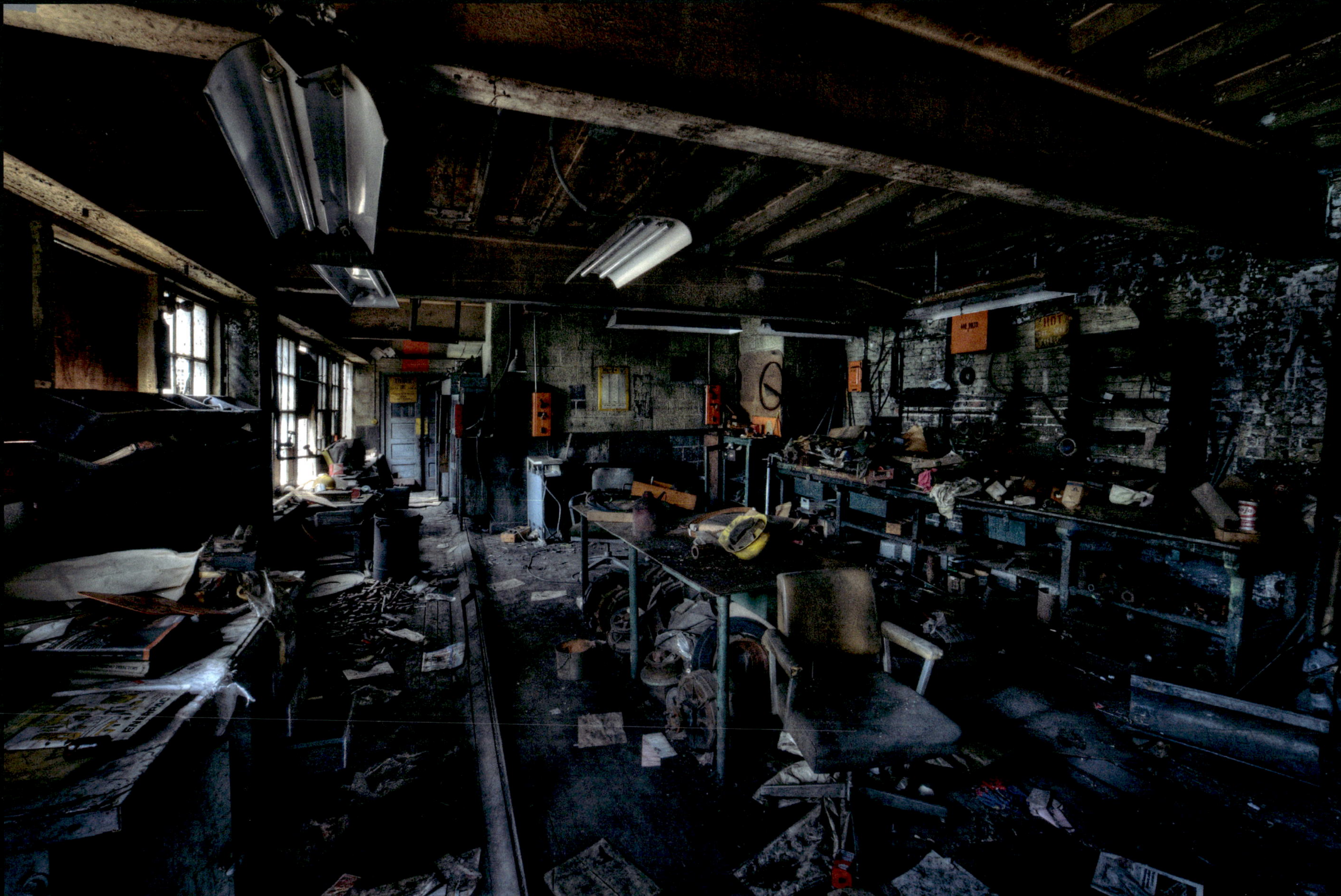

PHOTOGRAPHER'S JOURNAL:
I shot a number of pictures in the Engineers' Office—there had been a brawl or a skirmish with eternity—a binder of specifications lay open and scattered about. Then I discovered a narrow doorway at the far end and investigated. I descended a few steps to a passage that went on like a long, dark tunnel. Dust grew like fur on screen-covered windows on my left. They lined one side of the tunnel letting in muted, gray illumination. It took some moments before my eyes adjusted and I saw the parts. For all my explorations into the corners of the building, I was looking back down the same rabbit hole from the end I hadn't reached, or had the rabbit hole of parts become an endless loop where vermin teem, and there is no way out? The parts were here; whatever they were for was gone.

ENGINEERING DEPARTMENT

Farrel foundry, Ansonia, CT

OUR STORIES:

Mergers and Mayhem

Aaron Benedict partnered with Gordon Burnham in 1834. Benedict & Burnham Manufacturing Company was the first in the valley to incorporate, and they became the largest manufacturer of copper appliances and fixtures in the world.

Israel Holmes was a consummate entrepreneur involved in many partnerships. In 1853 he teamed with the ingenious inventor Hiram Hayden. Holmes, Booth & Haydens became the first company to manufacture planished copper-silver photographic plates, brass lenses, and other photographic equipment, but it was the oil lamps they made in their lampworks that lighted homes throughout the country.

The tiny company started by the Grilleys and Porters became Scovill Manufacturing, a giant in fasteners. Between 1880 and 1892 Scovill grew from 400 to 1,200 workers and from 340 to 1400 horsepower. Scovill made fasteners of all kinds, including a famous set of gold buttons with the head of George Washington on each button that was presented to Major General Marquis de Lafayette in 1825. They made the buttons for the North and buttons for the South, and the ubiquitous "gripper," a staple of children's sleepware to this day; they were known as the fastener company. With Ansonia Brass & Battery in the south, Wolcottville Brass in the north, projects of Anson Phelps and Israel Coe, the Naugatuck had truly earned the title Brass Valley. The large companies had spun off numerous smaller companies whose interests were often confusingly at cross purposes amid shifting alliances.

At the end of the nineteenth century, Holmes, Booth & Haydens, Benedict & Burnham, Wolcottville Brass, Ansonia Brass, and a host of smaller companies were merged into the giant American Brass Company. They told us it was to better manage cycles of supply and demand, and Brass Valley continued to prosper. By 1909 American Brass alone was responsible for two-thirds of brass manufacturing in America, consumed one-third of all the nation's copper, and was the largest producer of non-ferrous metal in the world. The so called "Big Three"—Scovill, American Brass, and Chase Brass—controlled brass manufacturing. All were located in the Naugatuck Valley and selling to the world. The men who ran the mills also ran the towns and wrote histories of the valley in which they told their own stories, and they put their names in stone or brass or bronze on public buildings and street signs, and some of us dreamed our children might do that, too. For most of those men, time was a glass always half full. Whether they sought money, power, command, or respect, they knew how to get things done, and they mostly had faith that the future they wanted belonged to progress.

It's hard to know when the families who built the mills lost command. In the 1920s Chase Brass was acquired by Kennecott Copper and American Brass Company was bought by Anaconda Copper, but it began long before that. Without us noticing, copper manufacturing had become an appendage of wealthy mining and oil conglomerates waging monopoly wars and perpetrating economic schemes, culminating in the Rockefeller-Ryan "pump and dump" scandals that some say led to our Great Depression. The neglect had begun even before the flood of 1955 scoured the valley floor. We didn't know it then, but the mills were running down, rusting, being sold off piecemeal as scrap or left to rot. That was long ago, and today in the US, whole cities have become as expendable as dull razor blades.

Scovill, the last independent brass maker, long ago moved headquarters to Clarkesville, Georgia. In Waterbury, empty brass mills linger as toxic ruins; Scovill's main factory complex vanished like the culture it bred, replaced by Brass Mill Mall and acres of parking, as stone and brass give way to neon, fluorescent, and fields of jiggling LEDs, and even that yields to online shopping.

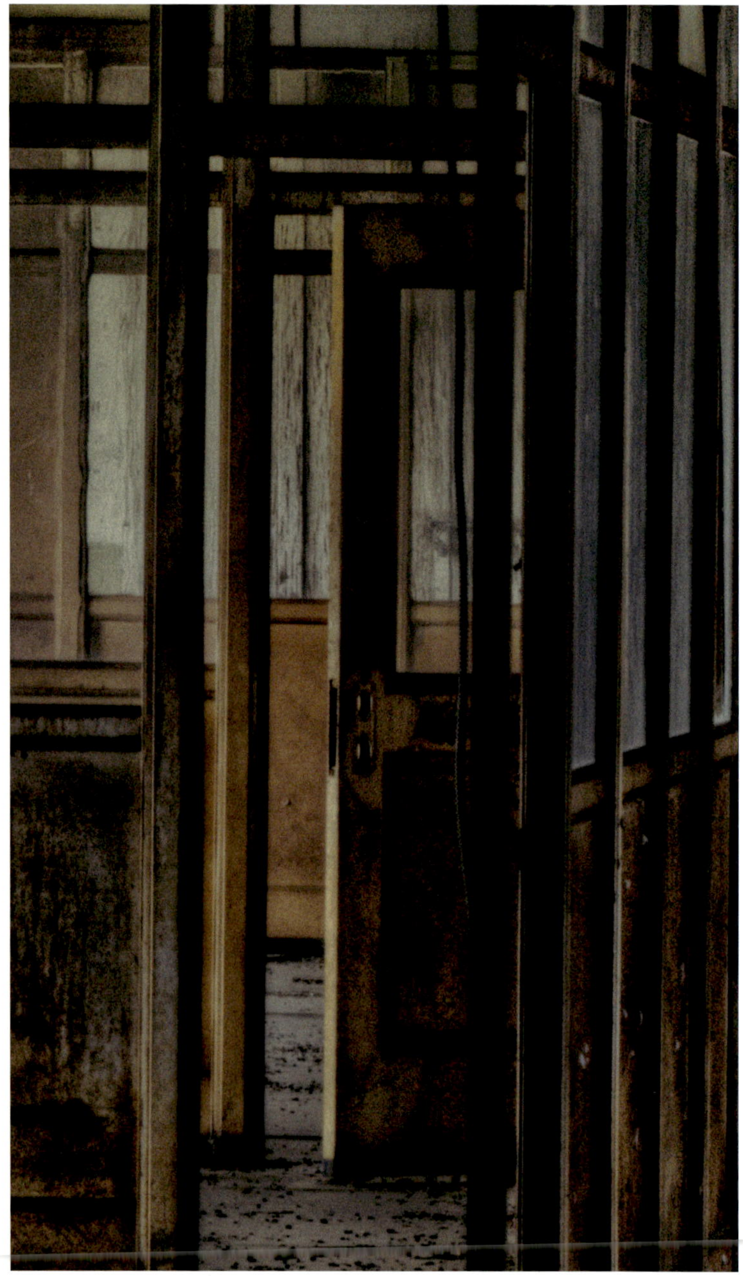

BRASS PASSING

American Brass (Holmes, Booth & Haydens), Bank Street, Waterbury, CT

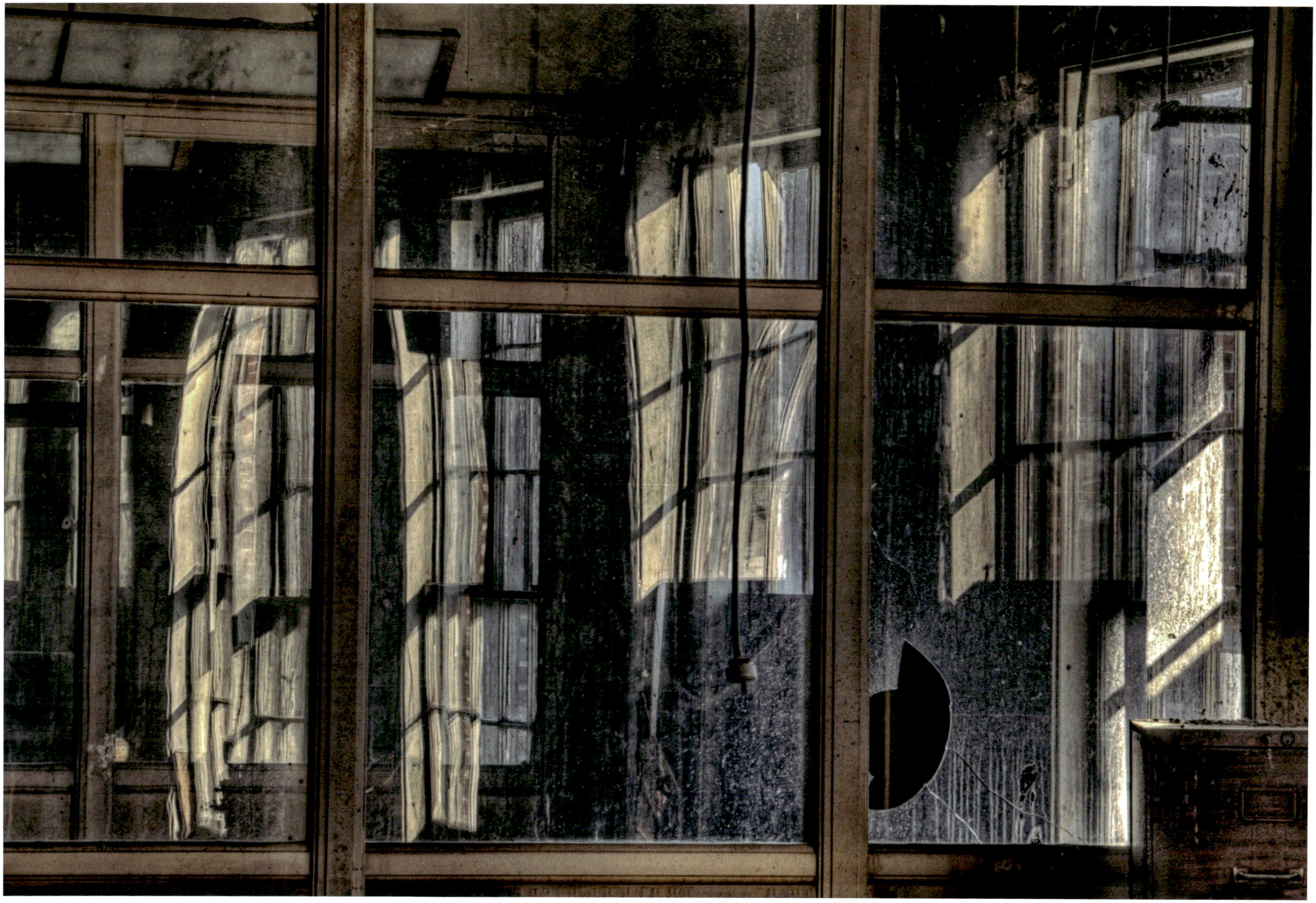

"EXEGI MONUMENTUM AERE PERENNIUS,"

(I have built a monument more lasting than bronze) —Horace

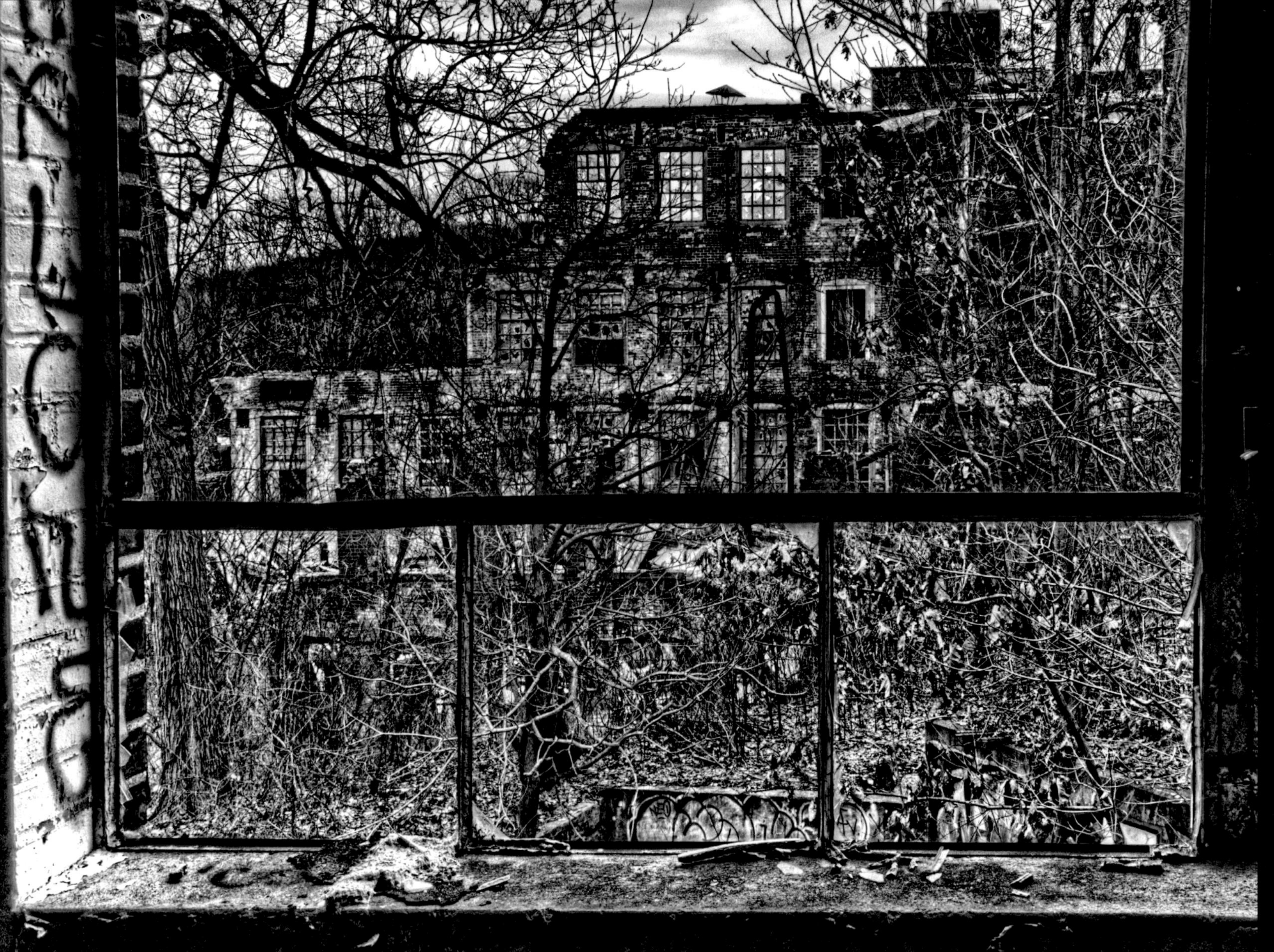

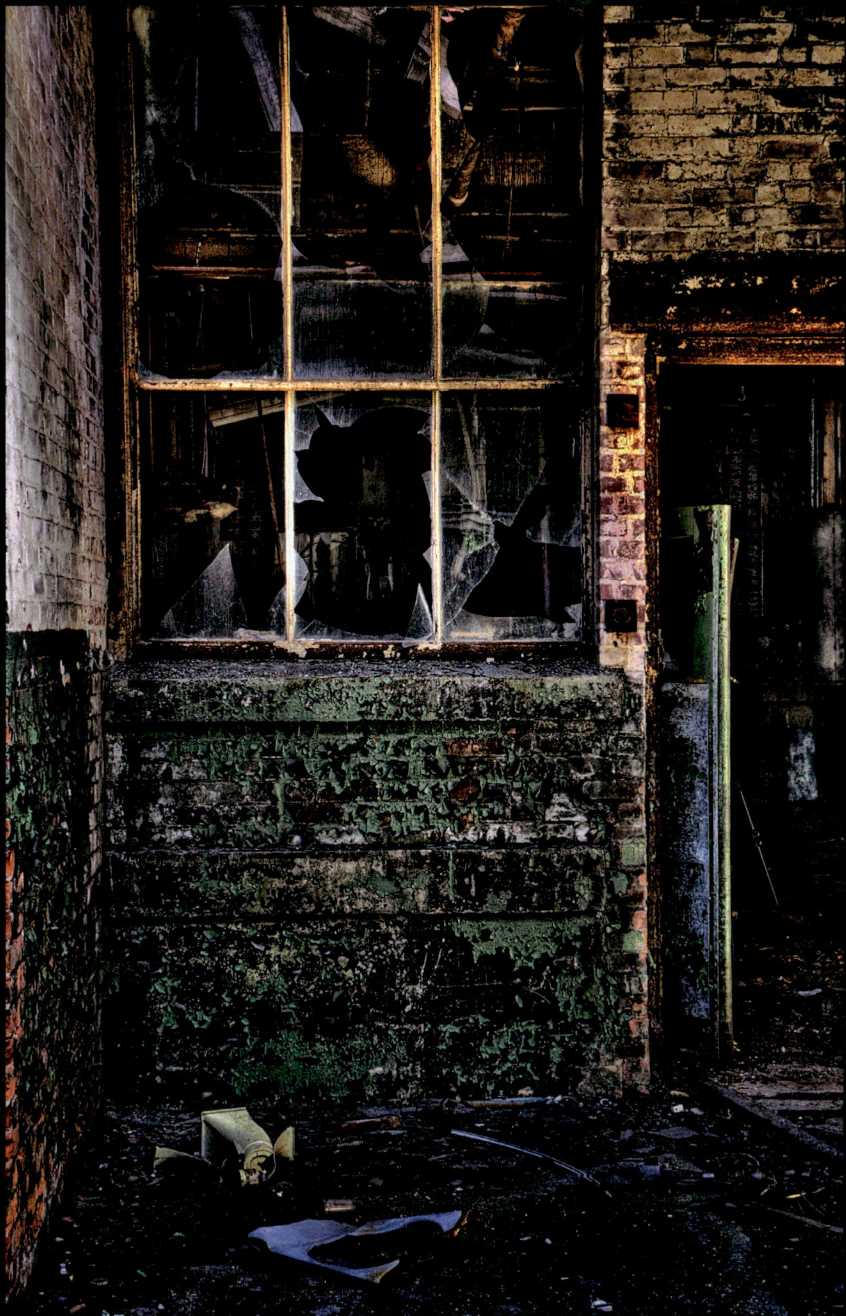

BROKEN
The Bristol Company, Waterbury, CT

EMPTY FACTORIES

They are like cloisters
battered and broken,
time feels bigger here
space grander
than walls imply

When time stops,
instants are eons,
and a drop
of river's flow
is oceans overflowing

They are like cloisters,
I walk by stained and broken glass
ponder how things decay,
my tripod aligns and spreads the rowed columns,
my lens fixes each time-sculptured brick in its crystal grip

When motion ceases
silence rumbles,
by and by
the quickness
of black night

They are like cloisters
When it rains the ceilings run,
and ducts and pipes channel fountains,
and cascades from broken skylights fall
to pools, and tin roofs thunder.

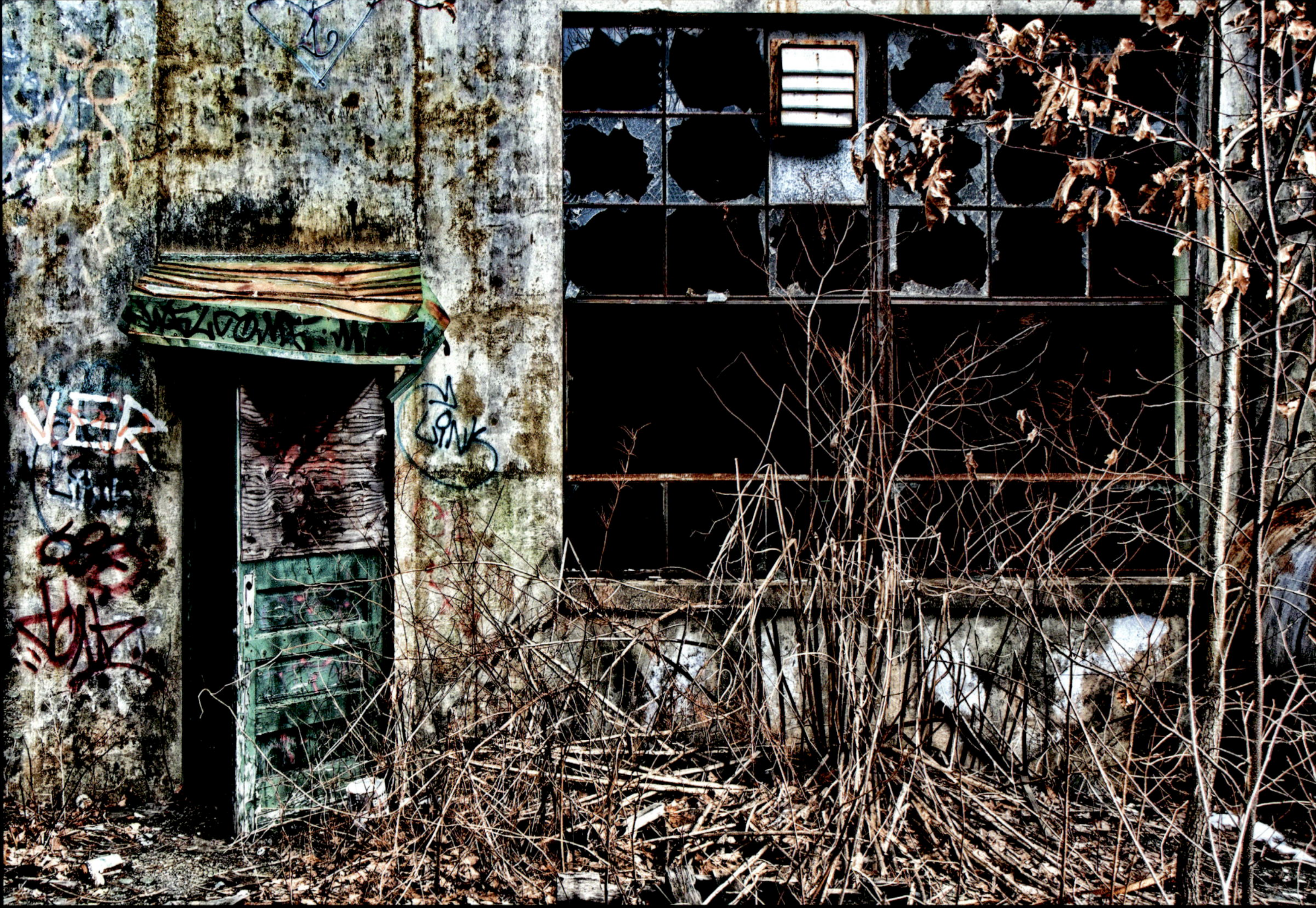

WELCOME
The Bristol Company,
Waterbury, CT

PHOTOGRAPHER'S JOURNAL:

The sign says, "Welcome," and it looks like a midway of freaks and fun and dizzying rides. There is no finer ruin in Connecticut. I've explored what's safe to cross and no clues reveal what went on here. On my first visit I had no idea that this is one of the holy places of engineering and technology. Here Professor William H. Bristol invented and produced devices that won him prizes and were among the miracles displayed in the pavilions of the White City, St. Louis, Philadelphia, San Francisco, and Paris. World commerce spread his genius around the globe long before he made movies speak.

Professor William H. Bristol recorded things. That was his life's work. If it ebbed or flowed, jiggled or weighed, smelled, swelled or sweated, Professor Bristol found a way to record its changes. His works sought to master time, trepidation, and the electrons that materialize them, in machines that multiplied and magnified our five senses.

The Bristol Company began in 1889, manufacturing steam gauges that recorded fluctuations in pressure. Driven by a thousand challenges, Bristol eventually built a catalog of more than two thousand devices to see, sniff, or otherwise sample and record data. His was a powerful magic

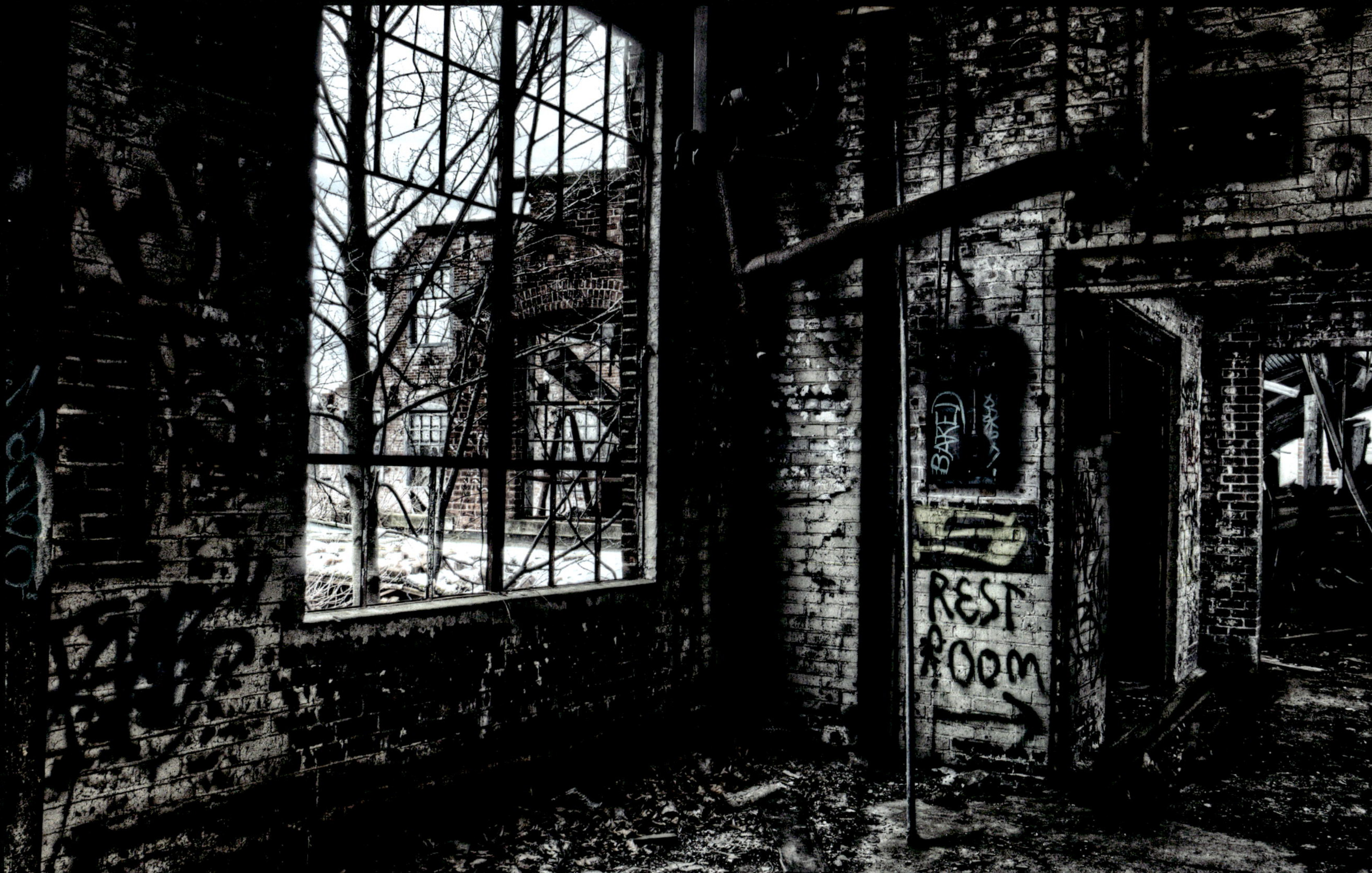

to industries seeking to regulate production and, as Professor Bristol knew, a useful tool for environmentalists trying to tame its effluvia. He was an industrial leader and an environmentalist and the fountainhead of data-driven industrialization.

When universal phone service became popular, Bristol Audiophone also retailed the Professor's magic to the ears of fathers struggling with tinny messages inside the wires of Mr. Bell's new instruments. The Professor's ads advised, "He'll have to get a loud speaker some day, so why not get the right one first." His research and manufacturing filled fifteen interconnected buildings covering seventeen acres in the Platt's Mill section of Waterbury.

It seems an odd, though productive, focus for a life: recording stuff regardless of its nature; was his time made up by puzzles and the challenges of solving them? William H. Bristol earned an engineering degree from the Stevens Institute of Technology in 1884. A bachelor's degree in engineering was a new idea. The school was just fourteen years old; Massachusetts Institute of Technology was only a decade older. Bristol began his working life teaching at the Working Man's School of the Ethical Culture Society in New York City, a school that provided free, quality education to children of working families. He spent the rest of his life developing and teaching the charms and spells of data recording to a generation of "professional" engineers long before data became golden.

THIS WAY
The Bristol Company, Waterbury, CT

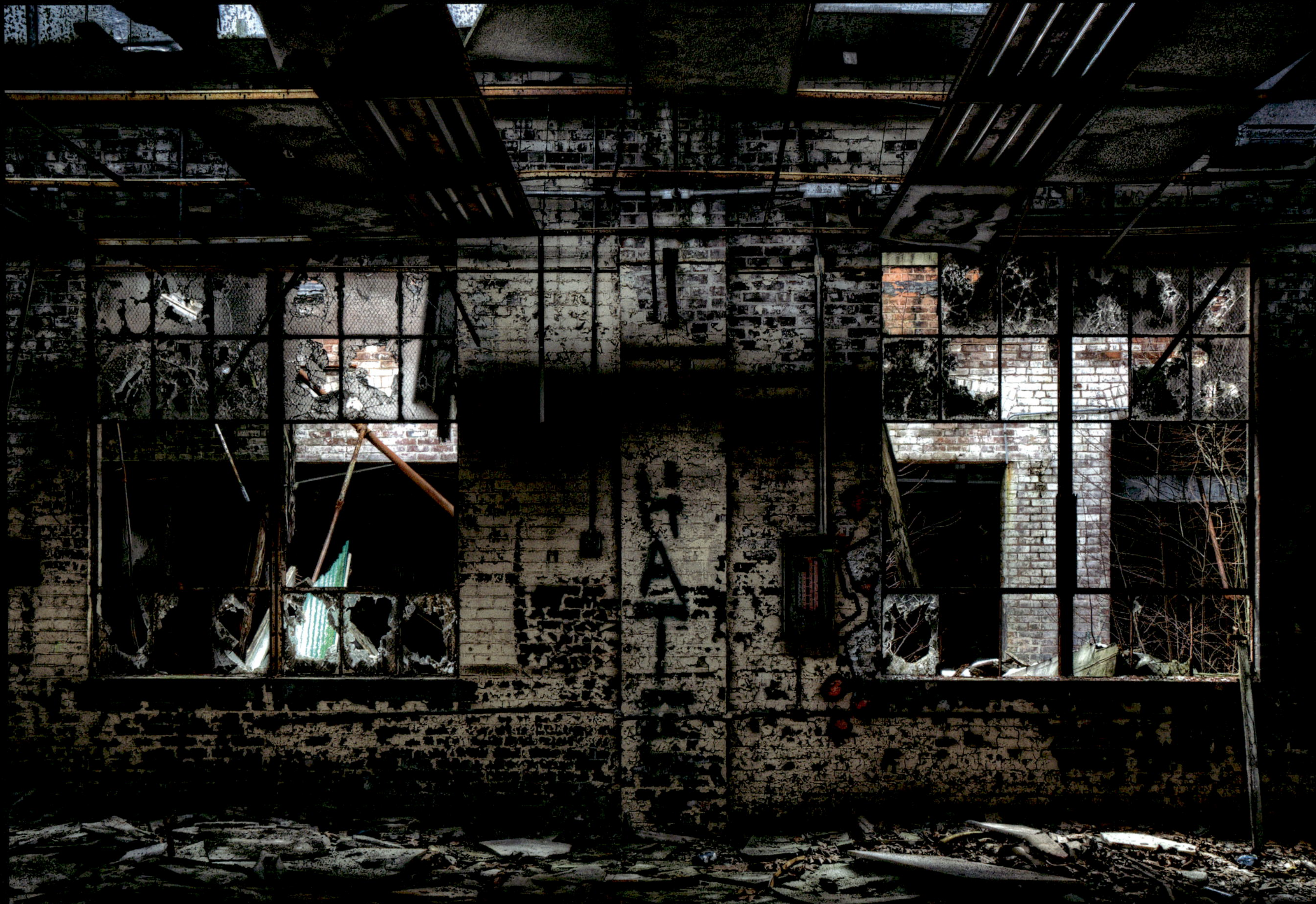

FLOWERS OF RAGE

The Bristol Company, Waterbury, CT

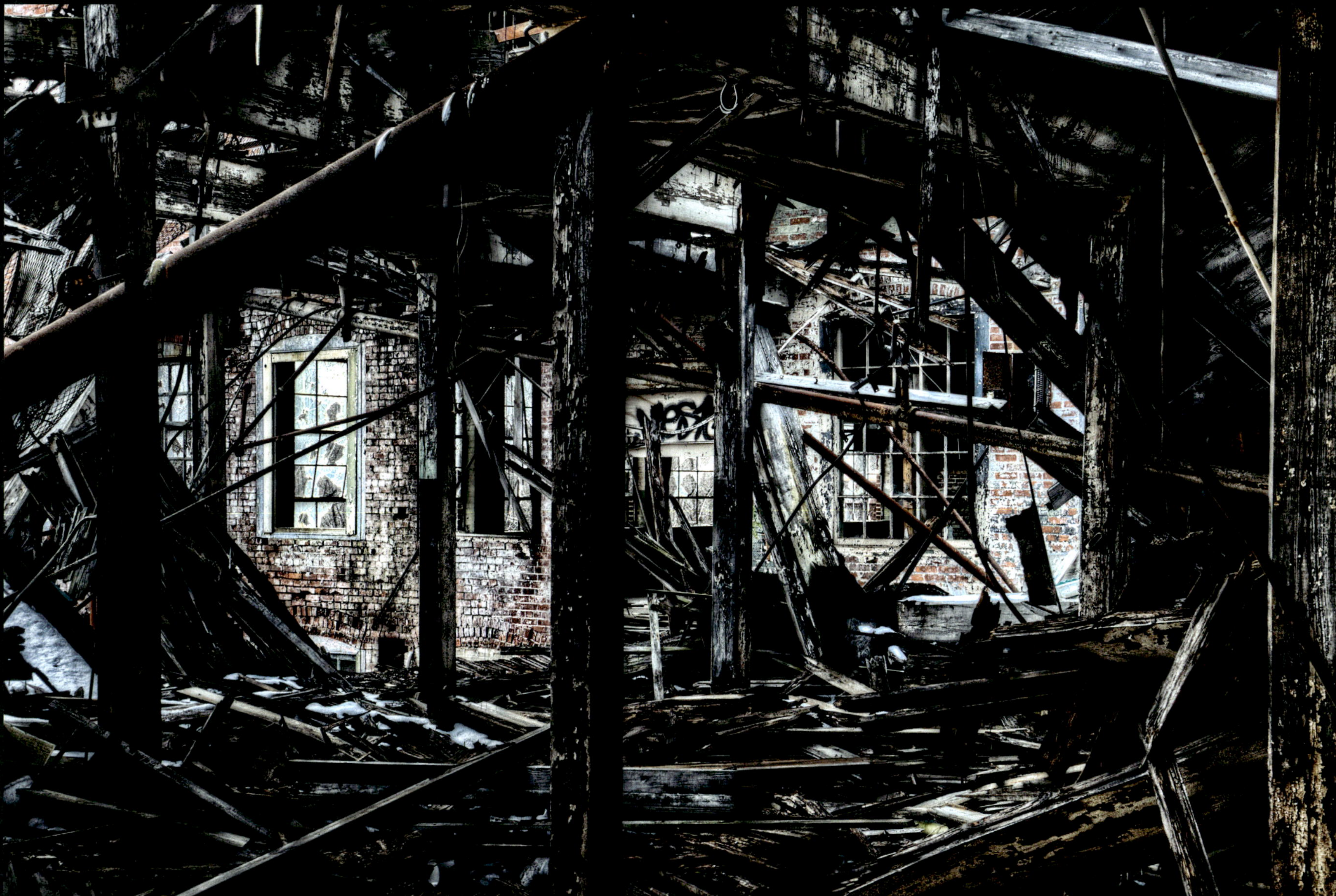

PHOTOGRAPHER'S JOURNAL:

It is one of those ironies that though Professor Bristol spent life deconstructing vitality into recordable components, he was a humanist, and it is fitting he is most remembered for his work on reassembling life-like reality. By 1915 he was at work on ways of making movies talk, to hold on to yesterday and master time. On December 21, 1927, at the Franklin Institute in Philadelphia, members of the motion picture industry assembled while Professor Bristol demonstrated the Bristolphone, "A New Device For Synchronizing And Re-Synchronizing Motion Pictures and Sound." They came to watch the first, full-length talkie two years before *The Jazz Singer*. Evidently the professor's movie and its name are lost to history, but it was recorded here at Bristol's in Platt's Mill. It is one of the holy places of industrial technology.

THE END

The Bristol Company, Waterbury, CT

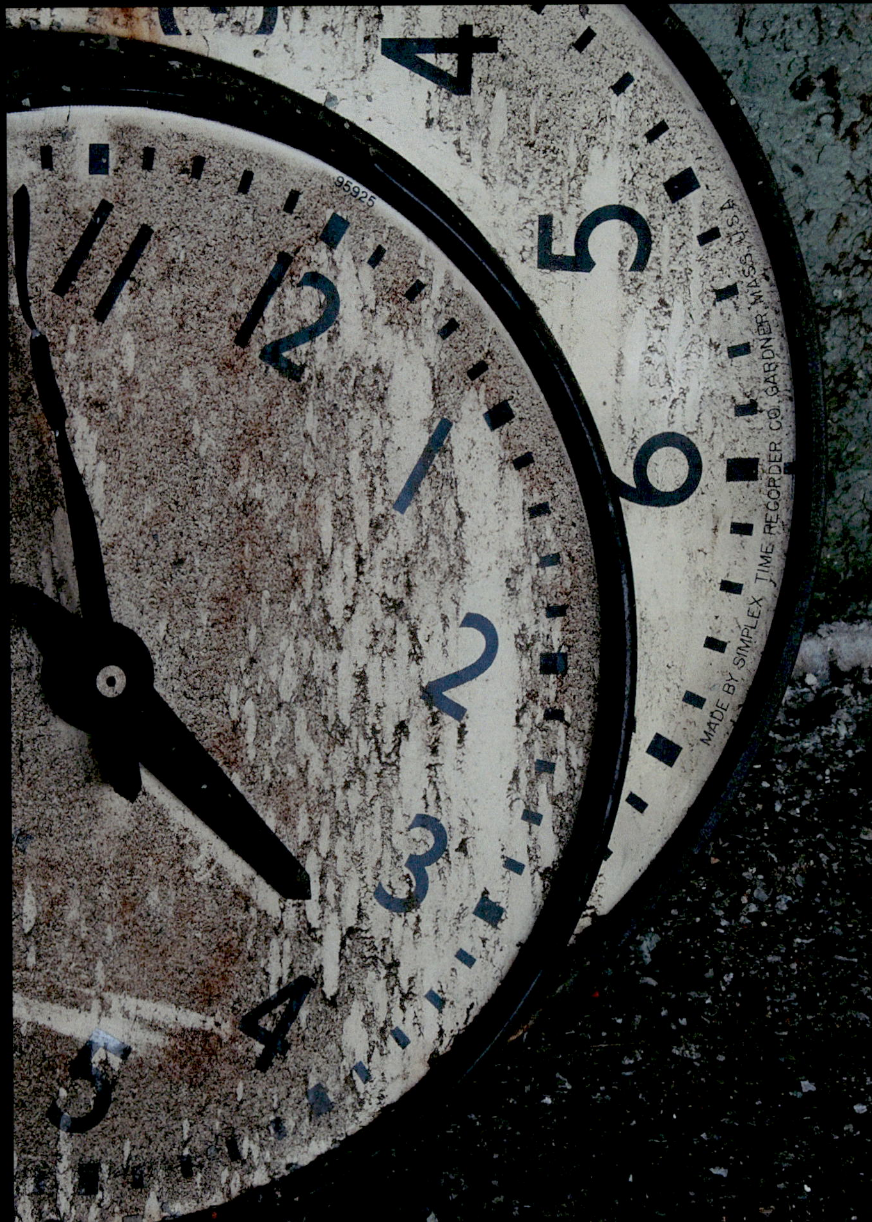

TIME TRAVEL

The past is always here,
always elusive,
like a familiar smell
that lets you know
you're home,

though you are a half-world away,

and when you finally
get back to
the disfigured
place that had been

home,

you search for that smell,
crave it,
even as you
sip mouthfuls of heartless dust and
savor mildew's inky sting.

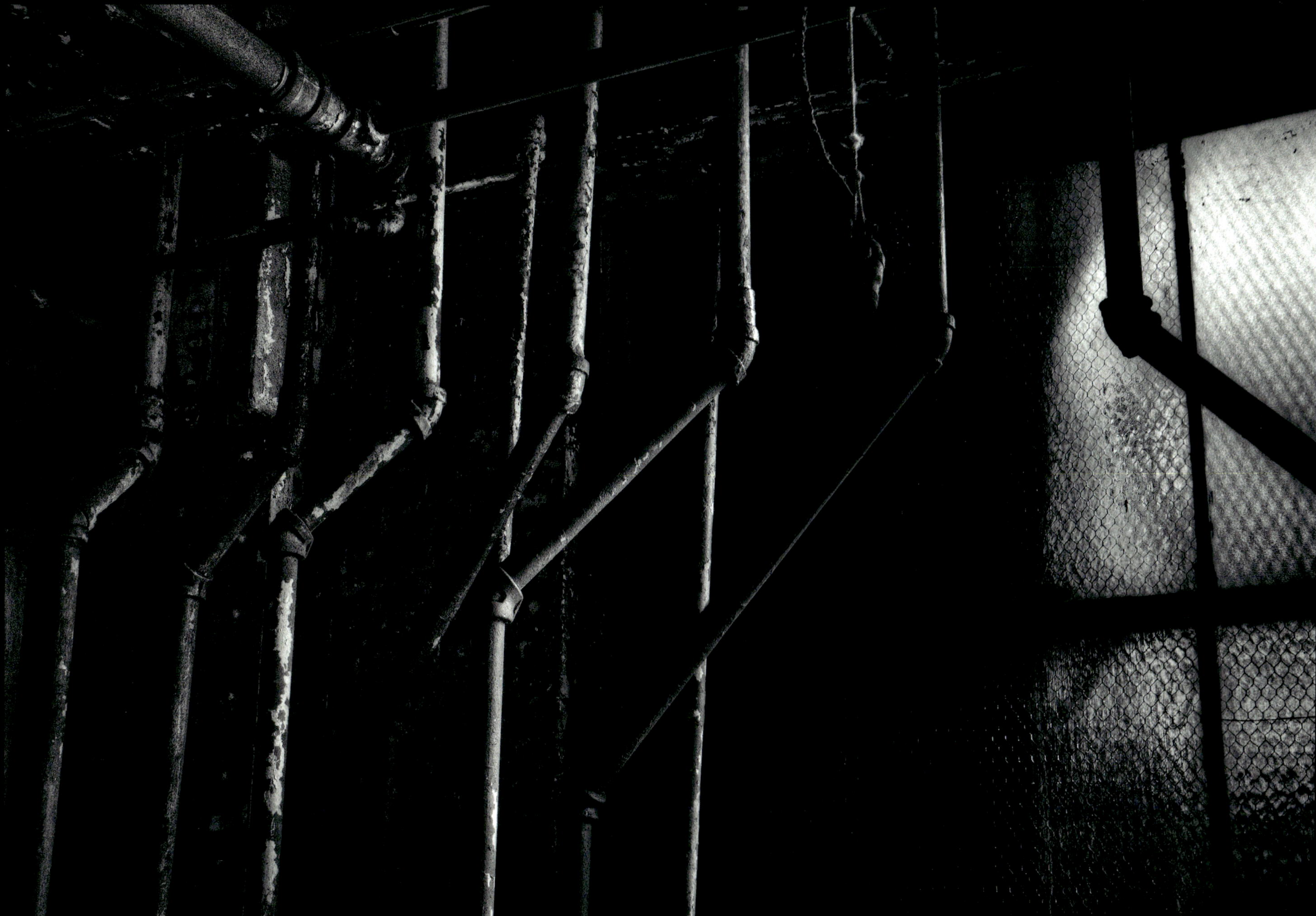

DOWNSTREAM NO. 1

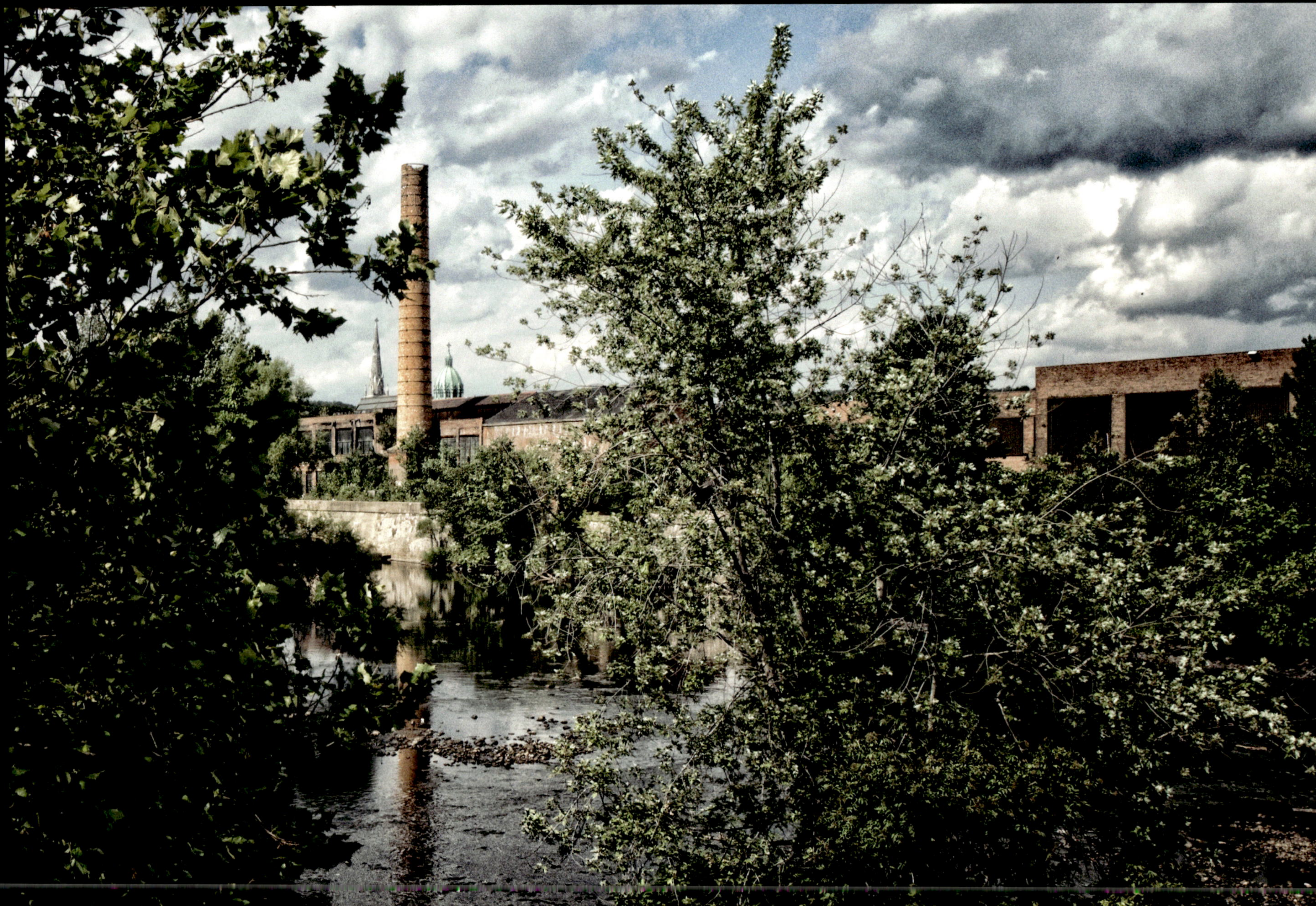

HOLY WATER, HOLY SMOKE, AND THE SHRINE OF ST. ANNE

The Naugatuck through American Brass from Washington Street, Waterbury, CT

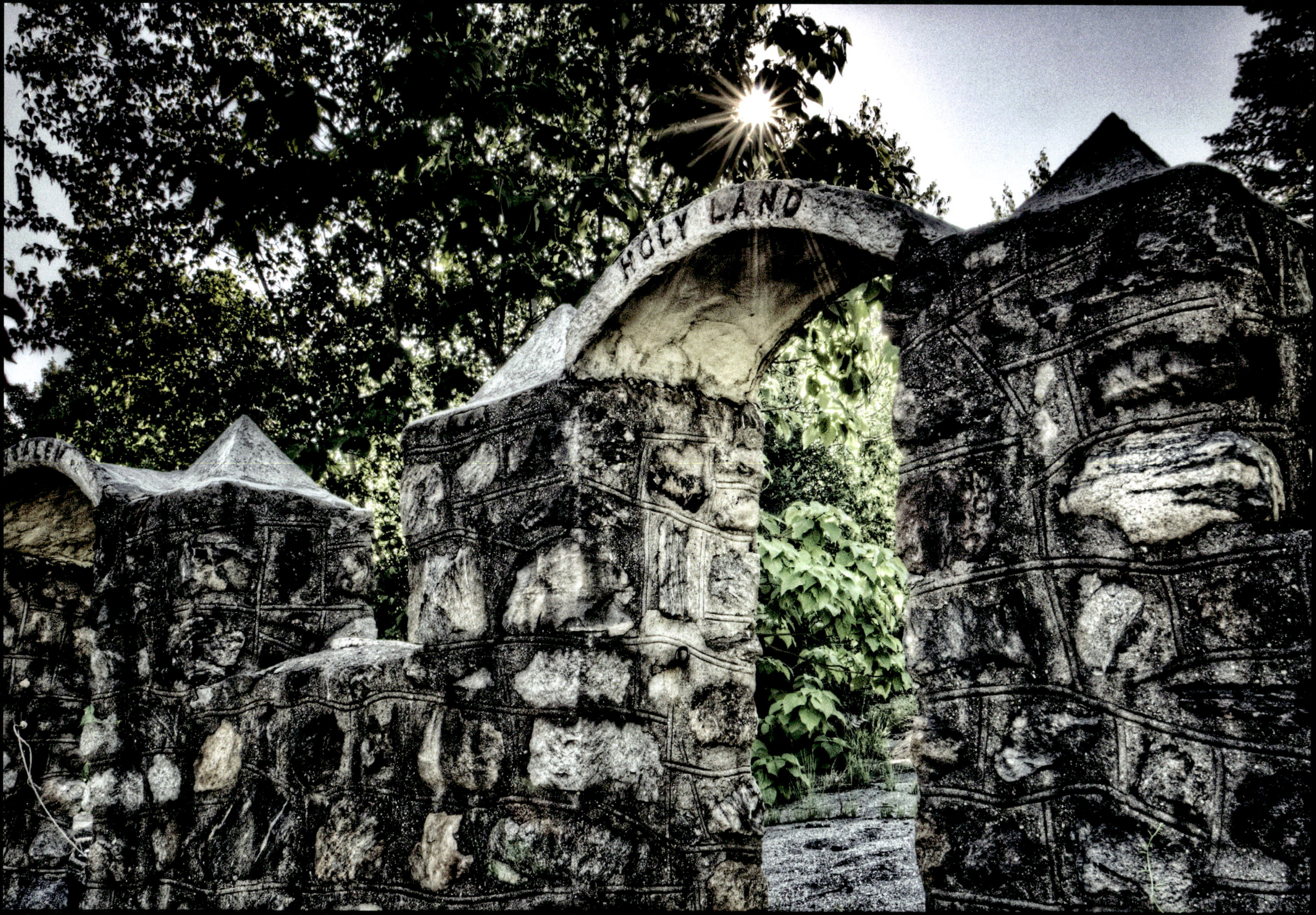

WELCOME TO HOLYLAND

The Entrance to Holyland, Waterbury, CT

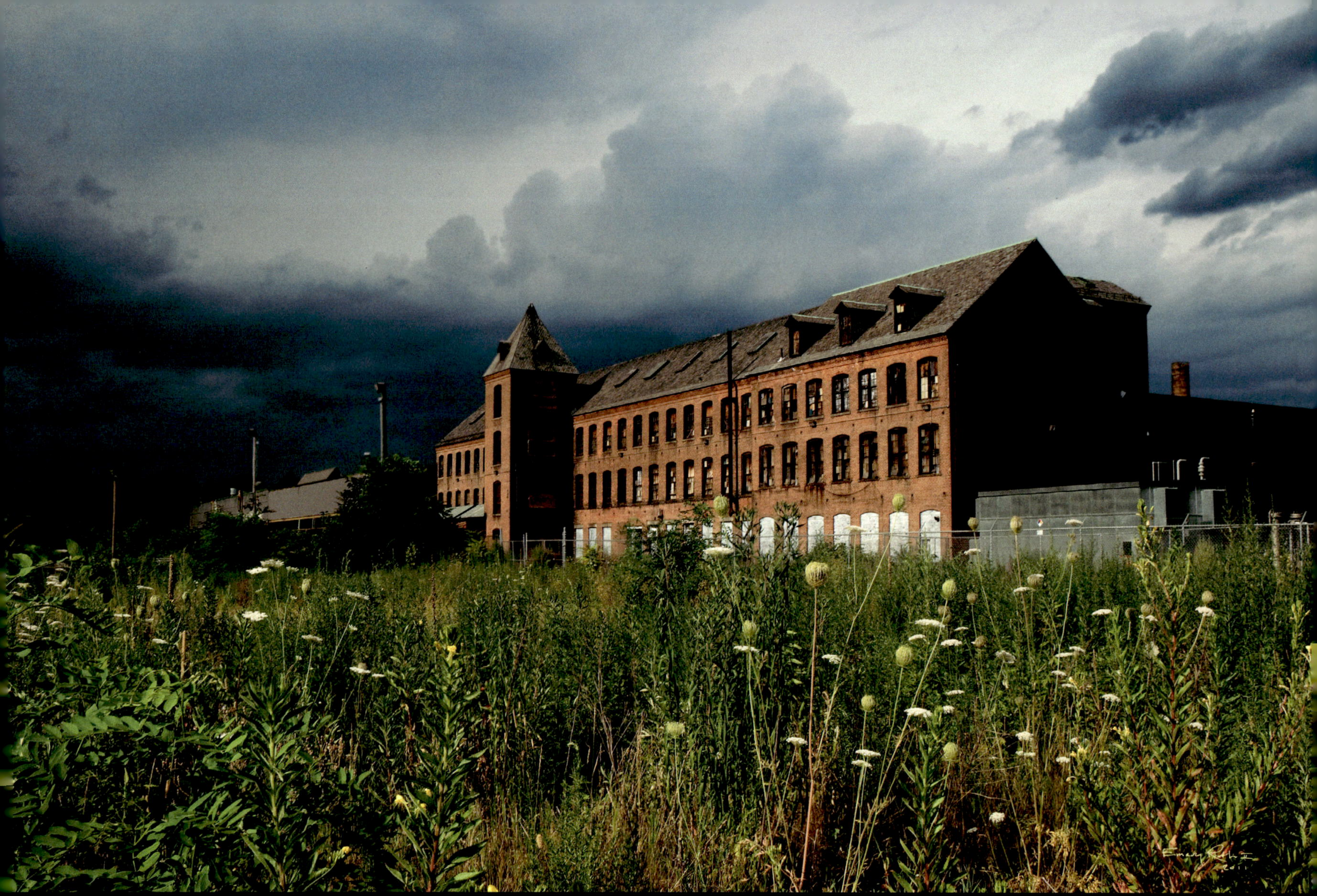

PART FOUR:

FAUST'S DRAGONS

Spinning and squirting Victorian brass in Waterbury

ROLLING MILL PLAYGROUND

Holmes, Booth & Haydens Lampworks, late American Brass, Bank Street, Waterbury, CT

HOTOGRAPHER'S JOURNAL:

hey call it, "Rolling Mill Playground" on Google naps and label it as "Public Parkland" that must be rotected. Someone must have a good sense of humor. 'm back on the west side of the Naugatuck. This is where John will deliver the freshly minted billets rom Ansonia. He'll drive his truck around back, past ne rolling chain-link gate, and into the World War I hed with the sawtooth roof, where Ansonia Copper & Brass keeps the old American Brass extruder queezing out new brass tube.

Democracy may demand a Brooklyn. They tell me nat before the Route 8 freight corridor slammed nrough here, the land beside Rolling Mill Playground was part of Waterbury's Brooklyn. Irish, Lithuanians, talians, Russians, Poles, and Jews all lived nearby. They still talk about the mix of spices gathered by ne winds along Bank Street and rising up the hillside rom back alleys and along the streets where the men nixed on their way to work in the mills. The playground was part of the factory then, and Brooklyn was a elf-sufficient community with five grammar schools, ight bakeries, twenty-two taverns, and churches with ervices in a variety of languages. People walked or rollied directly down Bank Street to the Waterbury green and dreamt that their kids would follow the rolley across the tracks and on up Willow Street and own one of the fine new houses on Cracker Hill or ater, in the twentieth century, in Overlook; that was where a middle class was ripening. Brooklyn was ardest hit by the flood, and the highway came through o fast it narrowly missed St. Pat's. Rows of triple-deckers and six-family blocks were gone, and a wasteland of concrete was erected, with multiple evels of roadway and dark underpasses, between what remained of Brooklyn and the rest of Waterbury.

spotted this angle across Rolling Mill Playground oward the old Holmes, Booth & Haydens lamp actory while walking along Washington Street where thickening for a photo op, but I was on the wrong side of a chain-link fence, trying to shoot between the links. Washington Street today is a cheerless, crumbling transverse funneling cars and pedestrians toward a gap through dark underpasses beneath the north-south infrastructure of highways and partially abandoned train lines. Determined pedestrians use it, though in places the sidewalks give out, and pedestrians must follow the highway's gutter. It is the only place where people in the South End and in Brooklyn can cross for a visit. I have learned to appreciate their trek. Getting to the playground from where I stood on the wrong side of the fence was a long way around, though only a few feet away. The way led me beneath bridges and beside fast-moving roadways.

The "playground" is in back of a lighting and building supply store, not that there's anything there with which to play, and you must pass through the retailer's chain-link gate to get in. Inside, the ground appears a mix of rubble and sand, but it's struggling to be meadow anyhow. It was late, and I was probably invisible through the boscage. Nobody goes there. As I photographed Rolling Mill Playground and the old Holmes, Booth & Haydens building in the dark storm light, the store owner came out to lock his gate. A moment more and I would have been in the playground for the night and unable to follow John and his load of billets through into the busy brass mill where, around the clock, billets are processed into seamless tube.

I first saw the name "Rolling Mill Playground" on plans of the mill from 1957. By then the Great Flood had devastated the area, and planners were already at work designing the six-lane, elevated Route 8 that would pass by the "playground." Amazingly, more than a half-century later the mill is still churning out tube, and still nobody plays at the protected "playground" where meadow bravely blooms under

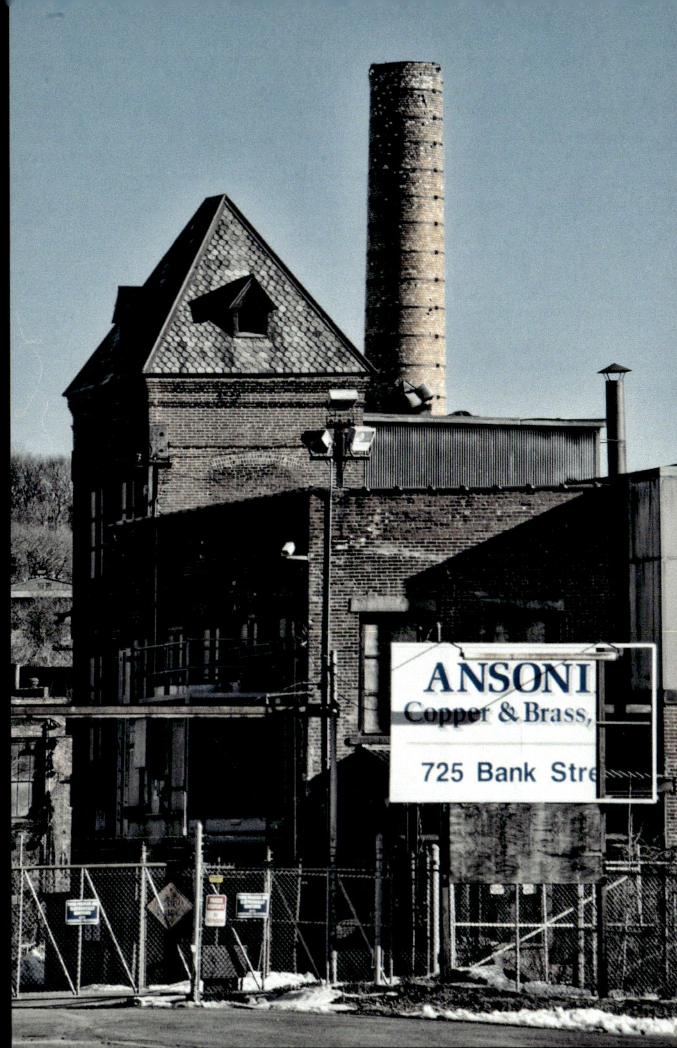

ANSONI
North Wall, American Brass extrusion tube mill, Bank Street, Waterbury, CT

PHOTOGRAPHER'S JOURNAL:
Inside the shed with the sawtooth roof, billets fly through the air, though it's anything but easy. Billets have mass and minds of their own. Carlos estimates each weighs two or three tons, and several hang balanced beneath his crane on a narrow base of straps. He has learned to move evenly and to guide their bulk the way a captain moves a ponderous ship. There's magic in such touch, and there's a dreamlike quality to life here, as if everything moves in gravitational harmony to Carlos and his billets.

I watch Carlos guiding the suspended mass toward Dave's saw bench with concentrated steps. It looks a little like sleepwalking, but his eyes are wide open, looking one way, watching another, as he choreographs his path toward Dave's saw bench accompanied by the shop's familiar, measureless hum and the cadenced drone and lazy moan of a soloist in the northeast corner of the shed; together, theirs is an incongruous largo, dignified and eerie.

When I first visited here I mistook it for a dirge, and I'm still hoping I was wrong. Fraught tranquility! Did it feel that way in the days when four times as many men worked here?

Dave has just measured off the first block from a new billet. He will wait while his saw cuts off the rough end. Sometimes he reads from his newspaper while the saw saws. After the end is smooth, he can stamp the number, advance the billet to his mark, and start the saw cutting again. A pyramid of sawed, numbered blocks waits for Carlos or Dave or Fred or Dennis to move them along to Fred's lathe. Fred is waiting while his lathe bores a hole through one of Dave's blocks, end to end. It is a precision process, and further on Dennis waits while his lathe turns and peels the outside of Fred's bored block evenly so that the hole is centered, and the diameter of the block true to one-hundredth of an inch. Beside each machine are pyramids of blocks, some waiting to be milled, some to be moved, like dancers in a dream, to the shop's largo.

Fred, Dennis, and all who follow will record into grimy computers the numbers Dave has stamped on the blocks. It is a tiny concession to technological progress. Finished, each block weighs about 300 pounds, and when Carlos moves them next, it will be in a bundle of a half-dozen or so hanging from straps. Each block will wear its number until the heater man records the number for the last time before extrusion.

The men keep the line of blocks moving, gather the filings, and keep machines precision-tuned as they monitor the progress of the blocks.

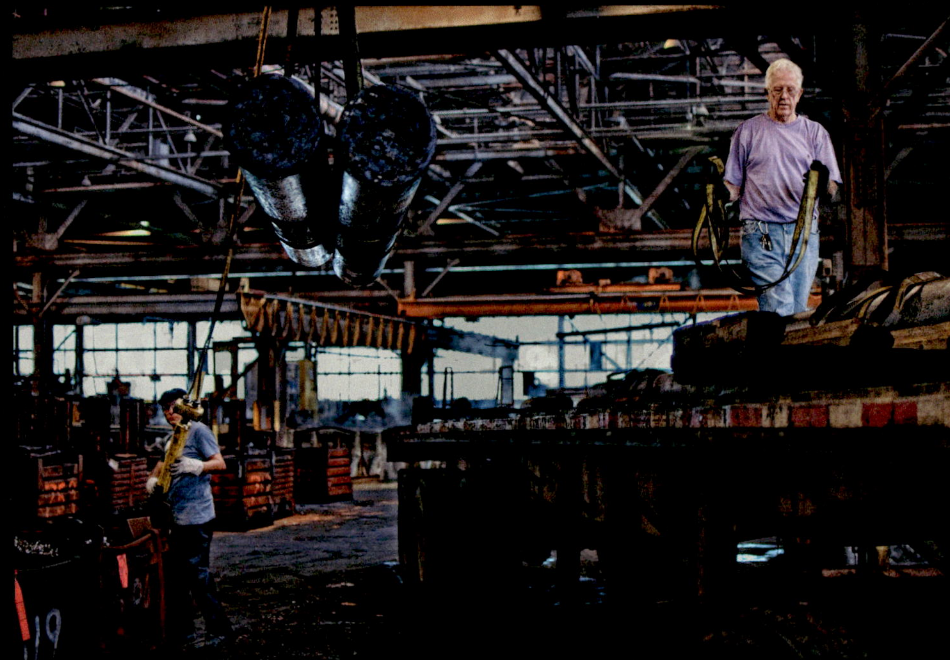

UNLOADING BILLETS

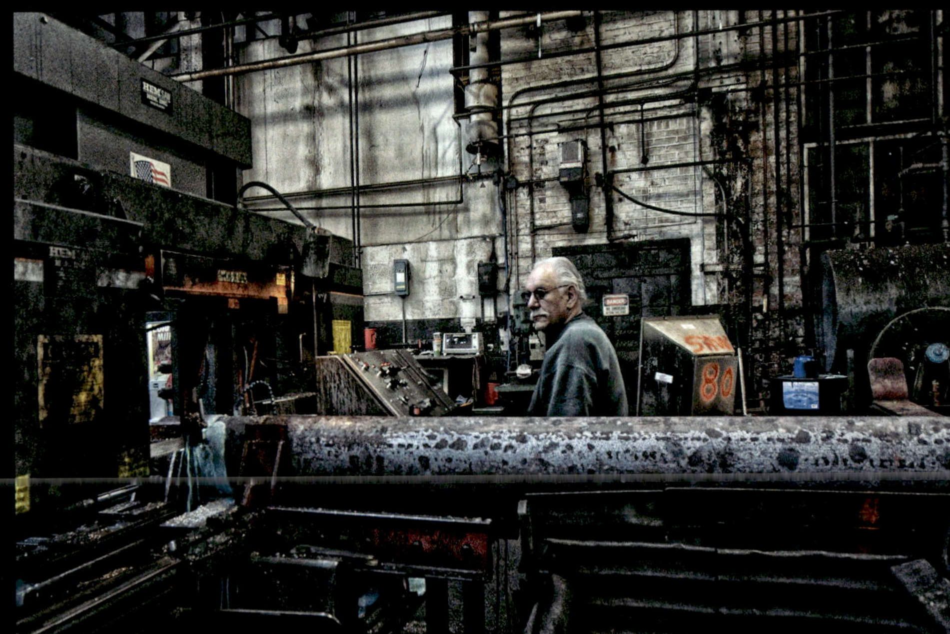

BILLETS TO BLOCKS NO. 1

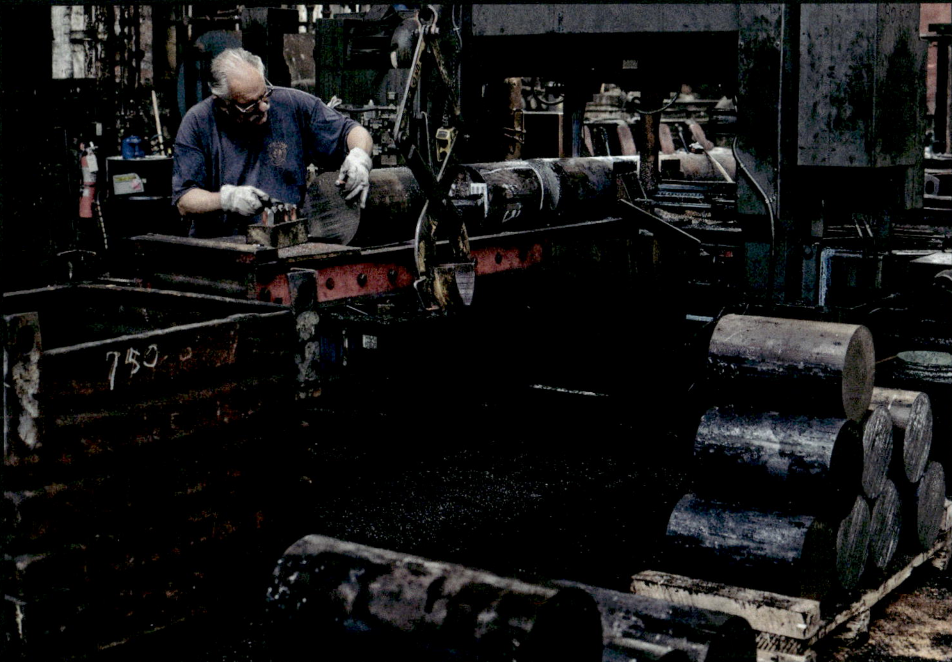

BILLETS TO BLOCKS NO. 2

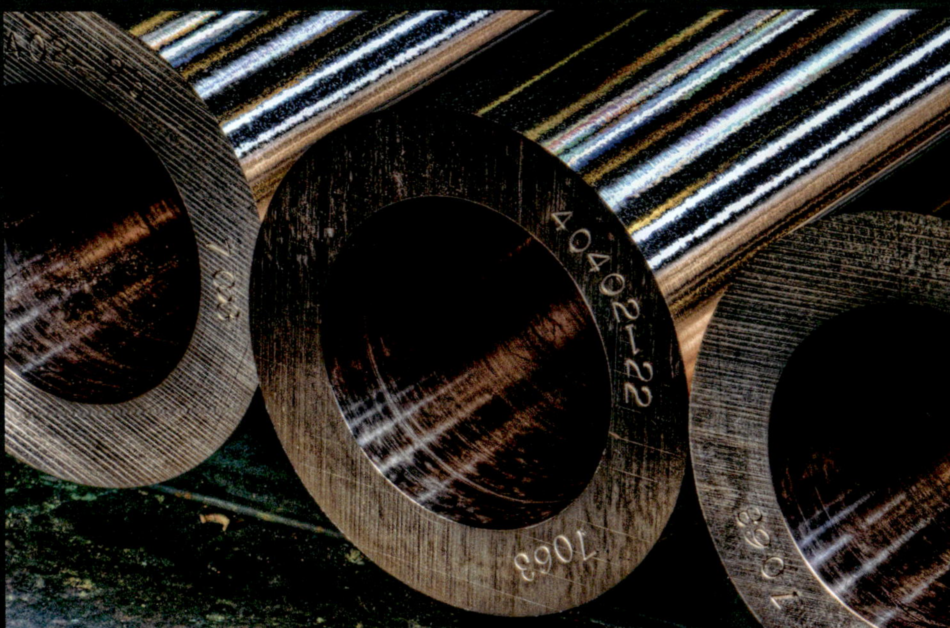

TOUCH IT

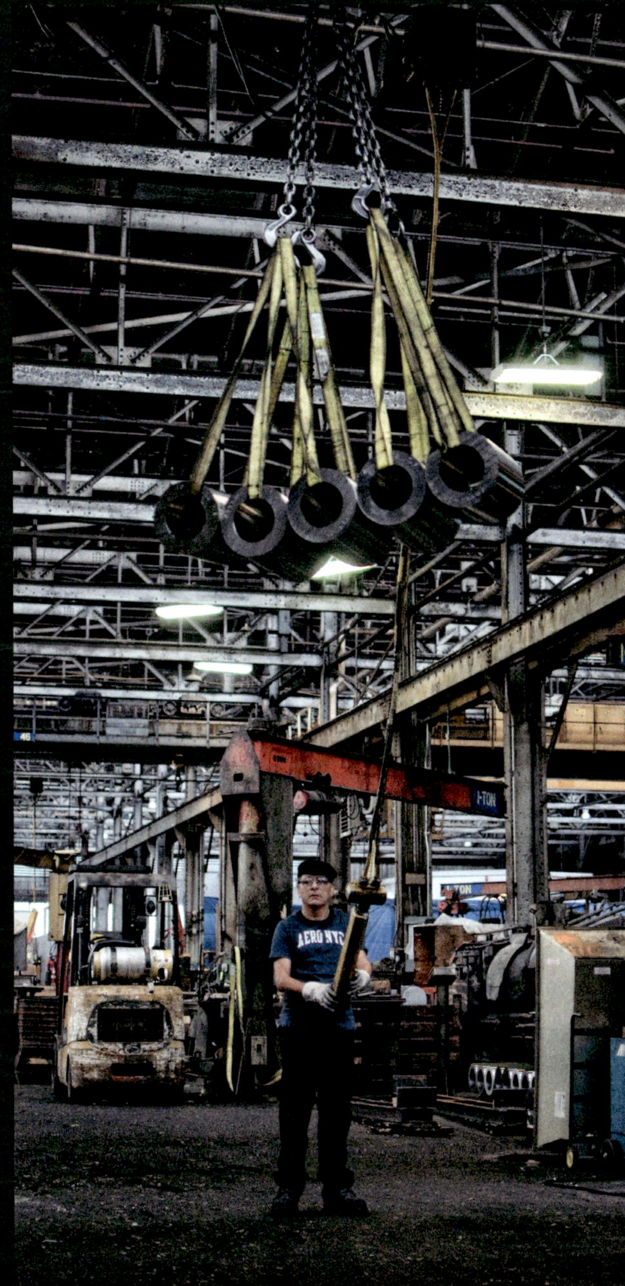

BRASS BALLOONS

Extrusion mill, American Brass, Bank Street, Waterbury, CT (all images)

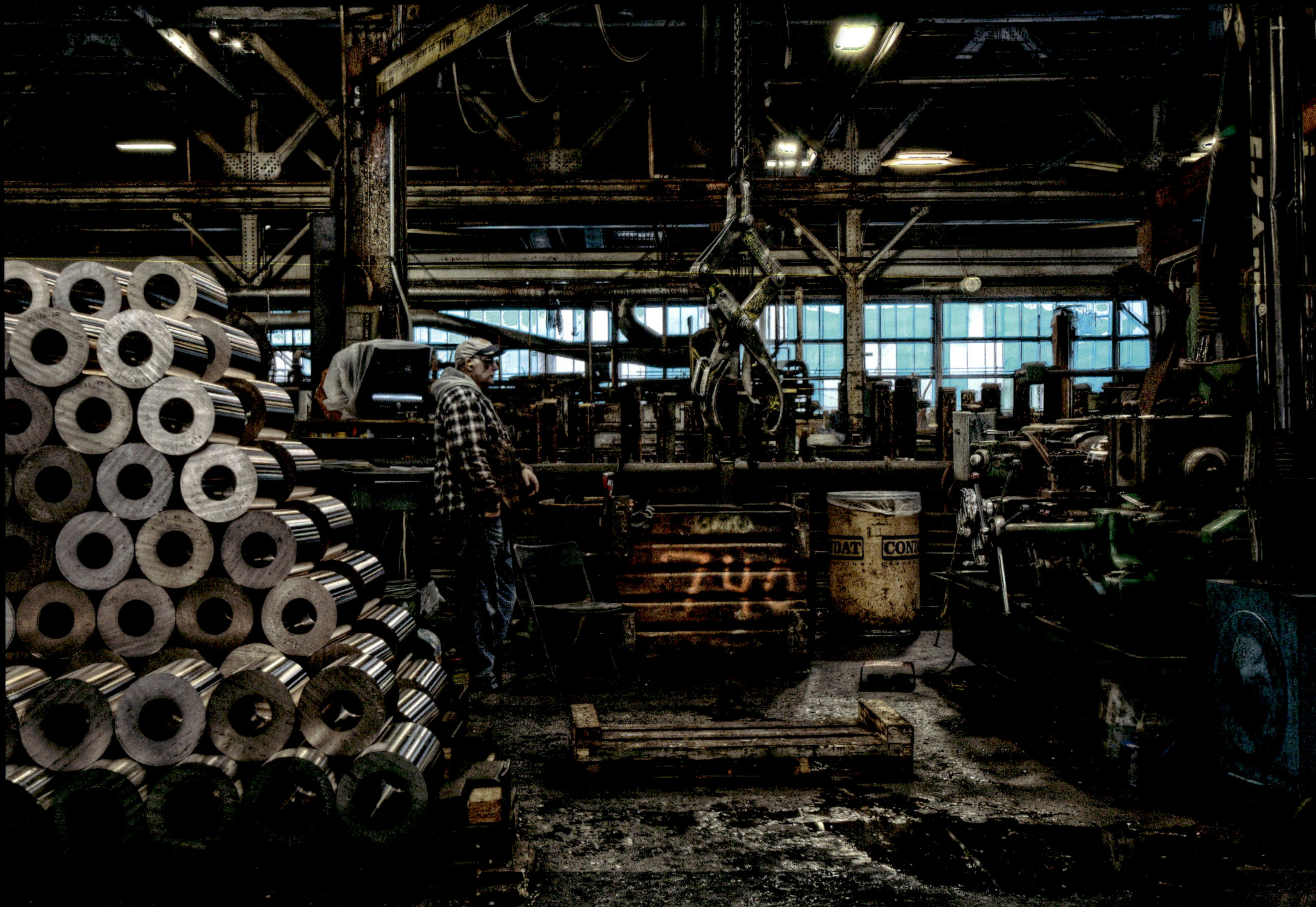

LATHE-ING

Extrusion mill, American Brass, Waterbury, CT

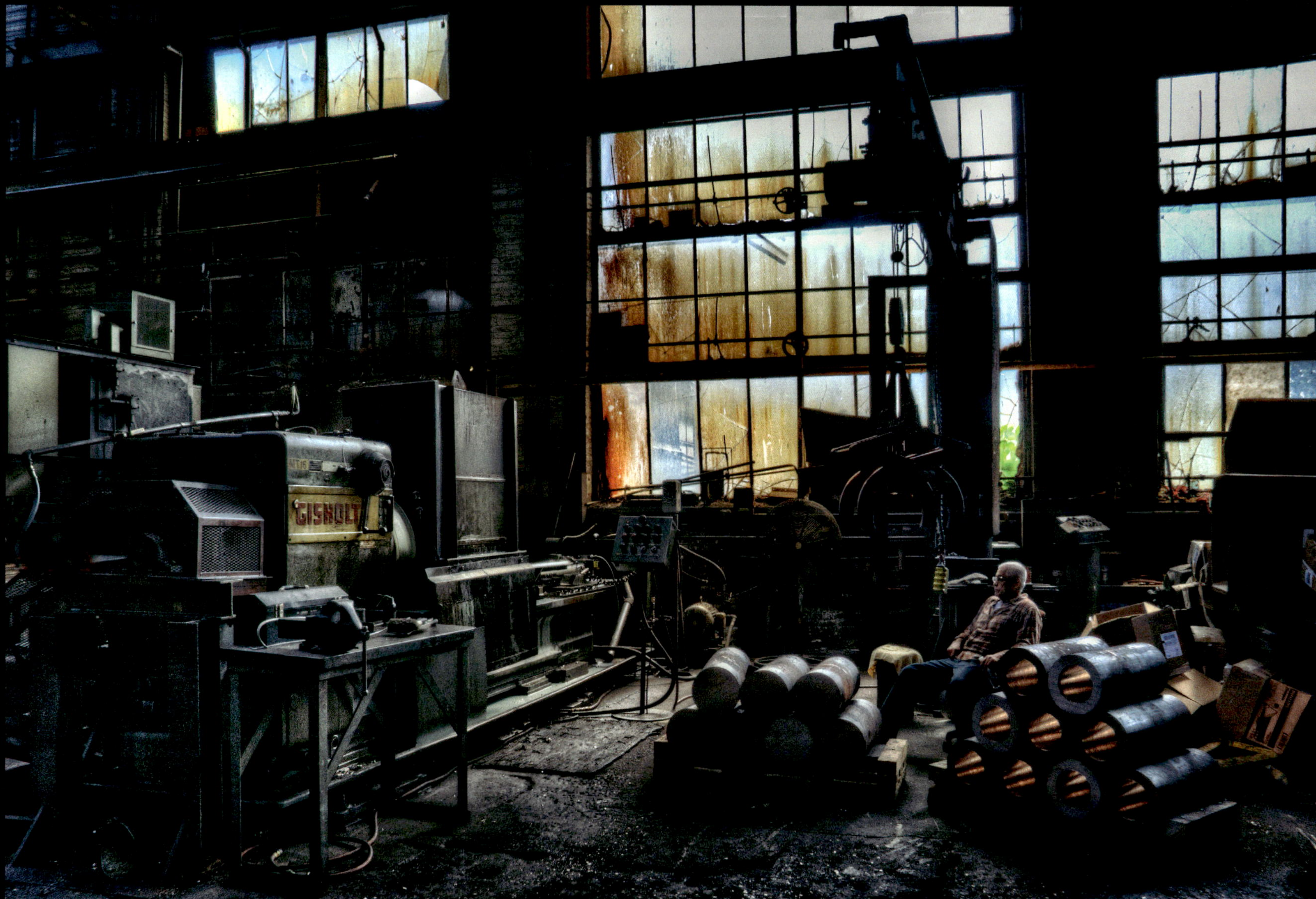

BORE-ING

Extrusion mill, American Brass, Waterbury, CT

"Although primarily a World War I structure with equipment probably installed after 1930, the Ansonia Copper & Brass plant retains the scale of an integrated 19th-century brass mill better than most other extant plants in the Naugatuck Valley, and has part of the original plant's c. 1853 casting house/foundry and c. 1880–1886 factories for lamp-burner manufacture. The c. 1917 components are also well-preserved examples of the steel-framed, sawtooth-roofed mills erected quickly to meet World War I demands."

—Raber & Associates' engineering report on Ansonia Copper & Brass, Inc., plant, Waterbury, Connecticut, December 2007

"WE BECOME WHAT WE BEHOLD. WE SHAPE OUR TOOLS. AND THEN OUR TOOLS SHAPE US." —Marshall McLuhan, *Understanding Media*, 1964

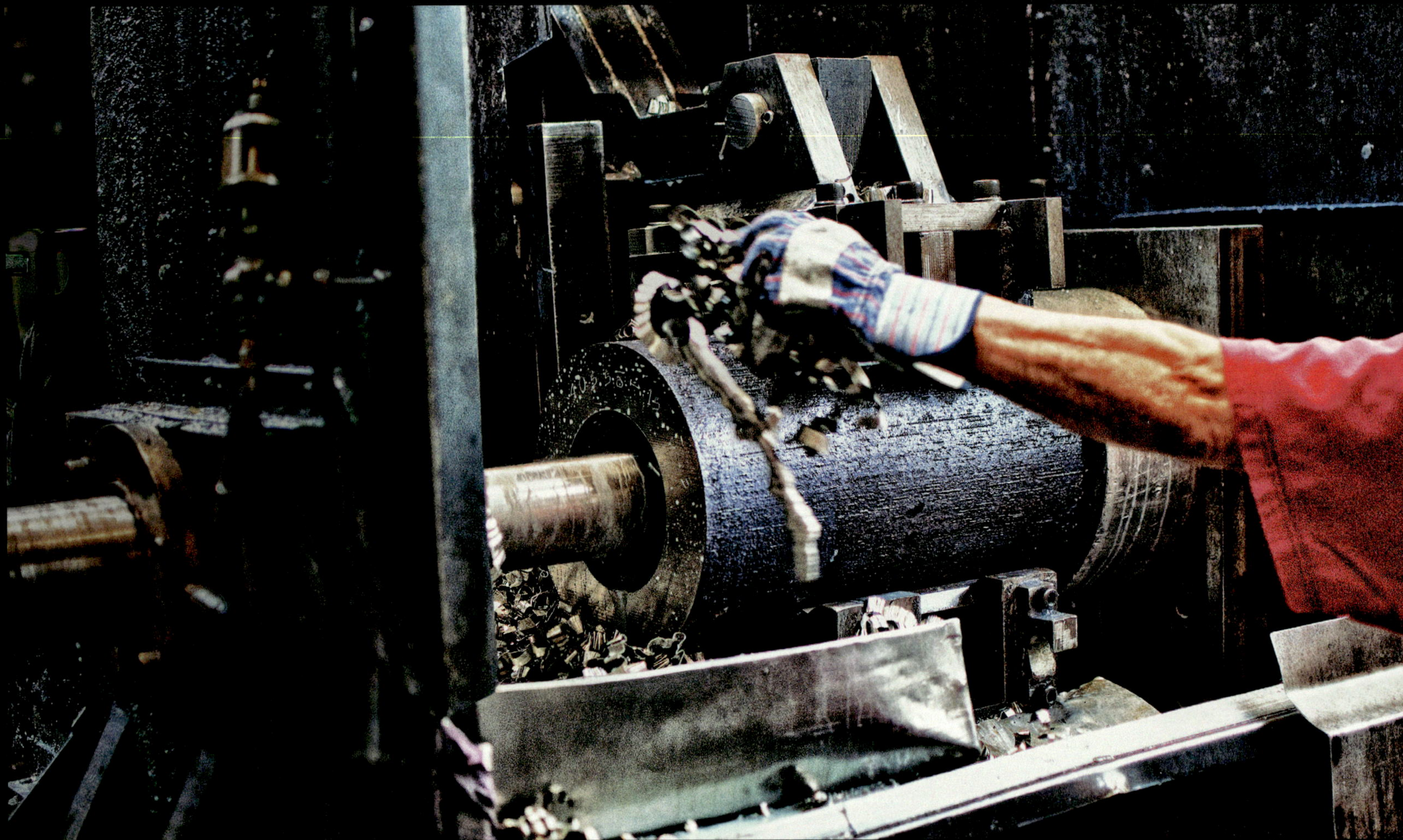

SCRAP
Extrusion mill,
American Brass,
Waterbury, CT

PHOTOGRAPHER'S JOURNAL:
I've been thinking about the meaning of, "hand-made," and the utility of the thumb which came to us by way of the trees and gave us tools and fire and the brains to use them and so brought us here to the wonders of nineteeth- century tool making capped by twentieth-century button making that allows the thumb some leisure while the index finger alone stops the boring when the hole is complete. Strike that—now the drill is programmed to stop automatically; no index finger needed. The lathe's open door reveals a nest of brass shavings, a feast for the gloved hand. The lathe's spin makes shavings drop like nickels and dimes until they fill scrap hampers on their way back to Ansonia to be recast, and the flow of brass continues, while thumbs and index fingers everywhere are moving on to iPads and dissolving as digits twinkling in cyberspace.

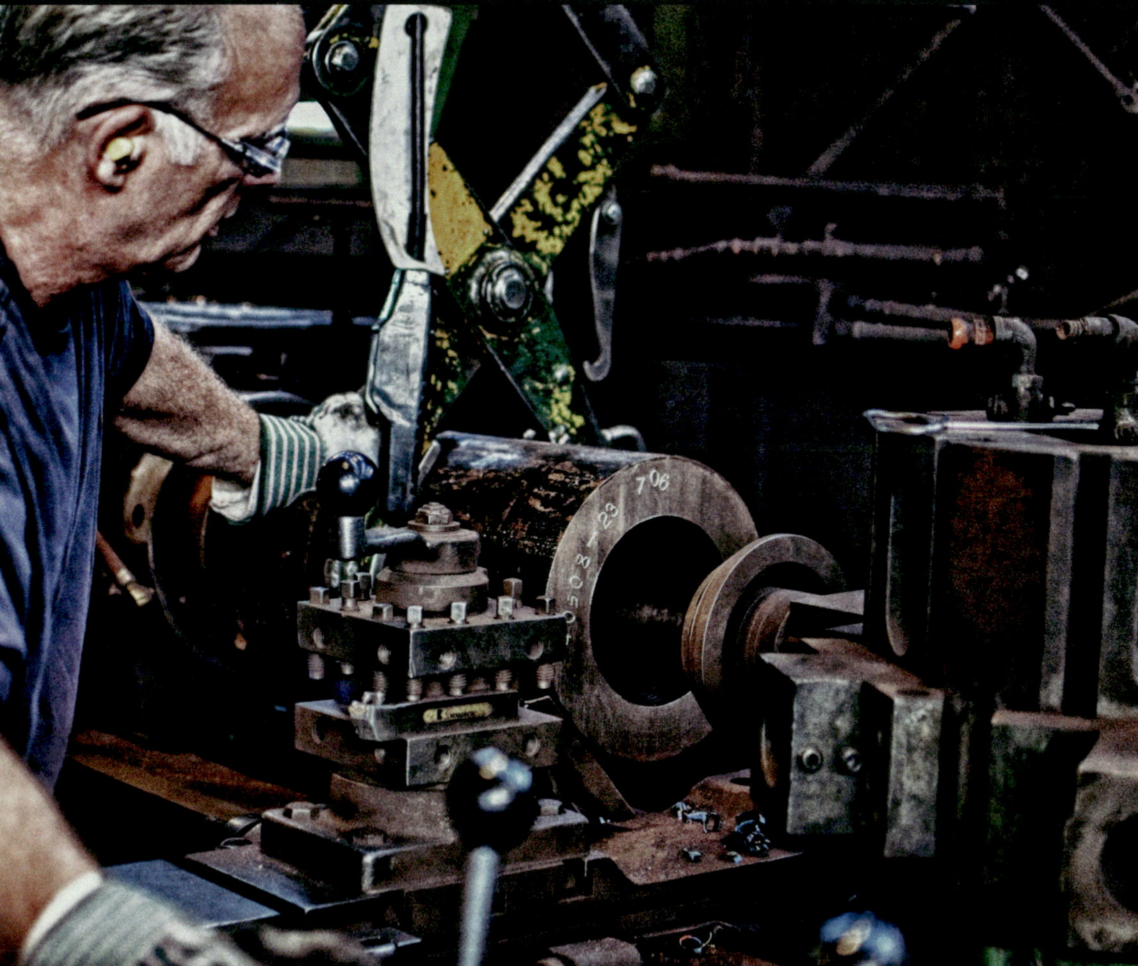

LATHED

Extrusion mill, American Brass, Waterbury, CT

PHOTOGRAPHER'S JOURNAL:

Lathes and drill presses, like potters' wheels and compasses and gyroscopes, and the music that used to gyrate from phonographs and hip-swinging Hula Hoops, and that carnival game where kids paint on whirling plates—all partake in the magic of spin. Spin has the feel of life. The wheel is only a circle until you feel the forces spiraling out, rotating, translating, revolving into corkscrew sprays of centrifugal blossoms. DNA, I'd like to think, is the way galaxies spin into our marrow.

When I was a kid, of all the tools in our high-school shop, it was the lathes that received the most respect, and each of us looked forward to a turn at making something on one. Until we got to the lathes, shop was square. I can still feel the jolt of that spinning, the current of vibration, while steadying my chisel on the fixed ledge and my eye on the spinning block; and then I drew a smooth curve that instantly sprung into three dimensional space. It was the exquisite physics of circular motion that turned boxy wood into fluid shapes, sent pedestal trays and bowls home to mom and dad, and occasionally sent shards of bowl and classmates flying across the shop. There's alchemy in spin.

Dennis centers the 300 pound block around the hole and positions the cutting blade. He must be precise. When he starts the block spinning, the blade will move steadily, evenly, automatically along the surface of the spinning mass, peeling away excess brass and leaving a perfect cylinder, shiny, smooth, and precisely centered.

Dennis enjoys the precision of his work and knows the lathe behind him is a better match to his task, but there is no money to repair it; he says little but there's frustration in his eyes. He hates waste as much as he likes precision. When the drilled and lathed block meets specifications, it is ready for transmutation and the extruder's crush.

OUR STORIES:

Hiram Hayden and the Spinning Kettles

Touch it. Freshly lathed and drilled blocks are irresistible. Run your hands over the crisp edges and across the smooth, gently rippling surfaces. That's what we all do the first time. Rap one with your knuckle to hear its density; try to roll it to feel its mass. It's always more massive than we expect. But the brassmen who formed Holmes, Booth & Haydens had a deeper understanding of their metals. They knew brass, even cold, heavy brass, was made of crystals and flowed like liquid when squeezed, but that squeezing deformed the crystal lattice. Their understanding of how to affect changes they couldn't see allowed them to make simple things better, cheaper, faster.

Hiram W. Hayden was an inventive genius and held more patents for manufacturing processes than anyone else in the industry—patents for machines and processes and, because he was an artist as well, decorative motifs. On December 16, 1851, he received his first patent revolutionizing one of life's most ubiquitous essentials, the common, copper kettle. The traditional way of manufacturing a copper kettle was on a machine that stamped a disk of metal between a succession of dies, gradually stretching the bottom and compressing the sides up and in, until the final set of dies stamped the kettle into kettle shape. It was called "the battery method," perhaps because of its assault on one's eardrums.

As Hayden explained in his patent renewal, the battery method is always trying to knock the bottom off the pot, damaging the metal and making it thin at the bottom where it needs to be thick, and thick at the top where it should be thin. The metal is pounded and damaged at precisely the points where daily use will give it greatest stress.

Hiram Hayden's patent calls for spinning a disk of copper and a succession of forms together on a lathe-like machine while an appropriate tool gradually presses the metal and draws it into the desired kettle shape. This method reduces the number of steps in the kettle-making process and the number of times the metal must be heat-annealed to relax the crystals between tooling, and it produces a kettle thick at the bottom where it takes punishment and thin at the top where it should be light. The metal is not abused while being processed, and the resulting kettle is better, cheaper, and more durable. Hiram Hayden understood the fluid nature of his metals, the value of spin, and how to engineer a machine that would take advantage of these, and he sold his patent to Aaron Benedict and the Waterbury Brass Company, and it revolutionized the industry.

Hiram Hayden held many patents, including patents for a breach-loading rifle, a magazine rifle, and machines for making seamless, brass tubing. He held one of three patents for daguerreotypes, and Holmes, Booth & Haydens and Scovill Manufacturing Company were the only US manufacturers of the popular, silvered, copper photographic plates on which daguerreotype images magically appear.

When in 1851 Hayden became the first person to successfully make such an image appear on treated paper, it was big news, and we read about it in the *Waterbury Republican*, though the newspaper had no way to reproduce the three landscape images Hayden had created. We hardly realized then how important his invention would be in the Civil War, when we carried and left behind precious paper images of faces we would never see again. Holmes, Booth & Haydens were among the first to manufacture cameras, lenses, and other photographic equipment, with precision, brass parts of course; Hiram Hayden showed us how we could make things from light, air, a bit of paper—from almost nothing.

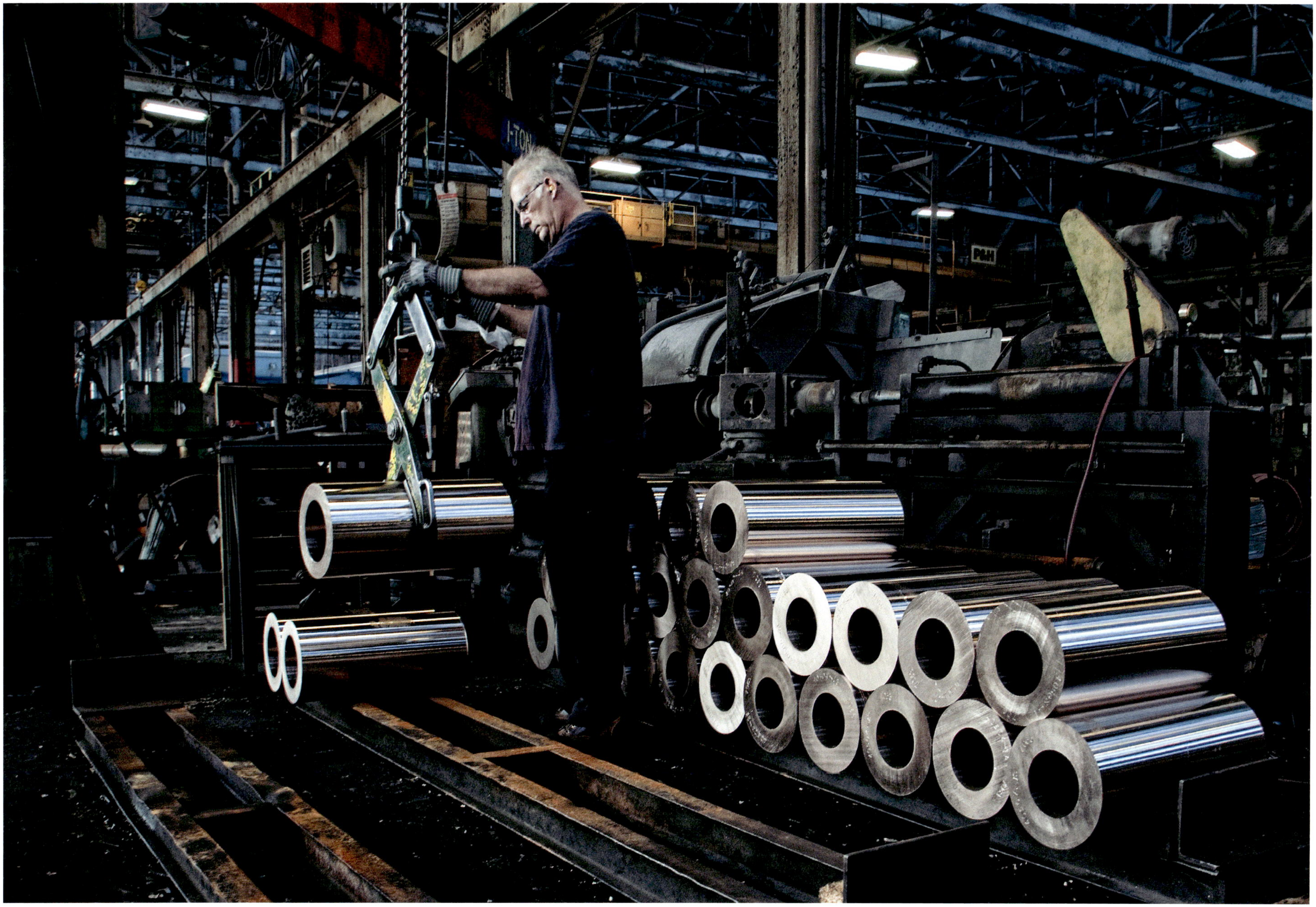

STACKING

Extrusion mill, American Brass, Waterbury, CT

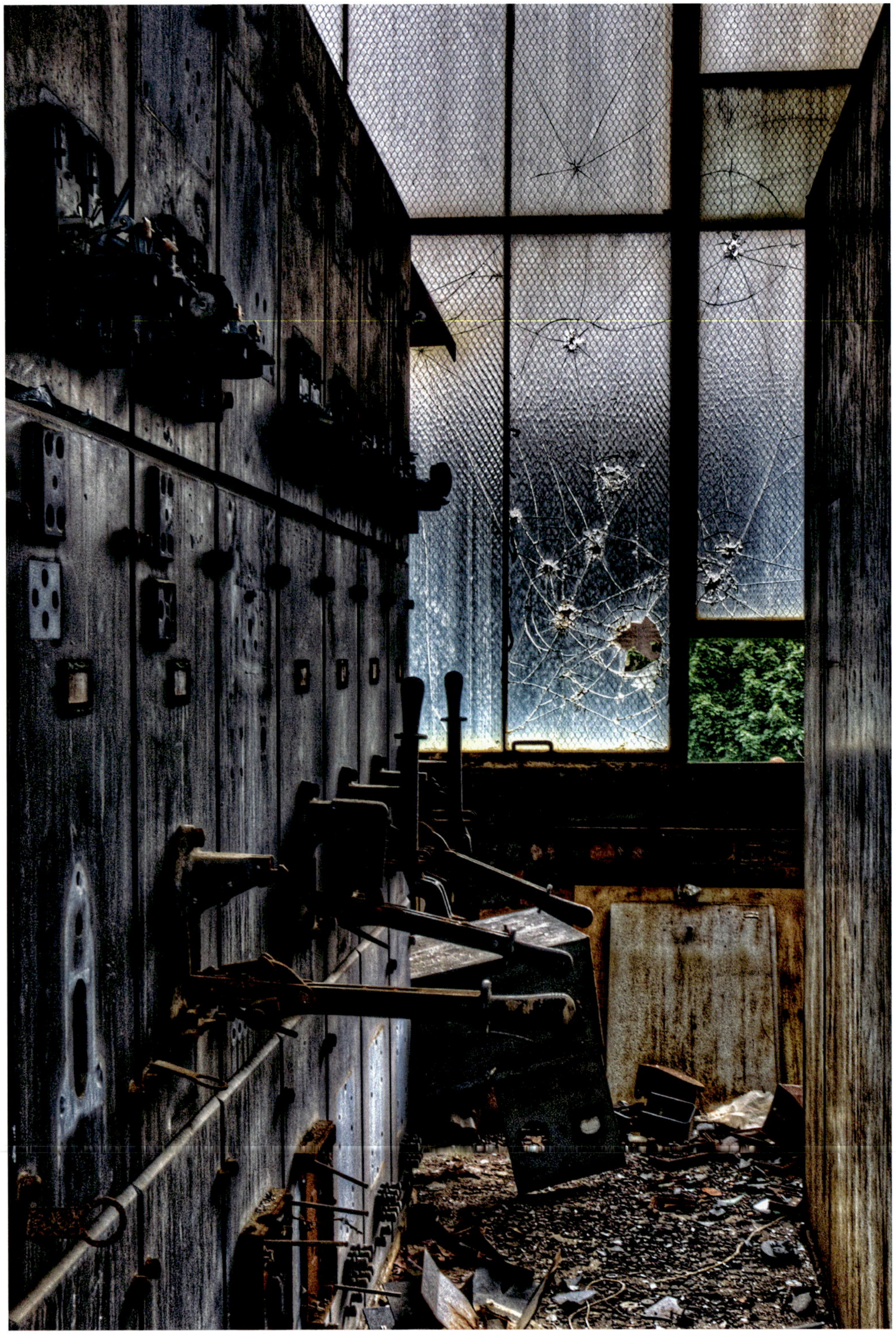

The Smithsonian Institution

In the Smithsonian Institution in Washington, DC, were prototype models of many of the machines and systems that drove industry in America. There were thousands of them, made to accompany patent filings. They stretched back to 1790 when the US patent law began requiring working models to demonstrate patent rights. Never before had a government sought to honor its genius in this manner. In 1840, the US Patent Office took up residence in a building that Walt Whitman, our poet, proclaimed as "the noblest of Washington buildings."

People who could take the train to DC would always talk about the models, looking like expensive toys, but they actually ran. Some were the seeds of commercial empires, and others were pipe dreams. By 1869, nine-foot-high glass cases at the Patent Office held more than 200,000 working patent models, as the collection grew to contain everything from artificial limbs to dancing dolls, from hoop skirts and a velocipede, to the first washing machine. They made the eyes of our children sparkle with delight. Sadly, after 1880 much of the collection was seen as a national nuisance and dispersed.

Although the models were legal documents, many had about them the pride and passion of the tinkerer. Arrayed in oak and glass cases in the old museum, the models took on hallowed significance. Those that earned fortunes, those that made life better, and others whose time never came were often indistinguishable on the shelves. All were vestiges of a culture of milling and tool making and were embodiments of its thought—some would say of the progressive spirit in our DNA. It was an unprecedented effervescence of genius, and the current of Brass Valley flowed vigorously in those glass cases, but it was here at the mill where we met and worked that most of it was cultured, flowered, and flourished.

UNPLUGGED

Powerhouse, American Brass (Benedict & Burnham), Benedict Street, Waterbury, CT

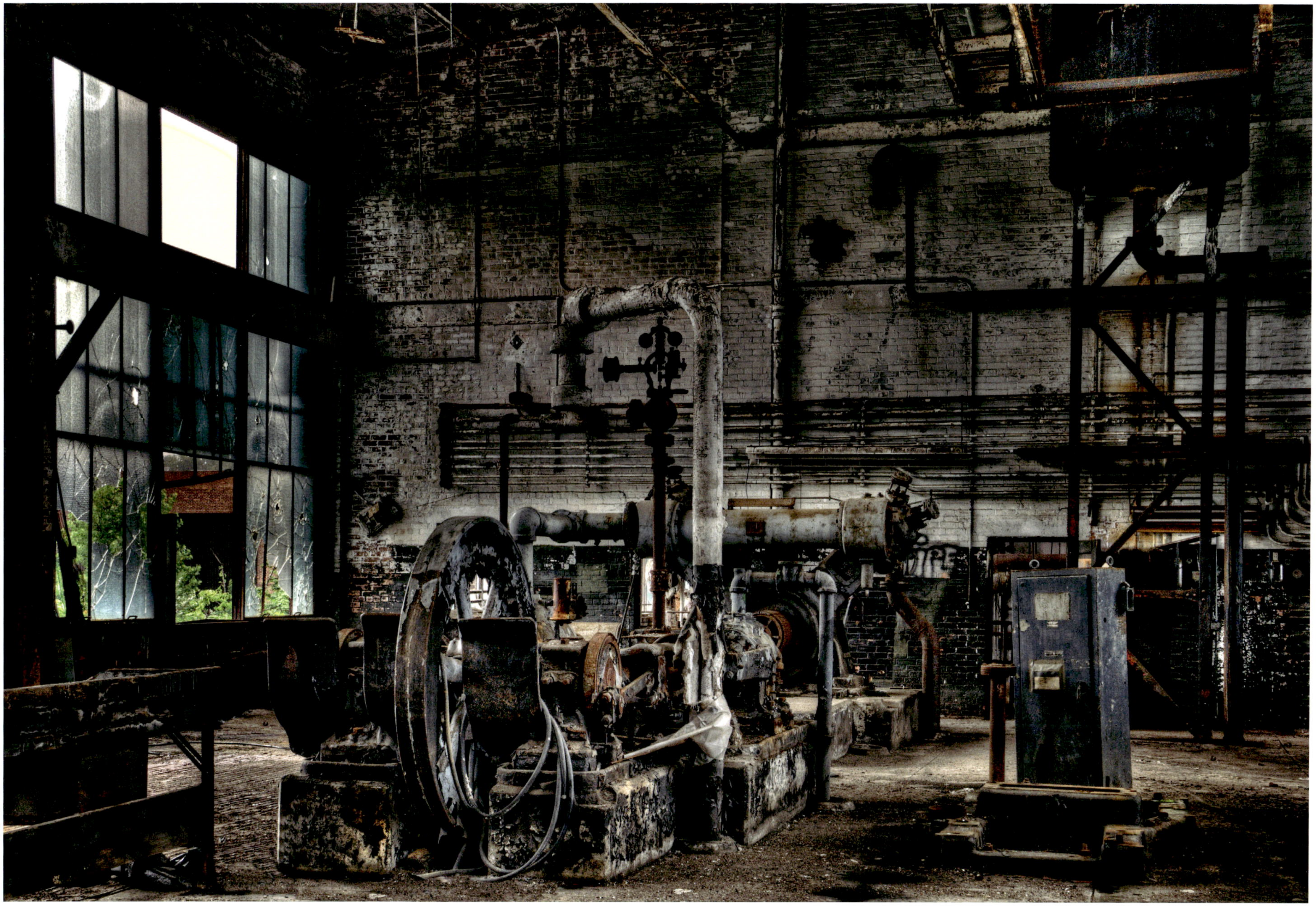

UNSPUN
Powerhouse, American Brass (Benedict & Burnham,
Benedict Street, Waterbury, CT

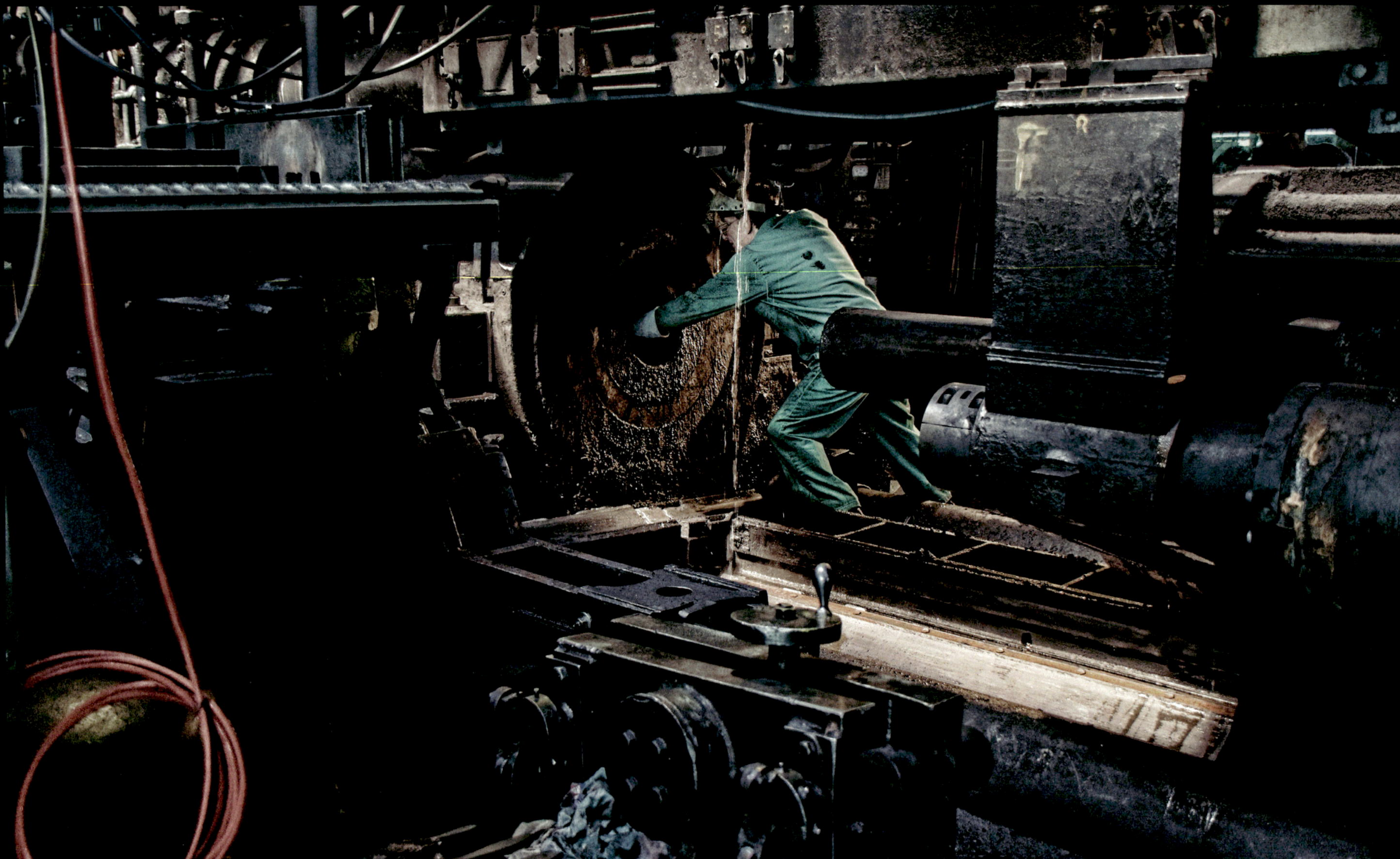

PINTO GREASING THE BIG SQUIRT

Under the extruder, American Brass, Waterbury

PHOTOGRAPHER'S JOURNAL:
In the 1820s extrusion, a new technology, was called squirting. There's a distinct mewling and whining when the extruder begins to squirt. It rises over all other choruses; the extruder requires five men to make it run.

The conveyor system that feeds blocks to the extruder begins at four ovens. On its way from oven to extrusion, each block is carried on track through interchanges and over bridges; they are engineering fantasies, and there must have been some fun when the engineers and machinists got it all working. My Lionels never carried glowing hot metal. The orange blocks ride on a metal tread, at right turns they become 300-pound hot wheels rolling to the next conveyor and advancing again. On the way to the extruder the hot block is first lowered and then raised and turned on elevators until it is finally positioned between the extruder's maw, commonly "called the container," and its giant "ram." The ram is powered by fifty feet of hydraulics that make a throbbing, sad, metallic moan as they squeeze, like a message from eternity.

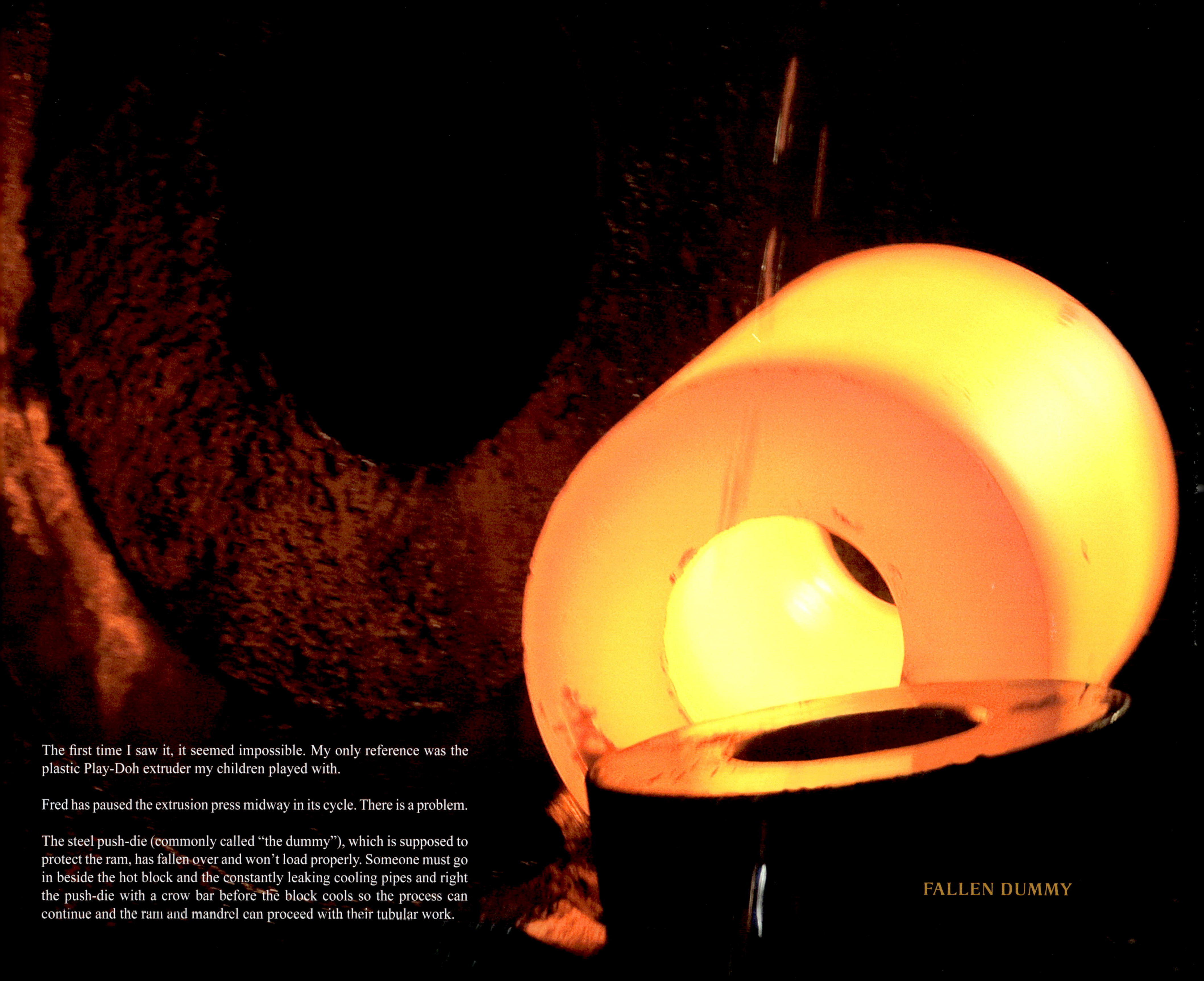

FALLEN DUMMY

The first time I saw it, it seemed impossible. My only reference was the plastic Play-Doh extruder my children played with.

Fred has paused the extrusion press midway in its cycle. There is a problem.

The steel push-die (commonly called "the dummy"), which is supposed to protect the ram, has fallen over and won't load properly. Someone must go in beside the hot block and the constantly leaking cooling pipes and right the push-die with a crow bar before the block cools so the process can continue and the ram and mandrel can proceed with their tubular work.

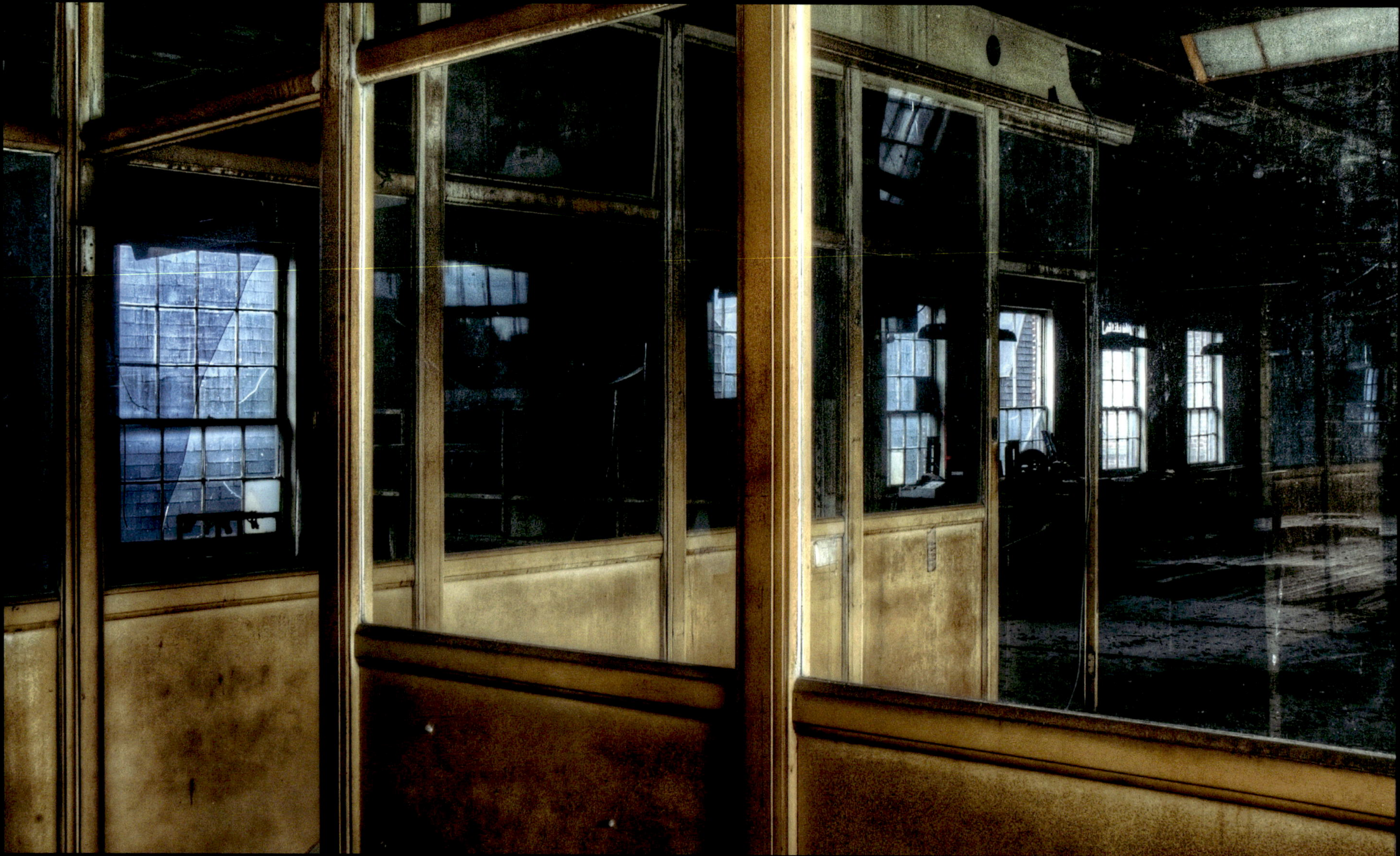

UPSTAIRS

Holmes, Booth & Haydens, Lampworks, Bank Street, Waterbury, CT

PHOTOGRAPHER'S JOURNAL:

In the shed below, the extrusion crew works to right the push-die behind the block, and brass tubes soak in vats of blue acid, and buckets of scrap sail downstream on the hooks of cranes. Everyone there wears ear plugs, but up the dark back stairs to the old, brick Holmes, Booth & Haydens lamp factory, only creaky risers and my shuffling footsteps bestir the quiet.

On the abandoned second floor, the filtered, gray window light is a pall over reality, which lives in the shadows. I strain to hear the source of distant buzzing, perhaps the complaint of an errant electrical circuit, back from the dead. Further up, beyond the broken clock with the crippled fingers, the world is increasingly pigeon haunted. It's best to creep when traversing time. Up there, other than pigeons, there are only drafts, drips, and the creaks of age; then on the third floor, Flash! commotion; the flapping of black wings flying at white light.

It is like crossing to the other side. The windows are high but the light through stained and broken windows is soaked up by dusty walls in

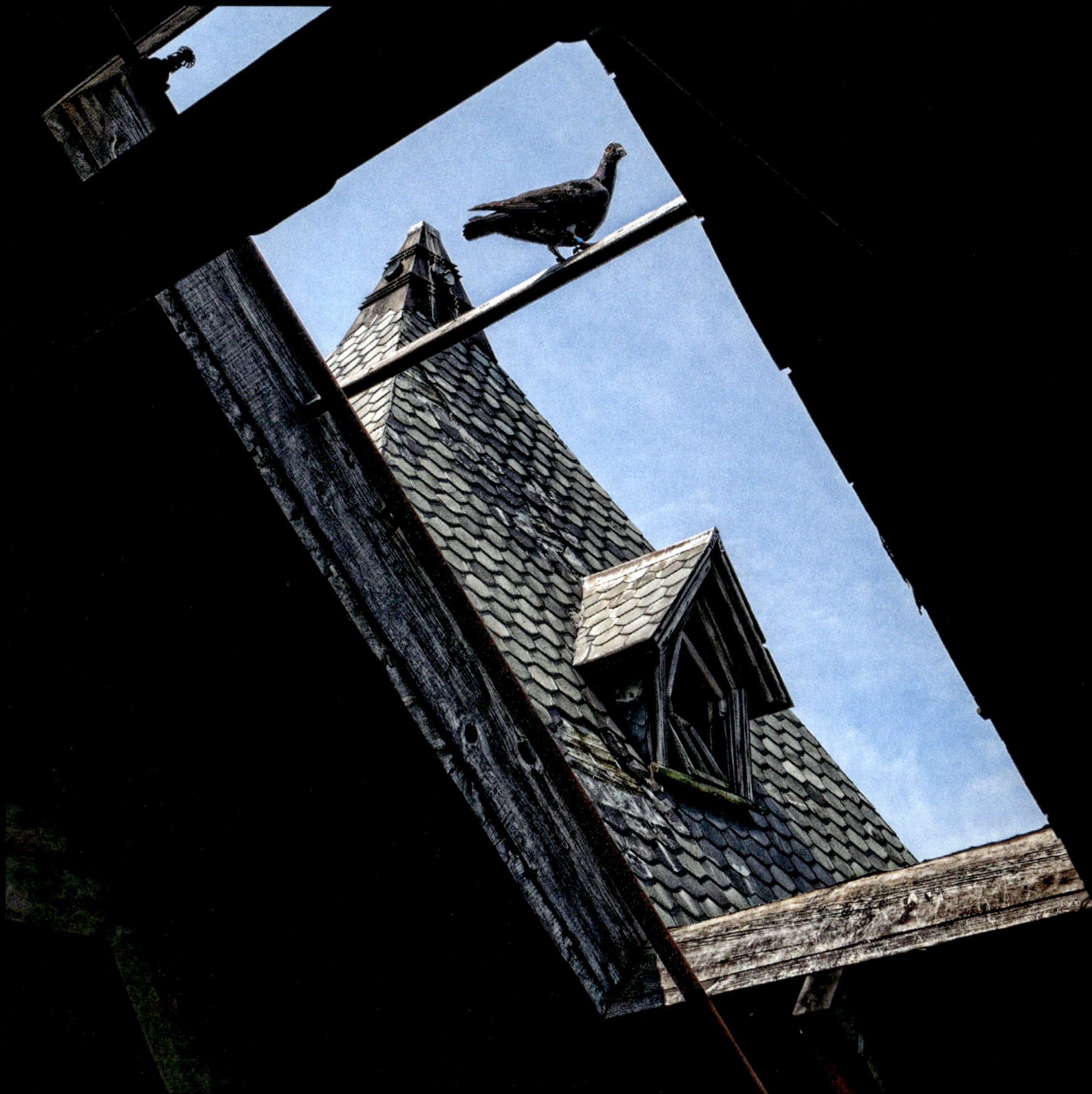

shadowy offices where clerks with fine hands keep accounts for Holmes, Booth & Haydens. Dutifully they enter into ledgers the sales of planished copper-silver photographic plates that will capture the daguerreotype faces of a generation. The clerks' flowing letters also record production and sales of crisp, brass oil burners, whose delicate gears, touched by countless fingertips, control the glow of lamps around the world (Hiram Hayden held more than thirty oil lamp patents). And later, when fine and flowing pens were obsolete, typewriters could spit orders faster and stayed abreast of new products and new demands.

The shadows of clerks flicker in the broken, glass cubicles built in some subsequent reform to achieve new, strategic efficiencies, and you can hear whispers in the rustling of feathers and occasional murmurs, clucks, and coos. A rusted Address-o-graph stands amid a scattered heap of stamped address plates spilled from file drawers and rusting, the forgotten contact list of Anaconda Copper, frosted in pigeon droppings, never to be re-alphabetized. A nervous pigeon watches me from his hiding place beside his empty file drawer as I shoot photographs. He will not come out and pose. I return to the mill. This world belongs to him.

ATTIC PIGEON

Holmes, Booth & Haydens,
Lampworks, Bank Street,
Waterbury, CT

It was the age of steam, hydraulics, oil lamps, and gas street lights. Brass valves, tubes, fittings, gears, cams, and widgets lubricated life, changed us and made brass essential for all our needs. Then, on September 4, 1882, at Mr. Edison's Pearl Street Power Station in lower Manhattan, a switch was thrown that sent a river of direct current flowing over copper wire. It lit 3,000 lightbulbs and made copper and electricity valued commodities. Four months later, on January 18, 1883, with a meter to record electron flow, the first electric bill was generated and sent to the New York offices of Ansonia Brass and Copper in the amount of $50.44 cents. Nobody minded. The future looked good in Brass Valley.

With ever-increasing frequency trains carried goods we made in Brass Valley to Bridgeport, where they were put on boats and sold around the world. The trains came back loaded with minerals and chemicals and metal. Much of the stuff the trains brought to the valley was pumped out into our river or up into our air. In foundries, melting scrap was mixed with oil in a process that spewed thick, black smoke and particles of metal. It settled into everything, made the river smell and the air taste bad, and in Waterbury and Naugatuck, people with money lived upwind of its stench. In Derby, whenever we approached the river by the Hull Dye Works, our children guessed at the "flavor of the day." We worked fourteen-hour days, and when we came home, our wives and children did piecework instead of homework to make enough money for food and shelter. Those who worked at the pickle tubs got metal fume fever, and rollers lost fingers and arms in dangerous machinery, but the guys with the pains argued whether oatmeal, hot cider, or pepper best cured spelters' shakes, young cocks crowed, and old-timers told us how much of an arm we might lose in the grip of each machine.

Mergers and Parlors

Newspapers in our native tongues brought news of the homeland, but we also read about the Sherman Act as it was being debated, and street corner talk followed, and by the time the Sherman Act was law in 1890 we'd learned about Haymarket in Chicago. Something was happening in other mill towns, and we were thinking about the meaning of "fair play." There was talk of unions, and rights, and unrest led to small strikes. In 1901 women making underwear walked off the job at the Paugussett Mills and didn't return to work until Samuel Gompers came to Derby, and we gathered at the Sterling Opera House and cheered when he announced a settlement. In 1903 the trolley workers shut down transit for two months. It was so serious Governor Chamberlain deployed the National Guard to Waterbury, sending divisions from as far away as Hartford, New Britain, and Bristol to join those in Waterbury, and he also sent six Gatling guns, just in case! We wished our friends who ran the trolleys success, but we were divided by our languages and homelands, jealous of each others' jobs; we bickered, got cheated, and our gains were few and the companies consistently refused to talk to our unions. It was that way until after the war.

By then the companies had merged in order to balance production, they told us, and to keep the flow of work steady. The old brass families still ran the shops; they lived beside us, were invested in the communities they had helped build. We knew the decisions they made here were rooted here; good will or ill will had nowhere else to flow, and the bargains stuck, ordered relationships and lives, and stamped their imprint on every enterprise. Local laws and governments were structured by that imprint, schools were run by the patterns of the mill, and the day was regulated by the factory whistle and the punch clock. It was even the mill whistle that told our kids, "No school today," when the expected snow would be more than knee-deep.

The first punch clock was invented in 1888 by William Bundy, a jeweler in Auburn, New York. It's a date worth noting; we began counting minutes. The railroads had already forced us to relinquish local control of the time, synchronized us into time zones. The punch clock boss was a merciless bell ringer even as we flashed our Ingersoll Yankees, a one-dollar pocket watch for the masses, and aspired to a Seth Thomas clock and a parlor to put it in. There's a curious relationship between punch clocks and parlor clocks: as more punch clocks were installed, more parlor clocks were purchased. Punctuality was a virtue newly sharpened. From McGuffey on, we were told clocks' authority came from the almighty sun, though the two rarely agreed, and we obeyed the machine.

With an Ingersoll Yankee everyone could afford not to be late: "The watch that made the dollar famous." They were manufactured by Waterbury Clock Company, a spinoff of Benedict & Burnham, which later brought us Mickey Mouse time that lifted us through the Depression and kept on ticking as Timex, which is still headquartered in nearby Middletown.

Few of us noticed in 1902 when certain smelting operations near the Great Lakes had been put out of business by the mining companies, nor would we have known the failed operations were the only ones in which the Waterbury brass men controlled the processing of raw metal. Waterbury brass barons had long been aware that brass could be manufactured into stuff anywhere. Our value in Brass Valley lay in know-how and experience.

But from the remote perspective of Anaconda mining headquarters in Montana, all our work in Brass Valley was just a channel for merchandising raw metal by the pound. Copper could be poured, rolled, and pounded, parts stamped, and assembled anywhere, even in countries with no Seth Thomas parlors.

THE CUTTER'S PARLOR

Extrusion Mill, American Brass, Bank Street, Waterbury, CT

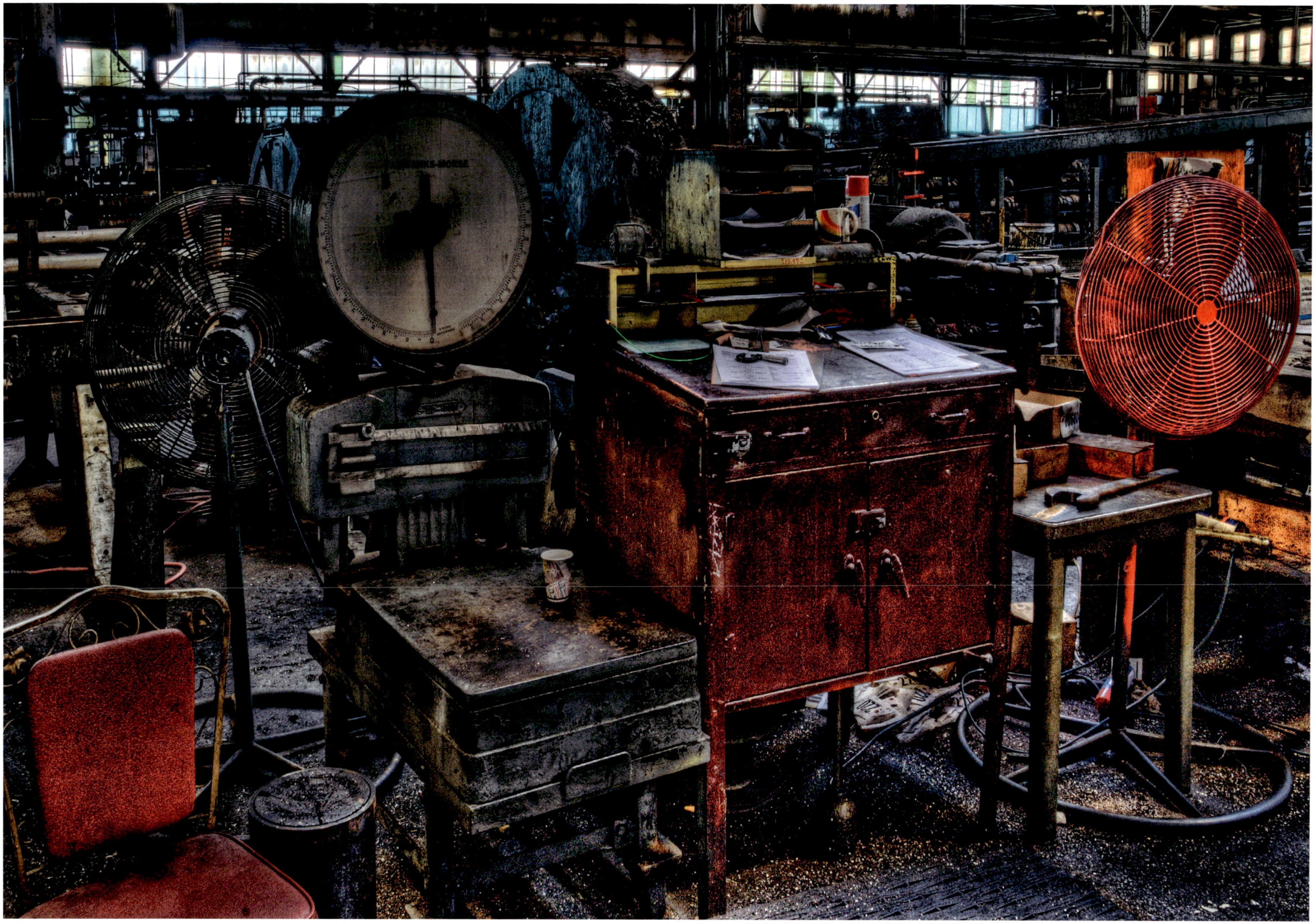

"Our industries might be gathered into the grasp of giant corporations whose controlling spirits, destitute alike of local affiliations and decency of sentiment, would cold-bloodedly close down many factories on the ground that Waterbury was not a logical site for an industry." —William Pape, Waterbury, 1918

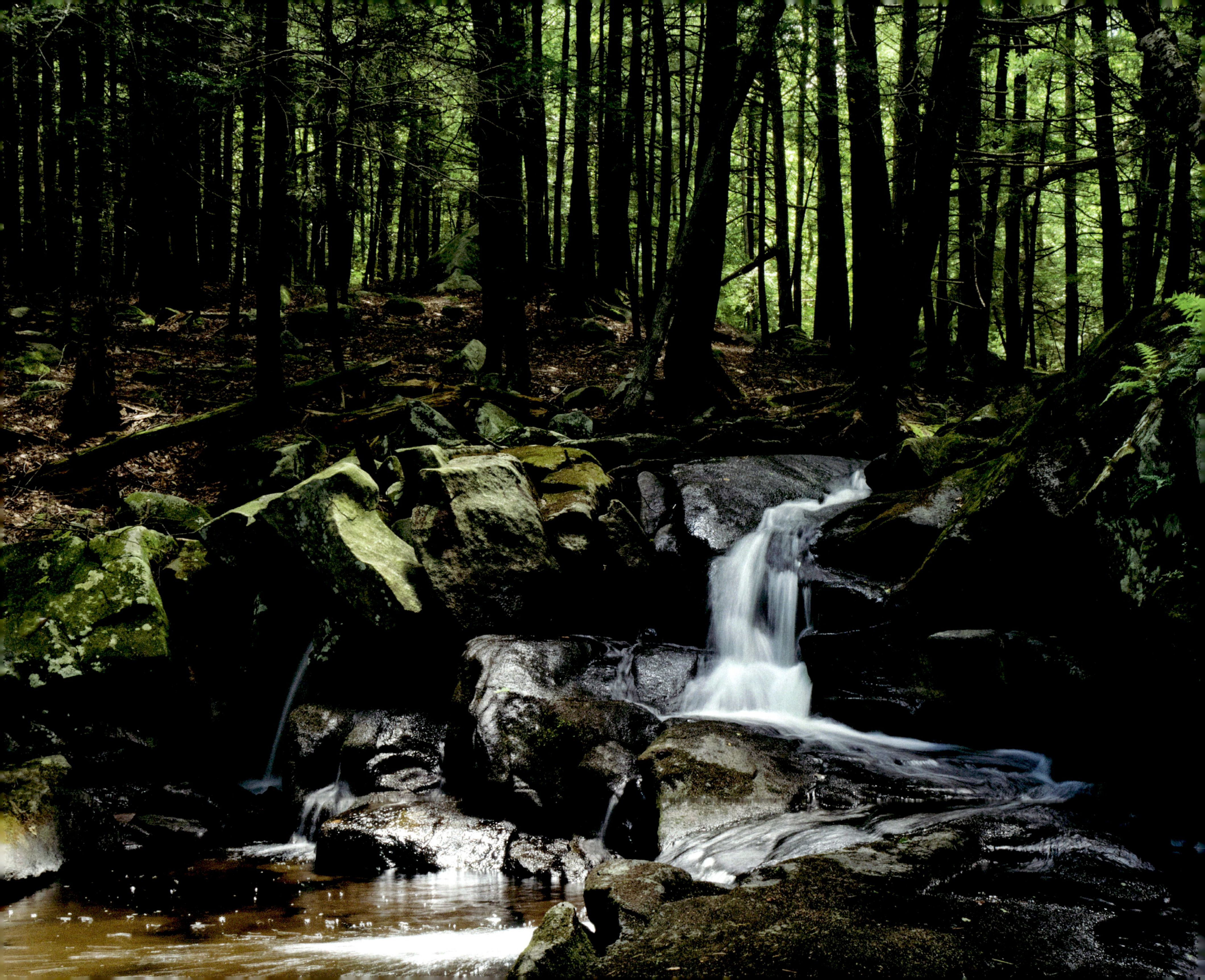

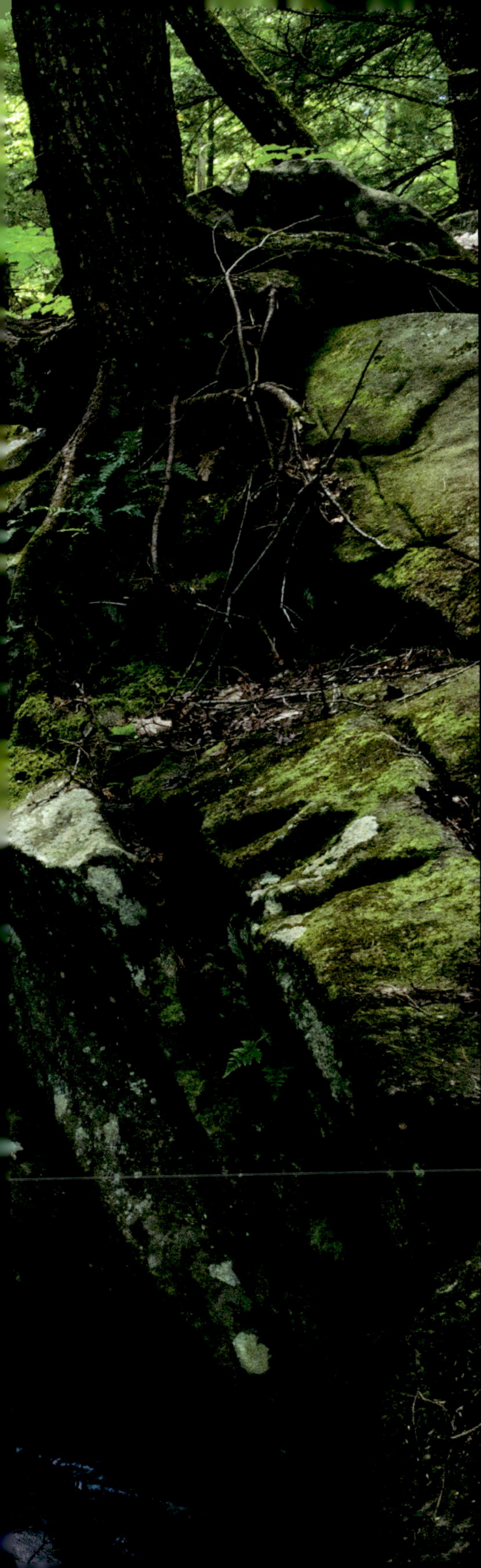

WILD RIDE

Winters tumble stones
that wrestle twisting roots,
and forests heave to stay
the tumble of time and
the flow of summer storms,
the oscillations of cosmic winds,
and restless eruptions of human soul,
as deep as painted water.

To be as nimble as the stream
and as rooted as rock.

HEADWATERS
Shepaug River Headwaters,
Upper Shepaug Reservoir, Warren, CT

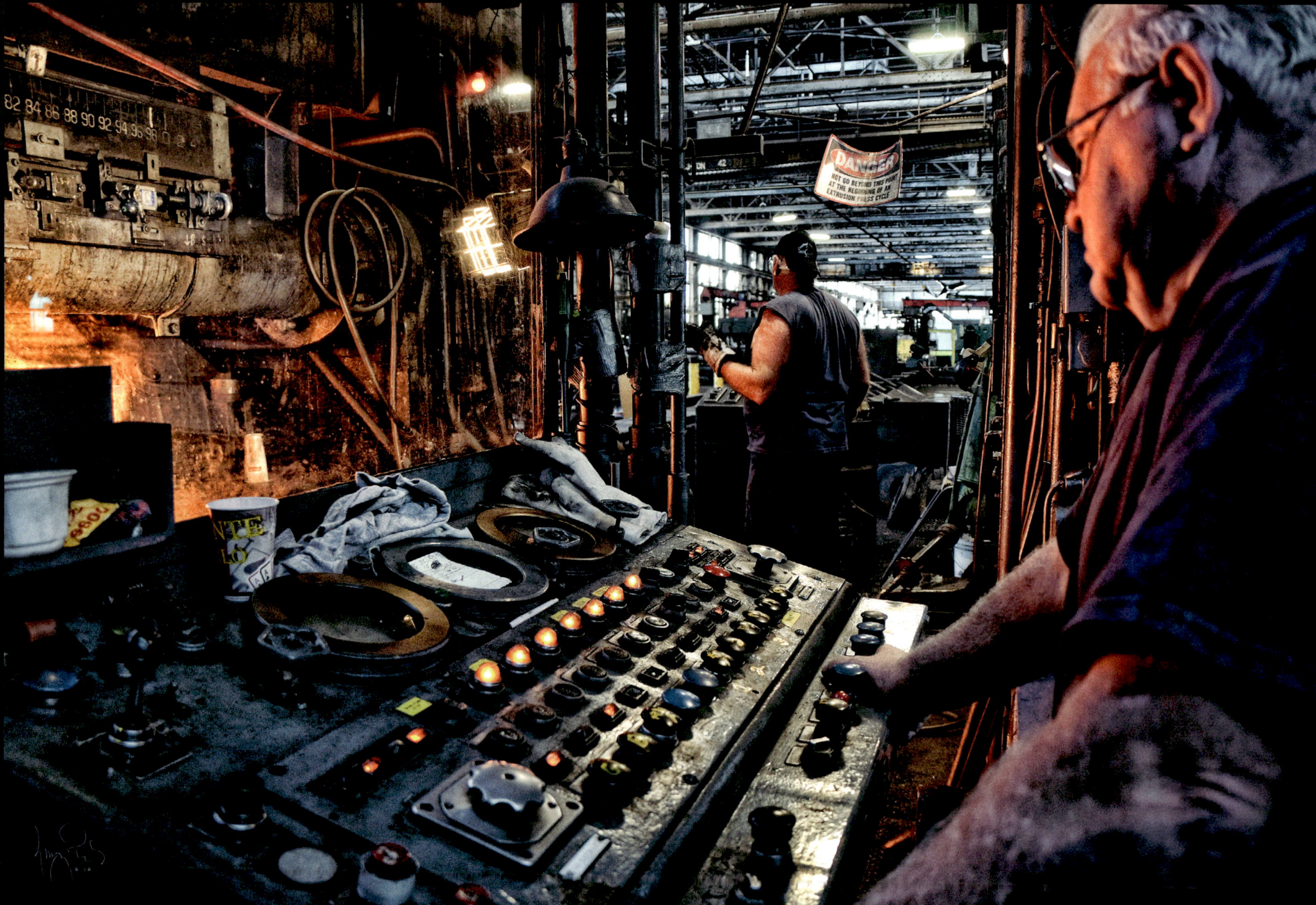

AT THE MASTER CONTROLS, FRED & KEN

American Brass, Bank Street, Waterbury

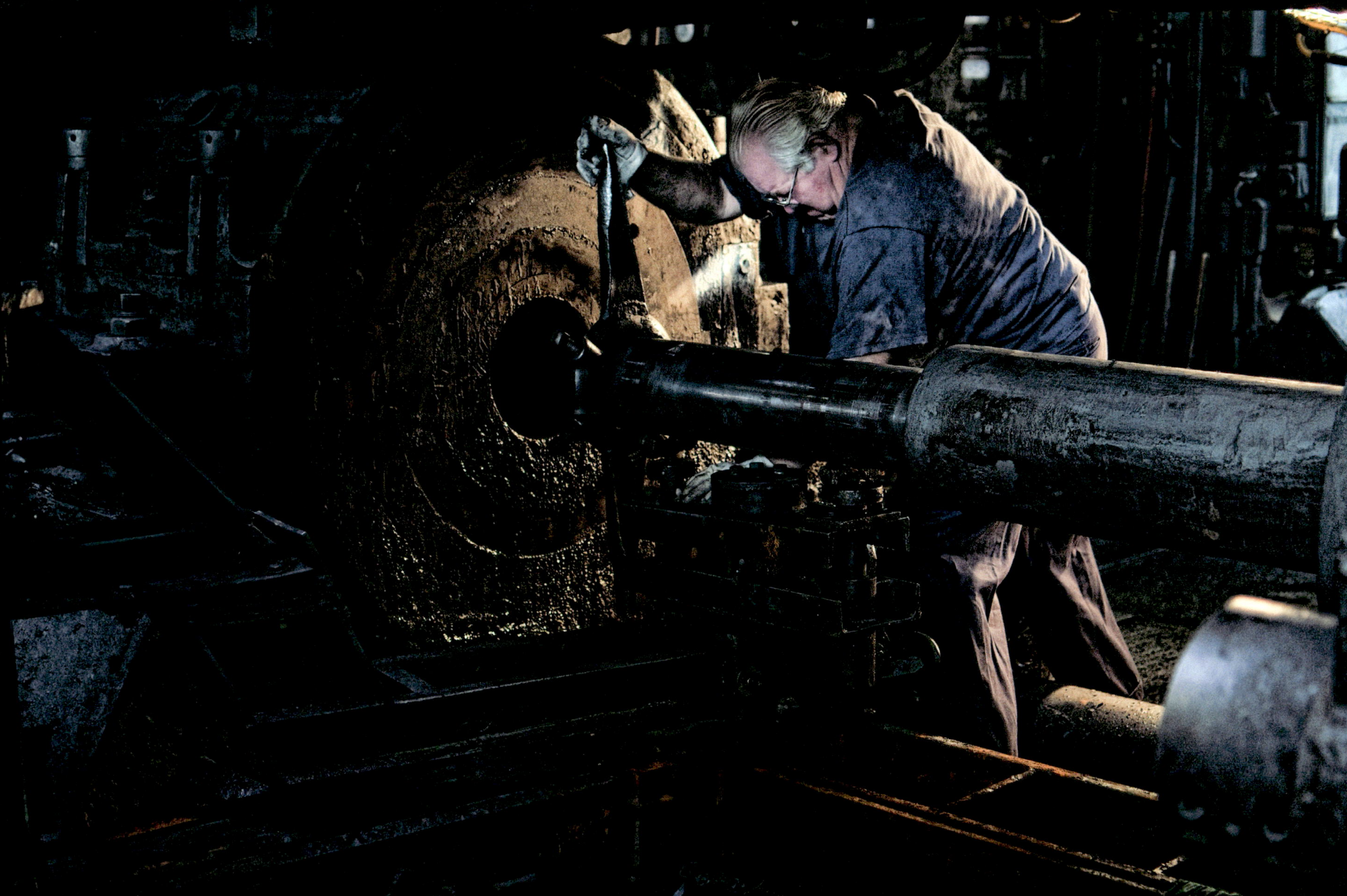

FRED LOOSENING THE MANDREL
Container, Mandrel, Ram, American Brass, Waterbury

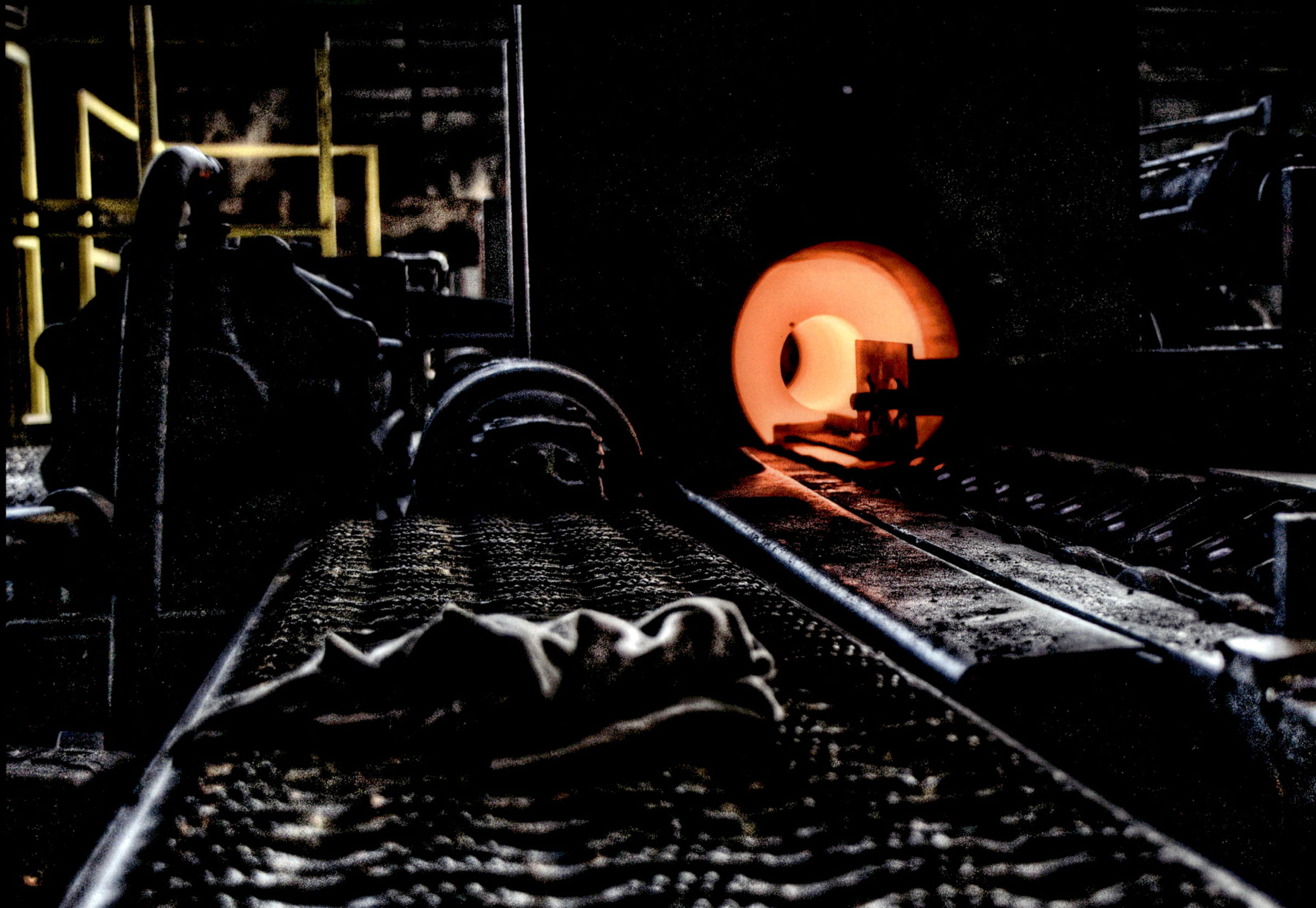

BLOCK WARMING IN AN INDUCTION FURNACE
American Brass, Waterbury

PHOTOGRAPHER'S JOURNAL:
Miguel, the heater man, is the first of five—the men of the extruder. The heater man works back, behind; it's hard to find the heater man, and if I pass through his narrow corridor, he has few words—he nods, his gunmetal mustache stays even, his thoughtful eyes acknowledge. Behind ovens and conveyors: a stool, a desk, controls, and two disks each as large around as a human face. The disks spin imperceptibly as pens spit faint scratches on their turning surface. They are cryptographs tracking data only Miguel can read and interpret. He's usually waiting in his corridor when I pass, where there's barely pacing space and others pass only at break time, but taped next to his controls is a small, metal shaving mirror—to comb that inscrutable mustache, I suppose.

When Miguel decides a block is hot, somewhere behind the ovens he pushes a button, and 300 pounds of hot brass moves down the track, along the conveyors, until the block arrives and stops, a glowing, orange beacon in front of Fred, the system operator, but by then Miguel is already attending to the next block.

SONG OF THE HEATER MAN

(to be accompanied by steam puffs, white noise, clanking steel and the sultry alto of the straining extruder, all set to a Latin beat)

Heater man,
where does he stand?
watching the graphs
watching the heat

Behind the ovens,
watching, waiting,
one-seater, man,
for the heater man.

When the button is pushed
the hot block rolls
meter man,
the heater man.

Nobody sees
In the mirror he keeps,
neater man,
one-seater man.

Next block broils
next block rolls
neater man,
meter man,

(THE VOICES:
heater man, following the heat,
heater man, always neat
heater man, neater man
neater man, one-seater man..., etc.)

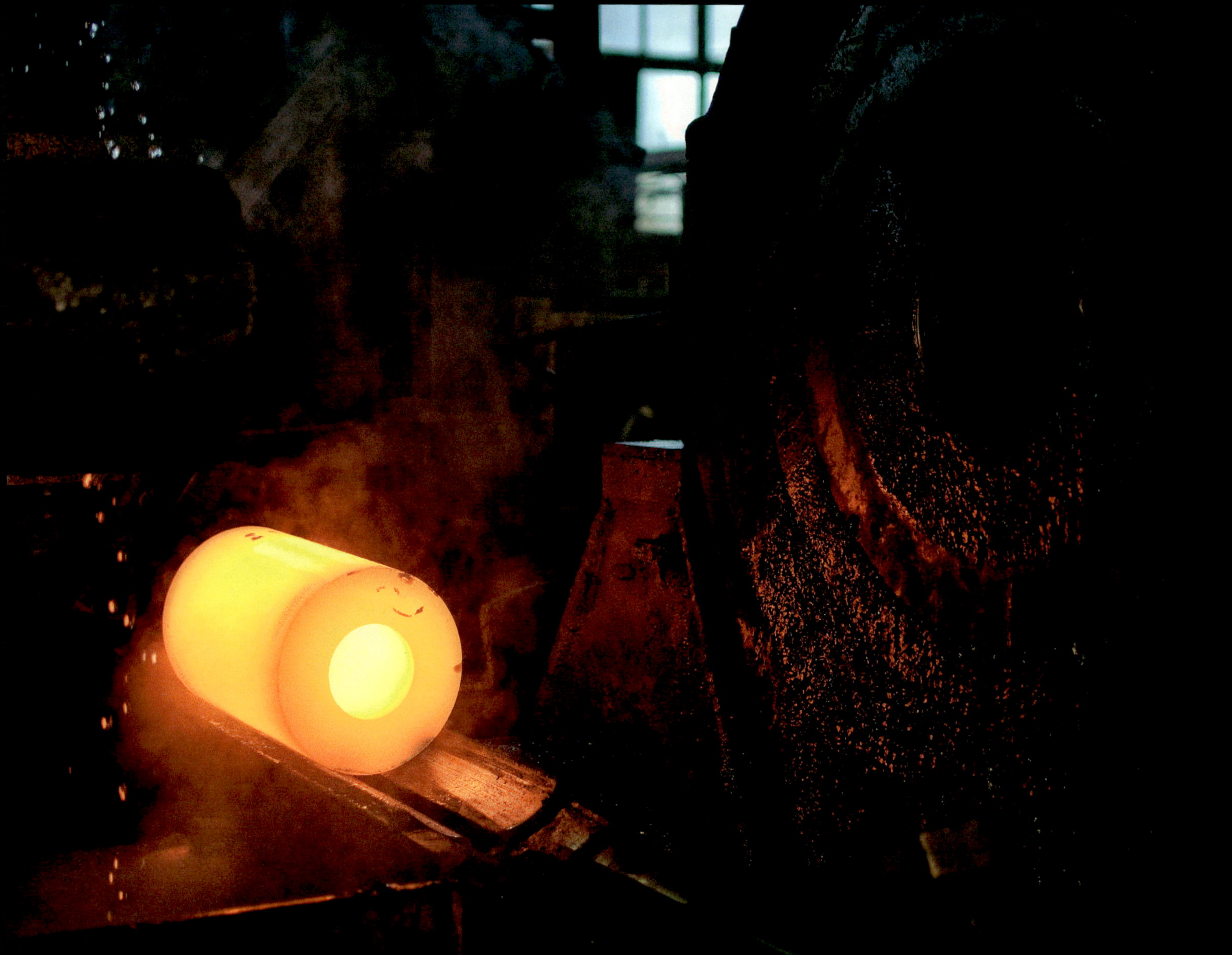

READY TO LOAD, A MOMENT

PHOTOGRAPHER'S JOURNAL:

There is a pregnant moment after the heater man has sent the block, and Fred, the machine operator, takes control and loads the extruder. The elevator with the glowing block drops, and the die-man rolls the steel dummy down the slot and it whirs into position behind the block. The machine operator hits a button, and a plunger pushes the push-die and block over a bridge to the last elevator. Another button lifts the elevator which rotates 90 degrees as it rises and leaves block and push-die ready between the ram and the container, everything is set to begin. Finally the machine operator pulls on the long, steel lever that comes out of the floor, and hydraulics the size of a large, freight truck engage for action. The dragon of the foundry was a tin dragon with a pot of gold. This dragon has the muscle and hot fury to transform this short gold block into a long, glowing tube. They call that squirting.

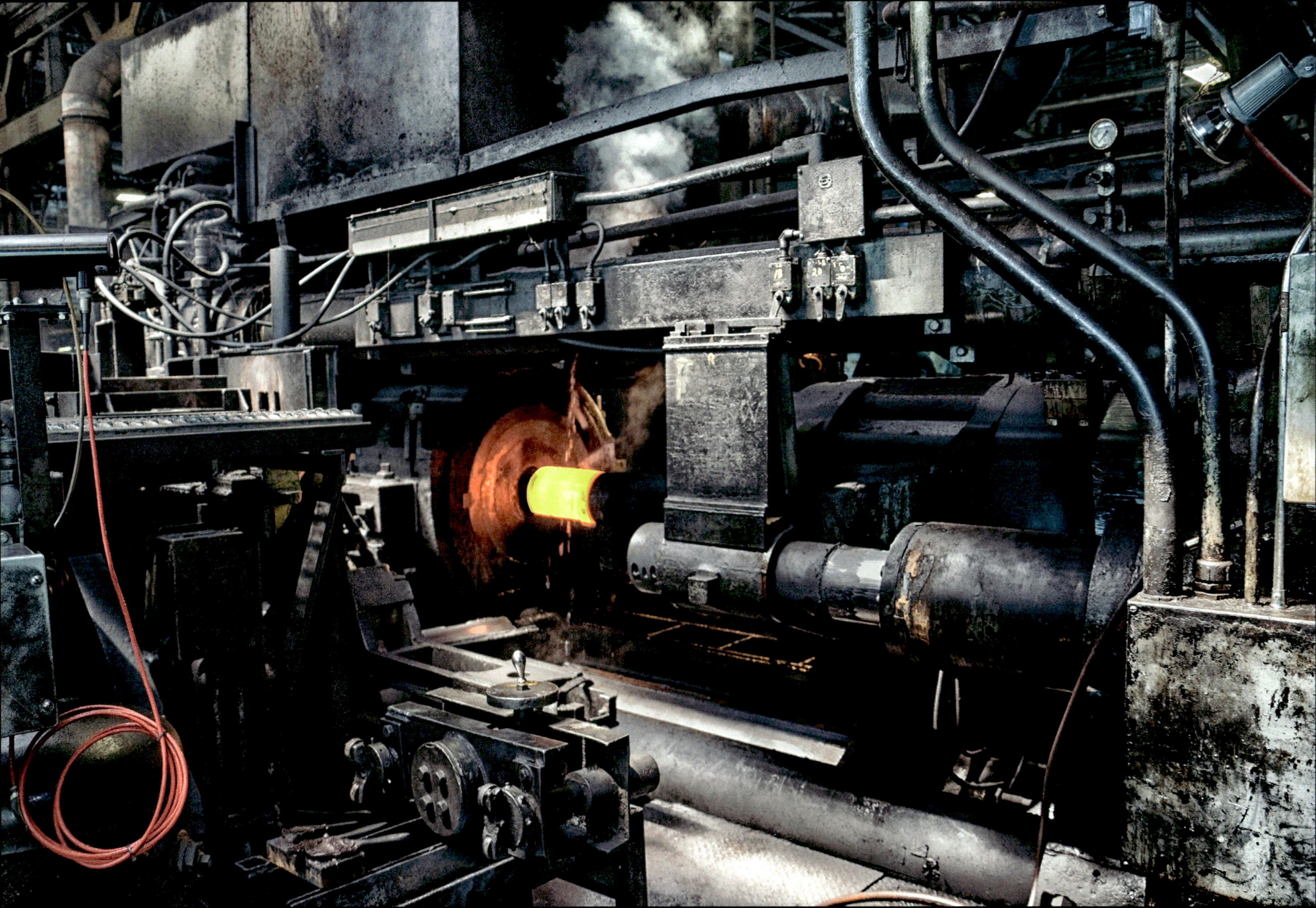

SQUIRTING

The ram has just begun pushing the block into the container

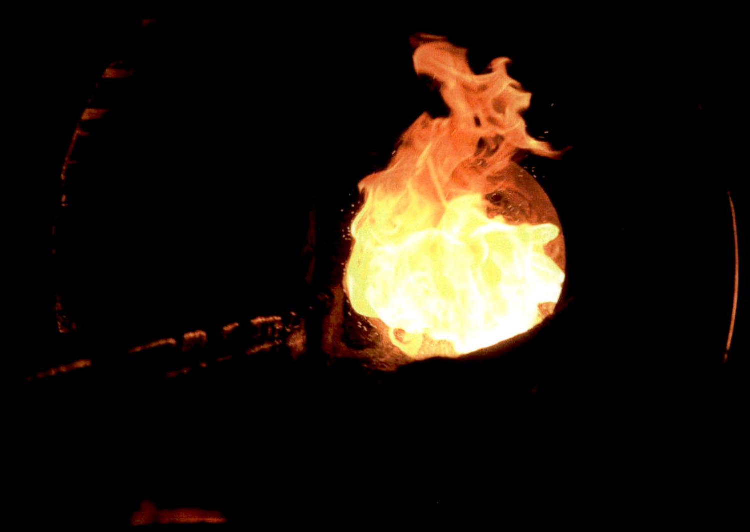

PHOTOGRAPHER'S JOURNAL:

When the crank is pulled the dragon tenses, clanking begins, a funnel of steam puffs from a stack, and hydraulic muscles thrust shining forearms that impel the ram. The ram forces the push-die and the hot block into the greased container. The extruder moves like a living thing; torso segmented, the groin pushes forward as the chest hunches back to take in the block. As the block slides into the container the ram inserts a mandrel, like a long tongue, down through the center of the push-die and block so that the semi-molten donut of brass is filled and contained by hard steel.

And then the dragon whines and wheezes, squeezes and whines, 2,700 pounds per square inch of pressure squeezing, wheezing brass as if it were paste through the small open ring at the cutting die at the end of

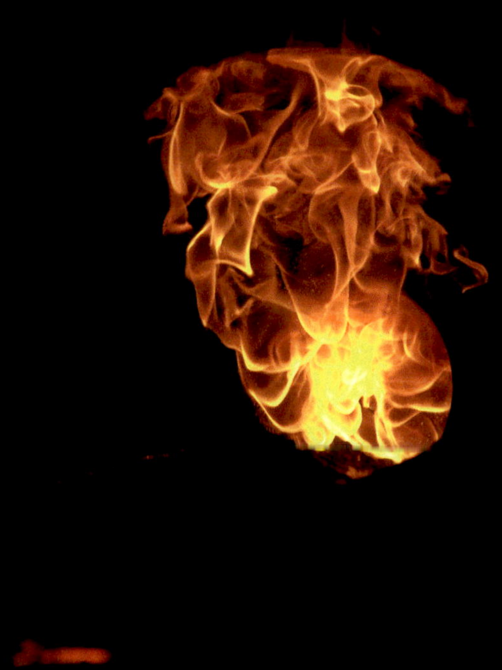

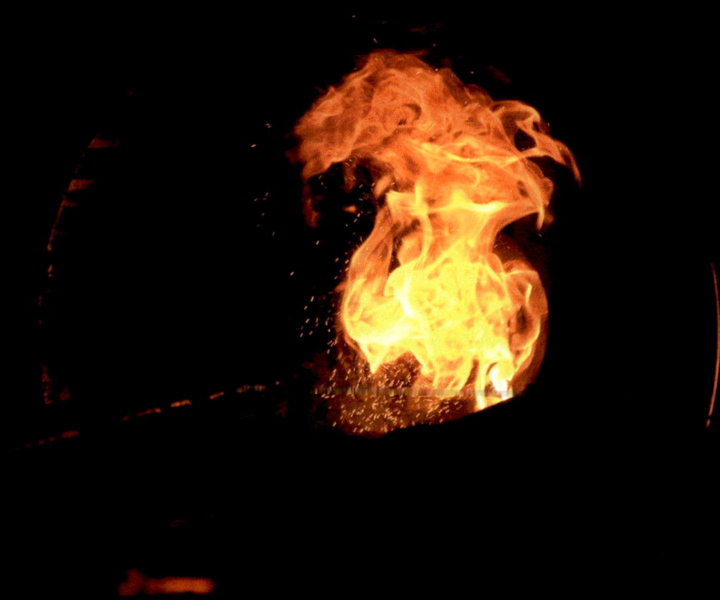

the container. From the sides of the ram come puffs of smoke and licks of flame as the grease inside the container is seared away, but at the front, the dragon's mouth is growling flames, puffing sparks, breathing fire as a glowing tube of brass slowly grows.

Those who were there recall the day the extruder exploded like a gun shooting the block and shrapnel down the factory floor to the south where men were working.

At the end of the conveyor that leads from the extruder, there is an iron plate to intercept such trajectories, though it is little match for what might be fired at it. On the iron plate someone has drawn a panicked face in chalk.

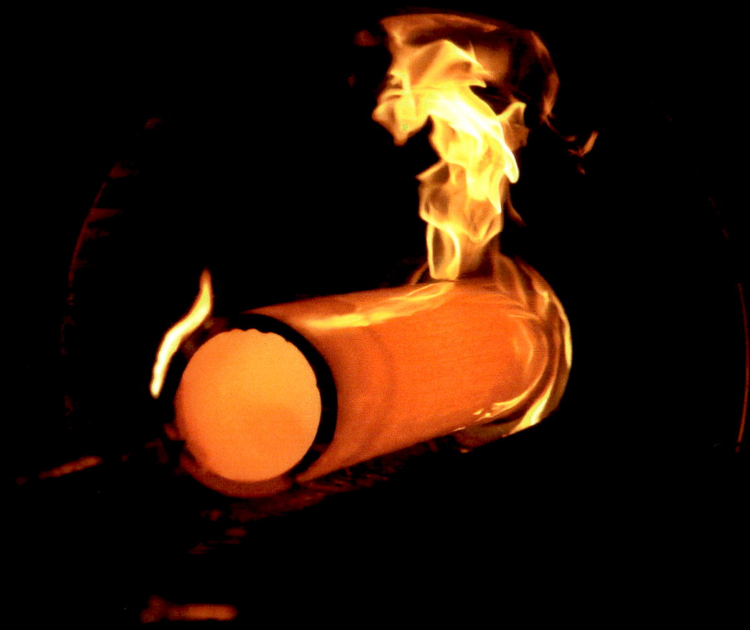

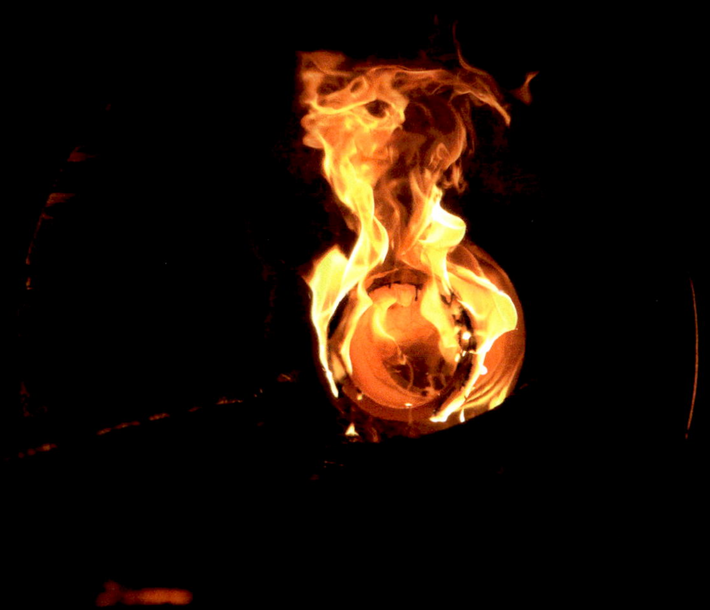

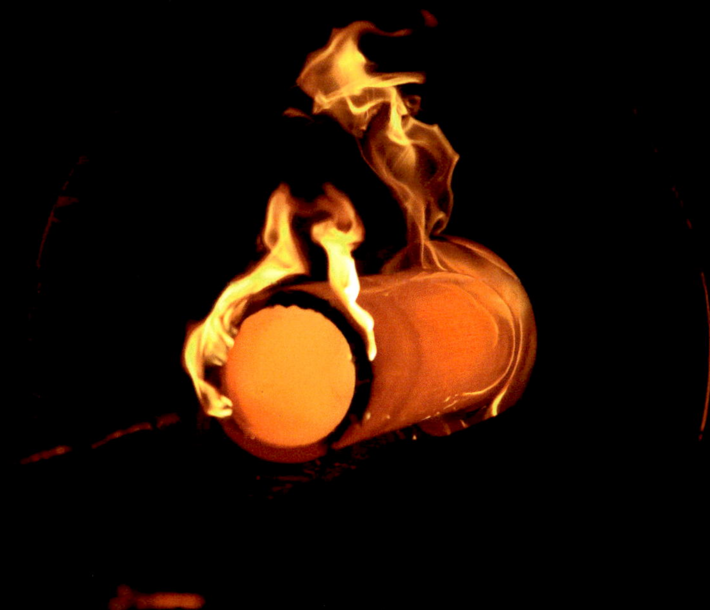

"Man is equally incapable of seeing the nothingness from which he emerges as the infinite in which he is engulfed."

—Blaise Pascal, *Pensées*, 1670

PHOTOGRAPHER'S JOURNAL:
Pascal's Law is the magic spell of hydraulics—not this epistemological law, but his physical law, which tells us that pressure exerted anywhere in liquids exerts its force equally in all directions. It explains why, when we squeeze the trigger on the Windex bottle, we get a jet from the tiny nozzle. It's why the force of a toe can stop a car, and how the extruder can develop the force needed to squeeze a solid block of brass as if it were only paste.

Hydraulic pumps also provide huge power to draw benches and to expanders that can work a brass tube when it's cold, stretching or dilating it, making it long or stout. The secret spell that opens the mysteries of hydraulics is Pascal's Law. With this knowledge we control hydraulic leverage and design machines to squirt brass.

Knowledge is leverage.

Arguably, Pascal's most radical idea was that the mind provided the leverage to elevate humanity above the infinite in which it is engulfed, a truly Faustian idea from his agnostic spirit. In the end, however, Pascal chose salvation, confessed his sins to God just in case. He made a merchant's wager, but those who followed took the Faustian leap anyway.

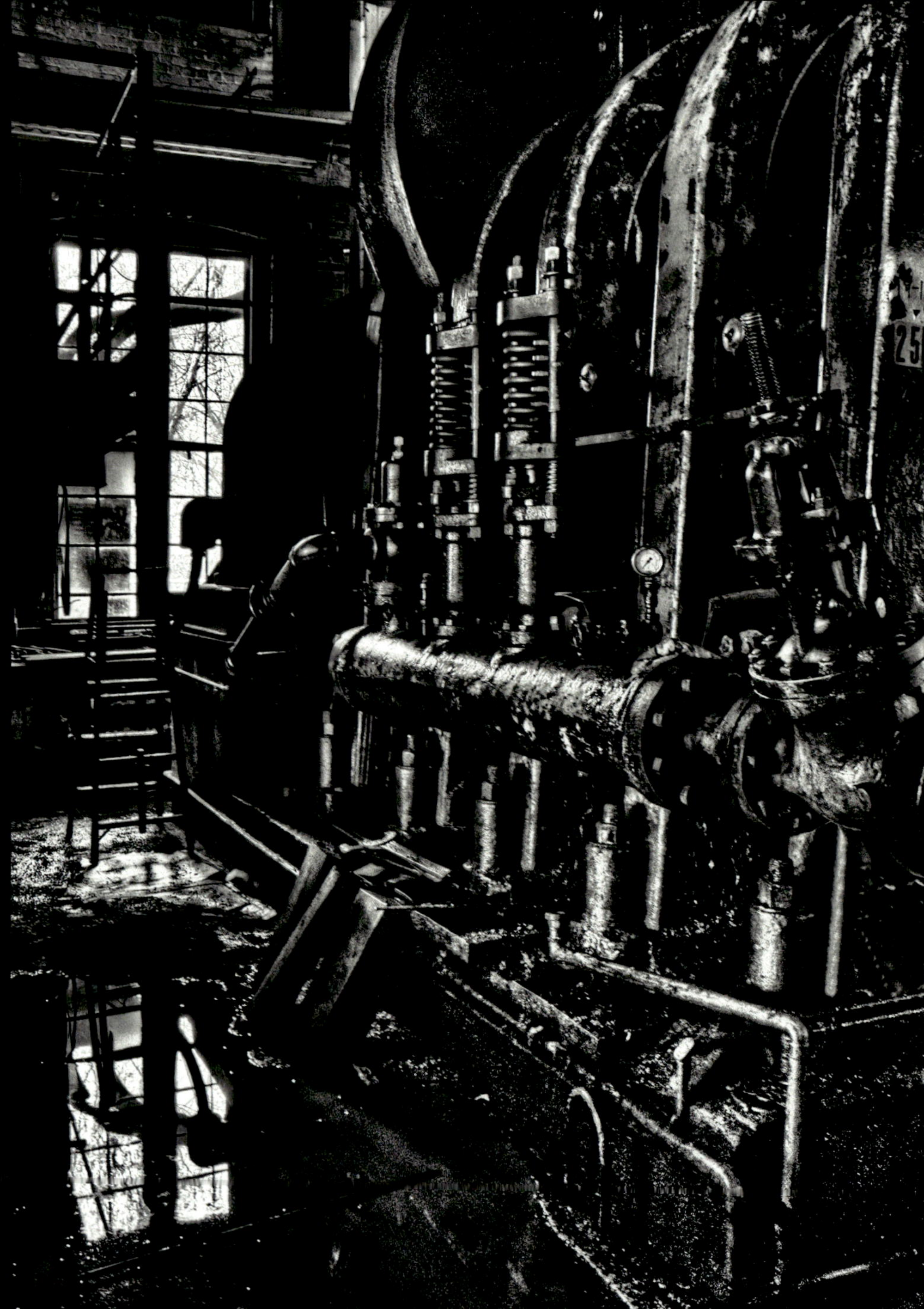

HYDRAULIC PUMP
(stamped patent 1917) American Brass, Extrusion Mill, Bank Street, Waterbury, CT

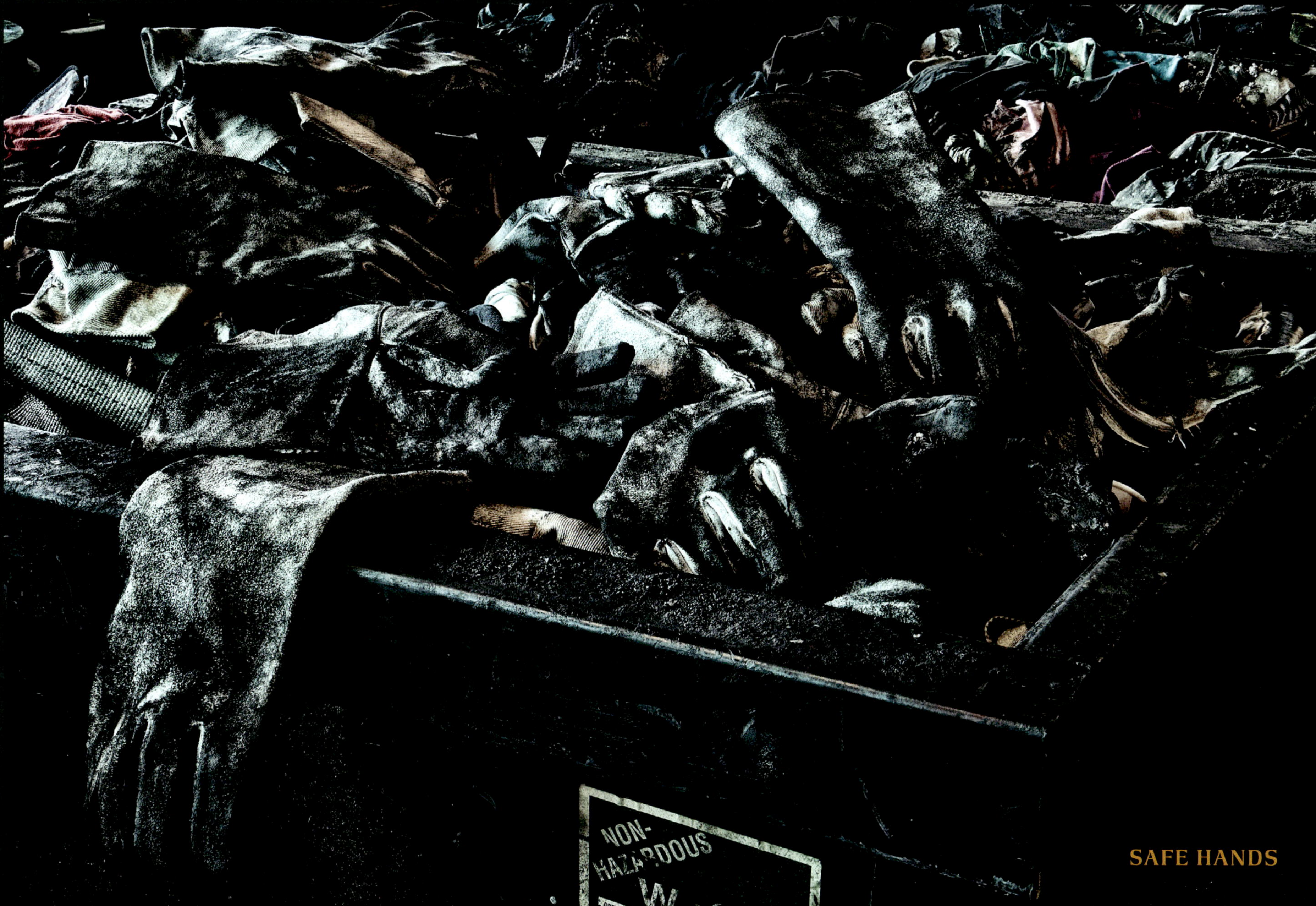

SAFE HANDS

"Labor was the first price, the original purchase-money that was paid for all things. It was not by gold or by silver, but by labor, that all wealth of the world was originally purchased."

—Adam Smith, *The Wealth of Nations*, 1776

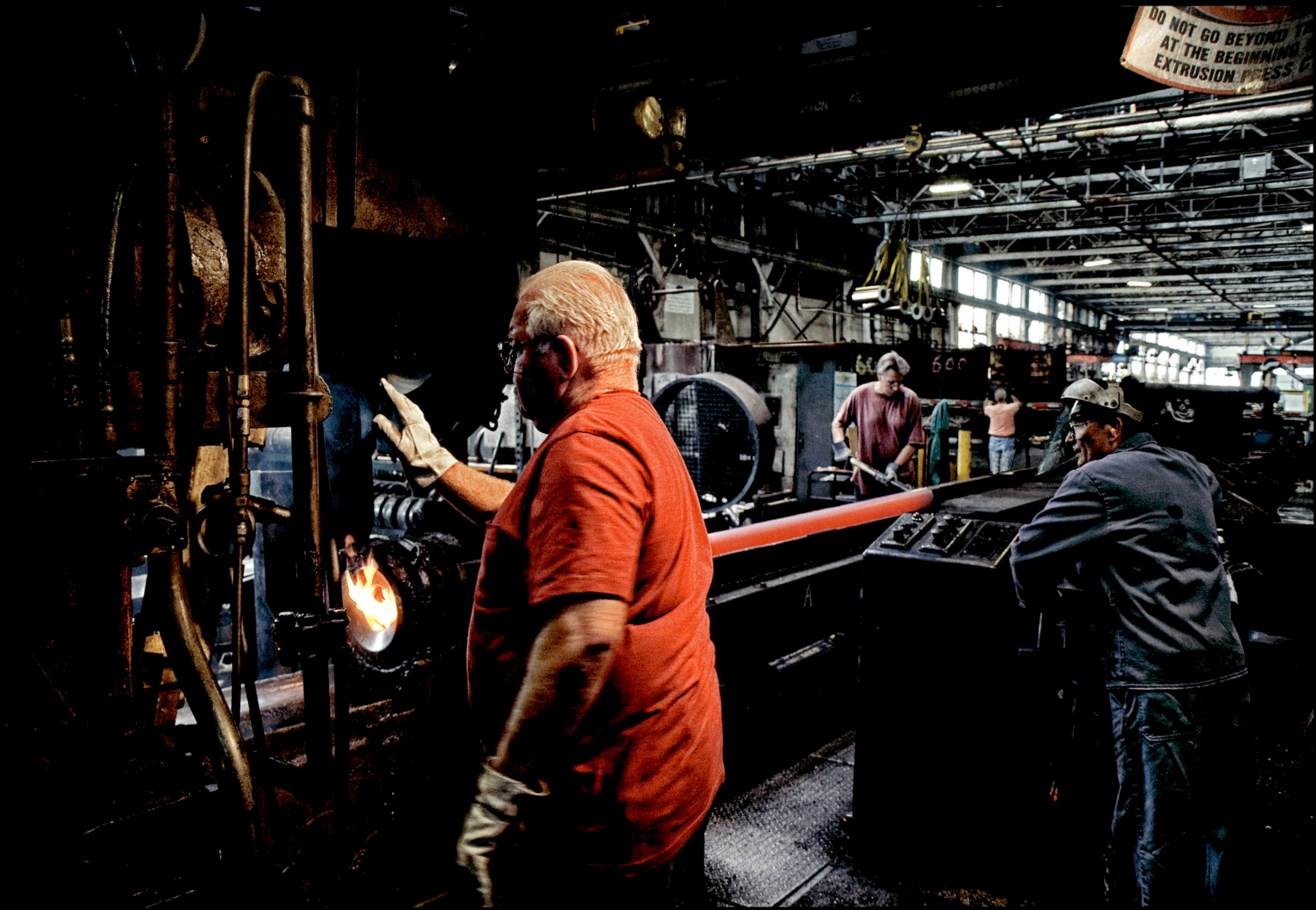

EXTRUSION BOOGIE-WOOGIE:
FRED, BOB, CARLOS, JOHN & PINTO

Fred the sysop has finished the cut, Pinto the die hanger has loosened the die, Bob the die puller has pulled it free, Carlos passes under a cloud of brass balloons, and John unloads billets, fresh from the foundry

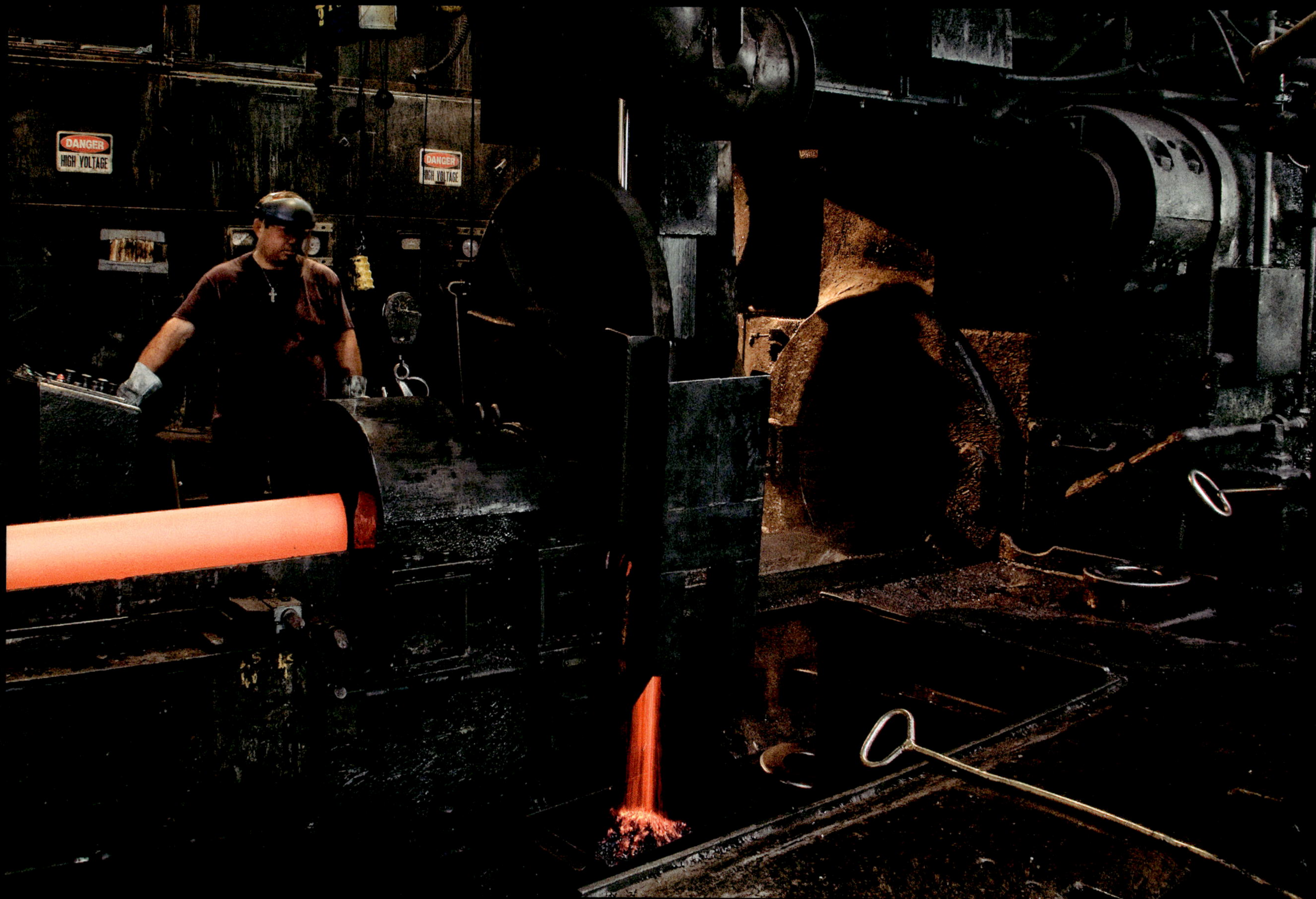

SPIKE, THE DIE HANGER

PHOTOGRAPHER'S JOURNAL:
If the block was hot enough when the ram began squeezing, only a bit of rim from the block will remain at the end of the new tube; one can never squeeze out that last bit of toothpaste. If the block was not hot enough, the ram will seize up before it is done pushing all of the brass through the cutting dies. Whatever is left of the block will hang like a stump on the new tube. It will be an awkward, hot, 300-pound nuisance to remove. It is another of the little things that can go wrong in the mundane routine of extruding tube. Some of the men say it happens more when the equipment is old and tired. Others hold their tongues and shrug. A mechanic's shrug is the duct tape of emotion.

All's well this time, and Spike, the die hanger, works the controls that slide the die head assembly forward exposing the tiny stump expected at the back so it can be cut off and the cutting die freed.

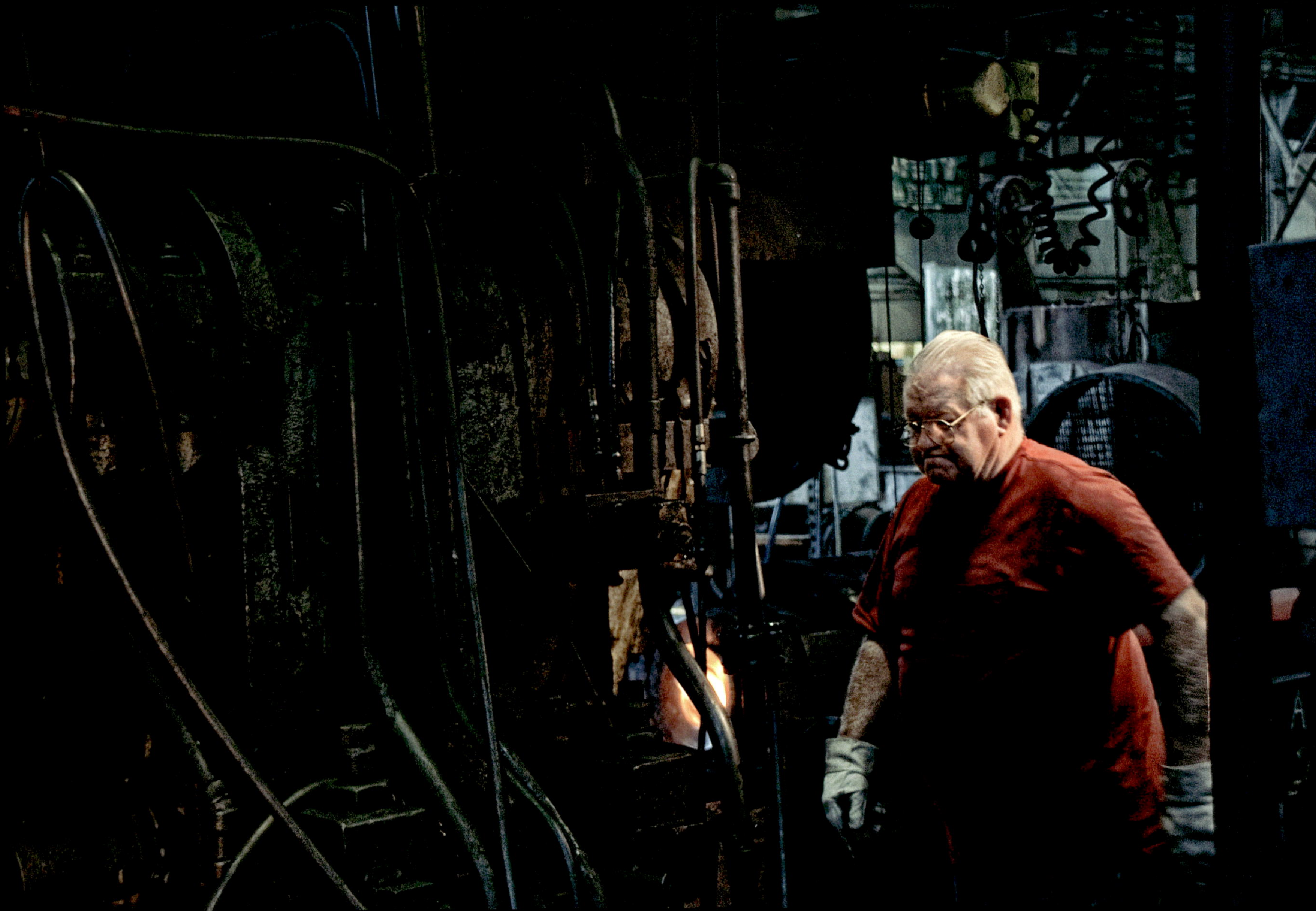

FRED, SYSTEM OPERATOR

PHOTOGRAPHER'S JOURNAL

Fred, the system operator, is dragon master. He tunes and adjusts the beast and oversees operation from the master controls. Each job requires a different configuration of dies and other interchangeable parts, and the machine is enveloped in pneumatic and hydraulic lines and pipes for cooling, heating, and switching systems. Fred must watch and manage them all, and there's a bit of Irish in everything he says, and it adds authority to the weight of his opinions.

How does one learn to feed and care for an ancient dragon, the last of its species? Fred says he learned from the previous operator. Before that he worked as a tool maker, the syllables pronounced with special pride. He tells me there's a back-up system operator if Fred has to be out, but I've never seen him. Is Fred also the last of his kind? When asked why he's the one working the extruder Fred says, "None of the other guys wanted to."

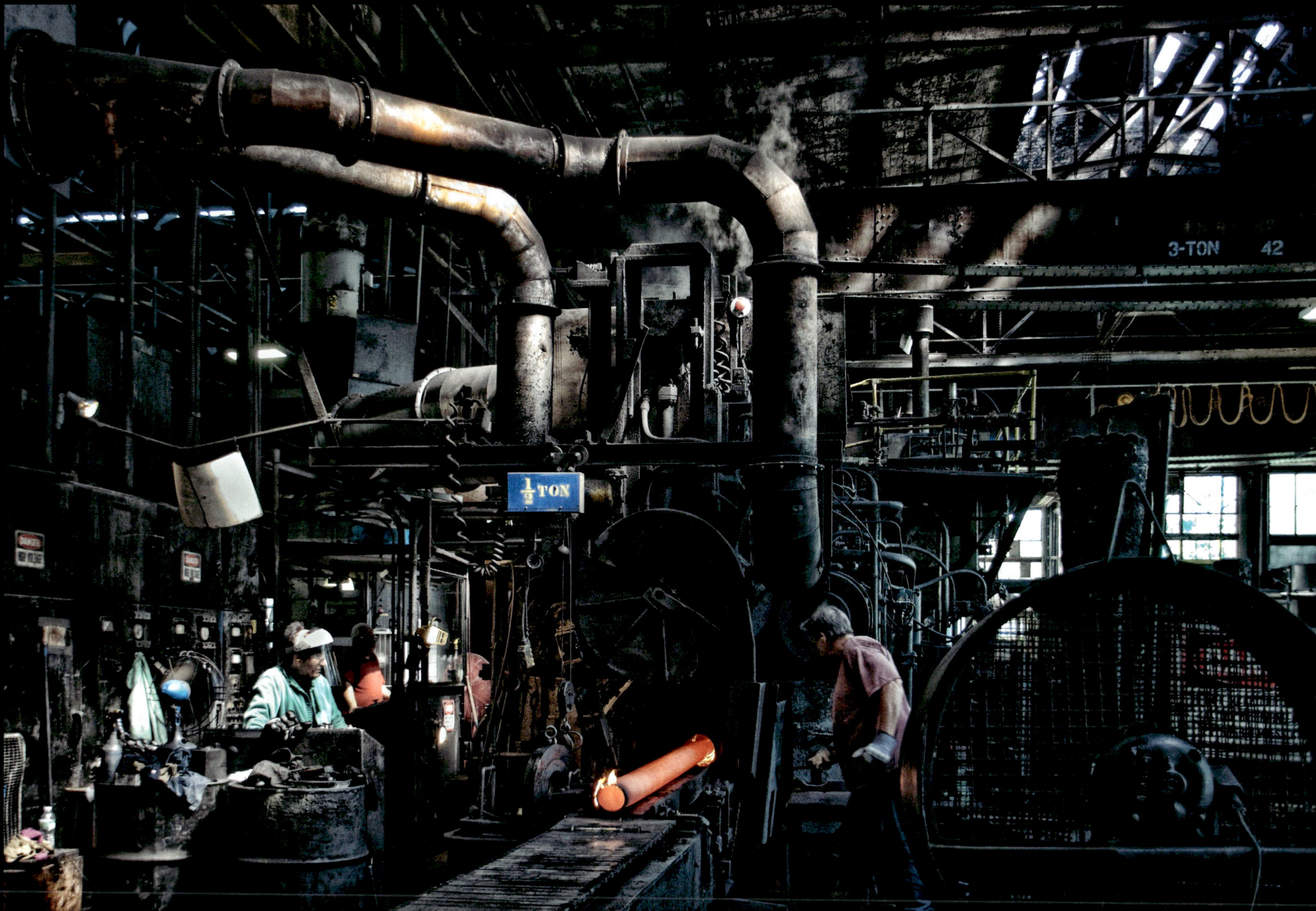

DRAGON CALM

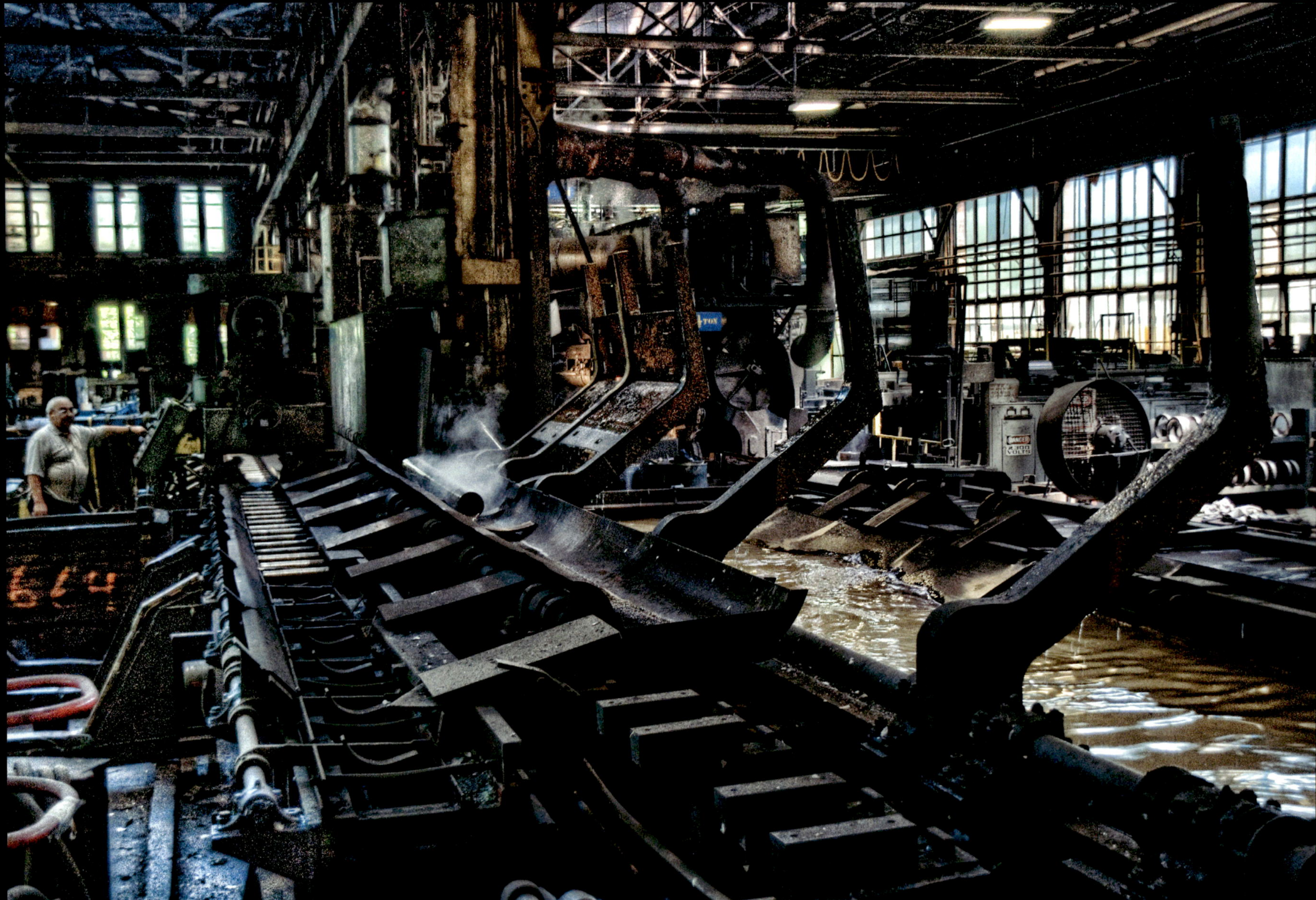

COOLING AND CUTTING

PHOTOGRAPHER'S JOURNAL:

Finally, Gil, the cutter, the last of five, removes the new length of pipe from the cooling tank. At the same time Spike, the die hanger, returns to the steamy belly of the dragon to re-grease the container and mandrel in preparation for extruding the next block. On a good day they'll keep running until they finish a job, and the machine needs to be refitted for different specs.

The rough tubes just extruded still need more work before they meet specification. For that they will move on to one or more of five long benches on which long, cold tube can be pushed and pulled in a variety of ways and the metal stretched like taffy.

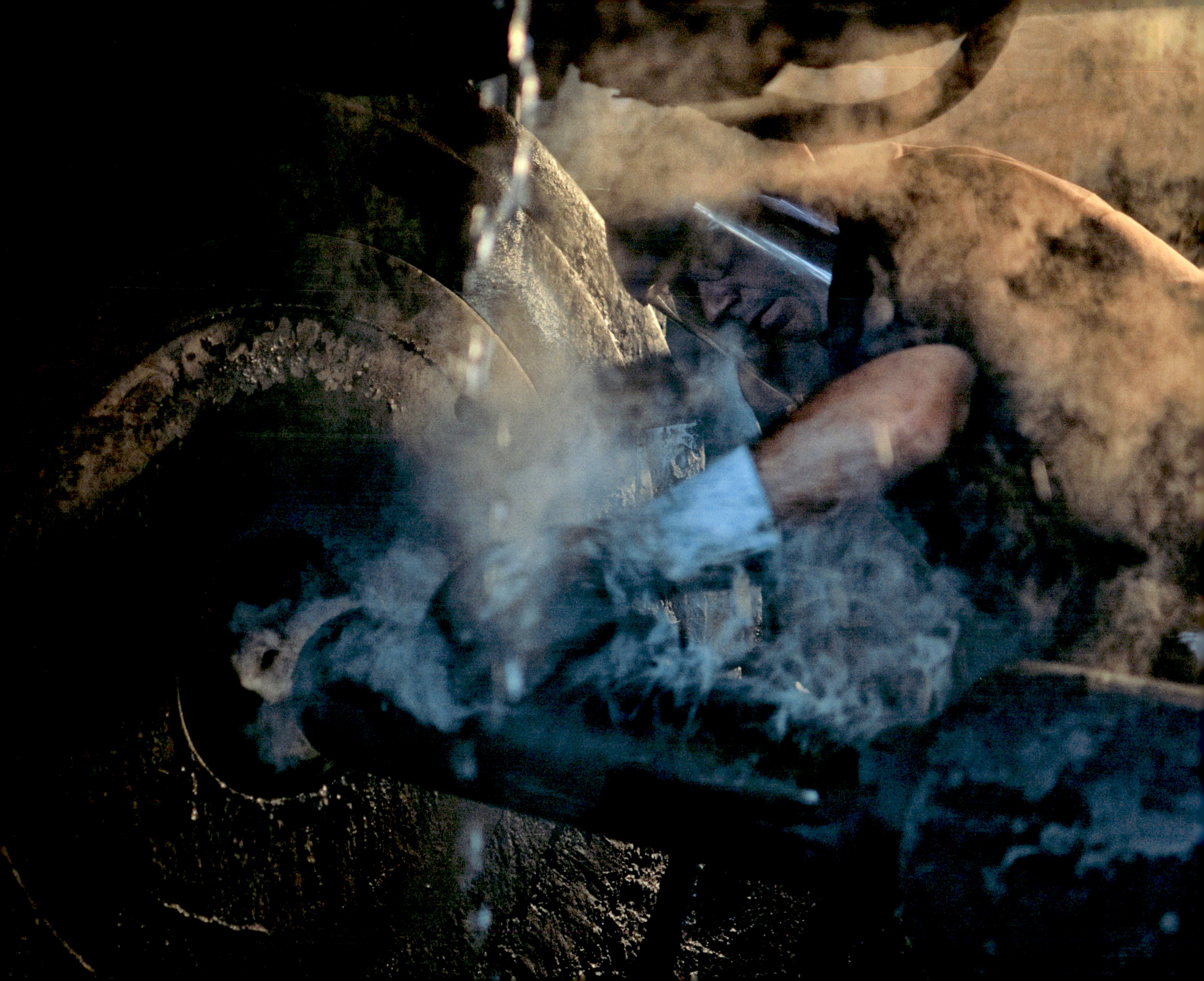

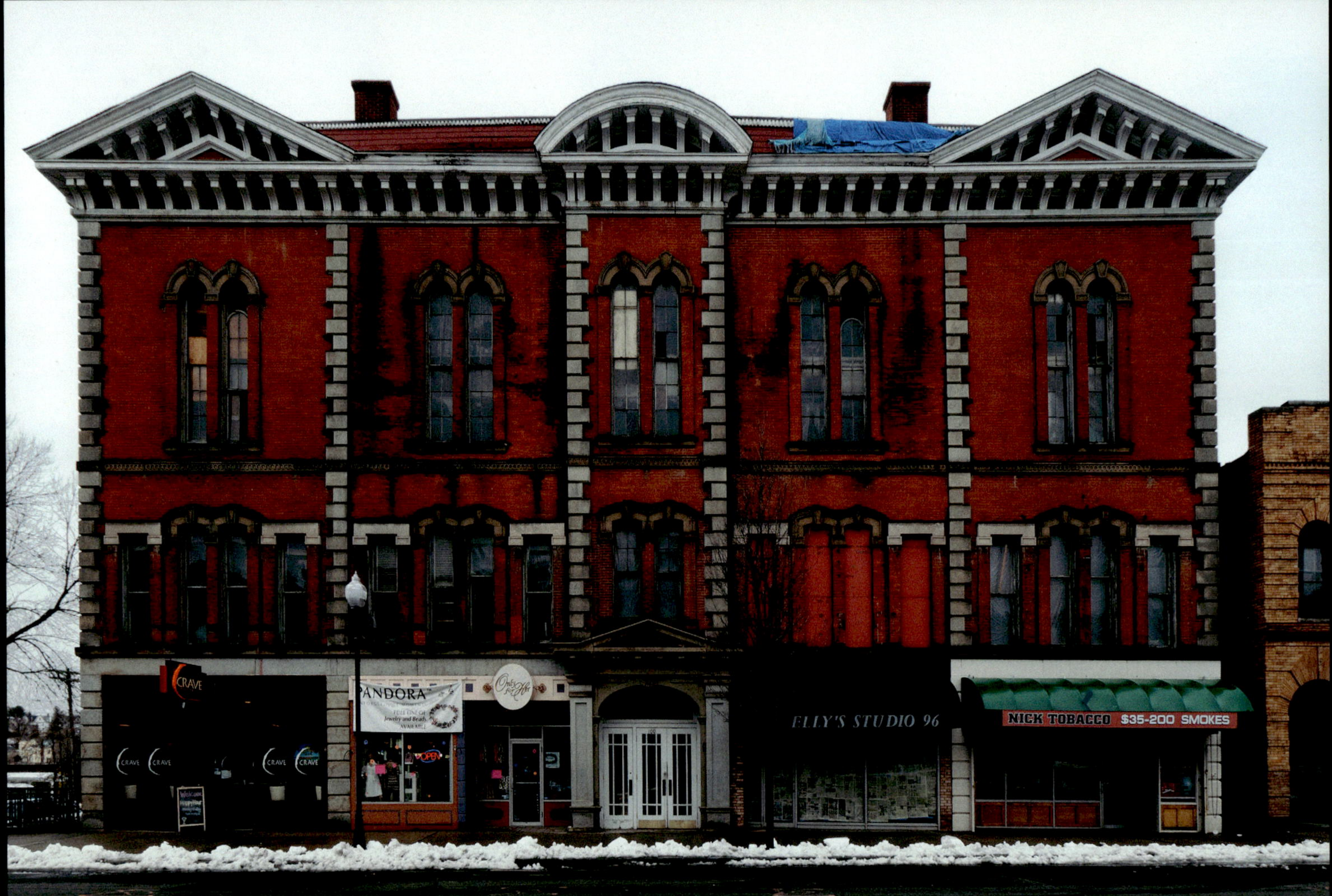

AT THE OPERA HOUSE

Ansonia Opera House, Main Street, Ansonia

PART FIVE:

SOUSA TO DECO

The opera house is no longer for skating

PHOTOGRAPHER'S JOURNAL:
Sometimes buildings call to me. Even from the back, this one had class. The front is in the middle of Main Street, Ansonia, and I passed it whenever I went to the foundry. I was not surprised to learn it was the 1870 Ansonia Opera House and became determined to get inside. I found out that the architect, Robert Hill, had designed buildings throughout the valley, including the famed opera house upriver in Thomaston.

Two years passed before I finally got my wish. It turns out the head of maintenance at the brass mill could've gotten me in anytime; his brother-in-law Walter owns it. When I finally met Walter he told me how his father had purchased it at a tax foreclosure auction; it was a gift to his mother, who recalled the days when everyone went skating there on Saturday afternoons. After Walter's parents died, he inherited the building, still unrestored. Walter cherishes his parents' dream of making it a center once again, and he patches the roof regularly.

SKATERS AT THE OPERA HOUSE

Everything important happened here,
weddings, graduations, and town meetings.
Romeo passed word to meet Juliet here,
Mimi died,
Uncle Tom suffered annually
while we held hands.
We loved
especially the magicians and their magic rabbits.

Saturday afternoons everyone roller-skated here,
roller-skating at the opera,
and in the evening men sang and danced and juggled.
If only spices could embalm a recollection
or memories could be pickled, smoked, or dried?
The voice cadences of childhood pals,
one's narrow-eyed assertiveness
and little-rat voice,
the way he slightly stammered
mischief in a grin,
her lattice of endless laughter
that filled spaces between friends
and the secrets we forgot,
smiles that wrinkle and dart
sometimes
almost
nothing
we can name
yet a crystal cadence
etched in memories' smoky glass.

We fall nameless
like oval photos
from flaking albums,
and our spirits return to the old opera house,
eternally circling there as when we were skaters.

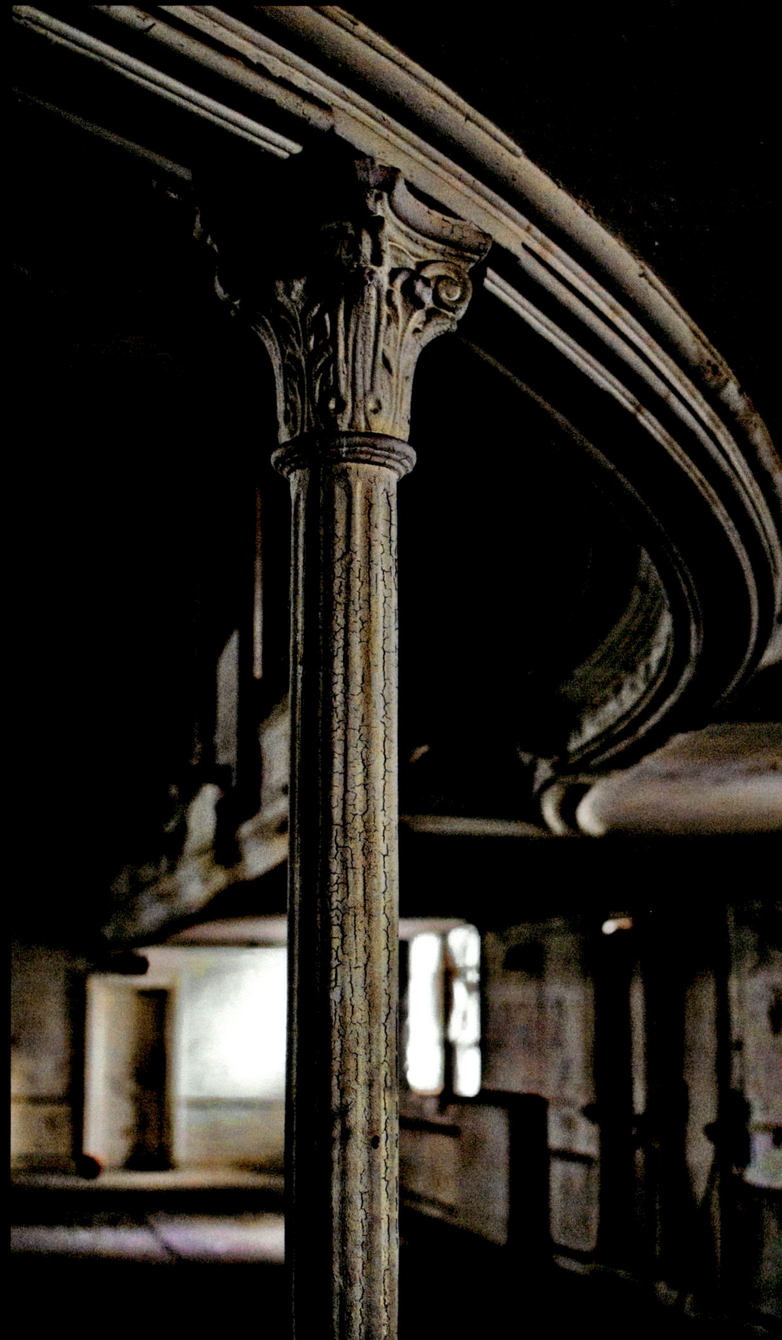

SKATERS' PROMENADE
Ansonia Opera House, Main Street, Ansonia

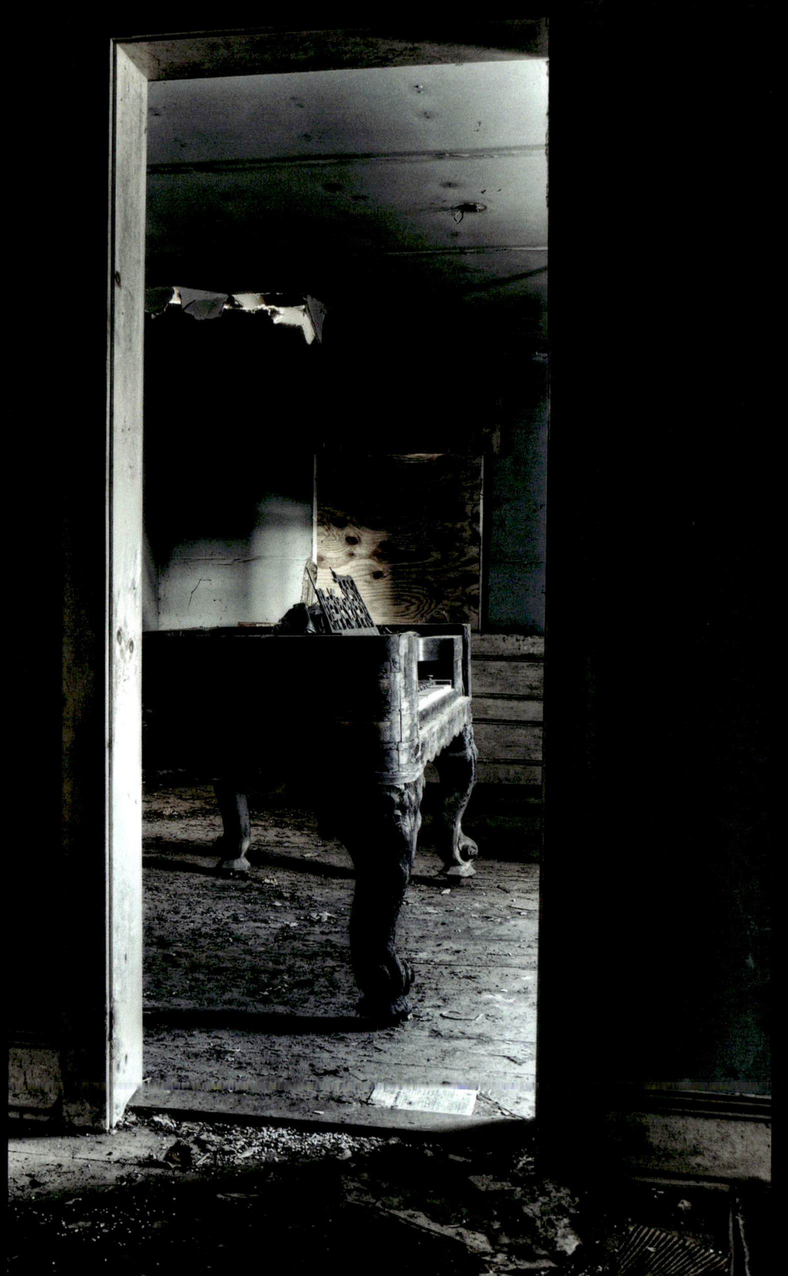

FORTEPIANO

Abandoned house, Dover Plains, NY

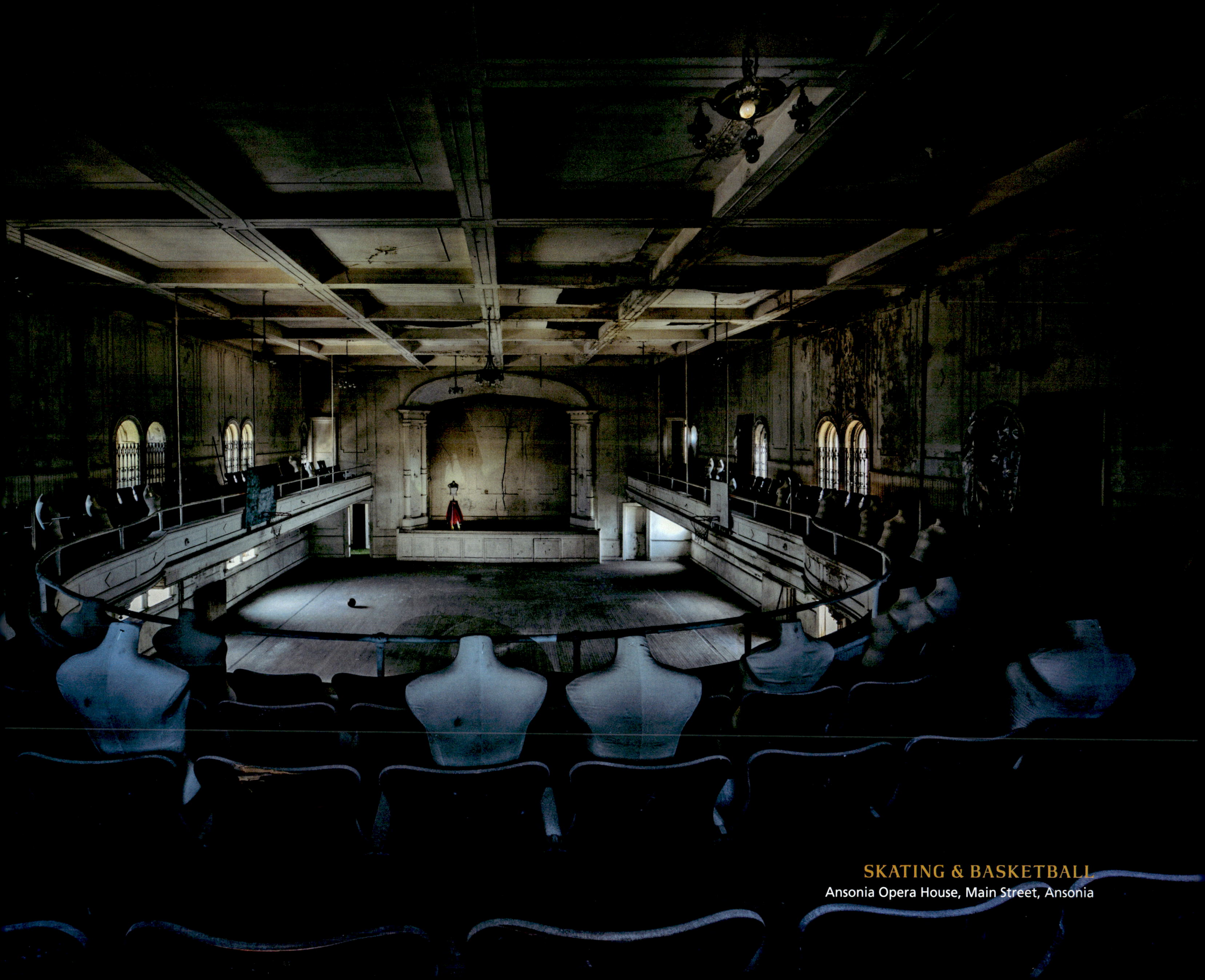

SKATING & BASKETBALL

Ansonia Opera House, Main Street, Ansonia

OUR STORIES:

Alchemy

They thought real wealth was material; it lay in a plot of ground and the stuff we picked from it—corn, coal, iron, gold—and from which we made things. The country's network of railroads nationalized the economy, and those who owned the coal fields or the copper mines or the exclusive means to bring the rock to market had a golden goose by the neck.

Big change happened with unusual speed; electricity surged into our lives in two forms. It lit light bulbs that gave us more time, and it powered motors that quickened the day. Electric trolleys are Frank Sprague's forgotten revolution. Though we spent years hanging the overhead wires and laying the iron claws, few of us recall how the change began, how quickly it washed over us.

In 1886 Waterbury's first horse trolleys trotted out, and the street-rails from Exchange Place began reaching into neighborhoods. The nation had built 526 horse railways since the Civil War, but Waterbury, apparently conservative in such matters, was just getting its first. In the same year, a horseless trolley with an electric motor to make it go, the first in New England, began shuttling freight between the Derby docks and the American Brass factory in Ansonia. It was the twelfth electric trolly in the nation, a bold experiment here in Brass Valley, a tipping point, and few guessed the swiftness of the revolution. Within a year Frank Sprague had built a city-wide electric trolley system in Richmond, Virginia, and 180 cities were building electric "traction" systems, transforming lives, quickening the tempo around the world.

In 1886, however, as many cities were electrifying, Waterbury was just getting horse rails. It wasn't as if things moved faster by horsecar than before, but the commitment of rails made drivers follow a route and a rough schedule; teams of horses didn't strain as when setting an omnibus in motion, and the steel wheels made the ride smooth for conversation, even with a friend strolling along the sidewalk.

A horse trolley along any of Waterbury's main streets wasn't much faster than walking, but the space of the horsecar was democratic, and we came to know folks we rode with. It was a poor conductor who didn't know everything worth knowing about the regulars and their neighbors. The conductor and driver were men of steady habits and friendly banter who added security to our lives as they passed through our neighborhoods throughout the day. Of course the streetcar could also sometimes be a place of class and racial tension, and conductors had to be good diplomats and, occasionally, enforcers of the law. The trolley set the tempo of the street. Its conductor brought us the news of the valley before our newspapers could. The ladies and the elderly appreciated the way conductors stepped down to help them aboard, and they knew us as regulars. And if we overslept, we appreciated when a driver waited at

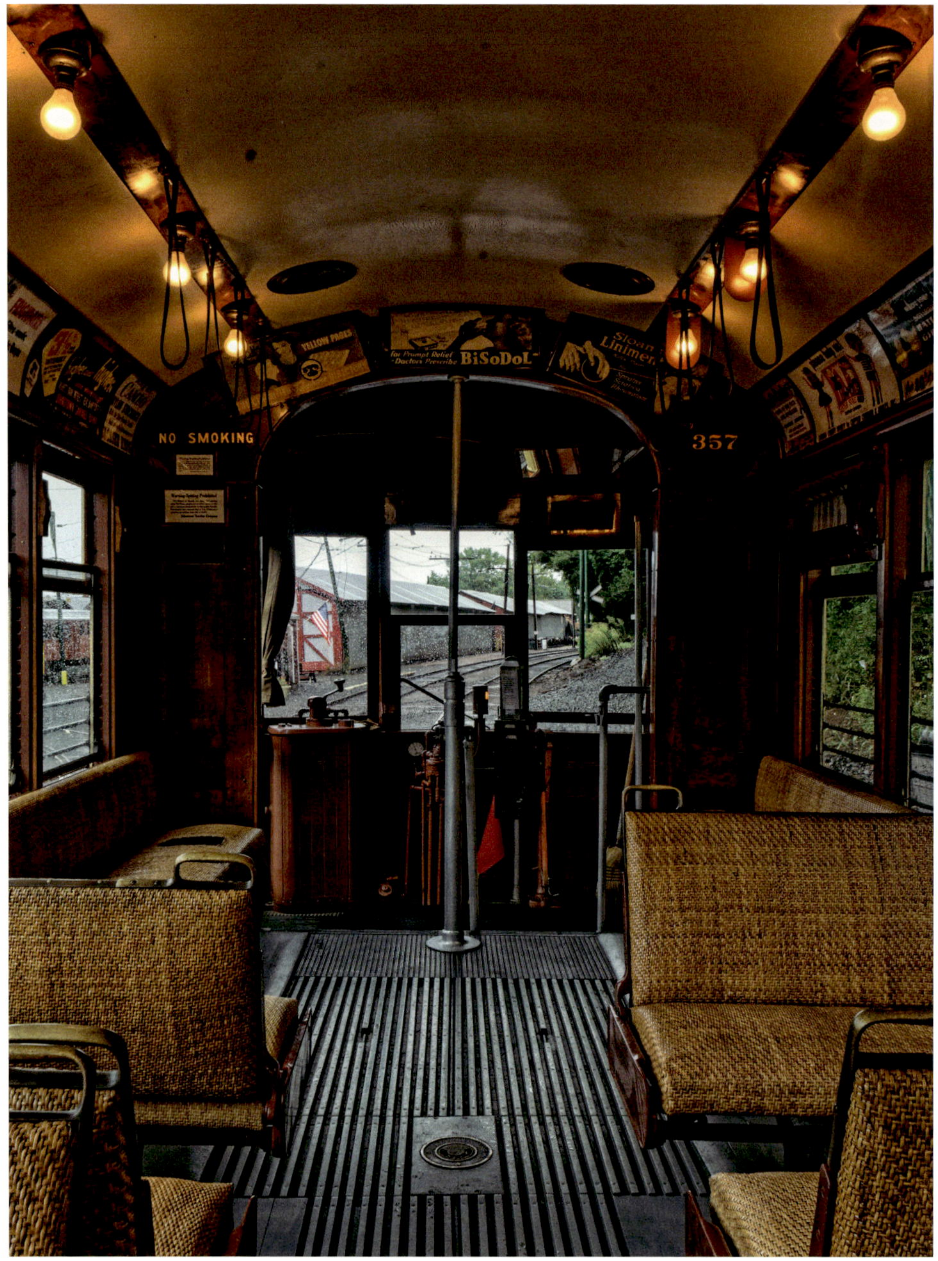

BISODOL

Shoreline Trolley Museum, Branford, CT

the stop an extra few minutes, and the conductor knew how much getting to our job meant to us.

When traction workers retired or died our newspapers ran stories about their careers, and their lives added continuity to our own. They were "Knights of the Road" in the great laboring city, solidly "middle class," and some little boys, seeing the respect a conductor was given, couldn't wait to start as "hill boys," and thought nothing of fourteen- and sixteen-hour workdays. But a few old-timers had driven in stage coach days when they owned their own rigs, and profits were theirs and shared only with the horses.

Of course nobody appreciated the mess, especially in the middle of Exchange Place, where the horses all passed and waited and passed some more. What cost and labor to remove what they passed! And then the cost to feed and stable eight or ten constantly passing horses for every horsecar! There was much political in-fighting over the right to use the public right-of-way. Despite the cost and mess of horsecars, it took until 1894 for the Waterbury Traction Company to be chartered by the legislature to begin electrification. By then many cities had electrified transit, and there was a growing move toward interurban lines. When Waterbury finally electrified our trolleys, it changed life's tempo: schedules were kept more crisply, conductors couldn't hold the car or step to the street to help ladies board, and then the crew was reduced to just a driver with a bell, and the banter was flat.

Even so, by 1910 we were taking trolley holidays to see relatives two towns away, and taking the family to a distant ball park to cheer on the home boys or to the circus in Bridgeport or to an electric trolley park filled with rides and amusements. Trolley parks kept us riders riding. It was George W. Beach's old "High Rock Park" idea, electrified.

A trolley line linked Winsted and Torrington in 1897 with a spur to a park at Highland Lake. In 1908 a trolley line even connected Waterbury to Woodbury, and at Lake Quassapaug they built a trolley park to draw riders from as far as Meriden via Cheshire and Exchange Place. City folk tried suburban living, and downtown Waterbury, lit up and bustling, was a golden spectacle for farm folk. Main Street in all directions was thriving, but the greatest profits came to those who knew first where the new trolley lines would be built as the age of electrification began.

The rest of us enjoyed the trolley's chime, and in summer the breezes of the bloomer cars. A few adventurers, we've heard, sought to ride out the system by hopping trolleys, town to town, from New York City to Boston with only small gaps to be crossed behind the heavy chugging of steam trains.

After 1906 trolley track finally snaked the wild, narrow stretch of valley between Beacon Falls and Naugatuck. It united service from Waterbury with the lower valley trolleys from Seymour to Derby and on to Bridgeport and by passenger steamship service daily to New York City, but the last valley link between Thomaston and Torrington was never built. After 1920 trolleys were in decline, and autos began claiming more roadway to move us faster. Trolleys had changed us: tightened our schedules, brought us closer, spread us apart, mixed us, crushed us, jumbled us, and caused us to see each other in new ways.

In 1901 the Superior Court of Connecticut ordered the Connecticut Lighting and Power Company to change its name to the Connecticut Railway and Lighting Company, so much had their business grown beyond the selling of electricity. They had devoured many small traction companies, until all the trolleys and the Naugatuck Steam Railway and the steamship from Bridgeport and more were finally controlled by the New York, New Haven, and Hartford Railroad. If it traveled with a motor, usually they moved it, and their push came with considerable mass.

Unlike railroads, trolleys mostly ran on public rights of way, and raised new questions about the role and behavior of local and state officials in negotiating contracts for their use, and about our public right to public transportation. Trolley service also provided a very public battlefield upon which unions and management frequently waged war and sought to woo our opinion regarding the value of our labor and our right to work, and some of us in the mills were becoming union members ourselves, and many of us refused, but American labor was exploring and testing its power.

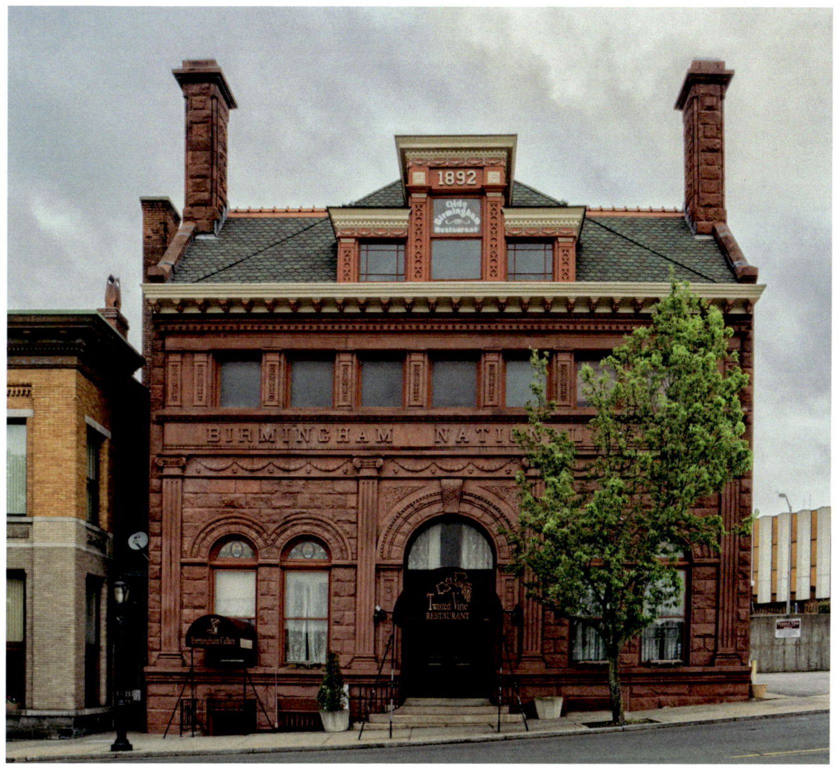

BIRMINGHAM BANK
Derby, CT

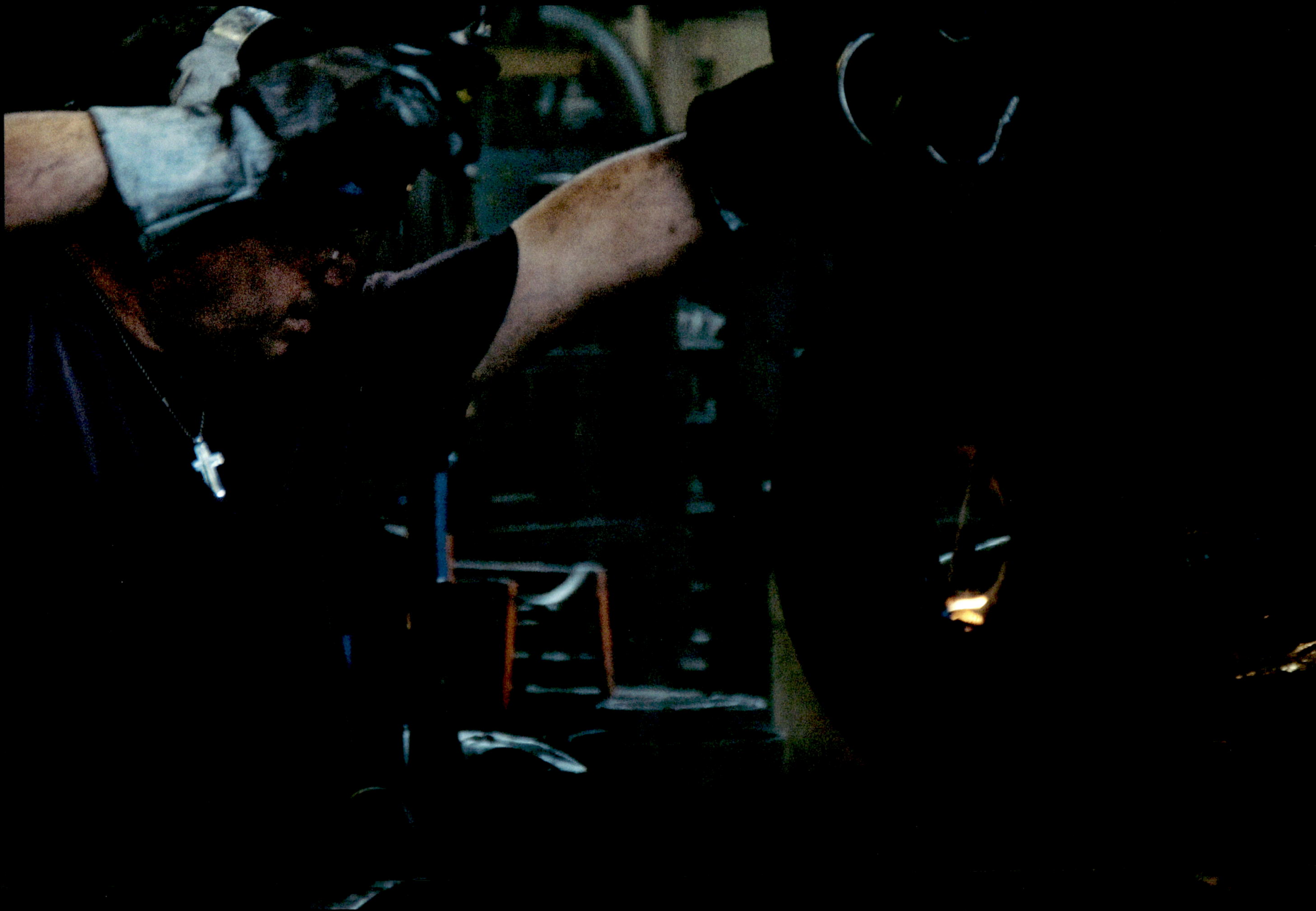

SPIKE, THE DIE HANGER & HIS DIE
American Brass, Bank Street, Waterbury, CT

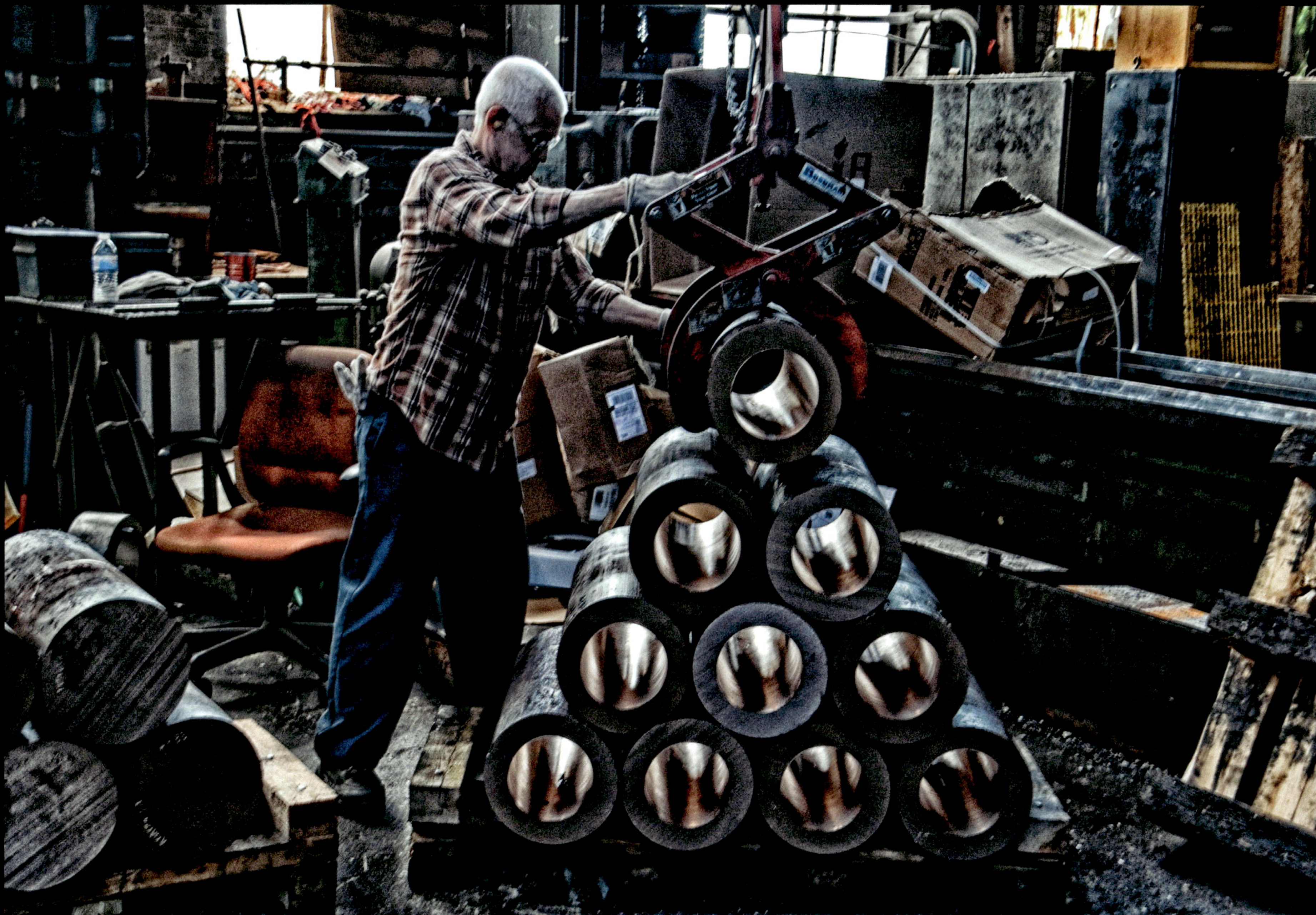

FRED THE MACHINIST & HIS PYRAMID
American Brass, Bank Street, Waterbury, CT

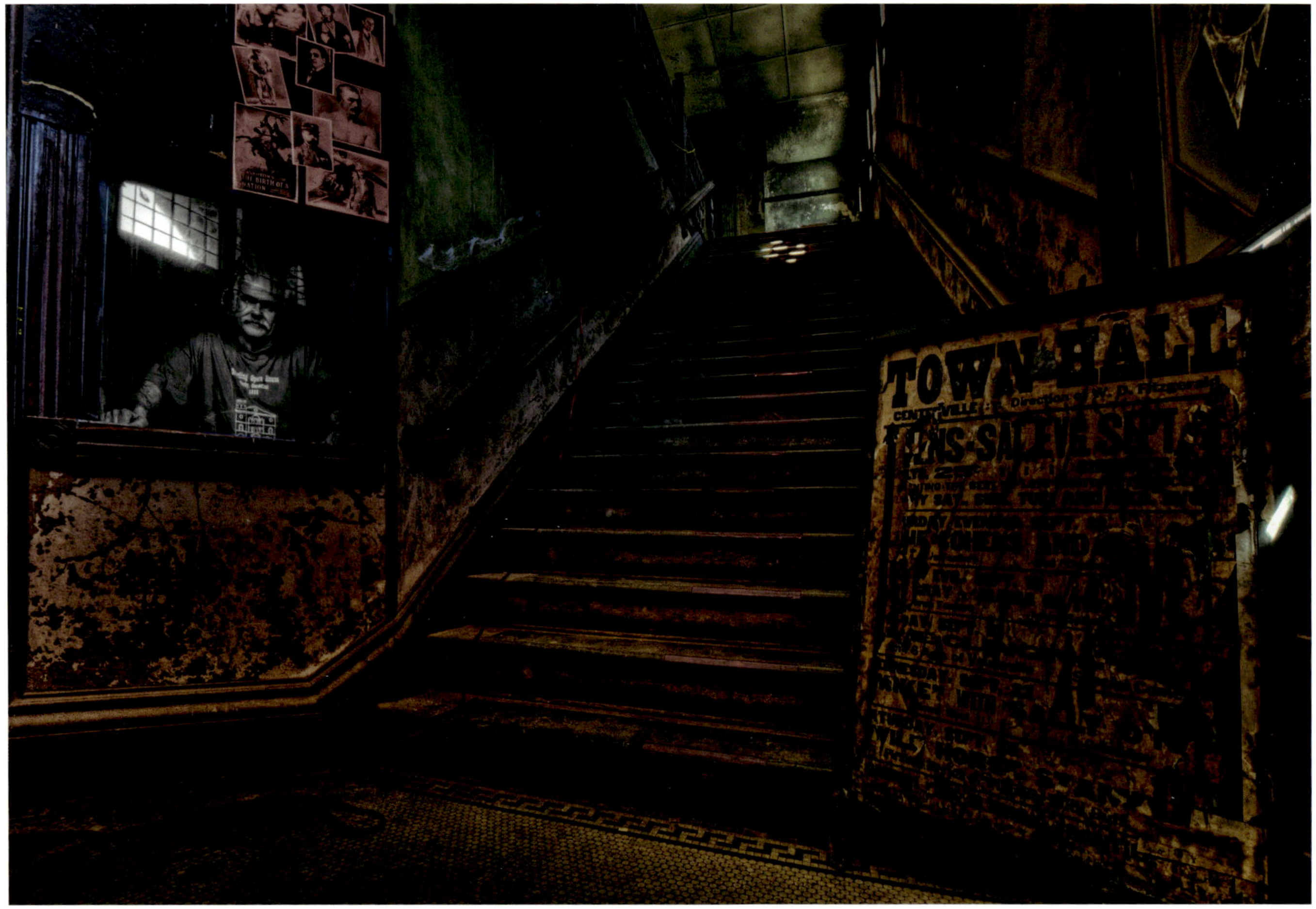

OUR STORIES:

Lower Valley Quarrels

MARK ANTHONY AT THE OPERA HOUSE

Lobby, Sterling Opera House, Derby, CT

It was 1889. One had only to step inside the vestibule of Borough Birmingham's new Sterling Opera House to feel how aspirations have swelled since 1870 when Ansonia's Opera House was built. Some said the Sterling is unconscionably extravagant, the product of overweening pride.

Others called it civic pride, and claimed to have vision. They told us Sterling Hall was a tribute to the memory of an esteemed citizen, the late Charles A. Sterling. What could be more natural than partnership between citizens of Birmingham and the Sterling Piano Company, a major Birmingham employer that has put up a good part of the money for the new hall? The results spoke, or rather, sang for themselves—acoustically perfect! It had been built following principles developed personally by Richard Wagner and his architects at the Festspielhaus in Bayreuth, Germany. They said that in one step the hall was making Birmingham the cultural center of the whole Northeast. With a hall even better than Mr. Steinway's, on 14th Street in New York City, the greatest artists of the day would flock to Birmingham.

Birmingham town fathers insisted Birmingham's new status demanded the upgrades to public infrastructure and to the town green that were recently completed. They said most people in Birmingham, including many mill owners there and across the Housatonic in the newly incorporated Borough of Shelton, were envisioning a united region, with the shining town green on the Birmingham hill as the political and cultural center of a prosperous Derby.

Across the river, along the heavily populated hillsides of Borough Ansonia, people were not ready to pay for Borough Birmingham's frills. They grumbled, what good is an opera house where you can't skate? Our opera house was designed for practical people and it is as good as it ever was, except for the shows lost to the Sterling, and it was built without town money. It still earned investors a tidy profit. They reasoned Ansonia is the economic center of the township of Derby, and they worried, when the debt came due, would they be stuck paying for Birmingham's beautification? Some people even talked of seceding from the township. Mostly, however, people were galled by the bombshell that dropped from the front page of *The Transcript* on the day after Christmas: Birmingham was petitioning to become the "City of Derby" with Ansonia and Shelton to be made boroughs thereof. No one saw it coming.

People in Ansonia were shocked at the swollen arrogance of it all; in Shelton they were stunned. Shelton and Birmingham were even in different townships; Birmingham was in Derby Township, but Shelton was in Huntington. Of course, all the land in Shelton was owned by the Ousatonic Water Company of Birmingham, which built and ran the dam on the Housatonic River between them. Everyone in Shelton was aware that the power company and its slick lawyers had always done as they pleased in Shelton with little opposition from the rural hill farmers of Huntington, legal governors of Shelton.

In Shelton they began contemplating all the mills on their side of the river and their outstanding record of growth, while making snide comments about, perhaps, Shelton becoming a city sometime soon and annexing Birmingham.

It was a classically tumultuous year, 1889. There were many parties of interest to the doings in the lower valley, and the whole region was soon embroiled. What you thought probably depended on where you lived. The *Evening Transcript* supported the Birmingham plan and editorialized, "United in one community we would soon advance to the front rank among the prominent and progressive towns of the State." *The Sentinel* opposed it and supported Ansonia's own petition for separation from Derby Township and incorporation as an independent town, unshackled by Birmingham's over-reaching debt. Wherever you lived, you were entitled to claim moral indignation and outrage against the other side with certainty that high ethical principles were at stake.

Of course there are also those who believed that it was always just about ego, greed, and lust for power, and there are those who look back and wonder if it mattered much at all. Up and down the valley, town streets were being paved and lighted, and new trolleys took a growing leisure class to places that had not existed a few years before, even as new immigrants arrived looking for work. Whatever you believed, one felt the aspirations of the age inside this hall. The opera house was no longer for skating.

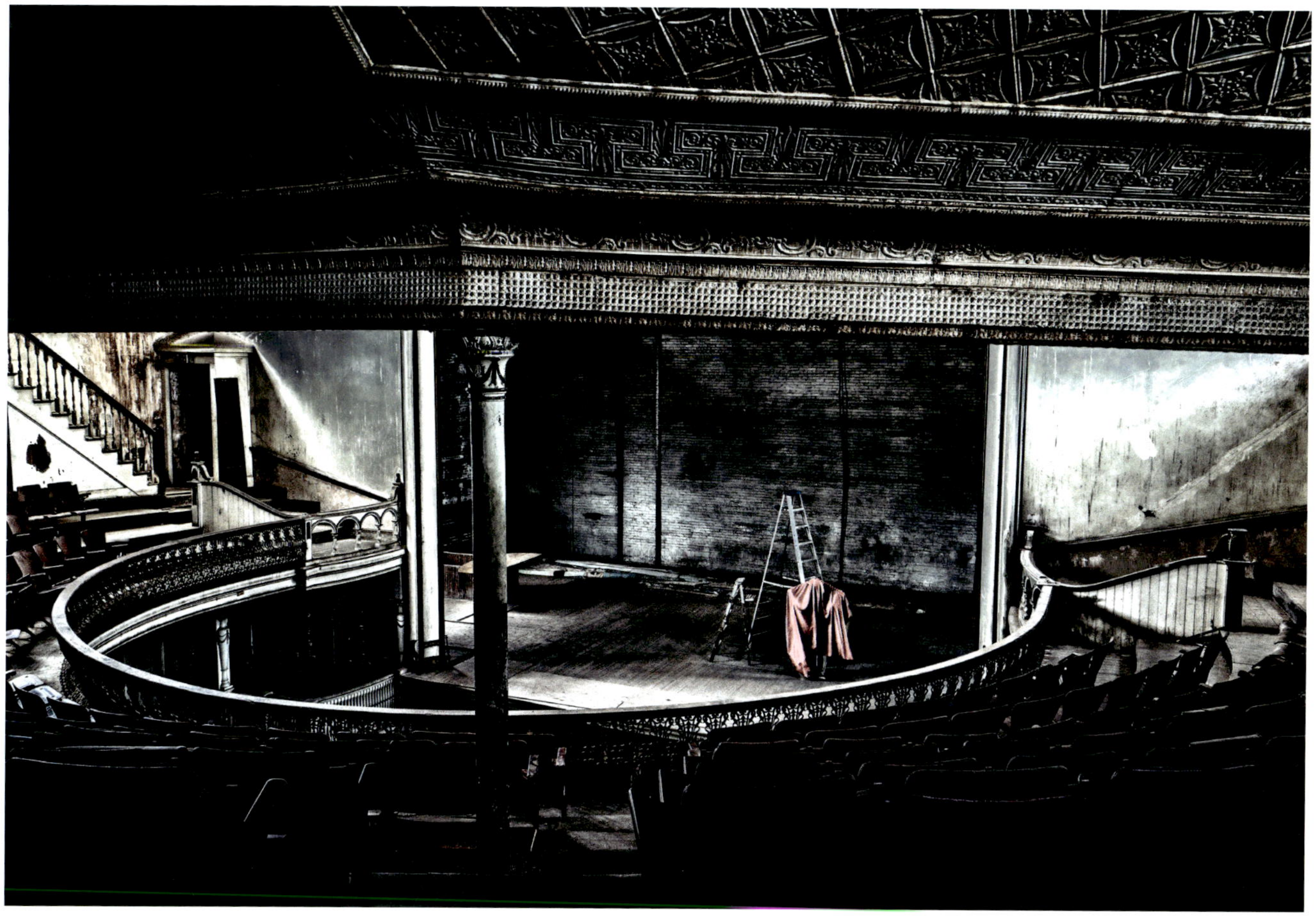

AT THE STERLING
Sterling Opera House, Derby, CT

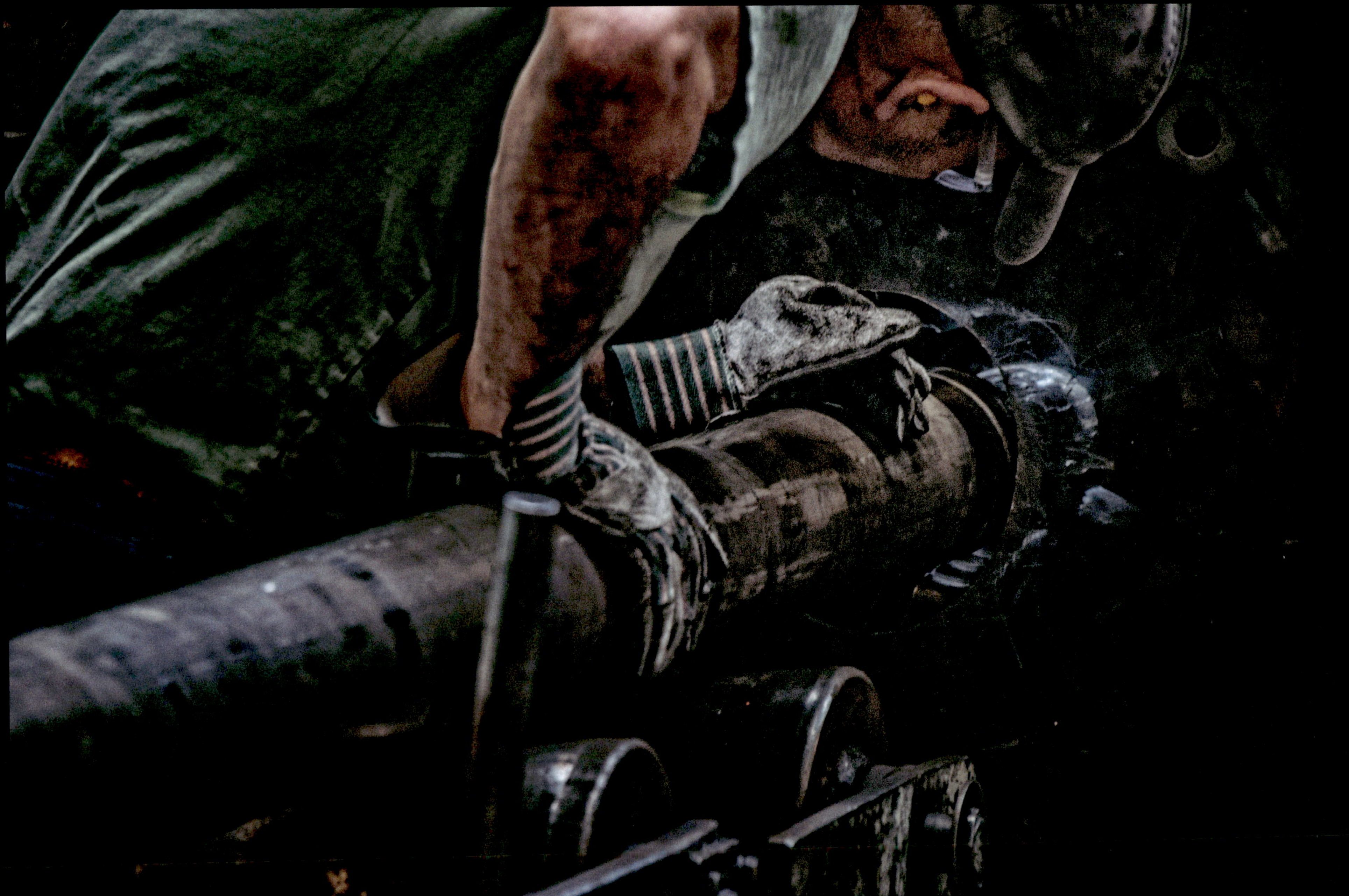

GEORGE THE POINTER MINDING HIS POINTERS
American Brass, Bank Street,
Waterbury, CT

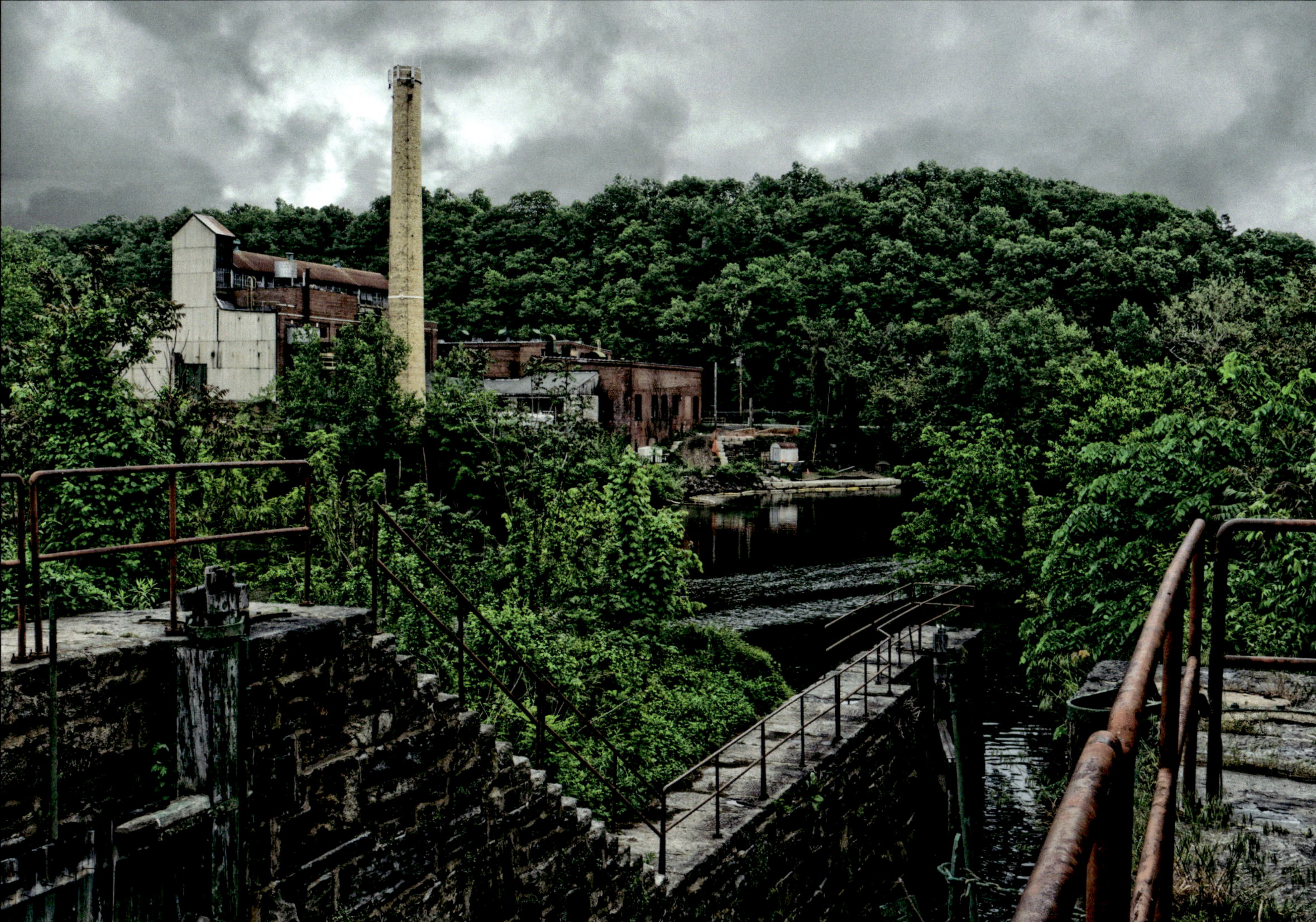

PHOTOGRAPHER'S JOURNAL:

These locks and the old power company across the river, and the dam just upstream from here, were built in 1867 by the Ousatonic Water Company of Birmingham. The water company belonged to a group of Birmingham businessmen. It was the first of many power generation dams across the Housatonic, though there was little industry upstream after the dam was built.

I've walked the canals that still flow on both sides of the river. They were built, I'm told, to power the last unharnessed mill sites around the basin where the Naugatuck meets the Housatonic. The owners of the water company were shrewd businessmen and knew what they were doing when they bought the future mill sites in the sleepy Borough of Shelton; they knew what the dam would mean. It was an odd arrangement. Even though Shelton was a borough in the rural township of Huntington, much of the profit from Shelton's mills went to the Borough of Birmingham, and taxes went to the township of Derby. The township of Derby once stretched all the way to Newtown, but by 1900 many towns had been settled and achieved self-government, until Derby and Birmingham had become nearly synonymous and there is still confusion over names.

REAL POWER

Ousatonic Water Company locks and power plant from Shelton, CT

Promenade

It is literally true, the opera house is no longer for skating. Wagner's principles of theater design required raked seating. Inside the Sterling Hall one feels the sensibility of the age swelling, striving to be urban and urbane. It features clear sound and unobstructed views for all, a democratic plan. Although the inexpensive top balcony seats are only benches, hard like church pews unless you bring your own cushion, those seated there and standing behind them are promised equal access to the proceedings.

More importantly, the truth, barely concealed, about the extravagant opera house was that half of the building was to be a new city hall with offices for a mayor, a meeting room for the city council, facilities for a city treasurer, police chief, even a jail, though there was no mayor, no city council, no city. Architect Henry Ficken had delivered to the town fathers exactly what they had specified: City Hall for the swollen vision that included annexing the independent boroughs of Ansonia and Shelton, now rejected and, alas, little more than a skirmish and revision of the water's bounties.

Though their vision of Derby never came to be, the building gives the ideals and deceptions lasting form in stone: their vision was of a metropolis whose extent encompassed all the shores where the rivers meet and where we toil, and where trolleys let us exercise our liberty by carrying us to markets and entertainments that yield us happiness. Meanwhile, as we spend, Derby's leaders manage the profits from atop the hill in the very center of the town in the square laid out a half-century earlier by Sheldon Smith and Anson Phelps for their industrial village. Sterling Opera was to become town center, city center, cultural center, on the town green beside religious centers; it was the capstone of a democratically ordered and, sometimes, benevolently corrupt life.

It is a vaguely Italianate town hall, a latter-day Uffizi for Yankee Medicis. Add whatever H. G. Wells visions turn-of-the-century Yankees might also have imagined, perhaps a tin can rocket shuttling us back and forth to Mars with names engraved in brass on saucepan spaceports. Even after the vision of City Birmingham was forgotten, it would be a long time before anyone realized quite how wrong the borough leaders were, but it set the tone of lower valley competition and high-school football for the next century as all three boroughs soon became the independent cities of Derby, Ansonia, and Shelton, smallest cities in the state. It was a framework for cooperation and competition.

Meanwhile, whether we came to see the latest melodrama or vaudeville show or to hear the great Paderewski or Caruso, the master of ceremonies at the Sterling and in auditoriums everywhere was often a new mechanical contraption of levers and strings stretched over a heavy, iron frame called a fortepiano, or "loudsoft." They had to be loud to fill a concert hall and soft to caress a tear and evoke a hush. Like clocks, pianos use many brass parts, and many craftsmen, machinists, and laborers are needed to make them.

Look inside the fine houses on the Birmingham green and along the town's central streets, named a half-century earlier for Sheldon Smith's daughters, Caroline, Minerva, and Elizabeth, and for Anson Phelps' wife, Olivia. There, inside the velvet and crystal parlors

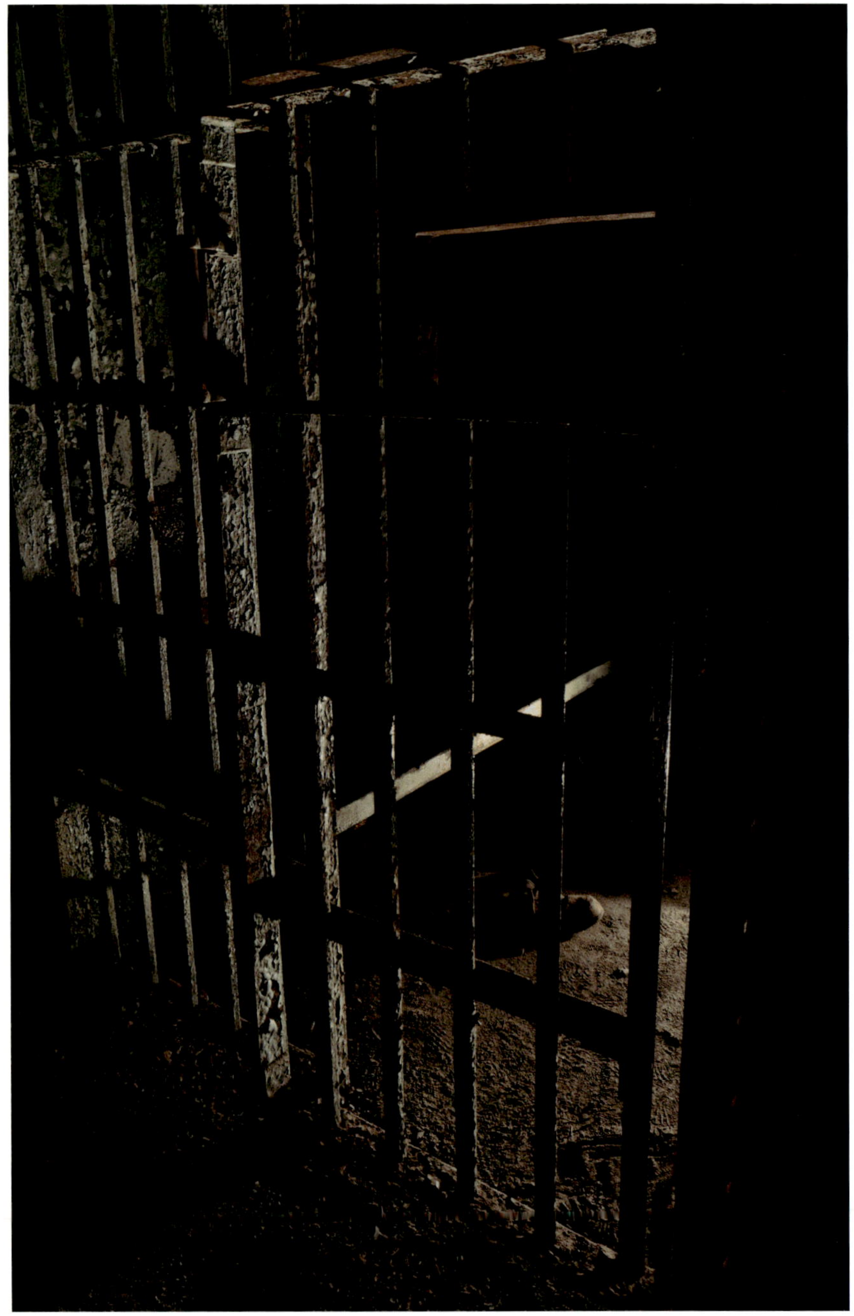

WAITING 1
City jail, Sterling Opera House,
Derby, CT

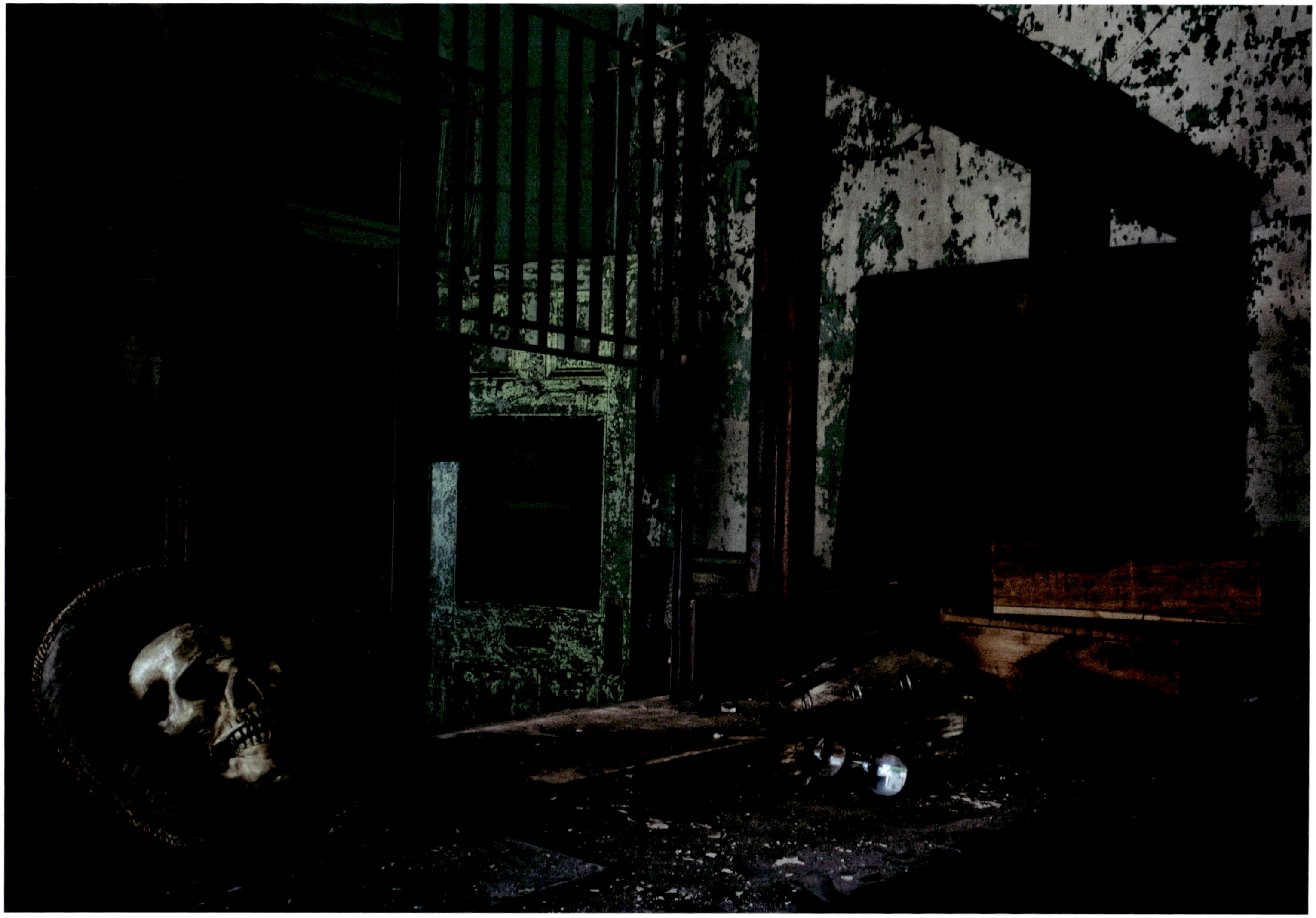

with their chiming mantle clocks, were pianos and often children practicing, and in Derby and Ansonia and towns throughout the northeast, merchants and professionals also had parlors, and once we had a parlor with a clock ticking, our next acquisition was often a piano with a bit of tatting and a ceramic compote rattling on the top, and lessons for the young ones.

The piano had become more than an MC; it was one of the stars, and we cheered even before the music stopped. The great age of the piano had begun, and virtuoso pianists were striving to succeed the great Franz Liszt by performing feats of pyrotechnics at the keyboard, and they were followed by legions of fans; entrepreneurs staged Monster Concert spectacles with dozens of pianos shaking walls and trying to stay together through a Strauss waltz or a Sousa march. The Sterling Piano Company had grown to occupy fifteen buildings, and just across the river in Shelton, the Huntington Piano Company was making inexpensive pianos with machines inside that let the keys magically play themselves, an eerie effect, no lessons or talent required, and lots of brass consumed.

Like the seating at the opera house, the distribution of swelling aspirations was similarly democratic with the toughest rump for those at the back but with prospects swelling for all. The new essential tech toy was a piano to pursue our happiness whether it was to play the old hymns or new rags, accompany ballads, or strive for the "Moonlight Sonata."

OFFICE OF THE CITY CLERK
Sterling Opera House,
Derby, CT

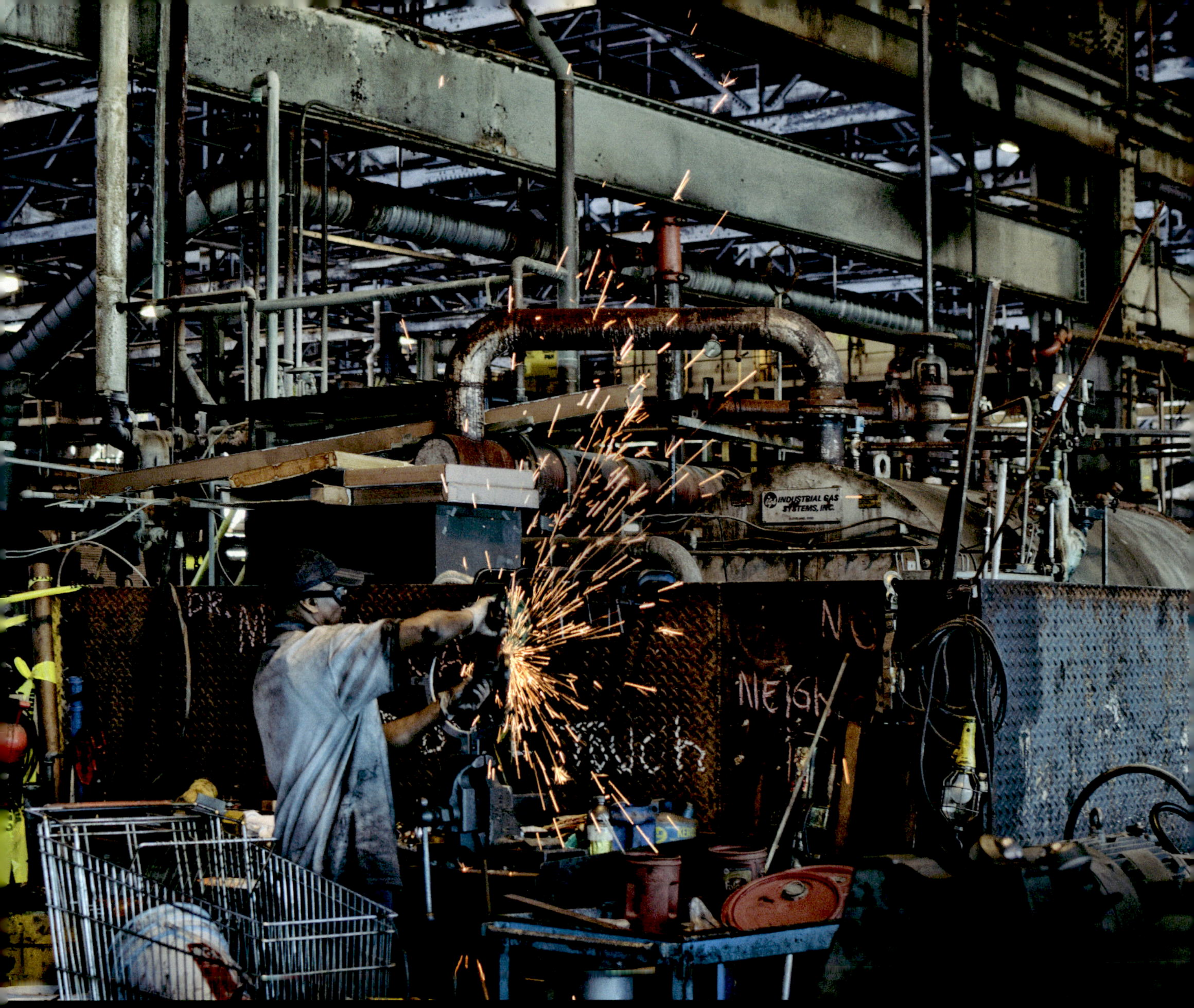

TOOLMAKER MEL'S TRAJECTORIES

American Brass, Bank Street, Waterbury, CT

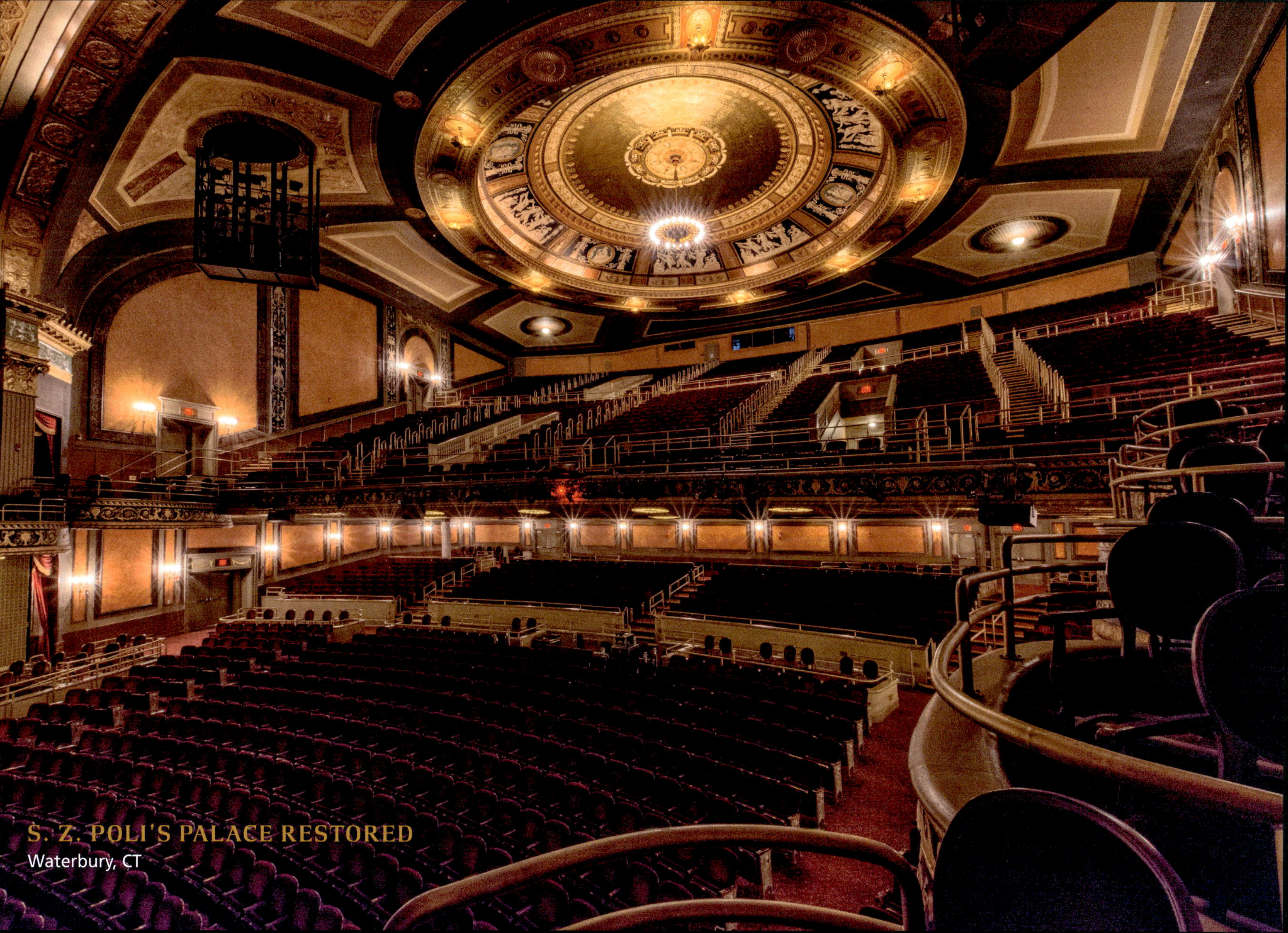

S. Z. POLI'S PALACE RESTORED
Waterbury, CT

The construction of an opera house or theater, whether in 1882 or 1922, proudly celebrated the community's sense of distinction and heralded a sense of civic achievement—just as protecting these theaters from demolition or conversion to a parking lot or an antique boutique and instead restoring and renewing them affords each community with a renewed sense of pride today." —Brian Leahy Doyle, *Encore!: The Renaissance of Wisconsin Opera Houses*, 2009

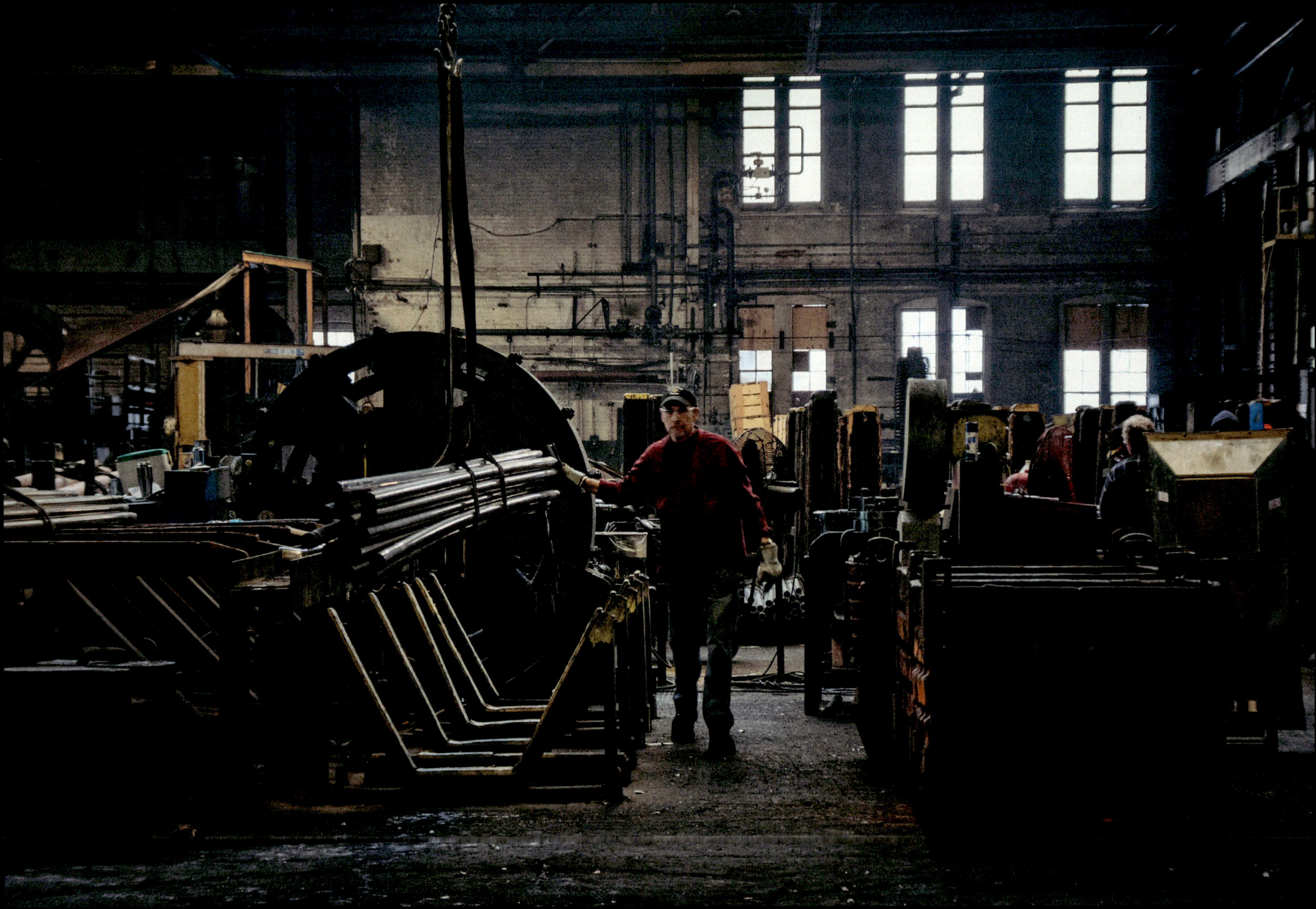

CIRCLES, SQUARES & TRAPEZOIDS OF LABOR

American Brass, Bank Street, Waterbury

PHOTOGRAPHER'S JOURNAL:

I rarely miss a chance to climb to the top of almost any tower to catch the view. In 1889, when the new Sterling Opera House opened its doors, the view from the third floor vestibule, behind the top balcony's hard pews, must have left the gents and ladies awed. At intermission there would have been just enough time to climb the stairs to the fourth-story tower room, no higher spot in town and a full panorama; factory smoke often makes for pretty sunsets. It would have been a romantic place, a place at the hub, above the original harbor where the Naugatuck found the Housatonic, where sailing ships took shelter and in times since, the source of Derby's industrial might. By 1889 there were lights at night in the city below, and people might be forgiven for thinking they saw the future twinkling. Freud and Einstein had not yet posed their hidden mysteries, and couples looking toward Long Island Sound from the tower of the Opera House dreamed the future might end their nightmares haunted with the specter of epidemics: influenza, consumption, dysentery.

Derby's Sterling Opera House, though distinguished by the three-borough battle over Derby's power grab and the repute of its acoustics, is in many ways of the era. City fathers sought a dignified building to fill multiple needs in a vision of harmoniously integrated civic life, corporate life, and government stability—a vision that was producing civilizing collaborations.

Immediately below the window's bunting was the old town green, and it's still there, looking much as it did a hundred and fifty years ago. If this were a hill town, there would once have been sheep grazing there, the town's common livestock, but this was a "valley" town planned for valley industry. The land had been a gift to the people by Sheldon Smith, the town's founder, the streets named for his daughters. Smith and Anson Phelps had also given land for building the Congregational, Methodist, and Episcopal churches there around the green, and the green in the middle was deeded to the town as common land on the expressed condition that it be fenced to keep sheep and people off the grass. Whatever it actually looked like, the idea was immaculate, Yankee Americana with an industrialist's twist.

Smith and Phelps were gone when the town fathers added vaudeville and politics to the green and visits by Houdini and Amelia and eventually Bing, but nobody could have foreseen Bing and radio's waves. Radio! The dream-magic of Nikola Tesla that made Marconi famous, provided FDR with a fireside, and tuned whole cities and the nation to a common cultural frequency as never before, but when Bing was at the Sterling, magic came to town.

The corner door at the base of the odd tower led to the opera house, but the doors to democracy were on the central axis through a classically columned, pedimented entry beneath a deeply shadowed, pedimented roof. It's not clear if the town fathers paused to contemplate democracy before giving it form in brick and stone; the full exterior is a hash of contradictions in which observers have found Italian Renaissance, Venetian, German, and English details. How oddly the roof's pediment hugs the building's squat tower as if they were best friends who always argued. The tower is topped by a Victorian, Federal, cupola-confection behind a white picket fence. Such ecumenical heresies seemed unimportant. Maybe ethnic hash was the point, as old wooden democracy was rebuilt in brick and stone to project new legacies into a new century that would stretch from crooning to Hendrix to a hip hop beyond.

Whatever the meaning of the architecture, whenever Sousa came to town, thrilling, chilling, exhilarating marches shook the windows and filled the town green, and the mayor and his friends had front row seats as the band played before their new town hall.

Imagine! It is entirely possible that a cacophonous young Charles Ives, who would write music peppered with remembered marching bands in musical collisions, traveled south from Danbury or north from Yale to hear the March King play in Derby's fine new hall. Ives was finishing his teens and entering Yale in the 1890s, playing organ in church and experimenting with the sounds of a century about to explode. The spirit of a time is written in its art; here in Derby, I'd like to think, was a point of curious intersection where Ives and Sousa might have collided.

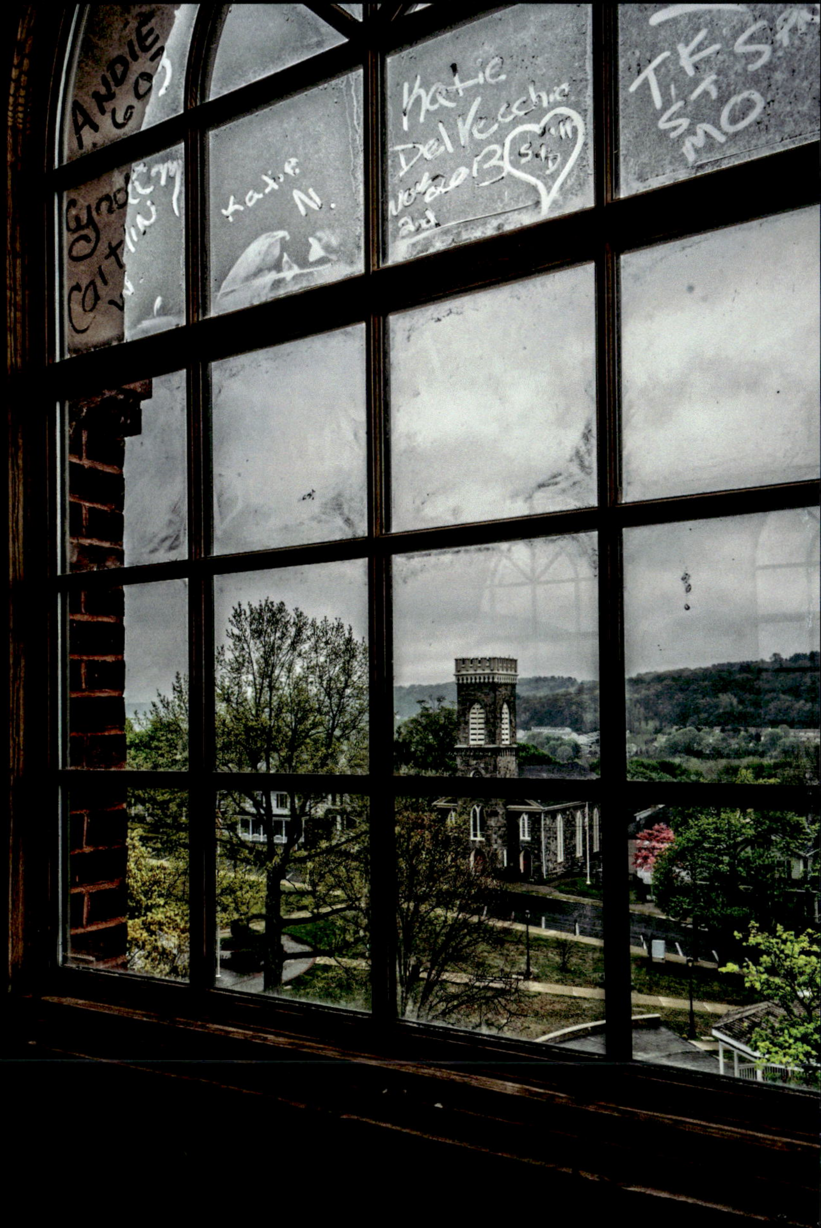

DERBY "TOWN GREEN"

As seen from the tower of the Sterling Opera House, Derby, CT

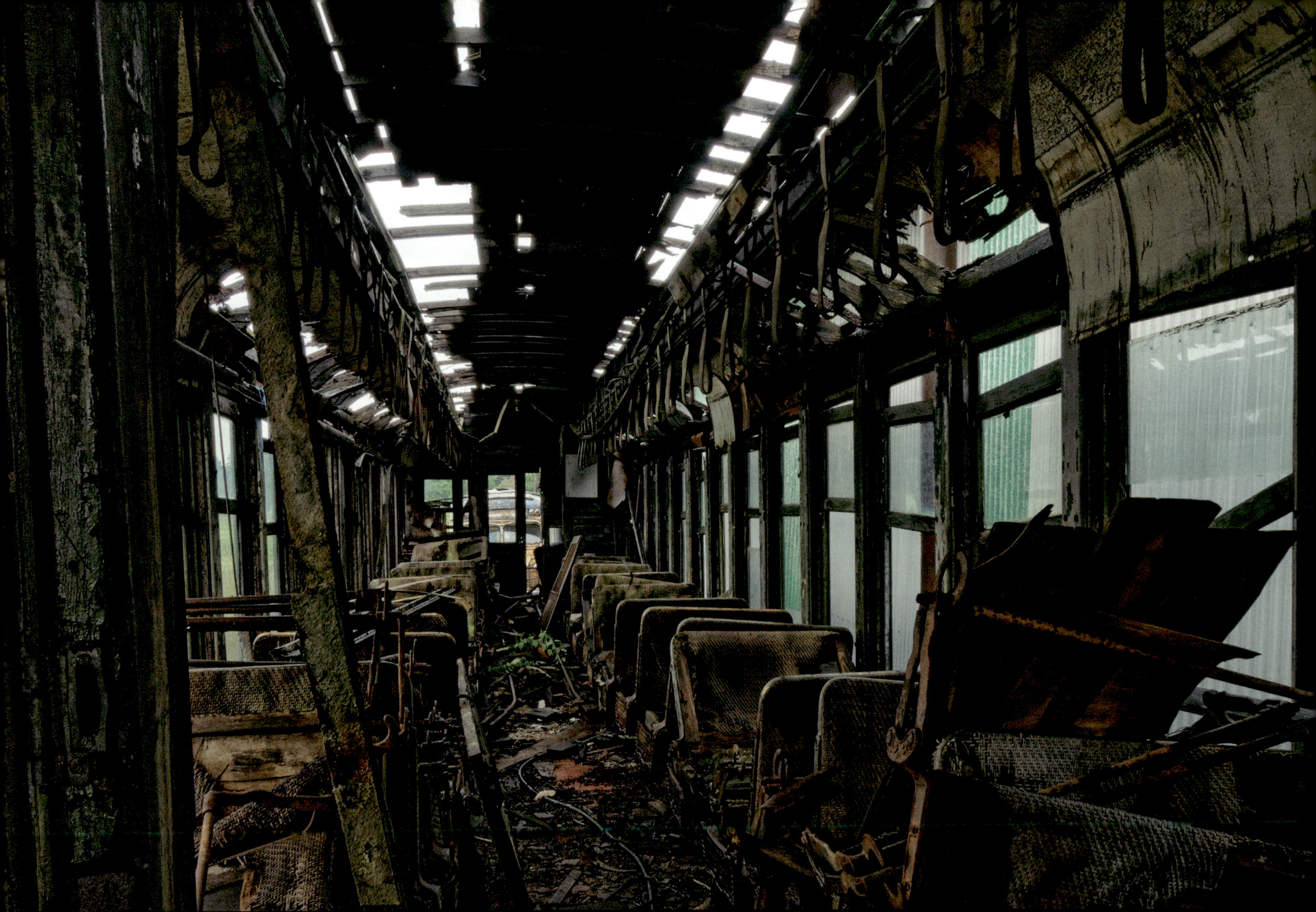

LAST STOP

ALCHEMY'S TOUCH

Toothsome particulates hang in the air,
the tongue knows first what simmers there
or if casting has begun,
and on the nerve ends round the nose
asperities of sooty harvest,
touchstones,
before eyes see the furnace glow.

WILLY THE FOUNDER,
MADE IN THE USA
American Brass, Ansonia, CT

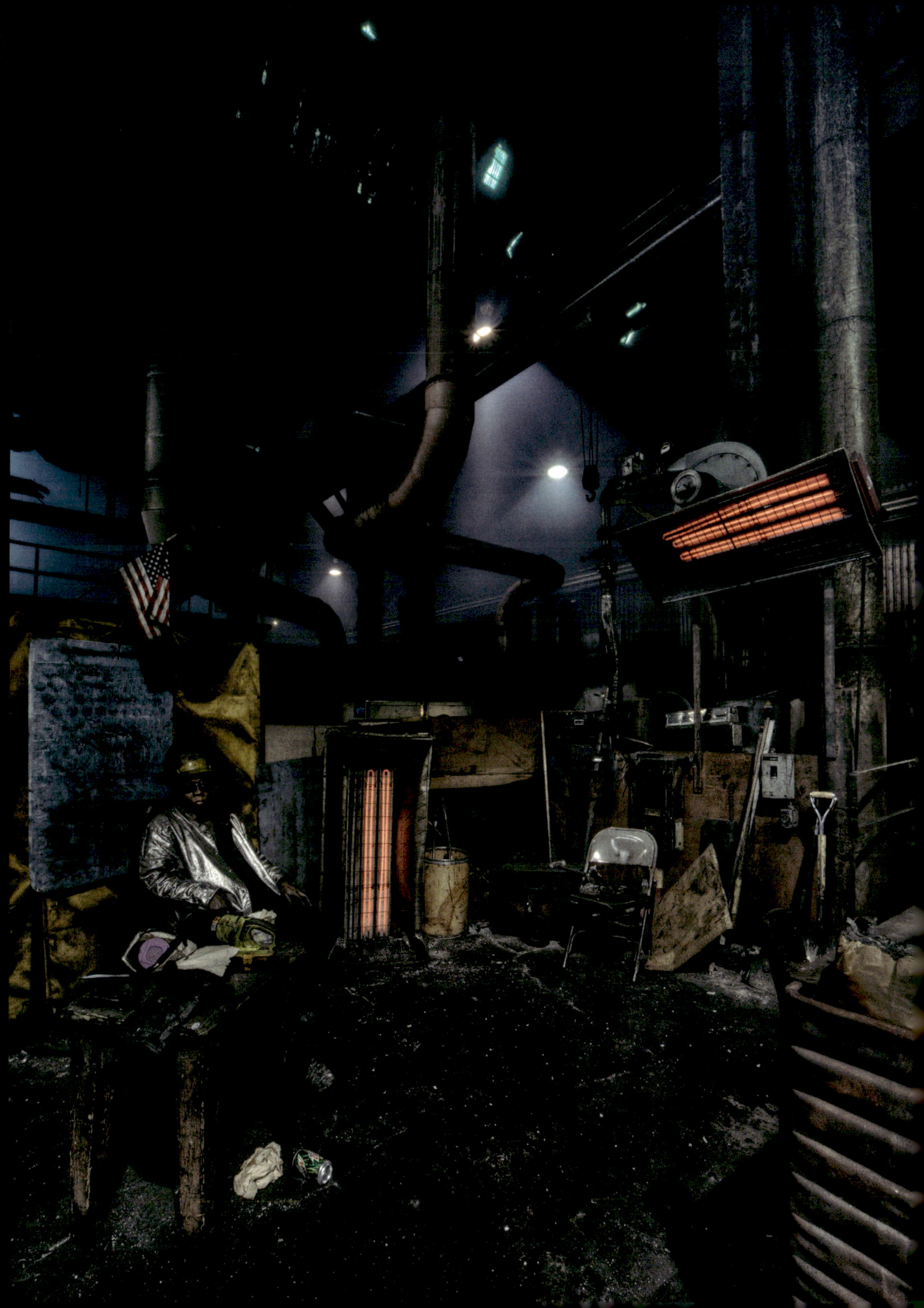

NEXT STOP HIGH ROCK GROVE, JULY 12, 1876

The train is sidetracked, loitering, killing time while the rails rust. They say the conductor died, but I've heard his voice, the conductor who became superintendent of the railroad and spoke with quiet authority.

"Tickets, fifty cents. Children under twelve half price. Leaving the station at 9 a.m., please deposit picnic baskets in the special baggage car provided at the rear of the train, and watch your step. Proceeds will help support the Poor Children's Excursion Fund. Ten minutes to board."

He served as agent in every station along the road from Long Island Sound to Winsted. "All aboard the Brass Valley Special with stops in Shelton, Birmingham, Ansonia Station, Seymour, Beacon Falls, and final destination, for today High Rock Grove, 1876."

The black track that runs along the river passes the Kinneytown Dam before it slips back in time, 'til we near the hiss of steam and the whistle's white shriek, and slip behind the surging hum of production for two world wars. As we pull out of Seymour, once Humphreysville, we watch for lovely Rimmon Falls beside the dam and the woolen mill where once, it's told, there was a tree.

That's where Superintendent of the Railroad George W. Beach was born, and now he has built a people's park upstream at that point in the river where the hills narrow to a gorge. It's a cool spot in the shadow of the valley, a green spot above Beacon Falls Dam, a quiet spot where the dam channels the water to make rubber shoes and woolen shawls and bronze piano-panels and leather belting and laces. We're near High Rock Grove when we see Rock Rimmon, like a plug in the valley, 400 feet high, but the train slips through, and as we slide back in time we glimpse Mr. Olmstead's landscaped workers' homes as rubber shoes are fading, but as the train coasts past the centennial, the gardens blend to a musical welcome. It's the Home Woolen Band's daily noontime concert and we lurch and stop.

"Beacon Falls! All aboard!"

Beacon Falls that brought fire to America. The first strike anywhere matches had been a flickering light, sometimes abandoned, but as we start again, sliding back before the town's incorporation we're almost to our destination, High Rock Grove, opening ceremonies, 1876. Above the dam the river narrows to a deep defile, pauses so young men flaunting mutton chops can row while gazing into the eyes of women reclined under mushroomy parasols to the harmonies of Scovill songsters on the shore. "High Rock Grove, last stop."

A simple platform tames the wilderness and the letters "HRG," spelled in floral planting and children's laughter. We follow the music of the Thomas Full Orchestra to a grand pavilion and a shady grove where we spread blankets, picnic, and play croquet. There's skating at the roller rink to the Wheeler and Wilson Band and meals by Mr. Marsh, our gentlemanly caterer furnishing refreshments at reasonable rates.

"Joy and gladness is the order of the day."

We follow trails deep into Sherman's Gorge, a precipitous course, past thick-thighed cataracts, dark pools, and mossy caves to where the world still grows wild, and adventures might yet be (though the Indians have gone, there is talk of a wild giant), until we arrive atop Lookout Point from which they say an Indian Princess jumped to her death, and where a grand pavilion rises above the hills so our eyes can follow the full arc of the day.

At the opening celebrations even the well-heeled of Norfolk and Winsted Yankees have come in coaches down the rails to mix with us, the more recently scrubbed, and occasionally on the 4th of July.

At the Naugatuck Railroad's peak, one could catch several trains daily to Bridgeport and catch the steamship to New York City, but High Rock Grove was where families went and especially children until 1905 when the Consolidated Railroad closed the park, blaming the smell of the river.

By the time the rink burned, the park was forgotten. Today commuter rail service as far up as Waterbury passes by the fabled gorge. The grove is forest, the station and the dam with its mutton-chopped rowers are gone, and there are kayakers in the rapids and on the top of High Rock; instead of a pavilion is a hash of graffiti and shredded American flags.

When the trains pass down the black track, where do they lead? Can we still find the rails to the valley where George Beach grew wise in David Humphreys's school, and where he later built not only the railroad but the pavilion atop High Rock with the park at its feet, a New Parthenon for picnics and parasols, songsters from Scovill and rowing behind the dam? Or was it only an American dream? And what new, magical transport is sidetracked and waiting to whisk us away? Where is the black track leading?

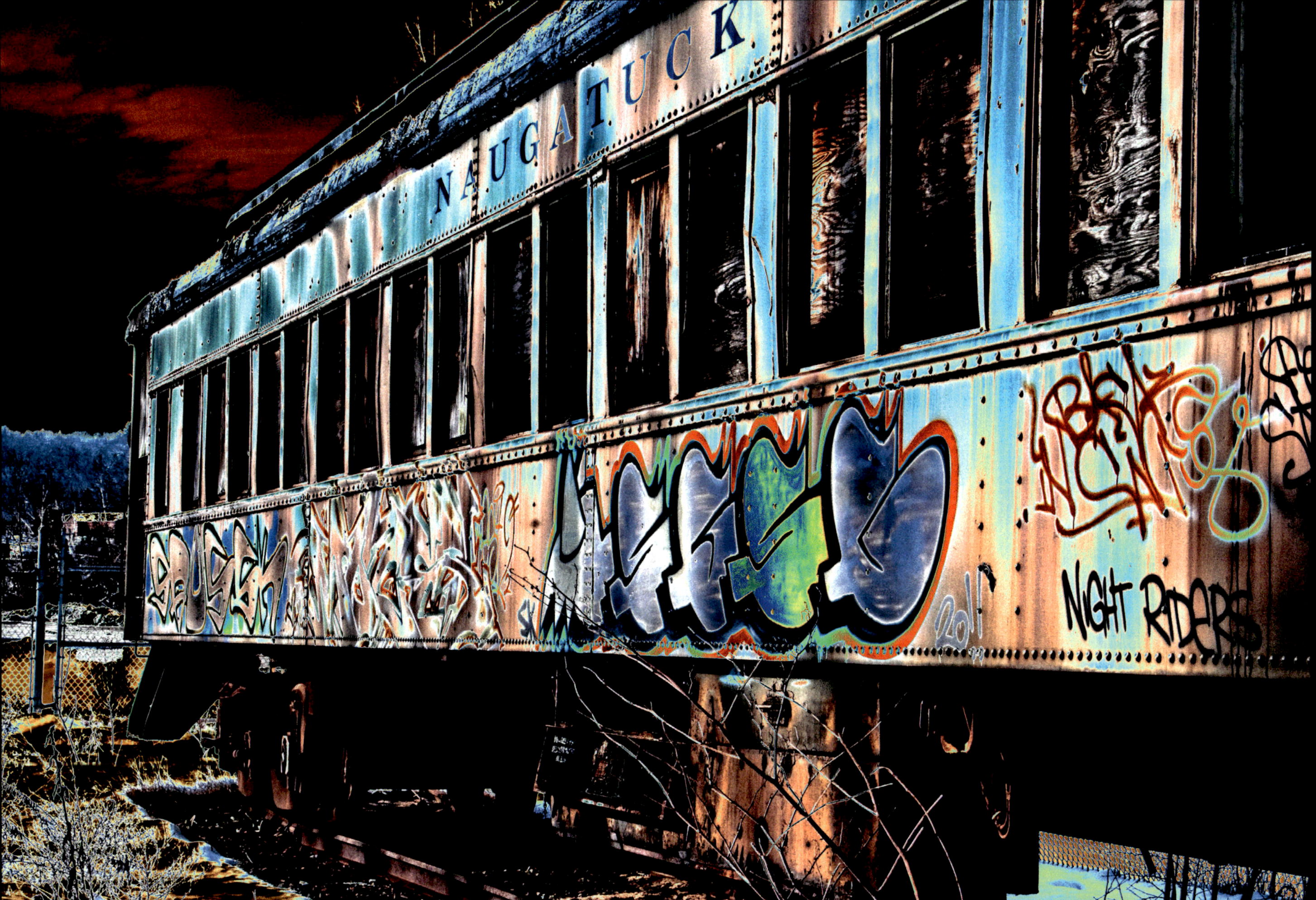

NAUGATUCK EXPRESS

Abandoned, Thomaston, CT

WATCH YOUR STEP

Watch your step,
Move to the rear.
Hold on to the hand rails
when stepping up or stepping down.
Please keep your bags out of the aisles.
Don't crowd.
Let departing passengers pass.
Watch your step getting off.
Move to the rear.

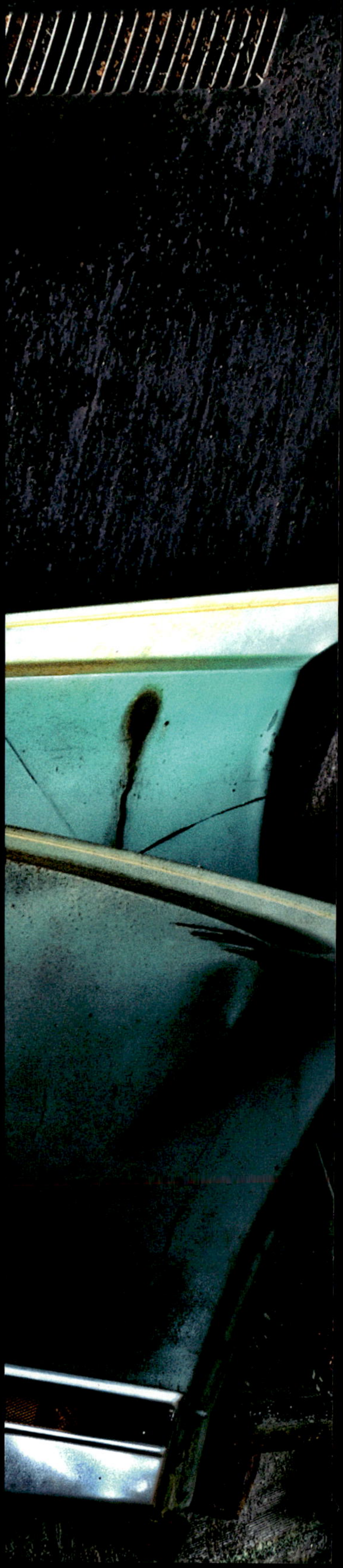

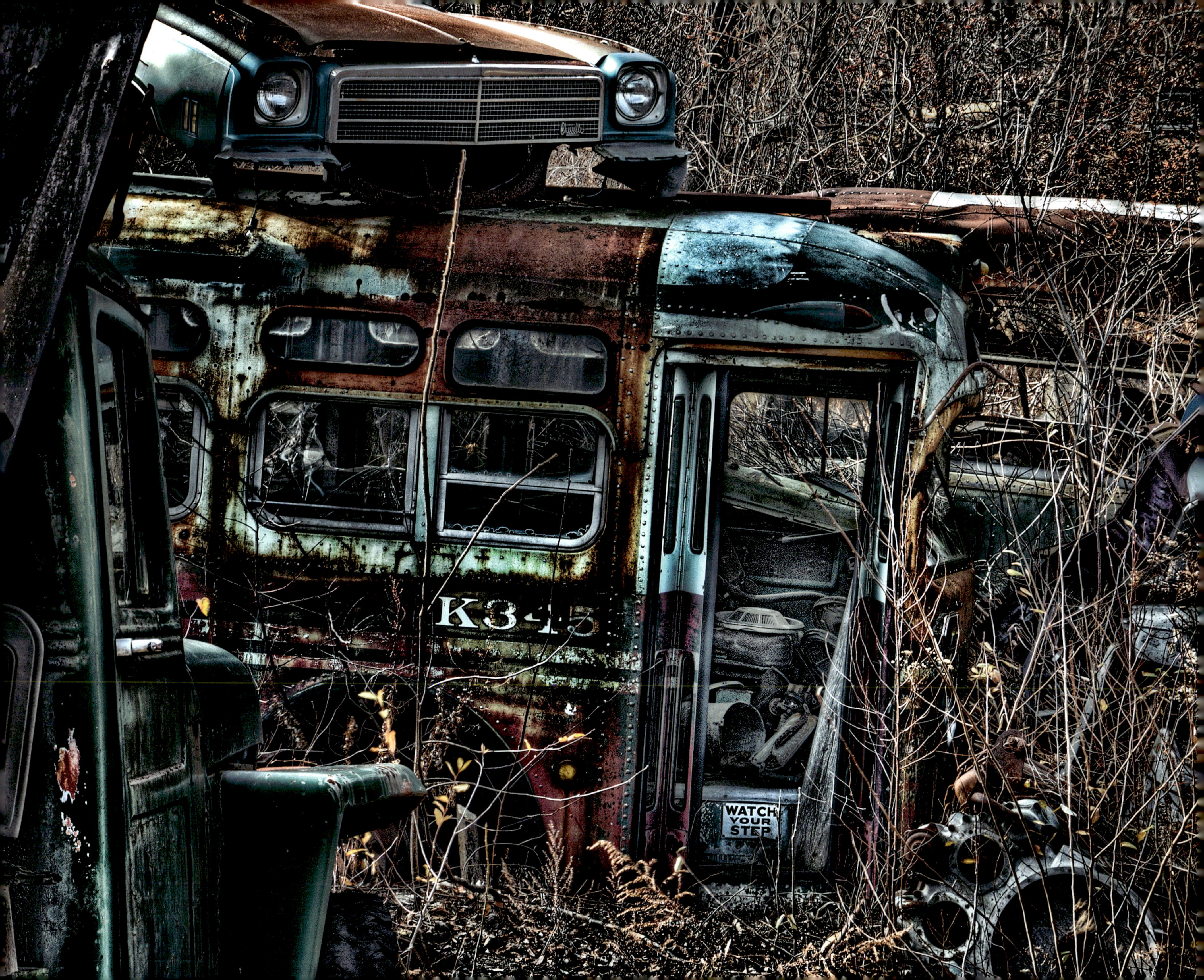
K345
WATCH
YOUR
STEP

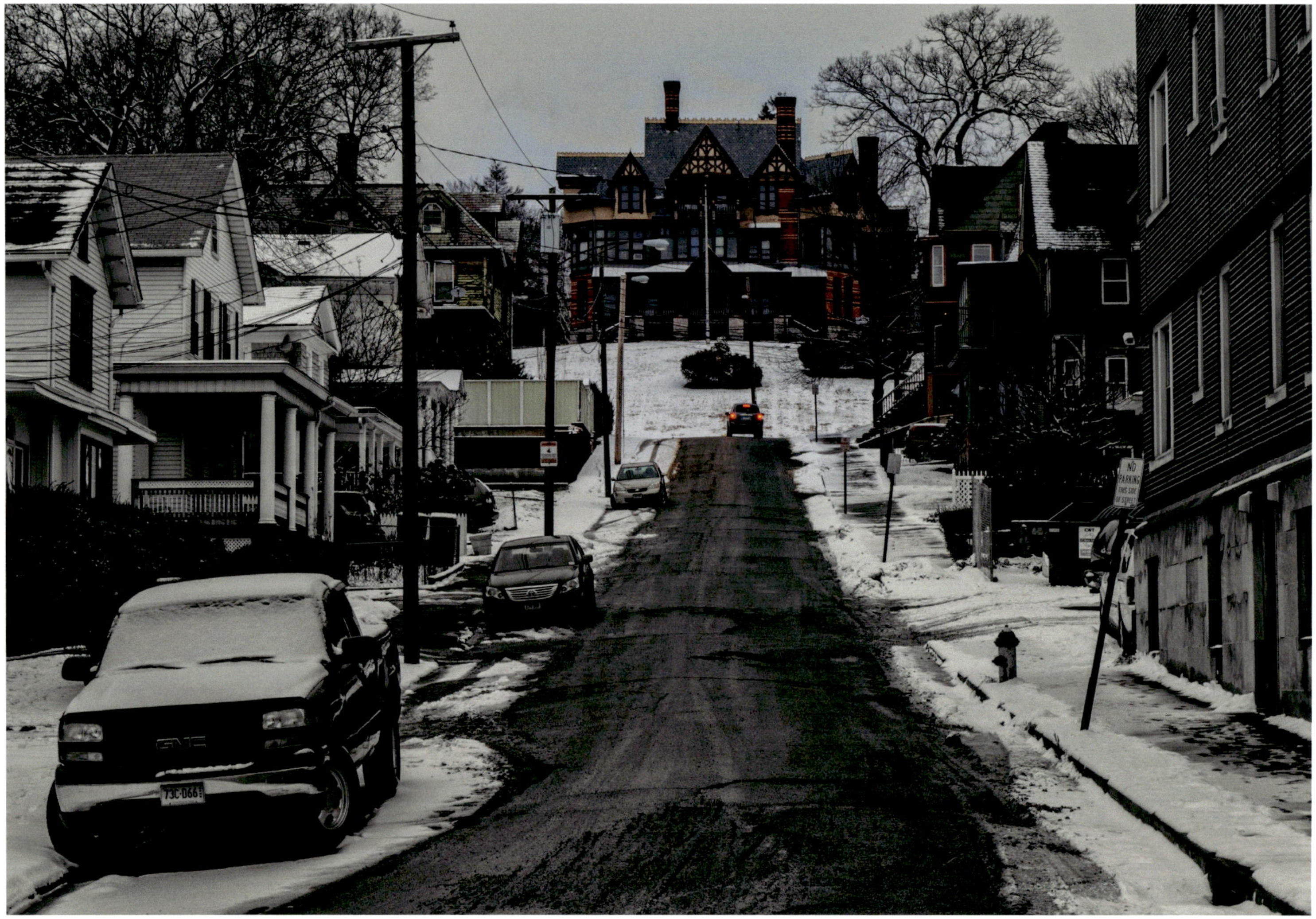

OUR STORIES:

Grove Hill

UP FIRST

Looking up First Street to Grove Hill, Waterbury, CT

The Birmingham green in Derby was a gift, formal and fenced against livestock, by Sheldon Smith and Anson Phelps, the town fathers. Waterbury's green evolved in the way of hill towns, from a town common with meetinghouse at the center and shared flock grazing rough turf all around. Does it make a difference for democracy?

Up and down Brass Valley, power was distributed among so called Brass Barons, the children of Yankee entrepreneurs, tinkers and tinkerers who had wrangled with new technologies and primitive systems of finance and built a valley of brass. And their children sought to embellish the legacy with new buildings designed to be venerable. They were often the children of privilege who went to the best schools, but in their factories we had to make it with all kinds of people. Up and down the valley affluence and confidence were spreading on a network of relationships, and the view we could get from the top of Derby's Sterling Opera would soon be almost as good as the prospect we imagined from the front porch of regal Grove Hill, on Hillside Avenue, high above the Waterbury green.

Grove Hill was the home built by Charles Benedict, Aaron's son, in 1876, after his father had died, and he had succeeded to his realm. Designed by the architects Palliser & Palliser, there wasn't a house to match it anywhere in the state except the one P. T. Barnum asked Palliser & Palliser to build for him. The style was called "Queen Anne," or "American Cottage," or even less grandly, "Stick Style." Palliser &

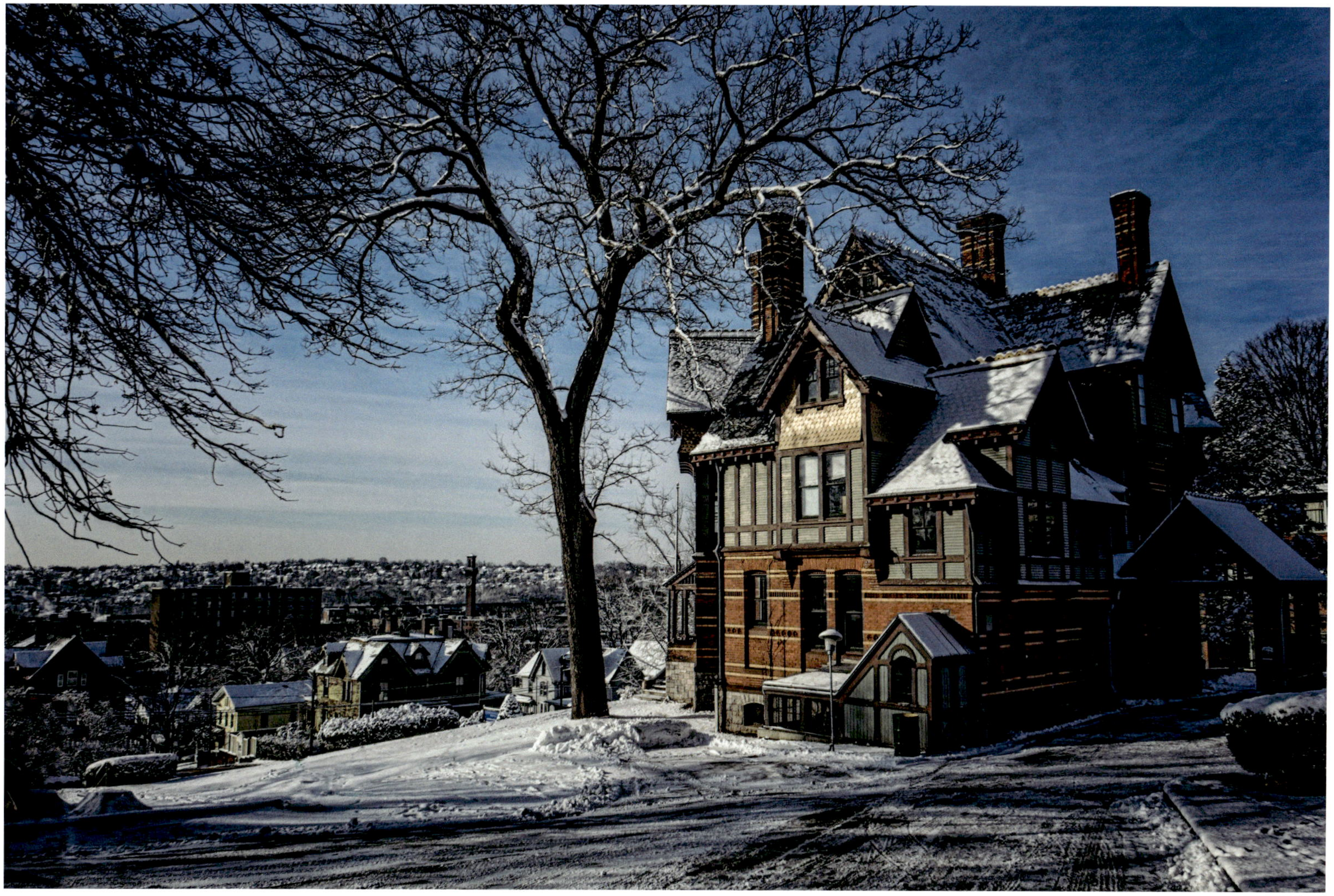

Palliser had begun their architectural lives by putting together a kind of do-it-yourself pattern book so every man could afford "Queen Anne," and the streets climbing the hill to Hillside Avenue were filling up too with the homes of managers and lawyers and merchants, some, even, with exotic accents.

There was nothing everyman about Grove Hill. It was a statement of all that the Benedicts had achieved. Some said Brass Valley began with Aaron Benedict. We imagine Charles standing on that porch looking down the steep slope that spread beneath Grove Hill, past the trim homes of professionals and managers to the flats, where once agriculture failed, and that were now covered by the factories he controlled and the homes where we lived and the shops where we shopped in the town where he was sometimes mayor, feeling the streets flowing down the hill and outward as if they were the silk lining of robes fashioned by his father and flowing from him to the horizon. When Charles Benedict died, before the new curtains were even hung in the windows of Grove Hill, and before town government was rebuilt in marble and brass, we thought of his family, and it made us sad, and flags were lowered and the drums rolled and the bugle played.

THE VIEW FROM GROVE HILL

Looking southwest toward Union Station, factories, and downtown Waterbury, CT

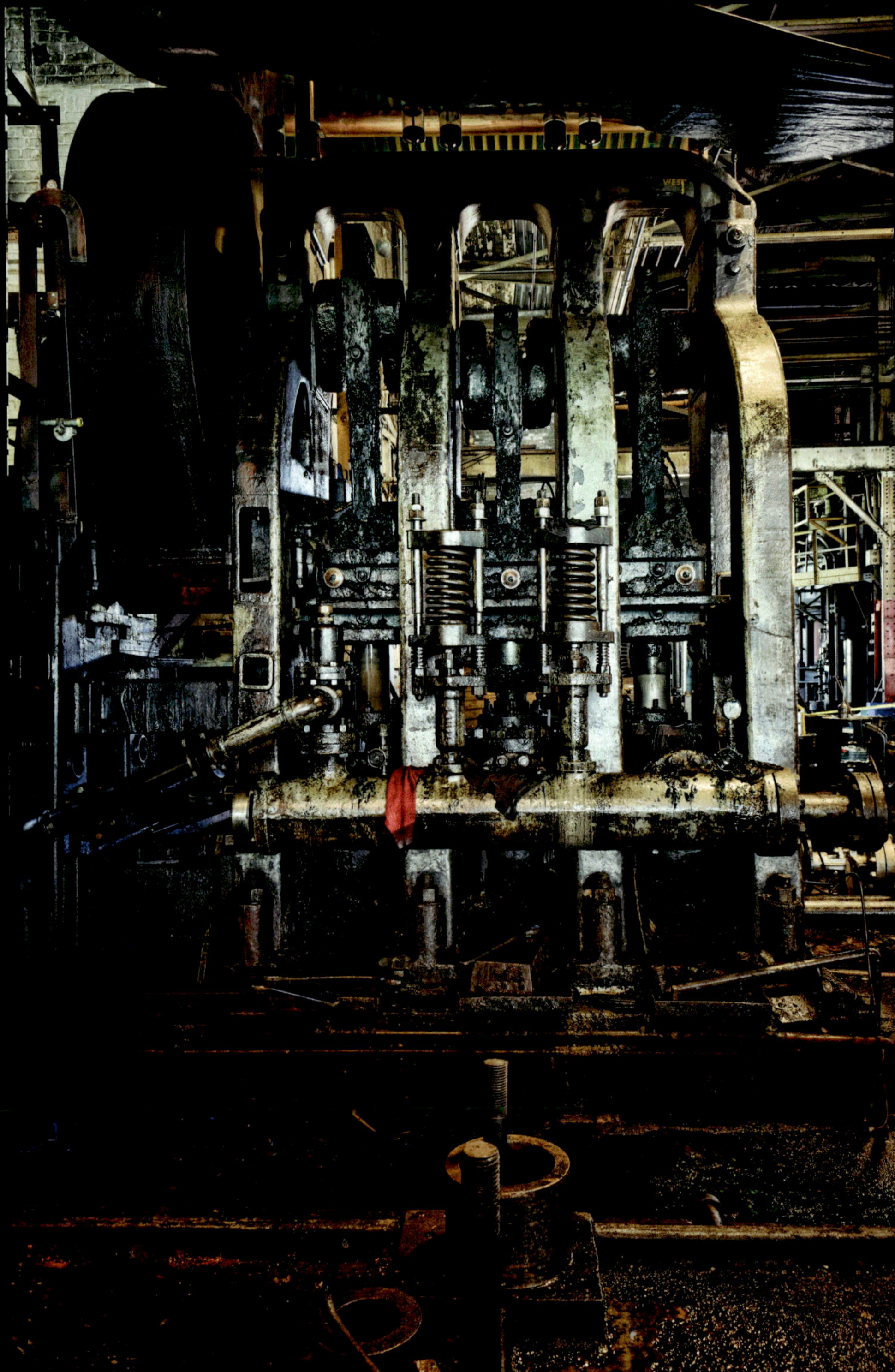

PHOTOGRAPHER'S JOURNAL: Art deco—was it a style or a fashion? There are always fashions; they change as quickly as the clothes that embody them. Style is, as one friend recently put it, the outward form of spirit.

What led so many artists from before the 1920s through the '40s to draw their imagery from the utilitarian forms of commerce and industry? Art deco often proclaims mass production as the key to Utopia. Radio City, the Chrysler Building, and the Empire State are not only triumphs of technology but radiant, deco cathedrals of optimism. At the Bauhaus the materials and forms of industry were elevated to principles of Beauty even as they drove Lyonel Feininger and others into shadow worlds.

What does all this have to do with radios designed to look aerodynamic, and places that appear at the mention of white tie, top hat, and tails and whirl on to Gershwin's taxi horns and saxophones still strong when Gene Kelly dances to them at MGM? How does that sleek, heroic imagery resonate in the satire of Chaplin, and how is it transformed by Hopper and in numerous dystopian visions, whether Lang's *Metropolis*, Kafka's *Amerika*, Huxley's bottling plants and decanting rooms....We all know roads through Gotham. Art deco is an art style that didn't even have a name until the 1960s, and we can still put it on like a fashion, but is it still really ours with our iPhones and iHeads? Or have we already become something never seen before?

Can style be sought or must it be left unwatched to germinate and grow as we wriggle within our cultural cocoon? ...and how much style does it take to make culture and tradition, and what is it all worth, and can it be conserved?

DECO

Hydraulic Pump, c. 1917, American Brass,
Bank Street, Waterbury

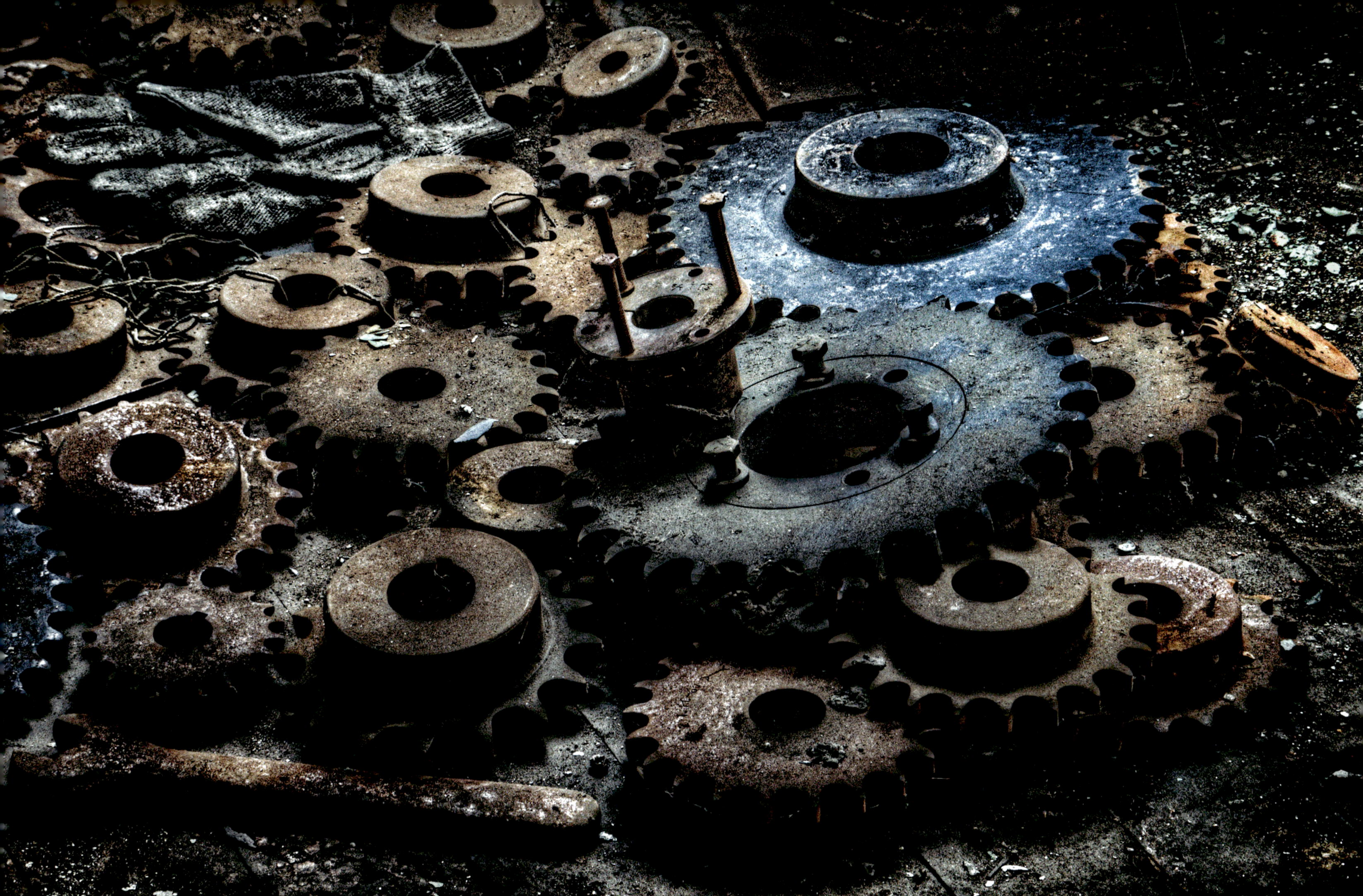

"IT TAKES AN ENDLESS AMOUNT OF HISTORY
TO MAKE EVEN A LITTLE TRADITION."

—Henry James, The American Scene, 1905

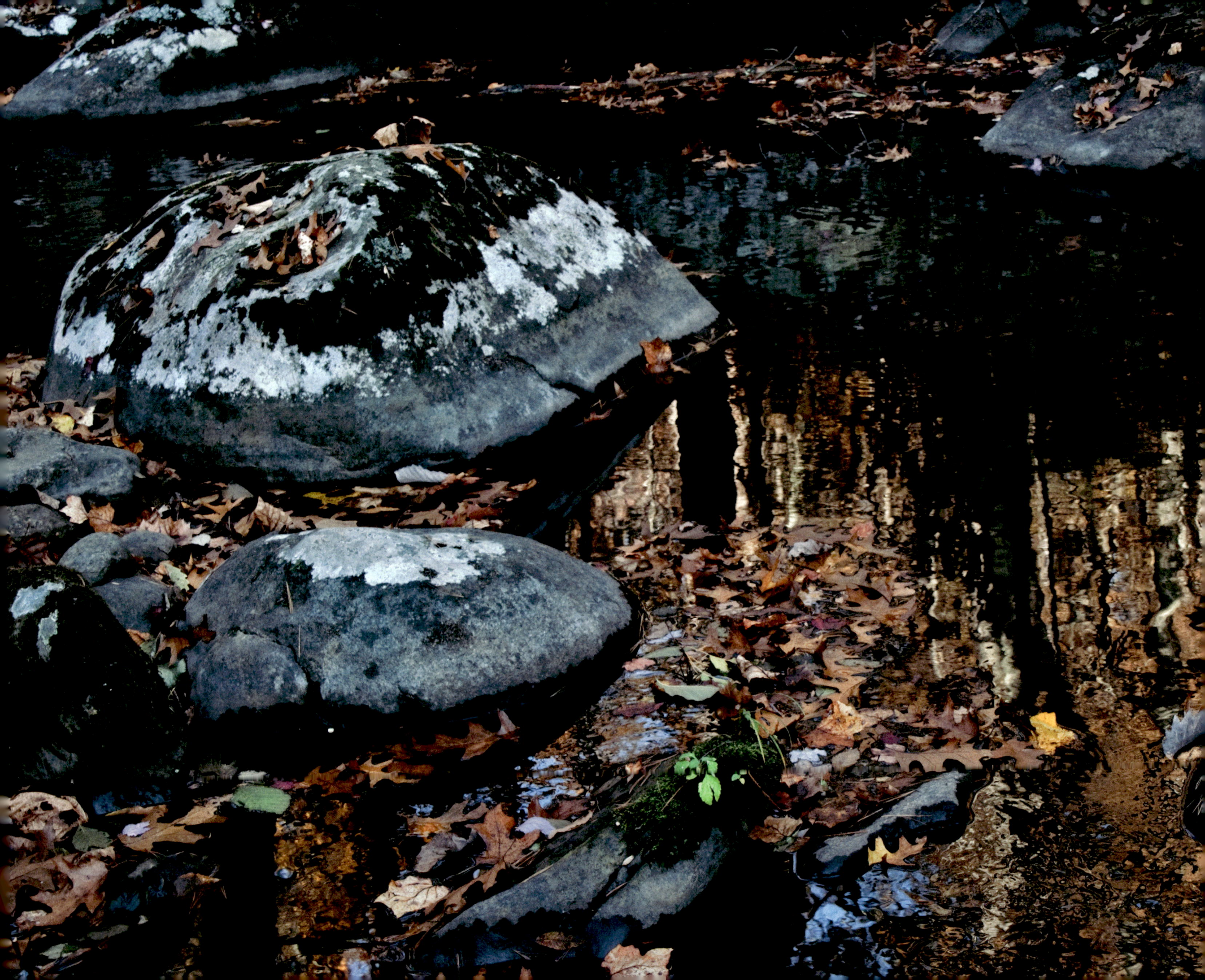

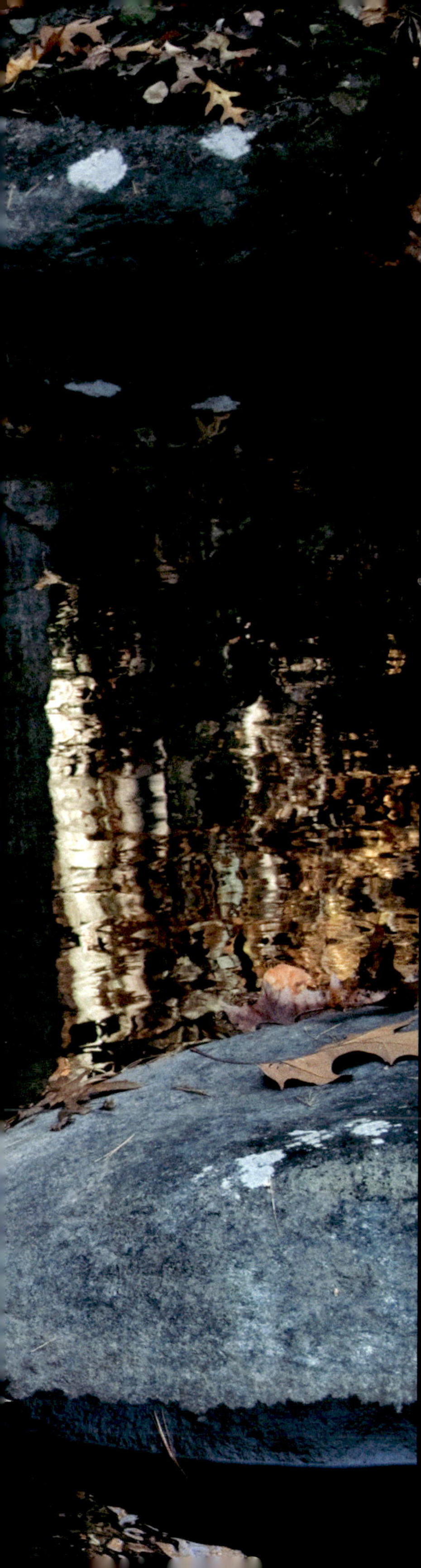

WATERCOLORS

In the copper pools of autumn
thought accumulates and falling leaves
while the stream itself still surges and cascades
across old stones and wind-blasted hills.
What is there in us that is not of that crush?

PART SIX:

ON DOWN THE TRACKS

Of machine operators, machinists, tool makers, and summer storms

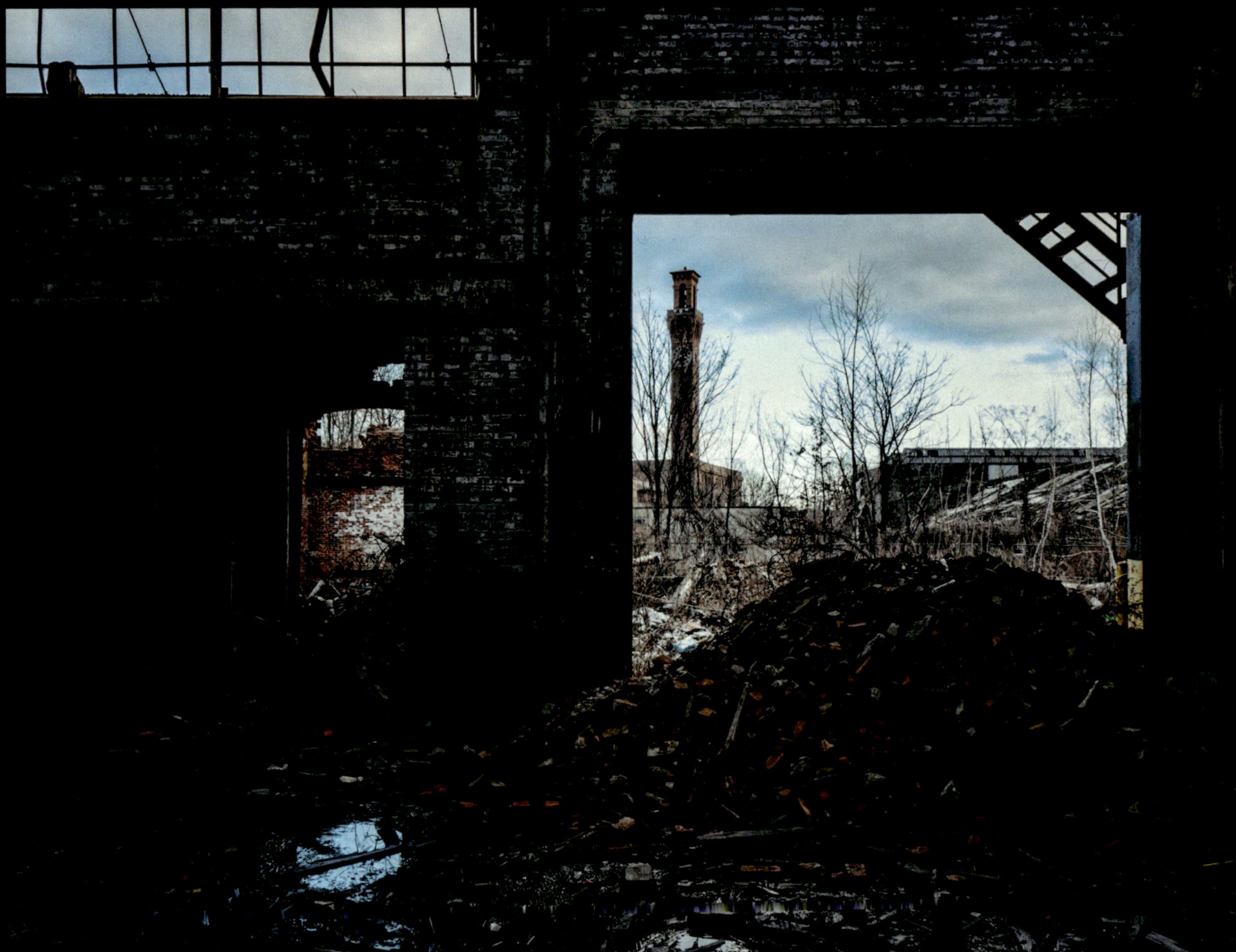

UNION STATION FROM AMERICAN BRASS
Freight Street, Waterbury, CT

In 1906 planning began on the country's grandest railway terminal, Pennsylvania Station in New York City. In the same year the New Haven Railroad flexed its muscle with its own landmark project, a new railway station for Waterbury to begin the rebuilding of downtown after the Great Fire of 1902. The project would inspire the Chase family, owners of one of the "big three" brass mills, to initiate a massive redesign of Grand Street, realigning streets, destroying some of our homes that the Great Fire had not already claimed. In their place we would have a fine grand concourse of government and industry on which to stroll and parade. Everyone loves a parade. City fathers chose Cass Gilbert, architect of America's Supreme Court Building in Washington, DC, to design buildings of marble to outlast time, and to enshrine civic virtue and Chase Brass in the fashionable forms of Ancient Greece and in quotes from Lincoln carved deep into the marble. Gilbert's most important impact on architecture, however, came with New York's pioneering Woolworth Building, once the tallest in the world. We called it a needle in heaven and it was decorated with swastikas of hope.

However, first came the railway stations. In both New York and Waterbury, civic and railroad leaders chose the nation's most prominent architectural firm, McKim, Mead, & White. Cass Gilbert had been a novice in the McKim office. Stanford White was a design wizard who had long reigned as tastemaker and visionary to the most wealthy and powerful people in the country. He was a showman and a true artist. It was an age when no building in town was more important than the railway station. It proclaimed a town's status as it welcomed the world, and it solidified the railroad's place in the center of it all. In 1906 both New York and Waterbury chose the tastemakers as their architects.

A pharaoh once advised, if you want to know where power lies, look for the tallest building. The most distinctive feature of Waterbury's Union Station is its 240-foot-high bell tower. Although history tells us the tower was an afterthought, added at the insistence of an uneducated railroad executive after a trip through Italy, it's likely the railroad executive was under the spell of Stanford White, whose power of suggestion might bring forth a tower just as surely as rabbits lay Easter eggs. Whether seen in original drawings and photographs or live with the modern addition, the proportions are superb, the treatment, simple and restrained; the tower is the necessary vertical that completes the composition; it is a model of classical poise and, unlike the original in Siena, there is a Seth Thomas near the top to manage valley time.

New York's Penn Station and Waterbury's Union Station both opened to crowds in 1909. Union Station made Waterbury a busy place with sixty-six trains every day from all points of the compass; twelve tracks served arrivals and departures, with spurs splitting off into a sizable rail yard behind. Much of it is still there beneath highway interchange ramps and covered in a garden of brambles. The clock tower became grandfather clock to the city. Try to imagine it when it was new, granddaddy above a field of puffing smokestacks filling the air with progress, as Seth Thomas and the New York, New Haven & Hartford Railroad chimed the sooty hours, their echoes peeling from the valley walls, and a century suddenly eager for travel fell nose-deep in time tables and rushing after trains chugging and puffing in and out of town. People were clamoring to see the world, but Stanford White, the man of the moment, was already just as dead in Waterbury as he was in New York, famously shot on Eastern Time as he dined in public by Harry Thaw, the crazed husband of White's lover Evelyn Nesbit—most beautiful woman, some said, of the century, and Thaw was tried in "the trial of the century," in a century barely begun.

And a century later McKim, Mead and White's Union Station is home to the *Republican American*, still owned and run by the Pape family. It has survived or absorbed all the former great newspapers of Waterbury. Still fiscally conservative and generally critical of unions, like the rest of us, it is seeking to find its voice in the digital cloud. Nearby factories along Freight Street are rubble-filled refuges for the homeless. Trains and commuters are few, and the grand spaces along Grand Street can sometimes make emptiness echo, but McKim, Mead, and White's re-creation of Siena's Torre del Mangia has the crisp vitality of the original. The buildings look as modern today as when Siena was new; the tower has become the most recognizable structure to motorists up and down the valley, a place to clutch roots, to anchor with Seth Thomas and Siena against the ravages of time.

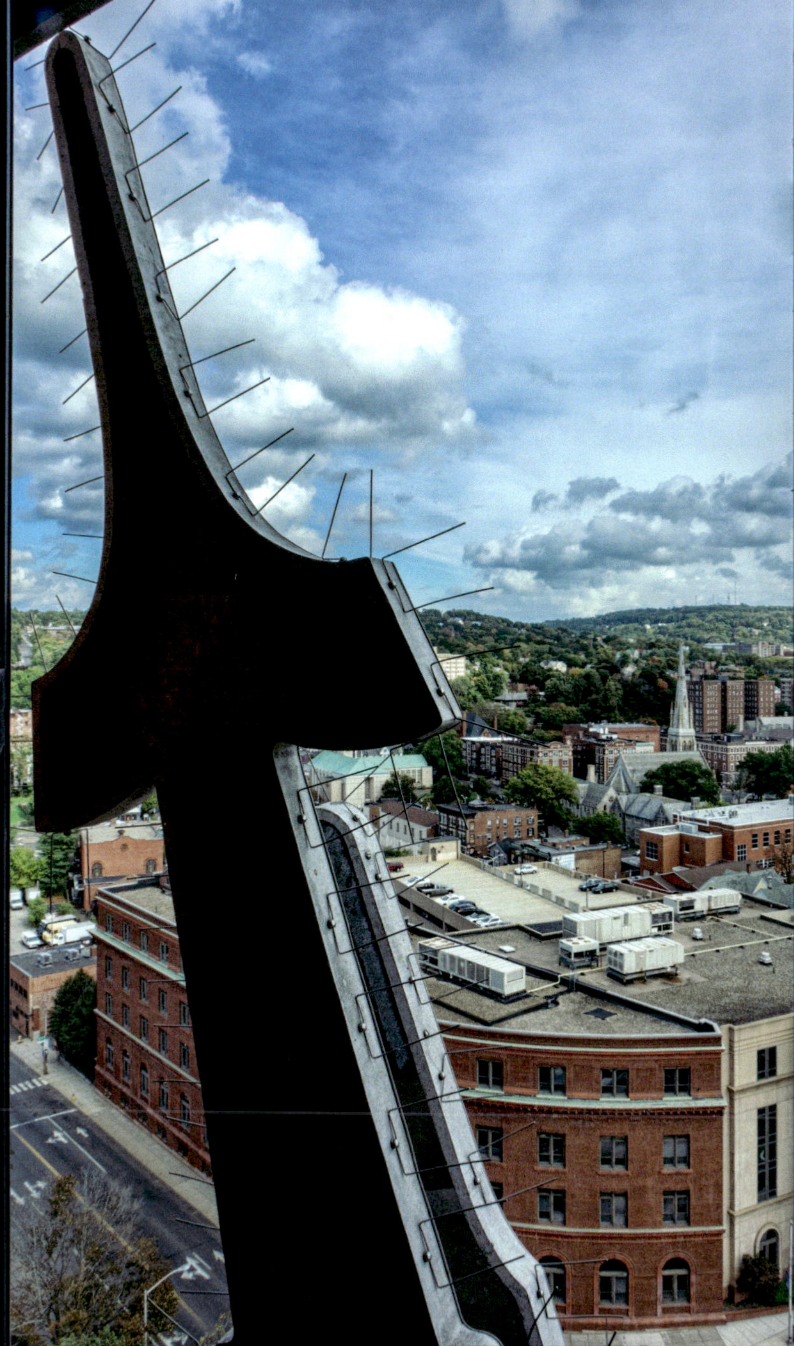

RAVAGES OF TIME

American Brass and Waterbury Green from Union Tower Station

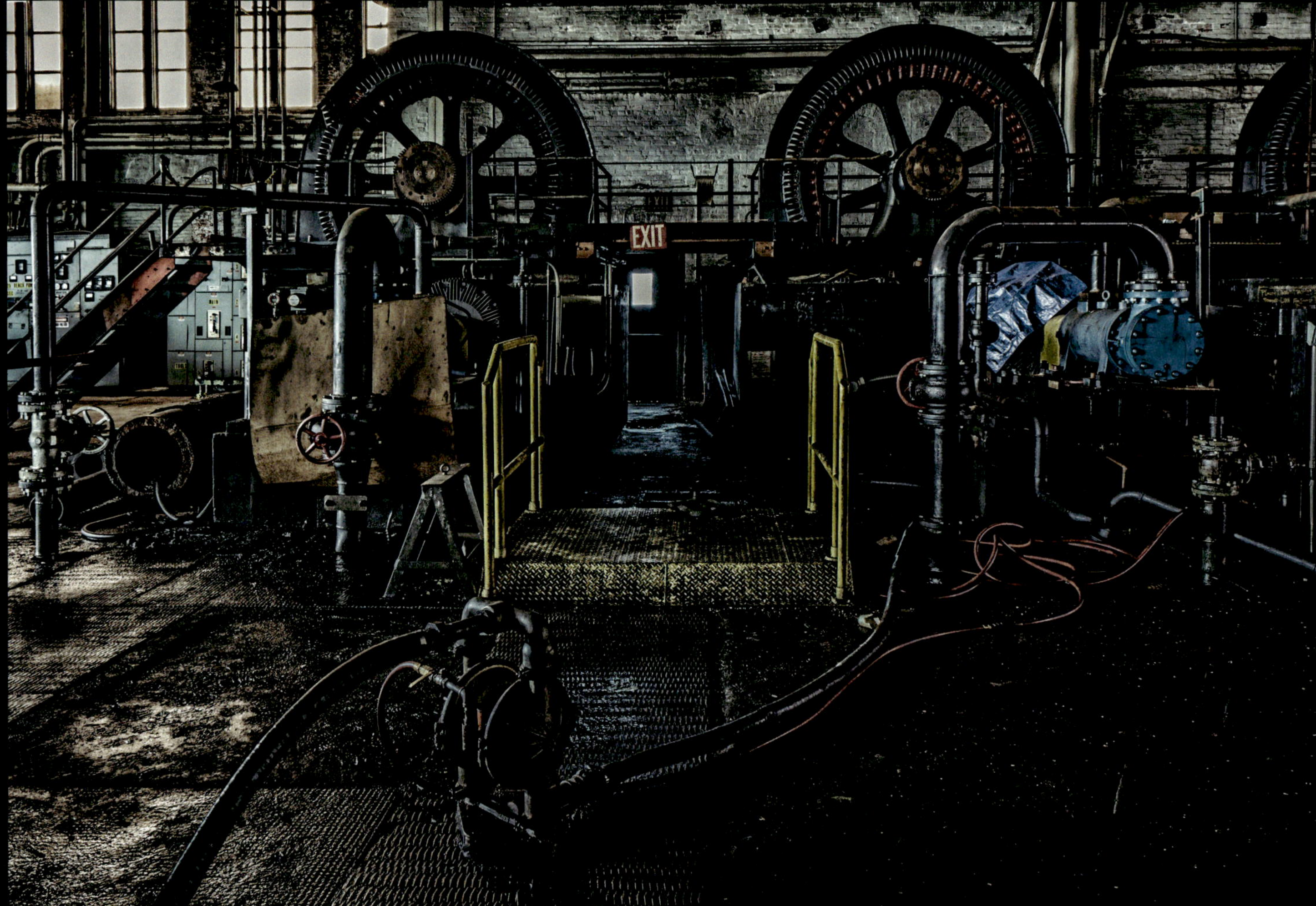

ENGINES OF POWER

Electrical motors c. 1897, American Brass, Waterbury, CT

PHOTOGRAPHER'S JOURNAL:
They are the single most striking feature of the brass factory. I've stood on the catwalk beside them, seen how the double-ring of copper coils might almost envelop me, imagined the sparks they must have given off when the magnetism of the pulsing current made the great wheels spin, but an electrical contractor who'd seen them spinning told me there were no sparks. He said they were smooth and silent, not so fast you lost sight of the flickering spokes, but a lot of mass spinning. "Beautiful!" he exclaimed. "Definitely nineteenth century." He told me it was only six or eight years ago when he saw them running. I was surprised. He knew the guy who maintained them and kept the careful schedule for adding oil, and he knew the guy that took over after the first guy retired, and how a few months later the motors burned out. They tried to repair them, but nobody knew how.

The first practical electric motors were made by Frank Sprague in 1886 when everything was still direct current. These motors were made a few years after Nikola Tesla's 1893 victory over Edison in the "War of Currents" at White City. Tesla, whose flexible mind understood not only that light was only another form of electricity, but also that so are we, versus Edison, who closed his mind and fabricated fear of alternating current to protect his DC business interests.

Wally, the current maintenance chief, explained how it all worked: Along the far north wall of the extrusion shop there once stood three large hydraulic pumps that provided the muscle for three long expansion benches that made cold brass flow. These three motors drove the hydraulic pumps. Wally

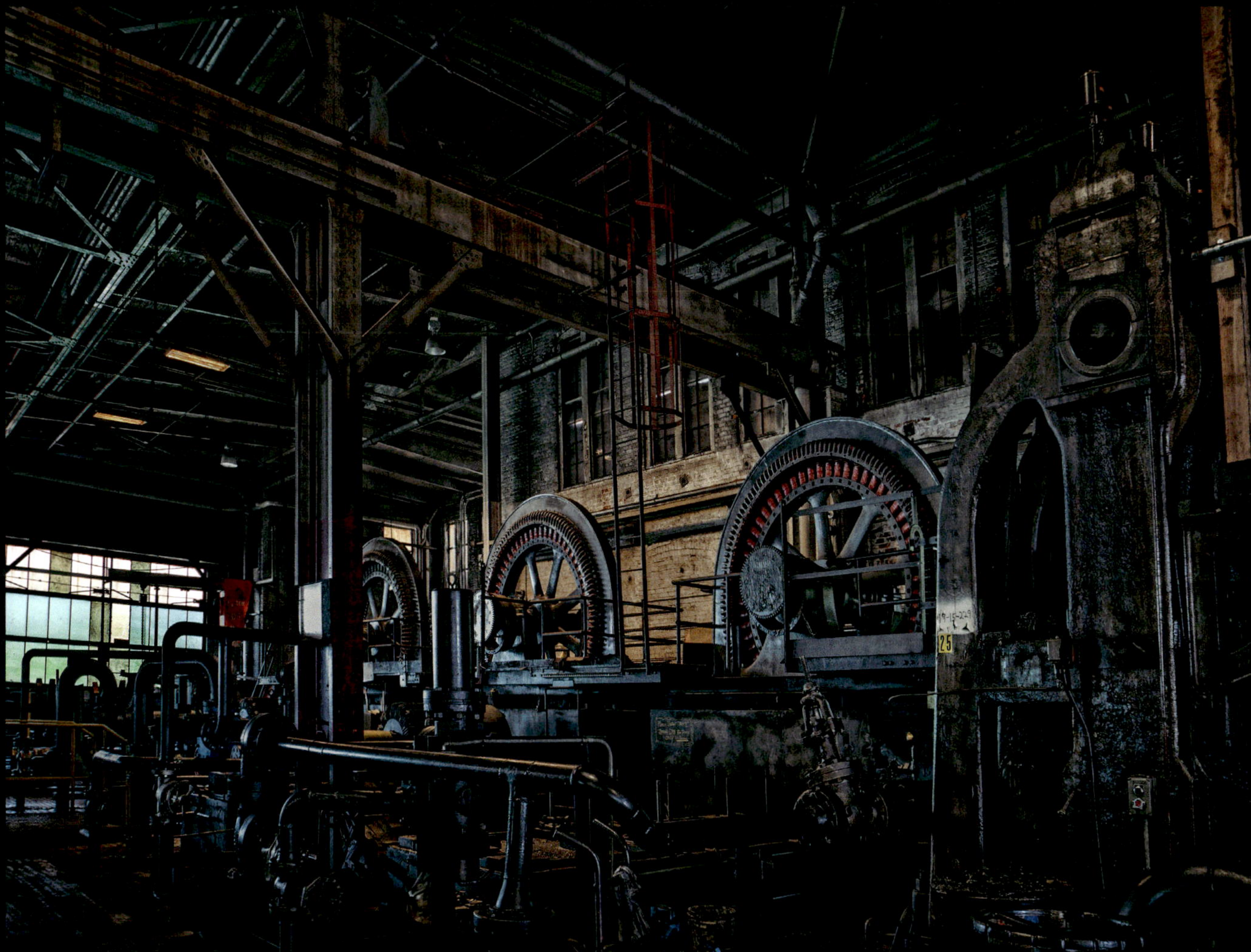

explained how the missing hydraulic pumps once leveraged the motors' steady spin and turned it to superhuman push, and how in removing the pumps the motors' shafts were cut off. Now they look like three enigmatic altars in a ruined temple.

Much of the industrial revolution was built upon Pascal's Law, but so, of course am I, from the blood that flows in the rivers of my veins to the waters that carve rivers through the mountains to the shores. That was the plumbing system Pascal's Law modernized in order to leverage, he said, through God's Laws, God's power. Tesla, Einstein, and others were the inheritors of the Faustian powers. Are these their sacred shrines? And what do they tell us about who we just were as we spin faster into what we will become?

Newer pumps, with internal motors, muscle the same benches still; they are hi-rev things, purring insidiously, squeezing out new efficiencies from ancient technology; Charlie, chief engineer, showed me plans for the motors dated 1897. They could have produced ordnance for the Spanish-American War and specification tubing for all the wars after, through to Iraq.

Further down, a fourth, older, hydraulic pump remains in place, smaller cousin, Wally says, to the ones now removed. A brass plaque indicates it was built in 1917, perhaps when the mill was rebuilt and refitted for the Great War. The old pump still muscles a draw bench, and when it turns it swings and rumbles. To an age that saw progress gleaming just ahead, this must have seemed an idol. From another angle it was the demon Moloch beside his spawn.

SPIN & PUSH

Three electric motors c. 1897, and a hydraulic pump c.1917
American Brass, Bank Street, Waterbury, CT

204

OUR STORIES:
Strike

When Teddy Roosevelt came to power we began calling for a "square deal," too, and some of us began to organize. During the Great War there were plenty of jobs, twenty-four hours a day, and, as we worked, American Brass went on a buying spree, acquiring working mills in Kenosha, Wisconsin, and Buffalo, New York; and William Pape, our conservative, Republican newsman from Liverpool, England, son of a ship's captain, worried about that buying: How could the market sustain the superfluous expense of shipping new copper from Montana to Connecticut in order for us to make things that are sent back to Chicago? He was our witness to news, and also the first publisher to make comic books in color. Some of us learned to read inside those comics.

The Great War blocked the flow of workers from the homelands just when we needed more hands. Rules barring blacks from the mills were lifted, and a new wave of immigration began from the South to Brass Valley. Workers were in demand; we had power to exercise, though the companies complained of enemy subversives undermining the labor force. We were told that management had snitches and rats, and kept files on our activities, especially people they thought were "troublemakers and radicals," and everyone was warned of communist plots.

After the Great War production slowed, and inflation grew quickly. There were strikes and violence around the country. In Brass Valley in 1919, they say, a spontaneous job action at Farrel Foundry in Ansonia spread from the slitters to the rollers and then to American Brass, next door. As word spread, Waterbury joined the job action, and 3,000 unskilled Russians, Poles, and Lithuanians from the mills joined the strike. In the end, the mill owners backed down. We heard later of the order given. If things get out of hand, the police were told, "Aim for the gut." And we wondered who was giving those orders.

It's hard to say when exactly the influence of the mining giants came to dominate Brass Valley, but in 1922 with their booty from the Great War, Anaconda purchased American Brass, which was responsible for at least half of all US brass production. Kennecott Copper later bought Chase Brass, and so when we were finally organized into a union in the 1930s, it was on a national level and in concert with miners we'd never met, and we were all starving for a new deal. The mills were already spinning when Pearl Harbor was hit, and as men went to battle once again, we needed women's arms to meet quotas at home, and many of us had family still in the old country, and we felt rage at the aggressions and we worked to support the men on the front lines of battle and claim freedom and democracy for the globe.

By the end of WWII, 25,000 men and women in Brass Valley were casting molten metal, pressing it into rods, wire, strips, and sheets, and fabricating those materials into finished parts. Our work supported butchers and bakers and the people who sold us ice, and many more small businesses up and down the valley. We had been born here, worked beside people we'd gone to school with, and after the war there was the GI Bill, and new schools and programs to get ahead, and our children were going to colleges and technical schools, and we saw them settling down, opening businesses in our community. We rarely looked back; we belonged.

That was a long time ago when brass was cheap, and the decisions about brass production were still influenced by people who lived in Brass Valley. Those were very different times. Now we import our brass and export our pollution to places far away, where labor is cheap, and laws are lax, and the world has gotten smaller and faster, and it's wired to our brains and flashed before our eyes. Time spins like a speeding car's odometer, as news is breaking.

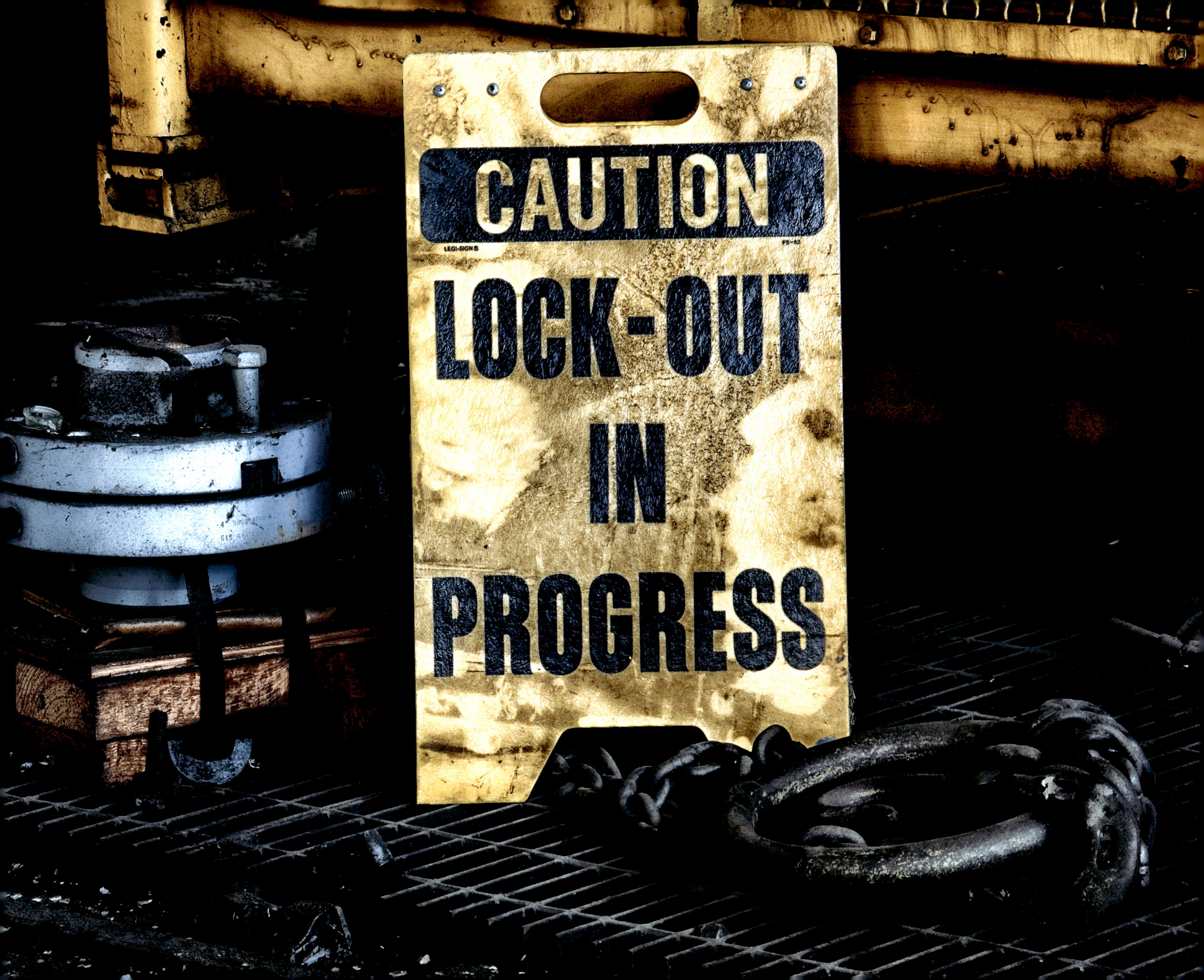
CAUTION
LOCK-OUT
IN
PROGRESS

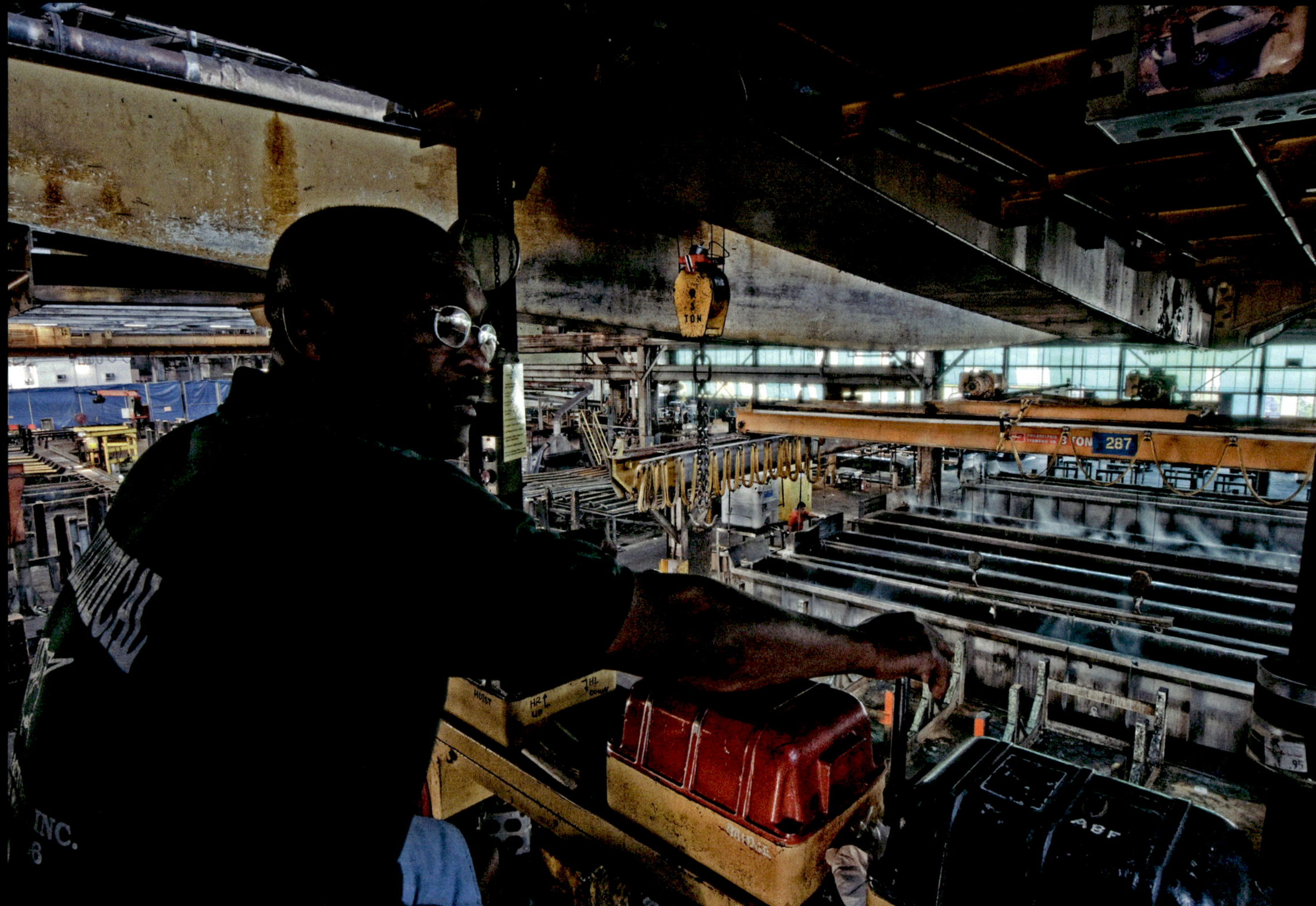

ALFRED ABOVE THE PICKLING TANKS

American Brass, Bank Street, Waterbury, CT

PHOTOGRAPHER'S JOURNAL:
Where factory sheds survive, the big ones, there's always at least one large crane straddling every bay, sometimes several. I've seen and photographed dozens of them, rusted and frozen in place, but they are meant to move. The big ones can be run from a cab above or on a leash from below—biggest muscles in the room. Running one is an ennobling responsibility.

I've photographed Carlos walking cautiously, leash in hand, beside his delicately balanced load. Alfred runs the main crane from above. His seat is just below the roof trusses, and for many weeks we had a waving, honking relationship until I finally hauled my gear up the ladder, and rode and photographed from his rig.

He spends the day shuttling the length of the central bay, moving bundles of tube between stations: the extruder and draw benches in the north, pickling tanks and annealer in the center, testing and finishing stations in the south. Here at the pickling tanks a smaller crane moves tubes east and west from tank to tank. Things are always moving in the central bay, and Alfred honks his horn to alert traffic below. "MAXIMUM LOAD 3 TONS" is written on the side of Alfred's crane. Although I've seen cranes in factories marked for twenty or thirty times that load, this is one of very few I've seen still moving in Brass Valley.

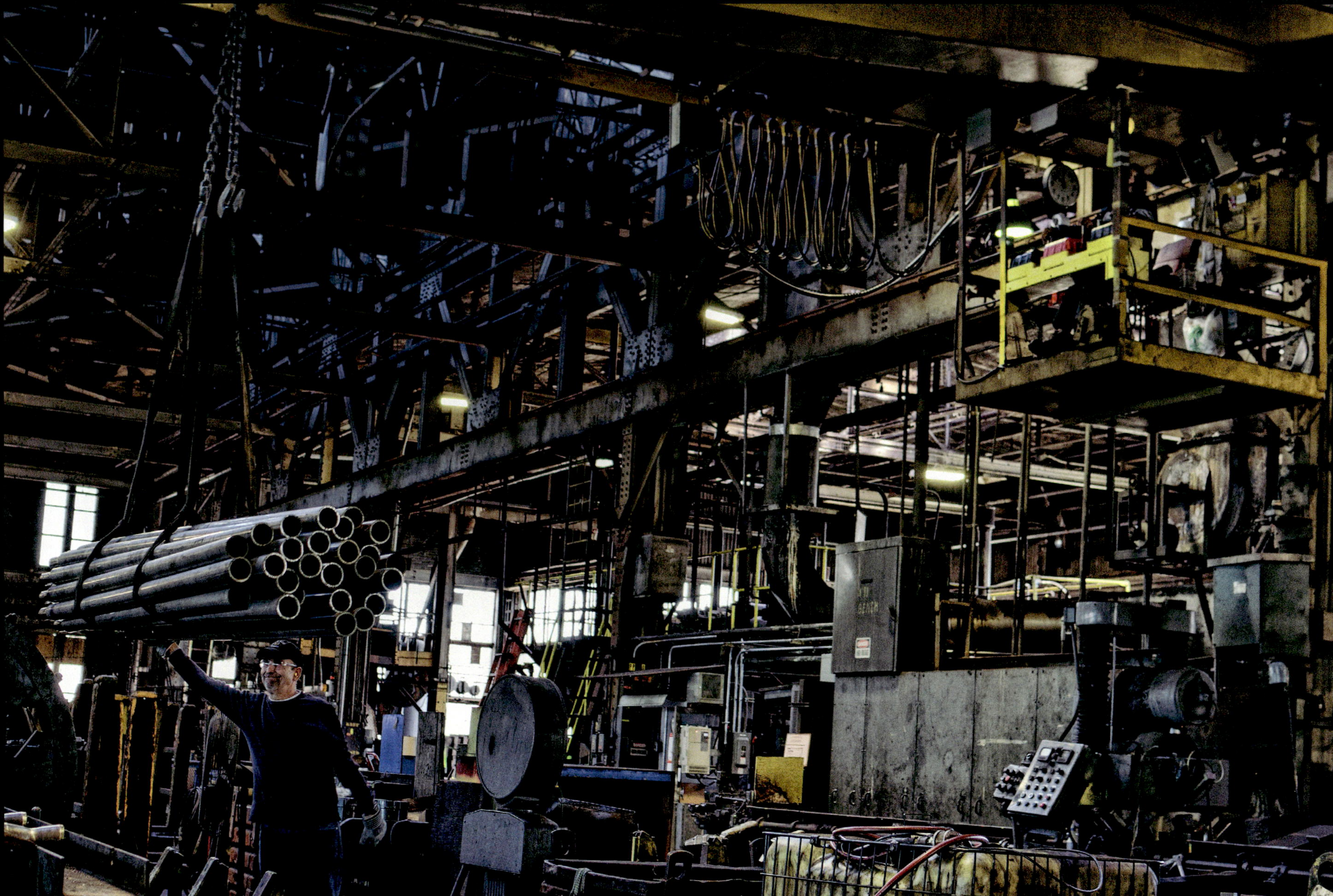

TRUNDLING BUNDLES

Alfred drives from above while George guides from below,
American Brass, Bank Street, Waterbury, CT

PHOTOGRAPHER'S JOURNAL:
The extruder mashes molten metal into tube, but this draw bench stretches cold, hard tube as if it were taffy. Riccardo has climbed on top to free pipe that has become caught in the loader. Below him is a flat area that looks like a conveyor belt. It is really a giant chain, like the tread of a large construction crane. The chain runs for about thirty feet, looping and disappearing below the floor on the way back. Each link is massive. The chain is turned by an electric motor as large as a truck and half submerged below the floor.

A small car rides above the chain. It is pulled along from above by a thin wire. It looks a bit like an arcade rabbit as it is pulled into position, or like a giant steel grasshopper with big wheels where hind legs might stick up. Riccardo climbs down and hits buttons that tip the tables to load the tube into a bigger tube, as if into the bore of a cannon. Then Riccardo sets the arcade rabbit in motion; it grips the pipe by what I imagine as teeth, and its large hind claws lock onto the chain, which is rolling backward. The rabbit grips the tube, grabs the chain, and the tube stretches invisibly over a mandrel and through cutting dies that make it longer, leaner, warmer. Each time Riccardo ejects a tube I'm surprised to see it is half again longer than when it went in. It is a process quite invisible to my camera and to me. Only the results reveal what happened.

Meanwhile, at a bench called a "pointer," Ray crimps pipe bound for an expansion bench. Safety glasses may be required, but it's his fingers Ray watches as he tugs and shoves on heavy tubes to position them in the jaws of the pointer. These jaws are eight steel wedges. Two large donuts of hydraulic fluid provide the muscle, when flexed, to drive the wedges hard into the sides of a tube, pointing it so it can be gripped on the expansion bench.

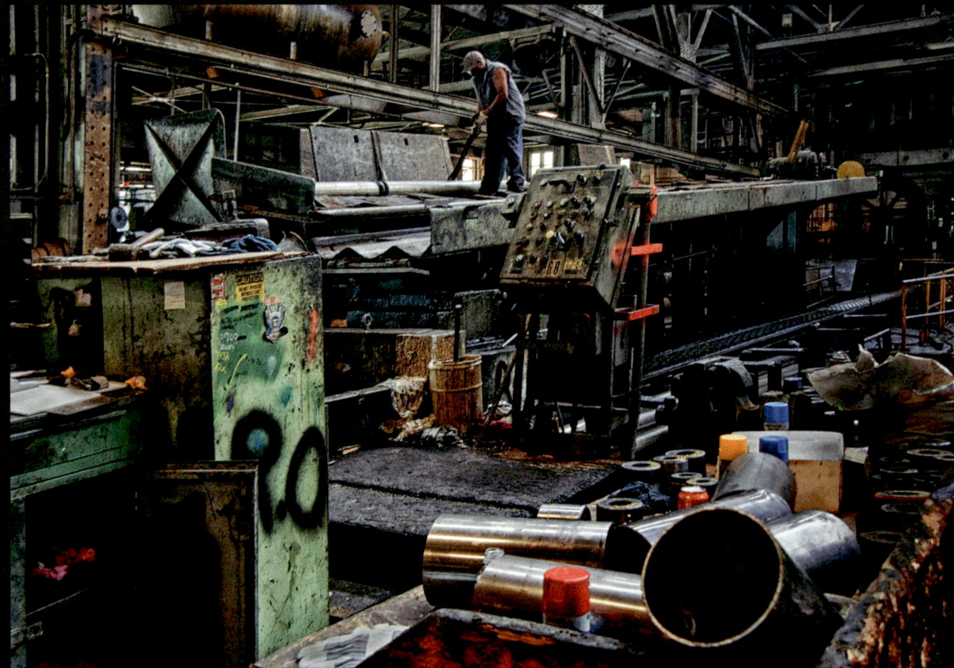

THE DRAW BENCH

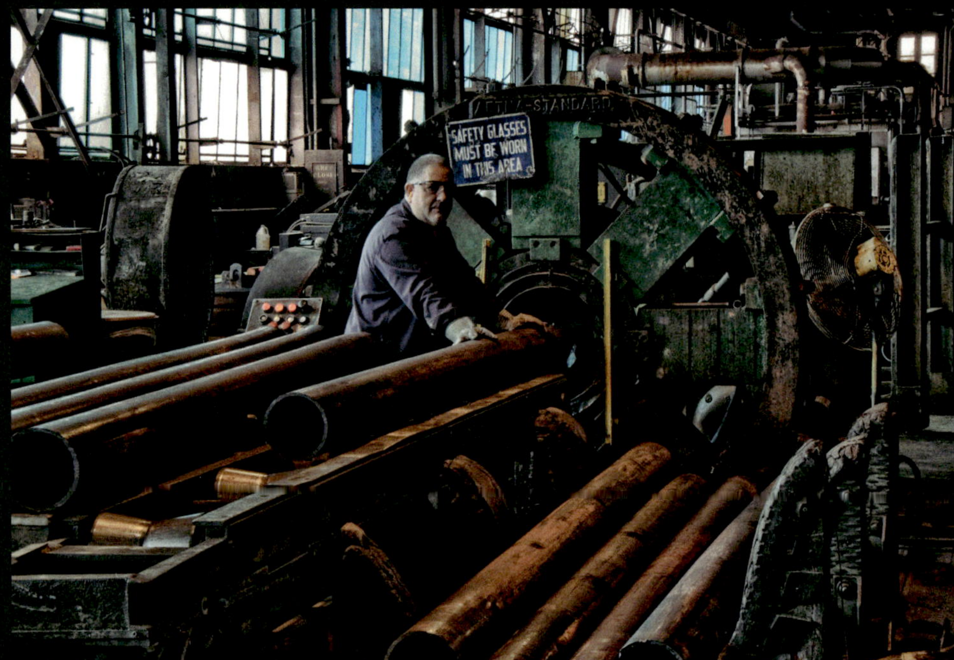

THE POINTER

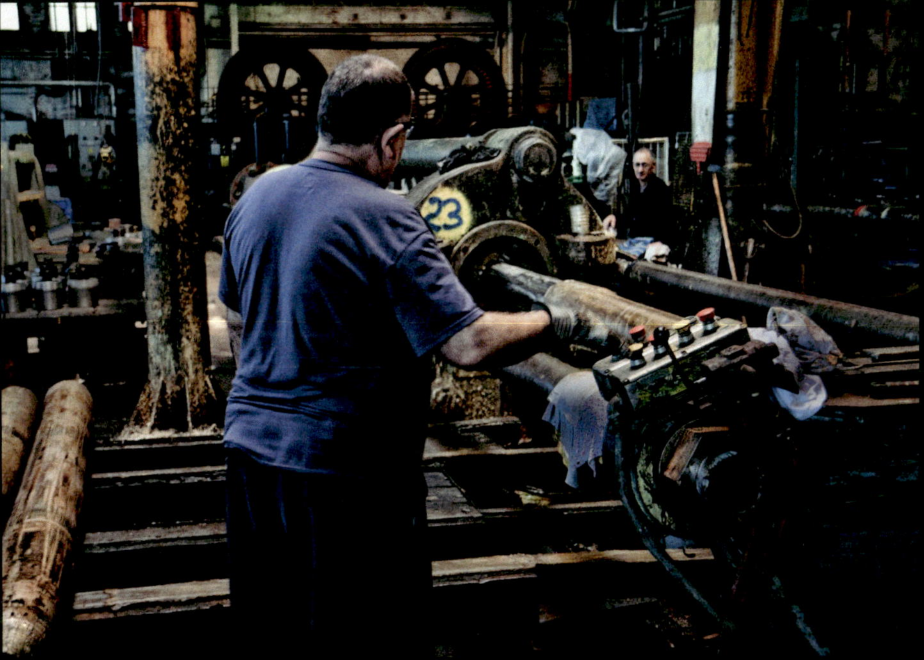

THE EXPANDER

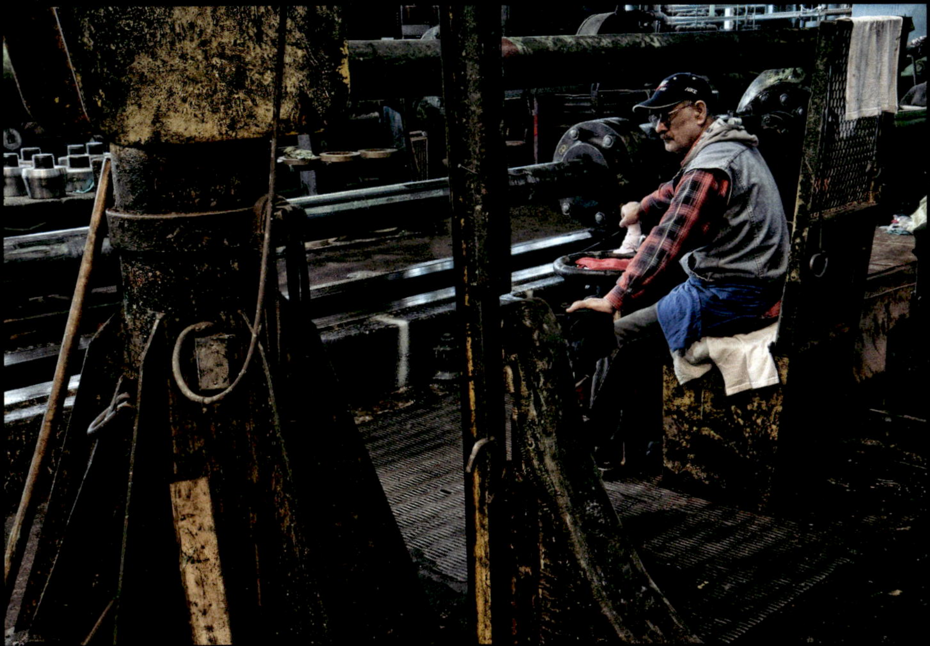

PHOTOGRAPHER'S JOURNAL:
As the expander's ram pushes through the length of brass tube, the tube looks like a snake swallowing a mouse. It takes under five seconds for the mandrel to expand a cold brass tube, and make it longer, wider, thinner.

Ray and Rudy must coordinate their efforts to thread the mandrel into the tube. Ray's buttons work hydraulic elevators that lift the tube up and down so that Rudy can thread it with his hydraulic ram. The elevator lifting the tube moves in jerks, and unfinished pipe is a clumsy passenger.

Ray's controls set the target while Rudy advances the ram. Rudy watches Ray while seated on a singular metal throne of unknown origin. He turns a large iron wheel, set flat like the steering wheel on a bus; it rotates a shaft disappearing into the floor. The wheel controls the pressure in the hydraulic system that forces the ram and swells the tube.

Plans for this bench are dated 1905, and workers may have sat on Rudy's throne running this machine for well over a century. The throne is an odd thing, inhuman in its engineered rigidity, and with a high back out of all human proportion. The back panel is made of expanded metal, a product developed, patented, and first marketed in 1889. It is a parody of wicker only an engineer or a machinist could conceive.

What is the story behind this homemade chair? Perhaps the swing of the great wheel requires such force that chairs made of wood were being turned to matchsticks. Or maybe the great wheel was at one time turned by a "big wheel," who the shop engineers thought to honor with a throne. If so, it is a story that's lost.

American Brass, Bank Street, Waterbury, CT

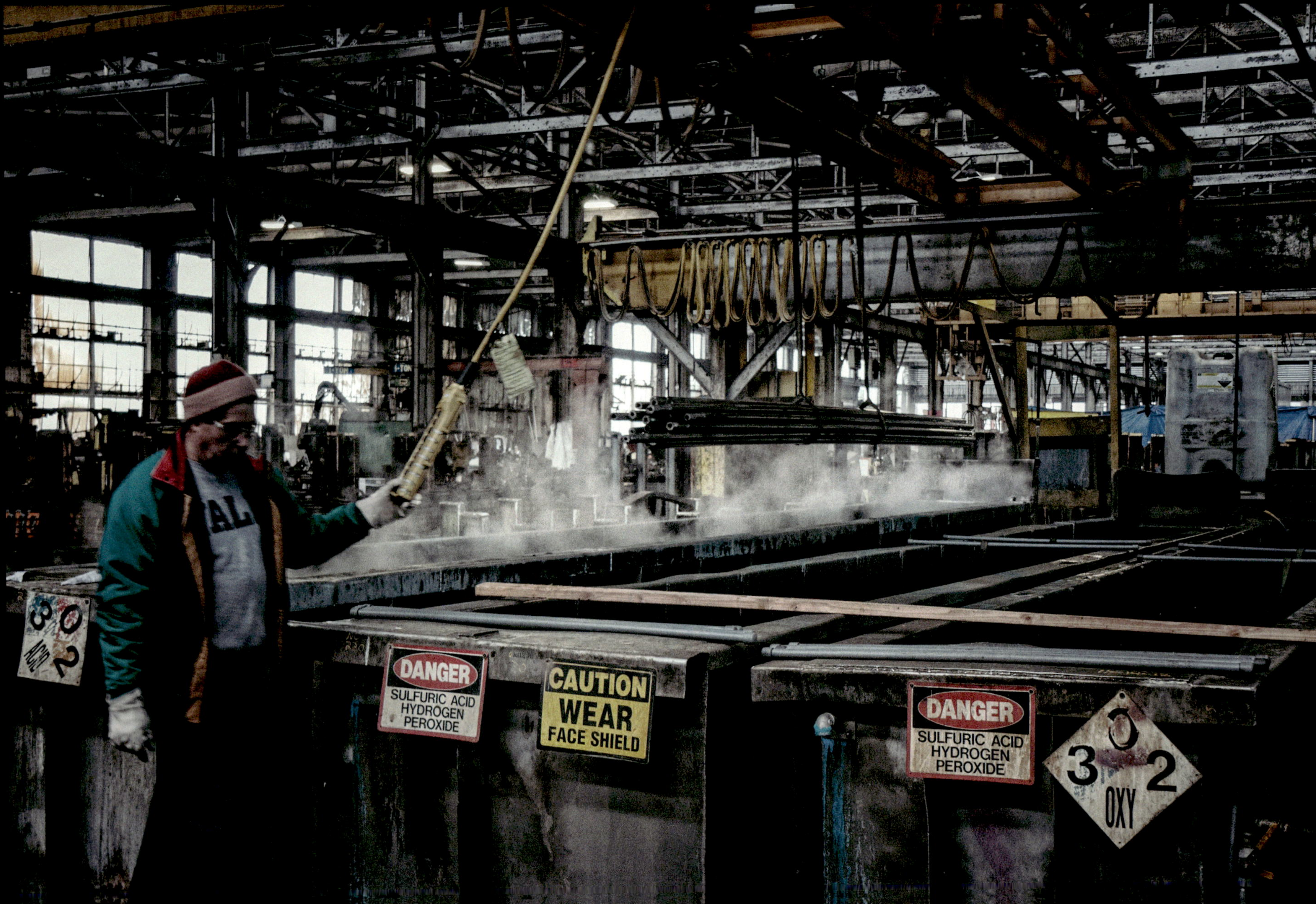

THE PICKLE TANK

American Brass, Bank Street, Waterbury, CT

PHOTOGRAPHER'S JOURNAL:
Periodically Alfred leaves and retrieves bundles of tube from racks at the foot of the pickling tanks, and José spends much of his day pacing back and forth and waiting beside the pickle tanks to move bundles of tube from bath to bath. Each tank contains a different tonic.

PHOTOGRAPHER'S JOURNAL:
Tube must often be run through the benches multiple times to bring it to its specified dimensions. Between each pass on the benches it's rinsed. José guides each bundle through the proper sequence of baths, before leaving the washed tubes in the bins at the foot of the tanks for Alfred.

The thickness of the clouds that envelop the pickling tanks varies by the season, but the rhythm never stops. For José, time is mostly about waiting for tubes to bathe and scrupulously tracking multiple jobs. José never picks up his newspaper when he thinks I'm photographing. Perhaps, when your job is waiting, you worry the boss may think you're loafing, and it took awhile before he trusted my camera.

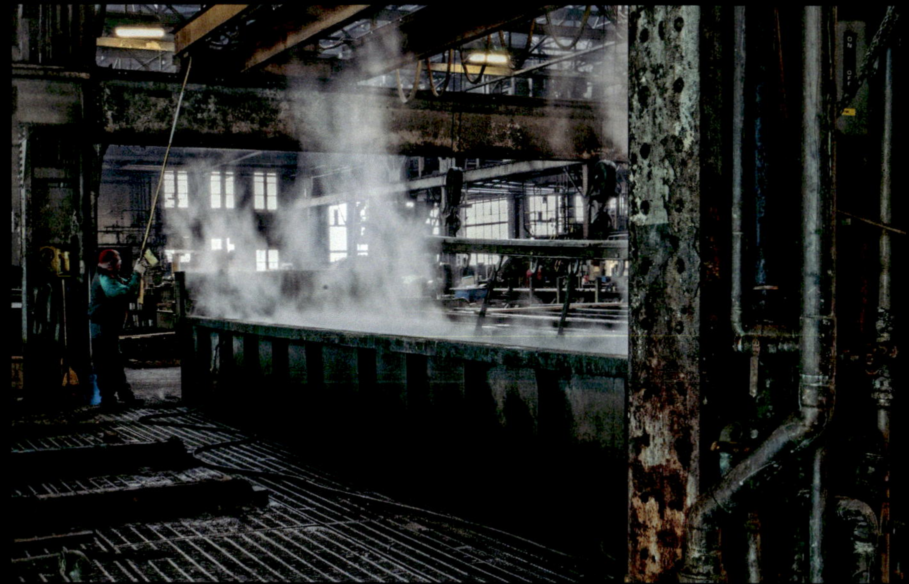

WINTER PICKLING
American Brass, Bank Street, Waterbury, CT

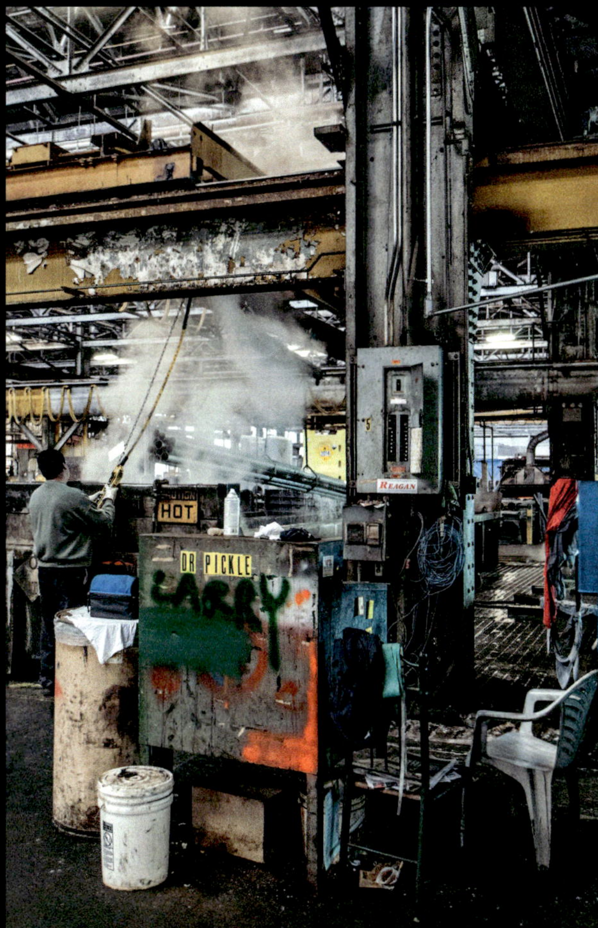

HOT DR. PICKLE
American Brass, Bank Street, Waterbury, CT

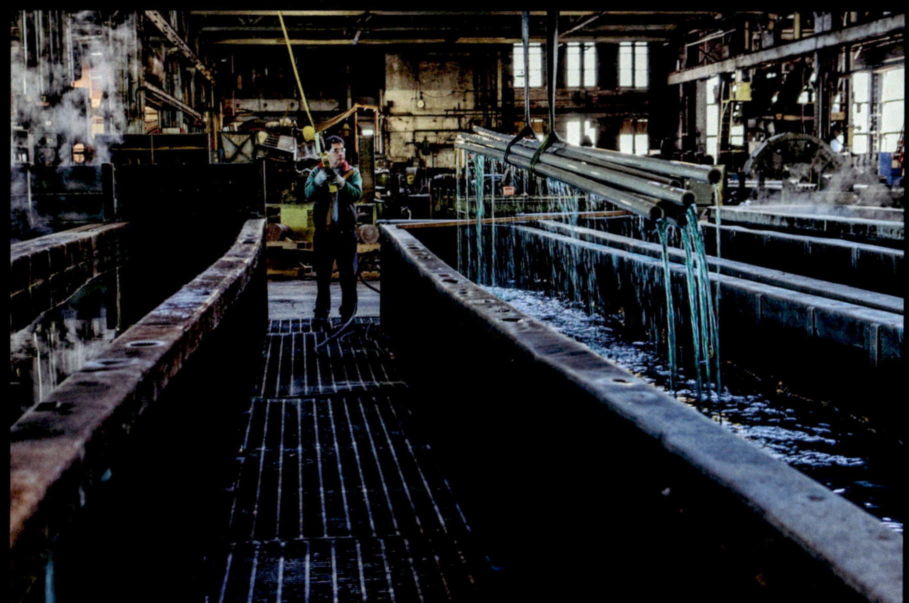

BLUE RAIN
American Brass, Bank Street, Waterbury, CT

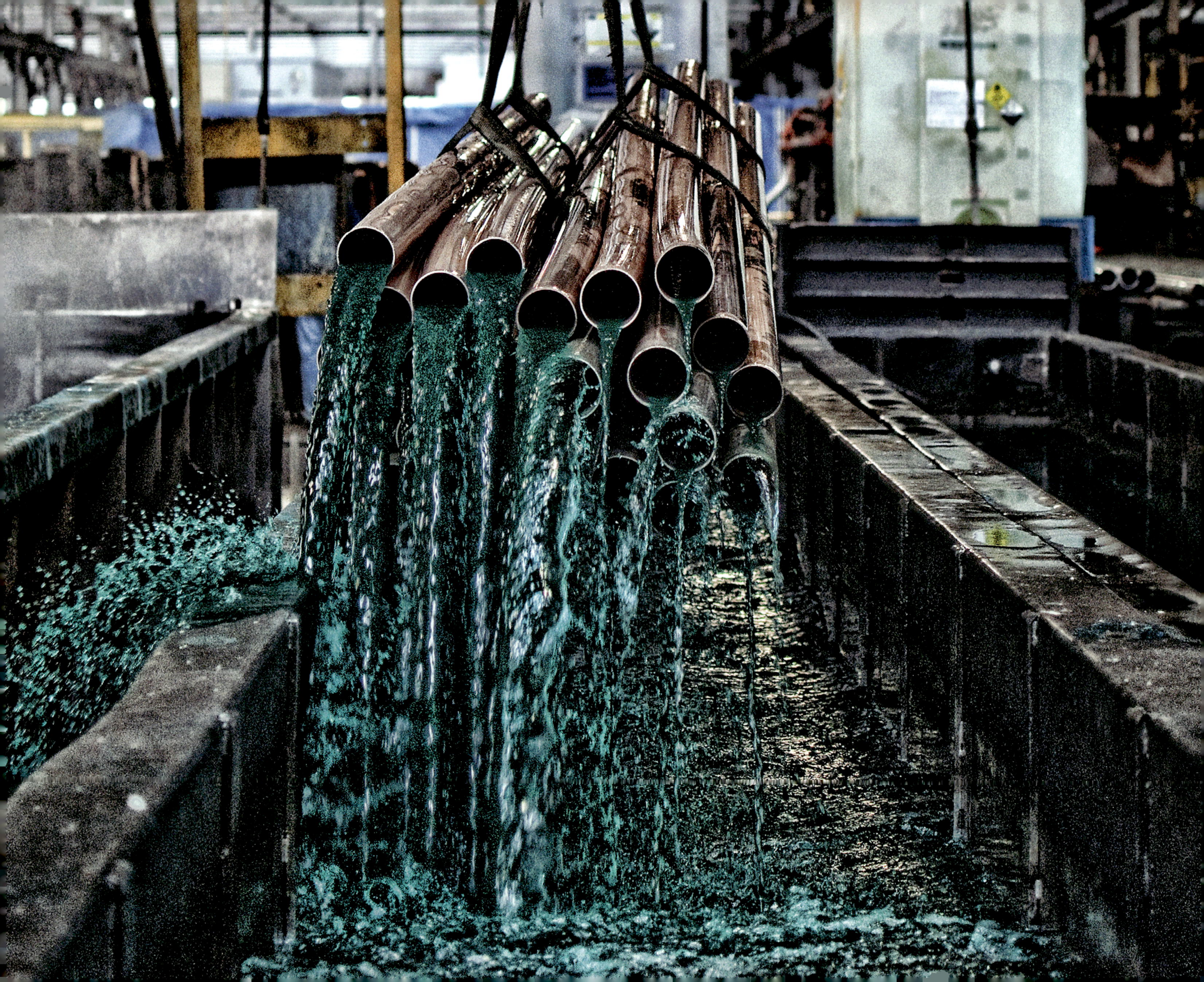

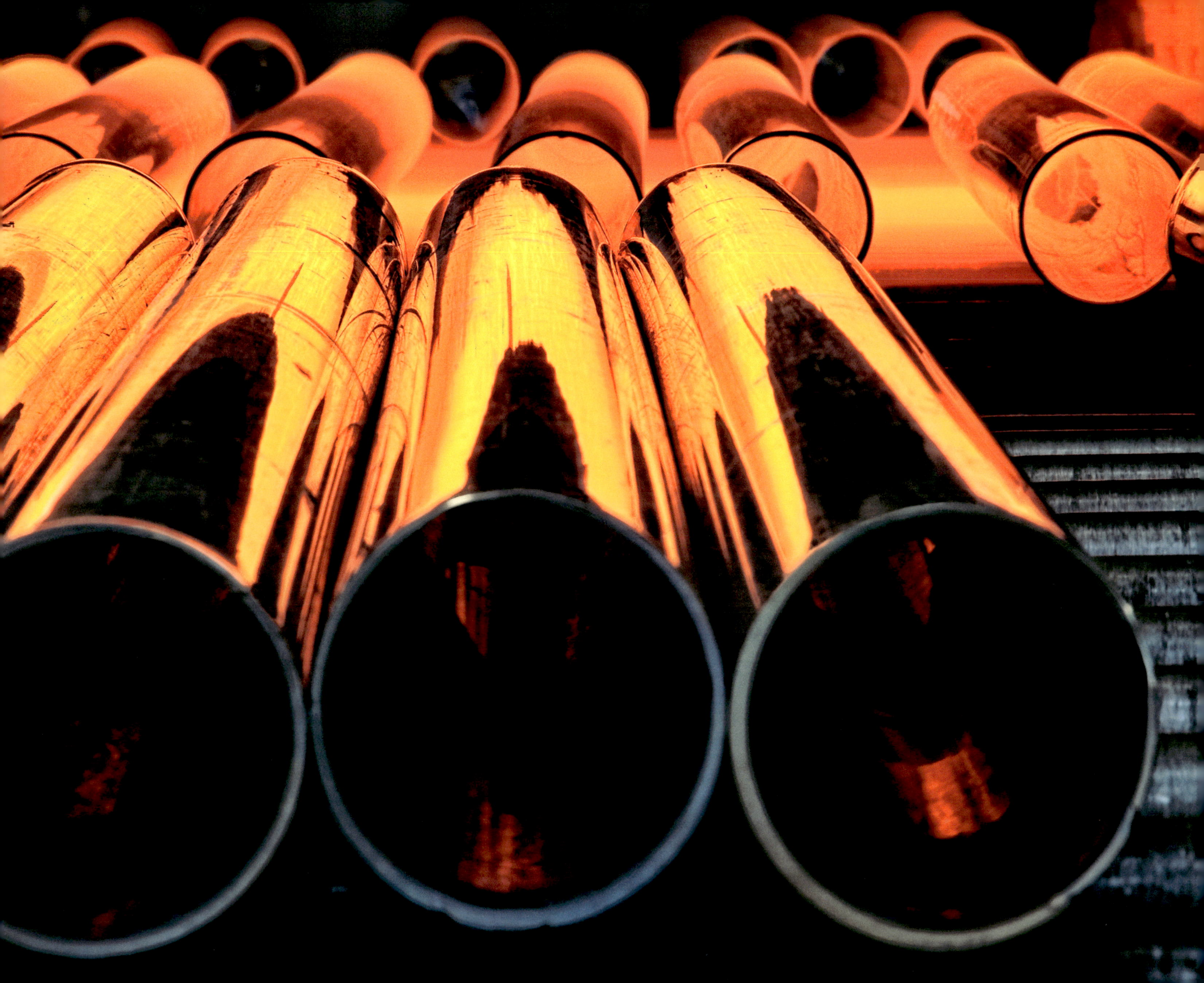

PHOTOGRAPHER'S JOURNAL:
Paul is the youngest guy on the job. His father, Gil, sometimes runs the extruder's saw. Paul looks around and sees there are no others like him. He must worry about the future, but he just shrugs cheerfully, and monitors the annealer. When work is slow, he works other stations and José fills in here.

After a good soak in the pickling tubs, a slow trip through the annealer lets the brass crystals relax and fall back into latticed order as if they were living things whose muscles relax in steam after a hard day. When tubes come out, they are no longer brittle, and they are fit for more stretching and expanding on the benches. Paul says annealing prevents pinholes from forming in the tube. He performs the sorcery he has learned from his elders to heal crystal structures he has never seen.

As the annealed tubes emerge, Paul bundles them for Alfred, who knows where the tubes go next.

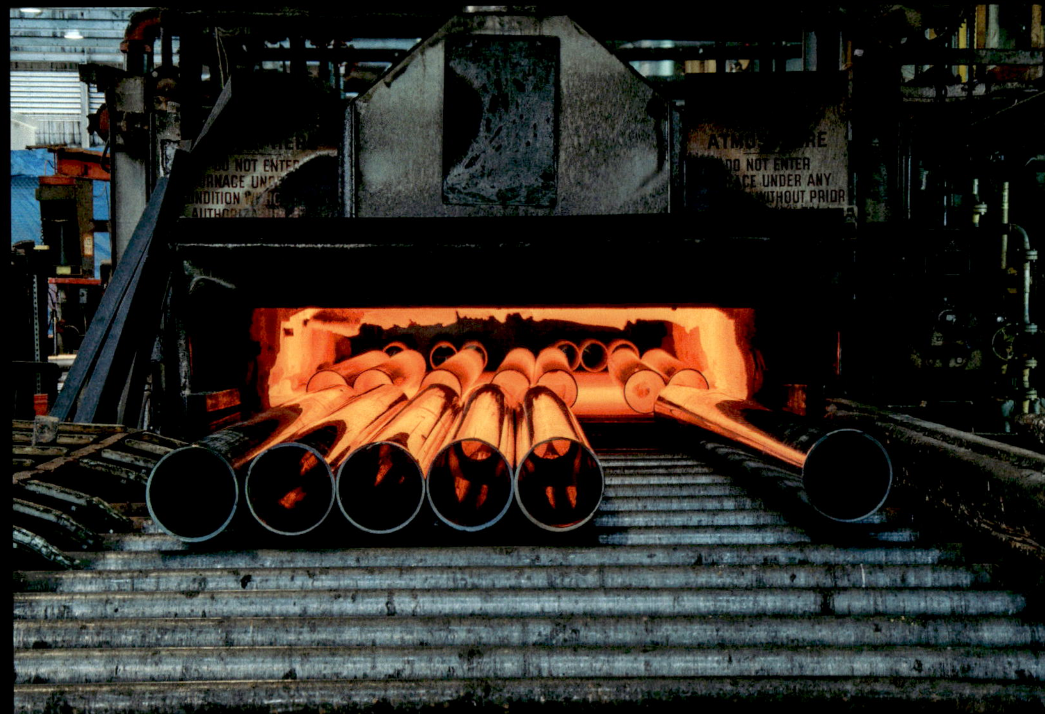

DEEP HEAT
Annealer, American Brass, Bank Street, Waterbury, CT

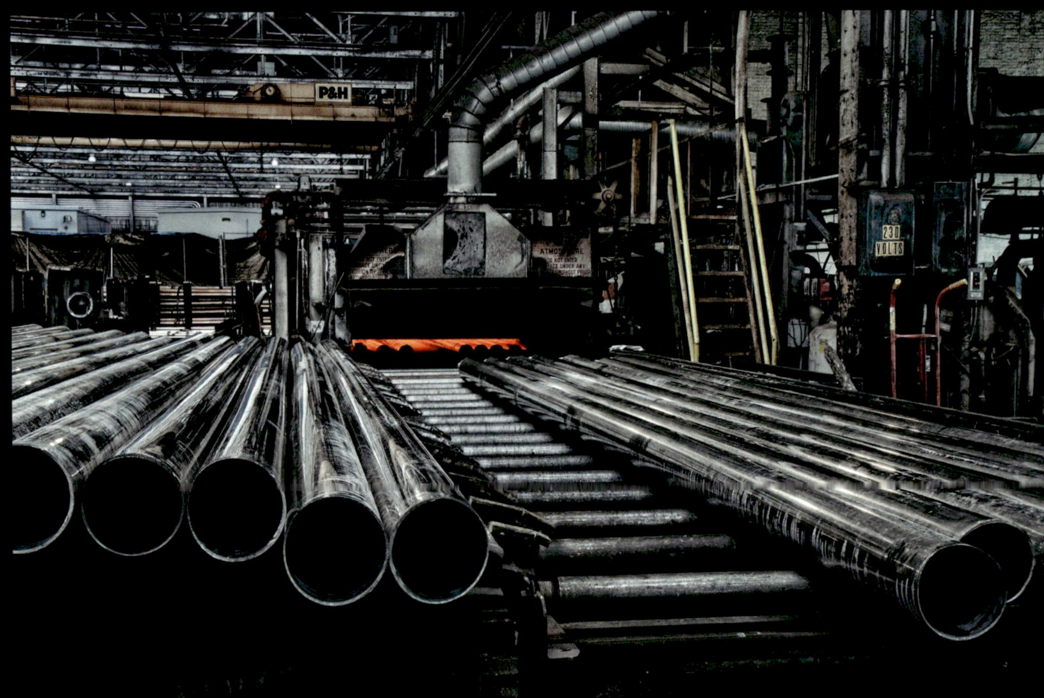

BRITTLE CRYSTALS
Annealer, American Brass, Bank Street, Waterbury, CT

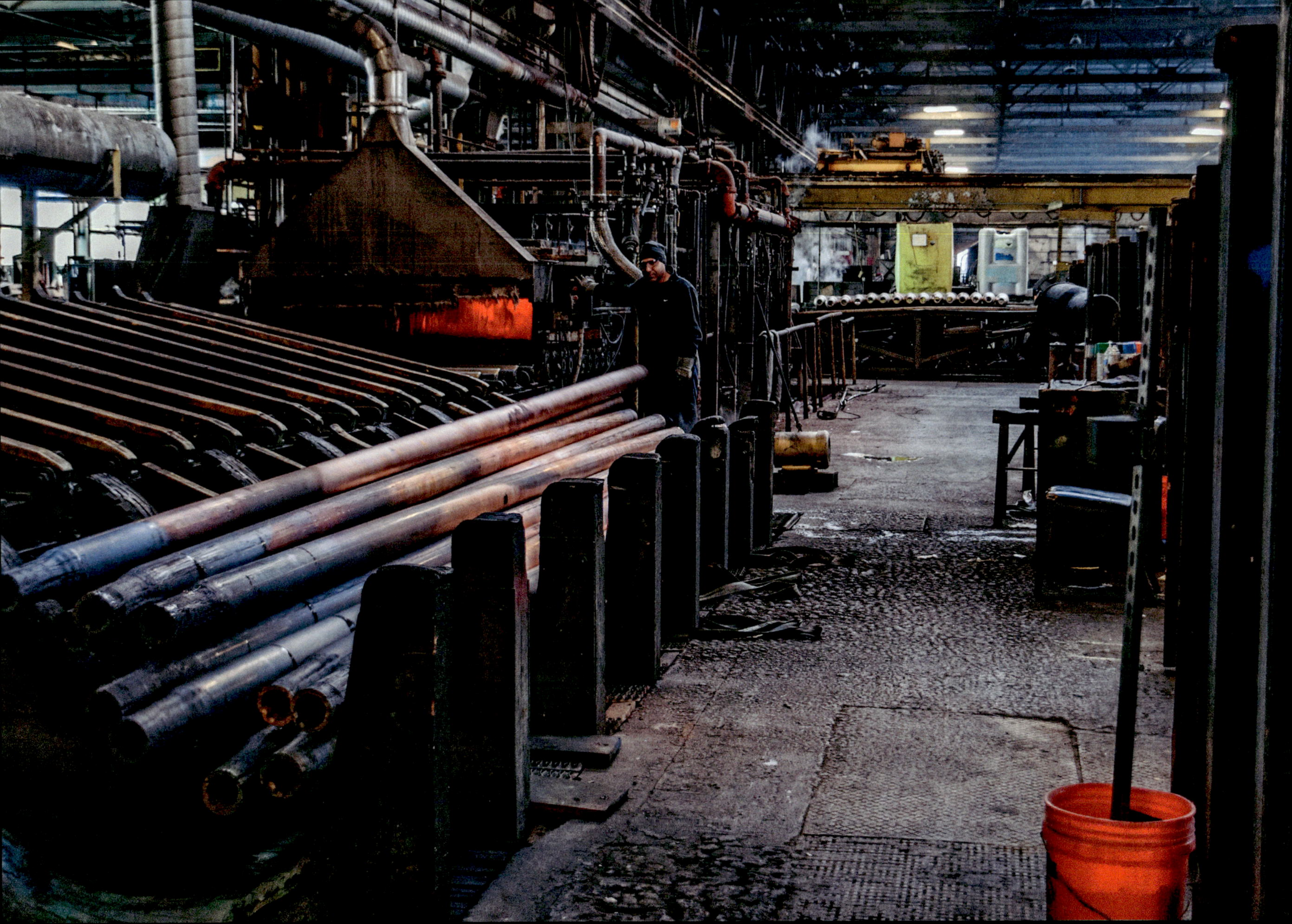

RELAXED CRYSTALS

Annealer, American Brass, Bank Street, Waterbury, CT

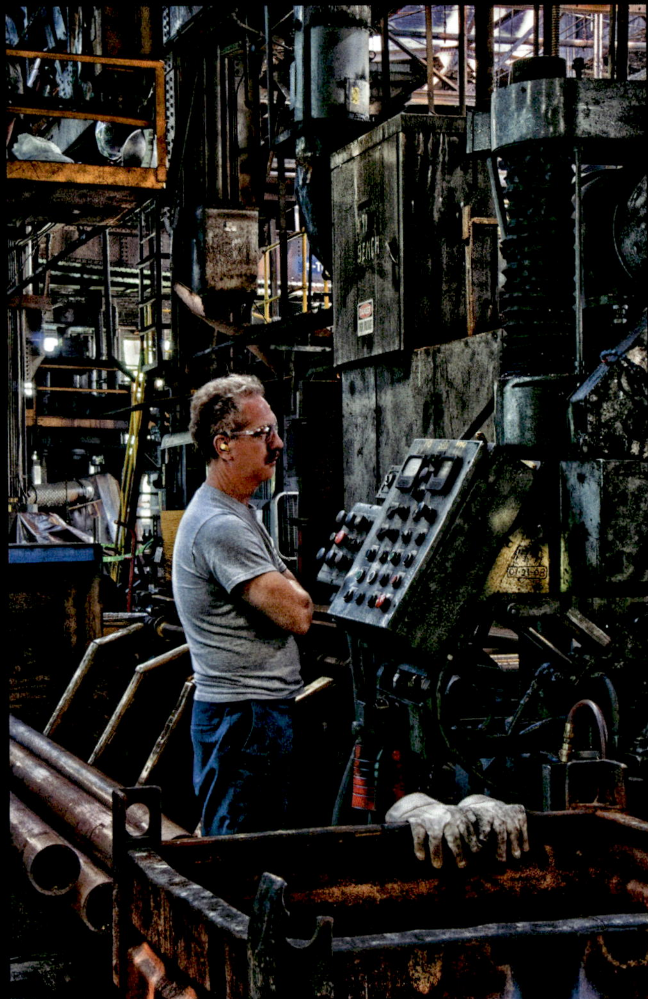

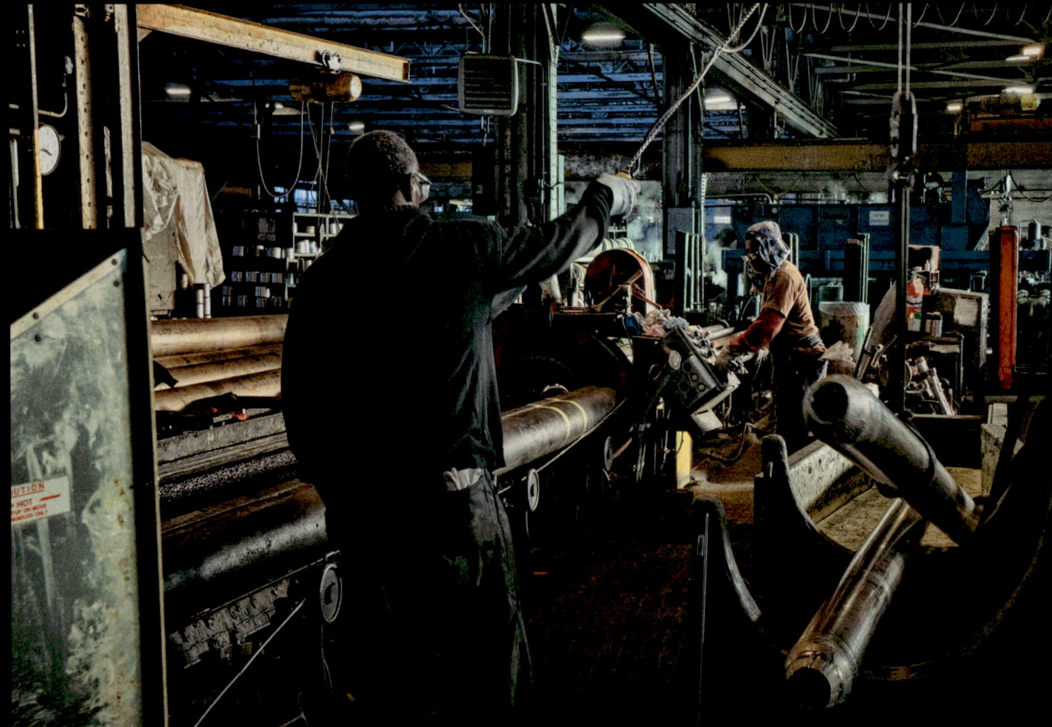

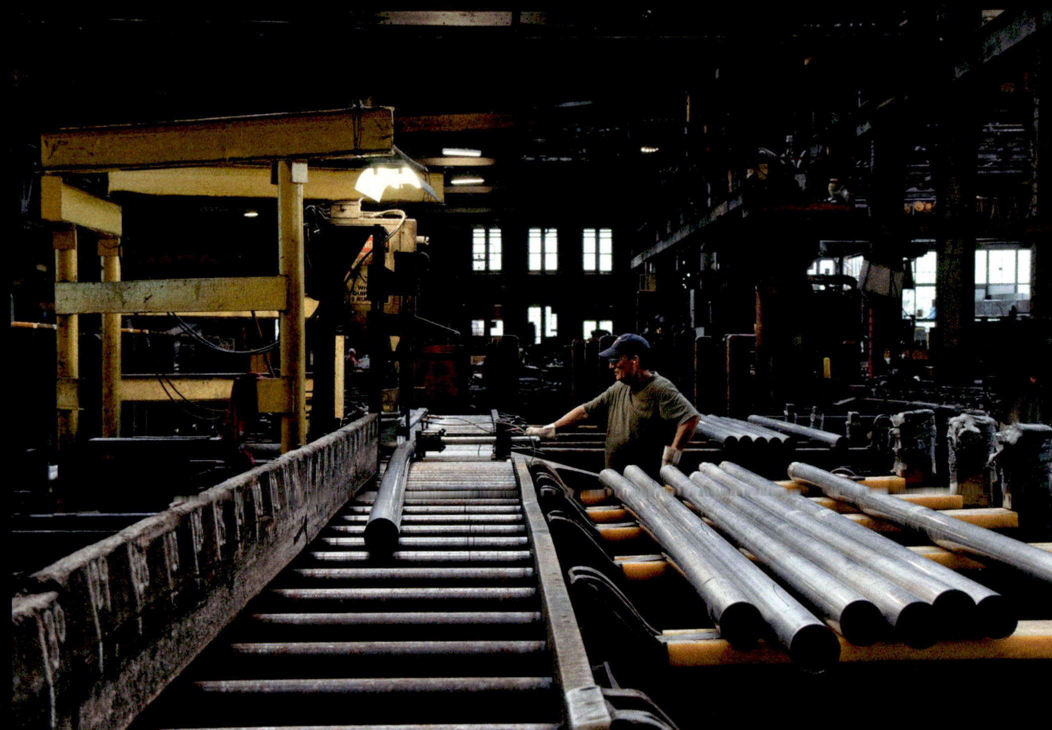

MAESTRO NO HANDS
Saw 179, American Brass, Bank Street, Waterbury, CT

SYNCOPATION & TEAMWORK
The expansion bench, American Brass, Bank Street, Waterbury, CT

EVEN TRIMMING
American Brass, Bank Street, Waterbury, CT

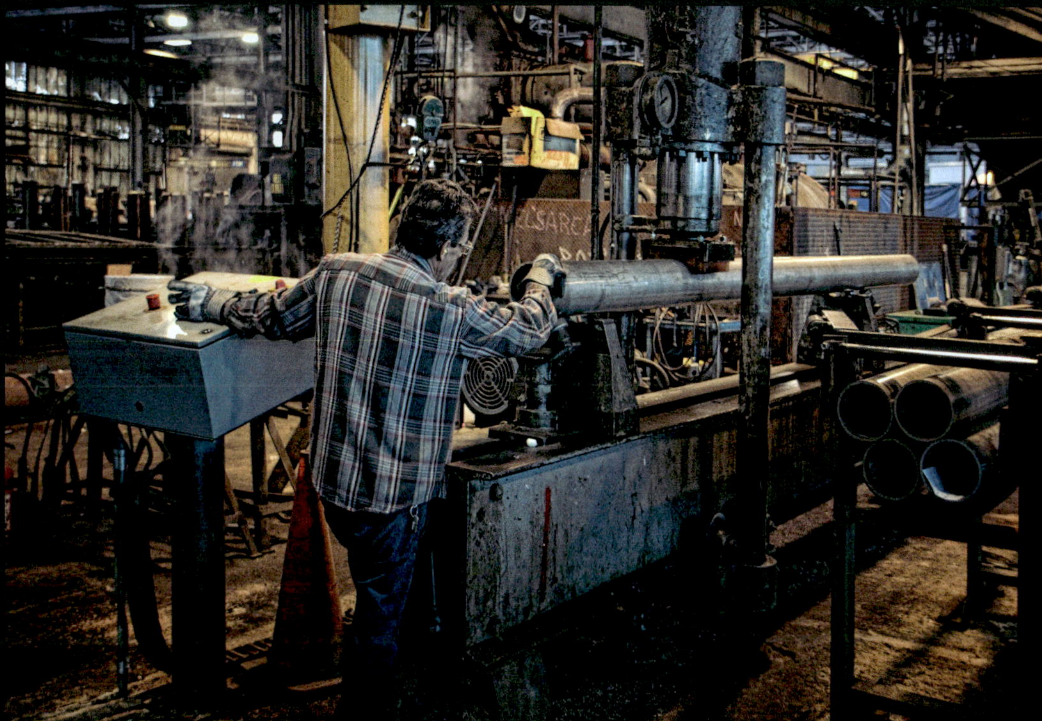

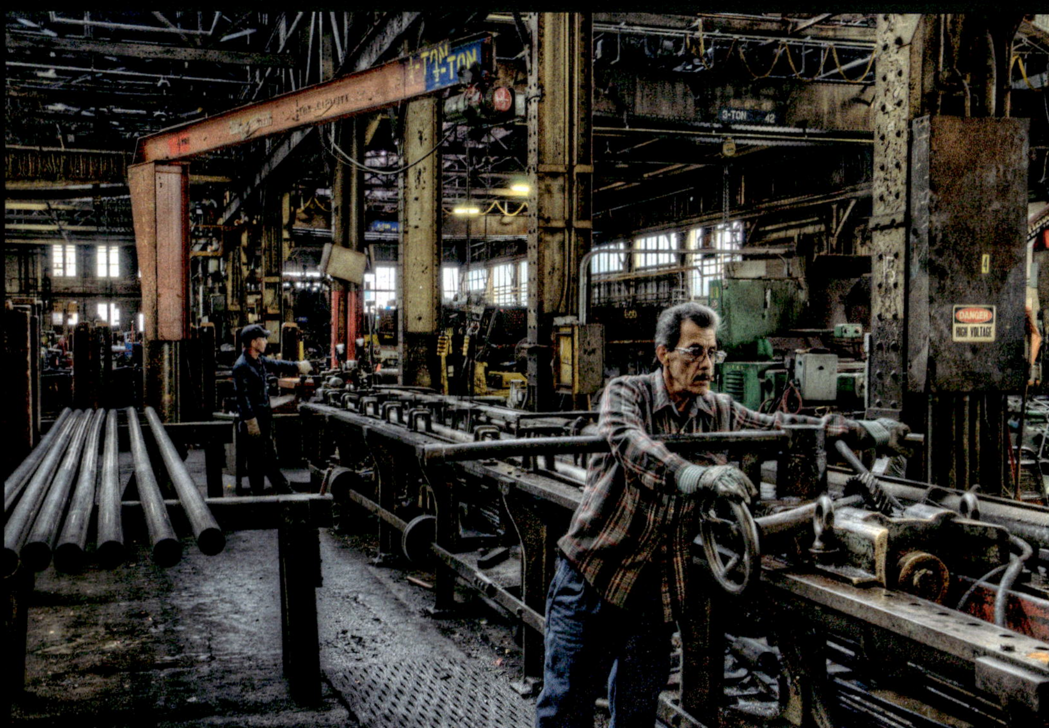

PHOTOGRAPHER'S JOURNAL:
When the tubes meet specification for size and gauge, they make their final trip through the pickling tubs. Then Miguel checks each tube for alignment and makes it true, and Pinto makes the final cut to length. It is ready for final testing.

Miguel and Paul test for porosity by filling each tube with water under high pressure; testing certifies everyone's work. No pinholes!

At last Arthur and Ed will inspect each tube with ultrasonic waves that shake the crystals to see if they're tight; findings appear in a printout from the machine that can see through crystal structure.

Only after all inspections are passed is the custom tube ready for delivery, even as the scrap from the new tube may already have found its way into new billets to begin the round again. That's pretty much the way it's been here for a century or so.

ALIGNMENT
American Brass, Bank Street, Waterbury, CT

HYDRAULIC TESTING
American Brass, Bank Street, Waterbury, CT

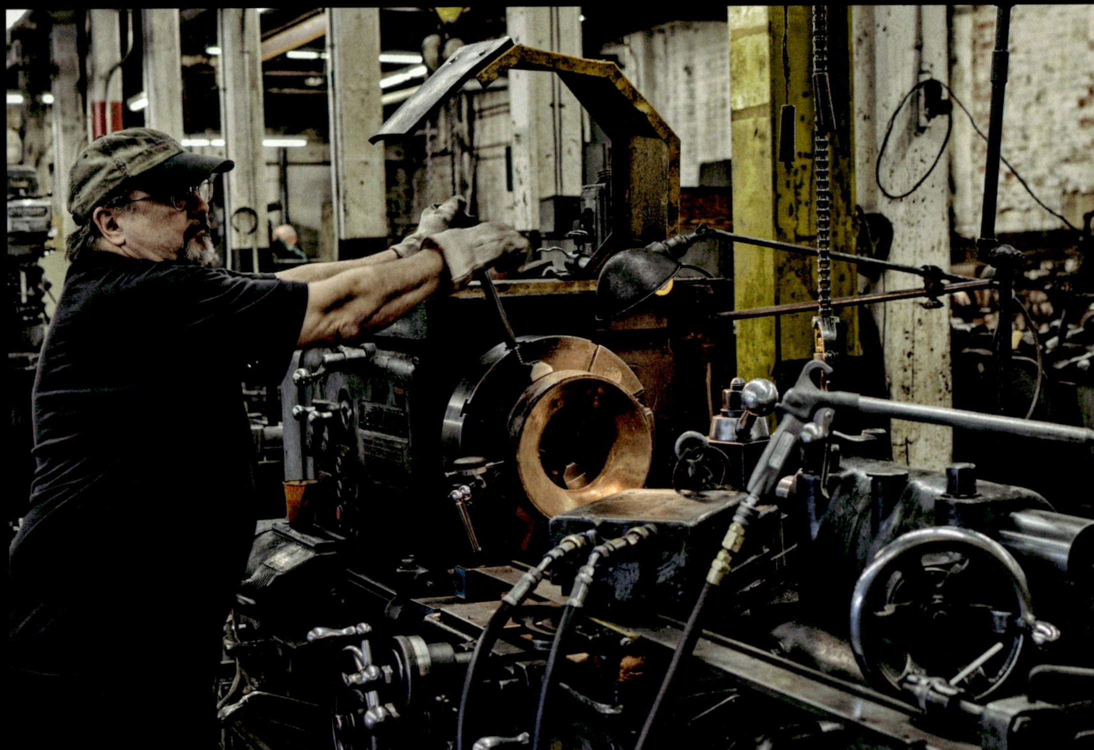

MACHINIST, DAVE

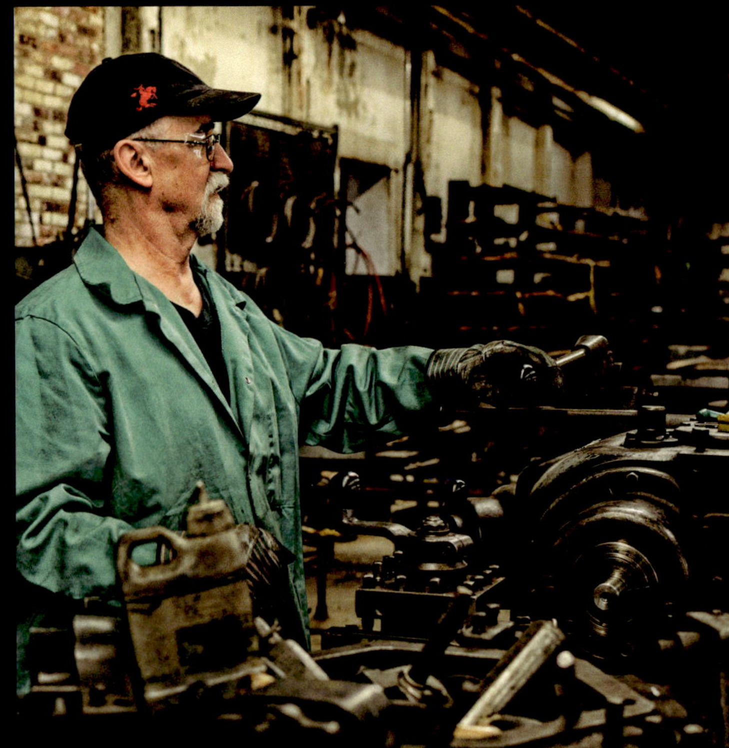

MACHINIST, JOE

PHOTOGRAPHER'S JOURNAL:

Behind the working tube mill, on the first floor of the otherwise abandoned Holmes, Booth & Haydens building, is the mysterious world of the tool makers. It's a Merlin's den of instruments: precision lathes and powerful drill presses, racks full of bits, and bins full of widgets, rods, and plates, cutters, grinders, wheels, bobs, chucks, and occasionally one of a crew of tool makers.

They keep dies sharp, remake what breaks, and sustain the heating, cooling, pushing, turning, or standing firm of everything everywhere in the factory. They also fix leaks. It is a place of problem solving and collaboration, and work stations may appear at a moment's notice and disappear as quickly; a problem will be solved.

These were prized jobs, and the need for men to work here led to technical schools and colleges and degrees in engineering, but until after the war, many men got their college on the job. Even as heavy industry was being systematically de-skilled by technological advances, those advances were creating new jobs at all skill levels, and opportunity must have seemed infinite. The tech ed schools in Connecticut led the nation, and they rested on the tool-making culture that thrived here in the machine shops of industry—a powerhouse of expertise and creative problem solving.

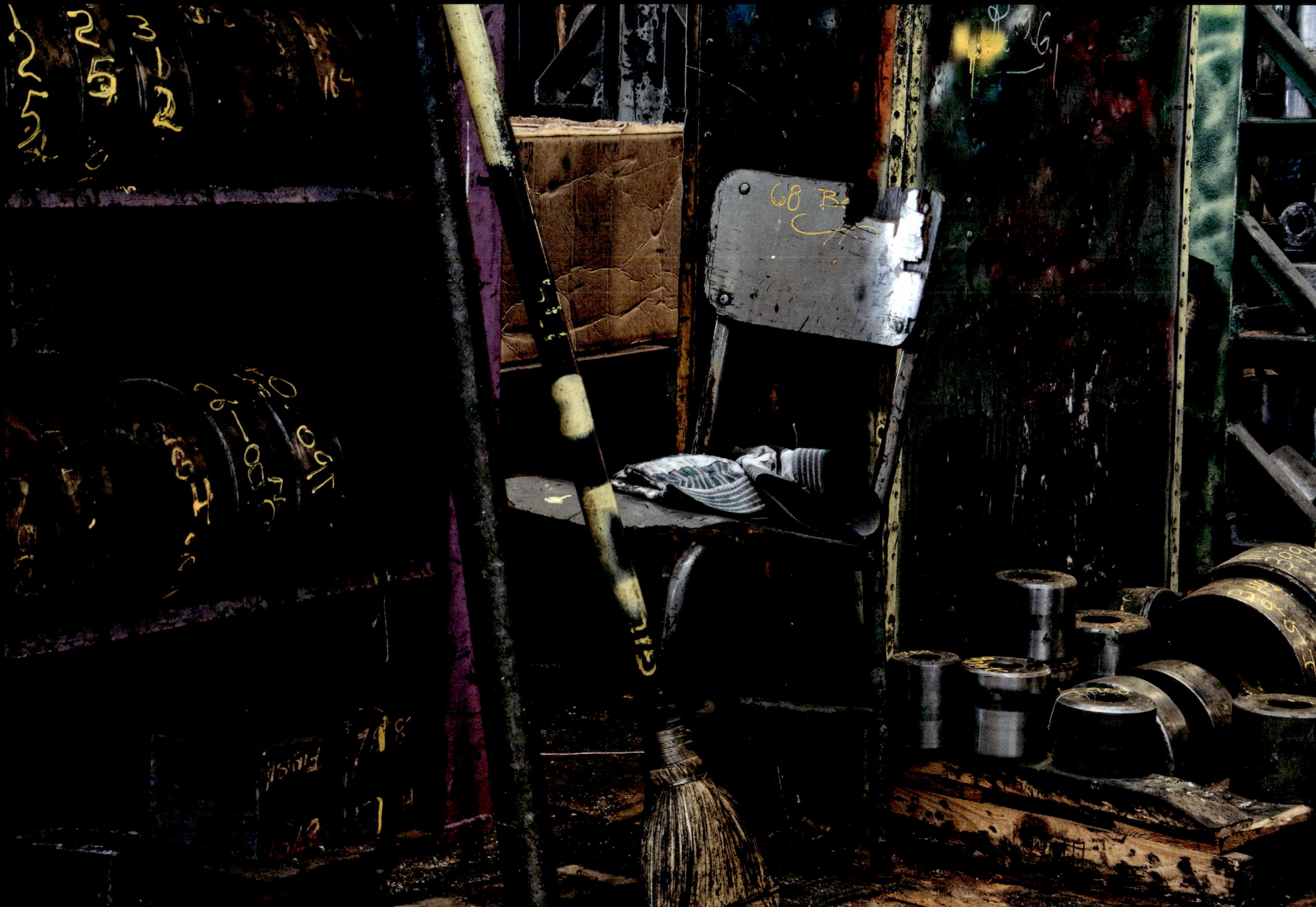

"Deindustrialization liquidated not only factories and jobs; it liquidated a legacy of community building in the Naugatuck Valley and in working class America. While family networks, unions, churches, ethnic associations, and other working-class institutions had been able to establish considerable control over daily life, they had hardly even attempted to influence the basic decisions of capital. Those decisions, it turned out, could lay waste to everything they had gained."

Jeremy Brecher, *Banded Together: Economic Democratization in the Brass Valley*, 2011

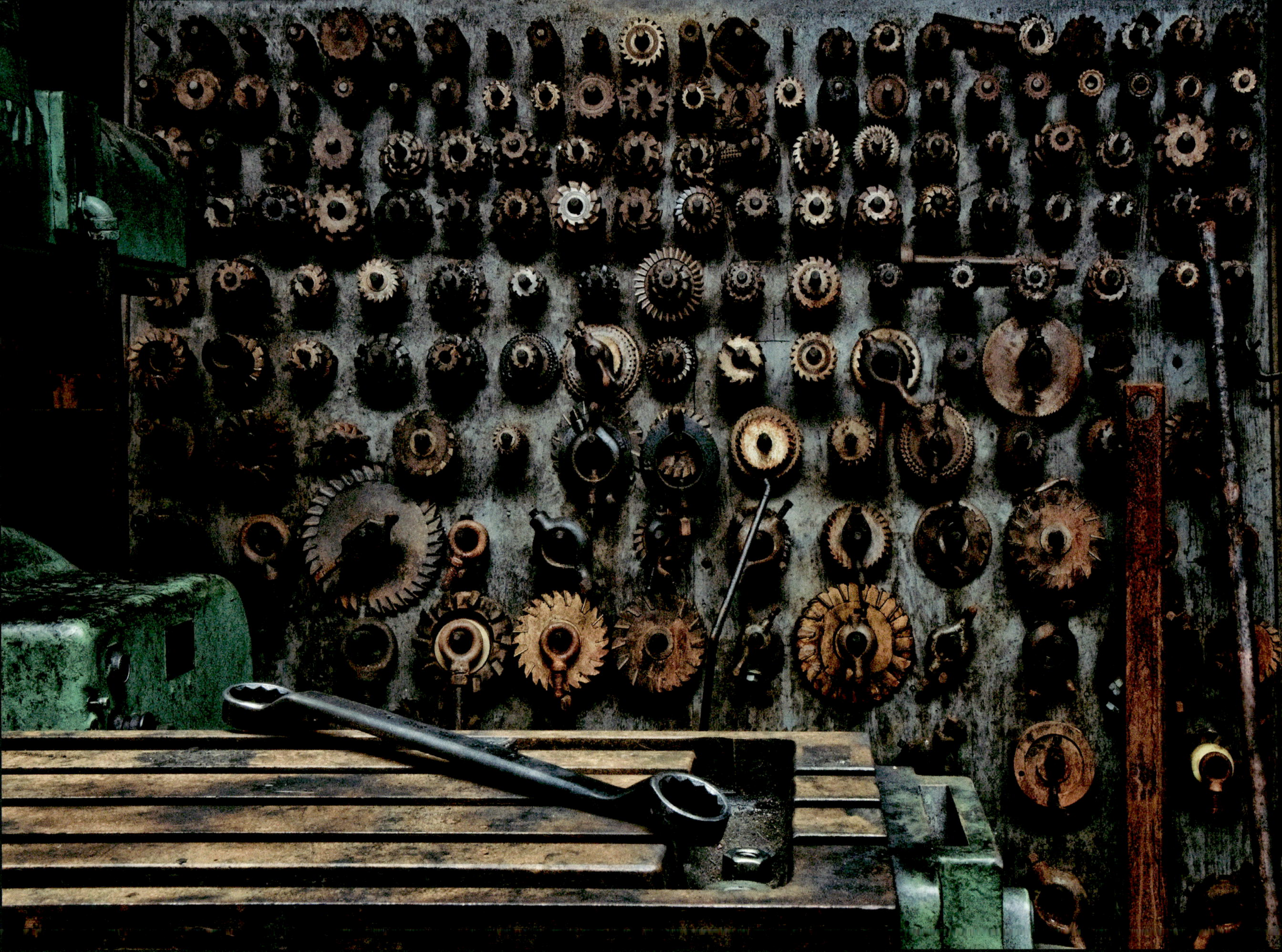

THE ORDERLY MIND

Cutters at the toolmakers' shop,
American Brass, Ansonia, CT

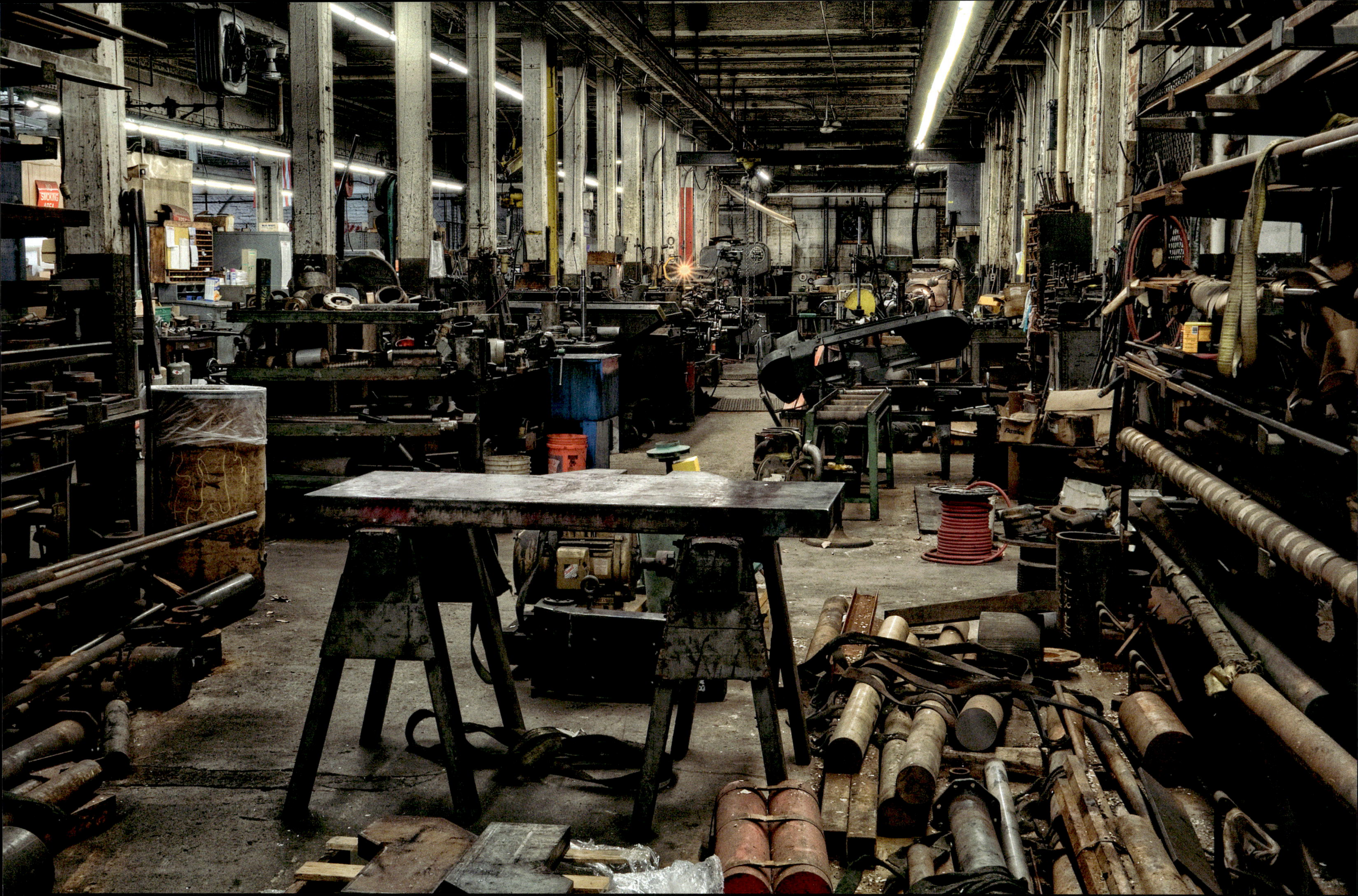

WORKSTATIONS APPEAR
AT A MOMENT'S NOTICE

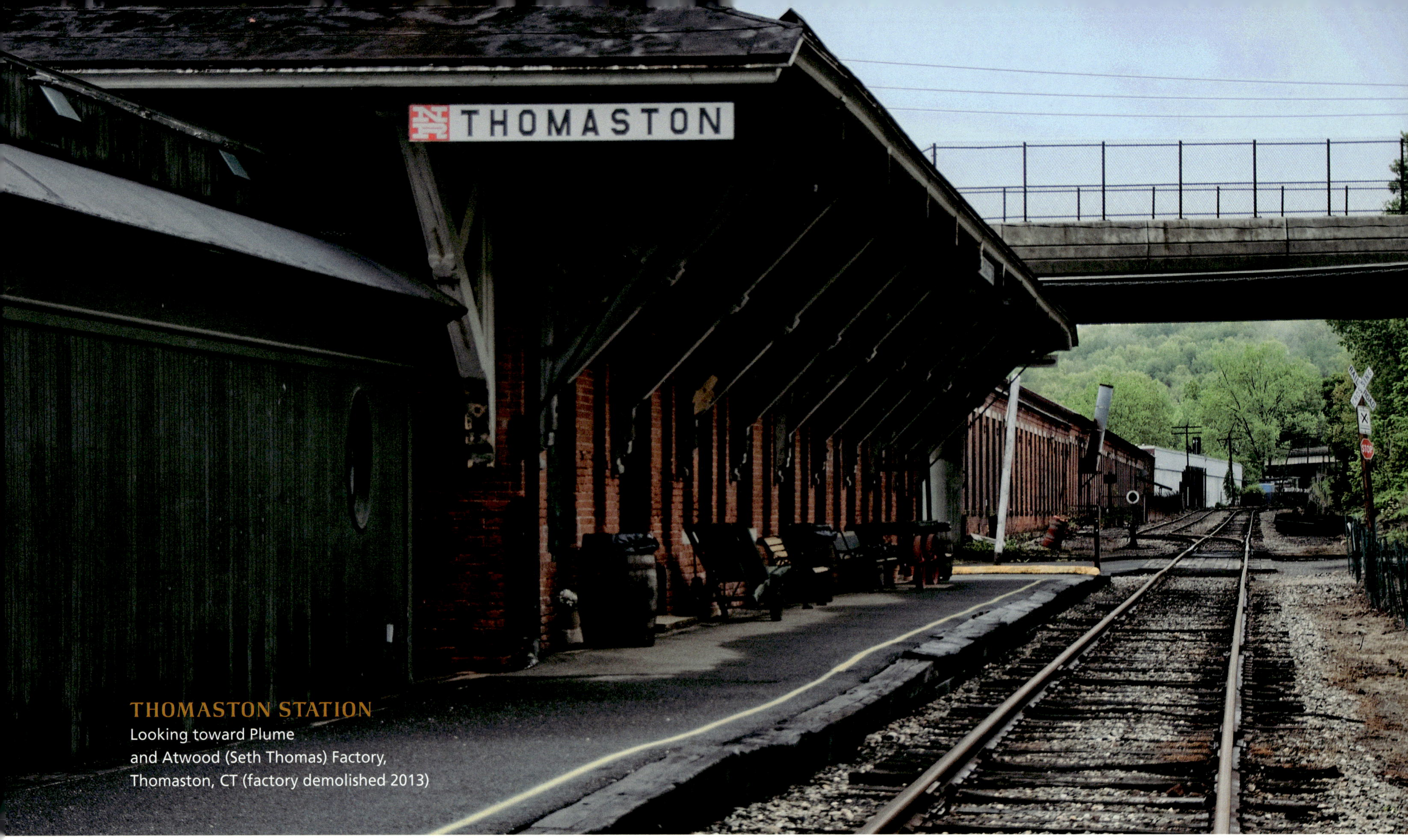

THOMASTON STATION
Looking toward Plume
and Atwood (Seth Thomas) Factory,
Thomaston, CT (factory demolished 2013)

OUR STORIES:

Warp Time

Surely, few transformations of consciousness have been more mysterious than that brought on by Eli Terry's four-dollar clock. His partners—Seth Thomas, Sirus Hoadley, Chauncey Jerome—ramped up the production of Terry's clock, and we've been learning to step to clocks' marching beat ever since. Hoadley finally owned Terry's first company and became a state legislator. Jerome was an innovator, and after the railroads came through, he took Terry's methods and translated them for manufacturing clocks of stamped brass. He made time even less expensive and more accurate, but he was widely imitated, his patents and his profits stolen. Benedict and Burnham finally hired him to set up and run the new Waterbury Clock Company that later became known as Timex.

When clocks were made of wood, we spent half our time in darkness; before the Civil War we hadn't lit night to resemble day, and as you traveled east or west, clock time changed in every town to suit the sun, but we were buying clocks and leaving Circadia. Eli Terry made timepieces that people treasure as antique machinery. Seth Thomas made fine furniture that told the time as clock time permeated our lives, and he did it so well that they changed the town's name from Plymouth Hollow to Thomaston.

In 1881 the New Haven Railroad took control of time; Connecticut legislated a single time zone for the state so that the local railroad could make time tables. It would take three more years before the nation would legislate four time zones, but angry debates and law suits about what time it was continued for half a century. Of influential clocks in public places, few can vie with the famous four-sided clock that sets the pace in the center of Grand Central Station; it is a Seth Thomas clock. Most people think it is powered by electricity, but Seth Thomas never made an electric clock. It is run by an ingenious self-winding mechanism.

The hands of Seth Thomas's Grand Central clock still gracefully circle like planets orbiting a star, as we circle round the clock's faces toward our trains and planes and cars, coming and going. How are we changed by our orbitless digital watches blinking disconnected seconds, as we wait for our train? Or by time in our cell phones all pulsing in harmony with the Internet that can split a second to a millionth part and always know where each of us is? How do our tools change us, and how much time have we got?

But it was Eli Terry's magic that first led us from Circadia; How did the harmonies mingle, as we engineered our first steps into a "well-tempered" world with rigid, twenty-four-hour intervals and no allegiance to sunlight? There is a curious incident, a marker in the history of human consciousness that relates: in 1826 citizens of New Haven were outraged when Eli Terry set his new clock into operation on the town green. What was it about Terry's clock that upset their steady Yankee habits?

Eli Terry was a master at building wooden tower-clocks, and one was needed on the New Haven green to mark time for the daily firing of the canon by which the residents of the town might tune their sundials. The clock that Eli Terry provided had a complicated mechanism that operated two sets of dials. One of these dials was operated by Terry's equation mechanism that varied the length of hours throughout the year in order to mimic the correct sun time. The other dial offered what we call clock time.

New Haven citizens protested—wanted nothing of clock time, wanted it gone. Heated letters debating the nature of Time were exchanged in New Haven newspapers. Terry himself contributed anonymously to the exchanges, but Terry still owned the clock; he showed his disdain by removing the equation mechanism leaving only warped clock time. Today the difference is as invisible to us as telephone wires along the highway.

Of course, in reality the matter had been settled long before. It was decided by the many clocks of Terry's design that had seduced us and that had been mass-produced, inexpensive, and ubiquitously chiming the hours in homes and parlors since 1808, a decade before the New Haven squabble, and more than a half century before the lights came on.

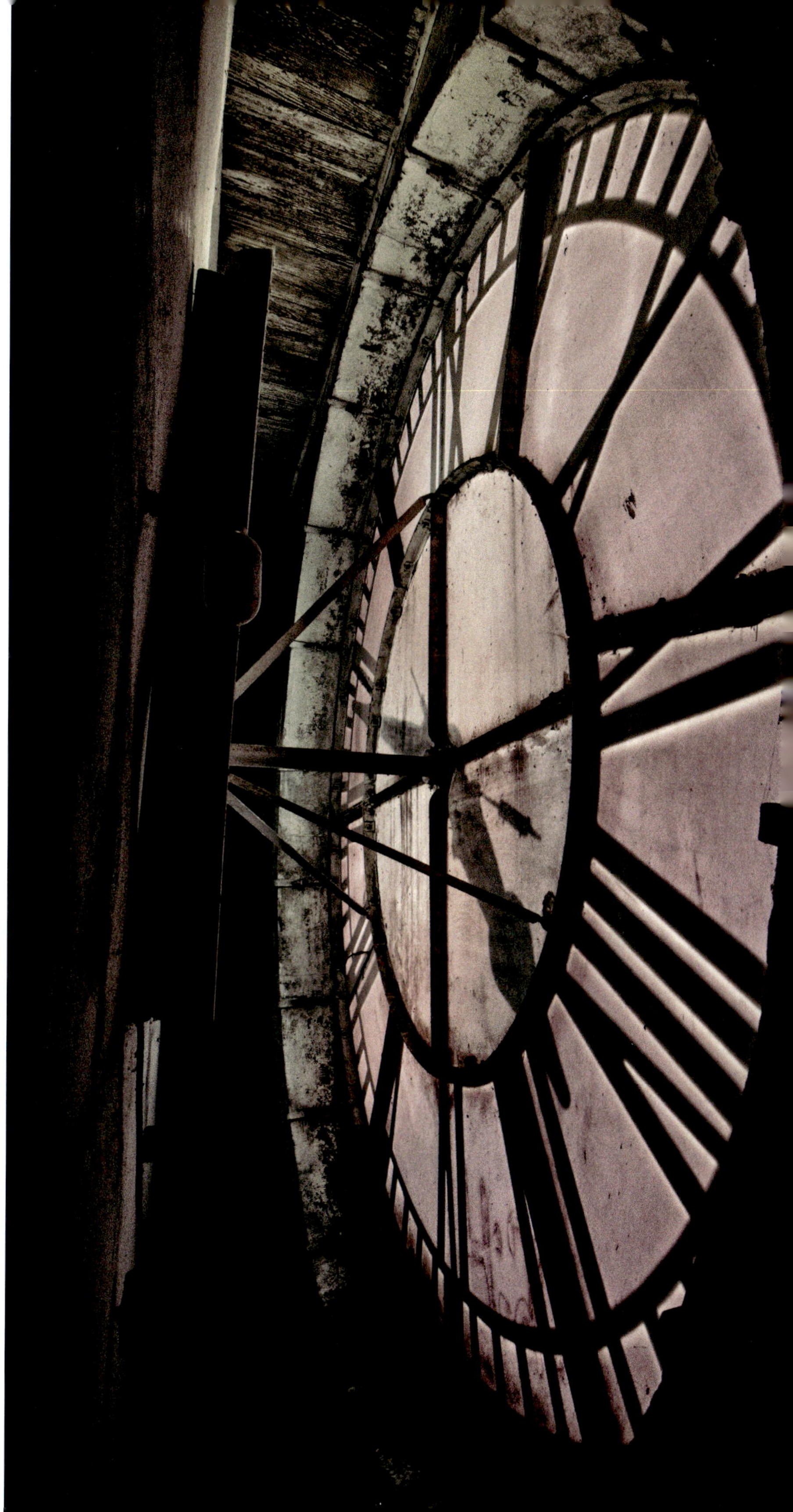

INSIDE TIME

Seth Thomas clock tower from inside, Thomaston, CT

TO ELI TERRY AND HIS FOUR-DOLLAR CLOCKS

We rode the even gait of time
like cowmen on the drive,
easy in the saddle;
or like turnips and beans
in the black earth.
Daybreak opened our eyes
as the cock opened our ears;
we made music
when there was moonshine.

'Til those wooden wheels of time,
the even clenching of their teeth
reset the axis of the earth
so equal moments fill each hour,
snug as cans sealed in a carton.
We sleep while the sun shines
or party 'til dawn
or work the nightshift
to moonlight at daybreak.

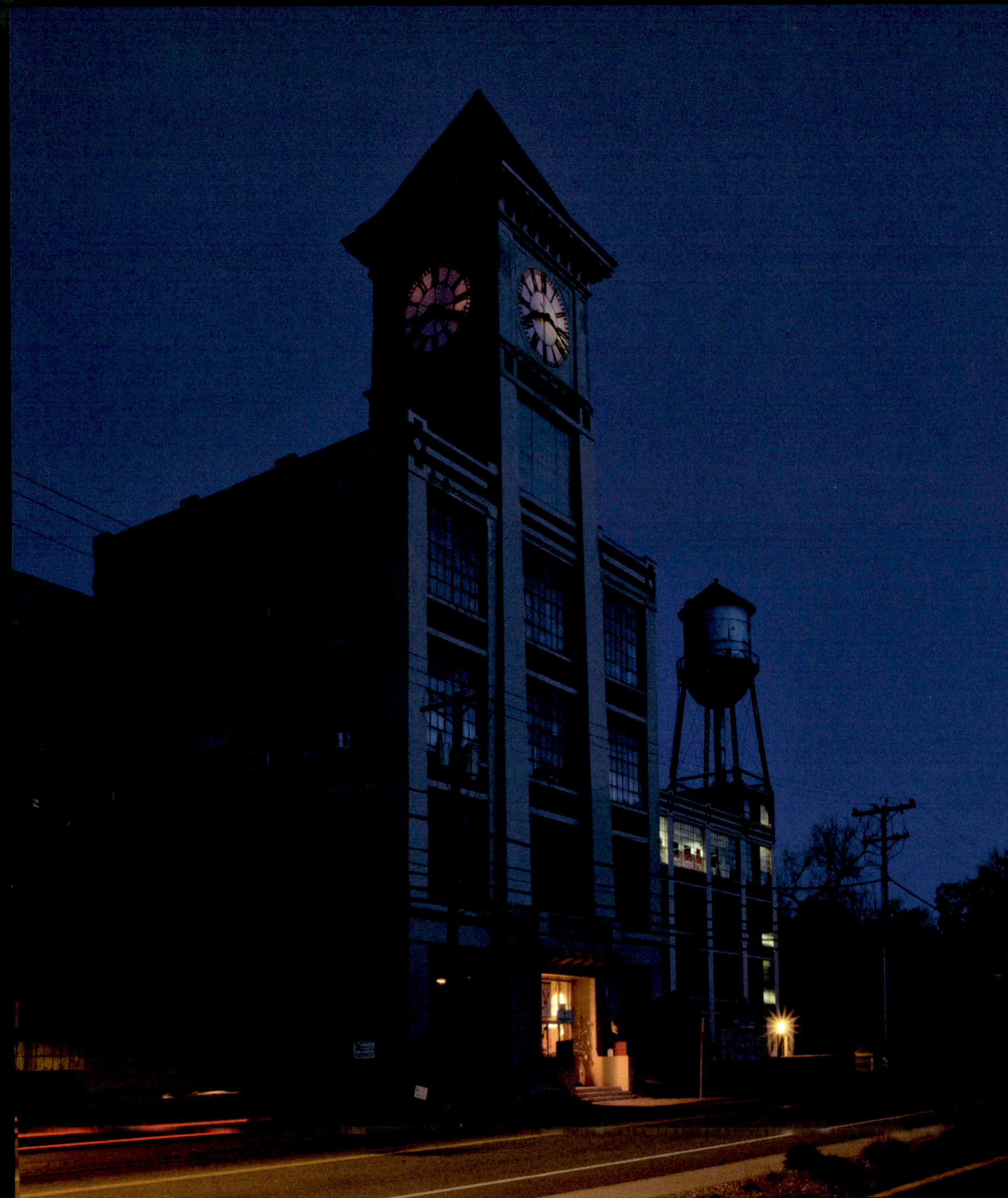

SETH THOMAS BY NIGHT
Seth Thomas factory, Thomaston, CT

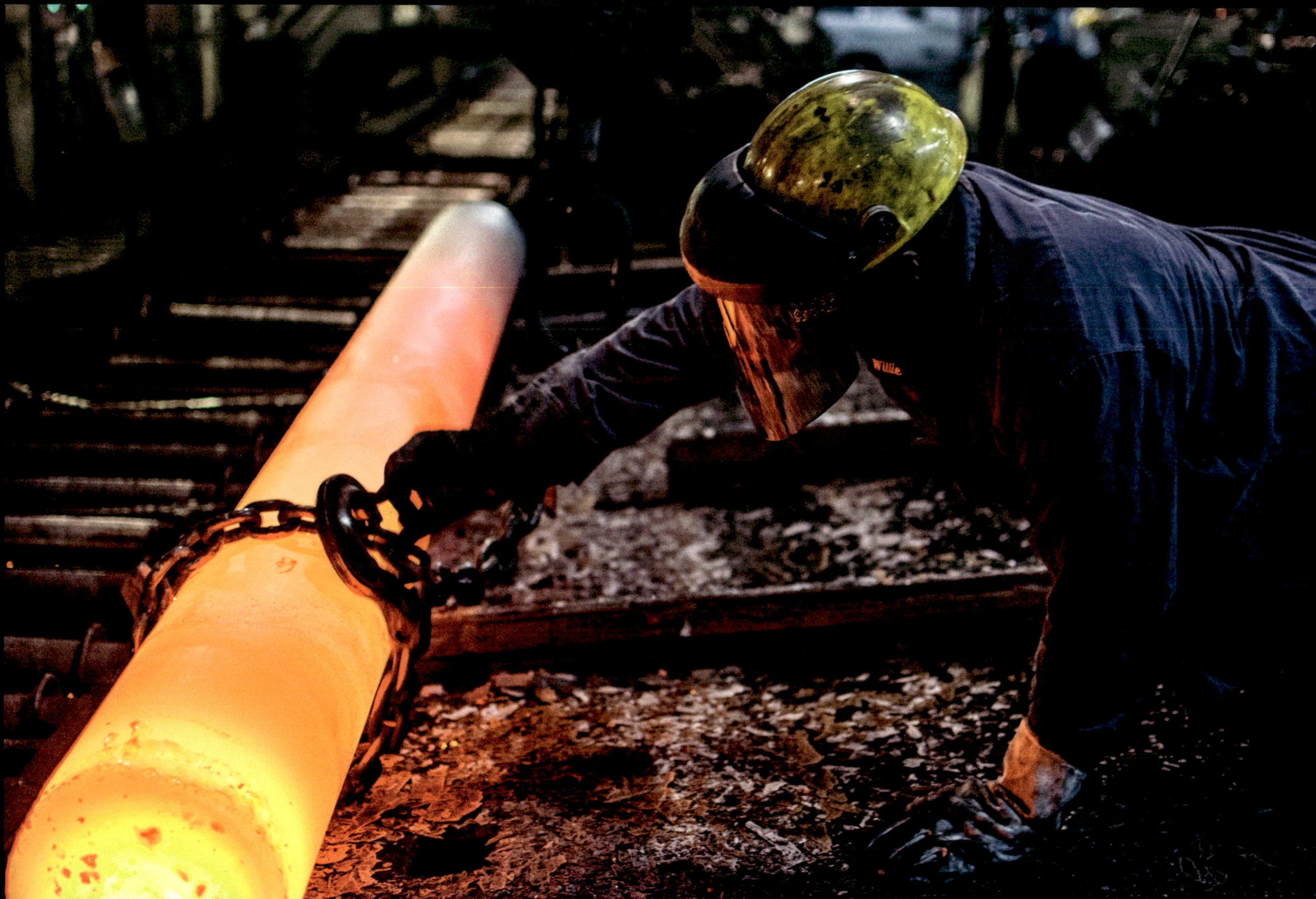

PHOTOGRAPHER'S JOURNAL:
It was winter when I learned the factory would close. Three years had nearly passed since I first saw the extruder puff white gas and began photographing. I'd waited since fall for news that casting would resume to meet new orders, but it had already been clear for a while, they had finished casting out, and time had foreclosed. There would be no last-minute order to save the mill. Still, everyone hoped for a miracle, and many shrugged and pretended not to care. As the last metal made its way through the production stream, the men were gradually laid off. I tried going back, but I couldn't shoot to the dirge in which the men and metal moved. All at once the spirit was gone.

The old Plume & Atwood buildings in Thomaston, which once made parts for Seth Thomas, had collapsed over the summer—bulldozed and carted off as fill. Taylor & Seymour finally failed and closed but their valley shops were rusted over long ago.

I went back to American Brass again after the mill closed, and I was there when a salvage man came by. He said there's not another like it left, and he's seen them all. As always, what can be sold will be sent where labor is cheap, and rules are lax, and we have yet to learn that all land is holy.

I feel sorry for the friends I made at the mill, and the lives they leave behind, and the way of living that seems almost gone; I'm grateful I could snatch images of the men and the place, that they may be saved from the torrent of time, and I'm grateful to all my friends at the mill for opening a story for me to tell.

TOIL & TROUBLE
Willy removing the chain from the billet after casting, American Brass, Ansonia, CT

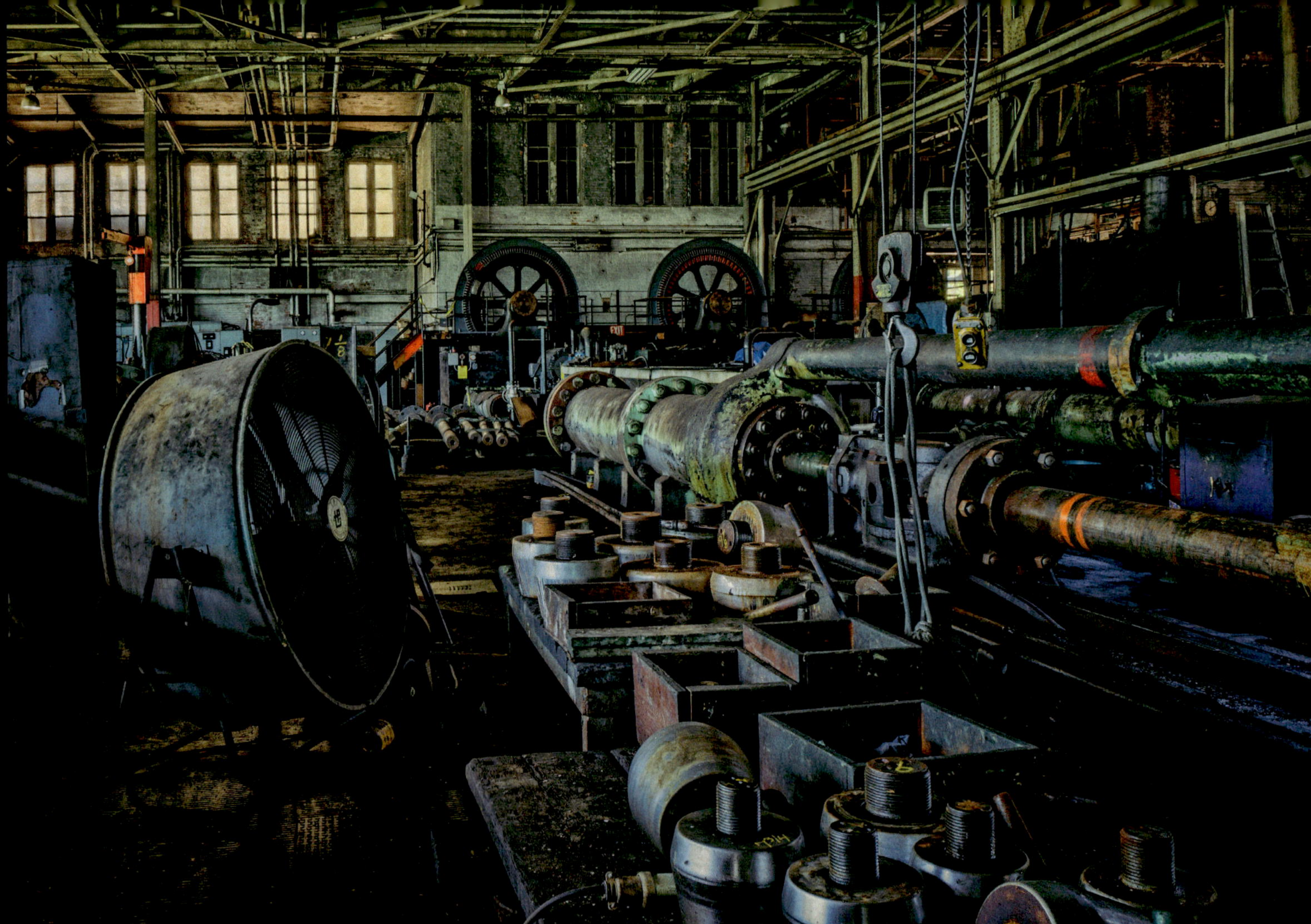

ORIGINAL TUBE MILL

Fittings and hydraulic cylinder for Draw Bench 23 with 1897 electric motors behind

PHOTOGRAPHER'S JOURNAL:

If there is a place called Brass Valley lingering in time, then for awhile its center of gravity must have been here. Looking this way in 1905 would have been little different than this 2014 photograph. However, in 1905 all this would have been cutting edge.

The giant hydraulic cylinder at the center of this shot is the muscle end of an expansion bench used to work cold metal as if it were taffy. Three expansion benches of graduated sizes lay parallel here. The benches could be refitted with different mandrils and dies to customize tube of all shapes, sizes, and gauges in alloys for every environment. I've read that Benedict & Burnham developed these technologies; this seems to be the place. The electric motors along the back wall are pioneers. The plans give their date as 1898. Each of the electric motors here turned a hydraulic pump strong enough to crack that cylinder wall.

The mergers that created American Brass began to be implemented in 1899. By 1917, the new American Brass had assembled a state-of-the-art tube mill here, no doubt figuring it all out as they expanded, and the finished tube mill was all still functioning, turning out specification-critical tube for nuclear submarines, they say, until 2014. On my first day photographing in this mill one of the men here referred to it as "paleolithic."

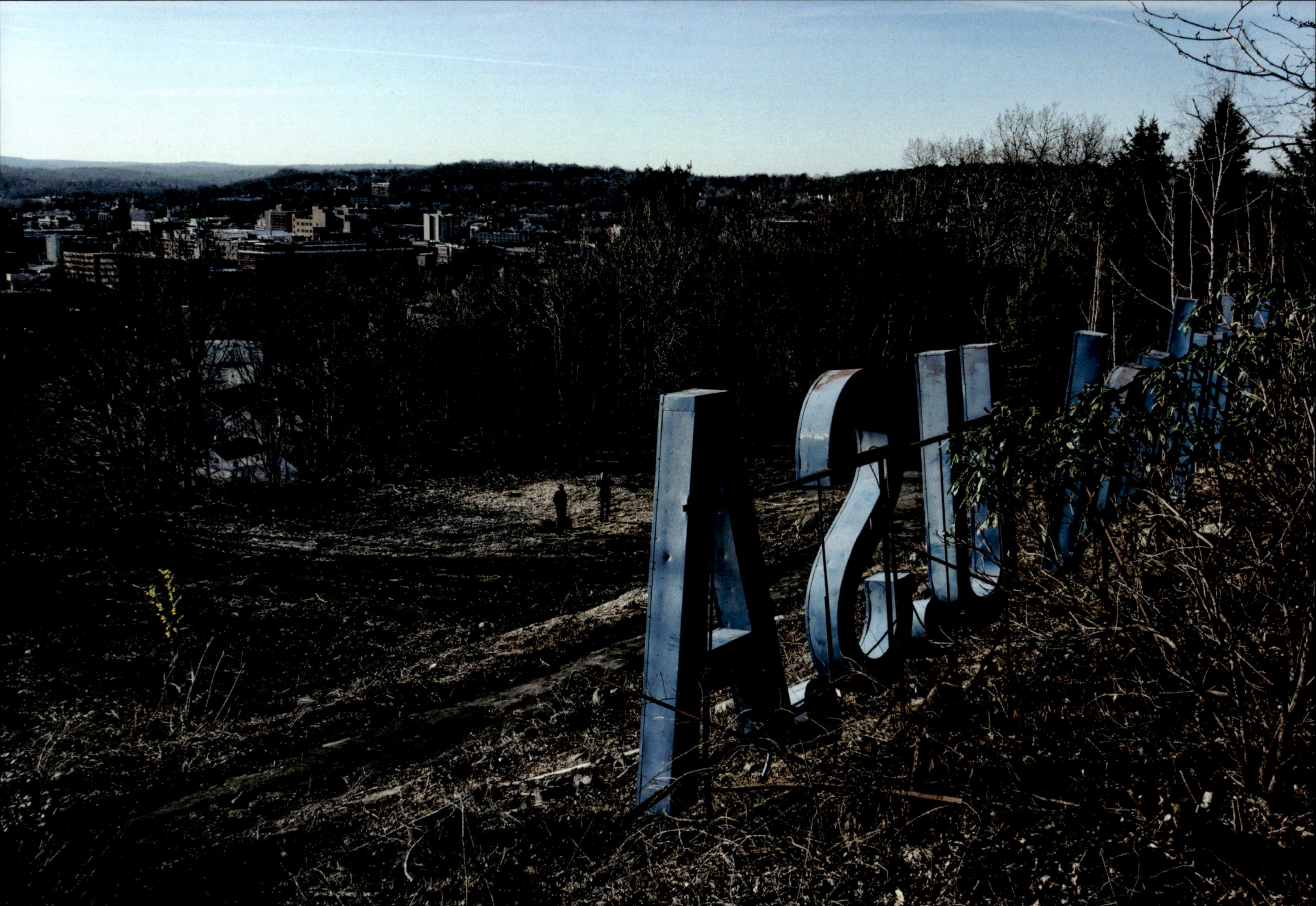

WATERBURY FROM
HOLYLAND USA, 2014

"WHO HOLDS THE DEVIL, LET HIM HOLD HIM WELL,
HE HARDLY WILL BE CAUGHT A SECOND TIME."

—Johann von Goethe, *Faust*, 1808/1829

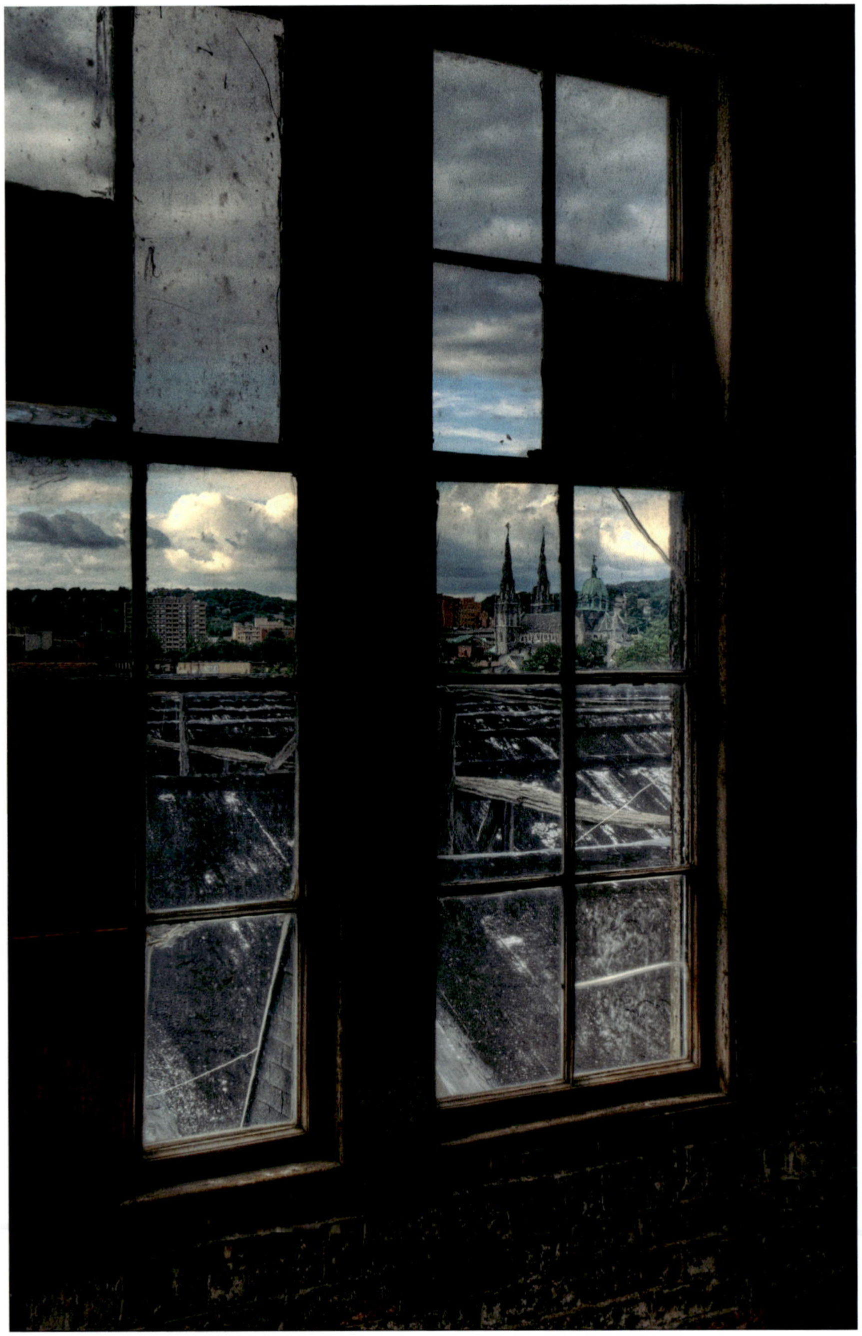

FACTORY LANDSCAPE
From stair tower, Holmes, Booth & Hayden Lampworks, Bank Street, Waterbury, CT

OUR STORIES:

Mixmaster

Interstate 84 heading east leaps from the western bluff of the Naugatuck Valley, and motorists find themselves looking down across the City of Waterbury from the top deck of a gangling, graceless structure known as "the mixmaster," which spans the valley at its center and speeds us east–west along I-84, or if we choose, it connects us along careening ramps to the north–south valley highway or into downtown Waterbury way below on the valley floor. First-timers find it a harrowing ride.

When we are not dodging lane-shifting commuters, we always glance over at Waterbury's three tall landmarks: the campanile above Union Station, our bit of Italy; the paired spires and dome of St. Anne's, our petit soupçon of France; and Holyland's cross, beside our crumbling Jerusalem.

Through this window in the stair tower of Holmes, Booth & Haydens's lampworks we watched Waterbury grow. St. Anne's was partly built when the old lampworks burned, but by the time the bells pealed for the topping-off ceremony upon completion of the dome, we were French Canadians standing at this window cheering the church built with pennies we scrimped from our salaries! That was shortly after World War I. It was the sort of day one might not even notice smog.

January 8, 1920, was cold and smoggy. They told us the men seized were "reds," and put them aboard the Soviet Ark and sent them back to Russia, but from here the truth was hard to know, and we returned to our work and little talk of unions.

The air only thickened in the 1930s, but the "reformer," former mayor T. Frank Hayes, and his former pals and their formal appeals, wouldn't reach prison until 1941. We hoped that would clear the air, but we were focused on the war in Europe, and more of us were women passing this factory window then, and some of us prayed, and some hoped, and most of us pitched in.

And then came the flood. In '55 as waters rose, we heard this window was a doorway. The high water mark we painted afterward is still high on the wall in the shed below. There were people in boats, climbing over the rooftops, salvaging valuables. And everyone pledged to rebuild.

On November 6, 1960, at 3 AM, we stopped here on night shift and listened at the open window to hear the crowds, three thousand strong, waiting on the green for John F. Kennedy to come through town and reaffirm visions of Waterbury's revival.

After the earth movers began their thunderous digs, and the ground shook with frequent blasts, this was a front row seat, as dizzying highway interchanges rose over Meadow Street and Mill Street and became the Mixmaster, and we dreamed of neat suburbs where every house has a double garage.

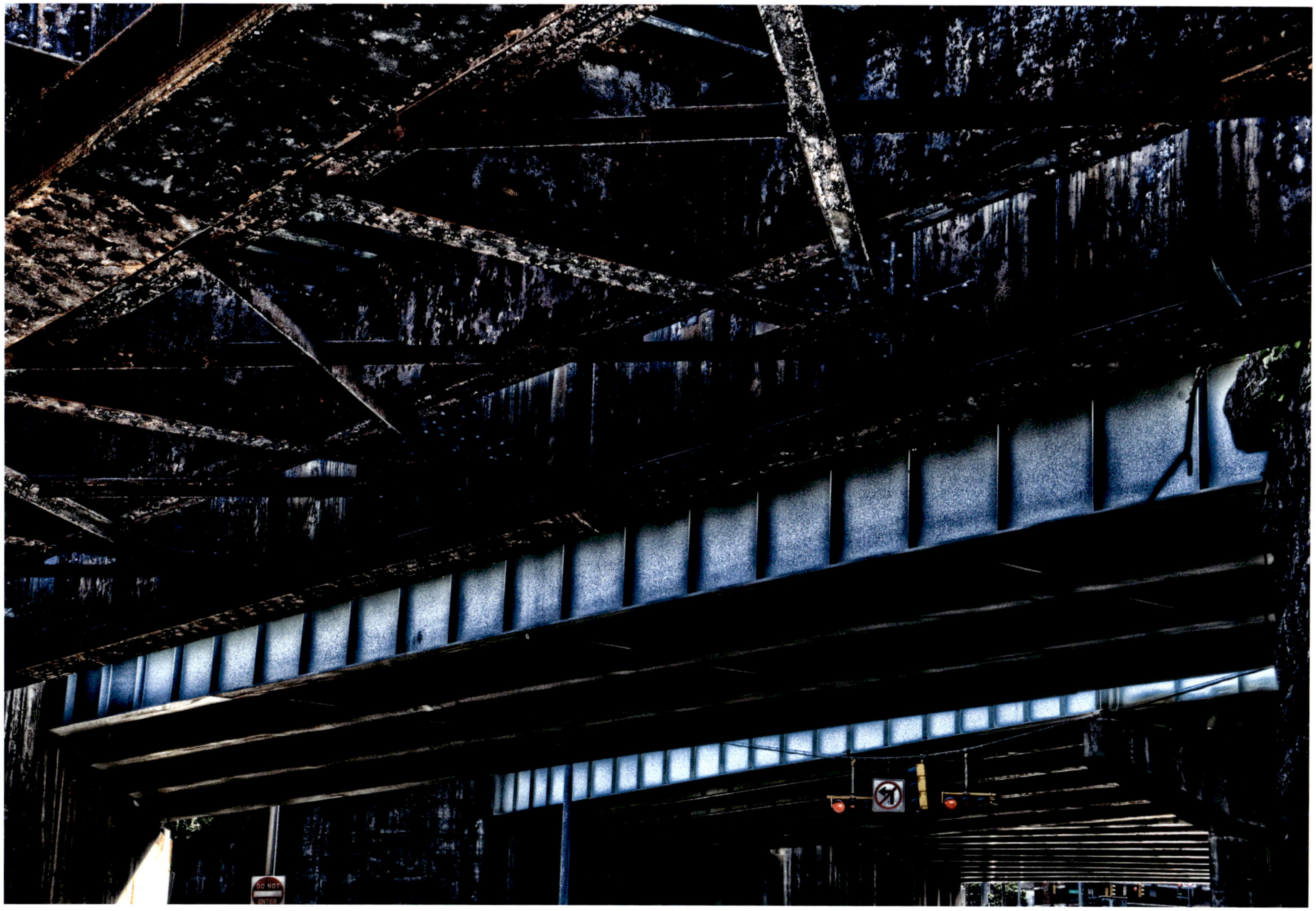

There was other talk as well, of neighborhoods bulldozed to let highways through, and afterward Ronald Reagan stood where JFK had stood. He came to draw a line, and Waterbury's leaders envisioned an inner city as jet age as the highways whizzing by, towers of glass and gleaming aluminum. Whatever we all dreamed, we were all about to step on the gas, and highways were gold.

When the spires of St. Anne's caught fire the first time in 1971 we came to this window to look, though it's been awhile since many French-Canadians were among us. The services at St. Anne's are regularly in Spanish now, but neighborhood churches have always spoken the language of the new community.

This was Brass City at the very center of Brass Valley. To those who cross the mixmaster frequently, the spires of St. Anne's Church, the tall, slender tower of Union Station, and Holyland's cross on top of the eastern bluff of the Valley are familiar landmarks. Unless traffic is snarled, motorists have a two-minute window on Waterbury and then it's gone. It's almost the blink of an eye.

ROUTE 8 UNDERPASS

Bank Street,
Waterbury, CT

TRAIN DEPARTING

The past is a cacophonous tumult
a maelstrom of melodies
some singing
some wailing
some marching defiantly.

A railroad coach abandoned halfway up the Naugatuck Valley
its ruined upholstery a nesting place for rodents and small birds
the meaning of the train
the track
the valley
whiplash through time
factory gears flash
amassing brassy fortunes
sparking dreams
winning wars
grinding lives to ash
populating suburbs with two-car families.
If not quite music, may it be chaos akin to the orchestra tuning up!
The black track along the river, where does it come from, where does it lead?

On the side of the coach a swastika has been spray-painted, an ancient tune.
Who put it there and when?
How does it reverberate out of the valley's past?
How does it partake of the valley's bigotries and rivalries,
its compromises and its compassion?
Or is it the scornful howl of those who have come unhinged from history,
beside the walls of Bedlam
while the rest of us try to remember the past?

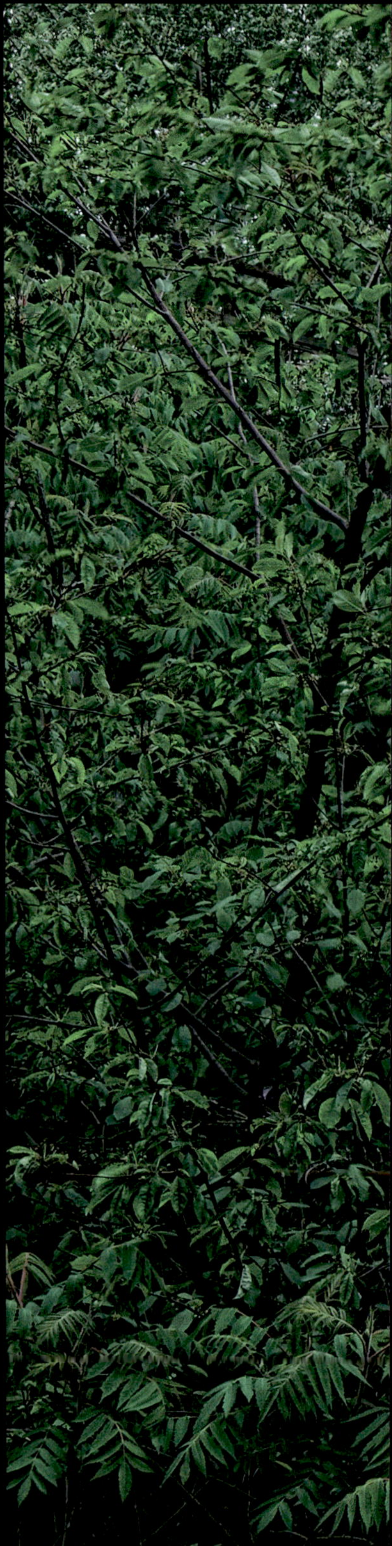

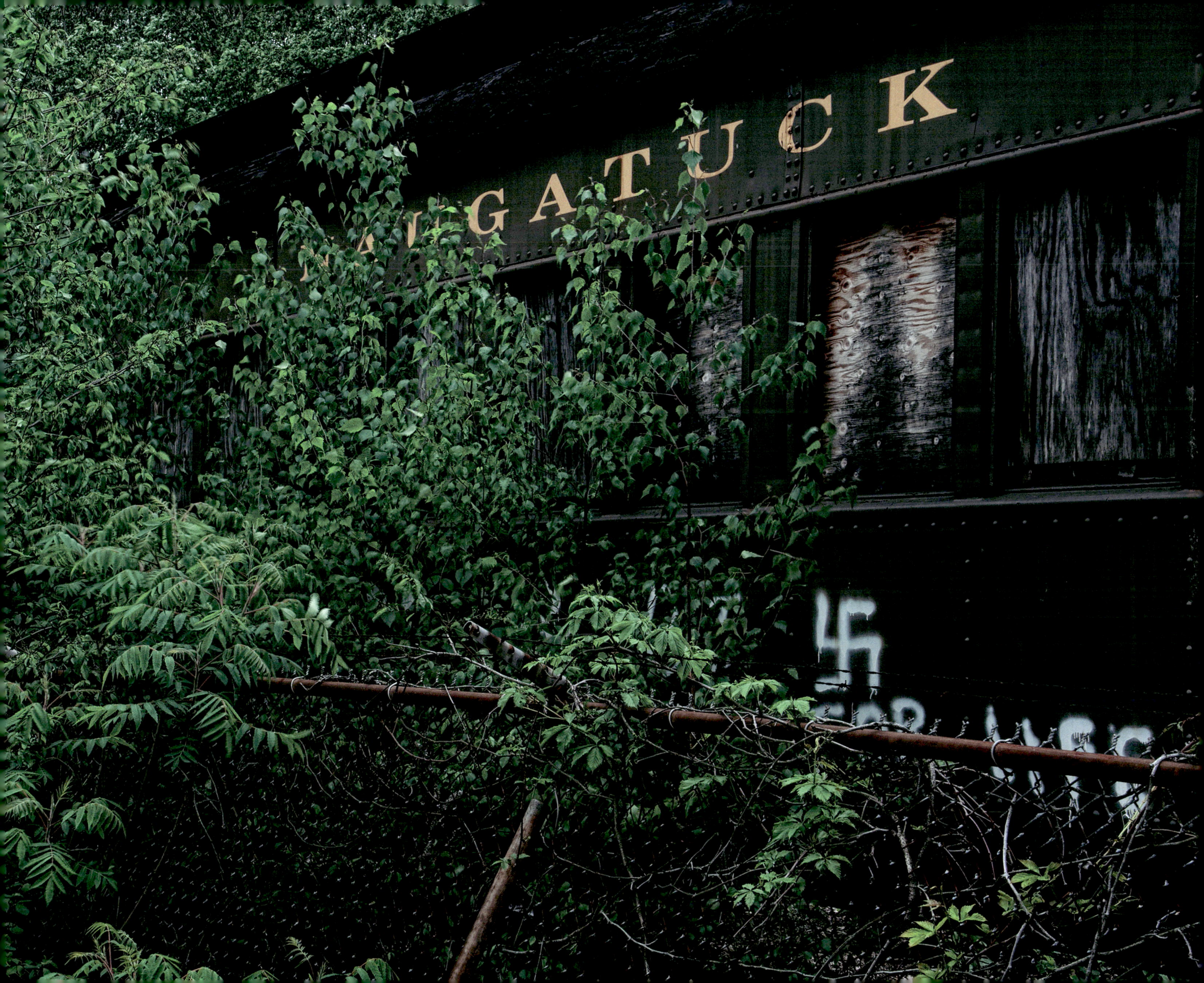
GATUCK

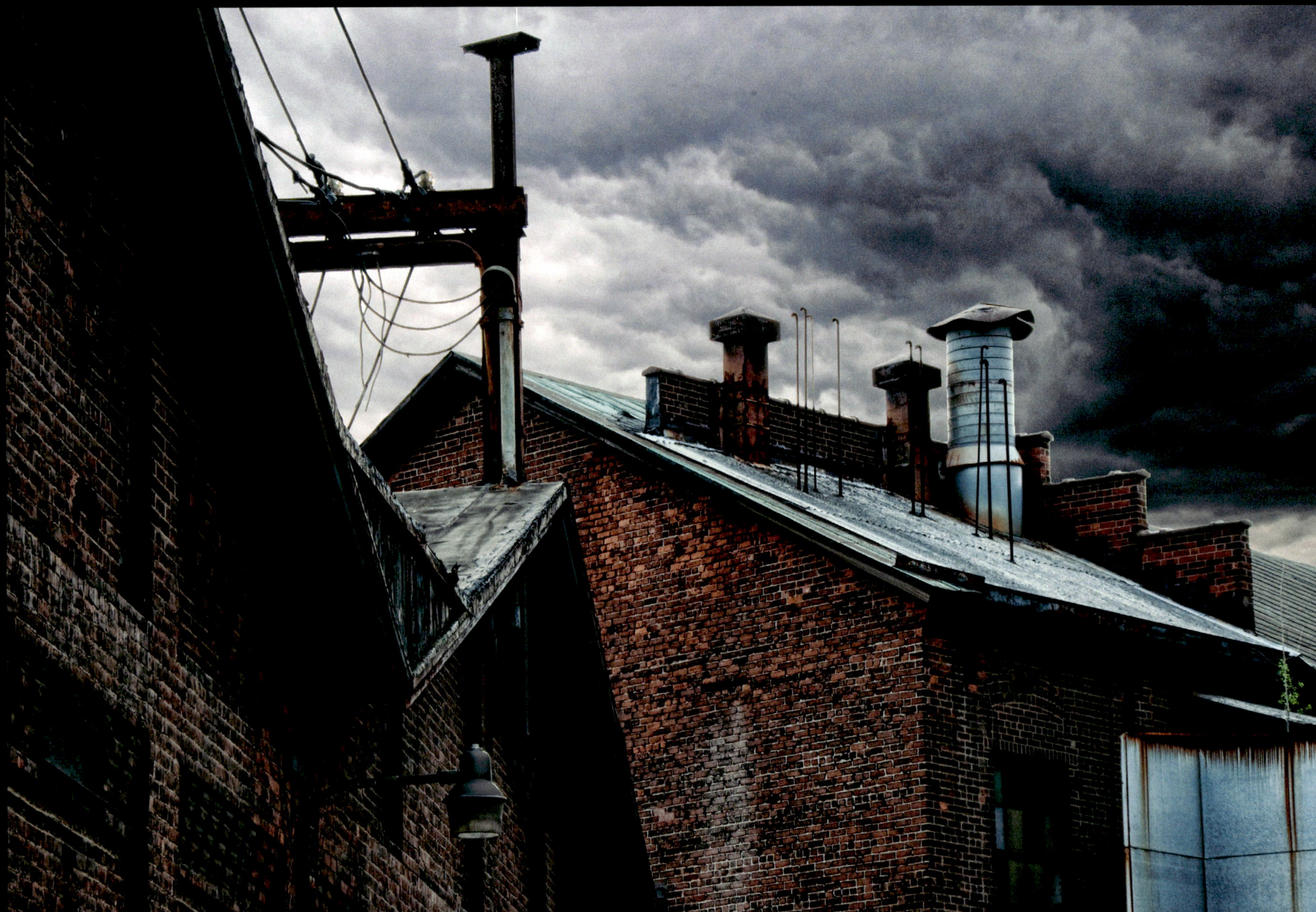

APPROACHING THUNDER
Farrel Works, Ansonia, CT

AN ARPEGGIO OF CORBELING LIKE A RIPPLE OF WIND
A TINY FLOURISH OF MASONIC ART AND IMPRINT OF THE MASON'S HAND

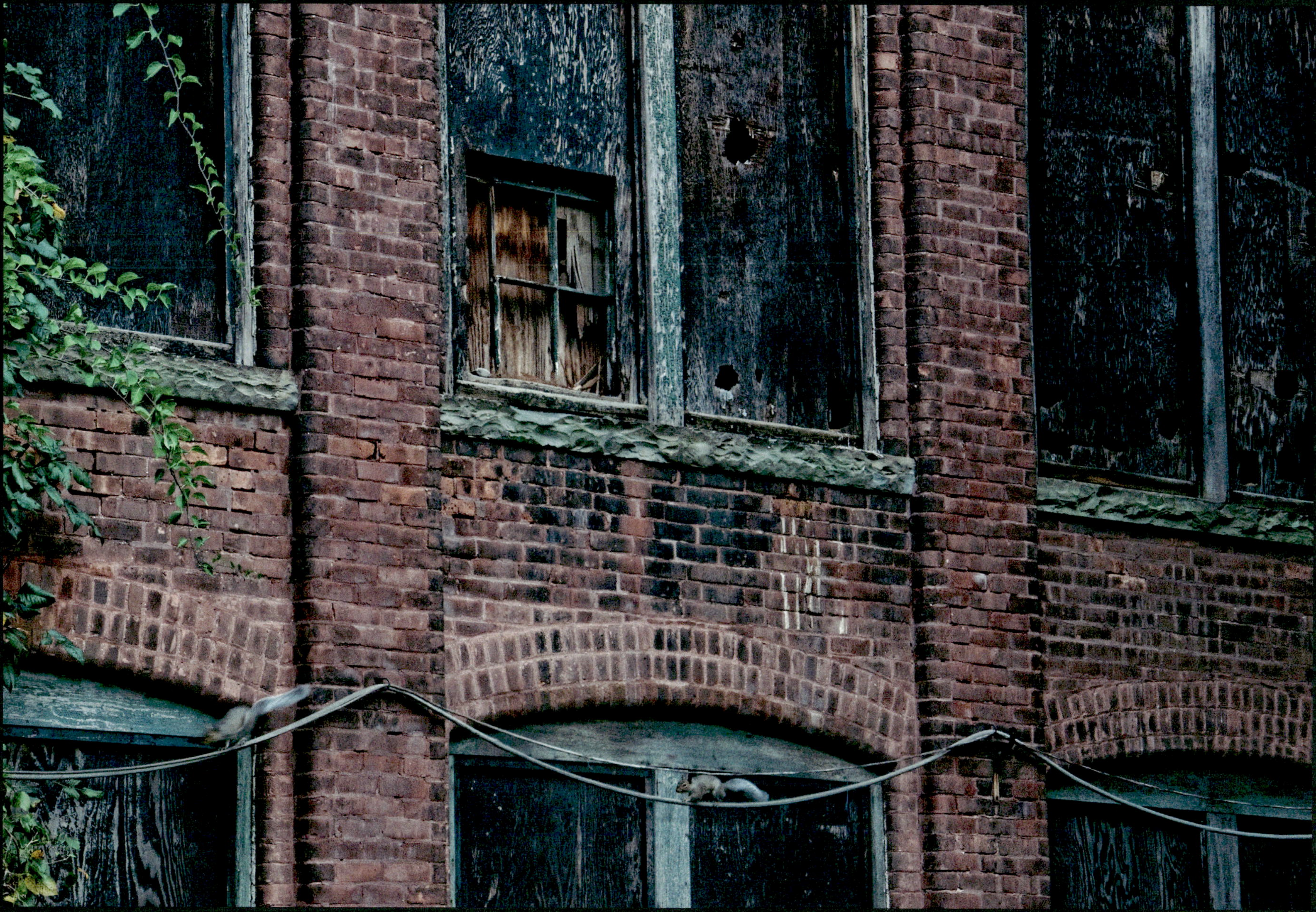

SCIURINE PERFORATIONS
Hendey Company, Torrington, CT

UPSTREAM SCHERZO

Upstream,
rivers
begin
as
raindrops.

They fall,
splash,
gather in puddles, over
flow into rills
and creeks,
runnels and freshets,
minnows and frogs,
beetles and water bugs,
scarabs and butterflies,

they tumble down cataracts,
cascade along fissures and hobble over rocks,
fishtail through woods and moony grasses before,
like salamanders to serpents,
white in spring rains surging
racing
swirling
spilling over
waterfalls,

pause.

In deep pools where trout lurk
and hawk-eyed shadows
they carry on the fugal singing
ever downstream
or along the gulf stream
or upswept seashells and
fish scales in an airstream
of fogs and clouds and drops of rain
born at thirty-two feet per second per second.

They dance in
an engine of spin and gravity,
surging and coursing through
the industries of our kind
and whirling scorpions of Mind
and the maelstrom of
whatever's next.

We are children of raindrops
longing for spring's genial rains
as we desecrate holy shores.

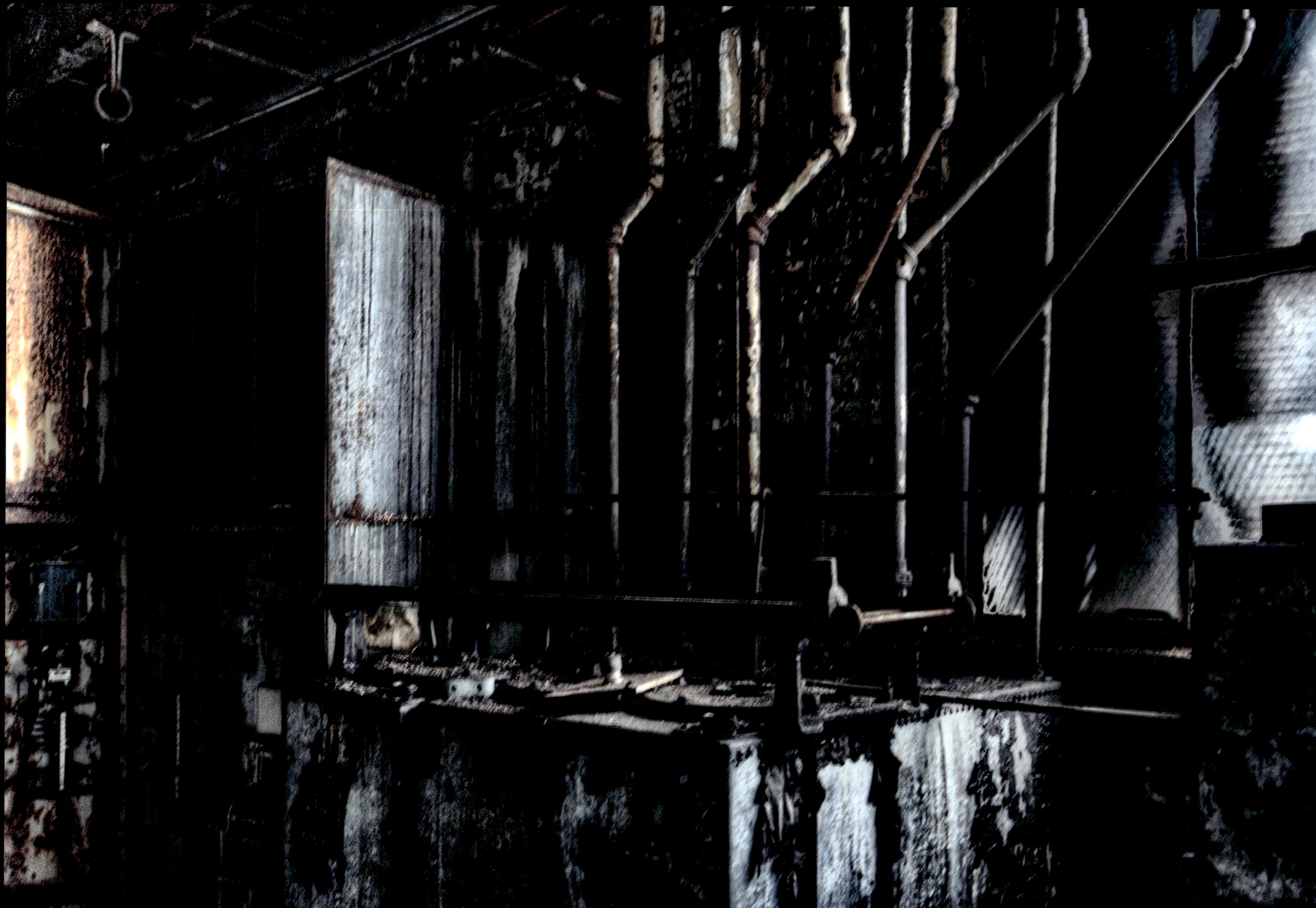

DOWNSTREAM NO. 2

OUR STORIES:

Humphreysville

Once, we're told, there was a sunny spot in the deep woods, where the river was loud and swift, and fish leapt from the water; where rock snagged the river's rush beneath the spread branches of that old tree, Nawkatunk. Eagles came to fish, and the spot was cherished by Chief Joseph, called "Chuse." When the white settlers came we fished there, too, and when there were too many of us, Chuse moved on.

In 1804 the legislature designated the area previously called Chusetown, by Rimmon Falls, as "Humphreysville." By then, David Humphreys, former aide de camp to George Washington, was raising sheep.

Born in Derby, where he learned about sheep, and educated at Yale, he was friend and confidant of Washington during and after the revolution. He was honored for his bravery at Yorktown, chosen to receive the enemy's colors at the surrender of Cornwallis, and to convey them to Congress in session in Philadelphia.

For a hundred years before the revolution, many towns employed a sheep master to oversee the breeding of sheep and the duties of the town shepherd; they understood the quality of the wool was vital to our economic well-being. In spite of these efforts, throughout the young nation the quality of our wool was coarse, and the yield, poor. And those of us with the means counted on expensive, imported English textiles, and the rest of us wore hand-me-downs and home-spun and patches.

After the revolution Humphreys became our first ambassador to a foreign land, and served in Spain and Portugal securing treaties. After Jefferson recalled him, and he finally disembarked at Derby Landing from his travels in Europe, he was accompanied by ninety-one Merino sheep, prized still today for the fineness and abundance of their fleece. While abroad Humphreys studied English woolen manufacturing. In 1803 on the banks of the Naugatuck River beside Rimmon Falls, Colonel Humphreys began laying out what has been called the first factory village in the United States.

There, using the power of the Naugatuck's waters, we converted the wool of his Merino sheep to woolen cloth. By 1811 there were nearly 300 of us working and living in Colonel Humphrey's industrial village. A channel cut in the rock on the eastern side of Rimmon Falls provided power for all the mills. In the four-story fabric mill we learned to work the spinning jennies and the slubbing billies and the carding machines, and some of us were developing a new shearing machine, while others made our thread into fabric, and there were even clothiers turning out fine new woolen coats and cotton frocks. There was also a grist mill and a paper mill, and for any of us with a knack for mechanics or carpentry, there was plenty of equipment that needed to be kept in repair.

Colonel Humphreys surrounded our village with gardens where we produced our own food; graced with plentiful bounty we always ate heartily. He even built a school where our children learned. Humphreys paid the schoolmaster's salary and offered prizes for scholarship and prizes for outstanding job performance in the mill. He went before the state legislature to lobby for bills to enforce factory safety and cleanliness. Colonel Humphreys was consciously building a model for American industrialization. When Madison took his oath of office in 1809, he was dressed in a full suit of American woolens from Humphreys's Merino sheep, and Colonel Humphreys's factory produced the coat.

Humphreys's was a Utopian vision put into practice on the Naugatuck River when men still remembered Chief Joseph fishing from its banks, and its waters still contained fish. Today, the town is Seymour, and busy Route 8 has put its great footprint on our falls. Little is left here of our factory past and less of the fabled Nawkatunk tree. We come and we go, and we go on.

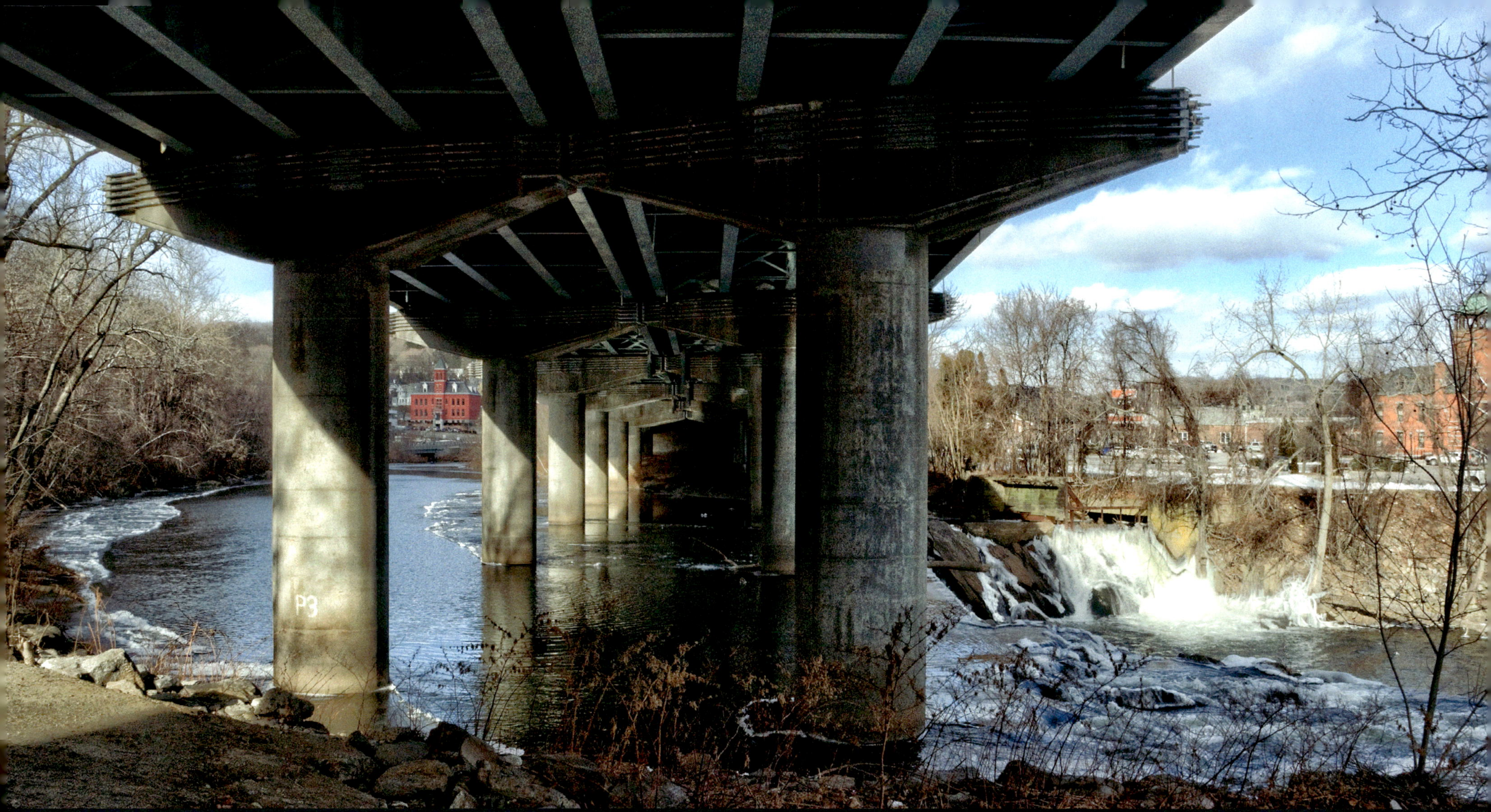

PHOTOGRAPHER'S JOURNAL:
By Rimmon Falls, in the shadow of the highway, lie remains of an old dam and sluiceway. It is a thin deposit onto slaty eons, culture stratified, as we dissolve to fossils. I look for words to explain, but time is too slippery for words, always sliding away to a place that's already vanished with the ground beneath our feet.

As I photograph I hear the commuter train struggling up the track nearby, and the roar of Rimmon Falls is often merged with trucks rattling on the highway overhead. Nearby, citizens are building a new park below the expressway, and I spoke with a volunteer setting paving stones. It's a park to honor veterans, and to salvage from ceaseless, dissonant agitation, moments of trust, harmony, and common purpose. He told me it brings us together and reclaims the river and the falls. "We have plans," he said. "It will be beautiful."

Somewhere within the merged din of highway, railroad, and falls, I try to feel the river within, and I imagine the wind in the leaves of that old tree, to the Pequots: "Naw-Ka-Tunk." Fish are back in the river again, and wheels still spin, as we struggle to evolve new ways to compete and to belong. Beneath the seas new alchemists have built a great fiber optic girdle of shooting light that hovers like a cloud and spins like a whirlwind through our thoughts; while here, on the Naugatuck's banks, waters still wash across our feet and toward those seas. May they teach us balance and flow that our humanity may flourish.

RIMMON FALLS, NAUGATUCK RIVER

Seymour, CT

ACKNOWLEDGMENTS

It is impossible for me to thank all who helped in the preparation of this book. I'm indebted to Chuck Blackledge, who went beyond the call of duty in connecting me to John Barto, and but for John Barto, President of Ansonia Copper & Brass, who gave me and my colleague unfettered access to every building from rooftop catwalks to grease pits below the floor, this book would show only Brass Valley's ruins.

The men from the mill are all dispersed, too many to name without fear of leaving someone out. What little I know about manufacturing brass comes from their patient explanations. I am especially grateful to Wally Hartsburg, chief of operations, and Charlie Essex, chief engineer, for always doing their best to answer every question, no matter how arcane, and meet any request, no matter how outlandish. It was Wally who connected me to his brother-in-law, Walter Kenderzierski, who matches him in graciousness for providing easy access to the old Ansonia Opera House; thank you, both Walters. Across the river at the Sterling Opera House I want to thank Markanthony Izzo for the constant loving care he gives the building and for his joy in sharing it with us.

Of all the men at the mill, none was more open-hearted and welcoming than Mike Lorenzo. Many mornings when I arrived at the foundry his Sicilian-cadenced "Hey, Ted!" would reverberate in the rafters before I saw, through smoky haze, the man it was coming from. Mike's voice was an aria. We made two draft copies of this book with his picture on the cover, even as the furnace was running, and I was still taking photographs. A month after the mill closed in Decemeber of 2013, Mike died suddenly. He never saw the book finished. However, his explanations, always a walk-and-talk experience of how it all worked, are preserved in these pages. His presence is with me now, though if he were here, I'd have more questions for him, but mostly I'd welcome the embrace of his Sicilian song of greeting.

Finally, I want to thank Jena Gerard, Don Giroux, Gene Horrigan, and especially, my wife, Jane, for their patience reading and sometimes re-reading countless manuscripts and offering valuable suggestions. And my thanks to Lazlo Gyorsok, frequent companion in these photographic adventures and in all questions related to the fate of humankind and the planet Earth. Thanks are hardly adequate to express all I owe Jane, my muse, friend, and life companion who always has dinner waiting.

RESOURCES

Anderson, Joseph, Sarah Johnson Prichard and Anna Lydia Ward. *The Town and City of Waterbury Connecticut.* New Haven, CT: The Price Lee Company, 1896.

Black, George. *The Trout Pool Paradox: The American Lives of Three Rivers*. Boston, New York: Houghton Mifflin Company, 2004.

Borrup Roger, editor. *Trolley Days in Connecticut* (magazine). Windsor, CT: Roger Borrup, c. 1984–6

Brecher, Jeremy, Jerry Lombardi and Jan Stackhouse. *Brass Valley: The Story of Working People's Lives and Struggles in an American Industrial Region*. Philadelphia: Temple University Press, 1982.

Bronson, Henry, MD. The History of Waterbury, Connecticut. Waterbury, CT: Bronson Bros., 1858 (https://archive.org/details/historyofwaterbu01bron).

Crapo, Raymond F. *The Environment of the Traction Era*. Short Beach, CT: Branford Electric Railway Historical Publications, 1978.

Daniels, Jim and Jane McCafferty, Charles Brodsky (photography). *From Milltown to Malltown*. Grosse Pointe Farms, Michigan: Marick Press, 2010.

DeLuca, Richard. *Post Roads & Iron Horses: Transportation in Connecticut from Colonial Times to the Age of Steam*. Middletown, CT: Wesleyen University Press, 2011.

Doyle, Brian Leahy. *Encore! The Renaissance of Wisconsin Opera Houses*. Wisconsin Historical Society Press, 2009

Jerome, Chauncey, *History of the American Clock Business for the Past Sixty Years, and Life of Chauncey Jerome*. Bookjungle.com.

Kingsbury, Frederick J. *Old Connecticut.* Waterbury, CT: Mattatck Historical Society, 1928.

Landes, David S. *Revolution in Time.* Cambridge, MA: The Belknap Press of Harvard University Press, 1983.

Lathrop, William Gilbert. *The Brass Industry in Connecticut; A study of the Origin and the Development of the Brass Industry in the Naugatuck Valley*. Miami, Florida: Hard Press Publishing (reprint of 1909 original).

Marcosson, Isaac F. *Anaconda*. New York: Dodd, Mead & Co., 1957.

Matricaria, Elizabeth Crossland. Anson's Glory. Trafford Publishing, 2013.

Molloy, Scott. *Trolley Wars: Streetcar Workers on the Line*. Durham, NH: University of New Hampshire Press, 2007.

Novak, Robert Jr., "The Creation of the City of Ansonia and today's Valley in 1888–1889," *Huntington Herald*, March–April, 2003 (http://derbyhistorical.org/Derby%20 Division.htm).

O'Malley, Michael. *Keeping Watch: A History of American Time*. Viking Penguin, 1990.

RESOURCES cont.

Orcutt, Rev. Samuel. *History of Torrington, Connecticut, from its first settlement in 1737, with Biographies and Genealogies*. Albany, NY: J. Munsell, 1878 (https://archive.org/details/historyoftorring1878orcu).

———— & Ambrose Beardsley. *History of the Old Town of Derby, Connecticut, 1642–1880*. Springfield, MA: Springfield Printing Company, 1880 (https://archive.org/details/historyoftorring1878orcu).

Pape, William J. *History of Waterbury and the Naugatuck Valley*. Connecticut. Chicago, New York: The S. J. Clarke Publishing Company, 1918.

Presnell, Barbara. *Piece Work*, Cleveland State University Poetry Center, 2007.

Prichard, Sarah Johnson. *The Town and City of Waterbury, Connecticut, Vol. 1*. Accessed through Google Books.

Raber, Michael S. and Robert B. Gordon. *Documentation of Ansonia Copper & Brass, Inc., Plant, Waterbury, Connecticut*. Raber Associates, prepared for FireLight Power Resources Services, LLC, Dec. 2007.

Shelton, Jane deForest. *The Salt-Box House; Eighteenth Century Life in a New England Hill Town*. Initial publication 1901. Memphis, TN: General Books, 2010.

Stevens, John R. *The Derby Horse Railway and the World's First Electric Locomotive*. New Haven, CT: New Haven Colony Historical Society, 1987.

ONLINE

Aerial survey of Connecticut 1934 photograph 03275 (scalable), Connecticut State Library, http://cslib.cdmhost.com/cdm/singleitem/collection/p4005coll10/id/7710/rec/4.

American Brass corporate archives, University of Connecticut, Thomas J. Dodd Research Center, http://doddcenter.uconn.edu/asc/findaids/American_Brass/MSS19970996.html#ref3.

American Clock and Watch Museum, http://www.clockandwatchmuseum.org.

Connecticut Antique Machinery Association, photo essays, http://www.ctamachinery.com/photo-essays-old-website/.

Connecticut Trolley Museum, The, http://www.ct-trolley.org.

Farrel Company history, University of Connecticut, Thomas J. Dodd Research Center, http://doddcenter.uconn.edu/asc/findaids/Farrel/MSS19890053.html.

Gregorski, Bob. "Brief History of the Restoration of The Naugatuck River and its Tributaries," Naugatuck River Watershed Association, January 2007, http://www.naugawatshed.org/Naugatuck%20River%20History.htm.

"Improvements in Brass Kettles" patent grant to Hiram W. Hayden, United States Patent and Trademark Office, http://www.google.com/patents/USRE3996.

"Lamp Company Historical Profiles, The Lampworks, http://www.thelampworks.com/lw_companies_main.htm.

New Britain Industrial Museum, The, http://nbindustrial.org.

O'Malley, Michael, *Keeping Watch: A History of American Time* (detailed account of Eli Terry clock controversy), http://chnm.gmu.edu/courses/jackson/mill/1R.html.

Raechel Guest's Waterbury Thoughts Blog, http://waterburythoughts.blogspot.com.

Shore Line Trolley Museum, The, http://shorelinetrolley.org.

Sterling and Huntington piano company archives, The Plumb Memorial Library Sterling Collection, Derby, CT, http://www.pages.drexel.edu/~dwa27/final/sterling/Sterling%20Piano%20Page.htm.

Timex Museum, The, http://www.timexpo.com.

Waterbury Time Machine, http://www.freewebs.com/waterburyct/.

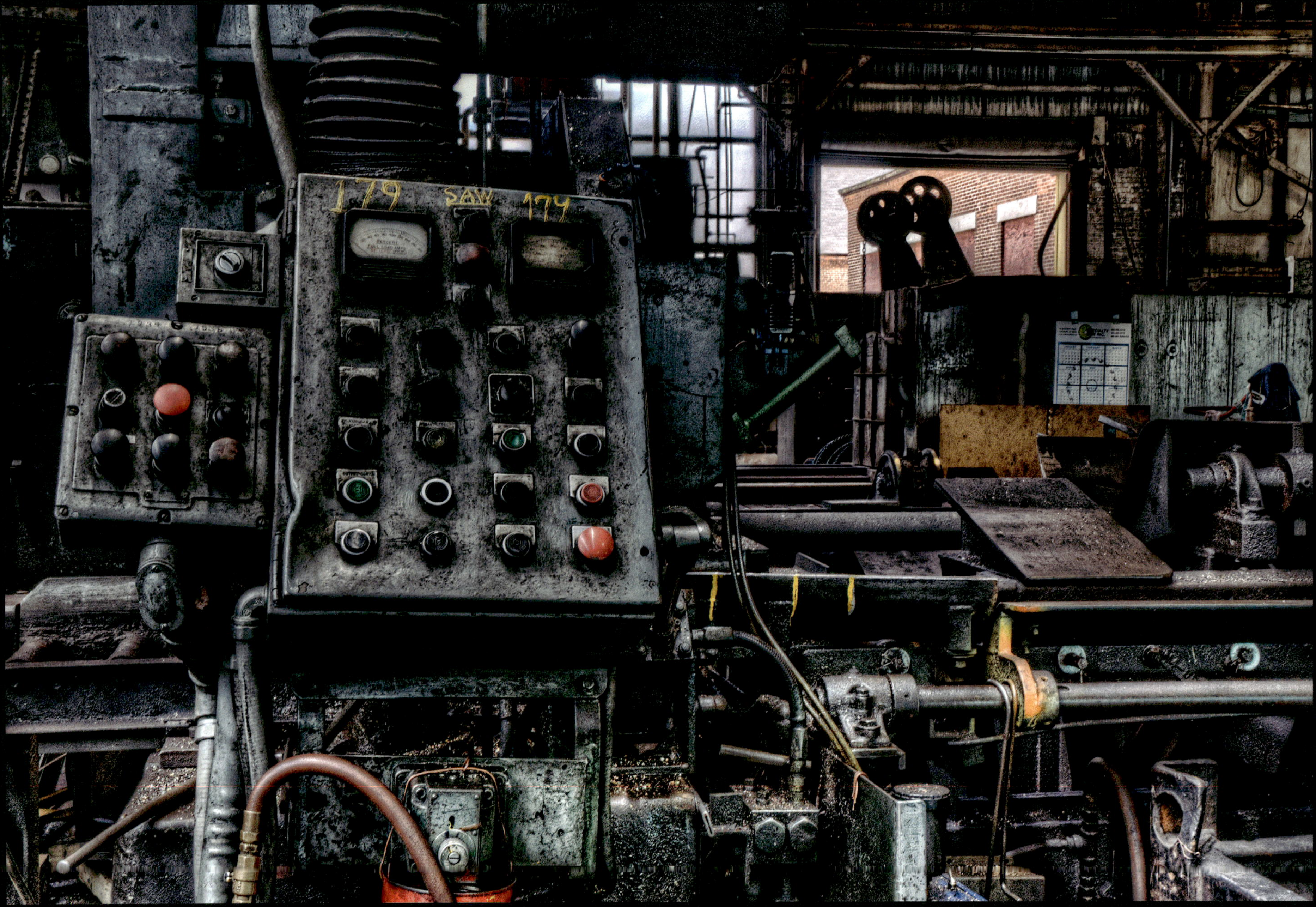

SAW 179

AN OLD SAW

Not so much about what it sawed as what it saw.

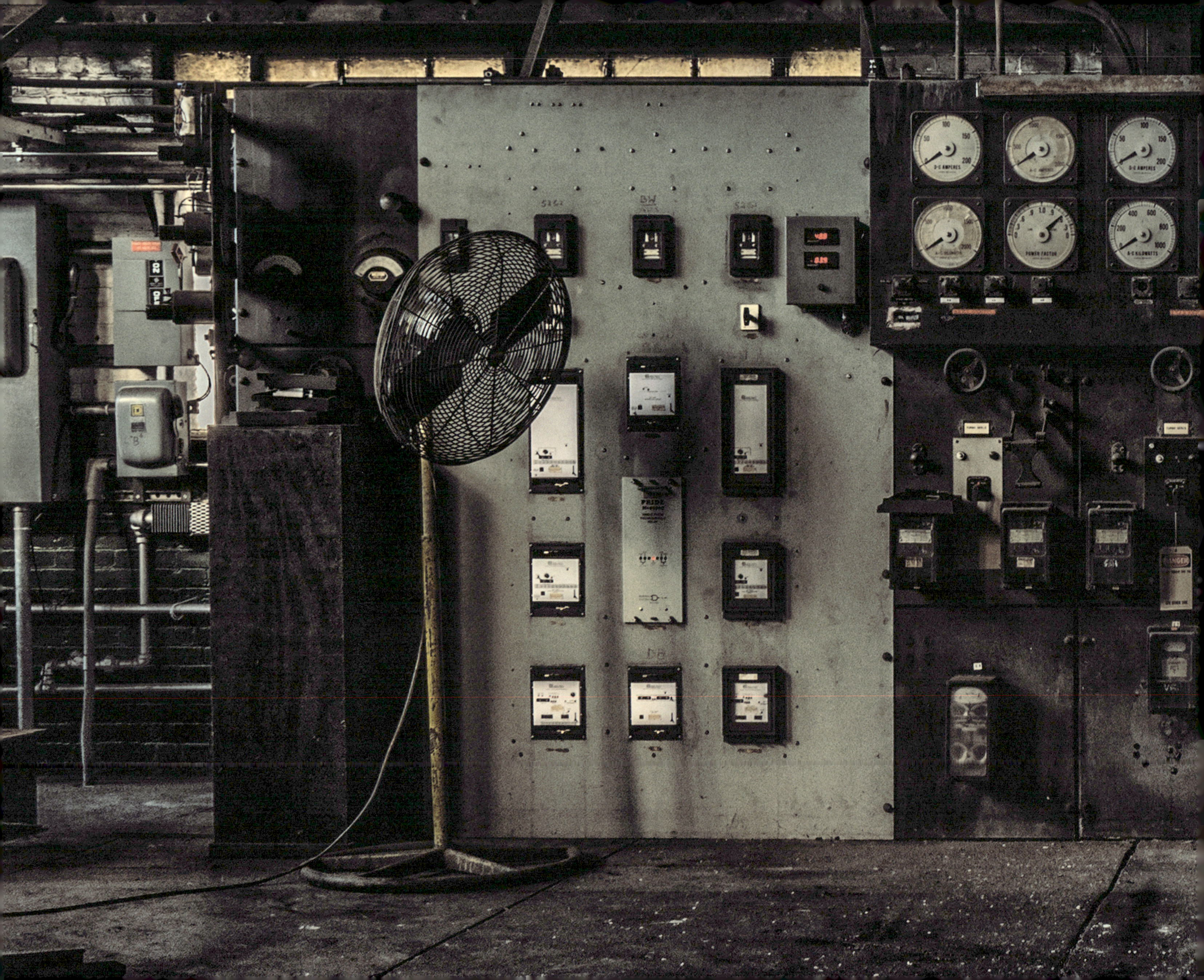
D-C AMPERES
D-C AMPERES
POWER FACTOR
A-C KILOWATTS